R/-/

MARY TUDOR

Also by H. F. M. PRESCOTT

THE MAN ON A DONKEY (*Historical Novel*)

'THE LADY MARY AFTER QUEEN'
By Hans Holbein the Younger. Windsor Castle.
Reproduced by gracious permission of Her Majesty the Queen.

MARY TUDOR

BY

H. F. M. PRESCOTT
M.A. (Oxon.), M.A. (Manchester)

Revised edition, with a new introduction
on the social background

EYRE & SPOTTISWOODE
LONDON

First published
  (as 'Spanish Tudor')   1940
Second, revised edition   1952
Reprinted   1953

This book is printed in Great Britain for
Eyre & Spottiswoode (Publishers), Ltd.,
15 Bedford Street, London, W.C.2 by
Jarrold & Sons Ltd., Norwich

To
JAMES

Acknowledgements

I wish to thank again the following who helped me when this book was being written: Miss C. Garrett for much counsel and encouragement: Misses Francis and Westland for help in translation: the Rev. H. M. Lang for his kindness in showing me the ruins of the Manor House at Woodham Walter: my brother and Mr. Ian Robertson for help with the Index. In addition I would thank those who have, in various ways, helped in the preparation of this re-issue: Mrs. J. Shipley, Mr. J. Woodward, and Mr. A. C. Wood.

Contents

Illustrations

Foreword

SINCE the first publication of this book a considerable amount of new material relevant to the subject has appeared which it has been possible to use in the preparation for a re-issue.

Of contemporary sources, the collection generally known as the *Calendar of State Papers–Spanish*, has been extended at both ends. A Supplement to Volumes I and II has been published, edited by Dr. Mattingly, in which there are a few, but lively, notices of Mary Tudor as a little girl. The *Calendar* previously ended with Volume XI and the year 1553, though among the Transcripts at the Public Record Office were those in which Dr. Royall Tyler had continued the collection and translation of the sources to the end of 1554. In 1949, Volume XII of the *Calendar* was published, with Dr. Tyler as Editor, and this covered the first six months of 1554. It has thus been possible to refer the reader to this printed collection instead of to the Transcripts, or to incomplete copies printed by Tytler in *England under the Reigns of Edward VI and Mary*.

Of modern works consulted, and listed in the revised bibliography, I should like to mention four which I have found particularly helpful for my purpose. Two are biographies: Garrett Mattingly's *Catherine of Aragon*, and Wilhelm Schenk's *Reginald Pole, Cardinal of England*. The *Reformation in England*, Volume I, 'The King's Proceedings' by Philip Hughes includes not only a richly documented account of 'the King's Matter' and the changes in religion consequent upon it down to 1540, but also a survey of society and the Church in England before the Reformation. *Rival Ambassadors at the Court of Queen Mary*, by E. H. Harbison bears even more directly upon my subject, consisting as it does of a study of Mary's short reign from the point of view of politics and diplomacy. This is based upon much unpublished material, the author having used not only MSS. of the de Noailles brothers preserved in France, but also Dr. Royall Tyler's untranslated transcripts, also in France, which continue the series in the Public Record Office down to the year 1558.

Introduction

ON November 2nd, 1501, a Spanish princess, come to be married to the King's elder son, rode into London. Henry VII had already inspected her; a careful man, he was not one to take delivery of goods without inspection. But this was the first sight that London had of Katherine, daughter of Ferdinand and Isabella the Catholic, and the streets were full. She rode a mule, its saddle and harness the finest that Spain could send; she herself was dressed richly and in the Spanish fashion; 'upon her head a little hat, fashioned like a cardinal's hat . . . with a lace of gold at this hat to stay it; her hair hanging down her shoulders, which is a fair auburn, and . . . a coif between her head and her hat of carnation colour.' After her came her Spanish ladies, each paired off with an Englishwoman of the Court, who rode alongside 'to keep her company in manner of a leader of her horse'; but, as Spanish side-saddles had crutch and stirrup on the off-side, these sisterly couples must have ridden back to back.[1]

After the marriage there was a pageant, and after that dancing at Court. Prince Arthur, the bridegroom, his brother Henry, Duke of York, their sister Margaret, Lady Cecil, the Spanish bride and one of her ladies danced together: Duke Henry, a ruddy, sturdy boy of ten, vehement in all he did, perceiving himself to be encumbered with his clothes, suddenly cast off his gown and danced in his jacket, so that even a homesick princess may have smiled at his light heels and lighter heart.

When the shows and jollifications were over the Court left London, going by barge up the river as far as Mortlake, and thence on horseback to Richmond through the dusk, arriving 'very late in the silence of the evening', with the flames of 300 torches tossing and flickering along both sides of the cavalcade.[2]

So Katherine was married, though later she declared that the marriage was never consummated, to the delicate youth whose storied name was never to be added to those of the English kings. Prince Arthur died next spring, and that brief marriage became, for Katherine as for England, but a prelude to another which was to last for nearly a quarter of a century.

Six years after Katherine's arrival she became the bride of the boy who had danced so merrily at her wedding, Henry, the King's second son, and now his heir. To him it was hoped she should bear a son who would perpetuate the Tudor line. For Katherine, as for England, more turned upon the birth of that son than any could have guessed, and the fact that after twenty-four years of married life she and Henry had only one surviving child, and that child a daughter, was to have an incalculable effect upon the future of the nation.

But before we turn to the history of Mary, daughter of Henry and Katherine, of England and Spain, the only crowned Tudor who had a parent not English, and who, by her father's doing, became all her mother's child and the Spanish Tudor–before we turn to the history of Mary, it is well that we should look round upon the England into which she was born.

Since the Court, the household of the King, still retained, like other great households, much of the peripatetic humour of the Middle Ages, the Princess, born at Greenwich, must soon have learnt to know many other houses, from such great castle-palaces as Windsor or Richmond, to the royal manor-houses in Essex and Hertfordshire, and distant hunting-boxes such as Wood-stock; in London, there were, besides the remains of the great palace of Westminster, little St. James, and Baynard's Castle on the river. Two other great houses were growing into splendour during Mary's childhood; White-hall and Hampton Court, both the work of Wolsey, Cardinal of York, Legate of the Pope, minister of the King; both at his fall judged by that King to be fit for royal palaces.

Of Richmond Palace, the pride of Henry VII, built by him and called after his own Yorkshire Richmond, we have a contemporary description. The plan was four-square, with angle-towers, and towers half-way along each wall. That was after the old style, but the material was brick, and the new age showed itself in gallantry above the towers, for each of these bore a weather-vane 'with the King's arms painted and gilded with rich gold and azure . . . that as well the pleasant sight of them, as the hearing on a windy day was right marvellous to know and understand'.[3] Inside the walls were the quaint-ness, the colour, the fantastic decoration of a fairy-tale. A fountain in the midst of the marble and freestone paving of the second court had 'in the upper part . . . lions and dragons, and other goodly beasts, and in the midst, certain branches of red roses, out of which flowers and roses is evermore running a course of the cleanest and most purest water in the cistern beneath'. The Great Hall with its glazed windows, coloured tiles, and timber roof craftily carved with 'proper knots', led on to the King's chambers, whitewashed–a new fashion then–and chequered with azure, 'having between each check a red rose of gold and a portcullis'. Beyond, in long ranges, lay the pleasant dancing chambers, 'the galleries for games, and beyond again, the gardens, tennis-courts, bowling alleys and archery butts'.[4]

What Henry VII did at Richmond, Cardinal Wolsey, and later Henry VIII, outdid at Hampton Court. Here the profusion, the magnificence, the gusto of the age broke all bounds in a riot of painted and gilded classical medal-lions let into the brickwork of the walls, in painted and gilded terra-cotta escutcheons of arms, initials, mottoes, emblems; above upon numberless crocketed pinnacles sat a sculptured menagerie of beasts, 'the King's beasts', that is to say the heraldic badges of every family from which he traced his descent. These beasts, whether of wood or of stone, were painted in colour, and, as at Richmond, held rods upon which gilded vanes turned.

The splendour of the exterior was more than matched within. In the roof of Henry VIII's Great Hall Italian and English fancy met and mingled. The beauty and wealth of its carving remains, but not the colour which emphasized and enhanced its riches; for the panels were painted blue, the carved pendants and the spandrels were painted and gilded; the great louvre in the centre was blue as the sky and spangled with golden stars, and all was lighted from windows so cunningly placed as to prevent those shadows which lurk in the vaulting of a roof.[5] This roof, though the crowning, was not the only splendour of the Hall. There was colour and ornament in the painted glass of the windows, in the painted and carved cornice, and colour in the green and white tiles of the dais.

The Great Hall was part of the ancient domestic plan. But in these houses one form of room was new and peculiar to the period. 'Galleries', the Venetian ambassador informed the Lords of the Signory, . . . 'are long porticoes or halls without chambers, with windows on each side, looking on gardens or rivers, the ceilings being marvellously wrought in stone with gold, and the wainscot of carved wood representing a thousand beautiful figures.' Such an apartment, lending itself so easily to display, became immensely popular, so that it is to be found among the magnificent additions made by Henry VIII at Hampton Court, where the gallery of the Queen's Lodging, later pulled down by Wren, had along its eastern wall eleven windows, three of them bays, all filled with heraldic glass, and above these a cornice and frieze of fretwork painted and gilded, with a ceiling that bore '1256 balls of burnished gold, with the leaves gilt'.[6]

This prodigality of ornament, colour and gilding must have been sumptuous, but may well have been overwhelming, and one is inclined to agree with the criticism which Wallop reported after a conversation with Francis I on the subject of Henry VIII's new buildings. 'He', said the ambassador, 'heard that your Majesty did much use gilding in your said houses, and especially in the roofs, and that he in his buildings used little or none, but made roofs of timber finely wrought with divers colours of wood natural, as ebony, brasil and certain others that I cannot well name to your Majesty, which he reckoneth to be more rich than gilding and more durable.'[7]

The gardens which lay about the palace of the sixteenth century were as 'high fantastical' as the buildings themselves. At the beginning of the century fashions in gardening were changing. The older style of garden, still to be found at such great but remote houses as Thornbury, the West Country home of the princely and unfortunate house of Stafford, was, for all its rose trellises and fountains, a rather haphazard place where fruit-trees and flowers grew together in the grass, and flowers upon the built-up grass bank which surrounded the garden. So, at Thornbury, the 'privy garden' was an 'orchard full of young grafts well loaden with fruit, many roses and other pleasures', though the new curiosity of workmanship showed itself in 'goodly alleys with roosting places covered thoroughly with white thorn and hasill . . .'[8] which were perhaps an early form of Bacon's 'covert alley upon carpenters' work by which you may go in shade' through the 'green' to the garden proper.

The King's palace gardens were of the new fashion. At Richmond

Henry VII made one with 'royal knots alleyed and herbed, many marvellous beasts as lions, dragons', and the like, 'carved in the ground, right well sanded and compressed with lead'.[9] This was that style which Bacon was to condemn with all the acrimonious scorn which we bring to our denunciations of the Victorian fashion of carpet-bedding. Sir Francis will have none of 'the making of knots or figures, with divers-coloured earths . . . they be but toys; you may see as good sights many times in tarts'. And we cannot but share his sentiments, when we read of the methods of this strange type of the gardener's craft, how various substances were pounded to powder–chalk, plaster or lime for white, lime and coal mixed for 'a perfect blueness', broken bricks for red, and so on;[10] an arid style indeed. It is a garden of this newer fashion that can be seen beyond the Ionic columns of that large, straggling, composite portrait of Henry VIII and his family which is at Hampton Court. There you get a glimpse of the wooden pillars, painted with the Tudor white and green, and supporting heraldic beasts. There were 'puncheons' too, supporting the uprights of rails, all white and green, and in the picture can be seen the neat-cropped edges of the intricately shaped beds of this royal 'knot garden'.

In those days even the quiet little sunk garden at Hampton Court was crowded with the heralds' fantasy; '38 of the King's and Queen's beasts in freestone, bearing shields with the King's arms and the Queen's', that is to say 4 dragons, 5 greyhounds, 5 harts, 4 'innycornes', stood 'about the ponds in the pond yard', all of them carved by Harry Corant of Kingston, and painted 'in oil and colours'.[11]

Another fashionable device of garden design was 'the Mount'; such an artificial hill as Leland saw in the garden at Wressel Castle, 'writhen about with degrees like turnings of cockle shells, to come to the top without pain'. The King made one at Hampton Court, and adorned it not only by more of his ubiquitous 'Beasts' but also by plantings of pear trees, of rosemary and quick-set hedges.[12]

For the two first Tudors took an interest in the more legitimate arts of gardening: Henry VII stocked Richmond with 'many vines, seeds and strange fruits'. His son, always with one eye upon the fashions in France, sent John Leland to bring back a hundred pear and apple trees from Rouen.[13] And for all their strangeness of ornament palace gardens were full of our simplest and most familiar cottagers' flowers. The King bought 'gilliver slips, mints and other sweet flowers', sweet Williams at 3d. the bushel, and Alis Brewer and Margaret Rogers were, apparently, sent out to rifle the woods for '34 bushels of strawberry root, primrose and violets'.[14] Besides these there would be cowslips, bachelors' buttons, snapdragon, columbine, larkspurs, pansies, poppies, carnations, pinks which were called 'sops in wine', tall hollyhocks and roses.

When we turn to consider the furnishings of these palaces we find, as might be expected, gorgeous colours, sumptuous materials and intricate workmanship. Chairs of estate covered with red cloth of gold or with blue cloth of gold, and fringed with blue silk and gold of Venice; counterpanes of satin, silk or embroidery, of 'red russett silk with Venetian gold'; pillow-cases stitched with black silk, and fleur-de-lis of gold; such are a few of the entries in the huge inventory of Wolsey's goods appropriated by the King. Articles still more strange and bizarre appear in this and other inventories. One of the Cardinal's beds, listed as a 'trussing bed', that is one designed for packing up and transport, is 'of alabaster with my lord's arms in flowers and gilt upon the sides'.[15] The King possessed a bed of which the posts and head were 'curiously wrought, painted and gilt', and surmounted by four 'bullyeons of timber work, gilt' from each of which rose a vane of iron painted with the King's arms.

The great Cardinal's sets of hangings were judged worthy of comment by ambassadors in their letters home. The Venetian ambassador reported that all the tapestries in Hampton Court were changed each week. Gresham in Flanders was buying for his master on a grand scale; at one purchase he acquired hangings for eighteen rooms, and these would probably run into well over 100 pieces. For Wolsey's own closet nothing was good enough but cloth of gold. Not only the opulence but also the secular, not to say pagan, subjects of some of the Cardinal's tapestries gave a handle to his political enemies. Skelton in his quick, tumbling verses rebuked this prince of the Church for what must have been the still existing 'Triumph' tapestries.

> Hanging about the walls
> Cloths of gold and palls
> Arras of rich array
> Fresh as flowers in May
> With Dame Diana naked
> How lusty Venus quaked
> And how Cupid shaked
> His dart, and bent his bow.
>
> With triumphs of Cesar
> And of Pompeius war
> How they ride in goodly chairs
> Conveyed by elephants
> With laureate garlands
> And by unicorns
> With their seemly horns. . . .[16]

Skelton was shocked; or said that he was; but it is only fair to remark that the Cardinal had bought the tapestries second-hand from the executors of the Bishop of Durham.[17]

Of all the Cardinal's magnificent possessions his collection of plate was perhaps the most notorious. In every great house on festival occasions the plate – silver, silver-gilt or gold, would be brought out from locked chests and set upon the 'cupboard' in the hall. Most noblemen when entertaining had to dip into that display for use, but not so the Cardinal. Foreign visitors, boasted Cavendish, were amazed to see the ranks of gold cups, gold mazers, gold salts set with pearls or enriched with enamel, remain upon the cupboard, untouched throughout the meal, and duplicated upon the tables. That glorious collection passed into the King's hands, and was from time to time supplemented by other confiscations; many of the political and matrimonial vicissitudes of the reign left their traces, in initials, badges or emblems of the late owners still visible upon the King's plate, and these marks are noted with meticulous care in the records of the Jewel House.

Yet still, for all their splendour, even such great houses went short of three types of furnishings which nowadays and for long have been taken for granted; that is to say carpets, tables and chairs. Rushes, sweetened as much as might be by flowers and sweet smelling 'strawing herbs', or occasionally rush matting, were universally the ordinary floor covering. Carpets were kept for special purposes; to lay over furniture, or beside beds, or in windows.[18] Though tables of small size are fairly common in inventories, it is clear that the table at which even the King sat down to dine was a board set upon trestles, removed after the meal, and tucked away out of sight behind the hangings of the room.[19] As for chairs, though a very up-to-date and travelled man, Master Thomas Cromwell, might have standing in his Hall three 'little gilt chairs for women', it was still usual, even for royal ladies, to sit as Skelton's company of noble embroideresses sat, on 'tappets and carpets' and on cushions. When, in 1554, the Duchess of Alva visited Mary herself, just after the Queen's marriage, there appears to have been only one chair, the chair of estate, in the room, for until two velvet brocade stools were fetched the only alternative seat was a cushion on the floor.*

If we try to reconstruct the life that went on in the King's palaces, or in the houses of those great nobles who kept a state which was the same in kind though less in degree than the King's, we must imagine three conditions as common to all; perpetual crowding, chronic disorder, and elaborate ceremony. 'Shortage of man-power', that thwarting phrase, was one entirely unknown in the sixteenth-century household. Service then was both honourable – a Percy's younger sons would serve before their father as Carver and Sewer – and advisable, for a man found a master useful, not so much, as in the Middle Ages, to defend him against violence, as to save him from the pinch of changing economic conditions. On the other hand England was still near enough to the medieval tradition for a large meiny to be a source of pride to any rich man. Stow, writing at the end of the century, gives, with manifest admiration, the numbers of some great households: Wolsey's comes easily first with 'near about 400, omitting his servants' servants, which were many', but West, Bishop of Ely had 100 servants, and Edward, Earl of Derby 220;[20] in 1512 Henry Percy, Earl of Northumberland, had a household of 166; in 1542 Sir Thomas Lovell, by no means a personage of the first rank, had one of

* See below, pp. 276–7.

97.[21] It was indeed the aim of the household reformers of the time, and these, owing to the dwindling value of money, were many, to regulate and reduce the swarming population of the house. At Court servants' servants were to be discouraged; old and decrepit officials pensioned off, 'boys and vile persons' who had no business there at all should be excluded, 'vagabonds and mighty beggars' punished and driven out.

It was not the burden of the wages, for these were neither large nor regularly paid, which was the chief expense of great households, but all that the officer or servant or hanger-on received in kind. Each man in the King's service had the right to lodging, to food in hall at dinner-time and to what was known as 'Bouche' or 'Bouge of Court', that is to say a livery, or allowance, of food, fire and light in his own rooms. This charge was normal and must be borne, but much of the lord's substance might leak away through sheer careless waste, and to check this the Counting House, or its equivalent office, must audit regular accounts, not only at Michaelmas, but monthly and weekly; even daily, before any might have their breakfast, account must be taken of all the stores consumed during the previous day. Wolsey and Cromwell were particular to regulate the exact amount of the Bouche of Court for the King's Household; the number of 'messes' eaten in Hall with four men to a mess, must be recorded; in the fifteenth century the steward had been expected to notch a tally for this purpose.

Loss by dishonesty was harder to prevent. Unscrupulous officers found a ready means of profit in a manipulation of those perquisites which were their right. The Yeoman of the Pantry got all the bread chippings, and as crusts had a bad reputation for engendering 'melancholy humours' these would in any case be considerable in amount; but it was tempting also to 'chop off great pieces of the bottoms of the loaves' and then sell these back to the household for feeding the master's dogs. The Yeoman of the Ewery, having the right to all unused candle-ends, was liable to persuade his friend, the Chandler, to make candles 'to be longer at the great ends very near 3 fingers' breadth than the bottom the wick doth reach'.[22]

Lesser servants, hanging about at the 'dresser', that is the kitchen hatch, were known on occasion to make off with dishes intended for their betters. So there must be a 'Surveyor of the Dresser' to prevent this. Other more important thefts, of silver, of pewter, of napery, must be guarded against by the regular locking up after every meal-time of every household office.

But it was not only against loss, by carelessness or by deliberate dishonesty that many of the regulations of the late fifteenth- and early sixteenth-century household ordinances are directed. Only Angels, according to Coventry Patmore, may be familiar; in a rude society, climbing arduously to politeness, elaborate ceremonies flourish; nothing but ceremony, rigid and complicated, will be strong enough to prevent mere nastiness of behaviour. And this age was indeed rude, though some men's eyes were already fixed upon the politer societies abroad; upon France, still more upon Italy. Mess and disorder therefore come in for their share of rebuke from the household reformers.

Nobles, say the King's Household Ordinances, 'do much delight to dine in corners and secret places'; especially, it appears, they desired to slip away to the Office of the Cellar; but this privilege, it was laid down, must be reserved for important strangers alone.[23] Or they would eat in their own apartment, and then allow their servants to put the dirty dishes outside the door. This was forbidden for various reasons; such a practice wasted food, and made the palace untidy, and it was likely that dogs would get those broken meats which, in the properly regulated meals in Hall, would be put in the alms-dish for the poor.[24]

Such disorders were however peccadilloes compared with the misdemeanours of lesser servants. It was necessary to forbid scullions in the royal kitchen to go about 'naked or in garments of such vileness as they now do'. Those serving meals in the King's bedchamber must be warned against wiping greasy fingers upon the King's tapestry hangings, or putting dishes down 'upon the King's bed for fear of hurting of the King's rich counterpoints that lie thereon'.[25]

It was at meal-times that ritual and ceremony were most elaborately displayed. All the Hall officers had their part in the laying, serving, and clearing away of the meal. The Sewer must see to the fire and to the hanging of the cloth of estate above his master's chair; he must set four cushions upon the bench at the high table. If it was winter, and, as was becoming more frequent, the lord's meal was to be eaten in some private room, the Usher must set up between this bench and the fire such movable screens as those which the four sackbut-men gave to the Queen as a New Year gift in 1556–'seven fannes to keep off the heate of the fyer, of straw'; and one 'of white silk'.[26]

The Yeoman of the Ewery was responsible for bringing out the tablecloths and the long towels which Carver and Sewer or Panter wore over one shoulder, and with which the Sewer must cover his hand before he might take up bread, or even knives, spoons, and the great covered salt for the high table. If the lord's bread was to be wrapped up 'stately' the Panter did this, according to instructions which are elaborate as any for the folding of tablenapkins in a Victorian cookery-book. Elaborate too was the whole ritual of Assay, by which salt, water for washing, food and wine were all tried for poison if the lord were the blood royal. To assay the salt, for instance, the Carver must uncover the salt-cellar, 'and with a cornet of bread touch it in foure parts and with your hand make a floryshe over it, and give it to the Panter to eat, for assay'. The same must be done for every dish; sauces, 'baked meat closed', custards, tarts, and 'Gelly', and always with a flourish of the hand.[27] And so the meal would go on with its fantastic cookery–half a capon stitched with needle and thread to half a pig; with its refinements of carving–you may touch beef or mutton with your left hand when you cut it, but must not touch venison;[28] with, if it were a great feast, its astonishing 'subtleties'–erections of wax, sugar and flowers representing perhaps 'St. Eustace kneeling . . . under a great tree full of Roses, and a White Hart before him with a crucifix between his horns and a man by him leading his horse'.[29]

So far we have not concerned ourselves with that household department which had become pre-eminent above all others – the Chamber. In the Royal Household this, with the growth of refinement, with the increasing insistence on the pleasures of privacy, had come to be divided into the Outer, or Presence Chamber, and the Privy Chamber. Here the officers, besides duplicating the Hall officers so as to provide Carver, Sewer, Panter, and the rest for the King's table, had been again duplicated by the addition of Gentlemen and Grooms of the Privy Chamber, to the Gentlemen, Yeomen and Groom Ushers of the 'Outward Chamber'.

These officers of the Privy Chamber were the close personal attendants of the King; they were chosen by him, either as the Marquess of Exeter was chosen, because 'he is the King's near kinsman and hath been brought up of a child with his Grace in his Chamber'[30] – but this was in the early years of the reign when as yet men of the blood royal did not go in danger of their lives – or because of their 'pregnant parts and quick inventive brain', so that we find such men as Sir Francis Bryan, brilliant and disreputable, prominent among them.

Their duties were all about the King's person; it was they who dressed him in the morning, undressed him at night, accompanied him in hunting, masking or playing if he wished, or remained on duty in the Privy Chamber in his absence. Their day began early; at seven o'clock they were awakened by the Pages, for those on duty slept in the Privy Chamber, and this must be made ready for the time when the King would enter it. It was the business of the Grooms of the Privy Chamber to take away the Gentlemen's pallets, to make up the fire, to 'dress and straw the Chamber, purging and making clean the same' against the King's coming. When awakened, the Gentlemen were dressed by the Pages of the Privy Chamber, nor must their own servants approach any nearer than the door, but there should hand over their masters' clothes to the Pages. If any of the Gentlemen slept on through all this activity, they must, when at last awakened, 'depart out of the King's Chamber in their night gowns' (i.e. dressing-gowns) so that 'by their long lying in bed the dressing of the King's Chamber be in no wise letted'.[31]

It is from the Courtesy Books that we learn the routine of the Gentleman's duty in the Bed Chamber. If it was winter he warmed the King's linen at the fire (and it must not be a smoking fire), set ready chair and cushion before it with a second cushion for the feet, and a 'foot sheet' over all. He prepared clean water, comb, and a kerchief to lay over the shoulders when he combed the King's hair. The King's clothes, clean and well brushed, were handed to the Gentleman by the Grooms of the Privy Chamber, and by him to the King. The Household Ordinances warn the Grooms that none shall presume 'to lay hands upon [the King's] royal person, or inter-meddle with preparing or dressing the same . . . except it be to warm clothes or to hand these to the Gentleman; both Grooms and Ushers must keep convenient distance from the King's person, not too homely or bold advancing of themselves'.[32]

Other exhortations are to be found in these 'Ordinances', which use a high moral tone when speaking of the behaviour which should be found among all those who served in the King's Privy Chamber. These should be 'loving together'; they must not tattle about 'such things as shall be done or said' there; when the King goes out they remain on duty, and must 'leave hearkening and enquiring where the King is or goeth . . . not grudgeing mumbling or talking of the King's pastime, late or early going to bed, or anything done by his Grace'. While they idled away the hours in the King's absence they are not to use 'immoderate and continual play, or dice, cards or tables'. If they must play high, there was 'the Groom Porter's house' where, for some reason, 'immoderate play' was not forbidden.[33]

When bed-time drew near again there was the function of making the King's bed. A Groom or Page of the Chamber, bearing a torch, went to fetch a Gentleman Usher and four Yeomen of the Chamber, lighting them to the Wardrobe of Beds, and back again with their load of bedding, to the King's Chamber. Then, spreading out 'the stuff of the King his bed upon a fair sheet', they got to work, the Groom standing at the foot of the bed with his torch, the Gentleman Usher a little apart to give directions, two Yeomen on each side to make the bed. First one of the Yeomen must prod the straw palliasse with a dagger; then, when the feather-bed was laid above it, another must 'tumble over it for the search thereof'. After that, bed-making proceeded much as it does today, with bolster, 'fustians', sheets, and 'two little small pillows', until it came to the final touches, when the Yeomen each made a cross, and kissed the place where their hands touched the bed. Then, when the curtains were drawn and the King's sword set up at the bed-head, the work was done, and each man might go off to draw his 'livery' from the buttery and pantry, a loaf of bread, 'a pot with ale, a pot with wine'.[34]

This, the last livery of the day, was known as 'the livery for All Night', and was served, at the warning cry of the Usher–'Have in for All Night! Have in Sirs!'–to all who had the right to Bouche of Court.

In the King's Bed Chamber a Gentleman prepared 'the Cupboard', laying it with cloth, basin, ewer, candle and towel, as well as the 'livery for All Night'. He tended the fire, set clean water ready, turned down the bed, and warmed 'the night kerchief'. When he had helped the King to undress, laying the discarded clothes over his own shoulder, had combed the King's hair, put on his kerchief and cap, and seen him to bed, he must draw the curtains, set in place the light that should burn all night, and having driven out all cats and dogs, bow, and withdraw in a seemly silence.[35]

So with the Huntsmen up in America, the Palace might fall asleep, with only the 'Wayte' to prowl about it, who 'nightly from Michaelmas to Shere-Thursday pipeth the watch within this Court 4 times, and in summer 3 times; and he to make bon gayte . . . as well for fire as for other pickers or perils'.[36]

Beyond the world of the Court lay all the lonely miles of the half-tamed country. To a Frenchman the English countryside appeared to be set so thick

with trees that 'in travelling you seemed to be in one continued wood'.[37]
Ill-kept, almost unkept roads straggled through these encroaching woods,
through heath and marsh, to emerge among the age-old open fields and
commons about the villages, and to run for a little between the hedges or
park-pales of newly enclosed lands. The village, except for church and manor-
house, was a collection of thatched small cottages, mostly of wattle and daub
– 'the English build their houses of sticks and dirt', said the Spaniards
scornfully.[38]

To these villages, buried deep in woodland or waste, news came slowly and
by snatches. A tramping sailor, an abbey bailiff riding on his rounds, a pedlar,
would bring word of the King's doings, of the Spaniards, or of the French.
Soon such wandering Protestant preachers as that elusive person who passed
under the alias of 'Trudgeover' would be bringing other matters of high
explosive nature, the Gospels Englished, or ballads and broad-sheets against
the Pope, monks and bishops; stuff to set the thoughtful, the restless, the
perverse to debating upon the alehouse bench beside the village green.

Less dangerous diversions there were in plenty among those country
customs that went far back beyond the memory of man, to the times when,
perhaps, a circle of tall stones stood in the place of the parish church. On
May Day or Whitsunday the women and children would go out by night
'some to the woods and groves, some to the hills and mountains . . . where
they spend all the night in pleasant pastimes, and in the morning they return,
bringing with them birch boughs and branches of trees' and as well, drawn
along by 'twenty or forty yoke of oxen, every ox having a sweet nosegay of
flowers tied on the top of his horns' the maypole, covered with flowers and
green leaves, 'bound round about with strings from the top to the bottom,
and sometimes painted with variable colours'.[39] When it was set up, decked
with flags and streamers, and saluted with dancing and music, the pleasant
summer had begun. Besides this early summer festival there were rejoicings
after sheep-shearing and at harvest home, when 'a garland of flowers crowned
the captain of the reapers' and the last load came home decked likewise with
flowers, and with a load of singing men and women on top.

Every Sunday too – a pause in the hard, unremitting labour of field and
house – the village turned out after Mass was over to enjoy itself. Long after
the Latin had been replaced by the English liturgy this custom continued, and,
as George Baxter complained, 'the rest of the day even till dark night almost,
except eating time, was spent in dancing under the maypole, and a great tree
not far from my father's door. . . . One of my father's own tenants was the
piper', and great and unwelcome to Baxter, that man of the new Puritan
England, was 'the disturbance of the tabor and pipe, and noise in the street'.[40]

Other intermittent diversions came with the neighbouring weekly market,
or, for those villages round about, with one of those great seasonal fairs, to
which the officers of large households came from far and near, to buy wine,
wax, beef, mutton, wheat, salt, and at which was sold also much strong ale to
fuddle country heads: 'Huffe cap' men called it, 'mad dog' or 'dragon's

milk'. Along the roads, when the fair closed, might be seen droves of cattle, horses laden with salt fish, and a great hue and cry as local pinders on the way took part in 'helping to keep . . . hogs from the corn as they drove thorowe the fields'.[41]

So, between long hours of labour, and nights spent on straw with a good round log for a pillow; under the shadow of death and, worse still, of sickness unrelieved by anything but the crudest medical science; in great discomfort and many fears; in the midst of beauty untouched by any ugliness save that of dirt, disease or death, the common people passed their lives.

But in England it was not only the common people who lived in the country. Already the English gentleman, to the surprise of the foreigner, and especially of the town-bred Italian, was a country gentleman, and, if he did spend part of the year at Court, longed for such country sights as that of 'the young rabbits that in a sunny morning sit washing their faces', or for the flowers which we may be sure he loved with as much tenderness, though inarticulately, as did the poets of his age.

It was in stone-built, moated houses, dark and cramped by the necessities of defence, that the gentlemen of the fifteenth century had lived. At the beginning of the new century, though houses were no longer built with an eye to war, yet the general plan did not change. The buildings surrounded a court, or, if the house were a great one, a series of courts. Forming, almost universally, one side of the chief of these, stood the Hall, entered from the courtyard by a door which led into a passage between the Hall itself and the kitchen offices, in the manner still preserved in use by Oxford and Cambridge Colleges.

All this was traditional. Only in the details of decoration, in terra-cotta medallions and classical ornaments applied to Gothic tower or gateway, did houses of the period show that English builders were beginning to look to alien models. Here alone the signs are to be seen of the new age when building in England would not be a thing native and natural as the whitethorn in the pastures, but an art to be learned from books.

But whether it were a house entirely of the old, or showing traces of the new age, round about it were to be found all the buildings of a farm of today and many more beside. For, as well as barns, stables, shippens and dairy there must be a brew-house, a malting house, a slaughter-house, wood-yard, and saw-pit; shops for blacksmith, carpenter and painter; and, standing stalwart in the midst, the old traditional dovecote. Tools, food, drink and clothes were made at home. Now and then a travelling cobbler or tailor would arrive on his rounds, stay for a while working in the house, and then depart. But all the time the manor-house must provide its own grain, and bake its own bread; fatten, slaughter and salt down for winter eating its own cattle; brew its own beer, make its own medicines and country wines, its jams, its carts, ink, furniture and candles.

In Mary Tudor's childhood there were many villages which had, instead of a manor-house, a monastery as its Great House, and monks and nuns, in those days as ordinary as eggs and bacon, and seemingly as little likely to disappear out of England, for neighbours and landlords.

After a thousand years, the first enthusiasm and devotion of monasticism had, except among a few of the Orders, been largely transmuted into qualities not widely removed from those of respectable but humdrum secular life. For good living, the proverb ran, take hunters' breakfast, lawyers' dinner, and the drinking of monks. In spite of the highly coloured reports produced by such tendencious Visitors as Legh and Layton, it is probable that most monks passed comfortable, peaceful, and harmless lives, enjoying the simple and robust pleasures of other English countrymen, and that monastic life, in its sheltered ease and corporate selfishness may have closely resembled that of Oxford and Cambridge Senior Common Rooms before the strenuous and conscientious reformers of the nineteenth century had done their work.

With dwindling enthusiasm went dwindling numbers, and in many abbeys only a handful of monks inhabited the great buildings of an earlier day. Nor were all rich, for the Visitation which preceded their dissolution found many whose revenues were pitifully small and finances sorely confused and embarrassed. But, as Robert Aske said, having in his mind, doubtless, great and noble churches of which now not one stone remains upon another—'the abbeys was one of the beauties of this realm to all men passing through the same'. Nor was the beauty only that contrived by generations of master-masons and their men, of pillar, arch and vault, carved capital and traceried window. Almost all monastic houses could boast of some costly example of goldsmith's craft, in gilt or jewelled chalice, or cross, or reliquary. In the greater abbeys, and particularly in those which were centres of pilgrimage, there were to be seen treasures of almost unimaginable splendour which the Prior would point out to distinguished visitors, touching each jewel with the tip of a white wand as he told its name, its value, its donor. Edward the Confessor's shrine seemed to a travelled Italian as rich or richer than that ancient and famous shrine of St. Martin at Tours. If the Confessor's was splendid, the shrine at Canterbury 'surpassed all belief', being covered, huge though it was, with plates of pure gold, and these again 'scarcely visible for the variety of precious stones with which it is studded, such as sapphires, diamonds, rubies, balas rubies and emeralds . . . but everything is left far behind by a ruby, not larger than a man's thumb which is set to the right of the altar. The church is rather dark, particularly where the shrine is placed, and when we went to see it the sun was nearly gone down, and the weather was cloudy, yet I saw that ruby as well as if I had it in my hand.'[42] The ruby, 'the Regal of France' was its name, had been the gift of Louis VII to the shrine of St. Thomas à Becket, that 'turbulent priest' for whose death Henry II had done public penance. Soon the shrine would be desecrated and torn down, and the jewel would shine in the thumb-ring of another King Henry, who had avenged, and more than avenged, his predecessor's defeat.

To the simple countryman London, if he came there, must have seemed a marvel. A city rising beside the long curve of the great river, with green banks beyond, and on the clear stream flocks of tame swans sailing unconcerned among the painted barges of the great, and the smaller wherries which plied for hire–London was a beautiful city to approach from the Kent shore. London Bridge, that strange monster, was built above twenty arches of squared stone, was lined with shops on each side, and had its own particular officers and warders whose duty it was to oversee the structure.

Once across the bridge the countryman was close to the Tower, still the key to London, still on occasions a palace, and always a prison, looking down over the river at its feet and the ships, gay ships painted and carved at bows and poop, that would set all their coloured sails and pennants to the sound of drums and trumpets. To the left and ahead lay the tangled narrow streets of the city, houses of the great merchants and nobles with their gardens, monasteries enclosed within walls, booths with the blue-capped apprentices at the open counter, all cheek by jowl after a history of a thousand years. Here would be a fine stone house that had once belonged to the Black Prince, now an alehouse, there a new palace was rising for the accommodation of the Emperor Charles on his approaching visit; soon there would be new houses of noblemen built on the site of this or that house of monks, friars or nuns; and stones from their churches would be going cheap–6d. or 7d. a load, carriage paid to the door.[43]

Except for the beauty of its position, foreigners, especially Italians, did not greatly admire London, since they considered that the English cared little in their building for anything but their own convenience, so that the outside was all anyhow, whatever might be the comfort inside. It was not often that men built as Thomas Wood, goldsmith, had built in 1491 that range of houses upon Cheapside which was called Goldsmiths' Row, and which was still for Stow a century later 'the most beautiful frame of fair houses and shops in England', ten houses and fourteen shops 'all in one frame, uniformly builded four storeys high' with the arms of the Goldsmiths' Company and the likeness of woodmen riding on monstrous beasts, all cast in lead, and painted and gilt.[44] For the most part the humbler houses, stone-built often in the lower storey and timbered above, were content for adornment with a coat of whitewash.

And if the Italian visitors decried the outward appearance of the Londoner's house, that great Dutchman, the scholar Erasmus, left a harrowing description of the accumulated dirt and stench inside. Windows, by now for the most part glazed, were not made to open, and even if all that he said were not generally true, enough is corroborated from other sources to explain the prevalence of epidemics. Outside the streets were filthy underfoot with refuse; as an easy, though only partial remedy, flocks of birds were allowed to breed undisturbed in order that they might reduce the piles of offal thrown out by householders; the kites were so tame and bold that they would sometimes snatch the children's butties out of their hands.[45]

But if the town were foul, it was gay. Even the scourer of the palace sinks received, as part of his yearly pay, a scarlet coat.[46] Even a funeral, if the dead man had been rich, was a show of colour, light and sound, with its priests, heralds, and escutcheons of arms, its standards, banners, and bannerets, its dozens of burning torches, its poor men in procession carrying white staves, its singing clerks and choristers. And besides being a show, a funeral was a feast. Master Henry Machyn–an undertaker himself–records meticulously every considerable funeral in London, and, as though with a sigh of satisfaction, concludes each account alike–'and there was a great dinner, and a great dole'.[47]

Feasts of the Church meant more processions, more candles and crosses, more singing in the streets. Sermons at Paul's Cross in Easter week brought the Lord Mayor and aldermen in scarlet or violet liveries. If your business took you by the Cathedral on either of the two feasts of St. Paul, you could loiter and watch the forester who brought in to the Canons the old bequest of a buck, listening while he 'blowed the death of the Buck, and then the horners that were about the city presently answered him in like manner'. Meanwhile within the great church, the Dean and Chapter, in vestments embroidered with a pattern of running deer, and, if it were the summer festival, wearing garlands of roses, received the dead beast, sent it to the kitchen to be cooked, and, after, went about in procession with the antlered head borne on high before the cross.[48]

In addition to all these amusements, there was the stir, bustle, and display that was in London when the King came to one of his palaces. Then the Earl of Oxford would ride in 'to his house by London Stone with 80 gentlemen in livery of Reading Tawney and chains of gold before him; 100 yeomen in the same livery without chains after, all having the blue boar embroidered on the shoulder'; or yeomen of the upstart Cromwell would swagger by, the skirts of their coat, 'made of very good cloth . . . large enough for their friends to sit on them';[49] or ladies of the Court might rattle past in a carriage 'fringed with red silk, and lined with red buckram, painted with red colours, collars and draughts of red leather', and hammer-cloths with the royal arms and badges.[50] Or, outdoing all in splendour during his day, there was Wolsey, the Cardinal, magnificent in scarlet or fine crimson taffeta, with his red gloves and hat, his shoes of silver and gilt set with pearls and precious stones.[51]

From the splendour of these chance displays can be guessed something of what could be done when men of that age of magnificence and pageantry set out to stage a show. Royal marriages, or coronations were opportunities never missed; these failing, there was always the Christmas feast, for the revelries of which young nobles about Court anxiously devised their costumes, conferring weeks beforehand by letter, and in the letter enclosing, perhaps, a pattern of a blue velvet 'which hath a kind of powdered ermines on it'; mightily earnest about the whole frivolity.[52] On one of the twelve days of Christmas down would come the King's Lord of Misrule from Greenwich to the city, and many young knights with him, a riot of yellow and green, to

the accompaniment of 'guns and squibs, trumpets, bagpipes and flutes' to
broach a hogshead of wine, and, after morris dancing, to dine with the Lord
Mayor.[53]

A crowded, noisy, bustling town it was, yet childishly small to us, the only
thing in it like to our London, those glimpses of the river, seen down every
narrow southward-running street from St. Paul's to Charing Cross. But
in London of the sixteenth century, besides those constant glimpses of the
river and the ships, you could not go far without seeing the tree-tops in the
gardens. Nor indeed was any part of London far from country sights and
sounds. A great deal–a shocking great deal–of building was noted by that
observant man, Master John Stow, during his lifetime; but in the earlier
part of the century fields and farms were close to the doors of Londoners.
Stow could remember how, when he was a boy, he would be sent to a farm
of the St. Clare sisters just outside Aldgate, to bring back milk 'hot from
the kine'. He remembered too the country-like pastimes in the streets of a
holiday evening; when the 'prentices used to fight with 'wasters and bucklers'
outside their master's door, 'and the maidens, one of them playing on a
timbrel, in sight of their Masters and Dames, to dance for garlands hung
thwart the streets'.[54] On Midsummer Eve, and St. Peter and Paul's Eve 'every
man's door being shadowed with green birch, long fennel, St. John's wort,
orpine, white lilies', and trimmed with garlands, 'had also lamps of glass with
oil burning in them all night'.[55] Londoners were in fact in those days only
countrymen living in town, and, like the villagers, had their own maypole,
set up yearly, until the 'evil May Day' of 1517, at the top of Cornhill, and
laid by again under a penthouse roof along the wall of a row of houses near
the church of St. Andrew, named for its sake 'St. Andrew Undershaft'.
Along the banks of the town ditch, that ran close to where now the trains
rumble into Holborn Viaduct Station, anglers sat on summer evenings, and
caught good fish there too; 'as many men yet living' Stow declared 'who
have taken and tasted them, can well witness'.

Yet it was in this century that London took one more step towards
becoming a great town, and to judge from Master Stow's regretful tone,
that step was a long one. For Stow could recall the loss of such pleasant
places as the 'large highway with fair elm trees on both sides' that he saw
built over even as far as Limehouse; or the common field at Aldgate so taken
up 'by building of filthy cottages' that there was no 'fair, pleasant and wholesome way for people to walk on foot, which is no small blemish to so famous
a city to have so unsavory and unseemly an entry thereunto'. Another of
Stow's laments finds a curious echo today, for he thought the streets of
London abominably crowded, noisy, and dangerous by reason of the
coaches, which 'are now made so common, as there is no distinction of time
nor difference of people observed; for the world runs on wheels with many,
whose parents were glad to go on foot'. Already London was being fed by
the counties round about, so that an Essex farmer's wife 'twice or thrice a
week conveyeth to London milk, butter, cheese, apples, pears, frumenty,

hens, chickens, eggs, bacon, and a thousand other country drugs, which a good housewife can frame and find to get a penny';[56] and, early in the mornings, the long carts of the bakers of Stratford le Bowe would jolt in, with their cargo of fresh loaves.

The extravagance of Englishmen, and their hearty appetites, especially for meat, were already proverbial. In times of prosperity 'you may commonly see artizans such as hatters and joiners, play at tennis for a crown ... and continually feasting in a tavern on rabbits and hares'.[57] When a citizen of London spent an evening out, supping with friends at Henley on Thames, the vast meal, enlivened by '12 wessells ... and maidens singing with them wessells', concluded with dishes of spices and fruit 'as marmalade, ginger bread, jelly, comfits, sugar plate'.[58] That same worthy citizen, Henry Machyn, the undertaker, recorded another feast in his diary–surely on the night itself and not on the morning after–how, he 'Monser the Machyn de Henry' had, with other cronies, devoured ½ bushel of oysters in Mr. Gitton's cellar, eating them from the tops of hogsheads, by candlelight, with a relish of onions, and draughts of red ale and claret ale.[59]

To wash down these meals, that mingled so strangely sweet things and savoury and masked all tastes under the flavour of spices, the ordinary drink, for King as for ploughman, was beer. Wine indeed came, along with such strange fruits as oranges and lemons, in the holds of merchantmen from Spain, France, Italy and Cyprus. But foreigners found the English sparing in their offers of wine, even if wine were served. Beer was always in plenty. Good country housewives brewed it every month, 'yellow as the gold noble, as our pot-knights call it', and this home-brewed would serve at 'hock carts, may poles, wassails, wakes', or at village bride-ales, where the goodman of the house needed to provide only 'bread, drink, salt, house-room and fire', since each of the guests who came tramping in from farms and lonely cottages would bring with him a dish of his wife's making, to furnish the feast.

As for its people, England, with its woods and rivers, its abundance of flocks and herds, was, to one exasperated foreigner, 'a Paradise inhabited by devils'.[60] Convinced, as Englishmen always are, 'that there are no other men but themselves, and no other world but England',[61] the untravelled, unlettered English gentleman of the early sixteenth century was an aggressive, unmannerly fellow, haughty and quarrelsome with foreigners, even though an Italian ambassador might find the great nobles perfectly polite. As for the poor commons–'the people of England is more given to idle gluttony than any people in the world', says Reginald Pole in Starkey's *Dialogue*. Laziness was a congenital sin. The French, when they were planning the attack on Calais, reckoned on the known English aversion to winter campaigns. An Italian noticed that there was hardly a peasant who did not manage somehow to raise a mount, 'and miserable must that man be who follows his cart on foot'.[62]

In appearance Englishmen were all, both nobles and commons, to the view of the stranger, big, ruddy, and handsome. The women, for the most part 'the greatest beauties of the world, and as fair as alabaster',[63] shocked aliens by the length of black stocking which they casually displayed on horseback and afoot, and even more by their free ways. It was English fashion for a woman to greet by a kiss any man she knew passably well. Ladies of rank, instead of travelling sedately in carriages, preferred to ride, with their women and footmen going before and behind. These same ladies thought nothing of dining in taverns with a friend, even if that friend was a foreigner; and it annoyed an Italian to see that should the husband come into the same tavern and find his wife in such compromising company, 'Not only does he not take it amiss, but will shake hands, . . . returning thanks for the invitation to his wife.' So staggering an indifference to propriety was hard to account for, but then the English 'have no idea of the point of honour. When they do fight it is from some caprice, and after exchanging two or three stabs with a knife, even when they wound each other, they will make peace instantly, and go away and drink together.'[64]

This casual, almost slovenly good humour, this easiness of temper, did not however extend very far. When hard times came with the growing economic changes of the century, with enclosures, rising rents, and rising prices, with the King's wanton debasement of the coinage, English character showed at its worst. Undisciplined, greedy, and selfish, the nobles preyed upon the poor; poor men repaid the treatment with bitter hatred. The great religious upheaval of the new century shattered the old conventions of behaviour, and when they were gone the hardness of men's hearts was apparent. 'Faith, not works', was a convenient cry for the selfish or miserly. 'These decaying times of Charity' Stow calls his age–an age in which King and nobles had conspired to snatch the goods and revenue, not only of abbeys, but of hospitals, alms-houses, schools. Very truly there was one law for the rich and another for the poor. 'Thousands in England,' cried Bernard Gilpin, 'Thousands do beg from door to door who once kept honest houses. They come to London . . . seeking for justice, but they find not justice. They cannot get speech of the great men to whom they are suitors, because they cannot find money to bribe their servants. Barabbas was a notable thief, says St. Matthew, a gentleman thief, such as rob nowadays in velvet coats. There were two other thieves when Christ suffered; but they were little thieves, like those that steal from necessity nowadays. The rustical thieves were hanged, and Barabbas was delivered.'[65]

If such was the Englishman's character in his social relations, politically he was, by the common consent of Europe, a man fickle and rebellious, always in and out of treason. Most gentle families had been involved at one time or another in unsuccessful treason. When an Italian idly inquired of an English acquaintance whether any of his kin had suffered death as a traitor, and received the answer–No–another Englishman, plucking the foreigner by the sleeve, whispered 'Don't be surprised. He is not a gentleman.'[66] The Tudor Princes had, in fact, a sinister history of kingship to look back upon. The deposition of Richard II was distant from Henry VIII's accession only

110 years. Men like Stow, who had heard their fathers remember to have seen Richard III as a young and comely prince, were removed only by one lifetime from those unquiet years when the saintly Lancastrian had been deposed, then murdered; the innocent Yorkist heir proclaimed King, and murdered; the usurping Richard crowned King only to fall in battle before his successful rival.

There was in Englishmen of that day a store of vehement but unused energy. England was a country in the trough of the wave, between crest and crest; the nation, remembering the days when the Crown of France had seemed hardly more than a mark for the arrows of the English archers, was ill-content with the second rank in which it found itself. A high-spirited people wounded in its pride and goaded by economic distress becomes an ugly tempered beast to ride. The England of Mary's reign was such a country, at odds with itself, its ruler, and its neighbours. It was necessary that English self-confidence should be restored, that the abounding vigour and daring of the nation should find an outlet, and the commercial genius of the people should be set to work; only then would the jarring interests be harmonized, the ill-temper of the people humoured, and in the new and unhoped for renaissance of Elizabeth's reign, out of the strong, sweetness come forth.

Chapter I

I T was April 1509 when the young Prince succeeded his father as Henry VIII, and his accession was, for England, like the coming of spring. To make joy complete it only needed that Katherine should bear a son. In 1510 her first child, a daughter, came into the world, stillborn. The King was cheerful, but the people thought it an ill omen; and they were right. During the next six years Katherine indeed bore four sons, but if they lived at all none survived longer than a few weeks.

At last, on February 18th 1516, at Greenwich Palace, a daughter was born, who did not die. They christened her at the Friar's Church there on the 21st carrying her down a lane enclosed with tapestry, to a little wooden pavilion, arras-covered also, where her god-parents waited. From there the Countess of Surrey bore her into the church under an embroidered canopy, in the midst of a procession of the greatest lords of England. In the church, hung with needlework in which jewels glinted and pearls gleamed, stood the silver font brought for this christening from Canterbury. The child, baptized with the name of Mary, was afterwards confirmed, the *Te Deum* was sung, and the little girl's title proclaimed to the sound of the heralds' trumpets.[1]

When Mary was born her father was twenty-five, and her mother thirty-one. Henry, excelling at all sports, playing tennis to the admiration of on-lookers, hurling himself with a fen-man's pole over ditches after his hawks, wrestling, singing, dancing, dicing with his courtiers, seemed still to care for nothing but for spending his father's hoarded wealth. He would get up at four or five in the morning, and hunt till ten at night, sparing no pains, as Pace ruefully said, 'to convert the sport . . . into a martyrdom'. At Court, and the Court was the one centre of all polite society, he set the fashion and led the revelry. If the King hurt his foot and could wear nothing straiter than a velvet slipper, all the gentlemen of the Court came out in velvet slippers too. When Cardinal Wolsey gave a masked dance to celebrate a treaty with France, 'after supper . . . twelve male and female dancers made their appearance in the richest and most sumptuous array possible, being all dressed alike . . . They were disguised in one suit of fine green satin, all over-covered with cloth of gold, under tied together with laces of gold, and had masking hoods on their heads; the ladies had tires made of braids of damask gold, with long hairs of white gold. All these maskers danced at one time, and after they had danced they put off their visors, and then were they all known.' The leader of the men was the King, of the women the Queen Dowager of France, Henry's sister Mary, whom the French called 'la reine blanche', and of whom a sober Fleming said, 'I think never man saw a more beautiful woman, nor one having such grace and sweetness.'

Whatever Henry did he must do strenuously. When a royal ship was to be launched, he himself acted as pilot, in a sailor's coat and trousers of cloth of gold, and a gold chain with the inscription 'Dieu et mon Droit' on which hung a whistle, 'which he blew as loud as a trumpet'. Not that, even in these first years of gaiety, he cared only for pleasure; ships always seriously interested him; he was devout in his attendance at Mass, and a question in theology immediately caught and held his attention; there is something of comedy in the thought of Henry, studiously bent over his refutation of Luther; while Thomas Wolsey, Cardinal of England, conducted affairs of state.

The Court was by no means that of a magnificent pleasure-seeker. Henry was far too truly a child of his age for that. Erasmus said that it was more like a home of the Muses than a Court. Erudition in Kings was the fashion, but it was for Henry a sincere pleasure too, and on this side of his interests his wife could join more easily than in his more frivolous pursuits. She, who had spent most of her childhood in Granada, knew at least as well as Henry what refinement could be. Her nephew Charles, after 1520 Emperor of the Holy Roman Empire, lord also of the riches of the New World, was a potentate of immeasurably greater wealth and state than the King of this small island. Englishmen had perhaps never yet come so close to those new lands of wonder as they did when they saw the presents that the Treasurer General of the Indies sent to the Queen–a gown such as the Indian caciques wore on great festivals, and a saddle which a cacique's wife would ride on; he would have sent parrots, too, but he feared that they would not, in winter, endure the change of climate.[2]

Katherine had been well educated, and scholars considered that the King of England had a worthy wife. They were right, but, gracious, amiable, and dignified as she was, she was ill matched with the splendid King. Older than he by six years, plain in face, short and heavy in figure, a stout little woman as time passed, she would have found it hard in any case to keep the King constant. But she did not even take care to make the best of herself, lacking as she did all her husband's and daughter's love of fine clothes. Rising at midnight for Matins, she would dress for the day 'with what haste she might, saying that the time was lost which was spent in apparelling herself'.[3] So high-minded an indifference was counted unto her for righteousness, but it was not the way to hold the fancy of a man like Henry.

Such were the parents of the child who was to be Queen of England, and through whom Mary inherited mind and temper. Little of her indeed was her father's. From the King, vain, lustful, merciless and masterful, yet with that magic touch of personality that made men like Gardiner love him as Elizabeth's servants loved her, Mary inherited perhaps nothing more than a quick temper, a high courage, imperiousness, and a passion for jewels and gay clothes. From her mother she drew far more. Katherine was the daughter of those Spanish kings who, by blood and steel, had defended Christianity against Mahomet; who had, step by step, carried forward the banner of their belief till Spain was a Christian land from the Pyrenees to the Rock. Unwavering belief and a bitter courage were the two halves of the spirit that had brought them through the struggle; a spirit that knew no compromise, that was as willing to die as to kill for the Cross against the Crescent. With her capacity, for patient, untiring affection, her unquestioned purity, her piety, Katherine had that same union of inexorable courage, and unquestioning loyalty to a creed. Along with her mother's gentler qualities Mary inherited it too.

Whatever might lie in the future, at present all was fair weather for the Princess and her mother. Although the longed for heir was a daughter, Henry took it so cheerfully that Katherine thanked God for giving her such a husband. Henry, always fond of children, took pleasure in showing off the little thing to visitors, carrying her about the room in his arms and bragging, as any father might–although in Latin–'Per Deum immortalem ista puella nunquam plorat–this girl never cries'.[4] The Venetian ambassador Giustinian, waiting upon the King one Sunday with Cardinal Wolsey, was presented to her, a child of two, and solemnly kissed her small hand. The rest of the interview was less formal, and reads indeed much like the account of a Sunday afternoon visit to any family when a baby is present. One of the company there was Master Dionysius Memo, the Venetian priest who was Henry's chaplain and choir-master. Catching sight of him the child began to clamour 'Priest! Priest!' and would not be satisfied till Memo had come near, and played for her. Afterwards Henry, holding his small daughter in his arms, stood chatting with Giustinian in polite Latin. 'By God! that is an excellent fellow, and one we value highly', he said of the musician.[5]

At two years old Mary undertook for the first time one important duty of female royalty–that of being betrothed. The bridegroom selected, the first of a very long series, was the little Dauphin, an infant even younger than Mary; indeed the marriage had been suggested before it was known whether the French royal child would be boy or girl. It was a boy, and in October Bonnivet, Francis I's personal friend and Admiral of France, came to the palace of Greenwich for the formal betrothal.

There in the Queen's great chamber, which was decorated with special magnificence, stood the King before the throne, the Queen beside him, and the tiny Princess, dressed in cloth of gold, her little cap of black velvet twinkling with jewels, in front of her mother. Bishop Tunstal, a man of forty-four who was to outlive the child, addressed to her a sermon upon the honourableness of the married state, and formal consent having been given and received on both sides, the child was lifted up, and Cardinal Wolsey set on her finger a small ring with a very big diamond.[6] She was now, for the time at least, the betrothed wife of the baby who lay in his cradle in France.

As such, the French took an interest in her. Next year, the Queen Mother of France was inquiring anxiously after her health. In the summer of 1520 three French gentlemen came to Richmond to visit the Princess, now four years old. She received them in the Presence Chamber, the Duchess of Norfolk, and her Governess the Countess of Salisbury attending her. She entertained the visitors 'with the most goodly countenance, proper communication and pleasant pastime in playing at the virginals, that they greatly marvelled and rejoiced at the same, her young and tender age considered'. When the little girl had played her piece and retired, the Frenchmen were regaled with a summer feast of 'strawberries, wafers, wine and hippocras in plenty'–in plenty certainly, for they drank four gallons of hippocras and the bill for the cherries they ate came to 7s. 4d., for old apples 2s., for wafers 5s. 3d., and for strawberries 10s.[7]

But already, and for some time, Mary's father had been considering for her the possibility of another bridegroom and a greater, her cousin, Charles V, a young man of nineteen, King of Spain, and from 1520 Emperor of the Holy Roman Empire. Charles, though contracted to a French princess, and considering marriage with a Portuguese, could not bear to see England brought to the side of France by a marriage alliance, for the brief friendship between Charles and his life-long rival Francis, sealed by the treaty of Noyon, was already waning. Henry and Wolsey were for their part only too pleased to be able to play two great fish, though the Emperor proved difficult to land.

It was impossible that the French should be unaware of the project, and Francis was already growing anxious about the English alliance, and must have been relieved when, in the summer of 1520, the day arrived on which Henry was to meet him at Ardres; all the more so because the Emperor had just paid a visit to England, and no one in France knew what had then been concluded, or even discussed. Henry and Francis met, but from that meeting at Ardres, from the splendour of the Field of the Cloth of Gold, from the glass pavilion hung with white satin, and all the rest of that ruinous and lovely display, Henry went to Gravelines to meet again Francis's great rival, and at Calais Chièvres made a formal proposal that Henry should drop the Dauphin and take up Charles as a suitor for Mary.

From that time the bargaining went on seriously though secretly, while to keep up appearances to France, Henry with affectionate candour, informed Francis that Charles had twice made offers for the marriage of Mary, but he, so he said, would not hear of it. In the same spirit Francis replied that he did not for the moment believe the rumour and added that 'he had liever have my lady Princess . . . than the King of Portugal's daughter, with all the spice her father hath'.

Only two months after this, however, Wolsey was commissioned to treat finally of the marriage with the Emperor's envoys. But, though he thought Charles's ambassadors to be 'marvellously desirous of it', they were not so eager as to be anything but hard bargainers. But at last after 'many difficulties and much difficulties' and a last four or five hours of debate, it was agreed that Mary should be handed over when 'of perfect age' and with a dowry which was to be increased if Henry should have another heir. On August 25th, 1521, the treaty was signed, Mary was to be the bride of Charles, and in two years' time the King and his son-in-law to be should declare war on France.

Next June the Emperor came to England to visit his betrothed and to conclude with her father the treaty of Windsor. This time the two affianced parties, the child of six and the quiet slow young man of twenty-two, with the heavy chin and very intelligent eyes, met at Greenwich, and again, when the Emperor was about to leave, at Windsor. Mary's mother had sent for her to say farewell to her betrothed; Charles was, when older, a kindly man with children, and perhaps even now he managed to make the little girl fond of him, so that she remembered him with affection and confidence all her life.

The Emperor had not been gone six months when rumours began to get abroad that a new bridegroom had been found for Mary–this time it was to be James V of Scotland. To Charles the English denied the rumour strenuously as a great lie, but next year Scots lords came from the Dowager Queen Margaret to her brother's Court to propose that marriage, which, though so much less magnificent than either the French or the Imperial, had yet its attractions. Henry seemed to be willing. The English ambassadors were instructed to tell Margaret, but as a great secret, that the King intended to break off the Imperial match, and give Mary to James. They also carried presents for the young King–a coat of cloth of gold and a sword. James was delighted with both; he put them on at once and wore them all afternoon.

But though in November 1521 James and his mother actually sent commissioners to treat of the marriage, the plan hung fire. In Scotland only the Dowager Queen was in favour of it, and though Henry's ambassadors might do their best, they could not warm the Scots lords towards the marriage. Louise of Savoy too, the Queen Mother of France, did her best, in a confidential letter, to discourage Margaret, declaring that Henry would deal with Scotland as he had dealt with France and Spain.

She was right. Henry by no means intended so soon to make up his mind to any bridegroom. Sons and daughters were not only arrows in the quiver of a royal father, but also cards in his hand. Unplayed, they could be used again and again for a temporary advantage; once the child was married the card was lost, though a good dowry and a solid alliance might make the loss worth while. In addition to these considerations, there was for Henry another more weighty and more anxious. Mary was still his only heir. Giustinian believed that the solemn betrothal of the little Princess to the Dauphin would not have taken place in 1517, if Katherine had not been pregnant, and a male heir again hoped for. Above all things, he believed, Englishmen dreaded to have a Frenchman for their King; hating all foreigners, with the possible exception of their kinsmen the Netherlanders, they hated Frenchmen worst. Certainly Henry would think twice before he married his heir to any foreign prince. Not that he would neglect to show off his daughter's accomplishments to visiting ambassadors. In 1522 the Emperor's envoy, paying his respects to the Queen, was told that he must see the Princess dance. The child of six 'did not have to be asked twice . . . she twirled so prettily that no woman in the world could do better . . . then she played two or three songs on the spinet'. Two years later her father was boasting to another Imperial ambassador that she played better on the instrument than he did, and was beginning to learn the lute.[8] But it was a long time yet before a final decision need be so much as thought of.

At the beginning of 1525 there was fresh talk of a French marriage, though Tunstal and Wingfield were ordered to deny to the Emperor that Henry had breathed a word on the subject, either to France or to Scotland. But in this year, which saw the crushing defeat of Pavia and the capture and imprisonment of Francis I, Henry's affection for Charles suddenly flagged. The Emperor, swollen by his rival's downfall, was over-mighty for Henry's taste; a complete break would not be safe, but Charles might be made to feel that England's friendship was not entirely uncritical. Let Charles, Henry coolly suggested, hand over to him the royal prisoner, meet him in Paris and see him crowned King of France; then Henry would at once deliver the Princess Mary to her bridegroom. This audacious suggestion was followed up by another reminder of a different nature. The English ambassador received a packet and orders to deliver it to the Emperor. It contained a ring, and a letter, both from the Princess; the ring was set with an emerald, a jewel which is known to prove the truth of lovers, for it changes at inconstancy; the letter declared that the Emperor's betrothed suffered much from jealousy, this 'being one of the greatest signs and tokens of hearty love and cordial affection'. Henry and his ministers were not so simple as to expect Charles to believe in the jealous pangs of a child of nine; the letter was rather a pretty device to hint to the Emperor that the child's father had got wind of his renewed negotiations for a Portuguese bride.[9] Still, for some time, with lessening cordiality, but perfect propriety, the two sovereigns played the game of prospective father-in-law to prospective son-in-law.

Charles came out into the open first, and let it be known that he had determined to marry Portugal. Henry had no great objection, but before formally relinquishing the Spanish match, he made an effort to get some profit out of it. If there was no hope of the Emperor marrying Mary, he might pay for not marrying her, could he be made to realize what Henry's complaisance cost in inconvenience and loss of prestige. So, when the Portuguese match had been made, the unfortunate English ambassador was instructed to try to wring from Charles some payment in lieu of the dowry promised to Mary. Neither the Emperor nor his Chancellor denied, in principle, that 'debt was debt between enemies'. But though the ambassador might movingly remind Charles that Henry had not pressed for the money till now, when, with the Portuguese dowry in his coffers, 'he floweth with money', all that the Emperor would say, when caught at a garden door was, 'Not yet', and the unhappy ambassador lamented 'that so I run in an endless circle, from one to another, without an answer'. There was, however, one compensation, as Tunstal pointed out, namely that Henry had, 'with much thank, the Princess in your hand, which is a pearl worth keeping'.[10]

Throughout all these vicissitudes there was perhaps no one at Court so totally unconcerned as the little girl whose future was being played with like a shuttlecock. What must have interested her far more than the distant and problematical bridegrooms, were her lessons, her companions, and her pleasures. Her lessons were copious and exacting, but such was the lot of every child of the age whose parents were cultivated, and Mary, intelligent enough, but not naturally a scholar, was never encouraged to acquire that immoderate load of learning which Renaissance parents so coveted for their young. Yet the child who could play on the virginals at the age of four, and write a Latin letter by the time she was nine, had made at least an early beginning. For her teachers she had good men, some of them noted scholars of the day. The Spanish Vives wrote, at Katherine's request, a scheme of education for her, while Linacre contributed a Rudimenta Grammatica. She was to read, Vives directed, Erasmus's secular works and More's *Utopia* to acquire a familiar Latin vocabulary, and to combine Latin with divinity in the Paraphrases of the Gospel by Erasmus; besides these she was to study the New Testament morning and evening. The Spaniard recommended that she should have fellow pupils, 'for it is not good to be taught alone'; so perhaps she shared with other small solemn girls the various lessons, and, as Vives advised, read over to herself when she went to bed anything which she had to learn by heart, as schoolgirls still do.[11] Besides the lessons in Latin and Greek, she learnt French, some Italian, though she never spoke it well, and Spanish, which she understood but did not speak. Apart from languages she learned to ride, dance, sing, and play upon lute and virginals; for music she had her father's natural bent.

Parents in the sixteenth century were not frequently indulgent. The harshness of Lady Jane Grey's parents is notorious. Vives himself thoroughly approved of the most rigid convention of severity. His own mother had been a stern, unbending parent; 'she never', he boasted, 'lightly laughed upon me, she never cockered me, and yet, when I had been three or four days out of the house, she wist not where, she was almost sure sick; and when I was come home, I could not perceive that ever she longed for me. Therefore there was nobody that I did more flee, or was more loath to come nigh, than my mother, when I was a child.' If such behaviour was desirable with sons, it was necessary for daughters; it was a wise man, Vives thought, who said, 'Never have the rod off a boy's back; specially the daughter should be handled without any cherishing. For cherishing marreth sons, but it utterly destroyeth daughters.'[12]

Yet in the sixteenth century, there were parents of another sort; among whom were William Cecil and his lady, whose little 'Tannikin' was evidently a person of so great importance that her welfare might forbid her parents a Christmas visit to an old friend; but, wheedled Sir Philip Hoby, 'I hope so to provide for her and her nurse as all the house shall be merry, and she notwithstanding at her own ease and quiet.'[13] Henry and Katherine were more like to these parents. Henry was an affectionate, teasing father, who would, even at a State Masque, pull off the little daughter's hood so that all her hair tumbled about her shoulders. Katherine too must have seemed, to the austere Spaniard, to be bent on 'destroying her daughter', for when Mary was nine, and away from her mother in the west, Katherine wrote a letter which plainly showed how she longed for the little girl.

'As for your writing, I am glad ye shall change from me to Master Fetherstone, for that shall do you much good to learn by him to write right but yet sometimes I would be glad when ye do write to Master Fetherstone, of your own inditing, when he hath read it, that I may see it, for it shall be great comfort to me to see you keep your Latin and fair writing and all.'[14]

There was no stern concealment of affection here, but the candid expression of a mother's desire to hear, in anything artless, quaint, or even incorrect, the little girl's own voice speaking in absence.

So it is likely that Mary's childhood passed pleasantly, sometimes in the splendour of the Court with a father who must have seemed to a little one a very wonderful person, and with a mother whose heart was divided between her magnificent husband and this one surviving child of theirs. When she was parted from her parents it was to experience the variety and interest of the constant journeys between palaces and manors, which were still the necessary routine of the royal household. The packing up, the start, the long cavalcade down the country lanes, the excitement of arrival–all must have been pleasant to a child. In October 1520 she moved from Ditton to Windsor, and in the same month to Hanworth, Martyn Abbey, Greenwich, and Eltham. In December she was back at Greenwich where the King kept Christmas, and where his Lord of Misrule got a New Year's tip of 20s. from the Princess. Next Christmas, Mary being nearly six years old, she spent at Ditton with her own household, and her own Lord of Misrule, John Thorogoode, one of her valets. For the Christmas jollities in her household there were careful preparations; painters had to gild the Boar's Head, parchment must be bought for 'subtleties', there must be ready two taborets, a man to play the Friar, another to play the Shipman, and a whole cargo of properties–'visors, coat armour, hats, gold foil, cony skins and tails for mummers, four dozen clattering staves, gunpowder, frankincense, ten dozen bells and nine dozen morris coats, straw to cover twelve men in a disguising', and–a gruesome and obscure entry in the accounts–'a man to kill a calf behind a cloth'.[15]

In the midst of the Twelve Days of Christmas came New Year with its gifts. On her first New Year's Day the Princess had received a gold mug, a pomander of gold, a gold spoon, and a primer, this last from the Duke of Norfolk. Lord Mountjoy gave two smocks, and 'a woman' some Queen apples.[16] Three years later Cardinal Wolsey repeated his gift of a gold cup, the Duke of Norfolk gave silver snuffers, Mistress Margaret, the child's nurse, presented what was probably much more appreciated a purse of 'tynsent satin'. But, of all the gifts that the Princess received, that of a poor woman of

Greenwich was calculated to please her most. For the woman brought 'rosemary bushes *cum spangillis de auro*'. [17] Golden spangles on a bush would go straight to the heart of any child of four.

In 1525, still her father's only legitimate heir, Mary was provided with a special household and Council, so that she might play her part as Princess of Wales. Ludlow Castle was repaired for her, and in August she set off for the Welsh Marches with her retinue of house servants, very brave in their new liveries of blue and green damask or cloth, and her gentlemen and ladies still finer in black velvet or damask.[18] After them rumbled a long train of wagons with all their household and personal stuff, such a miscellaneous assortment as –'3 brass pots, one brazen pestle and mortar; a frying pan and with a flesh hook . . . a chest with irons for keeping prisoners, a chest with three locks containing divers books of the extent of the lands of the Marches'.[19] Yet before next Christmas the President of Mary's Council was writing to the Cardinal for more. He wanted 'a ship of silver for an alms dish', spice plates, trumpets and a rebeck.[20]

Although Mary had left her mother, her life was still regulated by the same spirit of open affection and tender care that had always till now watched over it. Careful directions were given to her Council for her education. She was to learn, first of all, to serve God; after that, 'at seasons convenient, to use moderate exercise for taking open air in gardens, sweet and wholesome places and walks . . . and likewise to pass her time most seasons at her virginals or other instruments musical, so that the same be not too much, and without fatigation or weariness to intend to her learning the Latin tongue and French. At other seasons to dance, and among the residue to have good respect unto her diet, which is meet to be well prepared, dressed, and served with comfortable, joyous, and merry communication in all honourable and virtuous manner; and likewise unto the cleanliness and well wearing of her garments and apparel, so that everything about her be pure, sweet, clean, and wholesome.'[21]

Mary's life under such a scheme of education, carried out by her Lady Governess, the Countess of Salisbury, daughter of George, Duke of Clarence, a woman of royal blood and royal heart, could not fail to be happy. For a year or so longer, while the storm was brewing which was to wreck her girlhood and darken her whole life, she travelled pleasantly through the lovely Marches of Wales, from Ludlow to Tewkesbury, from Gloucester to Chester, with John, Bishop of Exeter as the President of her Council, Edward Lord Dudley her Chamberlain, and a full complement of household officers–chancellor, treasurer, receiver, steward, and the rest; but also, because though a princess she was still a very young one, with her schoolmaster, Master John Fetherstone. It was presumably too in these journeyings that she first enrolled in her household those men of Welsh and Cheshire names such as Rice, Dodd, and Wilbraham, who stayed with her so long.

Meanwhile, jilted as she had been by the Emperor, another match was under consideration for the Princess. This time she was to be given to the French

King, now a widower, a man older than her father and with a far worse
reputation for incontinence. Henry did indeed give Francis a hint that he
'would have him now become and wax a good man', but Francis took it, as
perhaps it was meant, for a joke, passing it on to Henry's ambassador Clerk,
'with many good and galliard words'.

Whether indeed either party was at this moment serious in their proposition is doubtful; it is more likely that each opened the matter merely to annoy
and disconcert Spain. For Francis, though freed from his captivity, had been
forced to give as hostages to Spain his two eldest sons, who now must do
their best to amuse themselves by playing with their dogs and scrawling
pictures on the walls of their dreary chamber in Madrid. Francis had passed
his oath that he would marry the Emperor's sister; an oath meant little enough
to him, but his boys meant much–he probably spoke near the truth when he
said that 'he would rather, than fail of his children, marry the Emperor's
mule'.[22] Even the threat that he might see Mary married 'in such place as he
would be loth to see her', did not shake him. When it came to the point of
committing himself, the most he would say was that he would send to demand
Eleanor, and, if she were refused, he would be free. But Clerk was sure that
he hoped and believed there would be no refusal; he had seen and liked
Eleanor in Spain, and besides, he wanted peace.

Yet Francis would not say no to England either, and sent envoys into England begging for Mary's portrait, so in January 1527 Henry, by the mouth of
the Bishop of Bath, declared his terms. He would give Mary, he would join
the league against the Emperor that Francis was trying to engineer in order
to recover his sons, and would forego his title to the crown of France. But
in return Francis must pay him a pension, grant him an annuity, and
give him Boulogne. To keep up appearances, and a little to elevate the
business above this cut-throat bargaining, Henry also sent his own and Mary's
portrait.

For some time yet Francis played with the proposition. In March came the
Bishop of Tarbes with the Vicomte de Turenne, and people thought it significant that the Princess was sent for to come to London at the same time. But,
in the discussions that followed, whenever the French advanced, the English
retreated. Probably, for all that the French just now showed themselves
accommodating, Henry had in mind the words which Francis was reported
to have spoken–'The King of England would have me take his daughter and
give him Boulogne. Nay! Nay!'[23]

In the midst of these negotiations, as if it were to remind the envoys that
there was a real princess hidden in the midst of the diplomatic maze, the
French were invited to Greenwich for the feast of St. George. After dinner
the King led them into the Hall and presented them to the Queen and
Princess. Henry, acting the part of the match-making parent, urged them to
speak to the little girl in French, Latin, and Italian. One of the Frenchmen,
judging by her answers, and by her playing of the virginals, thought her the
most accomplished child he had ever seen.[24]

In May there were more festivities, a great masque in the Queen's apartments, in the course of which Mary, with other ladies of the Court, was
discovered in a cloth of gold cave, guarded by gentlemen wearing tall plumes,
and carrying torches. Down from the cave, to the sound of trumpets, stepped
the Princess, hand in hand with the Marchioness of Exeter, her hair in a gold
net, a jewelled garland about her head and a velvet cap upon that. After some
dancing, the King, the Vicomte de Turenne and others came in, all masked in
gold, and black satin, and tawny velvet, to dance with them, and the revelry
lasted till the sun was up, and the May morning upon them. Turenne admired,
so he said, the looks and conversation of the child, but decided, flattery forgotten, that she was 'so thin, spare and small, as to make it impossible to be
married for the next three years'.[25]

In August the friendship between France and England was cemented by
the treaty of Amiens, which, though it spoke of perpetual peace, was to prove
as brittle a thing as any treaty might be. According to the terms of the treaty
Mary was to marry, if not Francis, then the young Duke of Orleans. This last
was an interesting conjunction of persons, for Henry of Orleans, though
none knew it yet, was to wear the crown of France and to be Mary's most
dangerous, indeed her fatal enemy. Yet the two young things were not, in
character, ill assorted, for there was in both something sober, pedestrian,
conscientious, and both belonged to a sadder generation than their magnificent fathers. But this marriage also came to nothing, for in England there
was a certain matter now afoot which made the value of Mary Tudor's hand
too uncertain for Francis to desire it either for himself or his son.

Chapter II

THE Venetian ambassador who had seen the baby Princess carried about in her father's arms, and who found himself expected to kiss her hand, felt it a little absurd that the child should receive more honour than her mother, the Queen. But he could not remember, as Englishmen of fifty could, the anxieties and apprehensions of that August, thirty odd years before, when Henry of Richmond had landed to dispute the crown; and if middle-aged men remembered those days, very old men could remember worse times still when the 'irregular hewing and jostling' of the opposing armies of the two Roses had shattered the peace of the countryside. It was because these memories were so fresh that England was hungry for an heir. After the King's marriage had been childless for so long, the birth of even a daughter was a huge relief; but as the daughter grew up, and no other children, male or female, followed her, fresh anxieties began to rankle in men's minds. The English crown had only once, since the White Ship went down, been the inheritance of a woman, and Matilda's disputed succession was no pleasant precedent to recall. In one way too, the outlook now was worse for the lords of the Council, and all the irascible gentlemen of England, than it had been for the English barons in the twelfth century. It stood to reason, it was in the nature of things, that a Queen could not remain single; she must marry in order to bear children, and it was usual for royalty to marry abroad. But Matilda's Angevin husband was hardly a stranger, and certainly no alien to the barons whose fathers had gathered like vultures against England from every part of France. Now, in the sixteenth century, the marriage of a Queen was a very different question. That hatred of foreigners, the muddy soil out of which grows at last the comely flower of patriotism, was in Englishmen the very ground of all their feelings. If the Princess married an alien, that alien would be King, and it was hard to imagine a King who did not rule. If, on the other hand, she married an Englishman, for the sake of her dignity he must be of royal blood, and the marriage would waken again the lapsed but never forgotten claims of the last representatives of the White Rose. This was England's problem, and Henry's problem. It was to be Mary's too, and her solution of it was the rock on which she split. The solution that Henry chose was even more catastrophic, but it was not his ship that foundered; it was the great, ancient, and venerable Ship of the Church in England.

Long before Wolsey, and others in the King's closest confidence, had begun to talk, behind shut doors or in garden walks safe from eavesdropping, of the 'secret matter' or the 'King's matter', as long ago as 1514, people in Rome were discussing a rumour that the King of England wished to leave his wife because she could bear him no living children. Mary's birth a year and

31

a half later had put the thought out of the public mind; out of Henry's too, if it had ever been there. He and his wife, he argued, were young; if it were a daughter this time it might well be a son next. But when, nine years later, the King had still no legitimate child but the one daughter, Henry gave up hope. Katherine was forty; after so many miscarriages, so many stillborn, or sickly children who died, it was not likely that she would ever bear the lusty thriving son that Henry needed.

But before he committed himself to that course of action which was to have such stupendous results, Henry, when Mary was nine years old, seemed to be inclining to a different solution. An illegitimate son, three years younger than Mary, borne to Henry by Elizabeth Blount, and called Henry Fitzroy, was in 1525 suddenly acknowledged, and as suddenly promoted to honour. Mary might be sent off to the Marches as Princess of Wales, but the boy was made Lord High Admiral, Lord Warden of the Marches, Lord Lieutenant of Ireland, and created Duke of Richmond and Duke of Somerset; the titles were of old and significant association among the Tudors. At the same time he was given a household greater than that of Mary. When Katherine protested, the King took no more notice than to dismiss three of her Spanish ladies as a lesson in wifely obedience, and began to discuss with the Council a still more startling project—that of entailing the Crown upon this bastard son.

Two years later, however, Henry had returned to the more conventional idea of divorce and remarriage, but though such a step was by no means new among Kings, the results in this case lay far beyond the guess of men. For by it Henry was to set in motion that train of circumstances which drove England out from her secure place in the port of the Catholic kingdoms, to the hazards and profits of the high seas of schism; which cost lives in hundreds, both in the action and reaction of the shock; which brought changes undreamed of into the ceremonies and constitution of the Church, into the smallest of its customs and the most esoteric of its dogmas, so that the ploughman on Sundays ceased to perform those ritual acts that his forefathers had for generations performed, while the theologian cast back for his authority to ideas so old that they seemed entirely new.

Henry sometimes maintained that a word spoken by the Bishop of Tarbes in the spring of 1527, when the marriage between Mary and Orleans was being discussed, had first wakened a doubt in his mind. At other times he was equally emphatic that a study of Leviticus had made him fear that the divine anger had been kindled against him by his marriage.[1] What he never for one moment admitted was that his growing passion for Mistress Anne Boleyn had any connexion with his scruples.

Until this time Henry had found no serious obstacles set in the way of that enormous energy of his that poured itself into the strenuous pleasures of the hunt, or laboured to achieve the nice contentments of the scholar, that flowered into music, dancing or games, or went gaily and wantonly to work to seduce complaisant women. But now he was to be opposed, and upon every hand. Even Anne Boleyn, the lively, witty girl of twenty, brought up at the French Court, endowed by nature with more than a little of the French vivacity and grace; a girl who could sing, dance, and play on the lute; a slight young thing with a mass of black hair, a slim long neck, and eyes that were 'black and beautiful' and 'invited to conversation'; Anne Boleyn, in looks a piquant contrast to Katherine with her stout, heavy figure, reddish hair, and plain resolute face, Anne Boleyn resisted him. It was marriage or nothing, for her. Henry fell deeper in love for that resistance; his letters to her, frankly sensual though they are, have yet a sincerity, an almost boyish ardour and simplicity, that partially redeems the sensuality, and makes somehow pitiful that headlong, illicit love.

Anne's decision, and England's need of an unquestionably legitimate prince, threw Henry back upon divorce as his only hope; and in this he was to find opposition from wife, daughter, nobles, and people, from Pope and Emperor, almost from all the world. This opposition called out all the volcanic forces of his character, taught him his own strength and his subjects his mercilessness.

It was in May 1527, the very month in which Henry received, with such splendid gaieties, the envoys who came from France to ask for his daughter's hand, that the King told Wolsey of his doubts about the validity of his marriage. Soon after, judicial proceedings began with a secret summons to the King to appear before Wolsey and Archbishop Warham to answer what the summons stated to be their doubts upon the subject. Such was the first move in that long legal battle which was to drag on for almost exactly six years.

In the early history of the divorce Mary had no active part, indeed hardly a part at all, and even when her time came to take a hand, her rôle was passive. But for the next nine years, that is until the death of her mother and Anne Boleyn, those critical years which saw her grow from child to woman, her whole life was keyed up to the tension of stubborn resistance. For some time she was neglected rather than persecuted, and the thing which must first have left its mark upon her young and plastic character, was not any injury to herself, but the gossip of her household, and the news that came from the Court, news that was always full of fresh and more bitter humiliations suffered by her mother, fresh and more glittering honours upon her mother's rival.

The decision of Wolsey's legatine court, that the King's marriage was invalid, might have been followed, had things in Italy been otherwise, by the same Papal confirmation that Henry's sister Margaret, Queen Dowager of Scotland, had once obtained in a like case. But though the Pope might have been willing to confirm any divorce, to dispense with any prohibitions for the King of England at another time, he could not do so now. In May, not a fortnight before the meeting of Wolsey's court, the Emperor's unpaid *lanzknechts* had stormed the defences of Rome, and for eight awful days systematically sacked the city in order to recover their arrears. Since then the Pope, abandoned by the French, could do nothing but obey the Emperor's

whistle. He would have gone as far as any man might either to secure the
English succession, or to allow Henry to have his desire; he would have
granted a dispensation for the Duke of Richmond to marry his half-sister
Mary; he would have been only too thankful for Henry to have had the case
tried by Wolsey-the sentence thus being a foregone conclusion-and so
have presented him with a *fait accompli*; but himself dissolve the marriage
of the Emperor's aunt he dared not.[2]

Katherine heard of what was afoot before it was intended she should, much
to the King's annoyance, especially as it was clear that she took it badly.
On June 22nd, however, the King himself told her that because of her
previous marriage with Arthur, his brother, they were not truly man and
wife, and that he could not continue to live with her in mortal sin. When the
Queen burst into tears, at this confirmation of all she had dreaded, Henry was
not unkindly; but even though she solemnly declared that her marriage with
Arthur had never been consummated, he did not for that give up his
intention. His marriage, Wolsey told him, might still be broken, if not
because of affinity, then on the ground of '*impedimentum publicae honestatis*';
Katherine's first marriage, whether consummated or not, had taken place '*in
facie ecclesiae*'. Henry was indifferent to the argument used, so long as it told
in the right direction.

Katherine, knowing Henry as she did, must have guessed from the first that
she was in great danger. She turned in her need to Fisher, the good old man,
Bishop of Rochester, sending word to him, so Wolsey reported to the King,
that she needed his counsel on 'certain matters . . . between Your Grace and
her'. Bishop Fisher, no coward, as he was to show, now replied only by word
of mouth that he would give counsel in nothing that touched the King's
Majesty. Later he was to die in her quarrel, proud to follow in the steps of the
Baptist who, he said, had 'regarded it impossible for him to die more gloriously
than in the cause of marriage'. But his conscience was not yet engaged, and
Katherine, receiving his answer, may well have felt that at a touch these
English, among whom she had lived for close on thirty years, had become
strangers, just as the husband whom she so deeply and faithfully loved, had
turned into a cruel enemy.

She turned then, and small blame to her, towards her Spanish kin. About
the beginning of July one of the Spanish servants, 'Francis Philips', asked
leave of the Queen to go home to Spain 'to visit his mother who is very sore
sick'. Henry let him go, but ordered Wolsey, who was in France, to have the
man seized over there. 'Francis Philips', however, got safely through to Spain
with his news, and before the end of the month Charles was writing to Henry
a very private letter in cypher containing a solemn warning which he hoped
would check Henry in his disastrous course. If, he said, the King divorced his
wife, the legitimacy of Mary would be in doubt, and James of Scotland
Henry's next heir.

That possibility, with all its unpleasant consequences, might have made
another pause, but not Henry. He rejected now, and continued to reject, the

Emperor's implied assumption that Mary would remain his only heir. Wolsey, working with the fury of a frightened man laboured to get a dispensation and divorce from the Pope; a dispensation that Henry might marry Anne, whose sister had once been his mistress; a divorce from Katherine because his brother had once been her husband. He got the dispensation, but it was useless to Henry without the divorce.

In the autumn arrived Cardinal Campeggio, after a very slow and unwilling journey. The Pope, badgered by Henry's agents, ambassadors, and special envoys, made apprehensive by Wolsey's alarming hints of the dangers to the Church that might follow from a refusal to oblige the King, had given way so much as to send his representative to try the case, but had at the same time given him injunctions to delay and temporize as much as was possible, unless he could possibly persuade Katherine to resolve the problem by retiring into a nunnery. It was not till June 1529 that Campeggio's Court met; a month later it was prorogued till October. During that interval news came to England that the case had been advoked to Rome. The King, who all along had doubted Wolsey's sincerity, and whose mind had been gradually poisoned against him by Anne's unremitting hatred, turned upon him in fury, and the Cardinal's fifteen years of power and splendour went down the wind with the autumn leaves. But the fall of Wolsey did little to advance the King's matter; instead of delays in England, there were now to be delays in Rome.

Up to this time Henry's relations with his wife had not been greatly different from those of any unhappily mated pair, of whom one is unfaithful but not willing to separate entirely, and the other obstinately attached—a state variable, stormy, and miserable. Although for the past year Anne had lived openly at Greenwich when the King was there, and Katherine had been his wife only in name, yet she was still Queen, he would still dine on occasion with her, and there was still at times a pretence, or perhaps not altogether a pretence, of kindness on Henry's part. He had, indeed, and he could confess it, no ground of complaint against Katherine. One day when they were at dinner together, he reproached her, as if half in jest, because, though the Princess was indisposed, the Queen had not sent to her any doctor from her own household. Katherine, whose overwhelming anxiety may have led her a little to forget Mary, brooded over the words, and saw in them suddenly a gleam of light. The King had always loved his daughter; if she were sent for, the sight of her might recall him to himself and to the past; next day she asked the King if the Princess might come to Court. But Henry's mood had changed and his answer was curt and brutal. She might go and see the Princess, he said, if she wished—and stop there. Katherine with a stubborn, gentle dignity, replied that 'she would not leave him for her daughter nor for anyone else in the world'.[3] She would not leave him, and it was the only thing Henry asked of her.

Sometimes the subject that must have been uppermost in both their minds came into the open, and they wrangled miserably together. At dinner on St. Andrew's night the Queen broke out suddenly. The pains of Purgatory,

she said, were what she now suffered; the King wronged her deeply by avoiding her company and refusing to come to her in her apartments. Henry,
uncomfortable and surly, replied that she had no cause to complain; she was
mistress in her own household and could do as she pleased. From that they
fell to disputing, and there the Queen had the best of it. Henry quoted his
almoner's opinion. He was not the Pope, cried Katherine, to judge in the
matter, and for one doctor that Henry got to pronounce against the marriage
she had a thousand to hold it good. The King, 'very pensive', left her for
Anne's company. But there he got cold comfort. He had better not, the young
woman told him, argue with the Queen, for he would always get the worst of
it. Then she began to lament that her own youth was passing, and chances of
good marriages, and hope of bearing children.[4] Between the two women
Henry cut a figure no more dignified than any common man ridden by his
passions; suffering, angry, ridiculous.

But with Henry such friction only inflamed his temper, hardened his
resolve, and brought him to a state of recklessness in which he was ready to
cast off the last rags of decent appearance. As, one morning, he set off with
Anne, riding openly beside him for one of those long, summer hunting expeditions, he paused to send a short message to Katherine–she was to remain at
Windsor, not to follow him. Katherine may have heard all the stir of departure, the trampling of horses and barking of dogs, but she did not know
officially that the King had gone until she received his order. Then she sent a
message, regretting that he had not given her the consolation of saying farewell. That gentle, insistent reproach touched Henry on the raw. Furiously he
bade the messenger tell the Queen 'that he had no need to bid her adieux nor
give her the consolation of which she spoke, nor any other; and still less that
she should send to visit him or to inquire of his estate, . . .[and] that he was
sorry and angry at her because she had wished to bring shame on him by having
him publicly cited'.[5] This citation to appear in person before the Pope, though
in itself an offence to his dignity, was in one way most welcome to Henry, for
it was Katherine's fault and he had this sop to quiet his conscience. She was
now no longer the blameless victim; she was the cause of this insult, and
henceforth an enemy to be hunted, humiliated, and trampled upon, her
helplessness and fortitude alike only adding a keener edge to his rancour.

Though separated from her husband, Katherine for a little while longer had
the comfort of her daughter's presence, for Mary had been allowed to join
her parents at Windsor, and now, with Henry gone, the Queen had the girl
all to herself; they spent the time together hunting, and moving about from
one to another of the royal houses; a mournful attempt at pleasure it must
have been, their hearts heavy, and their talks in the long light evenings, sad.

When Henry's hunting was over and he wished to return to Windsor, he
sent orders that Mary was to go to Richmond, and the Queen to the More,
that Hertfordshire hunting-box, pleasant enough in summer but a dreary
place now that autumn had come, with its broken park-pales and the
neglected, overgrown knot garden. There, and later at Ampthill, Katherine

could for a while do nothing but wait, and watch the progress of her cause
in England and in Rome.

Just when Mary had first learnt the unhappy secret of her mother's anxiety
it is impossible to say. In 1528, while she was on the Welsh border, her household was reduced, but the alleged motive was that of economy. In May of
the same year when she lay ill with smallpox at Greenwich, Mistress Anne was
there also, but lodging, while the infection lasted, 'in the gallery of the tilt-
yard'. In the late summer at any rate she must have known, for the news
became public property when Campeggio set out from Rome. It was perhaps
by Katherine's own choice that the Princess was not often at Court in these
troubled years, to watch, as she must have done, the King's favourite going
about the palace, or coming up into the Queen's own barge. For, unless Mary
as a girl of fifteen was far less outspoken and candid than she was as a grown
woman, it is inconceivable that she would not have taken every opportunity
to remind the woman who was her mother's worst enemy, that the Princess
of England was her enemy for that.

If she was Anne's enemy, so was Anne hers, and though the girl was still
Princess and Henry's only heir, even now Mary's feet were set upon a quaking
sod. In the autumn of 1529 Chapuys, the Emperor's new ambassador, dashed
off an alarmed and hasty letter to his master telling him that Henry was so
besotted on 'the Lady' that he had even agreed, at her desire, to marry Mary
to her kinsman, the Duke of Norfolk's son.[6] Master Eustace Chapuys, an
energetic, voluble, enthusiastic young Savoyard, whom his friends called
'Os', had a nose like a terrier for rumours, and smelt mischief whenever
Anne Boleyn had passed by. After this rumour he reported others – Mary was
to marry the Duke of Milan, the Duke of Cleves's son, or King James of
Scotland,[7] as her matrimonial value wavered up and down.

Henry indeed at this time was convinced that, with regard to Mary, he
could both eat his cake and have it. He might seem to be doing his best to
bastardize his daughter by the invalidation of her mother's marriage; but he
knew well that Mary's title to the crown would never be called in question
by a Council that had been ready to consider his bastard son as king. As for
Henry's own feelings, it is likely that he had still a good deal of affection left
for the girl of whom he had been so proud. In June 1530 she sent him the
present of a buck.[8] Next month, before he set off for his summer hunting,
which would last till the beginning of November, she asked permission to
visit him. Henry, perhaps for the sake of decorum, preferred to visit her, and
spent the whole of one long summer day with her at Richmond.[9] Even two
years later, when the breach with Katherine was complete, in October, just
before he went to France, with Anne as Marchioness of Pembroke in his
company, he happened to meet Mary walking in the country. He stopped
and spoke to her, asked how she was, told her that he would soon see her
more often. It was a strange meeting, a King and his daughter standing to
talk among the pale stubble of the autumn fields, and it did not last long. Henry
moved away, because, so Chapuys thought, a couple of Anne's servants came

up to overhear, and report the conversation to their mistress;[10] or perhaps because Mary let her father see that she was, as she always of necessity had been, utterly her mother's.

Separated, she and Katherine were still able to correspond, to send messages and inquiries. Every insult that Henry put upon her mother bound Mary closer to her, in a fierce loyalty, and Henry had gone out of his way to humiliate the Queen. At the end of September he sent to Katherine demanding her jewels, so that Anne might go gay to the meeting with the French King. Katherine, who must have known that nothing now remained that could be lost by plain speaking, replied with all the uncompromising pride of her Spanish royal blood, that she would not give them up to one who was the scandal of Christendom, unless she knew, by the King's own letter of credence, that it was his will.[11] Henry's hide was tough. The letter of credence was sent; the jewels, every one, surrendered; and the King was pleased.

No one, even at Court, pretended to like what for the Bishops had been from the first the 'benedictum divortium'. The Duchess of Norfolk, at Anne's request, had to be packed off home 'because she spoke too freely and declared herself more than was liked for the Queen'. Even her husband, the Duke, Anne's uncle, who probably knew already too much of the young woman's shrewish temper to be glad of her advancement, said that 'it was the devil and nobody else who was the inventor of this accursed dispute'.[12] In Parliament the Speaker had to rebuke those who suggested that 'the King pursued this divorce out of love for some lady and not out of any scruple of conscience'.[13] And, while country folk cheered the Queen and the Princess, the women of Oxford threw stones at the Vice Chancellor when he went to get the seal of the University set upon the document declaring the King's first marriage incestuous.

But such expressions of disapproval were less serious than the opposition which Henry was to meet when, by his action, the question of divorce merged into the far wider question of Papal authority in England. The first sign of his reckless decision was to be seen in the appeal to the Universities, which a Cambridge don, a Doctor of Divinity, by name Thomas Cranmer, suggested to Stephen Gardiner, that servant of the King who in Rome had been so resolute and persistent in demanding the Pope's acquiescence to the King's requests. The appeal to the Universities was only a beginning. Another step, this time a greater one, was taken when the clergy were forced, by threats of a praemunire incurred by their submission to the legatine authority of Wolsey, to acknowledge Henry as 'Supreme Head of the Church and Clergy of England'. To this they would only agree 'so far as the law or Christ allows'; Henry was content with this for the moment.

But in 1532 he went farther. The first Act of Annates was passed but was not to come in force for twelve months. Its withdrawal would be a *quid pro quo* to offer the Pope, its enforcement a wedge to drive in between his authority and the Church in England. The 'Submission of the Clergy' in the same year surrendered that independence for which Thomas à Becket had died. With these gains secured, the King was ready for a fresh advance, though he had as yet done nothing that he could not retract. But something was soon to happen which put all thoughts of compromise, if indeed he had any, out of his mind.

In February 1533 courtiers hanging about outside Anne's chamber witnessed a strange and interesting scene. That morning, as Anne came out, her eyes lit upon 'one she loves well, whom the King formerly sent away from Court for jealousy of her'; presumably, that is, upon Sir Thomas Wyatt the poet, who had been at least so much in her favour as to exchange tokens with her. In uncontrollable excitement, she cried out to this old friend, telling him 'that for the last three days she had had such an incredible fierce desire to eat apples, as she had never felt before, and that the King had said to her that it was a sign that she was with child, and she had said it was not so at all'. Having spoken, she turned with a burst of loud, hysterical laughter, and went back to her room, leaving all the men and women staring at each other 'abashed and uneasy' at such behaviour, and doubtless also drawing from it the same conclusion which the King had drawn.[14]

It was a strange way to announce the news to a Court, but the strangeness is perhaps some indication of the strain which the resolute, daring young woman had suffered, as she played her hazardous game, resisting long, and at last risking all by surrender. Now at last she knew that by that surrender she had won; and the crown was the prize.

Henry himself must have been told of that momentous pregnancy late in January, and as the immediate result, they had been secretly married; so secretly that Cranmer, Archbishop elect now, and Henry's right-hand man, did not learn of it till a fortnight later, and the Court in general did not officially know till Easter Eve, when Anne attended Mass at Greenwich in Royal state, dressed in gold tissue, and with the candle flames flashing upon the diamonds she wore.[15]

But once that strange and hasty marriage had been made and blessed, the marriage of a man still bound to his first wife, the divorce must at once go through if the coming child was to be the heir. If the Pope would not yield, then Henry would sweep the Papal authority out of doors, leaving, as judge in the King's case, the King's man, Thomas Cranmer. A pretence to Rome of softened feelings, a hint that after all the Act of Annates should not become operative, brought Cranmer's bulls from the Pope as fast as Papal messengers could carry them. Cranmer was now indubitably, unassailably Archbishop; and as such he should be, by the King's assertion, competent to judge the case. His Court was opened in May at Dunstable. He dreaded much that the defendant would appear, instead of her appointed, pliant counsel, thus delaying the sentence. He need not have feared. Katherine ignored the proceedings. On the 23rd he pronounced her marriage incestuous. On the 28th he proclaimed that Anne was Henry's lawful wife.

Henry, triumphantly expecting the birth of a son, began to harden his heart against his daughter. He forbade her now to write, or to send messengers to her mother. Mary, who cannot yet have realized how changed her father was, though what she knew was bad enough, replied begging him not to forbid either; let him ask her household, she said, if there was anything in these messages but inquiries as to her mother's health. As for letters—let him read them himself. Henry gave no answer to this, good or bad, but the correspondence did go on, and servants would come and go between Mary and her mother carrying letters that were, for safety, left without any superscription.[16]

It was at the end of April that Mary was officially informed of his new marriage. She received the news in silence, for already she had learned something of a self-control beyond her years; she even made shift to appear cheerful. But, refraining from any talk on the matter, she went off after dinner to her chamber, and there wrote a letter, which the King, when he read it, found very satisfactory. But when the messenger had asked for a verbal message, she would give none;[17] it comes more easily to an honest person to lie on paper than by the spoken word.

A month later Mary must have listened to news of the coronation of this new Queen; of the salute from the ships that broke the windows all about the Tower; of the progress through London, with Anne magnificent in crimson brocade with a link of pearls about her neck 'bigger than chick peas';[18] of the dinner in Westminster Hall with spices and delicacies served 'on great high plates of gold';[19] of the river procession which one of the onlookers described in an outburst of ornate prose, in which his excitement worked strangely upon his spelling. For, it was marvellous, he said, 'to see the good order kept by the barges, and how banars and penauntes of armis, the which were beaten of fine gould, yllastring so goodly against the sonne, and allso the standardes, stremares of the conisaunsys and devisis ventyling with the wynd, allso the trompettes blowying, shallmes and mistrielles playing, the which was a ryght symtiois and tryhumfantt sight . . . and to her [hear] the sayd marvelles swet armone of the said ynstermentes, the which soundes to be a thing of a nother world.'[20]

There was only one thing wrong with the celebrations, and that was the surliness of the greater part of the Londoners. 'Sir,' said Anne, answering the King's inquiries, 'I liked the city well enough, but I saw a great many caps on heads and heard but a few tongues.'[21] The common people of London looked on with disapproval and a sour humour. Everywhere the letters H and A had been set up by the city authorities among the decorations. 'Ha Ha!' the Londoners unkindly read them.

Now that Anne was crowned, it was outrageous, in Henry's eyes, that his first wife should obstinately continue to call herself Queen. Already, even before the divorce was pronounced, her new title of 'Princess Dowager' had been announced to Katherine and rejected by her. Henry must try again. But for some time Katherine would not admit to her presence even Lord Mountjoy, her own servant, knowing him charged with these messages. At last, however, on July 3rd, he was allowed to see her, and found her with a very bad cough, and 'lying upon her palet because she had pricked her foot with a pin'. When by her own order all her household had been summoned, Mountjoy announced the King's will.

Katherine had waited for this. It was her cue, and now she would speak. But when she spoke to Mountjoy she spoke to the King, the Council, the Bishops–indeed to all England. First she explicitly refused the new title, and denied the justice of the divorce. As for the fear that any danger might threaten Mary because of her mother's obduracy, the dauntless woman, no more Henry's dutiful wife, but the daughter of generations of desperate fighters, set it aside as irrelevant. Mary was, she declared, 'the King's true begotten child, and as God had given her unto them, so for her part she would render her again to the King, as his daughter, to do with her as shall stand with his pleasure, trusting to God that she will prove an honest woman'.[22] That was courage; the iron courage of Spain.

Next day Mountjoy and the commissioners came to her again. They had to take to the King a report of her words, and she questioned them sharply if they had them down correctly. 'As nigh as we could remember', Mountjoy told her. But she would not trust even his word, and bade them give her the 'book' they had made. When she had read a little she called for pen and ink, and, with an angry scribbling, she scored out the words 'Princess Dowager'. The furious scratches of her pen are still there to be seen in the very paper that Katherine read that day.[23]

When she had done this, she told them to read over the whole of it to her, but she did not listen in silence. The writing charged her with vainglory for keeping the name of Queen; she broke out–'I would rather be a poor beggar's wife and be sure of Heaven, than to be Queen of all the world and stand in doubt thereof.' The second time she interrupted was when she heard herself spoken of 'but as the King's subject'. That was too much for the pride of Spain. 'As long as the King took me for his wife', she cried, 'I was also his subject. But if the King take me not for his wife, I came not unto this realm as merchandise, nor yet to be married to any merchant, nor further to con- tinue in the same, but as to be his lawful wife.' She would never agree, she said, that her marriage was unlawful, for that would be 'to confess to have been the King's harlot this twenty-four years'. And what, she asked them next, was the court that had tried the case but one 'much more partial and suspect' than that of Rome could have been for the King? 'But', she cried, with mounting bitterness, 'I think the place to have been more indifferent to have been adjudged in hell, where as no truth can be suffered; for as I do suppose the devils themselves trouble to see the truth of this cause so sore oppressed.' After that outburst, and still more poignant than any anger, there followed words heavy with the full weight of her loneliness. For, calm once more, she told the commissioners–'I may err in any word, because I am no English- woman, but a Spaniard born, and have no learned council to advise me.' It was the same cry that had broken from her when she appealed for advice to Ludovic Vives, as to 'her countryman, who spoke the same language', when first she knew that 'the man she loved more than herself' [24] was not only untrue but cruel.

She was a Spaniard born. For years she had so much forgotten it that her father could reproach her with her Englishry. Now, by her husband's action, she was forced to remember. England during these last years had become for her a country of enemies, where only the helpless common folk and some few faithful ones were her friends.

Something at least of that loneliness and homesickness must have been understood by Mary, who now, more than ever, was united with her mother by an affection at once tender and fierce. Mary, the child, must have listened to tales of Spain; she must have remembered her grown-up cousin, the Emperor, who had visited England as her betrothed; Vives, a Spaniard, had taught her; Spaniards had often been about the Court; Spain was for her a country it was natural to love. It was not possible for the girl, with her quick temper and warm affections, to avoid confounding together now, and ever after, the remembrance of her mother, and the thought of Spain. But her mother, defenceless because an alien and a Spaniard, was wronged by the King, the Council, the Archbishops of England.

Soon, however, Mary was to experience for herself the anger of her father, and his new wife's hatred. Already Chapuys, whose quick ears were always pricking at any rumour from the Court, had heard that Anne bragged openly how she would make the Princess her waiting-maid. Chapuys, it seems, could never be sure whether he more feared or hated 'la Ana' as he called her, and this rumour terrified him because he was sure that something worse than petty malice lay behind it. He believed that the purpose was 'to give her [Mary] something to eat that will disagree with her, or else to get her married to some low fellow'.[25] Either purpose was almost incredible, considering that as yet the King had no other heir, but the ambassador believed that a terrible change had come over Henry owing to the influence of Anne. He did not realize yet that what he dreaded in the King had always been innate in him, and that not Anne, but opposition had brought it out.

Henry's new temper towards his daughter soon began to show. A little while after Mountjoy's painful interview with Katherine, Lord Hussey, newly appointed Chamberlain to Mary, received an order from the King that she should give up all her jewels into the hands of Mistress Frances Elmer. Hussey, whose sympathy was no more with the King than was Mountjoy's, found it a most unpleasant business. He had never, he declared, seen the jewels except when the Princess wore them. When he asked Lady Salisbury for an inventory, no inventory could be found. 'The most', Hussey wrote to Cromwell, 'that I could get my lady to do was to bring forth the jewels and set [her] hand to the inventory [I] had made.' For Mary was as obstinate as her mother, and from her mother had probably learnt her lesson. She would not give up the jewels unless she received the King's letter for them. 'Would to God,' cried poor Hussey, distracted by the flimsy but baffling defences of women, 'Would to God that the King and you did know what I have had to do here of late.' At the end of August he was still unhappily employed in trying to get possession of such of the King's plate as had been granted to Mary's use. But the clerk of the Princess's Jewel House had never seen it, and Lady Salisbury, when approached, replied tartly that 'it was occupied at all such seasons as the Princess is diseased, and cannot well be spared'.[26]

As things stood, neither Hussey nor even the King wished to press things further. The new Queen's child was not yet born, and upon the birth everything depended. Mary and her mother knew that well, and throughout the summer must have waited, with almost as much dread of the issue, as Anne waited with hope. Good women though mother and daughter were, neither was of that saintly submissiveness of temper which could wait without a longing that their enemy might be humbled, that she might fail to bear a living heir. Neither they, nor yet Anne had their desire. On September 7th the new Queen was brought to bed of a child. It lived, but it was a girl.

Chapter III

THE boy, the heir, for whose sake Henry had insulted the Emperor and defied the Pope, was as much, or almost as much a matter of uncertainty as ever. Henry had now two daughters instead of one, a young wife instead of a middle-aged. That was all his gain, and to compass it he had made enemies abroad, and offended his subjects at home. Obstinately silent, or openly unfriendly to Anne, these were as openly loyal to Katherine and her daughter. As for those two women, if he had ever hoped that they would, on his marriage, accept defeat, he must have known by now that the hope was vain. It was their will against the King's, and much turned upon their surrender. Unless he could break their will, this marriage of his, and the fruit of it, would never be accepted as legitimate by all those Englishmen who now began to see that, with the legitimacy of the King's first marriage, the Catholic Church in England would go down. These two women, unless tamed and broken, would be the natural rallying points of every discontented conservative. Brutal and despicably petty as the persecution was which the two had to endure it was not entirely wanton, not entirely and only a savage revenge taken by a tyrant against indomitable opponents.

As for Katherine and her daughter they fought undaunted, yielding no point, letting slip no opportunity, however trivial, of declaring their truceless resistance. To insist on a title which is questioned is not perhaps a very dignified form of protest, yet it was the only one open to them; in taking it they risked much; they themselves believed that they risked all, and they had some grounds for that belief. They were, however deeply popular sympathy might be stirred in their favour, alone as yet in their open opposition to the King. It was no more than sixty years since two boys, children almost, but one of them the King, had disappeared because they stood between their uncle and the throne; that uncle was the grand-uncle of Henry VIII. And now at Henry's ear was a woman, whom Chapuys at least held to be capable of anything. Vindictive, cruel, and unscrupulous, the ambassador believed her, and for the moment at least, supreme in the King's counsels. Little wonder that Chapuys feared for Katherine and Mary, and that they feared for themselves, imprisonment, execution, even murder.

If there is anything to choose between the courage of the two, Mary's was perhaps the finer. Katherine with all the assurance of her age was also armoured by despair, and, except through her daughter, was invulnerable. But the girl, unschooled at first in adversity, was throughout as stubborn as her mother. Only when Katherine was dead, and she left alone in a hostile world, did her nerve break. Till then, through years when she should have been thinking of her lessons, her play, and the splendours of a royal marriage, she learnt instead sorrow and humiliation. '*Moult ad appris qui ben conust ahan*', wrote the ancient singer of Charlemagne. 'Much had he learnt, being well acquaint with sorrow.' But that sorrow which comes from treachery or oppression can sometimes teach an ill lesson. Through these years Mary learnt, not, indeed, the bitterness of the cynic, but a deep and rankling distrust of those men who for fear or gain had acquiesced in the persecution of her mother; and these men were Englishmen.

A week after the birth of the new daughter, and before Anne Boleyn's child had received her name in that same church at Greenwich that had seen Mary carried in state to her christening, the heralds were blowing their trumpets at the Cross in Cheap and proclaiming to a silent crowd that Elizabeth and not Mary was Princess of Wales. To Mary's household, at Beaulieu in Essex, an order came from the King, and that day her servants' coats showed patches of brighter colour where her own device had been cut off, and where the King's was to replace it,[1] for now, though for a while the same people remained about her, they were to be the King's servants and not her own. Soon she was informed by Lord Hussey that her household was to be reduced because, he told her, she was no longer Princess of Wales. At once the challenge brought its answer–the answer Katherine had taught her. She would not, she said, believe such a message unless she saw Hussey's commission in writing.[2]

In October he brought that commission. Her household was reconstituted and reduced, though still she kept some old friends around her–the Countess of Salisbury, her cousin Margaret Douglas, Mary Brown, Master Fetherstone, and others.[3]

At the same time she was told that she must leave the pleasant house of Beaulieu–that is, the manor of Newhall Boreham in Essex, which the King wished to lend to Anne Boleyn's brother, Viscount Rochford. The third part of Hussey's charge was contained in a letter from Sir William Paulet, the King's own Comptroller. Mary was to be ordered no longer to call herself Princess of Wales.

She demanded at once to see the letter; it was given her and she read her own name–'the Lady Mary, the King's daughter'–that, and no title more, as if she were no better than young Richmond, the King's bastard; and not so good as he, for she was not a boy.

Without a word to Hussey, she left him, and going to her chamber wrote to her father. She could not, she said, believe him privy to such a letter, knowing herself, as she did, his lawful daughter. Then, with that same rigid, conscientious obstinacy of her mother–'If I agreed to the contrary,' she concluded, 'I should offend God; in all other things your obedient daughter.'[4] But it was this one thing that Henry required.

The answer to her letter was a commission of lords–the Earls of Oxford, Essex, and Sussex, and one cleric, Dr. Simpson, Dean of the King's Chapel. Meeting at Chelmsford they rode the remaining few miles through the autumn woods to Newhall, and there gave the King's answer to the words she had

written, words 'declaring that she could not in conscience think but she is
the King's lawful daughter and . . . believed the King in his own conscience
thinks the same'. Henry, by his mouthpiece the Dean, emphatically and
finally corrected her misapprehension as to the state of his conscience. He
warned her 'that she had worthily deserved the King's high displeasure and
punishment by law, but that, on her conforming to his will, he might incline,
of his fatherly pity, to promote her welfare'.[5] Mary did not conform, and a
few days after left Newhall for a smaller house.

The obstinacy of the two women, discarded wife and bastardized daughter,
goaded Henry on. He knew well that no servant in either of their households
but felt with them, and abhorred the orders to discontinue the use of the old,
and as they held, the rightful titles. Mary's household had replied to the
King's orders that they would obey 'saving their conscience'. Lord Hussey
as yet gave no sign of where his sympathy lay, but Mountjoy, Katherine's
Chamberlain, writing to Cromwell, did not mince his words. He had told
the household the King's orders that Katherine was no longer to be called
Queen, whereupon her Chaplain promptly replied that so they must in conscience call her; and her gentlewomen, with one accord, were of the same
mind. 'It shall not', wrote Mountjoy, 'be well possible for me to be a
reformer of folk's tongues in this matter; and for me to be a complainer
and accuser of them, the which, as I do verily think, bear their true heart's
service and allegiance to the King's Grace. It is not my part nor for me,
thus often to vex and unquiet her, whom the King's Grace caused to be sworn
unto, and truly to serve her to my power, she keeping herself true unto the
King, as I know none other. I have had divers times sore words of the Princess
for the messages I have brought her. . . . I had liever serve the King's Grace in
any cause, [even] if it were very dangerous, than further meddle in this.'[6]
It was the letter of an honourable man, but it moved neither Cromwell nor
his master. In December, with a greatly reduced household, Katherine was
taken to Buckden near Huntingdon.

Either because Henry believed that Mary could be more easily broken to
his will than her mother, or because her surrender, the surrender of the one-
time heir, was really of more value, it was now upon her that the King trained
most of his guns. Even before November those servants of hers who were
encouraging her in her obstinacy by their stubborn loyalty, were being
gradually removed from her household.[7] Now he declared that Mary should
become maid of honour to the child on whom Chapuys rarely bestowed a
better name than 'the little bastard'. This would be, not only to put upon her
an indignity which to any but a saint must have been bitter as gall; not only to
deprive her of the consolation and support of old and loyal friends; but also
to set her, lonely and unprotected, among the friends of the still triumphant
Anne. Chapuys, when he first heard of the plan, was appalled; God only
knew what they might force the girl to, in such a situation. At once he composed and sent privately to Mary a form of protest which he bade her sign
and keep secret, and another declaration which she was to learn by heart,

and which, if she must submit, she was to recite, in the presence of witnesses, to the messengers of the King.[8] Thus, though Chapuys could do little to protect her person, or her feelings, he thought he might have safeguarded her title.

For a while, the threat was only a threat. But before long one of those secret messengers that went between mother and daughter, put into Mary's hand a letter* from Katherine:

'Daughter,' wrote the Queen, 'I heard such tidings to-day that I do perceive, if it be true, the time is come that Almighty God will prove you, and I am very glad of it, for I trust He doth handle you with a good love. I beseech you agree to his pleasure with a merry heart, and be sure that, without fail, he will not suffer you to perish if you beware to offend him. I pray you, good daughter, to offer yourself to him. If any pangs come to you, shrive yourself, first make you clean; take heed of his commandments to keep them as near as he will give you grace to do, for then you are sure armed. And if this lady do come to you, as it is spoken, if she do bring you a letter from the King, I am sure in the self-same letter you shall be commanded what you shall do. Answer you with few words, obeying the King your father in everything, save only that you will not offend God and lose your own soul; and go no further with learning and disputation in the matter. And wheresoever and in whatsoever company you shall come obey the King's commandments. Speak you few words and meddle nothing. I will send you two books in Latin; one shall be *De Vita Christi*, the declaration of the Gospels; and the other the epistles of Hierome . . . and in them I trust you shall see good things. And sometimes, for recreation, use your virginals or lute, if you have any. But one thing specially I desire of you for the love that you do owe unto God and unto me, to keep your heart with a chaste mind, and your body from all ill and wanton company, not thinking nor desiring any husband, for Christ's Passion; neither determine yourself to any manner of living until this troublesome time be past, for I dare make sure that you shall see a very good end, and better than you even desire. I would God, good daughter, that you did know with how good a heart I write this letter unto you. I never did one with a better for I perceive very well that God loveth you. I beseech Him of his goodness to continue it; and if it fortune that you shall have no one to be with you of your acquaintance, I think it best you keep your keys yourself, for howsoever it is, so shall be done as shall please them. And now you shall begin, and by likelihood I shall follow. I set not a rush by it; for when they have done the uttermost they can, then I am sure of the amendment. I pray you recommend me unto my good lady of Salisbury, and pray her to have a good heart, for we never come to the Kingdom of Heaven but by troubles. Daughter, wheresoever you be come, take no pains to send for me, for if I may I will send to you.

'By your loving mother, Katherine the Queen.'[9]

* The letter is not dated, but it seems probable that it was sent about this time.

That heroic letter, with its lofty faith, its tender, careful affection, its gallant cheerfulness, tells a little of the mother that the girl knew. To a nature such as Mary's, like as it was to her mother's, its appeal must have been irresistible. Not only during the next unhappy months, but for years, she was loyally and with untiring fortitude to carry out her mother's commands, just as she was to cling to her mother's faith; never doubting nor questioning it, but accepting it as the one refuge of her soul, and only through its ancient windows looking out upon that light 'which lighteth every man that cometh into the world'. In these years of her troubled youth Mary's heart and mind took the impress of Katherine's signet, and never after lost it.

On December 16th the little Elizabeth was carried through London with some pomp to Hatfield, which was to be her residence, not in those days the stately and magnificent palace built by the Cecils, but a pleasant countrified manor on the slope of a wooded hill. Next day Norfolk waited on Mary. She was, he said, to make ready at once to attend the Princess of Wales. 'That', she replied, 'is the title which belongs to me by right, and to no one else.' It was for her far more than a title; it held, as it were in a cypher, everything to which she had given her loyalty.

Norfolk, whom his own wife accused of locking her up while he kept 'that drab Bess Holland' in her place, had a short way with Mary's protest. He told her he had come, not to dispute, but to have the King's commands obeyed. Mary saw that he meant it. She yielded, and asked only for half an hour's delay, and when she got it, retired to her chamber. Chapuys, when he heard of all this, believed that she employed the time in copying and signing the protest with which he had provided her, but he was mistaken, for by some mischance she had not yet received it.

She must have known that she could hope to take only a small number of her old friends with her, for when she came down she asked Norfolk to beg the King to be good to her servants. But she could not have guessed that the blow was to be so heavy as it proved. When she asked how many might go with her, he told her curtly that there would be plenty where she went; she could take two ladies only, and these of inferior rank. When the Countess of Salisbury, who had for so long been her Lady Governess, cried out that she would go, and bring servants at her own cost, Norfolk would not have it. It was none of Henry's plan to allow the girl any company of faithful friends, to hearten her resistance, and smuggle out letters and news to other friends outside. Mary had now to learn what it was to be alone–all but absolutely alone–among enemies.[10]

Yet, as she went jolting in her litter through the winter countryside, she had some encouragement, for Dr. Fox, the King's own almoner, rode up beside her when no one was near, and told her 'that she had answered as virtuously as any woman could, and begged her for the love of God to be firm', or else, he said, 'all the kingdom is in danger of ruin and perdition'. Already men were beginning to see the gulf that had opened at their feet, though they did not yet guess at its depth.

But for Mary that journey in the short December day must have been miserable, and the arrival worse. When they came into the house Norfolk asked if she did not wish to pay her respects to the Princess. Mary knew of no other Princess in England but herself, and said so. As for the daughter of Madame of Pembroke, she was none; though, said the delicate, forlorn, indomitable girl, if the King acknowledged the child as his daughter, she would call her sister, as she called young Richmond brother.

Norfolk, on leaving, gave her one more chance. Had she, he asked, any message for the King?

'None,' she said, 'except that the Princess of Wales, his daughter, asks for his blessing.'

Norfolk told her roundly that he dared not take such a message.

'Then go away and leave me alone', she cried, and rushed away to her strange new chamber, to give way to the tears that always came so easily to her. As for the Duke, when he gave his report, he was told by the King that he had treated her too mildly.[11] But Henry added that he would yet find a way of humbling her.

So Mary remained under the same roof as that half-sister whom as Anne's daughter she must have hated, and subjected to no one knows what pricks and scorns from the women about the new Princess. By February she had come to the end of any money she had brought with her; she lacked clothes too, and must needs send to the King to ask for them. She was so mewed up that she might not even go to Mass in the church which adjoined the house, and this lack of exercise, while the spring was coming in the country, must have been a sore trial to the girl who loved both walking and riding, and whose health moreover needed both.

Now and again she was reminded that she had friends, though they were only poor and helpless, for once as she walked along a gallery she was seen by some country folk, who shouted for her as Princess, and waved their caps; but the salutation did her more harm than good, for after it she was even more closely shut up.[12] It was small wonder that not only round about Hatfield but throughout all England, people in villages, who got their news in scraps, like sheep's wool from the bushes, thought and talked of her as if she had been the princess of a fairy-tale, shut up in Dolorous Gard. A Yorkshire girl, whose name was Mary, pretended that she was the Princess, and went about with a strange story of how Henry's sister Mary, 'la reine blanche', sitting one day in a bath, had told her niece's fortune out of a book; a hard fortune, for, said she who had been the French Queen, 'You must go a-begging once in your life, either in your youth, or in your age.' 'And therefore,' said the girl, explaining how she came to be wandering about the Yorkshire lanes, 'I take it upon me in my youth.'[13]

If Mary in these days got any news of her mother, it must have made her lot harder yet to bear. About the same time that she was brought to Hatfield, commissioners came to Katherine at Buckden, giving the Queen the King's orders to remove to Somersham in the Isle of Ely. Already, at Buckden, she was on the edge of that vast tract of waste—mile upon mile of pool, or fen, or rushy sodden ground, with its long watercourses bordered with reeds. Somersham was in the very midst of it, an unhealthy spot for anyone, and almost certain death for one whose childhood had been spent under the sun of southern Spain. Katherine believed that for this very reason she was to be sent there. She refused to go. She shut herself in her room, barred the door, and spoke to the King's messengers through a hole in the wall. She told them, they reported, 'that she would not go, unless we should bind her with ropes'; Suffolk, son-in-law of one of the Spanish ladies who had followed Katherine to England, hated the whole business, and was not likely to do that. After a few days, it seems, Katherine opened her door, but even then the commissioners, distracted between their stringent orders and their disgust at the task, quailed at the thought of what she might yet do, for, they complained, 'she may feign herself sick, and keep her bed; or keep her bed in health and will not put on her clothes; which extremities were not well remembered at the making of our instructions'.[14]

If the commissioners were acutely uncomfortable, Katherine was wretched. Chapuys received a warning from 'a worthy Englishman', which presumably he passed on, that she should take care always to have her room searched at night, and to lock the door before she slept.[15] After that, fear must have kept her company. In windy nights of winter when casements shook and doors slammed, she must have lain listening for footsteps, wondering, as Chapuys wondered, whether her enemies intended to murder her, or to stage a scene of adultery so as to give the King's cause some colour of justice.

Soon she was removed from Buckden, not to Somersham, but to Kimbolton Castle, and there kept to one chamber entirely, leaving it only to go to Mass. In that one room to which had shrunk the whole state of the daughter of Spain and wife of England, she slept, lived, and watched her few faithful women bending over the pots upon the fire, because, for fear of poison, they cooked all the Queen's food before her eyes.[16]

That fear was haunting Mary also. In the crowded household at Hatfield, where she was given, said Chapuys indignantly, 'the worst room in the house', discomfort was not the hardest thing she had to bear, nor yet the idle spite of ungenerous women, though it was said that Anne had sent a message to Mistress Shelton, who was in charge of the household, bidding her to give Mary a 'box on the ears now and then for the cursed bastard she is', and ordering her to see that the girl did not have her meals served in her own chamber, or anywhere indeed but in the crowd of the Great Hall. The worst, because it hinted at more sinister things, was the dismissal, before Christmas, of the two ladies she had brought with her, so that to serve her she had no one but a common chambermaid, lately engaged, who was not even ordered to taste the Princess's food.[17]

In England things were going ill for those who loved the old ways. In January 1534 Parliament met and set briskly about the work of pulling down the fabric of the old Church in England. No more payments, either of

Annates or of Peter's pence were to go to the Pope; no more appeals were to
proceed to any ecclesiastical court and so to the Pope–all were to be judged in
Chancery; no bishops should be chosen by the Pope, but instead by the King.
The Bishop of Rome was left no legal foothold in England. With all this,
the old heresy laws were repealed; it was now a commendable thing, that is
useful to the King, that a man should speak, and at the top of his voice,
against the Pope's usurped power.

No wonder that Castillon, the French ambassador, wrote alarming reports
to King Francis his master, still Henry's ally, but now a very anxious and embarrassed ally–'I write freely to you that you may show the Pope that things
are in a very dangerous state here; and I see no help unless the Holy Father
will in this matter have mercy more than justice, whereby he will restore a
King and country which is on the point of being lost and becoming his perpetual enemy.'[18] There was still just this chance; the Papal verdict in the
divorce case was not yet given, and men both in England and abroad, scandalized, fearful, but not yet despairing of a return to that old order that no one yet
could imagine as gone for ever, could still reckon that if the Pope would do
what Henry demanded, all would revert to its accustomed state, that the earth
tremor would cease and the crack close.

Their hope was vain. Just a week after Castillon wrote his letter, the case
was decided in Rome in Katherine's favour. Almost at the same time, Parliament in England passed an Act of Succession, bastardizing Mary, excluding
her from the crown and entailing the succession upon the children of the King
by his present wife. To this Act every member of Parliament was sworn
before he rode off to his home at the end of March. Nor was this enough.
Every man and woman in England must in person take that same oath which
demanded from each a disavowal of the age-old fidelity to the Pope, whose
original dispensation for the King's first marriage was, in the preamble of the
oath, declared invalid. All that spring and summer, and right into the autumn,
the King's commissioners rode about the country exacting the oath in villages
and towns. They visited also the monasteries, and by open threats or by the
persuasive sight of soldiers with their halberds and bows standing in the
cloisters, wrung from all but the bravest this repudiation of allegiance. No
blood flowed yet, except that of the poor, half crazy Nun of Kent, who
suffered for her visions and voices; but the King's Chancellor More, and Fisher,
the frail and saintly Bishop of Rochester, refused to swear, and were lodged
in the Tower. Monks of the Charterhouse also refused, though they, after a
short sojourn in the same quarters, took the oath 'as far as was lawful'. They
escaped for the moment, but that was all; over them and over every man who
could not 'without scrupulosity of conscience', deny his fidelity to that
Head of the Church whom he had always known, a dark cloud hung.

Even for those who cared little for the Pope there was yet their loyalty to
the young woman they had always called Princess. At fairs, at bride-ales, on
the way back from market, there were discussions and doubts. John Snap
of Horsingdon had said, so Henry Keble of Henley reported, that 'if he had

5

twenty thousand pound he would bestow his life and all he had upon my lady Mary's title, against the issue that shall come of the Queen'. More cautious neighbours who sat by cried 'Fie, Snap, fie! No more of these words.' But no one had contradicted him.[19] The Council felt constrained to assure those whose conscience was troubled, of the manifest righteousness of the King's cause. 'That God is pleased,' they argued, 'appears by issue so soon had of this lawful matrimony, so fair weather with plenty of corn and cattle, the purity of the air and freedom from pestilence for so long time.'[20]

They might so argue, but the spring and summer had been a time of fear and growing bewilderment for many, and not least for Mary, alone in that household at Hatfield which was governed by two of Anne Boleyn's aunts—Lady Anne Shelton and Lady Alice Clere. Now and again the King or his new Queen would come to visit the little Elizabeth. But Henry, Chapuys believed, had had to promise Anne that he would not see Mary, lest the 'king's weakness or instability' should not be equal to resist a meeting with his daughter. So, when the King arrived in the middle of January, he would not allow Mary to come to him. Instead he sent Cromwell to her chamber, to try again to persuade her to give up the title she claimed; the result was the same as ever. Yet, as the King mounted to ride away with the courtiers around him, something drew their eyes upward. There, upon a high terrace, the Princess kneeled with her hands clasped together. The King, perhaps involuntarily, nodded to her, and put his hand to his cap. The Court taking its cue, hastened to salute her.[21] Then they rode away leaving her to her enemies.

No one could tell with any certainty what the King's feelings were with regard to his daughter. He would abuse her obstinacy, which, he declared, 'she inherited with her Spanish blood', and then, when the French ambassador praised her education, his eyes would fill with tears.[22] When Chapuys had gone to the palace to ask of the King an unusual favour—namely that he, the Imperial ambassador, should appear before Parliament to state the case against the Bill that made Mary a bastard, Norfolk rushed out at him breathlessly from the door of the King's chamber, and warned him to speak mildly. Yet when Chapuys preferred his strange request, the King kept his temper surprisingly. Only when pressed for better treatment for Mary, the King took him up short. That was his own business, he said, and he would not be interfered with.[23]

He did not welcome interference even from his friends the French. When Castillon suggested to him that if Mary were to be married abroad it would take her out of the way, Henry asked him to dinner to talk about it. After dinner, however, he would not treat the suggestion seriously, but spent his time abusing and threatening his daughter, and running over the other girls who might succeed—all girls, alas, for never was there such a dearth of male heirs. He had indeed no intention of marrying Mary just now; to give her to an English bridegroom would stir up a hornet's nest of disloyalty at home; to give her to a foreign prince would put a stick into the hand of anyone who wished to beat the King of England.

Chapuys, though he could get nothing out of Henry, was indefatigable. He went to Cromwell, and here he had better fortune, or at least, more sympathy. The Savoyard got on well with that deep, conscienceless schemer, whose worldly experience was great, and whose wit both pleasant and ready. Cromwell, the Putney blacksmith's son, had knocked about Italy in his youth, learning there the morals of mercenary soldiers, and watching out of his small eyes the principles of Machiavelli's book put into practice; the book which Reginald Pole said 'had already empoisoned our country of England and ... was a story to empoison all the rest of the states of Christendom'.[24] Cromwell might not appeal to so high-minded and great a gentleman as Reginald Pole, a voluntary exile now because of his abhorrence of the King's ways. He might appear slightly ridiculous to an educated man of the world like Stephen Gardiner because of 'that conceit he had whatsoever he talked with me, he knew ever as much as I, Greek or Latin and all'.[25] Chapuys, equally a man of the world but no scholar, liked and respected him as an opponent; when they differed they could do it with a jest.

In the matter of Mary they did not fundamentally differ. Cromwell, before the divorce went through, had made a note in his 'remembrances', a note of a very cautious obscurity. 'Item', he wrote, 'Touching the judgement that the great person might be brought in to be noted *in bona fide parentum*';[26] that is, put plainly, that Mary, the great person, might be considered legitimate because her parents were honestly ignorant of the invalidity of their marriage. All through, Cromwell, not from either pity or principle, but from sheer common sense, tried by small and small and without ever risking his own position, to soften the fury of the father, and supple the obstinacy of the daughter.

After Parliament's declaration of Mary's illegitimacy the women and courtiers at Hatfield grew bolder against her. Towards the end of March Elizabeth and her household were to leave for another royal house. When all was ready to start, Mary refused to go. Perhaps the refusal was meant only as a desperate protest; perhaps she hoped that they dared not use force and that she might remain behind, in a quiet retirement, at Hatfield. If the latter, she was mistaken. The servants and idlers who watched the start that morning witnessed the spectacle of the King's elder daughter, she who had been Princess of Wales, seized by several gentlemen, lifted bodily, and thrust into a litter, where already sat Mistress Clere, aunt of Queen Anne, ready to start.[27] It is to be hoped that after such brutal humiliation, Mistress Clere was kind to her, for it was this lady who, when ordered by Norfolk to treat Mary more harshly, and as a bastard, replied hotly that if she were, aye, even if she were the bastard of a poor gentleman, the girl deserved respect and kind treatment, for she was a good girl.[28]

Chapuys, when he heard that violence had been used against the Princess, was not only scandalized at the outrage, but terrified lest Henry, stung beyond endurance by her obstinacy, should grant the girl's life to her enemy, Anne. But Katherine, once the obedient gentle wife, now reckless in her despair, thought that her daughter did well 'to show her teeth to the King'.[29]

In the spring or summer the commissioners came to the baby princess's household to exact the oath to the new succession. Mary, needless to say, refused it; and the explicit refusal brought more trouble upon her. Now, when the King visited Elizabeth, Mary was locked in her room, and a guard stood at the door. One of her chambermaids – it seems she had some personal attendants – who refused to take the oath, was shut up for a while, and threatened with prison until she yielded. That, at least, was the story which Chapuys believed. Mistress Shelton, Mistress of the Household, would jeer at, and threaten Mary by turns. The King, she told Mary, did not now care whether she surrendered her title or not, for by the new Act she was a bastard whatever she said. 'And', cried the woman, 'if I were in the King's place I would kick you out of the King's house for your disobedience.'[30]

Even if Mary met such abuse with an angry scorn, she must have felt the strain of it. When Mistress Shelton followed it up with a bald statement that only yesterday the King had said he would have her beheaded for disobeying the laws of the realm, Mary's nerve broke. She had already suffered enough to believe that almost anything was true. There was only one person in England willing and able to help her, Chapuys, the Emperor's ambassador. But the question was how to get word to him.

There happened to be in the house, how, Chapuys does not say, 'a physician who formerly was her tutor and usual doctor', perhaps Fetherstone. The Princess asked leave to speak privily with him. This was refused. Yet he was clearly the only messenger. Next time Mary saw him, it was in public, but she had devised a small bold scheme of her own. She began to talk of her studies; of how long it was since she had spoken Latin, so that now she doubted if she could say two words of it. Fetherstone, if it were he, bade her try. The women round about listened, doubtless with some respect, to the erudition of their betters, though, if they watched the doctor's face they may have thought his expression strange, and wondered if his old pupil could be making such mistakes as to appal her tutor. When she had finished he stammered only that 'her Latin was not very good'.[31] But it was from this man that the Imperial ambassador, shortly after, received word of the King's threat.

Upon Chapuys Mary had learned to lean, and the correspondence between them, though secret and risky, went on. In May, the King inquired of Mistress Clere if his daughter's rebellious spirit was subdued, and received the answer, 'no'. 'Then', he said, 'there must be someone near her who feeds these fancies by bringing news of her mother to her.' That person must be removed. The waiting maid who had at first refused to take the oath was packed off, without money or escort, to find her way home as best she might, and Mary and Chapuys were left without their go-between. Some time after, when the Princess was allowed more attendants, the correspondence was re-opened, but Mary had so thoroughly learnt the lesson of distrust that she believed this better treatment was only a device to lull her suspicions, so that they might find it more easy to poison her. She told Chapuys so, and told him too that her only hope was to die.[32]

The summer passed, and in August Mary was again faced with another removal, and the same problem of precedence, trivial in itself, but profound in its implications. With her frayed nerves she could not, this time, make up her mind what course to take. Three times in twenty-four hours she sent a message to Chapuys asking him what to do, and what to say, if, as before, they made her follow after her younger sister. Chapuys replied explicitly. She must protest, and he told her what to say; but she must submit before they again used violence. He also asked her if he should go to Greenwich to see her embark. Mary who must have longed for the sight of a friendly face, jumped at the offer.[33]

The day came when the start was to be made. Mary had already made her protest. The Comptroller, perhaps for peace' sake, allowed a compromise, for by now many may have dreaded, even if they respected, the young woman's obstinacy. When Mary came to the door there was little Elizabeth in her litter, and she herself must wait till it had moved off; but once in her own litter–and (significant trifle) it was not the leather-covered one of her unhappy journey to Hatfield, but another, gay with velvet–she might push on, and she did. Such good speed was made that when she came to Greenwich there was an hour to spare. She was able to go into the great barge that was moored there for their journey up the river, and occupy the chief place in it.

Among the little crowd that watched her stood Eustace Chapuys, but she did not recognize him; it must have been some years since they had met, and besides he was in disguise; one would be glad to know what disguise. But he saw her, and reported in demure diplomatic style to the Emperor that it had been 'a pleasure to see such excellent beauty and heroic bearing'.[34] Behind the words, and behind his daily cheering letters to her, behind all his passionate labours in her behalf, there was perhaps more than political feeling. It almost seems as if the Savoyard was the only man who ever felt for Mary a touch of the romantic devotion, half for her royalty, half for her womanhood, that so many men were to feel for Mary's half-sister, the one-year-old child whom he saw now arrive, an hour later, at Greenwich.

For all Mary's brave show that day, she cannot have been in good health, for soon after she was so ill that Henry sent his own doctor,[35] a large, serene, kindly man, a tower of strength to judge by his portrait,* Doctor Buttes. He at once asked permission to call in Katherine's physician and apothecary. The King permitted this upon conditions. Mary might see them, but not privately, and nothing might be spoken in any language but English.

For a while Mary's condition caused anxiety not only to Chapuys but also to those in charge of her, for the unfortunate Mistress Clere had long ago been warned by Chapuys, that it would be an ill thing for her if anything happened to the Princess. That warning the ambassador repeated now,

* In the National Portrait Gallery.

contriving somehow to get the King's doctor to tell her it was common talk in London that she had given the Princess poison. The wretched woman was reduced to a state of helpless tears as long as the crisis lasted.[36] She knew, as the Spanish physician – Miguel de la Sa knew, that even from an obliged government, and even on an unjust charge, the wages of the accused poisoner is likely to be death.[37]

Just at this time, and owing probably to Henry's errant fancy lighting upon a certain lady whose name is not mentioned, but who was probably Jane Seymour, Mary's treatment improved. At the More, in the autumn, some of the courtiers dared to visit her under the very nose of Queen Anne. In October, at Richmond, the Dukes of Norfolk and Suffolk, and, still more significant, some ladies of the Court who had come with the Queen, paid their respects to Mary. They found her in her room, where she stayed while there was any fear of meeting Anne.[38]

Once again too, when she moved from Richmond to Greenwich, she was able to avoid accepting the precedence of Elizabeth. The child travelled by road, and Mary had chosen the river. But she had not chosen it for this reason only. She had written gaily to Chapuys that she was going 'to have her revenge for my having gone to Greenwich to see her off'. This time she would see him, as well as be seen, and she bade him be at a small country house of his that he kept as a refuge for times when the plague was bad in London. It stood upon the bank of the river, and the country about it was lonely. There he waited, on a fine, late autumn evening, and the barge passed him, close in. On the forecastle, from which the awning had been taken down, the Princess stood for as long as they could see each other.[39]

Although Chapuys reported her as looking well and even plump, Mary did not recover her health the whole of that winter. In the low nervous state to which confinement, anxiety, and unhappiness had reduced her, the least thing was enough to upset her. Mistress Shelton was rude to her; her maids of honour were locked up and questioned as to who had made the assignation with the Imperial ambassador for the river bank. Mary fell sick again.[40] It was becoming a problem what to do with her. Then Dr. Buttes, humane and sensible, suggested that she should be sent to her mother. It would be cheaper, and her mother's doctors could not be suspected of trying to poison her.[41]

Katherine must have heard of the suggestion and snatched at the sudden hope. She wrote to Chapuys, begging him to go to the King again, 'and desire him on my behalf to do such a charity as to send his daughter and mine where I am; because, treating her with my own hands, and by the advice of other physicians, and of my own, if God please to take her from his world my heart will rest satisfied; otherwise in great pain. You shall say to his Highness that there is no need of any other person but myself to nurse her; that I will put her in my own bed where I sleep, and will watch her when needful.'[42]

That letter Chapuys took to Court, and read it standing before the King. But Henry would not do 'such a charity', and told the ambassador exactly why. For one thing, did he send the girl to her mother, her resistance, which he had gone about to break, would be strengthened. For another, he believed that there was a plot between some persons (he did not name Chapuys to his face) and Katherine, to steal Mary away from that lonely place and carry her out of the kingdom.[43]

It was Cromwell who, whether because Chapuys had worked on him, or because with his long political eyesight he always saw Mary as heir to the throne, managed to persuade the King to a concession. Mary should go to a house near by her mother so that Katherine's doctors could attend her. Katherine heard of his good offices and wrote:

'Mine especial friend,

'You have greatly bound me with the pains that you have taken in speaking to the King my Lord, concerning the coming of my daughter unto me. The reward you shall trust to have of God. For (as you know) in me there is no power to gratify that you have done but only my good will. As touching the answer which has been made to you that his Highness is contented to send her to some place nigh me, so as I do not see her, I pray you vouchsafe to give unto his Highness mine effectual thanks for the goodness, which he sheweth unto his daughter and me, and for the comfort that I have thereby received; and as to my seeing of her, you shall certify, that if she were within one mile of me, I would not see her. For the time permitteth not that I should go about sights, and, be that I would, I could not, because I lack provision therefore. Howbeit you shall always say unto his Highness, that the thing, which I desired, was, to send her where I am, being assured that a little comfort and mirth, which she should take with me, should undoubtedly be half a health to her. I have proved the like by experience, being diseased of the same infirmity, and know, how much good it may do, that I say. And, sith I desired a thing so just and reasonable, and so much touched the honour and conscience of the King my Lord I thought it not it should have been denied me. Let not for my love to do what you may, that this may be yet done. Here have I among others heard, that he had some suspicion of the surety of her. I cannot believe, that a thing so far from reason should pass from the royal heart of his Highness. Neither can I think that he hath so little confidence in me. If any such matter chance to be communed of, I pray you say unto His Highness, that I am determined to die (without doubt) in this realm, and that I from henceforth offer mine own person for a surety, to the intent, that if any such thing be attempted, that then he do justice of me, as of the most evil woman, that ever was born. The residue I remit to your good wisdom and judgment, as unto a trusty friend, to whom I pray God give health.'[44]

Chapter IV

THE King believed that there was a plot to smuggle Mary out of England. Katherine denied it utterly. It may be that so far as she was concerned, she spoke the truth; or it may be, that intrepid woman as she was, and pushed now to extremity, she lied; that she not only knew of, but intended to help the plan, and was ready, when the thing had been done, to suffer for it. If she knew, and so intended, she would consider the lie righteous. For the time was now passing—had indeed passed—when the safety of mother and daughter was a matter of only personal concern. At first Katherine had fought for her daughter's inheritance; Mary had fought for her mother's honour. Now the time was coming when both must fight for Mary only—for her safety and her legitimacy—because in her succession, immediate or eventual, lay the one hope of the restoration of the ancient Church in England.

Such things were happening in England, this late winter of 1534 and spring of 1535, that shocked to the soul Katherine, her daughter, and all those who believed as they did in the divine origin of the Papal power. In November Parliament declared the King 'Supreme Head of the Church in England'; as a broad hint of what was in store for those who would not stomach that novelty, it also passed a bill of attainder against Fisher, Bishop of Rochester, and against More, friend of European scholars, spiritual disciple of the Platonist Pico della Mirandola, one of the most lovable of all good men, and the very flower of that hopeful spring-time of religion and learning, that had given such fair promise in England, but was now to go down in gloom and blood. For the King was no longer the gay youth who danced and hunted nights and days away while Wolsey ruled for him; he was no longer that man of quick apprehensions and sympathy, who had walked with Colet in the Friars' garden at Greenwich, had borne his rebuke, and had drunk his health saying, 'Let every man have his own doctor. This is mine!' That Henry of the old days was gone, and there remained a creature suspicious, cruel, goaded rather than restrained by resistance or criticism, a man who must master or break every opposing will.

Henry had outraged decency by his second marriage and had been excommunicated. Once before an English King had suffered that sentence—John, the one King of such ill memory that his name has never again been borne by any of his successors. But King John had submitted to the sentence, and thereby checkmated his angry barons. King Henry did otherwise. He pulled down the whole edifice of the Church in England, and set it up again upon new ground. For the first time in the history of the country, the Church of England was cut off from the whole Church in Europe, as England itself is cut off by the sea; and against those men and women whose consciences could not budge from the ways of their childhood, the King turned the sword of the state. Now, for the first time Englishmen were to become familiar with the fact of persecution for conscience' sake. It was not now a few odd, half-crazy, dangerous people such as Anabaptists who suffered, but monks, noblemen, a bishop, the Chancellor of England. And these men died not for a new or strange notion, but for a thing which had always been held to be the truth.

For a time indeed, many people found it impossible to believe that the amazing change which had shifted the ground under their feet was a change that could last. Yet events were moving quickly. In the New Year 1535, Thomas Cromwell, the ex-mercenary soldier and money-lender, was made Vicar General; his work would be to visit monasteries and churches, and to direct bishops and priests into the way of obedience, seeing above all that they should preach suitably upon the King's new title. In May the Prior and some of the monks of the London Charterhouse, after close on three weeks of torment, suffered the awful death of the common traitor; next month, Bishop Fisher, just made Cardinal in Rome, lost his head upon the block; it might now, and welcome, said the King, go to Rome to fetch its hat. In July, More followed Fisher to the scaffold.

Such shocking events, coming after the King's unpopular marriage, stirred nobles and commons alike. 'A common stewed whore' for the King's wife; a bishop and the Chancellor of England put to death for upholding the marriage of the old Queen whom at least three-quarters of England never ceased to regard as Queen indeed – it was enough to make men both angry and afraid. An old labourer whose memory could go back to the days before the Battle of Barnet, trudging home in the rain from Worcester Market that dreary wet summer of 1535, would complain to a neighbour's wife of the season. 'It is long of the King', was his grumble, 'that this weather is so troublous and unstable, and I ween we shall never have better weather whilst this King reigneth; and therefore it maketh no matter if he were knocked and patted on the head.'[1] When he found himself in trouble for the words, he said that he was drunk when he spoke them; but many men were thinking them while sober.

Even among the King's own friends there was discontent and disgust. A courtier, by name Sebastian Nudigate, to all appearances no more than a gay young scapegrace, was moved among the rest. His elder sister Jane, the wife of Sir William Dormer, a strong-minded woman, and evidently used to managing her men-folk, was all for the old Queen. One day, about the time of the King's divorce, when Sebastian rode out from London to see her, she took the opportunity of warning him against the King's evil courses. He replied, mildly, that the King was not so bad as some thought. Lady Dormer persisted that he would do well to remember what she had said.

'"I shall", saith he. "I fear it", said she. At which word, pausing a while, leaning his head on his hand, he replied – "Sister, what will you say if the next news you hear of me, shall be that I am entered to be a monk of the Charter-house." "A monk!" she saith. "I fear rather I shall see thee hanged!"' Yet the next news she heard of him was just this, that he had entered the Carthu-sian order, that strictest order of contemplatives, who never touched meat all the year round. The masterful woman was not pleased with such independ-ence. Forthwith she went to the Charterhouse, demanded to see the Prior, and told him roundly that Sebastian was no fit man to be a monk; for one thing, she said, she knew that her brother could never eat fish without vomiting. At this point the story turns from gay to grave. The Prior, know-ing it would be enough answer, sent for the novice. At the sight of the change in him, even Jane Dormer was abashed. She left him there, a monk as he had said; and before very long, as she had said, he was hanged among the Carthusians who defied Henry.[2] It was a strange, unlikely end for a young courtier, but of this gay stuff, as well as of hodden grey, the opposition to the King was composed.

Nor were all prepared merely to be grumblers, or passive victims of the King's anger. Two years before, at the time of Henry's second marriage, Chapuys had reported exultantly to his master that 'every day his head was battered by Englishmen of birth, insisting by word or letter that "King Richard, the last one, was never hated as this King and yet he was put down by two or three thousand Frenchmen"'.[3] Respectfully but with ardour, the enthusiastic young man developed the implied invitation. Let Charles step in, rescue the Queen and Princess, and marry Mary to the King of Scots.

Chapuys was indefatigable. All round the Court he went; he had a word in some quiet corner with the Marquess of Exeter, whose only grief it was that he could not shed his blood for the Queen and Princess, but 'if there were question of anything, he would not be among the laggards'; he chatted with this one who told him that the Duke of Suffolk had gone off from Court without taking leave of the King—Suffolk might be Henry's old friend and companion in the joust but his new Duchess was the daughter of one of the Spanish ladies who had come to England with Katherine; he listened to another who said that a fortnight ago the Duke of Norfolk had grumbled to Lord Montague that he was held in small esteem, and 'nothing had he got from the King's lady'—though she were his kinswoman.[4]

Chapuys was indeed close friends with all the great lords whose loyalty to the old ways bound them also to Queen Katherine and her daughter. Lord Darcy, the tough old fighter of the North country, was in the habit of send-ing, presumably on New Year's day, a present to the Imperial ambassador. That was natural enough. But each of Darcy's presents had a meaning. Once he sent a 'gold penny, well enamelled'; a pretty trifle, but the device upon it was the badge of the Poles, and the purpose of the gift was to remind Chapuys of that marriage, always desired by Katherine for Mary—the marriage with one of the sons of the Lord Montague, who through their grandmother had royal Plantagenet blood in their veins. More than once in the old, happy days, the Queen had said that she hoped it might be by her means that the house of Plantagenet should come to its own again. This union of Tudor with Plantagenet which should have peacefully restored the crown to the older line, was now designed to be a lever to overset Henry Tudor, and to provide not only a Queen, but a King to supplant him. So Darcy's next gift was equally significant. He sent a sword. 'It meant', said Chapuys, that it was time for 'playing with steel'.[5]

The discontented were, some of them, old and tried servants of the King. Lord Sandys, Captain of Guisnes, was one of Henry's best soldiers; but his doctor told Chapuys that Sandys so disliked the way things went that he was shamming sickness as an excuse for avoiding Court; he believed too, that the Emperor had the hearts of all the kingdom. Chapuys recorded the information for his master's benefit, and with it a maxim for ambassadors–that it is well to make friends of doctors for they come and go unsuspected. Lord Hussey, a man so trusty in the King's eyes that he had been made Chamberlain of Princess Mary's household to carry out its reduction, had gone off into the North, grudging and ill-content. Before he went he paid a stealthy visit to Chapuys to tell him plainly that he, and all the honest men of the kingdom, were dismayed that the Emperor had not lifted a hand to help Mary and her mother. Chapuys, who felt much as he did, was rather at a loss for an answer, and could only suggest that Charles did not wish to plunge England into war. Hussey brushed the objection aside, and bade Chapuys go to Lord Darcy, whom Hussey called his own brother. Darcy was ready as Hussey to talk of rebellion. To their mind it only needed a few harquebusmen landed in the North, an attack from the Scots Border, a ship or two at the Thames mouth, and then Darcy would come out with 8,000 men, the other northern lords with their footmen and bowmen, and so 'raise the banner of the crucifix together with yours'.[6]

Already in the autumn of 1534 that was the way of it for the Yorkshire lords. Katherine herself did not, for another year, abandon her resolve that her wrongs should never be the cause of war. Only after the terrible summer of 1535 was she driven to believe that the Emperor's sword was needed, not to defend justice only, but that also which she and thousands of Englishmen believed to be God's holy Church. Mary felt as her mother. Writing to Chapuys in October, she begged urgently that he would send to the Emperor not only letters, but a messenger who could tell him all the truth of the state of things in England, and pray him 'to take the matter in hand and provide a remedy for the affairs in this country'. That remedy, she declared, was no less holy, no less a Crusade, than the Emperor's expedition against Mahomedan Tunis.[7]

With regard to Mary, Henry had done an ill work well. Now, and for the rest of her life, England, except for a few short spells of quiet weather, was a place of danger and treachery where heretics flourished and faithful Catholics were oppressed. She turned for help–she could hardly have helped turning–from England to her mother's land and people; to Charles, her mother's nephew, and to the Savoyard Chapuys now; to Simon Renard later, and to his master Philip of Spain. She wrote to these friends when she could, but at the foot of a hasty, scribbled note were the words—'Written in haste and fear.'[8] Often she dared not write at all, lest 'those who are constantly watching me should get hold of the letter'.[9] From such experiences a woman of a more elastic temperament might have recovered, little harmed; a less courageous woman would have yielded, and thus been spared the long rigour of persecution; Mary, with her stubborn loyalty and stout courage, endured, and never lost the mark of it.

If Katherine, Mary, Chapuys, and many Englishmen were of one mind as to an invasion of England, that very person on whose action all depended was not. Charles, the Emperor, slow-moving, cautious statesman, did not entirely disregard Chapuys's excited tales of all the threats hurled at his aunt and cousin, though he pointed out dryly that threats could be used on occasion without any intention of making them good. Hobbled though he was by complications of Imperial statecraft, he did not entirely neglect their cause. Apart from any natural feeling, Mary was to him a person of great potential value. But he was unmoved by any idea of an English Crusade, and his remedy for his cousin's present case was marriage outside England to a bridegroom who would fall in with Imperial schemes.

His first hope was a French marriage, but for this he must use the French King, Henry's ally, as a stalking-horse, since he could not himself approach Henry across open country. In the late summer of 1534 he ordered Count Henry of Nassau, his ambassador extraordinary in France, to introduce into his conversations with the French King the subject of the cruelties practised against Mary and her mother; to express surprise at the value Francis seemed to put on the English alliance; and then, as if it were a happy thought of his own, to suggest marriage between Mary and Angoulême. For there would be, he might say, advantages to France—Francis could set the pensions he paid to England against Mary's dowry, and Angoulême would hardly get such a good bargain anywhere else. And if Francis and Charles were to work together they would carry it; Henry would not refuse; no one abroad would support him, and at home there were murmurs and grudgings everywhere.

But though Admiral de Brion duly passed on Nassau's suggestion to Henry when he visited England, he did it in such a manner that Henry was able to trace in it what he described as the malice of the Emperor, and all it drew from the King was a counter-suggestion—that if Francis could get the Pope to retract the late sentence against him, he would consider a marriage between Angoulême and Elizabeth.[10]

Besides this he gave the Emperor a smart rap on the knuckles for his interference. He denied the alleged ill-treatment of Mary and her mother, 'whom', he said, 'we do order and entertain as we think most expedient, and also as to us seemeth pertinent, for we think it not meet that any person should prescribe unto us how we should order our own daughter, we being her natural father'. To this he added a further reproof. He was sure that if only the Emperor would leave carnal affection and vain worldly respects he would realize the righteousness of Henry's dealing.[11]

The Emperor, unable to take such an austerely impersonal view as Henry advised, did not cease from his efforts. Count Cifuentes in Rome was ordered to urge the Pope to insist that Henry should restore Katherine and Mary, and the Imperial ambassador in Scotland was to suggest that King James might find Mary a desirable match. The Scotsman thanked him politely for this suggestion but pointed out that Mary was not in the Emperor's power. Might he not, he suggested, have instead the daughter of the King of Denmark, Charles's niece?[12]

Meanwhile Charles had not given up hope of a French marriage. In February 1535 Chapuys went to see Cromwell with a variety of business. Partly it was to do with Mary's illness; after that, the two adversaries who yet had a liking for each other, being each of them of a nimble wit, and knowing the rules of the cut-throat game of diplomacy, settled down to a match. Chapuys asked if Nassau's proposal had come to Henry's ears. Cromwell denied it. Chapuys found this hard to believe, and no wonder, since Henry had undoubtedly known it for several months, and he told Cromwell so. The next move was to the Englishman. He said, *à propos des bottes*, that he heard rumours of a marriage between the Dauphin and the Infanta–but this would be an ill-assorted marriage because of the disparity in age. 'I said', Chapuys wrote home, '. . . that was true, and it would be well to prevent it by giving the English princess in marriage to the Dauphin.' Cromwell smiled. 'You pay me well', he said, 'but I do not want to remain long in your debt for fear of high interest, so I'll repay at once. It would be better to talk of the marriage between the Spanish prince and the King's last daughter.' 'At this', says Chapuys, 'I only laughed, saying that he overpaid me.'[13]

When the Imperial ambassador next had his audience with the King, he managed again to come off with a jest, but not before he had turned an awkward corner. For Henry, dropping pretence, complained that the Emperor was offering Mary here and there as if she were his own daughter. Chapuys of course denied it, 'and I said jestingly . . . that he ought to have asked whoever told him, "if he was not to be at the feast, seeing that he was to pay the reckoning?"' Henry let him go with only one more awkward question–what was the Spanish ambassador doing in Scotland?[14]

So far all the Emperor's efforts had been in vain. French theologians might decide that Mary's claim to the throne was not affected by her mother's divorce, and even the French ambassador complained that though he had seen all the sights of London, including the Tower, he had not been allowed to see Princess Mary, whose marriage to Angoulême was his ostensible business in England. But the Frenchman confessed that he had not mentioned the marriage point-blank, and his compliance with the Emperor's request was little more than show. Probably he was neither surprised nor disappointed when Henry declared himself willing for the marriage with

Angoulême to take place on condition that all Mary's rights to the throne were renounced–a condition which was the equivalent of a refusal. Six weeks later Henry received at Westminster another French envoy whose arrival he had impatiently awaited. He talked with him familiarly, leaning on a sideboard as he read his letters of credence. When they got to business the match they discussed was that of Elizabeth and Angoulême; the only difficulty was that Francis must be sure that she was Henry's only heir. She was that, Henry replied, by Act of Parliament, and 'everyone takes Mary for the bastard that she is'.[15]

By this time Charles was seriously alarmed. It was not only that Katherine and Mary, two unhappy women, were in the power of their enemies; nor that English Catholics clamoured that the Emperor should restore the Church in England; things were going beyond this. Henry had begun to tamper with the German princes, with the town of Lübeck, with Denmark; this was to strike at the Emperor's unprotected side, and Charles knew that in the suggested treaty between the Danes, the Lübeckers and England, Mary was to marry John Duke of Holstein. He must certainly have felt that something should be done quickly.

But what? James of Scotland had put his finger on the weak point in the Emperor's plans. Mary was in England, and it was not in the Emperor's power to give her to anyone. Gradually, by the beginning of 1535, Charles was coming round to that part of Chapuys's scheme which concerned the flight of Mary to the Continent.[16] As to supporting a rising in England, when, in the state of public opinion armed support from outside might have resulted in the over-setting of yet another King of England, Charles would not consider it, though Chapuys wrote heatedly of the seething discontent in Wales, in Lancashire and Cheshire, and among the North country lords.

The Emperor's approval once given to the plot for Mary's escape, Chapuys set to work, and so enters that motive which was to be heard again and again in Mary's life for the next eighteen years; until in fact that July day when, fleeing from the Duke of Northumberland, she drew rein at Kenninghall, and decided to ride no farther along the road that led to Yarmouth and the Low Countries, but stand and try her fortune against her enemies. She stood then, but she was a woman of thirty-eight, and knew herself the lawful Queen of England. Now, a delicate girl of nineteen, watched, threatened, and taunted, seeing the old world she knew coming down about her ears, seeing in high places nothing but spiritual wickedness, and everywhere else darkness and cruel habitations, the only thing she desired, she told Chapuys, was to escape, if so she might. Moreover, to go to the Emperor seemed as natural to her, and as little a betrayal of her birth, as it was to many in England and abroad. 'I intend to go beyond the sea to mine uncle the Emperor, as soon as I may get shipping'–such had been the talk of the Yorkshire serving-maid who had called herself Princess Mary. In Brussels at the end of 1533, when the Queen Regent of the Netherlands was ill, Henry's ambassador reported that the talk there was, that 'if the Emperor may recover the Lady Mary, other his aunt

Lady Arthur [i.e. Queen Katherine] out of England, that any of both shall be meet to have . . . governance of his Low Countries'.[17]

The fact that such a scheme was commonly discussed made Chapuys's work most difficult, but he was undaunted, and fertile of plans. It would be easy, he told the Emperor, to get the Princess away from any house near London. He could answer for getting her out of the house at almost any time of the day or night. All that was needed then was to bring her to the Thames, where there must be an oared boat, independent of the tides, and strong enough to fight its way, if necessary, through the small craft of the river to the mouth of the estuary, where ships of the Emperor must lie, waiting to receive her. She was just then at Greenwich, admirably placed for escape, but, unfortunately for the plan, Chapuys heard, and believed, that she was to be moved in a day or two; so there was not time to prepare, he thought.[18]

The rumour was false. The month of March passed, and Mary was still at Greenwich. For the last fortnight she was even allowed to stay there after Elizabeth had moved. Chapuys must have worked feverishly, for one day word came to her from him. La Renterie, one of the Emperor's admirals, with his galleons of the Netherlands was at the mouth of the river. It was time to act; would the Princess take the chance? She replied that she would; then heard no more. Twice she sent servants urging the ambassador to give her instructions. But Chapuys waited for the Emperor's final orders, and they did not come. Charles had bidden him, and would continue to bid him seek out all ways of preparing for Mary's escape, but he would not quickly make up his mind to a move which would certainly spill the fat into the fire. So that chance was lost.[19]

At the beginning of April, Mary was removed from Greenwich to a house inland. She was a good rider, and perhaps with a wild idea of making her escape unaided, she tried to leave Greenwich on horseback. But that was not allowed, and if her intention was flight, it must have been small compensation to her that her 'litter was covered with velvet and was far the most honourable that she had had since her misfortunes'. It may have comforted her more that, as she went, a great crowd of citizens' wives met her on the road, crying out that she was still Princess in spite of all.[20]

Escape had seemed so near that now she must have felt she could not endure to see eyes watching her, to listen for eavesdroppers, to fear the peril that lurked in every meal. She begged Chapuys by his servant 'that for the love of God . . . I should contrive to remove her from the danger which is otherwise inevitable'. There was no hope of her escaping by night from the house where she now was, but as soon as the weather mended she would walk out in the country and see how flight might be arranged. It would be best, she said, that horsemen should come upon her as if by surprise in one of these walks, and seem to take her without her consent. The house where she was lay twelve miles from the river, and Chapuys thought that it might be done— a few riders, a horse for Mary and then a dash for the river-bank, if possible below Gravesend and clear 'of the danger of this river'; and then a row-boat

to take her out to a couple of the Emperor's great ships. Only her guards
would resist, and perhaps here and there a few ill-disposed persons, but most
people, he was sure 'would help her, and those sent in pursuit would shut
their eyes and bless those who had carried her off'.[21]

But that walk in the flowery fields, the descent of the waiting horsemen,
and the wild ride never took place. The Princess fell ill again; welcome news,
it seemed to Chapuys, for her father and even for Cromwell, whose goodwill
was a fluctuating quality. When the ambassador made urgent inquiries about
her health he got some snubs from the King, and from Cromwell little
sympathy. Mary was 'the thing that made all the difficulty and upset the
whole affair, and would to God——', Cromwell did not dare say further,
but there was no need, for what he meant was clear enough.[22]

Mary recovered, but it was to a darkening prospect. For this was the month
of May, in which Bishop Fisher and the first Carthusians suffered. No one
could guess now, since Henry had tasted blood, what he might do next; and
always there was Anne beside him, a woman fast becoming desperate, since
she saw the King's passion wane, and could not secure his gratitude by bearing
him a son. In that state of tension to which she must have been wrought, it is
no wonder the excitable young woman talked wildly. 'She is my death and
I am hers', she said of Mary, and vowed that Mary should not be the one to
laugh last.

Katherine at Kimbolton feared the worst both for herself and her daughter,
but it was for the girl that she cared most. She managed somehow that gloomy
summer to get a letter out of England to her nephew the Emperor, another
to the Pope. In both she spoke as a woman daily expecting death. She wrote to
Chapuys too, telling him her greatest dread; that the King would again
demand the oath to the succession from Mary.[23]

Chapuys himself feared that something sinister was brewing. Neither he nor
his men were allowed to see the Princess. Cromwell was as blank as a stone
wall to all his protests and requests. All was well with Mary, he would say,
'seeing that no one feels more anxiety about her than her father'. The best
way to set her free, he said, would be to arrange a marriage for her, but it was
no use for Chapuys to talk of the Dauphin. Several petty German princes had
asked for her, but that, Cromwell added, after this gentle touch with the foil,
would be to lower her state. Chapuys came away convinced that the King
did not intend to marry her to anyone.[24]

Mary herself, seeing the autumn come, and hope of escape vanish with the
summer weather, turned to another slight and illusory hope. The common
people of England believed that the special envoys who arrived from France
just then had come to complete the marriage, long ago arranged, between
Mary and the Dauphin; the Frenchmen found themselves, upon this assumption, enthusiastically welcomed, and fervently prayed for. Mary must have
deluded herself with the same belief, for she was heard to rebuke one of
Queen Anne's friends who spoke of the Dauphin as about to marry elsewhere;
the Dauphin could not, said Mary, have two wives. When the French envoys

KING HENRY VIII

By Joos van Cleve.   Hampton Court Palace.
Reproduced by gracious permission of Her Majesty the Queen.

came to visit the little Elizabeth, the elder Princess insisted so hotly that she should see them, that she had to be almost pushed into her chamber.[25]

As the winter passed, things grew worse. Chapuys was sure that 'that she-devil of a King's mistress' would never be satisfied with less than Mary's death. There was the Princess, in the household of her half-sister Elizabeth, with Anne's aunt as her Governess, only three women to wait on her, and no access allowed to Chapuys. Katherine, ill and desperate, was afraid still that the next Parliament would put her and her daughter to the touch with the oath of succession. She wrote, and wrote again to Charles, imploring him to help them. He, clogged as he was with the weight of his kingdoms, could only reply, that, except to save their lives, they must not take the oath, as that would be to break up their following in England.[26]

Before Katherine could receive that reply, her fears and troubles were over. At the very time that the Emperor's letter was written far away in Naples, Katherine, who had been ailing since the beginning of December, became suddenly worse. But, lurking in her rooms at Kimbolton like a sick animal in hiding, she did not allow the household officers appointed by the King to know her condition. It was the Imperial ambassador who told Henry and asked to be allowed to see her, and for permission for Mary to go to her. The first was granted. The second was refused.

Chapuys came to Kimbolton, and Katherine, who cannot have seen him for about three years, welcomed him—but it was a sad welcome. She could now, she said, 'die in his arms and not all alone like a beast'. But while he was there her condition improved. She was cheerful; smiled as she talked, in the old way; laughed at a joke that one of his servants made. He left her after four days, and for another day yet the improvement was sustained; she was able even to comb and tie up her own hair.[27]

When Chapuys went away, he did not leave her quite friendless. Another, a far older friend, made bold by the news of Katherine's illness, rode through the winter weather to Kimbolton among its dreary marshes. Lady Willoughby, once Doña Maria de Salinas, who had accompanied her from Spain thirty-five years before, came knocking on the gates of Kimbolton, asking if her mistress was yet alive, though dreading to hear that she had already passed. She was told she must show the King's licence to see Katherine, but she brushed that aside. She had had a fall from her horse, she said; she was in such case that she must, before anything else, come to a fire and warm and dry herself. The King's officers let her pass in, but 'since that time they never saw her nor any letter of licence'.[28] So she was with Katherine when on Friday January 7th, after a sudden relapse, Katherine died at about 2 o'clock in the afternoon.

What that loss was to Mary can be imagined. Her mother was dead, and she had not been there to say good-bye. Even the few poor trifles that Katherine could leave her daughter did not reach her for a time; some never reached her. Katherine had left her gowns to be cut up for vestments for a house of Observant Friars; the furs from them, and a chain and cross she had

6

brought out of Spain, were to be given to her daughter. Mary never received the furs; the cross and chain came to her, only to be sent for again by Cromwell. But he, looking it over with a pawnbroker's eye, and caring little for the morsel of the True Cross that the gold contained, decided that it was of small value, and returned it at last to Mary.[29]

Chapter V

A T the news of Katherine's death Henry dressed himself in yellow, wore a white feather in his cap, and led the dancing. Next Sunday, the day on which all the world came to Court, he carried about in his arms the small Elizabeth, just as he had once carried Mary, showing her off to ambassadors and courtiers.[1]

Anne appeared to rejoice as much as the King, but she was too clever a woman not to have divined that, in fact, Katherine's life was the one guarantee she had that her own marriage would stand. She may not have known that the King had already made private inquiries as to whether, if his second marriage were declared null, his first would thereby be again held valid. She may not have known that he was telling certain people, in the strictest confidence, that he had been tricked into marriage with her by the Black Art, so that it was really no marriage at all. But she knew certainly that the King's heart was gadding after strange goddesses; even a year ago, when she had tried to send from the Court a certain 'handsome young lady', Henry had told her roughly that she should be content with what he had done, for if he were to begin again he would not do so much.[2]

The days were long gone by when Henry would write her those passionate letters – 'No more to you at this present, mine own darling, for lack of time, but that I would you were in my arms or I in yours, for I think it long since I kissed you.'[3] The 'importunate rebel' he had then laughingly abused, had proved a very spitfire of a wife. People said that the King was so incredibly under her thumb that when she wanted anything he dared not deny her; that if she were thwarted 'she played the mad woman', and that Henry himself contrasted Katherine's gentleness with her railing tongue.[4] It had been between them for a time 'pull devil, pull baker', but even those days of uneasy sparring had passed. Courtiers whispered that the King had hardly spoken to her ten times within the last three months. One day when there was dancing at Court, she shocked and offended the French ambassador, who stood beside her, by a sudden burst of loud laughter. 'Madam,' he said sourly, 'you are laughing at me?' Controlling herself with difficulty the Queen assured him that she was not, but only laughed because the King, who had left her in order to find and bring to her the ambassador's secretary, had met on the way a certain young lady, and had forthwith forgotten everything else.

Knowing her danger, at any rate in part, Anne, like the unjust steward, resolved what she would do; she would make friends with Mary. If by diplomatic kindness she could soften the obduracy of Katherine's daughter, she might claim some gratitude from the King. The move would also make

for her friends among those who, as Mary's friends, had been her most
inveterate enemies.

Even before Katherine's death, Anne had made an attempt in this direction.
One day at Eltham, whither she had gone to visit Elizabeth, Anne and Mary
were both at Mass in the chapel. Mary was the first to get up from her knees;
she curtseyed to the altar and went out. One of Anne's women had seen the
curtsey, and perhaps mistaking it and meaning kindly, told the Queen that
the Lady Mary had done reverence to her. Anne at once followed it up. 'If we
had seen it', she said, 'we would have done as much to her.' She did not stop
there. At dinner Mary received a message. 'The Queen salutes you, and she
desires that this may be an entrance of friendly correspondence which your
Grace shall find completely to be embraced on her part.' Mary, however,
was perversely blank. 'It is not possible', she replied, 'that the Queen can
send me a message . . . her Majesty being so far from here. You would have
said "the Lady Anne Bullen" for I can acknowledge no other Queen but my
mother, nor esteem them my friends who are not hers. And for the reverence
I made, it was to the altar, to her Maker and mine.'[5]

However Anne might smart at the proud girl's words, she could not afford
to be as proud herself. After Katherine's death she sent another message by
Mistress Clere – if Mary would only obey the King's will, she herself would be
a mother to her, and Mary should come to Court again, not to carry the
Queen's train as Anne had once bragged, but to walk at her side. Mary, whose
sorrow had left her without the will to make a sharp retort, ignored the offer
of friendship, and replied only that no daughter could be more obedient than
she was, saving her honour and her conscience.[6]

This time it was Anne's sharp temper that flared. A little while after, Mary
saw an open letter lying on the floor of her oratory. She read it, as she was
meant to read it, and found it a letter from the Queen to Lady Shelton, who
was now Lady Governess to both the King's daughters.

'Mrs. Shelton, [Anne wrote]
'My pleasure is that you do not further move the Lady Mary to be toward
the King's Grace otherwise than it pleases herself. What I have done has been
more from charity than from anything the King or I care what road she takes,
or whether she will change her purpose, for if I have a son, as I hope shortly,
I know what will happen to her, and therefore considering the Word of God
to do good to one's enemy, I wished to warn her beforehand, because I have
daily experience that the King's wisdom is such as not to esteem her repentance of her rudeness and natural obstinacy when she had no choice . . . Mrs.
Shelton, I beg you not to think to do me any pleasure by turning her from
any of her wilful courses, because she could not do me [good] or evil; and do
your duty about her according to the King's command as I am assured you
do.'

When Mary read the letter she laughed with the cruel scorn of youth.
Whatever she had yet suffered – her mother lost and her name bastardized – she
kept that 'bird in her bosom', her own honour unstained and her conscience

clear. Not all her hard schooling had taught her to doubt that for any fear she could be brought to sacrifice these two things. So, in her harsh young confidence, she laughed bitterly at Anne's letter, copied it out for Chapuys's delectation, then laid it where she had found it, and gave no sign that she had ever seen it.[7]

'If I have a son, as I hope shortly——' In those words lay the reason for Anne's new carelessness of Mary's friendship or enmity and her hope of regaining, with triumph, the King's favour. If she could bear a son she might yet be what her chosen motto claimed–'The Happiest of Women'.

But on January 29th, the day that Katherine was buried at Peterborough, Anne miscarried; it was said that the child would have been a son. Even now the desperate woman did her best to wring some profit from the disaster by declaring that the catastrophe was due to Norfolk's stupidity in blurting out to her the news that the King had had a fall as he rode at the ring. Other people, however, said that it had been caused, not by any such loyal and loving terror, but by the Queen's chagrin at seeing one of her maids sitting on Henry's knees.[8]

That Anne's ship had begun to drive towards the rocks did not mean that Mary's was free to come into anchorage. These days must have been very dark for her. Her mother was dead, and, as she believed, by poison, and she herself was alone among enemies. Only Chapuys dared openly be her friend. He, who cared for her with a warmth of emotion that went beyond the duty of an ambassador, wrote to her almost daily and received in return such brave letters as only increased his admiration. She told him how much his letters comforted her, and his eager kindness must have meant a great deal at a time when each day brought not only fresh realization of her loss, but also, it seemed, warning of some new danger. For about the middle of January she heard again that the King intended to send commissioners to demand from her the dreaded oath. She managed to get a message through to the ambassador. What should she do? Chapuys was almost at his wits' end what to advise; perhaps, he said, a pathetic reply would be best, excusing herself upon the grounds of ignorance and incapacity, for after all she was only twenty this very February. Or perhaps she should give a half promise, that, if the matter might be shelved for a time, when she came of age she would take the veil.[9]

Between his fear of the political disaster that any prejudice to her title would be for the Emperor; fear for her safety; and real sympathy for her unhappiness, Chapuys's anxiety was acute. To make matters worse he heard at Court that same sinister prognostication that had preceded Katherine's death. Mary was ill and like to die, the courtiers said, of grief. When Chapuys tried to see her, he was refused; even his man, who till now had had access to her, was excluded. Bribes passed, but all that Lady Shelton would allow was that Mary might see his servant in her oratory, but with Lady Shelton present.[10]

That was no manner of good, for the matters which Chapuys wished to open to her were secret and dangerous. The ambassador had news to give her, and, as a solution of all her fears, a fresh plan of escape. He had to confirm her suspicions as to her mother's death, for after hearing the report of the physician who had helped to embalm Katherine, Chapuys believed that the Queen died of poison.[11] Many other people believed it too.

Yet even though Chapuys could not reach her, it is very likely that somehow or other Mary heard the rumours that were going about. Katherine's physician and apothecary actually visited her in the house where she was, though perhaps they did not get speech with her alone. But even without this added misery, she had suffered enough to make her only too ready to snatch at Chapuys's plans of escape, when he managed to convey the suggestion to her.

Up to January 1536 the ambassador had had great hopes. Charles's Regent in Flanders, the Dowager Queen Mary of Hungary, a very energetic and decisive lady, and much more ready to take risks than her brother, was enthusiastic about the plan.[12] Mary herself was still insisting that she could and must escape, though sometimes even now she would rally her courage and believe that she should wait, without giving Henry warning by her flight, for the Crusade against England that she hoped the Emperor would yet undertake.[13] Always she found it agony to decide between the wisdom of two courses; and now she halted between these. But the long strain, followed by the shock of her mother's death, and the added dread which that brought, had almost broken her down. It was for escape that she clamoured most often, ignoring the difficulties with an impatience which made even Chapuys's enthusiasm seem overcautious. She would, she told him, cross the channel in a sieve, if only he advised it. She would do precisely what he told her to do; he need not send her notice of any plan; she gave her approval to all beforehand. All she needed was something with which to drug her women. If he would send her that, she was confident that she could steal out one night, pass softly by Lady Shelton's window, and so through the garden to the gate which she could either unlock or break open.[14] But now Chapuys would not take the responsibility of bidding her try. He thought that her eagerness made her underrate difficulties, and that though she believed herself little watched, the seeming freedom was a trap. He was only the first of many men to set aside, with almost amused scorn, Mary's judgement; he was far more sincerely and affectionately her friend than many, but while he admired her courage, he thought little of her competence. [15]

And the Emperor began to withdraw even his qualified approval from the plan. Now that Katherine was dead, Charles thought it superfluously risky. He began to hope that, if Henry and he both consented to let bygones be bygones, they might agree very well. He would rather have had Henry as his friend than hazard men and money on an expedition which might very well fail; and which, if it failed, would drive England into the arms of France. He could not believe that the King would insist on persecuting the Princess still; he made first a gentle suggestion that she might be better provided for, then, coupled

with an offer of alliance, a hint that her title to the crown should be confirmed, and lastly a proposal, to be conveyed with the utmost delicacy, that
Henry might marry her to the Infante of Portugal. But one thing, he made
clear to Pate, Henry's ambassador, was essential to good relations between
Emperor and King; Mary's legitimacy must be recognized.[16]

To all this Henry turned a deaf ear. He was quite ready to discuss an alliance
with Spain and even to talk of a marriage for Mary, but when Chapuys
waited for some definite offer on the subject of her dowry, none came.
Instead, Cromwell had the bad taste to turn the conversation towards the
marriage of the King's 'little daughter', though it is true that he did it
'timidly, as one offering a coin to an elephant'.[17]

To all criticisms of Mary's treatment, the King and Cromwell had one
parrot answer. The King would treat Mary as his daughter 'if she will submit
to our Grace, without wrestling against the determination of our laws'. 'God',
Henry told Pate to tell the Emperor, 'has given us wisdom, policy, and other
graces in most plentiful sort, necessary for a prince to direct his affairs to his
own honour and glory.' He did not therefore want any help from the
Emperor in managing his own business. In fact, if by a foreign marriage a
King laid himself open to such interference, 'the servitude thereof would seem
so great that wisdom would allow no prince to marry out of his realm'.
As for the Emperor's demand that Mary should be declared legitimate, it
was ignored.[18]

For the moment Charles could do no more for Mary without taking a
decisive step. To that he was constitutionally and by habit averse, and the
reports of Court gossip which he was receiving from Chapuys during the
spring of 1536 may well have made him hope that no decisive step would be
necessary. Anne's miscarriage at the end of January had loosened the last
strand that held Henry to her. She was now only the mother of an unwanted
daughter, a woman of a harsh and stormy temper, and, to at least the great
majority of his subjects, little more than his concubine. A second divorce
would be the very opposite of the first. That had outraged all known laws
and the public opinion of Europe. This would make possible a return to
perfect respectability and a marriage that none could question.

All the Court was watching. One spring day lounging and chatting with
Chapuys at a window, Cromwell remarked demurely that, although the
King was still inclined to court and sport with ladies, yet he thought that his
Grace would henceforth live honestly and chastely in his present marriage.
As he spoke he hid a smile with his hand, but not so completely that Chapuys
missed it.[19] It was not only that the courtiers divined the King's disgust at his
present marriage; that had long been apparent. Now things were moving
further. After one or two passing fancies, Henry had determined upon his
next bride. The lady, Jane Seymour, was twenty-seven years old, had been
maid to Queen Katherine, and now served Queen Anne; it was said that
when the King's attentions became apparent 'there was often much scratch-
ing and bye-blows between the Queen and her maid'.[20]

Jane, no less than Anne at first, was careful of her virtue. But this time the King was careful of it too. He had had experience of the disadvantages that followed from a marriage with a woman whose name had been compromised. He would not repeat his mistake. Besides, Jane Seymour was a woman of a different stamp from Anne Boleyn. Though it is impossible entirely to acquit her, on the one hand, of calculation, and on the other of insensibility to the ugliness of Henry's sexual morality, it must be remembered in her favour that she probably did not regard Anne as truly Henry's wife, since her sympathies were always loyal to her old mistress; nor was there in the sixteenth century any suspicion that marriages were made in Heaven. In looks, as in all else, the fair-haired, pale, silent young woman was a contrast to the dark and sparkling termagant that Henry found such an uneasy helpmate. Of no great wit nor beauty, she had yet both conscience and courage. Not only did she refuse, though on her knees, a purse of gold sent by the King, and return a letter of his unopened[21]–such demonstrations of virtue might be mere moves in the game–but she dared to show openly her loyal affection for the memory of Katherine, and for Katherine's living daughter. It was said that when the King spoke to her of their own marriage, the gentle, quiet creature urged that he should restore Mary to her rights. Henry replied that she must be out of her mind; she should be thinking of her own children–the children she would bear to him. She answered, boldly and wisely, that she did think of them, and of their peace, for unless he did justice to Mary, Englishmen would never be content.[22] It must, almost certainly, have been at her suggestion, and to please her, that the King about this time sent Mary a present of a hundred crowns.

In church on Easter Day, April 16th, Chapuys, who was still trying to soften Henry's heart towards Mary, thought it worth while to show so much courtesy to Queen Anne as hand to her, with a bow, a couple of candles in the ceremonies of the feast, for, said he, 'if I had seen any hope of the King's answer I would have offered not two but two hundred candles to the she-devil'.[23] A fortnight later, on May Day, Queen Anne sat to watch a great joust at Greenwich, but the day was spoiled by the departure of the King, who suddenly took horse and rode away to London with only six persons in attendance. It was the signal. That afternoon men wondered at it. Next morning they understood, for the Queen was in the Tower. So too were her brother Viscount Rochford, three gentlemen of the household, and Mark Smeaton, 'a spinet player'. If Anne slept at all that night, she slept and saw the light come in the same room in which she had wakened to the sunshine on the morning of her coronation. It was, so she said to Kingston, 'too good for her' now.[24]

Outside the Tower, London buzzed with scandalous rumours. The Queen, never popular, was now safe game. Tales full of circumstance went round, relating her intrigue with Mark Smeaton, the musician. One morning, it was said, when the Queen lay in bed, he had been fetched in to play that her ladies might dance. The Queen, watching him, set her heart upon having him for her lover. But the man himself would not be bold, so she must take into her confidence an old waiting-woman of hers, named Margaret, who lay at night in the antechamber of the Queen's room, while, in the gallery beyond, and within hearing, slept all the rest of the ladies. In the antechamber there was a cupboard where sweetmeats, candied fruits and conserves were kept, and there, one night, old Margaret concealed Smeaton. When all is quiet the Queen calls out–'Margaret, bring me a little marmalade', and in comes the old lady leading Smeaton by the hand, 'Here', she says, 'is the marmalade my lady.' And Anne, aloud for all to hear–'Go along, go to bed.'[25]

Such stories went about the streets, and in the King's Hall at the Tower where she was tried, with her uncle Norfolk under the cloth of estate and holding a long white wand, the accusations were almost as irresponsible. She was charged with incest with her brother, adultery with the rest of the accused, with saying 'that she could never love the King in her heart', with laughing at his clothes, and calling his literary efforts 'stupid and clownish'.[26] She was, of course, condemned. But first it was declared, upon the authority of Cranmer, that her marriage with the King had never been valid. So, on May 19th, the woman who had never been the King's wife was executed, for adultery against the King. She came out to the Tower scaffold wearing a night robe of damask and a red damask skirt, with a netted coif over her hair, 'as gay as if she was not going to die'. [27] Her hysterical, wild laughter had shocked the Lieutenant of the Tower; she had never, till the last moment, abandoned hope of life. 'She has a stout heart', the King admitted, 'but', he added, 'she shall pay for it.'[28]

As she knelt praying, the Calais executioner, who had hidden the sword under a heap of straw, suddenly drew it out and took off her head. She had paid, the daring, dangerous woman, quarrelsome, imperious, witty, gifted, and fascinating. She left behind her, bastardized and disinherited, the little daughter who ought to have been a son.

Some of the consequences of her death were immediate. On May 20th Henry and Jane Seymour were betrothed. On the 30th they were married. Henry was riotously happy. While Anne was still a prisoner in the Tower he had been going out here and there to feasts. At the Bishop of Carlisle's house, he took from his breast a small MS. book which, he hinted, contained the tragedy he had written in anticipation of Anne's fall, for he had known, he said, which way things were going.[29] There was a water pageant up and down the river, and the King spent much of the pleasant summer days in his barge with the musicians playing.[30] Most people shared in his relief, but one thing that they had confidently expected did not yet come to pass. There was no sign that the King would do justice to Princess Mary, though the Queen herself had in public more than once gone upon her knees to the King begging him to send for his daughter and declare her again Princess. When the Countess of Salisbury, Mary's old Lady Governess, came to Court, a huge crowd gathered and hurried after her, thinking that she brought the

Princess. 'Why so many people?' the King asked, and when they told him, he replied with apparent good humour that Mary was not there; but they should see her soon.[31]

Mary herself was at Hunsdon. She let a week pass after the death of Anne, and then sent a letter to Cromwell.

'Master Secretary,' she wrote,

'I would have been a suitor to you before this time to have been a mean for me to the King's Grace to have obtained his Grace's blessing and favour; but I perceived that nobody dared speak for me as long as that woman lived, which now is gone; whom I pray our Lord of his great mercy to forgive.' But now, with confidence, she asked Cromwell 'for the love of God to be a suitor for me to the King to have his blessing and leave to write to his Grace'.[32]

At first all seemed to go as well as she undoubtedly expected it would. Cromwell got her the leave she asked for, and on May 30th she wrote thanking him. He would, she promised, find her 'next unto God . . . as obedient to the King's Grace as you can reasonably require of me'.[33]

Two days later she sent off her first letter to the King, written, 'in as humble and lowly manner as is possible for a child to use to her father and sovereign lord'. She acknowledged and repented of all her offences, and promised, as she had promised Cromwell, that 'next unto God I do and will submit me in all things to your goodness and pleasure . . . humbly beseeching your Highness to consider that I am but a woman and your child who hath committed her soul only to God and her body to be ordered in this world as it shall stand in your pleasure'. To conclude, and to show herself loyal and inoffensive in thought as in act, she congratulated the King on his new marriage and assured him that her daily prayer was that God should 'send your Grace shortly a Prince'.[34]

There was no answer to this letter, either good or bad. She waited till June 7th, and then sent off to Cromwell a letter with a token, the letter for himself, the token for the King. She was a little nervous at the delay. 'I think so long to hear some comfort from the King's Grace ; . . . whereby I may perceive his Grace . . . to have accepted my letter and withdrawn his displeasure towards me, that nature moveth me to be so bold to send his Grace a token.' This token she begged Cromwell to send on to the King, asking for one in return, as a sign that he had received and accepted her submission.[35]

That day or the next she must have received some letter or message which made her think that it was so. Perhaps Chapuys had written thus to her, for at this time he believed, taking Cromwell's word for it, that all was well. A week ago Cromwell had allowed the ambassador to see, and even to make a trifling alteration in a form of apology which was to be sent to Mary for her signature. Chapuys could find no harm in the formula, though it is true he suspected some 'bird-catching' in it. And on Whitsunday Cromwell coming to visit him in his lodging announced 'for his welcome' that both the King and Queen were pleased with Mary's letters.[36] Either Cromwell himself was deceived, or, which is more likely, he managed to hoodwink the usually astute ambassador, so that Chapuys should do nothing in the coming crisis to strengthen Mary's resistance.

For indeed the centre of the storm was advancing on her, and soon it would quench her hope of honourable reconciliation. Cromwell wrote to her, sending a draft which he advised her to copy and return to him for the King. The draft was abject enough, but in Cromwell's letter Mary must have read a hint of something more, of that which she had always most dreaded; a demand that she should swear to the Act of Succession. It was this threat perhaps which persuaded her to copy Cromwell's draft with one alteration– to make in fact two copies, one sealed for the King, the other open for himself. This time the King was to read how there lay, 'most humbly prostrate before your noble feet, your most obedient subject and humble child, that hath not only repented her offences hitherto but also decreed simply from henceforth and wholly, next to Almighty God, to put my state, continuance and living in your gracious mercy'.[37]

With the two copies of Cromwell's draft went a letter to him.

'Good Master Secretary,' Mary wrote,

'I do send you by this bearer, my servant, both the King's Highness' letter sealed, and the copy of the same again to you, whereby I trust you shall perceive that I have followed your advice and counsel, and will do in all things concerning my duty to the King's Grace (God and my conscience not offended) for I take you for one of my chief friends, next unto his Grace and the Queen. Wherefore I desire you for the passion which Christ suffered for you and me, and as my very trust is in you, that you will find such means through your great wisdom, that I be not moved to agree to any further entry into the matter than I have done. For I assure you by the faith that I owe to God, I have done the uttermost that my conscience will suffer me, and I do neither desire nor intend to do less than I have done. But if I be put to any more (I am plain with you as with my great friend) my said conscience will in no ways suffer me to consent thereto. And this point except, you nor any other shall be so much desirous to have me obey the King as I shall be ready to fulfil the same. For I promise you (as I desire God to help me at my most need) I had rather loose the life of my body, than displease his Grace willingly. Sir, I beseech you for the love of God to take in good worth this rude letter. For I would not have troubled you so much at this time, but that the end of your letter caused me a little to fear that I shall have more business hereafter.

'From Hunsdon the 10th of June.'[38]

That letter might have made a better man than the Chief Secretary ashamed, but Cromwell was proof against such weakness. Both Mary's courage and her scrupulous loyalty were to him qualities merely strange and inconvenient in politics; the gallantry of a young woman defending, with all her small might, her own untarnished honour of soul, probably seemed to him little better than silly perversity.

He received the letter and the copies of his draft, but he did not forward the sealed copy to the King, for when he read the open one he found that Mary had added four words which profoundly altered its content. There had been none of that reservation—'next to Almighty God' in his version. He wrote to her again, sharply this time, for his own position was becoming dangerous, as the King's anger rose against his daughter's obstinacy, and began to embrace all her friends. With the letter he sent yet another draft, in which, without qualification or reserve, she was to beg forgiveness, protest the 'humble and simple submission ... of my life, state and condition', welcome whatsoever the King should 'think convenient for me, without the remainder of my will in myself', and finally petition for 'some piece of your most abundant grace, that hath never wanted to them that have inwardly repented their offences, not committed by malice, but by young frailty and ignorance'.[39]

Mary received letter and draft. She must have known by now how imminent was the arrival of commissioners instructed to take her oath to the succession—an oath by which she would renounce the Papal authority, and approve the divorce of her mother. She could not, in this pass, afford to lose Cromwell's help; she could not any more boggle at a plain but general submission. She knew now that she would be fortunate if she could come off with no worse than that.

Obediently she copied out the draft. 'I cannot devise', she wrote to Cromwell 'what I should write more but your last copy without adding or minishing.' She thanked him 'with all her heart' for his trouble, and assured him that, as for the exception that he had misliked, 'I did not mean it as you do take it. For I do not mistrust that the King's goodness will move me to anything which should offend God and my conscience. But that I did write was only by reason of continual custom. For I have always used both in writing and speaking to except God in all things.' This time it was only one copy, left open and unsealed, that was sent back for Cromwell's inspection, 'because', she said, 'I cannot endure to write another'.[40] Toothache and headache were the excuses that she gave, genuine enough no doubt, but this last attempt at submission must have caused her also a mental and spiritual nausea. One copy was enough.

Again she must wait, but she had not to wait long. The King had done with delay. Cromwell had failed to produce that submission which he had covenanted for. Henry would take other ways with this obstinate daughter. A commission was appointed—the Duke of Norfolk, the Earl of Sussex, and the Bishop of Chichester—to carry to her articles for her signature. Those articles contained the very acknowledgement of the King's Supremacy and of her own bastardy which she had so dreaded.[41] They were the fruit of the King's triumph over Mary's sympathizers in the Council; Henry had also prevailed on the judges to give, as their verdict, that should his daughter refuse to sign she could be proceeded against under the law.[42]

At Hunsdon Mary, shattered by neuralgia and her sleepless nights, received the commissioners. They had come, they told her, to find out how far her submission went. She had, they said, 'of so long continuance showed herself so obstinate towards the King's Majesty . . . and so disobedient unto the laws conceived and made upon so just virtuous and godly grounds', that to them she seemed 'a monster in nature'. They put to her three questions. Would she recognize the King as her sovereign and submit to his laws? Would she acknowledge the King as Supreme Head of the Church? Would she admit the nullity of her mother's marriage?

She refused.

If she had had any doubts of the ferocity of the King's mood, the behaviour of his commissioners now removed it. At her refusal, they began to rail like fishwives. She was an unnatural daughter, they cried out at her. One of them doubted that she was even so much as the King's bastard. 'If you were mine, or any man's daughter,' he shouted, 'I would beat you to death and knock your head against the wall till it was as soft as a baked apple.' Lady Shelton added her shriller abuse to theirs, using yet more threats. When they had finished, they told her she might have four days to think it over, but during that time Lady Shelton should neither let her speak with anyone, nor leave her alone for a moment, day or night.

When the King received news of her refusal, his anger blazed up so dangerously and with such impartial fury that for a few days Cromwell, who had staked more than a little on his attempt at reconciliation, went about thinking himself 'a lost man and dead'. Ladies of the Court, suspected of disloyal sympathy with the King's daughter, were called up to swear again to the Act or Succession.[43] The Marquis of Exeter and Fitzwilliam the Treasurer were excluded from the Privy Council on suspicion of being at the back of Mary's resistance.[44] For a few days the Council sat from dawn to dusk.[45] The King even tried to prevail upon the judges, so Chapuys heard, to condemn Mary in her absence as contumacious. No one knew or dared to guess what fresh and startling atrocity the King might not commit. One of his Privy Chamber came to Chapuys to suggest a strange but ingenious device for allaying the King's wrath. Let the ambassador send five of his servants, good musicians all, to lie up in a barge under the palace and thence to salute the King's ears as he wakened in the early dawn. Chapuys would have done far more than this. He sent the men, and for several days they fiddled, sang, and fluted under the King's windows.[46]

Somehow Mary managed to send off a letter to Cromwell, and a message to Chapuys; desperate appeals they must have been, but Cromwell's answer, when it came, brought her no comfort, only more bitter reproaches, and a blank refusal of any help. 'Ye shall understand', he wrote, 'that how great soever your discomfort is it can be no greater than mine who hath upon your letters spoken so much of your repentance . . . and your humble submission in all things without exception and qualification, that knowing how diversely and contrarily you proceeded at the late being of his Majesty's counsell with you, I am both much ashamed of that I have said, and likewise afraid of that I have done; in so much that what the sequel thereof shall be, God knoweth.' Next he upbraided her for an 'example in the contempt of God, your natural father and his laws, by your own folly and fantasy, contrary to the judgement and determinations of all men, that ye must confess do know and love God as well as you, except you will show yourself altogether presumptuous. Wherefore, Madam, to be plain with you, as God is my witness, like as I think you a most obstinate and obdurate woman, all things considered, that ever was, so I dare not open my lips to name you unless I may have such a ground thereunto that it may appear you were mistaken, or at the least that you be both repentant . . . and ready to do all things that ye be bound unto by your duty and allegiance.' He sent her, for this end, the articles which she must sign. If she would not, he took his leave of her for 'the most ingrate unnatural and most obstinate person living, both to God, and your most dear benign father'. Finally, as if he bethought him of the temper of the woman with whom he had to deal, he added a persuasion apt for her case. He advised, so he told her, 'nothing (but I beseech God never to help me) if I know it not so certainly to be your bounden duty by God's laws and man's laws, that I must needs judge that person that shall refuse it, not meet to live in a Christian congregation'.[47]

Such was Mary's answer from Cromwell. But she had also managed to send off a message to Chapuys. And Chapuys, her true friend, who in this matter could do nothing to help, Chapuys also counselled submission. God, he said, looked not so closely at the actions of men as at their intentions, and he provided her with a protest, which, to his mind, would put all right; it would preserve her title unqualified, and absolve her conscience from loyalty to an oath exacted by threats of force. He was doing the best he could for her, but he forgot that her conscience was not that of an ambassador and man of the world.[48]

Threats, abuse, and argument had been used against Mary. She was ill and alone. Beaten at last, she gave in. Cromwell's letter and the articles he enclosed arrived late on a Thursday evening. At eleven that night, by candlelight, she signed the paper entitled 'The Confession of me, the Lady Mary.' In this she answered to the King's satisfaction the three questions which the commissioners had put to her. The King, she avowed, was 'Supreme Head of the Church in England'; she utterly refused 'the Bishop of Rome's pretended authority'; and in the third article she acknowledged 'that the marriage heretofore made between his Majesty and my mother . . . was by God's law and man's incestuous and unlawful'. Nothing was spared her. To make all sure she must sign her name to each clause. She signed it—'Marye'.[49]

The crisis was over which was to mark Mary for life. It had taken her almost unawares, so profoundly had she mistaken and misunderstood both the implications of her own position and her father's character, for it is plain that when she first approached Cromwell she believed that she had only to ask in order to obtain Henry's pardon.

It was an attitude illogical indeed in a woman who had, a few months earlier, clamoured for the Emperor to lead a Crusade against England. But she was not one to be governed by logic. For her, all wrongs that had come upon the faithful, upon herself, her mother, and loyal Catholics, wore one face—the face of Anne Boleyn. Anne's death, to her, changed everything. The very day that the news of Anne's imprisonment had come to her she had sent a message to Chapuys telling him that it was her wish he should help and not hinder in divorce proceedings, 'for the King's honour and relief of his conscience';[50] she did not, she said, care a straw if he had or had not children by another marriage. It is clear that she did not wish, now Anne was dead, to play the dangerous part that Chapuys had perhaps designed for her—the part of pretender against her father. She may well have thought, if indeed she thought clearly at all, that now Chapuys's 'she devil' was gone, Henry would return to the paths of righteousness, and that neither armed rebellion nor any very explicit submission on her part would be necessary.

She was utterly mistaken. For one thing, it was five years since she had seen, except casually or from a distance, the father whom she remembered as kindly, easy, and open, a devout and conventional Catholic too, and one who respected good men even if they opposed him. During that five years she herself had grown from girl to woman, but her father had changed no less. Portentous now both in guile and recklessness, no bonds could hold him; by no ordinary precedents could his actions be forecast. He had no intention of returning on his tracks; during this very summer his commissioners were visiting and suppressing the smaller abbeys of England which Parliament had given into his hand. For it had been discovered in Cromwell's previous Visitation that, with a remarkable uniformity, all abbeys of less than a dozen monks were plague spots of corrupt and scandalous conduct, while, for the moment, the 'great and solemn abbeys of the realm' were above reproach.

But beside her misapprehension of Henry's character and intentions, Mary forgot or ignored much that in justice to the King must be considered. What indeed, in his persecution of his daughter, had he aimed at? Was it merely that he must, in his tyranny, break any spirit that resisted him? Tyrant he was, but his cruelty was not, I think, so idle and wanton as that. Chapuys, though he never explicitly admitted it to Charles, knew quite well, as his master knew, what was at the root of Henry's behaviour. Only on two occasions did he even glance at it in his letters. The King, he said once, was angry with Mary because the nobles were encouraging her to resist. If—he said after Mary's submission—if she had continued her resistance, many would have died as a result of it.[51] It was what lay beneath these vague remarks that had caused Henry to use against his daughter such merciless pressure.

The King knew only too well that those who hated the new ways looked to Mary as their hope for the future; the questions put to more than one person arrested this summer show how tender he was on the subject of her title. Lady Hussey, who visited her at Whitsuntide and whose husband was so deep in the confidence of Lord Darcy, found herself, in August, in the Tower. There she was questioned by Wriothesley and Petre. 'How often', they asked, 'had she repaired to the Lady Mary since the time she lost the name of Princess?

Answereth that she never repaired to the said Lady Mary since the King's Highness discharged her from attendance upon her, but only at Whitsuntide.' Asked whether she had been sent for by Mary at any time, 'answereth of her allegiance that she was not so sent for'. Asked if she had called Mary 'Princess', she said 'that she first upon Monday, as she thinketh . . . called for drink for the Princess, and after, upon Tuesday, she said the Princess, meaning Lady Mary, was gone walking'. But that she did so was merely 'of custom'.[52]

In October came the Lincolnshire rising, followed by the much greater 'Pilgrimage of Grace' which brought out noblemen, gentlemen and commons of Yorkshire and the North. When the Pilgrims drew up their Articles at Pontefract these included a demand for the repeal of the Act which bastardized Mary, and those who examined prisoners after the 'Pilgrimage' harped upon just this string. George Throckmorton had to rake about in his memory for every circumstance of that afternoon on which, dining at the Horse's Head in Cheap with Sir John Clarke, 'in a little low parlour', he had borrowed a copy of the rebels' demands, and afterwards at supper when there was question of them and 'everyone looked upon other, and no man could make answer', had himself recited them – 'amongst others that to have my Lady Mary made legitimate, not approving that more than other'.[53]

In justice to Henry these things must be remembered. Brutal as was his treatment of his daughter, cruel the submission to which he forced her, and gallant her resistance, yet his relentless pressure was not mere wanton tyranny. His object, in forcing her to the complete surrender which he at last exacted from her, was not simply to break the pride of a creature who resisted him; it was to deprive rebellious subjects and foreign enemies of the use of her name and title, unstained by any submission. She herself must vitiate that birthright which she had so stubbornly and bravely guarded; it was for this purpose that Henry turned all his guns upon one lonely girl. That his calculation was sound, his opponents and even Mary herself tacitly admitted by their anxiety. When in the midst of her ordeal, a servant came from Sir Nicholas Carew with a letter to her, she took the opportunity of the messenger, had him copy out the letters she was even now sending to the King and Cromwell, and begged him to give the copies to the Imperial ambassador and to the Marquess of Exeter. When this servant brought the letters to the Marquess, Exeter immediately requested him, as the same messenger later confessed, for further copies that he might show them to 'other of her friends . . . and then brought me paper, pen and ink into a little closet at Westminster within his chamber'. There, in that quiet and safe place the copies were made which were to go round about among Mary's friends, and Exeter's friends, that they might know exactly the terms and extent of her capitulation.[54]

When, that summer night at Hunsdon, with all the household in bed and asleep, Mary signed her name to the three articles and wrote a letter to the King rehearsing their contents 'for the perfect declaration of the bottom of my heart and stomach', her spirit was, for the moment at least, as Cromwell

QUEEN KATHERINE OF ARAGON
Painter Unknown. National Portrait Gallery, London.

in his drafts had so often insisted for her, 'most humbly prostrate' at Henry's noble feet. The measure of her collapse can be read in a letter which she wrote to Cromwell soon after. 'For mine opinion touching pilgrimages,' she says, 'purgatory, relics and such like, I assure you I have none at all but such as I receive from him that hath my whole heart in keeping, that is the King's most gracious Highness.'[55] 'Pilgrimages, purgatory, relics and such like'–the old revered customs and beliefs of her childhood; she lumped them together and threw them in with surrender of her conscience and the honour of her soul.

When it was done she was smitten by horrible remorse. Chapuys might try to comfort her with casuistry, but she, an honest, most plain-dealing woman, found no comfort in it. Anxiously the ambassador assured her that she had done right, but she would not listen. It was nothing to her that if she had persisted 'she would have been dead and a great company with her'; it was little more that he insisted she had been preserved to do a good work. The only thing that could mend for her that which she had broken was the absolution that the Pope could give; the Pope who, for her, spoke as the very mouthpiece of God. She begged Chapuys to write for her, since she could not write herself, and ask for a secret absolution.[56]

But, though she might get the absolution and lay it as a balm upon her shrinking soul, the scar of her own surrender remained. Fisher, More, the Carthusian monks had died, martyred as surely as ever men were martyred. But she, in a fit of amazed panic, had been false to her mother and to her mother's Church. She knew what she was doing when she made her surrender. I believe that she never forgot it, and that in every crisis of her life afterwards she remembered it, and in the shadow of that memory, made her decision. She never could, now or later, weigh reason of state against reason of state; she could only try, groping and fumbling, to find out what was right for her to do, as a single human soul, like any other, before God's judgement seat, and then to do it, regardless of danger, regardless of wisdom, deaf to argument or persuasion, not daring to compromise or turn back, because once in her life she had known what was right, and had not done it.

Chapter VI

SHAMED and miserable, Mary waited at Hunsdon for the fruits of her submission, while Chapuys, really distressed at her palpable anguish, did his best to explain away to her the truth of what she had done. It was three weeks before Henry himself condescended to recognize her surrender. But one night early in July she was brought, riding secretly in the darkness, to the manor of Hackney. In the afternoon of the morrow the King and Queen arrived there, stayed the night and only left late next day. It must, for Mary at least, have been a strange, strained meeting, though Henry was gracious, and Queen Jane most kind. The Queen gave her a diamond ring; Henry put into her hands 'a check for about 1,000 crowns for her pocket money', and told her not to worry herself about expenses, for she would have what she wanted for the asking.[1]

The King and Queen left Hackney at vesper time, and Mary rode back to Hunsdon that same night through the hay-fields. She had money in her purse and a ring on her finger; and from now on she would be once more the King's dear daughter. Already Cromwell had sent her the present of a horse–a very acceptable gift, 'for', as she wrote to the new Lord Privy Seal, 'I have never a one to ride upon sometimes for my health, and besides that, my servant showeth me that he is such a one that I may of right accept not only the mind of the giver but also of the gift'.[2] Soon Cromwell was busy devising with a goldsmith a ring to be made for the Princess. In this ring there was a relief on the one side of the King and Queen, on the other of the Princess; round about was engraved a verse which extolled, above all else, the virtue of obedience. The beauty of the work and pertinence of the sentiment so pleased the King when he saw it, that he insisted on being himself the donor, and Cromwell was left to imagine some other device.[3]

Better than gifts for a woman like Mary was the re-establishment of her household, for this meant that she might ask for and obtain once more the service of those old friends whom she remembered always with affection. Cromwell inquired whom she would have about her. She told him–'I promise you upon my faith, Margaret Baynton and Susan Clarencieux have, in every condition, used themselves as faithfully, painfully, and diligently as ever did women. One other there is, that was sometime my maid, whom for her virtue I love and would be glad to have in my company, that is Mary Brown, and here be all that I will recommend.'[4] They were appointed, and with these, others who had served her before, men of Cheshire and the Marches, among them that Randall Dodd who had refused to serve in any other household but hers, and had gone instead 'in the place of a spear' to Calais.

For a while she remained in the country, but some time in the autumn she must have come to Court. Certainly she spent Christmas with her father at Greenwich, riding thither from Westminster beside the frozen river on a bitter winter day. In spite of the cold it was a gay ride through London at least, for the streets were strewn with gravel so that the horses might not slip, and the houses hanged with cloth of gold and arras. In Fleet Street stood friars of the four Orders in copes of gold, with crosses and candlesticks, and censers swinging to cense the King and Queen as they rode by. At the west door of St. Paul's the Bishop of London waited with the choir, and censed them again to the sound of its chanting. From the north door right down the hill to the foot of London Bridge stood priests of every parish of London each with the finest cross out of their churches, and candles, and censers. With them were the ranks of the city companies, 'standing in their best liveries with their hoods on their shoulders'.[5]

As she went through the crowded streets Mary may well have remembered her last Christmas, spent wretchedly in Elizabeth's household. Now, cast aside as a bastard, the little Elizabeth suffered the neglect which Mary had experienced, having 'neither gown nor kirtle, nor petticoat, nor linen for smocks, nor kerchiefs', as her Lady Governess wrote, while Mary rode with the King to keep the Christmas feast. Yet, for all that, Mary cannot have preferred the present to the unhappy past. A year ago her mother, though parted from her, was yet alive; she herself still preserved an unstained honour and a loyalty as scrupulous as that of any man. Now she had traded it in the hope of peace and security, and peace was precarious, security yet unattained.

Outwardly indeed prosperity might seem to have returned to her. Her household was as great as it ever had been. When at last she came to Court in the autumn, after the King's hunting season was over, she was second only to the Queen, and Jane, always fond of her, and loyal to the memory of Queen Katherine, kept Mary much in her company, and showed her all the honour that she could. Although the Princess at dinner-time presented the napkin to the King and Queen after the Marchioness of Exeter had brought them water to wash their hands, when that was done she sat down opposite the Queen and only a little lower down. Courtiers noticed also that when the King was not present, the Queen, to prevent Mary having to follow her through a door, would take her hand and pass through side by side with her.[6]

It mattered little that she was not again proclaimed Princess of Wales. That title had been a strange thing, due originally to some whim of Wolsey's; it was all one, thought Chapuys, whether they called her Princess of Wales or Duchess of Bedford or Duchess of York. As for her inheritance, until a son was born to the King, everyone held Mary for heir. Even though the King had by statute the power to bequeath the crown as if it were a ring from his finger, to whom would he bequeath it now? Young Richmond had died of consumption in July, and the outspoken question of Sussex—if both Mary and the lad were bastards, why not the male for heir?—had lost its point.

Yet for all Henry's large promises, his daughter was still at Christmas-time feeling the embarrassments of poverty. Looking forward to the expensive gifts of that feast she had to write to Cromwell asking him 'to be a mean to the King's Highness' to increase her allowance. 'I am ashamed', she said, 'always to be a beggar to you, but the occasion at this time is such that I cannot choose.'[7]

More serious than all this was the fact that her submission had not made the King trust her. On the one hand no one but a fool would have believed that the obstinately scrupulous young woman had yielded anything but a forced assent; on the other Henry always remembered that Mary's friends were his enemies. Even if she were innocent of rebellious intention, her orthodoxy and her birth made her dangerous. Before ever the King received her into his grace at Hackney there were rumours abroad that he intended to marry her in England, lest once safely married overseas she should retract her submission. Now the bridegroom was named by a persistent rumour, and he was, of all men, Cromwell.[8] Before she was allowed to return to Court Henry had insisted that she must blaze abroad the submission she had made. Not only the English nobles, but the Emperor must be sure of it. At the beginning of October Mary received a draft of a letter from which she was to make three copies, one for the Emperor, one for the Pope, and the third for the Queen of Hungary. The letter declared that, after study and reflection, she agreed with the statutes which decreed her mother's marriage incestuous. To the Emperor she was ordered to add a request that he should not, for her sake, trouble England, nor–the threat was barely veiled–reduce her to her late unhappy condition by bringing up her case at a General Council or anywhere else.[9]

Once she came to Court Mary had to endure in those long private talks with her father which to onlookers seemed such a proof of his affection, a probing inquisition into her private thoughts. Henry would tell her how he intended to hold the balance in Europe between France and Spain, and from that pass on to remark that though perhaps her obstinate resistance had been stiffened by her trust in Spain, yet Spain would never dare to help her so long as he lived. Then he would beg her to tell him whether indeed she had consented to his will cordially and without dissimulation. He himself, so he said with a monstrous bland effrontery, hated nothing so much as dissemblers. His Counsellors, he told her, sometimes urged him to dissemble with foreign ambassadors, but never would he do it. He asked her to show herself in this his very daughter, and to tell him the truth. What answer he wished or expected it is hard to divine, but Mary, having once thrown overboard honesty and plain dealing, gave him now, however she may have sickened at the repeated deception, the only answer she dared.[10]

In October 1537 Mary lost her loyal friend, the new Queen, whose affection must have meant much to her. In the June following Mary's surrender *Te Deum* had been sung in the churches because the child which the Queen carried quickened. The King was naturally delighted; always protective towards the Queen, he now was sending here and there to get fat quails for her; perhaps the quails were a pregnant woman's fancy, for Princess Mary also sent some–they cost her twelve shillings according to her accounts–to the Queen next month.[11] On October 11th a procession of priests and friars, with the aldermen and men of the crafts, were going about London 'to pray for the Queen who was then in labour of child'. At 2 a.m. on the Eve of Edward the Confessor, she was delivered of a son, that son for whom the King had waited for close on thirty years. Again all the churches rang with *Te Deum*, while outside there was clamour of bells, and great fires blazing in the streets, and the King's waits and the waits of London singing, and the Tower guns booming salutes. So the whole day and through the night there were more fires and guns, bells, and feasting in the streets 'with fruits and wine'.[12] But ten days later, the King was again a widower, and Mary, after standing godmother to the child, rode out from Hampton Court before dawn on a November morning, upon a horse trapped to the ground with black velvet as chief mourner for Queen Jane.[13]

Personal loss was not, however, by any means the worst thing that Mary had to bear in these years. With dismay and horror she and others must look on at attacks upon the Church to which their loyalty had been given. The Pilgrimage of Grace with its banner of the Five Wounds and its motto worked on crimson satin–'I love God, the King, and the Commonwealth', had been the reaction of the gentlemen and common people of Yorkshire to the King's doings, only become real to the North country by the suppression of the smaller monasteries. Far, for us almost unimaginably far from that centre of disturbance the King and his Council, hearing news by snatches, news often utterly false or distorted in its passage, the poor folk of these counties had at first cared little if the King disowned the Pope, divorced one wife, beheaded another, and bastardized his two daughters. The North did not at first argue or protest; its priests still prayed for the Pope, and people still held Princess Mary heir to the throne. There had been a growing uneasiness, suddenly intensified to fear and rage when the King's commissioners came to turn out those monks whom every man knew as old neighbours, from the abbey or priory that was as familiar to them all as the village alehouse. But when the King's commissioners had stripped the lead from the abbey roofs, taken down the bells out of the tower, carried away the silver rood and gilded chalice, the people realized what the King was doing. The night-long silence unbroken now by the clanging summons to prime and matins; the empty windows of the guest-house where firelight had cheered the eyes of travellers upon lonely roads, the weeds that choked the monks' flower and herb gardens–these were things that any ploughman, shepherd, or blacksmith could understand. If the monasteries went, what might not go next? That was the question asked, not only by poor and ignorant, and not only in the North, but by nobles like Lord Montague who hated the King's new ways. Many may have said, as he did, to some trusty friend at his own fireside–'I fear that within a while they will pull down the parish churches also', and received, as he did, the reply–'I fear the same.'[14]

But the Pilgrimage of Grace had failed. The summer of 1537 saw the trial and execution of its leaders, among whose awful treasons was that one, strange and new, of trusting in the King's promise of pardon. There had been a lull in the progress of religious change while Henry made his position secure, but now he could give reformers and innovators their head.

It was a very mixed army which the King called up against the old order. All sorts of men came together into the camp of this 'New Learning' as it was called, though scholars among them maintained that it was nothing but old truth rediscovered. Thomas Cranmer with his subtle, refining brain; Latimer with his cutting wit and his passionate resentment against social injustice; Hooper, austere and combative–such were the leaders of the movement. Besides these there were solid, thoughtful craftsmen and slow-minded husbandmen in town and country. Books went round about, passed unostentatiously from one 'known man' to another–Saint Luke in English or *The Prick of Conscience*–to be read behind shuttered windows and kept secure at the bottom of the master's ironbound chest. Such an ignorant but earnest student may well have been wrong-headed enough but he was often an honest searcher, an honourable adversary of the established order. Slowly and with stumbling he arrived at his conclusions; the sacrament was a remembrance only; the priest could not make the body of Christ; pilgrimages were unprofitable; images, candles, and the rest were superfluous or wrong. As for the Pope's power of pardon 'for some time he thought they had the power, and sometime he thought the contrary because they had so much money for it'. And again, he would ask himself, why should not all the mitres, crosses, and rings that gleamed in the sanctuary, be sold and given to the many miserable poor? The world, for such a man, was a world so pervaded by God that there was no room and no need for reminders or symbols of him. 'The water of the sea and other running water' was as holy as holy water in the church porch, because 'when Christ made the world and the water and other things He blessed them. Which blessing he thought to be sufficient. And so likewise he thought the blessing of Christ to be sufficient for the bread and all other ceremonies of the church.'[15]

Far as this way of thought lay from that of old Catholics such as Mary, and wounding as its stark rejection of well loved and venerable things was to them, its disciples were not the worst enemies that they had to face. There were wild spirits like Henry Daunce, the Whitechapel bricklayer, who would 'preach the word of God in his own house in his garden, Where he set a tub to a tree and therein he preached on Sundays and other days early in the morning and at 6 o'clock at night, and had great audience of people . . . which said person had no learning of his book neither in English nor other tongue, and yet he declared the Scripture as well as he had studied at the University'.[16] To the last statement all might not have agreed, but there is no manner of doubt that Daunce was an early example of that great army of preachers which grew with the years of the sixteenth century and which each of the Tudors, not even excepting Edward VI, was to find a public danger.

As one by one the monasteries were emptied and destroyed, monks, friars, and nuns who had fretted against their vows came out into the world, burning to attack all that had held them captive, proclaiming that 'the perfection of Christian living doth not consist in dumb ceremonies, wearing of a grey coat, disguising ourselves after strange fashions, duckings, noddings, and beckonings, in girding ourselves with a girdle full of knots and other papistical ceremonies',[17] but in freedom; too often they interpreted that to mean a freedom to destroy.

Besides these ex-religious, embittered with hoarded grudges, there were laymen, by nature violent and unruly, who, having taken a dislike, maybe often justified, to their parish priest, argued from it, after a very common human habit, to a condemnation of all which the priest stood for, and at last elevated their personal dislike into a principle. These men found the new learning much to their taste. Master Edmund Louth of Sawtrey in Huntingdon, after many brushes with the monks who were his neighbours, and with the parish priest of Sawtrey, 'conceived such a hate against that religion and that holy priest that he came into the church and plucked the fellow from the altar as he was about to make his God'. It is not to be wondered at that Louth met his death at the hands of the abbey tenants, who, when he was walking in the fields with his little son of three in his arms, set upon him, and killed him going over a stile, with a 'club gotten in Monks' wood, half a mile from Sawtrey'.[18] It is more surprising perhaps that John Fox saw fit to include him among the 'martyrs' for religion.

There were indeed plenty of such untamed, irresponsible spirits among the ranks of the so-called reformers—mockers, sceptics, rebels—they were of the same kidney as the carpenter who made a rood for the village church and gave to the figure of Christ a grinning, gaping face, saying that if the parish did not like it he would clap on a pair of horns and make it an excellent devil. It was such men as this that Cromwell specially encouraged and to whom he even gave some sort of organization. These 'Ribalds' forced upon the rest of the village or town plays of the crudest and coarsest satire, playing them openly in the church and churchyard; they shouted ballads at fairs, from the alehouse bench, down the village street, all in mockery, in blasphemous, vulgar mockery of ideas which, debatable or not, had at least a claim to sober and earnest criticism.

Mary, and others like her, watched with growing horror while the intellectual and moral ferment went on, for as long as it suited the King's purpose, almost unchecked. The smaller abbeys had been suppressed in 1536. Three years later the big religious houses fell, and monasticism, that ancient thing, as familiar as it was reverend, had come to an end in England. Roods and images went the way of the abbeys; they were pulled down and burned with mockery in market places. Thomas of Canterbury, old antagonist of kings, was summoned to answer the charge of treason, granted a counsel, tried and condemned. His dust and bones were raked out from under the fabulous treasures of his shrine and dishonoured. Monks and nuns wandered about the

country trying to find new homes, sometimes an abbot would marry an
abbess, or a nun; priests in Suffolk, thinking that in these new days they themselves might marry, took a wife 'and fell to occupations and husbandry to get
their living by, and their wives'. As Mary went about the country with the
King in one of the stately progresses, archers with bent bows going before
and behind, she must learn to sleep in a dismantled Yorkshire abbey hastily
rigged up with pavilions for the royal visit;[19] she must get used to seeing
upon Henry's thumb the great ruby, 'the Regal of France', which had gleamed
on the shrine at Canterbury.

In such a world it was no wonder if she were still unhappy. In the autumn
of 1538 the King, fearing much the growing cordiality between those old
enemies, France and the Empire, and determined to make safe his position at
home, turned against another group of old Catholic nobles, greater yet than
the victims of 1537, and more closely connected with Mary by ties of affection. In addition to their sympathies, these noblemen each possessed the
disastrous heritage of royal Plantagenet blood, for Lord Montague and his
brothers were sons of Margaret Countess of Salisbury, whose father had been
George of Clarence, brother of Edward IV. Henry Courtenay Marquess of
Exeter was the son of Katherine, Edward IV's youngest daughter.

Their connexion with Mary was as patent as their royalty. Margaret of
Salisbury, mother of the Poles, was Mary's old and dear friend; no one, least
of all the old Catholic lords, had forgotten the talk of a marriage between
Mary and Reginald Pole. Darcy had harped on that string; now John Worth
told Lord Lisle of a 'coat armour found in the Duchess of Salisbury's coffer',
which spoke of the same thing. The arms consisted of the leopards of England
impaling, as for marriage, another coat which John Worth did not describe
but which presumably was that of Pole, for round about the arms were
pansies and marigolds–pansies for Pole, marigolds for Mary. Growing from
the midst of the flowers there was a tree with a shield hanging on it, a shield
again party per pale, on the one side purple 'in token of the coat of Christ,
and on the other side . . . all the Passion of Christ'. It was in fact, as Worth
read it, as much as to say that 'Pole intended to have married my Lady Mary,
and betwixt them both should again arise the old doctrine of Christ'.[20]

If a Pole was counted by most of her friends as the best bridegroom for
Mary, there were others who looked to the Marquess of Exeter's family
instead. When news of the Pilgrimage of Grace came to Italy and brought all
travelling Englishmen together to talk it over, one Dingley, a knight of
Rhodes, who later was to die with the Marquess, Montague, and others, said
openly in the house of Ambassador Pate that 'if anything should fortune to
the King otherwise than good in this insurrection, then Lady Mary . . . might
marry with the Marquess of Exeter's son, and so they to enjoy the realm'.[21]
Whether the marriage was contemplated by Exeter himself or no, he certainly had been closely in touch with Mary at the time of her surrender, and
continued to be so until the date of his arrest. When in his examination he
found things going hard with him because the King's officers, searching for

treasonable correspondence, thought it suspicious that they discovered none, treasonable or other, he at once wrote a dozen or so letters to Mary which she might safely show.[22] The inference is that there had been others less innocent which she had destroyed.

Yet little that was actually treasonable came out in the examination; much that suggested there might be ground for treason in a deep discontent with the state of the kingdom. Exeter had said, 'Knaves rule about the King', and then wickedly and treacherously lifting up and stretching his arm and shaking his clenched fist said, 'I trust to give them a buffet one day.' He and Montague were certainly corresponding together; Montague's men knew well by sight the big fellow in a tawny coat who came with letters from Exeter. They had heard Montague lament the downfall of the abbeys, when the greater ones began to fall like ripe fruit into the King's insatiable hand. Especially Montague regretted Bisham, the Poles' well loved foundation, and would say sometimes that he hoped to see Bisham in as good state as ever. Sometimes there were forecasts of strife to come–'I like well', Lord Montague said to Geoffrey his brother, 'the doing of my brother Cardinal Pole. I would we were both oversea with the Bishop of Luke [sic] for this world will one day come to stripes. A time will come; I fear me we shall not tarry the time. If we may tarry the time we shall do well enough. It must needs come to this pass one day, and I fear me we shall lack nothing so much as honest men . . . I had liever dwell in the west parts than at Warblington, for in the west parts the Marquess of Exeter is strong . . . I am sorry the Lord of Bergavenny is dead, for if he were alive he were able to make 10,000 men.' 'Tush, Geoffrey', said Montague another day, 'thou hast no cast. The Lord Darcy played the fool. He went about to pluck down the Council; he should have first begun with the head, but I beshrew him for leaving off so soon.' Those indeed were hardly the words of a loyal subject. For the rest there was little against the accused but trivialities. Montague and his brother would walk forth alone in the gardens and fields adjoining the house; 'but what communication they have had' acknowledged the witness, 'this examinate knoweth not'; Jerome Ragland, one of Montague's men, remembered having heard it said '(but of whom he cannot tell) that it were a meet marriage for Reginald Pole to have my Lady Mary'.[23]

A fortnight before Christmas the Marquess of Exeter and Lord Montague, Sir Nicholas Carew and other less important persons were executed. Exeter's wife and young son Edward, a boy about twelve years old, remained in the Tower, in danger from time to time as events outside shaped themselves; so too for the moment remained old Lady Salisbury. Geoffrey Pole, Montague's brother, had his life and freedom, but he was unhappier than the dead, for under threat of torture he had given the information that served to condemn both his brother and his friend. While he was still in the Tower he tried to smother himself with a cushion, but he could not die; when they set him free the wretched man went about, lonely as a ghost, and seeming 'like one terror-stricken all his days'. For eighteen months longer, that is to say till May 1541, lasted the imprisonment of that lion-hearted old woman Margaret of Salisbury, whose hour came when the King was threatened with a rising in the North. In 1538 Southampton, Cromwell, and the Bishop of Ely had examined her, but could get nothing from her. 'We assure your Lordships', they reported to the Privy Council, 'we have dealed with a one as men have not dealed with before us; we may call her rather a strong and constant man, than a woman!'[24] On a May morning she was brought out under the arch of the Byward Tower and up the slope of Tower Hill where the circling gulls and the wide river spoke of the freedom of air and open sea. She sent a last message and special blessing to her old pupil Mary, and then the fellow who took the place of the regular executioner, busy just now at his trade in the North, hacked and hewed at her neck till he had at last severed her head.

After the death of Jane Seymour Henry remained a widower for a little over a year, but at the end of 1539 the King's fourth wife arrived from Cleves. Mary, with Elizabeth, who was now treated once more as the King's daughter, were there to greet her at Greenwich, at that stately entry where one of the foreign merchants, standing with his fellows, all in velvet coats and red caps with white feathers, relished the sight of Cromwell, looking more like a post runner than anything else, bustling up and down with his staff in his hand. It was indeed an anxious moment for Cromwell, since the marriage was of his devising, and even the bystanders could see as the King passed that he 'showed in his face that he was disappointed'.[25] His first words to Cromwell, 'spoken by way of lamentation, "What remedy?"' showed it still more plainly. Cromwell himself could not find a remedy, but the King did. In a few months he had married Katherine Howard; Cromwell's head was off; and Anne had retired, with a pension and four good manors, to the position, strange in the sixteenth century, of an independent woman of marriageable age without any husband, a position which she continued to fill with apparent satisfaction. For some time the courtiers speculated on the possibility of her return; once there was a rumour, serious enough for the King to have investigated, that she was with child; but neither was true. She never fell out with any of the royal family. She remained in an honoured retirement, having always a good place in royal processions, exchanging presents with Henry's daughters, placid and comfortable until her death.

Mary did not at first get on with the King's new wife, the young and gay Katherine Howard – the Princess balked at showing her so much reverence as her two predecessors; the result was that two of Mary's favourite maids were promptly removed; after that there was peace between them.[26]

But Queen Katherine's reign was short. On November 11th 1541 the Privy Council ordered that her household was to be broken up. She herself was to go to Syon. Princess Mary was to be escorted to the house where the little Prince lay. At Syon, whereas formerly the young Queen 'did nothing but dance and rejoice, now when the musicians come they are told that it is no more the time to dance'.[27] Archbishop Cranmer interviewed her, after she had been charged with treason, found her in a 'franzy' and was so much touched that he talked to her of mercy rather than of her faults. The King too, really wounded by the unfaithfulness of this lively girl, thought at first of separation only. But the charges against her were too serious. She went the way of Norfolk's other unfortunate kinswoman, Queen Anne, and again Henry was a widower.

In all these years Princess Mary was never a centre of interest, except when conspiracies made her potentially dangerous, or when Henry had on hand one of his many and various negotiations for her marriage. And these negotiations, in which a bewildering succession of shadowy suitors followed hard on each other's heels, were nothing but the ordinary stock-in-trade of Henry's diplomacy. He had no intention that Mary should marry either Don Luiz of Portugal, or the Duke of Orleans, or an Italian prince, or a German Protestant; but it was useful to talk of marrying her, now here now there. The negotiations for the Portuguese marriage, which had been begun by the Emperor in 1536, partly in the hope of getting Mary out of England into safety, continued for a couple of years. Henry would not hear of the Princess being declared legitimate; nor, till Edward was born, that she should leave the country. But at the same time he was inclining his other ear to the blandishments of France, and showing himself very coy on behalf of his daughter, for, as he more than once told the envoys when asked to make any definite offer, 'reason is the woman should be sought'. The French proposed the Dauphin, or Angoulême, but Henry would meet them in nothing; Mary should be taken as illegitimate or not at all.

In 1539 while the Emperor and France drew together, Henry was veering towards a German alliance, which was Cromwell's aim, and the cause of his ultimate disaster. While this was Henry's game, there was talk of marrying Mary to a son of the Duke of Cleves, and at the same time, for counterpoise, a sudden rumour that she should be given to the Emperor himself. As Pole wrote to Cardinal Contarini, it seemed likely that Henry 'darà parole a tutti et interim quaeret subterfugia'.[28]

In that same year appeared Mary's one and only visible suitor–the one man who came wooing for himself. This was Philip the Palatine of Bavaria, Philip 'the Fighter', a soldier thirteen years older than Mary, who had earned his nickname by his defence of Vienna against the Turks. He arrived in England just before Christmas, and went almost at once to Enfield, where Mary was living with the Prince, her little brother. There, though it was December, they met 'in the gardens of the abbey'. The Palatine–the news went the rounds of the ambassadors in London–kissed the Princess, a sign that there was marriage in the air, for since Exeter had died no one in England was near enough to her in rank to do so. Then they talked, partly through an interpreter–for Mary spoke no German and he no English–partly in Latin, and it is to be supposed that she thanked him for that gift which had been so carefully discussed between himself and Wriothesley, and which was later entered in the inventory of Mary's jewels, the 'cross of diamond set with four pearls and one pearl pendant at the same'. Wriothesley had considered it too valuable, so that Philip had promised to 'try all the friends he has in London to get a meaner', but presumably without success.[29] Mary probably was pleased with the jewelled cross. Whether she liked the lover or not was another thing. After their conversation they declared to witnesses, he, that he would marry her, 'if his person pleased her', she, that she would obey her father.[30] But Philip offended many, and Mary would certainly be among them, by saying openly that he had never heard Mass till he came to England. The Imperialists were shocked at the idea of such a marriage for the Princess, which, however, they feared would certainly take place soon; rumours even got about that it had already taken place. They need not have been disturbed. Henry had no real intention of giving his daughter to Philip, and though for the next five or six years the Palatine was kept dangling and hopeful, and though he visited England more than once, and on one occasion spent over an hour in conversation with the Princess, yet he never again came so near to attaining his prize as on his first visit.

While Henry played with the Palatine, he did not neglect other possibilities. The marriage between Mary and Orleans was once more discussed with France. Negotiations went on for months, sometimes brisk, sometimes languishing; but by May 1542 Francis was piqued at the coolness of the English, and when Paget went to see the French Admiral, the conversation, as the Englishman reported it, ran as follows:

' "What news?" quod I.

' "What news!" quod he. "The things be far asunder, which I am sure you know."

' "I looked for none other," quod I, "if you asked what was propounded to me; but what was asked and offered, I pray you?" quod I.

' "There was offered" quod he, "300,000 crowns; and what is that? Howbeit seeing things cannot go forward as we would we shall remain friends nevertheless."' But, though the Admiral tried to appear cheerful, Paget thought that the French were so much at a loss that they stood 'like deer upon a launde', not knowing which way now to take; even in the autumn the behaviour of the English was still such a sore subject with Francis that he abused Henry till Paget's loyal heart 'frobbed' to hear him.

Concurrently with these other suitors went the greatest of them all, the Emperor himself, now a widower, who set about his wooing with a caution and dilatoriness commensurate with his position. When Chapuys came back to England in 1540 the rumour went that it was to negotiate the marriage, and Henry was certainly, though by very 'indirect crooked ways', suggesting that the Emperor should suggest the match. In 1542 while the Orleans negotiations were actually on foot great wagers were offered daily in France that Mary would after all be given to the Emperor. In 1545 Stephen Gardiner Bishop of Winchester and another Bishop were actually sent to treat of the marriage and found 'that fox', Chapuys, most encouraging, for he reported that he had 'made the Emperor's mouth to water' for Mary as his bride.[31]

Other less notable suitors applied, or were rumoured to apply for Mary's hand. The King of Denmark's brother might have been a useful bridegroom, or the Duke of Saxony. The King of Poland would have been a more surprising choice, yet in 1546, when the Polish ambassador came to England, and Henry knighted him and hung a golden collar round his neck, people were talking openly about the marriage, and Mary was being teased about it by the Queen.[32]

But the Emperor, Orleans, Don Luiz, the lesser fry–all would not do. The truth was that no foreign suitor was acceptable to Henry, for he saw clearly, that once abroad and married, especially to a Catholic prince, Mary's surrendered claim to legitimacy might be revived, and her title as orthodox Catholic once more pressed, since for any logical believer in the Papacy she was, whatever he might call her, undoubtedly legitimate and heir to the throne, while he himself lay under the Pope's ban. He knew well that though logic might often be tempered by convenience, yet if Charles and Francis should find it possible and profitable to combine against the schismatic King of England, their logic would be surprisingly exact. His son indeed was as legitimate as Mary, and would for all but the most rigid and intransigent of the old Catholics take precedence of any daughter, but there were rumours already that the boy was not strong. Altogether, though it suited Henry to hawk his daughter's marriage round Europe, since none could be sure that he would not marry her, it did not suit him to come to any conclusion.

Mary herself knew it, just as clearly as her father. Here she was, in 1542, unmarried and with the best years of her life passing, for she was already twenty-six. She was a woman who loved children; she was also a woman, made, in spite of her royal courage, for the small world of a family and a household; but because she was Henry's daughter, when suitors came 'there was', she herself said, 'nothing to be got but fine words, and while my father lives I shall be only the Lady Mary, the most unhappy lady in Christendom'.[33]

Henry was not so fastidious about his own marriage. During the wild, wet summer of 1543 he decided to provide his family with a new stepmother, and in July he married Katherine Parr, a widow almost as often married as Henry himself. She was at once perhaps the least willing and the most satisfactory of Henry's wives. As a priggish girl she had once, on the strength of a royal fortune foretold for her, 'answered back' when bidden by her mother to do some sewing, 'My hands', she said, 'are ordained to touch crowns and sceptres, not needles and spindles.'[34] The prophecy had come true, but the intolerable child had grown into a witty, pleasant, cultured woman, musical and a good Latin scholar, a letter writer too who was able to keep a poise between teasing and affection almost as prettily as Dorothy Osborne a century or so later. As devout as Henry's first wife, she was believed to be rather of the advanced school of thought; perhaps, more truly, she harked back to the earlier days of the century, when it was possible to wish for reform without destruction. The last years of the King, though haunted by fears of plots, and by qualms of doubt as to whether the tide of change, so long encouraged, would check at a King's word, were free from domestic unhappiness.

As a stepmother, the third Queen Katherine must have been acceptable, not only to the two younger children, but to Mary herself. When they were not together, the two women—Katherine was only five years older than her step-daughter—would correspond pleasantly in Latin. Mary sent the Queen a present of a purse; Katherine replied in a letter borne by a messenger 'who', she said, 'will be welcome for the sake of his music'.[35] Both were well educated, both were devout; it was at Katherine's persuasion that Mary undertook an English translation of Erasmus's Latin Paraphrase of the Gospel of Saint John in whose preface Nicholas Udall wrote such praise of young and learned ladies that it might seem he spoke of a golden age. For, said he, 'Neither is it now any strange thing to hear gentlewomen, instead of most vain communication about the moon shining in the water, to use grave and substantial talk in Greek or Latin with their husbands in godly matters. It is now no news in England to see young damsels in noble houses and in the courts of princes, instead of cards and other instruments of vain trifling, to have continually in their hands either Psalms, homilies, or other devout meditations.'

There is one picture of Mary and Queen Katherine together which may be noticed since not only does it show the friendly relations between them, but also because, in it, an old friend of Mary's takes his last leave.

Chapuys was going home after a stay of sixteen years. He had for long been ill with gout, and now in 1545 was at last recalled. He was carried in a chair to the palace, to a final audience with the King, and as he went through the garden, the Queen and Princess Mary, walking there perhaps to enjoy the sweet airs of May, caught him up. Chapuys made his farewell to the Queen who kindly refused to let him stand, and then removed a few steps away so that Mary might speak with him privately. But the Princess, though he was so old a friend, and though their common memories went back through so much to her unhappy girlhood, would be equally obliging to the Queen. She only gave Chapuys a message of thanks for the Emperor, and briefly said good-bye.[36]

Chapter VII

A LONG chapter was drawing to an end when Eustace Chapuys took his leave of the Queen and Princess in the trim garden of the palace. The King was ageing and ill; there was now no thought in anyone's mind of another heir; Mary was twenty-nine, Elizabeth twelve, and Edward eight. For Mary the last years of her father's life were years of comparative peace. In 1544 her position had been assured by recognition of her right to succeed Edward, if no other children were born to the King. But, better than any title, must have been to her the natural family affection which she could feel for her father, for the little brother, and, if she chose, for the little sister.

During these years she lived a quiet life, now and again at Court, but for the most part with her own household in the country and often in company with one or other of the two children. Of that private side of her life the only recorded history is to be found in the pages of her account book, and these are full of pleasant trivialities. Here are a few entries.[1]

December	To my Lady's Grace for playing at cards	45s.
January	Given to a daughter of John Bell of Greenwich being my Lady's Grace's god-daughter and bringing to her Grace wardens ...	5s.
	Given to one bringing Bacon and Eggs ...	20d.
March	Given to the yeomen of the King's guard presenting my Lady's Grace with a leek. [Mary was always, to some, Princess of Wales.] ...	15s.
April	Given to the keeper of the King's gardens of Greenwich bringing herbs and flowers. ...	2s.
June	Given to Balthasar's servant for bringing Roses	12d.
	Given to a wife bringing strawberries ...	12d.
	To my Lady Page's servant bringing cream and strawberries ...	2s.
	Paid to Typkyn for cherries ...	20d.
December	Bought of Farnando at my Lady Grace's last coming to Court 100 pearls ...	£66 13s. 4d.
February	To George Mountjoy drawing my Lady's Grace to his Valentine ...	40s.

And a few years later, at New Year, 'Given to my lady Margaret's servant bringing ... a gown of carnation satin of the Venice fashion ... 20s.' and a whole list besides of presents received—a salt of gold, 8 yards of white damask, two wrought flowers, a ring with a diamond, a wrought smock and six handkerchiefs.

Many of the entries deal with games and amusements. Besides the frequent losses of money at cards, the Lady Mary lost her breakfast one day in a wager at bowls, and redeemed it for 10s. She would hunt in Waltham Forest, and the keepers got 5s. Perhaps she had been hunting one August day in Windsor Forest when John Wylde supplied her and her people with bread and ale. At home she had her sewing to occupy her, and made many of her New Year's gifts, a gold-embroidered 'qwyssion for Mr. Wriothesley', a silver-embroidered box for my Lady Elizabeth's grace, though when she gave the King a chair it was covered by Green of London and embroidered by 'Gwyllam Brellent'. Always too there was music and dancing in the house. Her lute, her virginals, are constantly in the account books; John Heywood came with his troupe of children and played an interlude–doubtless one of his own, merry, coarse, and robust; country folk, or perhaps even gentlemen of the Court, danced a morris dance before her in May time; she was herself so fond of dancing that her little brother, or the pedagogue who drafted his letter to Queen Katherine Parr, was alarmed for the state of her soul.[2] For more merriment she had Jane the Fool, whose head was regularly shaved, and Lucretia the Tumbler. Now and again she had the excitement of receiving packages which English gentlemen brought at her request from abroad. 'Eastern stuff' bought in France for her cost £12: 'certain Stuff' from Spain £3, and now and again there was a present–'10 pair of Spanish gloves in a coffer from the Duchess in Spain'.

Everywhere there is notice of gifts, for Mary was an affectionate woman, affectionate in these years even to little Elizabeth, giving her, one April, 20s. 'to play her withal', and at Christmas a kirtle of 5 yards of yellow satin at 7s. 6d. a yard.[3] The inventory of her jewels shows the same generosity. There was a 'Balas with one Diamond table over it and three mean pearls pendant at the same', which went to Lady Margaret Douglas at her marriage; a 'lace for the neck of goldsmith work with small pearls' was given to the young, accomplished, ill-starred Jane Grey to put about the throat that the headsman's axe was to sever. Sir Anthony Browne received as forfeit, when he drew her as his Valentine, 'a brooch enamelled black with an Agate and the story of Abraham with 4 small Rock Rubies'; little Elizabeth got a green Tablet garnished with gold having the picture of the Trinity in it, and a pomander of gold with a dial in it. The annotations, all in Mary's own hand, recording such gifts from among her jewels, sprinkle the margin of the inventory.[4] Nor, even before the King established her income, was she niggardly in charity. Old women, poor old men, god-children, the prisoners in 'the prison houses in London' all received something.

But there was a darker side hinted at in the entries of the account books. Mary had passed through years of fear, shame, and disaster; she had seen her friends, and the Church she loved, overwhelmed in the same catastrophe. The result of those years of unhappiness now showed itself at times in such a profound melancholy that Francis I thought it advisable that his ambassador should inquire if this could be the symptom of any disease that made her incapable of child-bearing;[5] at times in a weakness so absolute that her women doubted if she yet lived;[6] she suffered, as she had suffered long, from toothache and neuralgia, and there is more than one entry in her accounts of visits by her father's surgeon or others, to blood her, to prescribe for her, or to draw her teeth.[7]

So she went about the Court, and the country manors where most of these years were spent, a thin, frail woman with tight lips, low-bridged nose, red hair and a fair complexion that was still pretty. She had been born obstinate, and for courage she was every bit a Tudor, but to her father she must have seemed a quiet, inoffensive person, for he himself had taught her to be, as observers remarked, cautious and chary of speech. It was due to him also that her natural forthright confidence in other folks' honesty had been tainted with an anxious, uneasy mistrust that was often only too completely justified. Very fond of children, very much a woman too in her interest in dress and jewels, she was, as might be expected from her parents, well educated; reading in bed had, during her unhappiest years, given her solace in the long dark hours of sleeplessness; by day she had amused herself in teaching her women to play lute and virginals.

Like every Tudor, she was capable of passionate affection, but there never was a hint nor breath of scandal against her. Men spoke of her, and to her, as if to a nun. Her father, doubting such a reputation, once bade Sir Francis Bryan test it at a masque with who knows what bawdy talk; but Bryan was so received that both he and his master were convinced that the truth had been spoken.[8] The root and ground of Mary's character, flawed though it was with faults that her past suffering largely excused, was indeed a plain and humble goodness. She was a woman to whom God and the world of souls was the reality to which everything in the life of the visible world must be referred for judgement. Practical, housewifely little woman, with her neat, carefully checked and annotated account books, she was no mystic, but she was simply and deeply pious. Her religion did not make her judicious, nothing could do that, since her mind was narrow and by no means acute; but it did make her scrupulous, painstaking, disciplined.

Henry's younger daughter, even in these early years, was clearly of a different stamp. The child that Lady Bryan had found, in her teething, such a masterful young mistress, demanding at table 'divers meats, fruits and wine' that were meant for grown-ups,[9] was now a little girl of 'a singular wit', and a great favourite of her father. Her childish solemnity made a pretty comedy for men of importance such as Sir Thomas Wriothesley, who thought it worth while to report how, in answer to her father's inquiries and blessing, 'she gave humble thanks, enquiring after his Majesty's welfare and that with as great a gravity as if she had been 40 years old'.[10]

Last of all, but first in importance, came the heir, the Prince. Henry delighted in him. Always fond of young children, he would spend whole days with the little boy, 'dallying with him in his arms a long space, and so holding him in a window to the sight and great comfort of all the people'.[11] Even allowing for the enthusiasm naturally expressed by loyal subjects at the sight of their future King, there must have been something specially attractive in the pretty, unfortunate boy. At the age of eleven months he was visited by

8

Lord Audley, who told Cromwell that he 'never saw so goodly a child of his age, so merry, so pleasant, so good and loving countenance and so earnest an eye, as it were a sage judgement towards every person that repaireth to his grace'. The grown man and the baby regarded each other solemnly and with care; Audley thought that Edward was a little thinner than he had been, but then, 'he shooteth out in length and waxeth firm and stiff, and can steadfastly stand'.[12] What Edward thought, he did not disclose. Like all children he had his whims, interpreted sometimes with loyal jubilation by his future subjects. For after the visit of two German ambassadors, when the young Prince would neither look at them nor 'put forth his hand for no cheering dandling and flattering the nurse . . . could use', old Essex, 'to accustom him to a stern countenance and great rough beard', took his hand and thrust his own face near the child's. This was a different matter. The Prince laid hold of the beard 'and was therewith merry'. 'Now full well', cried Essex, 'knowest thou that I am thy father's true man and thine, and these others be false knaves.'[13]

Without care or thought of the crushing burden that was to fall upon his shoulders, the baby grew into a boy, riding, dancing, playing with little friends sent over to Ashridge, as Jane Dormer was sent, to amuse him. One day these two were at cards. 'Now Jane,' says the Prince, 'Your King is gone; I shall be good enough for you.'[14] The scrap of child's talk is a poignant thing to set beside the pathetic, schooled utterances of the boy King three years later, who had 'such a grace of posture and gesture in gravity . . . that it should seem he were already a father, and yet he passeth not the age of 10 years. A thing undoubtedly much rather to be seen than believed.'[15]

On January 27th 1547, in the early hours of the morning, King Henry died. He had for long been ailing, was in all probability syphilitic, and, though only fifty-six, was counted an old man. Edward Seymour, Lord Hertford, brother of Queen Jane Seymour, and thus the young King's uncle, rode off post-haste to Hertford Castle, with Sir Anthony Browne. They had the boy wakened and dressed, and brought him hurriedly to Enfield, where they announced to him the death of his father. Even in those later and more settled times, the death of a King meant an awkward break in the Government, and a few anxious, hard-driven days. But this time there was no disturbance from outside, no pretender to the crown. The little King came safely to his city of London and to the Tower, and the Council could settle down peacefully to alter the old coronation service 'for the tedious length of the same which should weary and be hurtsome peradventure to the King's Majesty, being yet of tender age, fully to endure and bide out'.[16]

On February 20th, the King, all in white velvet and cloth of silver, on a horse caparisoned in crimson, rode through London to his crowning. There were, of course, along the way, shows of great splendour and ingenuity at which the child must have stared with wide shining eyes. At Paul's he stopped for a long time to watch an Arragonese rope-dancer perform amazing feats. At the Great Cross in Cheap he rode under a triumphal arch made to represent the sky; from it an angel was let down through the air, who put into the boy's hand a purse containing £1,000. 'The little Prince said, "Why do they give me this?" and he had not the strength to hold it in his hands.'[17] At Westminster Cranmer recited the abbreviated order of service, and he led the child to the four sides of the stage in the Abbey, showing him to the people with the question – Would they have him for their King? To this the Council had designed

'The people taunser;
yea, yea, yea, King
Edward, King Edward,
King Edward.'[18]

And so they dutifully did.

The Council's new coronation service was not their only, nor their greatest innovation. Even while the King lay dying, Hertford and Paget were pacing up and down the gallery outside, in the chill of a winter's night, discussing whether it were not better to change the dispositions of the dying man's will. In the garden at Enfield, Hertford walked with Sir Anthony Browne, devising of the same matter. Hertford, and Paget had agreed, was all for a Protectorate rather than the equal council of Regency. To this Browne also 'gave his frank consent . . . thinking it . . . both the surest kind of government and most fit for the Commonwealth'.[19] Hertford himself, the King's uncle, was the obvious man for Protector, and so was accepted by the other executors; he also became Duke of Somerset, while a shower of compensatory honours descended on others of the Council; Sir Thomas Seymour the new Protector's brother was made Lord Seymour of Sudely, John Dudley Viscount Lisle received the Earldom of Warwick, William Parr, the rascal brother of Henry's last Queen, became Marquis of Northampton; the Chancellor, Wriothesley, Earl of Southampton; Sir Richard Rich, accomplished turncoat, and soon to be Chancellor in Catholic Wriothesley's place, Lord Rich.

With the death of Henry one of the most potent personalities that had ever ruled England passed away, and into the space that his portentous bulk had filled stepped a boy not quite ten years old. The world, which had held its breath for fear so long, and comported itself with care, moved quickly now. No one knows quite how soon after Henry's death, Katherine Parr, Mary's kind stepmother, married her old love, Lord Seymour of Sudely. The news, when it leaked out, must have been a shock to many; Mary, who was approached by Seymour with a request for her countenance after the marriage had been made, but before it was owned, felt the project as an insult to her father's memory. To her Henry was no longer as he had once been, the oppressor of her mother, her own tormentor, and the enemy of her Church. In the late years of his life he had been kind, and Mary, always warm hearted, was a woman to repay any kindness with good measure. Not only was the King her father, not only had he that same quick, immediate touch of mingled royalty and humanity that the child Elizabeth inherited from him; but also, in his later years he was a sick man; it was no wonder that such a woman as Mary was conquered by him, or that when he was gone, she looked back upon him with yearning. When Seymour asked her for her good offices in his wooing of the Queen she replied in a letter whose reserved tone shows far more real sorrow than Elizabeth's eloquent mourning – 'Of all other creatures in the world', she wrote, 'it standeth least with my poor honour to be a meddler in this matter, considering whose wife her grace was of late, and besides that, if she be minded to grant your suit, my letters shall do you but small pleasure. On the other side, if the remembrance of the King's Majesty my father (whose soul God pardon) will not suffer her to grant your suit, I am nothing able to persuade her to forget the loss of him, who is as yet very ripe in mine own remembrance.'[20]

It was not only for Mary a personal loss. From the very hour of the King's death it had been apparent how, now the strong hand had been removed, there would be a scramble of violent and greedy men for the sweets and profits of power. Seymour of Sudely did not long remain in possession of the oblique splendour of a dowager Queen's husband. Katherine died in childbirth in the autumn, and he was left to seek another bride. This time his ambition mounted even higher. He had already tried to win the affection of the young King, sending him, secretly, because by Somerset's orders 'his Grace is not half a quarter of an hour alone', very acceptable gifts of pocket-money. The King in return, hastily and secretly scrawled thanks and requests for more on small torn scraps of paper.[21]

Seymour, however, wanted something of greater durability than the brittle favour of a boy King. He now contemplated marriage with one of the King's sisters. But this suitor of Mary or of Elizabeth never got so far as to make any proposals to either. On January 17th 1549 he was sent to the Tower on a charge of treason. On March 20th he was beheaded, still undaunted and impenitent, if we may believe Latimer's sermon preached to justify the judicial murder. For Latimer said that on the scaffold just before his death Seymour bade the lieutenant's servant remind his own man to 'Speed the thing that he wot of.' The words seemed too significant to pass over. The servant was examined and confessed. Seymour, he said, while in the Tower, had written letters both to Mary and Elizabeth with the 'aglet of a point plucked off his hose', and with ink made 'as craftily'. The letters, hidden in the sole of a velvet shoe were discovered, and read. In them Seymour had urged that Mary and Elizabeth should oppose the Protector, since he was, of set purpose, determined to turn the King against them.[22]

Whether Somerset deliberately tried to alienate Edward from his elder sister is doubtful, but the whole of the boy's education had told that way. For the earlier part of that education the old King had been responsible, and Doctor Cheke, a notable supporter of the New Learning, had been Edward's tutor for the last three years of Henry's reign; Doctor Cox, another of the same way of thinking, for longer than that. Already Edward had absorbed, and now held with all the unquestioning conviction of childhood, and all the arrogant obstinacy of a Tudor, the views of the advanced reformers. Little as was his affection for either of his Seymour uncles, both of whom he saw perish without a protest, he was, in religion, Somerset's docile disciple. Hence, because really fond of his elder sister, the King had her increasingly upon his conscience by reason of her reactionary views. As yet, however, the responsibility did not lie very heavily upon the boy of ten. When, before the Admiral's marriage was made public, one of his friends asked the King 'whom his Grace would he [Seymour] should marry', his Highness said– naughtily–"'My Lady Anne of Cleeves," and so pausing a while, said after,' and we can imagine with what a splutter of schoolboy laughter, "'Nay, nay, wot you what? I would he married my sister Mary to turn her opinions."'[23]

Yet in the past the small boy had been used to follow his elder sister about, asking the innumerable questions of a child, seeking her company, and looking upon her almost, some said, as a mother. Sometimes it may even have been her answers that he quoted, if that story is true which Jane Dormer's biographer reports. For as he rode one day past one of the ruined abbeys, deserted but still beautiful, he asked what the buildings had been. He was told, and told also how, for the iniquity of the monks, his father had dissolved all such. Then, asked the King, 'Why did not my father punish the offenders and put better men into such goodly buildings . . . [and] so great an ornament to this kingdom.'[24] It was even said that once when Mary had been to visit him, and had talked to him of the changes that the Protector was making, he had burst into tears because things 'could not be according to her will and desire'. But perhaps it was only because he himself was fretting at the restraints Somerset laid upon him, that he 'besought her to have patience until he had more years, and he would remedy all'. The visit ended with kisses, the gift of a jewel, and a complaint by the King that his people allowed him nothing better to give her, and so farewell.[25]

But now, separated for the most part from her, and since the age of six taken from the care of women, the lonely boy was growing and hardening into that paragon of learning and Protestantism which was to be the theme of so many hymns of reformed praise. As for his learning, he was already grounded in Latin, Greek, and French, and men who found the child poring over his book in some retired gallery wondered at his diligence, as his masters admired his aptitude. Not that his education all came out of books. Ascham recommended for education dancing, swimming, archery, riding at the ring; and in these Edward sometimes relaxed himself. So in his diary, in March 1551, the King noted a 'Challenge made by me that I, with 16 of my Chamber should ride at base; shoot and run at ring with any 17 . . . gentlemen in the Court'. And on April 1st, which was the first day of the match, he recorded that 'the King wone'.[26] Nor was Edward so little of an ordinary boy that he did not pick up, from his companions, and proudly use, such bad language as shocked his tutors. Unfortunately he was not so much a gentleman–perhaps no royal child could have been–as to conceal, when questioned, the name of his teacher. The King received a lecture upon the sin of swearing; the other boy suffered in his person in the usual way.[27]

It was the fashion for a King to be erudite, but it was a necessity for Somerset that his nephew should be Protestant. For, no less than in the matter of the Council of Regency, he was determined in the matter of religion to reverse the late King's will. Henry VIII had changed much. As Gardiner put it, 'In my time hath come many alterations. First a great alteration it was to renounce the Bishop of Rome's authority, and I was one that stood in it. A great alteration it was that abbeys were dissolved. A great alteration it was that images were pulled down.'[28] Farther than this, however, neither Gardiner, nor Henry at the close of his reign, would have chosen to go. It is true that the Bible in English 'of the largest volume', ordered to be set in every church in 1538, was another and most dynamic alteration. But translations of the Scriptures had not been, at the outset of the Reform movement, or for a long time after, looked upon with suspicion. The earliest French Reformers, loyal Catholics like Lefèvre of Etaples, had translated into the vernacular of the people what Erasmus had translated into the common tongue of all European scholars. In England Princess Mary herself was busy upon the same task in her translation of Erasmus's Paraphrase of St. John's Gospel. Yet, for all that, in the last years of the reign, many books listed as heretical were burned at Paul's Cross–among them Coverdale's and Tyndale's versions of the Bible.

Except for his views on the Papal authority, Henry himself during his last years was rigidly orthodox, and he expected that others should be orthodox too. The Bishops' Book in which 'with his own pen' he had 'totted over the head' of this clause and that;[29] the King's Book; and the Act of Six Articles, left no one in doubt as to the King's opinions, or his will that they should be the opinions of all. Hooper wrote bitterly to Bullinger that 'as far as religion is concerned, idolatry is nowhere in greater vigour. Our King has destroyed the Pope, but not popery; he has expelled all the monks and nuns, pulled down their monasteries; he has caused all their possession to be transferred into his exchequer, and yet they are bound, even the fragile female sex . . . to perpetual chastity. . . . The impious mass, the most shameful celibacy of the clergy, the invocation of Saints, auricular confession, superstitions, abstinence from meats, and purgatory, were never held by the people in greater esteem than the moment.'[30]

Henry had indeed, when it suited him, set on every Protestant malcontent with the hunter's 'Hue! Hue!', and afterwards, when it suited him, had called his hounds off. He thought, with his superb power of self-deception, that they would obey him, even when he was dead. They had obeyed while he lived, but Stephen Gardiner, his tried and loyal servant, saw that with the old King gone, all those things which he had chosen to preserve were at once in danger. 'This I take to be true,' he wrote to Cranmer, 'that if the wall of authority . . . be once broken, and new water let in at a little gap, the vehement novelty will flow further than your Grace would admit.'[31] It was true, only too true. In days that were coming not only Gardiner, but Mary herself and others as loyal to the past, looked back upon the last years of Henry VIII, as a time when Catholic beliefs were safe, and the faithful at peace. It was to his settlement that they appealed, against all the changes that came pouring through that not so 'little gap' which Somerset had opened.

Henry's settlement contented the great mass of the people of England. Ploughman, weaver, butcher, miller's man, yeoman and squire, each heard the familiar Mass in the familiar, unknown tongue, and was satisfied. Each still saw the salt and oil used at his children's christening, oil again at his father's deathbed; at Candlemas the priest still blessed the candles; in church there was still the holy water for his fingers to dip in, and as he lay in his bed on the Vigil of All Hallows he heard the bells ring through the dark night. He had soon got used to the exclusion of the Pope from English affairs; he felt perhaps a short-lived, puzzled regret, a slight confusion of mind, and then forgot that things had been different, because so much – most indeed of what was closest to him – was still the same as it had ever been.

It was not now long to remain the same, for Henry, who had found the 'Whip of Six Strings' enough to bring his Protestants to heel, forgot that the will and testament of a dead man might not control the living. He intended the religious settlement to remain undisturbed till his son was of age; Somerset and the leaders of the Council determined otherwise. For the Council was a very lop-sided assembly, consisting largely of one school of thought, and that contrary to the views of the majority of Englishmen. Now was felt the lack of the peers who had gone down before Henry's anger; of old Catholics such as Montague and Exeter; of such a head of a great house as Norfolk, still alive, by the mercy of God and the death of the King, but a prisoner in the Tower. Gardiner, Bishop of Winchester, witty, choleric, practised man of affairs, conservative as a lawyer, was excluded by Henry's own choice from the Council of Regency; he was never afraid to express his opinions, even to the terrible old King himself, and express them he did when the changes began, and soon, after a sojourn in the Fleet prison, and a short retirement in the country, he joined Norfolk in the Tower. Wriothesley, now Earl of Southampton, was removed from the Chancellorship, which went first to Lord St. John, then to the pliable Lord Rich. There were of course some Catholics in the Council, who on occasion would resist in Parliament the work of the new party. But for the most part the influential members either inclined to the New Learning, whether sincerely, as Cranmer, or because it profited them, as Northampton; or were of such a temper as Paget and Warwick whose religious convictions were known to themselves alone.

For a while the government moved slowly in religion. Eager Reformers like Latimer deplored the delay; what good work could be done when 'there were so many put-offs, so many put-byes, so many respects and considerations of worldly wisdom'? [32] Yet it did move. That Lent there were sermons at Paul's Cross against images and ceremonies; at Court against the obligation of observing Lent, and when Gardiner wanted to take action against some persons unknown who at Portsmouth had hauled down the rood, and with ugly mockery had bored through the eye and into the side of the figure, all that Somerset would say was that if the Bishop himself was 'slack in such matters, he that removeth false images and idols abused, doth not a thing worthy of blame'.[33]

After a short pause changes came thick and fast. At the end of the year Parliament met and passed a number of laws for the Church without the formality of a reference to Convocation. Marriage was made legal for the clergy, all the old heresy laws were repealed; and the laity was to receive the Communion in both kinds. Half-way through January the Court by proclamation prohibited the ceremonial use of ashes, palms, and candles; in February it ordered the removal of all, not only of abused, images; in March it put forth a provisional order of Communion for the laity in English, though the old Mass at which the laity did not partake still remained untouched.

But it was not only by Acts of Parliament and by proclamations, not only at the instigation or by the advice of bishops and learned and austere men that changes were being wrought in the Church. The Council, which needed all the support it could get for its official reforms, inquired little, for the time at least, into either man's belief or his conduct, provided only he could contemn the Pope, cry down Images, and make a scoff of the Mass. Only a few, such as the Anabaptists, whose ideas were considered to be quite outrageous, suffered for their opinions. They were burned; the others taught, disputed, interpreted, unchecked.

It is not only Henry VIII, with his unscrupulous manipulation of religion, not only the fanatics of the Protectorate who must bear the blame for what is regrettable in the Edwardian Reformation. Churchmen themselves had much to answer for. That eruption of mental and spiritual forces which we call the Renaissance had overtaken a Church which had for long neglected any attempt at a thorough and general religious education. Before the suppression of the preaching Orders friars had gone about with some regularity as itinerant preachers; these failing Bernard Gilpin declared that among the Yorkshire parishes he knew, 'some had not four sermons in 16 years'.[34] And if there were a sermon it was long odds that the preacher was little more learned than his congregation. A priest of the parish near Scarborough was sitting one day at the alehouse talking with his neighbours. He talked of the Archbishop of Canterbury—the son of an ostler he said, 'and hath as much learning as the goslings of the green that go yonder'. News of this came somehow to Cranmer, who had the man fetched to him, and began to try his learning. The poor rogue found himself very soon out of his depths. 'I beseech your Grace to pardon me,' he said, 'I have no manner of learning in the Latin tongue; but altogether in English.' 'Well then (saith my lord), if you will not appose me, I will appose you. Are you wont to read the Bible?' (quod my lord). 'Yes, that do we daily,' said the priest. 'I pray you tell me (quod my lord then) who was David's father?' The priest stood still and said, 'I cannot surely tell your Grace.' Then said my lord again, 'If you cannot tell me, yet declare unto me who was Solomon's father?' 'Surely (quod the priest) I am nothing at all seen in these genealogies.' It was an unequal contest, but Cranmer's verdict was just. 'There are', he concluded, 'such a sort of you in this realm, that knoweth nothing, nor will know nothing, but sit upon your ale bench and slander all honest learned men.'[35] Cranmer's opinion of the clergy must have been founded on experience, an experience which other bishops shared. When Hooper made Visitation at Gloucester, out of the 311 clergy whom he examined, he found 171 who were not able to repeat the Ten Commandments. Of these, 31 did not know where in the Bible the Commandments were recorded, 10 could not repeat the Lord's Prayer, 30 did not know where to find it, and 27 could not tell who was its author. With pastors such as these, it is not easy to imagine the depths of ignorance in which congregations were plunged. A cathedral city, a great commercial town, might have more light; but for the most part the bulk of poor folk in the kingdom must have known next to nothing of the historical foundations of Christianity; and little more of the implications of those beliefs which they drank in from the performance of the old, accustomed ceremonies. Christian dogmas, unquestioned for centuries, and for centuries resting for most men upon oral tradition, were as rubbed, worn, and blurred as are the features of the effigies upon altar tombs in many a church—which only in general and roughly recall their first defined likeness to a human face.

Sermons, the chief means of instruction, were by now looked at askance by orthodox people as smacking of reform. Gardiner, who generally knew his Englishmen, thought little of sermons, and believed that they were not agreeable to the national taste. 'It is contrary to the inclination of us Englishmen', he said, 'to be long in the state of learners, . . . as appeareth in a parish church at Cambridge where, I hear say, it is ordinary, when the Vicar goeth into the pulpit to read that he hath himself written, then the multitude of the parish goeth straight out of church, home to drink. . . . So as I think that if the priests should be universally bound to read homilies, they should read them as bachelors do the "Institutes" at Cambridge for their form, even to themselves and the bare walls.'[36]

He was right in so far as the old-fashioned were concerned, and Latimer to his disgust found it so when, as Bishop of Worcester, he sent word to a certain town that next day, which was a holiday, he would preach there. But when he came thither the church door was locked and it took half an hour to find the key; and then, said Latimer, 'one of the parish comes to me and says, "Sir, this is a busy day with us; we cannot hear you, it is Robin Hood's day; the parish are gone abroad to gather Robin Hood; I pray you let them rest."'[37] Yet for those touched with the new thought sermons were already becoming, and were still more to become, meat and drink to the godly, and their appetite was to amount to gluttony. The England which Gardiner knew so well was England of the past not of the future, and he, and conservatives like him, erred profoundly in not seizing on this, the reformer's sharpest weapon, before it was too late. For the remedy, as Oliver Cromwell knew, is always

in the hands of that party which deplores its opponents' preaching–'Preach
back, then', said Oliver.

Among such a mass of ignorant, unthinking belief, new teaching ran like
fire in stubble; there was nothing but the inertia of dull minds to stop it.
Where it touched a mind not dull, a temperament eager to question, ready
to differ, the tinder blazed. The results of all the breaking of images, of all the
attacks on Papacy, priests, and Church, was both a readiness to question and
resent all authority but mainly that of the priests, and also a wave of levity
and irreverence. Even in Edward's reign the authorities sometimes thought
things were going too far. In the first year of the reign they found it necessary
to call serving-men and apprentices–the least responsible part of the population of London–to order for using 'such insolency and evil demeanour towards priests, as revelling, tossing of them, taking violently their caps and
tippets from them'.[38]

Worse than this unmannerly disrespect was the vulgar and blasphemous
irreverence which was, unfortunately, one of the favourite weapons of what
one might call the camp-followers of reform. Of the many ballads, aimed at
wounding the feelings of the old Catholics and intended also to detach others
from their views by making superstition ridiculous, there remains an example
in the story of 'John Bon and the Parson'–impudent, irreverent, and funny
with a blunt schoolboy humour. When the Parson mentions to John Bon
the feast of Corpus Christi, the Ploughman ludicrously stumbles over the
words. He cannot tell what is 'Copri Cursty', a man or woman? Or is it
'Cropsy Cursty'? Nor, when the Parson tries to explain doctrine is John Bon
more amenable.

The Priest says:

> 'And then we go forth, and Christ's body receive;
> Even the same that Mary did conceive–'

and John Bon replies:

> 'The devil it is! Ye have great grace
> To eat God and man in so short a space.'[39]

The same coarse and offensive mockery is to be found in the nicknames
with which the louts and loafers, the boys and persons of little reputation who
came in crowds to the sermons at Paul's, labelled the bread in the Sacrament,
calling it 'Round Robin' and 'Jack in the Box'; names in which the speakers
forgot both Christian charity and reverence, and which must have made
Catholics feel that the worser part of the reform party were ready, in the rage
of controversy, to spit in the face of Christ.

Such irreverence stank in the nostrils of the true reformers. Cranmer himself deplored the fact that 'by arrogant and ignorant men . . . the sacrament
hath been of late marvellously abused . . . the said persons contemning the
whole thing for certain abuses heretofore committed therein; reviling it and

disputing ungodly of that most holy mystery, and calling it by vile and unseemly names.'[40] Of such 'ungodly disputes' the style can be imagined from
a proclamation drawn up in December 1547 in which it was forbidden to
argue in such a vein as–'whether his blessed body be there, head, legs, arms,
toes, nails . . . whether he be broken or chewed or he be always whole. . . .
And what blood? That only which did flow out of his side, or that which
remained.'[41]

Apart from that fundamental disagreement with the old Catholics which
all of the New Learning shared–that is to say their denial of the Corporal
Presence–the Reform party had almost as many beliefs as heads. All the old
heresies sprang up again, as each man, a law unto himself, came to his own
conclusions, and once there, remained sure as death of their validity. There
were some who held God to be the author of sin; who believed that there
was no resurrection; who denied either that Christ took flesh of the Virgin
Mary or that he was the equal of the Father; who rejected both heaven and
hell. There were Anabaptists and Pelagians in Kent and Essex; there were men
who held that there was no original sin, or, perhaps more excusably 'that
learned men were the cause of great errors . . . for all errors were brought in by
learned men'.[42] An Italian, a trained observer, if not a strictly impartial one,
looking back on his stay in England during Edward's reign, remembering
the churches bare of all images, destitute of the gold and silver vessels which
had gleamed upon the altar, the walls no longer painted with stories that were
the Bible of the ignorant, but gaunt and glaring in their coat of new whitewash, the royal arms where the crucified Christ, the Virgin and Saint John
had been, saw little hope for England because of 'the endless diversity of
heresies which swarm there'.[43] Cuthbert Tunstal's nephew Bernard Gilpin, a
good Christian who could look beyond differences, and keep his cure of souls
through many changes, declared, when he preached in the King's own palace
of Greenwich, that 'there is entering into England more blind ignorance,
superstition and infidelity than ever was under the Romish Bishops'.[44]
Before the end of Edward's reign the crop of heresies which was springing up
so plentifully in the Church was giving the spiritual leaders some anxiety.
Cranmer, Ridley 'and other worshipful persons in Kent' were appointed
commissioners to inquire into the question there.[45] It was time indeed. If the
King's reign had lasted longer, and a Protestant settlement had succeeded to
Protestant flux, the government would have been forced to deal with the
undisciplined rabble which followed at the heels of reform. The wilder spirits
would have been restrained, coerced, punished. There would have been fresh
acts of Uniformity. There would have been more than Anabaptists burned.

For if the Anabaptists' beliefs were intolerable because they undermined the
foundation of secular society, so did the dogmas of many of the Reform party.
In 1548 the Council found it necessary to publish a proclamation against those
who put away one wife to marry another; those who maintain that the purity
of their souls was in no way contaminated by bigamy; or those, even more
daring, who conceived that a woman might lawfully have two husbands.[46]

Apart from these far-fetched notions there was always the doctrine of justification by faith, against which conservatives like Gardiner tilted with mingled scorn, fear, and rage, and which temperate scholars such as Redman deeply distrusted, on account, as he said, 'of a licentious life which some would be apt to take from it, if it should be taught the common people'.[47]

There was in fact, much truth in Gardiner's criticism of the effect upon public morals of the Reform movement as a whole. 'If', he said, 'in Germany such as have been brought up in these opinions had in their behaviour a more perfect reverence and obedience to the Emperor, who, whatsoever he be, is their superior, then I would think the learning might be good to teach obedience to princes; but I see it is not so. If I saw that part more civil, more honest, more reasonable, than they were wont to be, I might think the learning good for something in this world.'[48] But, in fine, Gardiner did not so see it, nor did many a Protestant preacher, horrified at the sins of the age.

The trouble with the Protestant movement was that, apart from those unworldly souls who welcomed the new doctrine as the light of the first day, both the secular leaders and the tail of the party were only too often men whose practice and theory were no recommendation to any Church. So far, except for a few unlucky extremists in Henry VIII's reign, Protestantism, or rather anti-Papalism, had been profitable rather than costly. Henry had seized the abbeys and many chantry foundations; Edward swept up what was left of the chantries, and the endowments of religious guilds. From the King the spoils percolated down to a horde of new men.

Not that the true Reformers approved of what Henry had done in the matter of Church lands. 'There was no reformation,' cried Anthony Gilbey, 'but a deformation, in the time of that tyrant and lecherous monster. The boar, I grant, was rooting and digging the earth, and all his pigs had followed him.'[49] Lever in 1550 used plain speech to those same pigs. 'If ye were not blind', he said, 'ye would see and be ashamed, that whereas 50 tun-bellied monks, given to gluttony, filled their paunches, kept up their house, and relieved the whole country round about them; there, one of your greedy guts devouring the whole house and making great pillage through the country, cannot be satisfied.'[50]

Denunciations, however, did not move the new landlords; much only wanted more. Sir Philip Hoby once made a suggestion to the Protector Somerset which showed how the idea of confiscating Church property was a thing with a growth like mustard seed. It would be well, he said, to divert the stipends of all English prebends to the provision of a force of horsemen for the defence of the realm.[51] How much of the money would have been spent on the avowed object had the idea been put into practice, may be questioned; the preamble of the act suppressing chantries spoke nobly of the destination of their endowments—they were to go to found schools, hospitals and the like, but as Mr. Tawney has wittily said, 'the grammar schools that Edward VI founded, are those which King Edward VI did not destroy'.[52]

The fact is, that whether the Reformers liked it or not, Henry VIII, by the dissolution of the monasteries and his distribution of the spoil, had once for all shackled together the cause of dogmatic reform and the self-interest of a grasping and unprincipled new nobility. The age, so brilliant, so rich in character, so fertile in thought, was yet not far in time from the sanguinary and unscrupulous days of the Wars of the Roses. The vices of the first half of the sixteenth century were simple and glaring–ambition, avarice, gluttony, cruelty, treachery. They were not confined to any one party, but the ambitious would be found on the side where profit was to be made; and the avaricious would accept with gladness the Protestant tenet that justification was by faith not works, so that, in what Stow called 'these decaying times of Charity', the poor might beg through the streets of London and have no relief, while on Fridays the Londoners walked no more along the street by Houndsditch where there used to be a row of small cottages 'with little garden plots backward, for poor bed-ridden people–there to bestow their charitable alms, every poor man or woman lying in their bed with their window which was toward the street open so low that every man might see them'.[53] The gluttonous found it pleasanter not to fast in Lent, and though, more for the sake of the fish trade than of the soul, the Council reimposed fish diet in Lent, licences could easily be bought by the wealthy; Lord Clinton bought such a one that he, his wife, and any six friends who ate at his table might be absolved.[54] Meanwhile, by the many vicissitudes of the times, ambition at Court had been robbed of any dignity it might have had; a man who wished to rise must be able to sacrifice loyalty to friends and loyalty to religion. As for cruelty, what that age did not know of it, Henry VIII had taught, and the lesson had been well taken to heart.

John Hales, the friend of the poor, who longed to see a Protestant England, declared that, 'if there be any way or policy of men to make the people receive and embrace and love God's word, it is only this–when they shall see that it bringeth forth so goodly fruit that men seek not their own wealth . . . but, as good members, the universal wealth of the whole body'.[55] That so goodly fruit was, alas, not displayed, and what attracted many of the poor to the doctrines of reform was an angry impatience and resentment at their wrongs and a hatred of all authority. The fruits of this were to ripen later, but Gardiner had seen them on the tree ten years before. Even in those days he would not even allow a new pronunciation of Greek to be used at Cambridge, insisting 'perhaps in a more severe fashion than the matter at issue would require, were it not that the tendencies of the age, the lack of discipline and uncontrolled license to which people are prone, call for stringent corrections . . . I will withstand fancies', he declared, 'even in pronunciation, and fight with the enemy of quiet at the first entry.'[56] So spoke that apostle of Toryism, faced with an equilibrium as shaken, and forces as incalculable as those of our time.

Gardiner was a statesman; Mary and many like her were no more than plain, devout, conservative folk who did not see far, but who held loyally by the old ways. To them the massed evils, economic, social, moral, which they saw about them, were parts of one mighty and irrefutable argument against the new religion, since whose inception, and therefore by whose means, these things had come to pass. Men and women of Mary Tudor's age, born when there was never any possible question of any church other than the one known and ancient Church, of any beliefs other than her beliefs, looked back upon the untroubled days of their childhood, and saw them steeped in the sunshine that lights those years; saw them also as an age of peace, unity, and plenty; of good order and great hope for the future.

Everything evil which had come since (apart from the prodigious rise in prices, the cause of which no one succeeded in diagnosing) had come because of change in religion. Comely observances, beliefs, morality, social and economic order, all had gone, devoured by the monster of iniquity. No wonder that simple men and women, recoiling from all change, longed to return, in every particular, to that state of things which they had known as good and safe. No wonder that Mary Tudor, with her limited mind, and her unshakeably loyal temper, clung to every tatter of the old seemly garment of ritual that had clothed the spirit, and in doing so was convinced, as human beings are always convinced, that it was the spirit itself she clutched. With her upbringing, her parentage, and her temperament, it was inevitable that she should be impervious to the verbal arguments of Reformers. She saw, as she thought, only too well, the visible arguments against them, written large in every church, and across the whole countryside. She saw, and judged the Protestant cause by the unwieldy army, with its rabble of camp-followers, that surrounded the standard while it was victorious. She had yet to suffer the sorrow and disillusion of seeing men of her own faith in prosperity, and behaving not so very differently.

Chapter VIII

ON January 7th 1549–the day that Parliament returned to its labours after the Twelve Days of Christmas, a Bill was read in the House of Lords. Before the end of January it had passed both houses, and the first English Prayer Book became law by the first Act of Uniformity. From Whitsuntide next it was to be the only service book in use, superseding all the old diverse uses; nothing must be added to it, nothing taken away, nothing substituted for it, or heavy penalties would fall on the offender. It seemed as if, after many vicissitudes, the rites of the Church in England were at last to be settled, arbitrarily indeed, but not unwisely, for the doctrine implicit in the book could be accepted by most Catholics, though of the old ritual there remained hardly even an identifiable skeleton. Now, for all, 'the Supper of the Lord, and the Holy Communion, Commonly called the Mass', was to be said in English, to be said aloud and plainly, instead of in secret murmurings; with audible, comprehensible prayers instead of the triumphant chanting of antiphons and that 'great rolling up and down of notes when the *missa est* is sung'[1] at which Latimer scoffed. Nothing was left of all the slow accumulation of symbolic ceremonies that had made the services of the Church a play in dumb show for the ignorant. Holy Water, Holy Bread, Palm crosses, Candlemas Candles, Ashes, and Creeping to the Cross, all these had gone already. Now in the Mass itself, where every act of the priest had represented a part of the Passion of Christ, the austere liturgy of the Reformers left little more than words to convey to men's reasoning souls the great event which formerly had been commemorated and rehearsed in 'the washings, crossings, shiftings, blessings, which had accompanied the Mass'. All these were gone, and in like manner 'the crosses, lights and bells' which attended the Communion of the sick, and the burial of the dead.[2]

On Whitsunday 1549 the new Prayer Book was to become universal and obligatory in England. That day at Sandford Courtenay in Devon the new order was used as it was everywhere else; there was no disturbance, but we may imagine what groups hung about in the churchyard after service, and what Sunday dinners were burnt while the goodman of the house debated with his neighbours the strange words, the new ways, and the untroubled past. Next day the priest, on his way to church, was met by a crowd of villagers. They asked him what service he intended to use; he told them, the new one. But, they declared, they would have nothing but 'the old and ancient religion'. Their priest was not unwilling; he went to church with the crowd, put on his vestments once more, and said Mass in the old, familiar words. From Sandford Courtenay the news spread; bells rang for joy and people clapped their hands; soon all Devon, and Cornwall too, were seething with revolt. What they clamoured for was the Act of Six Articles again, 'the Sacrament hung over the altar and worshipped and those who would not consent thereto, to die like heretics . . . the Sacrament delivered to the people only at Easter, and then only in one kind. . . . We will not', they added, 'have the new Service, nor the Bible in English'; they demanded in fact all the old ways to which they were accustomed.[3]

The Council, faced with rebellion not only in the West but in the Midlands, the East and in Yorkshire, had their hands full. It was only after some time and much bloodshed that the various risings were put down, and there was time to consider what had caused them, and whose was the blame. They were not all of one colour. Kett's rebellion in Norfolk, and the risings in the Midlands, came rather 'from idleness and grudging among the people who talked high, and were disposed to imagine and invent novelties, and devised mending this and that'.[4] Never perhaps were such 'devisings' more justified. For unfortunately these years of upheaval in religion coincided with a time of economic misery that added to every controversy ingredients of uneasiness, dread and hate. It would not be true to say that lines of religious cleavage followed those of economic differences; that the rich were Catholic and conservative, the poor Protestant and revolutionary. Far from it. It was the new landlords, the holders of monastic lands, and hence the bulwark of the anti-Papal party, that were most roundly abused by such social reformers as Latimer, Lever, and Crowley, and most hated by the poor. But, as in every time of great economic distress, sordid misery, or the fear of it, degraded and embittered poor men's minds; fear of violence woke hatred in the hearts of the rich.

On the one hand, going as flat against all the old scholastic theorists as against those who, like Latimer and Hales, were nicknamed 'Commonwealth men', stood the men who, as Crowley said, 'live as though there were no God at all, men that would have all in their own hands, men that would leave nothing for others, men that would be alone on the earth, men that be never satisfied'. These were the years in which capitalism and modern banking had their beginning. In the past men might possess many acres of land, head of cattle, and the like, but these were goods, the products of which could after all only be eaten and worn. Now it was possible not only to possess but to use money—money for luxuries and delicacies, money for power; an Imperial ambassador was to declare of England that 'more is done with money here than in any country of the world'.[5] All the old denunciations against the sin of usury fell on deaf ears. It had been held sin for a man to expect more than the value of his goods or his service; or to lay by out of his profits for a comfortable old age. Now the industrious apprentice was to be the pattern of worldly virtue, piling up savings on which to take his ease as an alderman at last. Needless to say there had been successful men, saving men, greedy and unscrupulous men in the past, but by the teaching of the Church, by laws, by regulations of the Guilds, they had been hampered, and certainly their ambitions had never been sanctioned by public opinion. Now, although from the pulpit such ambition was still denounced, a new theory of commerce, just as a new theory of the state, was growing up. Luther, who deplored as much as any the greed and cruelty of the rich, would have no laws to check it; for, 'as the soul needs the word alone for life, and justification, so it is justified by faith alone, and not by any works'; therefore there should be no duty of almsgiving laid upon men as necessary to salvation. In the perfect world which should have come so quickly after the purification of belief, there would have been no need of mentioning the duty; charity would have flown to the rescue before the word had been said. But unfortunately the perfect world did not come; and the Reformers, grievously disappointed, castigated the sins of the age, surprised and shocked as men always are surprised and shocked at human nature.

On the other hand there were the poor, a growing number of them in extreme want or actually destitute. Even in Sir Thomas More's lifetime, and long before the dissolution of the monasteries, the sixteenth century was faced with that same unhappy spectacle of unemployed men which we face today.

'Poor silly, wretched souls,' says More, 'away they trudge out of their known and accustomed houses; all their household stuff being suddenly thrust out, they be constrained to sell it for a thing of naught. And when they have, wandering about, soon spent that, what can they do but steal, and be hanged or else go a-begging. Whom no man will set a-work, though they never so willingly offer themselves thereto.'[6]

If that had been the state of things when Henry VIII was young, it had not, now his son was King, one whit improved; rather it had worsened. Not content with the spoil of the monasteries, Henry, departing from all English tradition, had tried to lighten the burden of debt by repeated debasement of the coinage. The rise in prices that was the necessary consequence struck hard at both yeomen and hired labourer. Latimer remembered the solid, cheerful comfort of a yeoman's house, whence one of the sons would go to the University and in time become a priest; where the daughters were given good portions for their marriage, and where there was always hospitality. He had seen also its decay. But if yeomen had suffered much, tenants and hired labourers suffered more. In addition to all the King had done, landlords had enclosed the commons, put up rents, resumed leases, and let 'sheep eat up the people' in their new pasture farms, so that tenants and labourers were reduced to destitution and came, as Latimer said, 'to beg in London, to lie sick at the door . . . and then perish from hunger'. So Hooper, writing to Cecil, called upon him 'to persuade and cause some order to be taken upon the price of things, or else the ire of God will shortly punish. All things be here so dear that the most part of the people lacketh. . . . All pastures and breeding of cattle is turned to sheep's meat, and they be not kept to be brought to the market, but to bear wool and profit only to their masters. Mr. Secretary, for the passion of Christ, take the fear of God and a bold stomach to speak herein for redress, and that the goods of every shire be not thus wrested and taken into a few men's hands. . . . The prices of things be here as I tell you, the

9

number of people be great; their little cottages and poor livings decay daily; except God by sickness take them out of the world, they must needs lack', and, he reminded Cecil, 'Ye know what a grievous extreme, yea, in a manner unruly evil hunger is.'[7]

Now it had shown itself so. In the risings in Hertfordshire, Somerset, Gloucestershire, Wiltshire, Hampshire, Sussex, Surrey, Worcestershire, Essex, Kent, Oxfordshire, Berkshire, Yorkshire, and Norfolk, gentlemen's park-pales were torn down, deer were killed, and the villagers' cattle driven in to pasture. As in all tumults there were among the rioters another type beside that of the honest men with a grievance. There were 'ruffians among them, and soldiers cashiered, which be the chief doers, [and] look for spoil, so that it seems no other thing but a plague and fury among the vilest and worst sort of men'.[8] But for all that, the grievances of the poor were real.

With such troubles came, inevitably, hatred on either side. 'Some cry, Pluck down enclosures and parks, some for their commons; others pretend religion, a number would rule and direct things as gentlemen have done, and indeed all have conceived a wonderful hate against gentlemen and take them all as their enemies.'[9] Such hatred was well repaid. Gentlemen, hearing the mutter of discontent, feared for the social order that secured their comfort. Paget urged the Protector to be stern, and contemptuously denied the reality of all the grievances that the rebels had put forward. Prices everywhere in Europe were as high or higher than in England, he said; enclosures had stood for sixty years. 'What is the matter then, troweth your Grace? By my faith, sir, even that which I said to your Grace in the gallery of the Tower the next day after the King's first coming there, "Liberty, Liberty".'[10]

But there was another cause of disturbance besides that of economic or social stress. In August Cranmer preached at Paul's Cross upon the rebellions, and, 'that the occasion came of Popish priests was the most part of all his sermon'.[11] This was true enough of the rising in the West, where all but two of the commons' demands were against the late changes in religion.[12] For a precaution all wrestling matches were forbidden that summer, and all plays and interludes; the former might be dangerous, as any assembly of excited men may be dangerous in a critical time; the latter might be used by the players as a convenient means of ventilating sedition. The risings also were dealt with; Warwick at Dussindale made a blood-stained name for himself in a victory over the Norfolk rebels, Kingston left a hated memory in the West; in the Midlands various ringleaders were hanged; if these were priests they were hanged from the steeples of their own churches; a grim exemplar and one easily to be understood by the worshippers next Sunday morning.

But there was one whom the Council suspected of being worse than a ring-leader, and whom they could not hang. Princess Mary was so obviously, even so ostentatiously in favour of all that the western rebels wanted, that it was not strange if the Council saw her hand in the rising. They wrote to her that two of the leaders there, Arundel and the priest of Sandford Courtenay, were known to be men of hers, while in Suffolk, Pooley, her receiver, was in great credit with the rebels.[13] It was true that even in Norfolk, though the rebels made no objection to the new Prayer Book, they had showed some tenderness of the Princess. They did indeed pull down her park-pales among the rest, but they did not further molest her, and they declared that she was kept more poorly than it was meet the King's sister should be.[14]

So it was natural that the Council, anxious, as rulers, for the peace of the kingdom, and, as landowners nervous for their own possessions, should turn on Mary as an agent in these tumults. In private letters men spoke of her complicity, disguising the dangerous accusation not only in Latin but under the masculine gender. So Sir Thomas Smith writing to William Cecil spoke 'de Mario vel Marianis' of Marius and the Marians, and of a fear which 'valde me angit, immo prope exanimat'. The fear which tormented, yea rather, almost destroyed him, can hardly have been other than the dread that Mary, hand in glove with the rebels, intended to overset the present rulers of England.[15]

Mary, in answer to the Council, denied all. She had, she said, no lands nor interests in Devon; no chaplain of hers lived at Sandford Courtenay. As for Pooley, he had not left her house during the revolt in Suffolk, and 'Arundel my servant . . . dwelleth within the walls of London', going only now and again on her business to Norfolk and Suffolk, and he was besides, she said, 'given to as much quietness as any man in my house'.[16] But even if Mary could rightly claim that Pooley had an alibi, and that Thomas Arundel of Lanherne was a man of peace, it did not mean that the Council's objections to her attitude were entirely without foundation. For, no more than the people of Sandford Courtenay, would she have anything to do with the new service book.

Her household had always been, and continued to be a refuge for Catholics, who, men as well as women, sought it as an oasis of peace and constant loyalty to their Church. Not all those who wished could take service with her; even when some made 'their earnest suit' to her, she must refuse, for her household could not be large. But among the old Catholic families that household was the one in the whole of England in which, both for virtue and orthodoxy, fathers and mothers who cared for such things wished to place their girls.

But beyond that known fact, Mary, from the very beginning of the religious changes of the reign, had made it clear to all that her face was set against the policy of the Council. Retired though she was from Court, living for the most part in those manors in the Eastern Counties which had been left to her in her father's will–and a miserable provision the Emperor's ambassador thought them–she was still, however much the Council might regret it, the second person in the kingdom. She knew it, and the knowledge was a burden to her that she could not put off. The girl who had broken down and yielded her soul and the honour of her word in fear of her father, was now a woman of thirty-three, and her brother, the King, a child. She saw it as her duty to prevent him from damaging, in his innocent nonage, the fabric of the Church as their father had left it. She alone in all England had the right to speak to the Council and King as she spoke; and she could not be silent. Fear she might, and fear she did, for she had known too many tragedies and outrages against justice to be confident that the worst *could* not happen. But, all the more because she had once failed, she would not now fail her faith, and the Church of her allegiance.

She was not a woman whose spirit rose to gaiety at the approach of peril; she had perhaps lain too long in her youth under the shadow of a danger that demanded a grim and passive courage; besides she was delicate, given much to tears, her nervous system deranged by her mental sufferings,[17] so that she was liable to sudden panics, and miserable indecisions. But in spite of all, and in spite of the profound discouragement and self-distrust which were the inevitable consequences of her surrender thirteen years before, Mary held on. Those who have tried to be true to a high intent and who have failed, will recognize in this her courage and her indomitable integrity. An unstained honour gives confidence; Mary, without that confidence, and with panic often at her heart, went grimly to battle with the princes of the people.

Before ever the Prayer Book was published she had written to the Protector –much of what she said can be gleaned from his reply, in which with a sort of resentful dignity he complained of her criticisms. She had told him, he wrote, 'that the most part of the realm, through a naughty liberty and presumption, are now brought into such a division as, if we executors go not about to bring them to that stay that our late master left them, they will forsake all obedience, unless they have their own wills and fantasies, and then it must follow that the King shall not be well served, and that all other realms shall have us in an obloquy and derision, and not without just cause'. Further she had reminded him 'that there was a godly order and quietness left by the King our late master . . . at the time of his death, and that the spirituality and the temporality of the whole realm did, . . . without compulsion, fully assent to his doings and proceedings, especially in matters of religion'. To the first, Somerset replied, as if more in sorrow than anger, that 'these words . . . soundeth not well'. The second accusation he rebutted more tartly, bidding her remember 'the great labours, travails and pains' her father had had in taming stiff-necked Papists; 'yes,' with a shrewd thrust, 'and did they not cause his subjects to rise and rebel against him?'

The months between the passing of the Act of Uniformity and the day upon which the new Prayer Book was to come into use, had been anxious ones for Mary. Mass meant for her, as for the Reformers themselves, the touch-stone of Catholicism. She, and every Catholic in England, had to choose whether she should accept the new book and obey the Statute. Many, like 'most politic Gardiner', could and did accept the book, but for Mary such acceptance was never in her mind. Narrow in her views she undoubtedly was, but narrow only in the common way of ordinary people. It was her position as the King's sister and heir to the throne that elevated her choice to the centre of public interest. On the one hand she was a woman who had not the mental powers–clarity of thought and impartiality–even to try to consider the Prayer Book on its merits; all she could do was to judge Protestantism by its fruits. On the other hand she knew that her submission would sanction not only the Prayer Book but all the actions of the Council in disturbing that equilibrium in religion which Henry had enjoined on his executors to maintain, and which, so Mary did not refrain from reminding them, each man of them had sworn to maintain. But again, just because of her position, any refusal or evasion by her of the Statute was impossible to conceal. She must therefore, before she made her decision, consider the dangers. She did so consider them; and they frightened her, sometimes almost to the pitch of panic.

The Act of Uniformity had been passed in January. Immediately the Emperor heard of it he had written to his ambassador Van der Delft, a Dutchman, bidding him go at once to the Protector and tell him roundly that if any attempt were made, under the Act, to compel Mary to alter her religion, the Emperor would not suffer it.[18] This, the Emperor's direct interference, was one of Mary's two weapons in this first engagement of the battle which was to take place between her and the Council; the other was her position as heir.

In March she sent for Van der Delft. She had a regard for the man; he seems to have been a simple, quiet, plain-dealing person such as she could understand and trust. In the presence of the Earl of Derby and the Lord Warden of the Cinque Ports–who had presumably ridden out with him to give formality to the interview, the Dutchman presented a letter from the Emperor, and received the Princess's thanks. Then he retired, but afterwards someone in the household must have plucked him by the sleeve and whispered; he was led away secretly to a private room, and there he found Mary waiting. This time both could speak freely, for they were alone.

Van der Delft gave her now a verbal message from the Emperor. He, so he sent word, loved her well, not only as his cousin, but also for her constancy in religion. He did not write often to her, for fear of rousing suspicion, but he would none the less look after her.

Mary seems almost to have broken down. She told Van der Delft that the Emperor was her only comfort. She believed that unless he helped her, the Council would soon try to force her to give up her religion, but she would die sooner. Then she took out and showed him an old letter, its folds worn and its ink faded. She told him that she had carried it about with her for twelve years and more. It was a letter from the Emperor, written in his own hand, and if she had had it as long as she said, she must have received it in those dreadful days just before she made her submission to the King. And now, she told Van der Delft, with a stiff little compliment in the Spanish fashion, the pleasure she had had in it was revived by the Emperor's last letter.[19] The words were formal, for it was a Princess who spoke of an Emperor, but the feeling that had made her keep that paper, scrawled over with Charles's jagged writing, was the feeling of a lonely woman who has kept a kind letter written by a friendly hand.

But though the Emperor's letters might comfort her, she was still frightened;

the more so as the time drew on towards Whitsunday, when the Statute was to come into force. In April she wrote in her own hand to the Emperor;[20] the letter does nothing but repeat what she had said to Van der Delft, but the very fact that she must repeat it, that she must make sure the Emperor knows and understands, tells its own tale of fear and anxiety. He is, she said, after God, and while her brother is so young, her only refuge; she has never been in such need of help as now when there are all these changes in religion; she has asked the ambassador what support she may count on if the Council should try to compel her by threats of violence; let Charles, she begged, somehow provide that she shall live in the ancient faith, or, as she has sworn, she will die in it.

The Emperor, who had been so tardy in his defence of her mother's marriage, moved more swiftly now. He wrote at once to Van der Delft, bidding him go again to the Protector, and demand a written and permanent permission for Mary to use what service she chose in spite of any innovations.[21] He followed this up a month later by fresh and full instructions; the ambassador was to tell Somerset, without precisely making a threat of it, that neither the Emperor nor the King of the Romans, nor any of Mary's kin, would suffer her to be deprived of the Mass, and that they insisted she should have, what he had asked for before, formal letters of assurance to this affect. As a *bonne bouche* for the Council he added that it was impossible for them to treat the Princess as others were treated, since she was the King's sister and his heir.[22] That was a thing which they knew only too well.

Van der Delft, on receiving the Emperor's first letter, had gone at once to Somerset. The Protector refused the assurance, which would run, he pointed out, against the laws of the land; he hoped, for the sake of England, where differences between the King and his heir could be dangerous, that Mary would conform. But, said he, if she did not agree with him, he, personally, would not inquire into her private conduct. Van der Delft found it easy to assure the Protector that she certainly did not agree, and added, rather wildly, that even had she wished to change her religion, the Emperor would not have allowed her to do so. 'Well,' said Somerset at the end, 'she shall do as she thinks best till the King comes of age, and meanwhile she shall find me her good servant, as I have always been, and I shall not cease to favour her in anything that does not prejudice the King.'[23]

So matters might have rested if Mary had had no other than Somerset to reckon with. For he spoke the truth; he was no enemy to her, while his wife was an old friend of hers, to be written to as 'my good Nan', and 'my good gossip' when Mary wished for some favour for 'my poor George Brickhouse', or for 'Richard Wood who was my mother's servant when you were one of her Grace's maids';[24] and these requests were only made to the Protector's wife and not the Protector himself because, as Mary said, 'I consider that it is in manner impossible for him to remember all such matters, having such a heap of business as he hath.'

But Somerset, though he might casually and in the arrogance of power give Mary 'license to attend Mass and have access to her sacrificing knaves', as John of Ulm put it, was not, though he sometimes mistook, the only ruler of England. Already the dark star of John Dudley, Earl of Warwick, had risen above the horizon. At the Council table he now questioned Somerset's licence. Mass, said he, was either of God or the Devil; if of the first all ought to have it; if of the second, 'should not the voice of this fury be equally proscribed to all'. Whether persuaded by Warwick's theology, or merely stiffened against the Protector by his example, the Council decided that commissioners should be sent to the Lady Mary to be with her at Kenninghall on Whitsunday, the critical day.

Mary heard of the appointed commission, but she did not know their full instructions and she feared a sharper attack than the Council intended. At once she wrote to Van der Delft, asking him, as she had so often asked his predecessor Chapuys, exactly what she should answer to the King's commissioners. Always, she told him, she received the Sacrament at Pentecost and what should she do if they used force to prevent her? Van der Delft gave what help he could. He suggested a mild but firm answer, promised the Emperor's protection, and offered to send her his own priest, if her English priests were afraid to officiate.[25]

So Mary waited for the commissioners, and just before Whitsunday they came; that is to say Mr. Secretary Petre, and Lord Rich, the Chancellor. Their orders from the Council, they told her, were to declare to her that the King's law was to bind even her and her household, and that they must declare the same to her people.

Mary answered them as Van der Delft had advised, but added, as a spice to the reply, words which were surely none of his, for she told the commissioners that she was subject to none of the Council; when they tried to insist that her servants must be told the penalties of disobedience, she retorted that her house was her flock and that she would stand by her servants in doing their duty; when Rich and Petre tried to argue she would not listen.

The commissioners were indeed sorely hampered in their action by their knowledge of the needs of England at this time, and Mary may have taken courage also from this. For at the moment the Council, at war with France and fearing for the safety of Boulogne, hankered much after the Emperor's alliance. Therefore their hands were tied when it came to putting pressure upon the Emperor's cousin, and the more so because they had, even now, a favour to ask her. So, though faced with her flat refusal to obey, they must most unseasonably introduce their request. They asked her to copy in her own hand a draft letter of recommendation to the Emperor introducing William Paget, whom the Council wished to send as ambassador to negotiate the much desired alliance. Mary, not unnaturally, caught at her opportunity. She would write the letter, she told them, but if they spoke to her servants as they had threatened, she would add to it, as news for the Emperor, an account of how she was treated for her religion.[26]

They yielded, as indeed they must, and the bargain was struck. Mary wrote the letter, cordially recommending Paget, and perhaps not unwillingly, 'for he is my friend, and as it seems to me, has a great desire to preserve the ancient friendship between Your Majesty and this realm'.[27] For their part the commissioners, that Whitsunday morning, made no attempt to prevent the Princess Mary's Mass. Perhaps they went off to the parish church, in which, bare and whitewashed, with scars on the stone-work where images and rood had stood, they heard the priest read for the first time that order of service which has since grown dear to the Church of England, for its age, dignity, and beauty. Meanwhile in the chapel of Kenninghall, with incense, candles and the chiming of the sacring bell, the old Office was sung by the poor priest who dared, when others would not, any peril that there might be in disobedience.[28]

This was on the 9th of June. Mary had won the first round of the game, but she was not long left in peace. Again, in spite of the parlous state of England, rebellions at home, war with Scotland, France in arms at the gates of Boulogne, the Emperor's alliance problematical – it appeared that the Council was divided. The tacit consent of Rich and Petre was rescinded, and less than a fortnight after Whitsuntide Mary received from the Lords of the Council orders to replace Mass by the new service, and to send to them her Comptroller, Sir Robert Rochester, and Dr. Hopton her chaplain, presumably that bold priest who had disobeyed the Statute.[29]

On June 22nd Mary replied to this demand in a letter which knows nothing of tricks of fence, but only of hard and straight hitting. She might, to her friends, to Van der Delft and the Emperor, confess herself afraid, but never to these men, her father's and her brother's subjects, and in her eyes either time-servers, or rank heretics. On the contrary, nailing her colours to the mast, she bade her chaplain sing three Masses instead of two, and to use greater solemnity in them than ever. Then she wrote to Somerset and to the Council.[30]

'My lord,

'I perceive by the letters which I late received of you that ye be all sorry to find so little conformity in me touching the observation of his Majesty's laws; who am well assured that I have offended no law, unless it be a late law of your own making, for the altering of matters in religion which in my conscience, is not worthy to have the name of a law, both for the King's honour's sake, the wealth of the realm ... and (as my conscience is very well persuaded) the offending of God, which passes all the rest.' From this she went on to remind the Lords of the Council, with a wounding bluntness, of a thing they very well knew, how 'all ye executors [were] sworn upon a book' to maintain Henry's late settlement of religion, 'and that I have obeyed and will do, with the Grace of God, till the King's Majesty my brother shall have sufficient years to be a judge in these matters himself, wherein, my Lord, I was plain with you at my last being in Court, declaring unto you at that time, whereunto I would stand; and now do assure you all that the only occasion of my stay from altering my opinion is from two causes; one principally for my conscience sake, and the other that the King my brother shall not hereafter charge me to be one of those that were agreeable to such alterations in his tender years. And what fruits daily grow by such changes, since the death of the King my father, to every indifferent person it well appeareth, both to the displeasure of God, and unquietness of the realm. . . . Notwithstanding, I assure you all, I would be as loth to see his Highness take hurt, or that any evil should come to this realm, as the best of you all. . . . And if any judge of me the contrary for mine opinions' sake (as I trust none doth) I doubt not in the end, with God's help, to prove myself as true and natural and humble sister, as they of the contrary opinion, with all their devices and altering of laws, shall prove themselve true subjects, praying you my Lord and the rest of the Council, no more to trouble and unquiet me with matters touching my conscience, wherein I am at a full point, with God's help, whatsoever shall happen to me. . . .' She concluded the letter by excusing from obedience the two men whose presence the Council had demanded, Hopton on the score of ill health, Rochester 'because the chief charge of my house resteth only upon the travails of my said Comptroller . . . so that if it were not for his continual diligence I think my little portion would not have stretched so far'.

But the Council insisted; more, they demanded with 'extreme words of peril' that she should send, not only these but also Master Francis Englefield.[31] Mary saw that she must yield, and, forgetting her fears, she lost her temper, and, having given leave to these three gentlemen to go, she wrote to the Council a letter that was little else than an angry woman's railing. It was the end of June, yet the life of her 'poor sick priest would be put to hazard by the wet and cold painful travail of this journey'. 'But', so she sums all up, 'for my part I assure you that since the King my father, your late master and very good lord, died, I never took you for other than my friends; but in this it appears to the contrary. And saving that I thought verily that my former letters should have discharged this matter, I would not have troubled myself with writing the same; not doubting but you do consider, that none of you all would have been contented to have been thus used at your inferior's hands, I mean to have had your officers, or any of your servants, sent for by force (as ye make it) knowing no just cause why.'[32]

'The King my father, your late master', 'none of you all',—the angry, contemptuous phrases show a Mary we have not before known, but she was after all, and for all her loneliness, the daughter of England and of Spain, and she knew it. Her father had been, heretofore, the only individual in the world whom she feared; she was soon to encounter another; but even him, John Dudley, Earl of Warwick, she did not fear as she had feared Henry. Now, with Henry dead she spoke to the Council de haut en bas, and did not trouble to restrain that sharp, hasty, but brief temper of hers.

The Council, since the men had come to them, did not need to reply. They hoped that the two servants would be more tractable than an angry Tudor. They were mistaken in Rochester, though Hopton, brave enough, but a man of peace, consented to carry back to his mistress articles devised by the Council which should answer all the points of her objections. To these, when they reached her, Mary listened, but only so as not to seem partial; so she told Van der Delft in a letter of appeal written when the chill of misgiving had succeeded her anger.[33]

Van der Delft, thus appealed to, did all that could be done; again he went to Somerset, complaining that this new pressure upon the Lady Mary was contrary to his promise. 'I see', said he bluntly, 'that you are trying to deprive the Lady Mary of Mass by taking her servants from her.'

Somerset, so tart in speech at the Council table, and so given to merciless snubbing of any discontent, was amazingly patient, reasoning mildly with Van der Delft and concluding the interview in much the same terms as those of the previous audience, 'I have told you', he said, 'all that had happened with regard to the Lady Mary'; and probably that 'all' included the Council's suspicions of her connexion with the rebels still up in the West. 'We must hold by the King and enforce his laws, and if she does not wish to conform, let her do as she pleases quietly and without scandal.'[34]

That might have been enough, if not for Mary, who felt it her duty to be a witness to her faith, at least for the Emperor and Van der Delft, if only they could have been sure that the promise would be kept. Not being able to be sure, Charles ordered Van der Delft once more to demand from the Protector letters of licence to which Mary could appeal if matters in England took a different turn.[35]

It was August. Kett and his men were still camped about the Oak of Reformation until the 22nd of the month; the West was not yet pacified, the Scots business had only been shelved. In the crisis Somerset yielded, apparently at any rate, and Van der Delft got something at least of what he asked for. A letter was drafted in which the King gave to Mary that promise of dispensation from his laws, which was for the next two years to be the subject of such vehement debate. For, when in the letter the King had expressed a proper surprise at his sister's obstinacy, he suddenly relented. 'And yet,' so runs the draft in the State Papers at the Public Record Office—'knowing your good nature and affection towards us, we cannot think any other matter in this your refusal than only a certain grudge of conscience, for want of good information and conference with some godly and well learned men.' Such men she might choose, and any chosen would be sent to her, 'and in the meantime, for the good affection and brotherly love which we bear towards you we have thought good in respect of your weakness to dispense both with you and your chaplain or chaplains and priests, for the hearing and saying ... any other service' than that in the new Prayer Book. Only, the letter added, the service must be in her private closet, and attended only by her servants, and these not to any greater number than a score, whose names must be sent to the King.[36]

All, in the letter, was brotherly love and kindness, and there is no reason to suppose that in young Edward's mind there was as yet anything else. But though a promise had been given, it was a provisional and temporary promise, explicit only for that time during which Mary should have the opportunity of better instruction. What was to happen if the 'godly and well learned men' failed to satisfy her conscience, was not stated, but left conveniently vague. If Van der Delft ever recieved the letter, he had in fact got little more than what he already had in the personal promise of the Duke of Somerset.

And the time was coming when the promise of Somerset would not be worth the price of a farthing bun. For change was in the air. In the gardens and galleries of the palace, and under the orchard trees where the fruit was ripening, there must have been gentlemen who walked with their heads very close together and talked in whispers. There must have been, after dark, cloaked figures who knocked at the garden gates of this Lord of the Council or of that, and were quietly let in. John Dudley, Earl of Warwick, was plotting against the Protector.

One of Somerset's last acts was to send to the Imperial ambassador Lord St. John and Mr. Comptroller Paget. These brought with them, not a written but a new verbal promise that Mary should be undisturbed. The Council, they said, would rather have found Mary wise enough to conform, but if she were not, she should not be troubled.[37] Somerset's goodwill could hardly be questioned. It was his ability to help which was becoming doubtful. The Emperor, hearing of the fresh promise instructed Van der Delft again to demand letters of licence.[38]

They were not obtained. On October 4th Somerset was arrested and sent to the Tower. Warwick, with Lord Arundel and a tail of Catholics behind him – Wriothesley, recalled for a few weeks from obscurity, Sir Richard Southwell and others – had seized the King's person and the control of affairs. For the moment few regretted the change, or indeed realized what it would mean. Somerset's policy both at home and abroad seemed to be responsible for nothing but disaster, and Edward himself had long fretted under his uncle's strict governance. The young King rejoiced to be able to leave Windsor, whither Somerset had brought him in a hurried evening ride. 'Methinks I am in prison,' he said to the malcontents who came to fetch him away, 'here be no galleries nor gardens to walk in.'[39] Most of the Council rejoiced, for Somerset had been a haughty colleague, and few of them knew him, as Paget did, so well that they did not mind being 'nipped' by him. All those who wished to have the old ways back again were glad, for Warwick himself was taken for a concealed Catholic, and there was no doubt about Wriothesley and Southwell, so that Protestants both at home and in the pulpit warned each other that the Mass would now be brought back.[40] Van der Delft, in his sober way, rejoiced, for he argued that 'religion could not be in a worse state, and that therefore a change must be for the better, and that it was not made by enemies of the old religion'.[41]

Mary, who had been taught most thoroughly the dismal lesson that it was impossible to trust anyone, was for a moment inclined to agree with him. In September while the plot was still in the egg, the confederates got in touch with her. She was too cautious, and as ever too undecided, to give any reply without a hasty appeal for advice from the Emperor. She sent, through Van der Delft, a message that in its uncertainties, contradictions, and despondency is a revelation of her harassed, bewildered mind. Were she known to be on the side of the plotters, she said, things would move faster. But if pressed she will say that she never has nor will interfere in matters of government. But it is sad to see the realm going to perdition so fast that there is no longer any knowledge of God nor of reason. Yet for this she can blame no man more than another, because it is by their common advice that things have fallen to their present disorder and desperate condition.[42]

The Emperor, who may have sighed and smiled over such a bungling practitioner in statecraft, sent an emphatic injunction that she must on no account interfere.[43] On reflection Mary herself decided that there was little indeed to hope for from the coming change of government. Even before Warwick and his friends struck, she had told Van der Delft that 'the Earl of Warwick is the most unstable man in England. The conspiracy against the Protector has envy and ambition only as its motives; for on all charges that may be moved against him, they are equally guilty, having given him their advice and consent.'[44]

They may all have been equally guilty, but they were not all equally to be feared. Somerset, with his dislike of bloodshed, his real feeling for the distresses of the poor, and his sharp autocratic temper; who, sincerely religious, had yet tried to pull down Westminster Abbey to build his palace; Somerset, that man of contradictions and qualifications, was a very different opponent from John Dudley, Earl of Warwick. For Warwick, more able than Somerset, though without his streak of cloudy greatness and his sensitive perceptions; the best soldier in England, hardy, masterful, vindictive, utterly devoid either of scruple or kindliness, was almost as dangerous to oppose as Henry VIII. The son of Henry VII's attainted minister, he had raised himself from the ruin of his father's fortunes by sheer ability. He was reputed the best lance, the bravest fighting man; when he chose he could appear gentle and affable; when he chose he could make men fear, so that at the end 'he ruled the whole Council as it pleased him, and they were all afraid of him (the more is the pity) so that such cowardness and fear was there never seen amongst honourable men'.[45] Over Edward he seems to have won complete ascendancy. At once he altered the system of the King's education. 'A soldier at heart and by profession', he encouraged the boy to ride and handle his weapons 'so that his Majesty soon began arming and tilting, managing horses, and delighting in every sort of exercise, drawing the bow, playing rackets, hunting', and the like.[46] Indeed the man's own personality and reputation were enough to win the affection and admiration of a boy of twelve. The Imperial ambassador noticed that at an audience, Edward would keep his eyes turned towards the Duke; when Dudley gave the signal the ambassador found himself dismissed. Sometimes, it was said, if the Duke wished Edward to do something which should not be known to have come from his suggestion, he would go secretly at night through the galleries of Whitehall, and into the King's bedchamber, and there instruct the sleepy boy as to what must be done.[47]

It may have been by his influence that the Court and the King himself became regrettably slack in attending sermons, so that Bernard Gilpin, ordered to preach before the King at Greenwich, had nothing more royal than his empty chair to address, and who therefore declared to those present that he was 'very sorry that they should be absent which ought to give example'.[48]

Those who had hoped, at the fall of Somerset 'that they should have again their old Latin service, their conjured bread and water',[49] were much deceived. Whatever Warwick's personal beliefs may have been, they did not interfere with his actions. First then, he got rid of the Catholics who had shouldered him into place–Southwell found himself in the Tower, Southampton (Wriothesley) was soon dismissed from the Council, and he and Arundel were confined to their houses. Arundel bought himself out for £1,200, but Southampton freed himself for nothing; a broken, disappointed man, he died soon after, and was buried as splendidly as if it were a triumph.

The next step for Warwick was to make sure of his alliance with another party. He turned from the Catholics to the extreme Protestants, to Hooper and his following; to men who considered Cranmer dilatory in reformation, and who scrupled at oaths, at vestments, at kneeling, at almost anything, till a man went about with his nose twitching like a dog's for the scent of idolatry, and found it in strange things. His conscience might be so tender that he would not even use a table in the church for an altar but must go outside and celebrate in sun or rain upon a tombstone; so tender that he could not even bear to call the days of the week by their old names, but must find out something which should not have been used in the days before the light of the Gospel had been recovered; so tender that for the same reason he would have fish days kept on any days but Friday, and Lent at any time but between Shrove-tide and Easter.[50]

After a flicker of optimism Mary faced the truth and turned to a desperate remedy. In September, even before Somerset fell, but when she had got wind of Warwick's plans, she sent the Emperor a ring, which he had given her some time before–perhaps even during their brief betrothal many years ago. It was to be a token to confirm the message that came with it, and that message was that now, as a dozen years ago, she wished to escape from England, and take refuge with him from the troubles of a world gone mad.[51] To Van der Delft in November she expressed herself more fully, explaining her necessity. She longed, she told him, now more than ever, that she might be safe out of England, where the common people were so infected and rebellious, and the nobles divided.[52] It must have seemed to her clear as a jag of lightning in the obscurity of a coming storm that God's punishment was over-hanging the country. Her only dream now was of a quiet life abroad. She would have been glad to be one of the Queen Dowager's maids in Flanders, so as to sleep in peace and wake without fear.

Van der Delft was very sympathetic. He told the Emperor, as a moving argument, of the difference there was now in the state of the King's two sisters. Elizabeth, brought up in as Protestant an atmosphere as her brother, was in high favour, and amusing herself at Court. Mary, not more than a day's ride from Whitehall, lived in country seclusion, utterly unvisited.[53] When he went to see her at New Hall, just before Christmas, after assisting at the christening of a child of Mr. Secretary Petre, he found that she was in a state of great distress. She told him then that she feared how Warwick's revolution 'may be only the beginning of our misfortunes'.

She had been invited, or summoned, to Court for Christmas, but she did not dare to go there, being sure that it was only a means to deprive her of her Mass at the festival; besides, the King would take her with him to sermons, and worse still, might even take her to his Holy Communion.[54] Van der Delft, listening, shared her anxiety, and wrote accordingly to the Emperor.

But the Emperor was not so easily moved as the good Dutchman. He had not responded to the token of the ring with any impulse of knight errantry. On the contrary, he gave his ambassador instructions as how to deal with Mary's idea of flight–'a matter in which, saving correction, the lady ought not to be encouraged, because of the great difficulty that would be met with in getting her out of the realm, and the problem of supporting her over here, for in such an event nothing might be expected for her from England'.[55]

But besides this unwillingness to take on the charge of a penniless princess, the Emperor had other plans for her rescue, more dignified than an abrupt flight and less awkward in their consequences. Before the fall of Somerset, when the English Council thirsted for his help against the French, and Paget had been sent to entice him into war, there had been talk between them of a marriage for Mary with Don Luiz, brother of the King of Portugal. The project had failed–a thing not to be wondered at since neither party wanted it enough. The ostensible reason for failure was that Don Luiz demanded that there should be no more religious changes in England till the Council of Trent had concluded its work. Somerset had then refused further discussion. 'If the Infante Don Luiz will not consider the marriage for that reason, our maid will have to have patience.'[56]

Now, in January 1550, the Emperor, who was by no means entirely unsympathetic with Mary's troubles, told Van der Delft to sound the Council on the subject of this old proposal. Van der Delft did so, and it was as if he had sown dragon's teeth in the Council Chamber. They asked him to withdraw, but he said afterwards that he might as well have stayed in the room, so loud did the wrangling voices rise.[57]

No answer to the suggestion was given until March, and then only indirectly. For Wotton told Van der Delft that the Council did not even know what Paget's proposal to the Emperor had been, because it had been Somerset's idea; but if it had been for a marriage between Mary and Don Luiz, that would never do. Had the Emperor suggested the King of Portugal's son it would have been a different matter. Wotton would not move from his position; Van der Delft could only tell him that the Council was misguided, and leave it at that.[58]

But indeed there was little likelihood that Warwick would, any more than Somerset, decide on a marriage for Mary. For one thing a dowry would have to be found for her, and Dudley was a man who 'thrusts his hand in deep wherever he can', but it was to draw out, and not to spend, and Edward's purse was a thing of many holes, out of which money ran fast into the greedy hands of courtiers. Besides all this, Somerset and Dudley, as Henry before them, might both consider that it was safest to have Mary under their hand; and if she must marry, a Protestant match would have suited them best. In April, as if for a counterblast to the Catholic Portuguese marriage, the Marquess of Brandenburg sent an ambassador to offer his men-at-arms for service with the King, and himself as bridegroom for the King's elder sister.[59]

So with the anti-Imperial bias of the English Council growing always more obvious, the Emperor found himself faced with the alternative of leaving Mary unmarried and unprotected in England, and of helping her to escape. Reluctantly, ungraciously, he began to consider the latter alternative. A Princess of England, the heir to the throne, to be smuggled out of the country –it was an enterprise against all his instincts. When, years before, he had heard that Francis of France, his prisoner after Pavia, had actually contemplated escape with his face blacked, and disguised as the negro who looked after his fire, Charles's first reaction had been one of shocked surprise at such an undignified idea. This was hardly better. In one way it was worse. As he pointed out to his ambassador, if Mary escaped, she would have to live at his expense.

Chapter IX

AT the end of April or the beginning of May 1550, Mary had warning from a friend that the Council intended to prohibit at least her household, and perhaps even herself, from hearing Mass. At once she sent to Van der Delft[1] begging him to come to her at Woodham Walter, near Maldon, the manor among the pleasant woods, the little hills and sheltered valleys of Essex. There is nothing left of the house now except the steep and moated site, and a few courses of the brickwork of the lower storey, but from the windows Mary saw beyond the trim garden, trees and gently rising slopes, and in the water of a pool, now drained, the reflection of the parish church which stood on the opposite side. All round, now as then, are woods, and narrow winding lanes; only in a few places the land lifts itself up to a tree-less, bramble-grown common that looks over the lower hills to where the wide salt-marshes lie, the winding river, and the sea.

By this time Mary and many others had realized that John Dudley's little finger was thicker than the loins of Somerset. The pace of religious change had quickened, and auguries of the future could easily be drawn from a fresh attack on the ancient customs of the Church. Images were gone; now the old stone altar slabs marked with their five carved crosses were being thrown out of church and a plain wooden table substituted. Two extreme Protestants, Hooper and Ridley, became Bishops. Ridley had to agree to alienate various possessions of his newly acquired Bishopric and these quickly found their way into the hands of courtiers. Fourteen years before, Erasmus had been glad to escape by death from 'this raving world'. The world was madder now, and Mary too young to hope yet for that way of deliverance; all she longed for, and she longed for it ardently, impatiently, was to escape out of England to the quiet and security of a Catholic country.

When Van der Delft came to her she clamoured to know if the Emperor had yet answered her prayer for help. What was she to do? she cried, and then told the ambassador that she had a plan of escape, all ready prepared. She had, she said, come to Woodham Walter from Newhall Boreham—or Beaulieu as she called it—so as to be near the sea, for now she was only two miles from the tidal Blackwater at Maldon. It had been easy to give out that Newhall needed the cleaning that all large sixteenth-century houses needed after a spell of habitation.

This then was her plan. Her Comptroller, Sir Robert Rochester, had, she said, friends 'of the religion' who often brought corn for her household by boat up the Blackwater as far as Maldon. Rochester had promised that he could have a boat ready, a boat belonging to an old and tried friend whose loyalty even Mary need not fear to trust. This man alone of the crew should know the destination of the voyage, but not even he should know, till Mary went on board, that he was to carry out of England anyone more important than Rochester himself. And not till the night itself when she was to escape, nor then till the very moment that she should ask them to follow her, would Mary tell her four most trusted women, and two gentlemen, of the plan.

Van der Delft may well have felt that events were running away with him. He answered her eagerness with the great question that exercised the Emperor's mind – Supposing Edward were to die? Folk in London in those days, watching the King ride by, saw a boy so slight and delicate that the weight of the great gold chain he wore bowed him down over his horse's neck; suppose Edward were to die, and she overseas? There would be no hope then of her succession, and unless she succeeded, religion in England was a lost cause.

Mary was, for the moment at least, beyond caring even for that. There was no one about the King who was not her enemy, she told Van der Delft. 'They would be so afraid of me', she cried, 'that before the people knew how it had pleased God to deal with the King, they would kill me by some means or other.' Remembering the old bad days when she had once before seen her only hope to lie in flight, she dreaded that the Emperor might again leave things until it was too late. 'If the Council', she said, 'had the same wit that the late King my father had, I should be too late even now to save myself.' She knew what would happen; she would be ordered inland, deprived of her servants, and left to face peril alone. If she fled she would not lose the crown, for the people of England would be true to her and accept no other ruler; from overseas she would justify her righteous cause in the eyes of the world. Working herself into a state almost of hysteria she talked on and on. 'I am', she cried, 'like a little ignorant girl caring nothing for my goods nor for the world, but only for God's service and my conscience.' She declared, and indeed it was true – 'I know not what to say', and then went on with hesitations, contradictions, qualifications. 'If there is peril in going and peril in staying I must chose the lesser of two evils.' Yet, if she went, there was her household to think of; they might become 'lost sheep'. 'But if,' – she turned to Van der Delft with a perfect example of the traditional obliquity of women – 'But if in your opinion I had better go, so be it in God's name, for I know no danger in going that will not be as great or even greater at any other time. ... I would willingly stay were I able to live and serve God as I have done in the past, which is what I have always said. But these men are so changeable that I know not what to say. What say you, Mr. Ambassador?'

Mr. Ambassador must have been hard put to it to say anything to such a hugger-mugger of contradictions. He replied hesitatingly that he could not answer, but thought that the Council probably would deprive her of Mass. Then, seeing her so distraught and being at his wits' end to comfort her, he protested that she must never doubt that the Emperor would welcome her, if once she could get away; yet the Portuguese marriage was a safer means

10

of escape, and he implored her at least to wait till his secretary had returned
from the Emperor. This secretary was a Master Jehan Duboys, of whom we
shall hear more.

Perhaps Charles was moved by her distress, or her arguments; or perhaps
he, like Van der Delft, feared that in desperation she would attempt to escape
unaided, and that so, 'the good lady, through her own incompetence, might
land herself in a worse scrape'.[2] At all event, some time during May he gave
his consent, not to Mary's compact, domestic, feminine plan, but to one
suggested by Van der Delft which provided for a more dignified, as well as a
safer exit for the Princess of England. By this plan the ambassador was to have
his recall. To avoid suspicion he was to give out that he was going into
Germany, but, once clear of the Thames' mouth, his ship, and two others
sent to be his convoy, should turn north to the Blackwater estuary and sail
up to Maldon. There Mary should join them in the boat belonging to
Rochester's friend. When the Princess was on board she would with two
ships as convoy, be safe from any of the swarm of small pirate vessels that
haunted the innumerable creeks and waterways of that flat and desolate coast.
Secrecy would insure that they should not have to face attack from anything
larger, that is to say from any English warships.

The plan once accepted by the Emperor, speed was essential. Van der
Delft was recalled, and his successor Jehan Scheyfve, a Dutch merchant of no
particular ability or standing, was sent in his stead. But just before Van der
Delft was to leave, he received a message from Mary. She would not, she said,
accept any excuses; he must take his leave of her in person. He guessed correctly that this message meant she had something to tell him regarding their
plan, and he went to see her. But he would not allow the new ambassador to
come with him. He told the man himself that he did thus to avert suspicion,
but to the Emperor he insisted that for Scheyfve's own sake he must know
nothing–absolutely nothing–of the plan. If it succeeded he would be in an
awkward corner enough; unless he were honestly ignorant of the whole
thing, it might be a dangerous corner.[3]

When Van der Delft rode down to Woodham Walter, Mary received him
with news of something that threatened to wreck their plan. Governments in
England always dreaded the summer, because men who met together for
markets and junketings might hatch such treasons as last year had broken out
into open rebellion. This year the order had gone out that every householder
should stand his term of watch and ward along the roads by night, so that
there should be no stealthy wayfarers going from village to village in the
short darkness, knocking quietly on cottage doors and giving word of a day
appointed.

With such an obstacle to fear Mary wanted to delay no longer, but to
seize the vanishing chance, before the order was put in force. But having
once got into her head the dread of pirates she was now craving for the
security which Van der Delft's escort would give her; and she proposed, since
Rochester's friend had at the last minute refused to sail, to use a fishing boat

which the ambassador had hired as a forlorn hope; to go to it on foot and in disguise, and thus join the Flemish ships now in the Blackwater. But Van der Delft was not to be hurried. There was no boat ready to sail from Maldon; and her four women would add to the difficulty of disguise; he much preferred another plan–a small ship of light draught to be sent from Ostend, as so many came there to Maldon with corn, and in it Jehan Duboys, his secretary, in the guise of a merchant selling his corn.

For a while they argued it this way and that; Van der Delft putting before the Princess all the difficulties, and explaining the necessity there was that the attempt, once made, should not fail; she objecting that 'It never will be safe, but I will trust in God.' At last he persuaded her to wait, even to withdraw from Woodham Walter if necessary; she could easily return again on some pretext of plague at Beaulieu. She would only have a few days to wait, and he promised her an escort. He also promised, so he told the Emperor, that 'as she seemed to cling to me', he himself would be in one of the ships. So they parted. Mary saw Jehan Duboys, the secretary, once more, just before he and his master left, and reminded him of Van der Delft's undertakings saying, 'But your master must have come for me as he promised me.' Then Duboys and his master left for the Netherlands.

On June 6th Van der Delft wrote to the Emperor from Turnhout telling him Mary's bad news.[4] Charles, in alarm, at last decided on haste; the thing, if it was to be done at all, must be done quickly or the secret would leak out. He ordered the ambassador to carry out the plan at once.[5] But Charles had, as Mary feared, waited too long. The ambassador was probably already a sick man when he wrote his report to the Emperor. Soon he took to his bed, and lay raving in his delirium of the plot that was so much on his mind. In less than a fortnight Van der Delft was dead.[6]

The Emperor might well have dropped the plan; but though slow to yield to persuasion, once persuaded he was obstinate. He waited for a few days, lest the late ambassador's ravings had betrayed the secret;[7] but in the marts of Flanders when the merchants drank over their bargains, there was no talk at all of the Lady Mary's flight. So the secret was not yet out. On June 21st Charles gave his consent to the Queen Regent's suggestion that with the Admiral, M. d'Eecke, or Scepperus, in support with two ships, Jehan Duboys, the dead ambassador's secretary, should sail according to his late master's plan and bring Mary back with him.[8] There could be nothing suspicious in an Ostend corn-ship, for many traded at Maldon; as for M. Scepperus, his presence was easily explained. He was there to hunt for Scots pirates in the creeks of the estuary.

When the Emperor made up his mind he did not do things by halves; one ship under M. Scepperus was to sail with Duboys as far as Stansgate, a hamlet five miles from Maldon, on the Essex shore, and there to wait; three more were to lie off Harwich, and four larger ships were to stand on and off at sea. And the Emperor could move quickly too. There can have been hardly a day between the decision, and the despatch, with a letter for Mary, of a man of her own called Henry, who was then in Antwerp. This letter, written by Jehan Duboys, promised his arrival before June 27th.[9]

It was at evening on the last day of June that Duboys and Scepperus's two ships found themselves off Harwich after a stormy crossing. Next morning they parted company, and in a flat calm Duboys pushed on, the sailors rowing with the coming tide along that featureless low shore that in a summer mist fades so imperceptibly into the sea. By the time they reached Stansgate the tide had turned and Duboys could go no farther till night. To save time, and in the hope that Woodham Walter would hear of his approach, he sent off in a small row-boat a sailor who could speak English, and his own brother-in-law Master Peter Marchant. So as to play their part convincingly, these took with them a sample of corn to show to the men of Maldon, and they were to promise the arrival of the ship by the next tide.

During the night Duboys weighed, and in the early hours of the morning, by a full moon, came to that long curve of quayside, hardly more indeed than a timber-shored bank, that follows the wide swing of the tidal river, where still the bluff-bowed coasters lie, smelling sharply of Stockholm tar, afloat at high tide, and at low lying on the bed of grey ooze that the river leaves. Above them, the ground rises sharply with little steep streets and flights of steps; there is a church, St. Mary's, on top of the slope, whose tower was, in the sixteenth century, and till long after, both a look-out and a beacon. Duboys passed this, and berthed farther up the river beside another smaller ship at which he looked with envious eyes, for his own ship was of deepish draught, but this much shallower and fitter for dodging the shoals of the river and taking advantage of every moment of the tide. Along the quay he could see no one at all who seemed to come from Woodham Walter. He went below, and in the twilight cabin, by the light of a ship's lantern, he wrote a letter – 'in my simple Latin', as he called it, to Mary's Comptroller.

'Sir,

'I believe you have received my letters sent with Henry from Antwerp. I arrived here with the corn about three this morning in a 6-oared boat. Yesterday I sent my brother, Peter Marchant, to announce in this town that we had brought the corn, and were coming with the next tide, and this I did in order that you might the sooner be advised of my arrival. However, as far as I know, there was nobody there to take the corn or receive the said Peter. Therefore I am obliged to write now to point out to you that there is danger in delay, especially as M. Scepperus is now coming to Stansgate with a war ship, and near Harwich there are 3 other ships waiting, and moreover 4 larger ships are out at sea. Consider therefore whether we must not hurry. There is yet another reason as well; the water will not be as high tomorrow night as tonight, and will be lower every night till next moon, and we now have the advantage that the tide serves our purpose late at night and towards morning, that is at 2 o'clock. By that hour or immediately afterwards, all ought to be here so that we may be on our way while the tide is still rising, and be carried out beyond the banks below Stansgate with the ebb, for my vessel draws a good deal of water. There is lying near me however, a smaller vessel which would be much better; I do not know whether it belongs to you. I will sell my corn at once, and will be ready tonight. Please let me know your intentions. There would be danger were there to be many women.'

He had got so far when a hail from the shore must have warned him of an arrival. It was Peter Marchant, and the man Henry. Once private in the cabin they gave him their news, and it was not good. The Comptroller was making difficulties. Duboys sat down again and continued his letter.

'But they [the women] might still escape in disguise, and I beg you once more to give me an answer in writing with which I may satisfy the Emperor. I must add that I see no better opportunity than the present one, and this undertaking is passing through so many hands that it is daily becoming more difficult, and I fear it may not remain secret. However, I will yield to a better opinion, and I pray God to inspire you now, for the Emperor has done all he could.'

Henry, who was to carry this letter to Sir Robert, was also given a verbal message. 'If the packet is to be sent off at all' he was to say, 'now or never is the time.' He was also to remind the Comptroller that Duboys had given him ample notice by the letters from Antwerp, and to warn him that it would be dangerous for the two of them to meet.

After a wait during the hour when the housewives of Maldon must have been lighting their fires, Henry came back to the ship. He had met the Comptroller coming from Woodham Walter, and Sir Robert now wished Duboys to meet him in the churchyard of St. Mary's, above the quay, a quiet airy spot looking out over the river.

Duboys, irritated, anxious, and unwilling, climbed the hill, and found walking together in the grassy churchyard, Sir Robert Rochester and a Master Schurtz, probably a Fleming living at Maldon, and the same who had formerly promised his boat for Rochester's scheme. Duboys greeted the Princess's Comptroller, with a handful of corn ostentatiously held out, and together they bargained loudly for the price of it. But when that was settled Rochester whispered that Duboys must follow them to his friend's house. Still more unwilling, Duboys obeyed, because he must.

In that garden, walking up and down together, the Emperor's servant and the Englishman came to grips. Rochester was full of discouragement. There was, he said, no earthly chance of bringing the Princess down to the river at night without grave risk, because of the watch that kept the roads then. Besides there were those in her household who would suspect, for 'some there are less loyal to religion than she thinks'. Nor was there any pressing reason now that she should fly, since she was as free as ever to have the Mass. If she did fly, there would be scandal, and, should Edward die, she would have lost her hope of succession.

That last lay at the bottom of Rochester's opposition; but to placate Duboys, he went on to talk now as if it might only be a matter of postponing Mary's escape. He was sure, so he said, that nothing would be done against her while Parliament sat. After that she would have the advantage of the long winter nights and could go to a house of hers on a branch of the Brightlingsea creek–to St. Osyths, only he called it and Duboys spelt it 'St. Ouses', as the country people nowadays call it 'Toosey'. To wind up with he told Duboys that he did not know what Mary would do when she knew that all was ready, vowed that he only gave warning of these dangers so that he should clear himself of responsibility, and finally asked when Mary should start, if she was to go.

Duboys was very stiff. 'I am not,' said he, 'a person to advise, and I can state no given time.' Scepperus was out in the estuary, and he here with his own ship. He would obey the Princess and go quietly away if she ordered it, but that she would do so, he said, he could hardly believe, when he thought of the last time he saw her, and of her letters since. He would need, he added, her letters to discharge him of his duty.

Rochester, an obstinate, but not a strong man, began to excuse himself. 'Sir,' he said,'I beg you do not judge me thus; for I would give my hand to see my Lady out of the country and in safety, and I was the first man to suggest it. And if you understand me, what I say is, not that my Lady does not wish to go, but that she wishes to go if she can.'

Duboys was not mollified. He understood well enough, he said, but all this had been discussed before. 'The thing is now a question of Yes or No, and you have the choice; you must be good enough to make up your mind and be quick about it, if it is to be done at all', for, he pointed out, there was risk of discovery when Scepperus's ships were sighted off Harwich. As for Rochester's plea that if Edward died Mary would lose her hope of succession, Duboys reminded him that that very thing had been the Emperor's main argument against the scheme, and that Mary, dictating to Duboys letters for his master had herself put it aside, saying that the greatest necessity compelled her to escape; and he concluded by quoting her hysterical outburst to Van der Delft in his last audience.

'You say well', answered Rochester, gently immovable, 'but this is not a matter to be hurried . . . and as for what you say of my Lady's words, they were that she wished to stay if she could, but to have all things in readiness.'

'Yes,' cried Duboys hotly, 'but you are putting the wrong construction on them.'

Duboys's frayed temper cannot have been improved when Rochester announced that Mary wished to see him. He asked curtly that Rochester should excuse him. He dared not, he said, go to her for fear of suspicion; besides he must keep his men together and ready. For all Rochester's urging he would not agree to a visit so dangerous.

'Well then,' said Rochester at last, 'let your brother come at one in the afternoon to fetch the answer.'

When Duboys had refused, as far too risky, an invitation to dine with Rochester, they parted; Master Schurtz was to come after dinner to weigh the corn.

Back at the quay the unhappy Duboys found that something else had gone wrong. The sailor sent to get permission from the town authorities to unload corn, had spent his time going from one to another, and all to no purpose. Duboys sent off a message to Schurtz, and went to dinner at some inn near the quay. But as he sat there with his brother, the English-speaking sailor, and the host, in came the bailiff and customs officer of Maldon. They had heard, they said, that this merchant had sold his corn to the Comptroller at Woodham Walter; he should not have done that before they had put a price on it; and they had rather anyway that he had sold it in the town. Worse than all this they had got hold of an idea that he had another ship in the estuary carrying more corn, for the amount they had heard of, as sold to the Comptroller, was far too great for his ship to hold.

Duboys was a ready man, and not easily abashed. He utterly denied having another ship in the Blackwater. And his sailor, he said, had spent all day trying to find them; so if they had not priced the corn, it was not his fault. As for corn to sell in Maldon, he would bring more. 'If I could make a decent profit,' he said, 'I would gladly bring more to Maldon, for they harass merchants so in London that I don't intend to go there for so little gain.'

That remark, playing on local patriotism, did its work. The Maldon men at once said he could come, and welcome. At Maldon he should sell as well, and get his money as quick, as anywhere in England.

Duboys was a bold, as well as a ready man. Another with so much to conceal might have been meek, but not he. Very well, he would bring more corn, 'but I don't understand', he said, 'why so simple a matter needs so much talk'.

'No, no,' said they, 'you are welcome and always will be', and they forthwith shifted the blame for that morning's transaction to Sir Robert Rochester. 'He should not have bought the corn', they said, but as they held the Lady Mary 'as high as the King's person (though she knows nothing of this business) we will let it pass this time.'

At just what point in the interview Duboys had taken the wise step of standing drinks all round, is not mentioned, but there is such a perceptible mellowing here, that one is persuaded some refreshment must already have gone down dry throats. Duboys was very pleasant too. He offered to sell them the corn, and said he was not bound to the Comptroller; and what duty, he asked, was he to pay?

The Maldon men were not to be outdone in friendliness. As for the duty, they said, 'it was nothing much, and, as the corn was for my lady, it should be nothing at all'. Nor, when Duboys offered them a tip, would they accept it, but thanked him for his good cheer. When he asked if he might unload, they told him, 'As soon as he liked.'

Perhaps it was just then that the clock of St. Mary's struck one. Duboys turned to his brother, told him it was time to be going, and bade him tell the Comptroller that the Maldon men were not pleased that he had bought the corn. So, under the bailiff's nose, Duboys sent him off to Woodham Walter.

But, daring as he had been and wily, all was not safe yet. Out on the quay with the bailiff, as he watched the weighing of the corn, he saw a boat come in with the morning's tide from M. Scepperus's ship. They had come for beer and provisions. Duboys looked them over with a glassy indifferent eye and never a sign of recognition. They gave no greeting either, for as they passed Duboys's craft they had looked for those signals which had been agreed upon as a sign that the plot had succeeded, and they had found none. But the bailiff came again to Duboys's elbow. 'Is that', he asked, 'the boat from the ship you have out at sea with more corn?' It was too near the truth to be pleasant; and Duboys needed all his courage. 'I have', he said, 'no corn other but what you see. But I saw the Emperor's ships outside looking for Scots pirates.'

'That is what I think', said the bailiff very wisely. 'They look as if they have come for supplies', and he went off to speak to them.

It was six o'clock when Peter Marchant and the servant Henry came back to the quay. Henry brought a horse for Duboys to ride; he was to guide him by a secret way (and there must have been many a quiet woodland path to choose from) to Woodham Walter. It was useless to protest; the Fleming's only hope of success was to go and persuade the Princess to make the venture. So, in the cool of the evening, he set off.

At Woodham Walter he was met by the Comptroller. The Lady Mary, Rochester said, was making ready to receive him, and had been told what had passed that morning. Then the two fell again, as was inevitable, into another haggling argument. Rochester told the Fleming 'as a mighty secret . . . that he was quite persuaded the King could not outlast the year; for he and others knew his horoscope to say so'. Duboys answered acidly. Rochester and his mistress must, he said, know what facts they had to consider, though on the very same facts my Lady had twice declared that she wished to go. And, he added, 'I am glad her letter reached Antwerp concerning this, or I might have been accused of giving a false account.' Then, with rising bitterness, 'God knows that my master's illness was partly brought on by his disappointment at knowing the attempt could not be made when he left the country. . . . However there is no reason why you should consider yourselves obliged to act in one way rather than another, and if my Lady wishes to stay she shall be welcome, and no harm done, except that the whole business is so near to being discovered that it is most unlikely it can be kept secret.'

Again, at a show of temper, Rochester grew apologetic.

'For the love of God', he cried, 'do not say that to my Lady. She is a good woman and really wants to go, but neither she nor you see what I see and know. Great danger threatens us.'

Duboys was dogged. He would not, he said, alarm the Princess, but must speak so that she should understand, and not afterwards have cause to regret his silence. The Emperor would soon be making peace with the Scots and there would then be no further excuse for the warships in the Blackwater. 'I can', he said, 'see no peril greater than letting this opportunity slip. Some of our ships' company have been heard to say that they suspected they were going for the Princess of England, as they had done ten years ago, as my Lady knows better than I.'

The sharp dispute was interrupted by a summons from Mary. Duboys was led to her, and, in some wainscotted or arrassed room, while one of her women kept the door, he must play his last cards to win or lose the game. Had he known Mary better he might have guessed it already lost, for Rochester had had plenty of time for persuasion, and Mary could so easily be persuaded to indecision.

It was the Princess who, naturally, opened the interview with inquiries after the Emperor and the Queen Regent, and thanks for M. Scepperus's and Duboys's trouble. She had, she told him, his last letter, 'and also the one you wrote before; but I am as yet ill prepared, and it seems you wish it to be tonight'.

At that Duboys's heart must have sunk. It was only too clear that Rochester had been at her. He could but reply politely–'Any time your Majesty pleases' –for Imperialists, she, and not a heretic lad, was sovereign of England–'but I have spoken and written to your Comptroller the reasons for which long delay seems to me dangerous.'

Mary, like her Comptroller, suffered from an uneasy sense of compunction. She hastened to tell Duboys, by way of clearing herself, of the preparations she had made, of 'great long hopsacks' packed with some of her stuff, 'which would not look as though they were heavy'. Duboys, picturing, most likely, a hasty ride through the dark woods burdened with enormous hopsacks, 'made so bold as to say that if once she crossed the water she should lack for nothing, and that her effects did not matter so much; the great thing was to bring her person to safety, and that was the point on which she must now make up her mind'.

She did not answer that, but spoke instead words that showed clearly enough both her discomfort, and the way her mind was turning. 'I do not know', she said, 'how the Emperor would take it if it turned out to be impossible for me to go now, after I have so often importuned his Majesty on the subject.'

Duboys, who could not take her up as he had taken the Comptroller, said only that the Emperor would be content with anything which satisfied her.

Would Duboys, she asked next, 'take her rings now?'

He replied that he would obey, but if news of such a thing once got about it would merely announce her intention of flight. Then he 'humbly begged her first to take care of her person, for as she was minded to risk her rings, she might as well go with, as after them'.

Mary was clearly shaken. She turned away and spoke for a while with Rochester and the woman at the door. Duboys, watching them, saw that they reached to a decision. Mary came back to him. She could not, she said, be ready before the day after next, but she could then leave her house at four in the morning 'under pretext of going to amuse herself and purge her stomach by the sea, as her ladies did daily'. Four o'clock was just the time that the watch retired. 'Would the tide serve then?' she asked.

Duboys answered that it would. Heartened by this new decision he was generous. The Queen Dowager, he told her, had preferred a plan by which she should leave in the morning and not at night.

'Well then,' cried Mary, evidently much relieved, 'the Queen and I are of one mind. And know you that the very day your master left London, two of the King's galleys, called the *Sun* and the *Moon*, also left and came up to Stansgate, where they stayed three or four days. And their Captain was the Vice Admiral, the greatest heretic on earth.' She was again swinging round to the idea of flight. 'It is more than time that I was hence,' she said, 'for things are going worse than ever. A short time ago they took down the altars in the very house my brother lives in.'

Harmony was restored, but that did not solve the problem of how to let M. Scepperus know that he must hale off until Friday. As they were debating it there was a knock at the door and Sir Robert Rochester went out. He came back with bad news.

'Our affair', he announced, 'is going very ill. There is nothing to be done this time, for here is my friend [Schurtz] who has ridden hard from Maldon to warn me that the bailiff and other folk . . . wish to arrest your boat . . . and suspect you of having some understanding with the warship at Stansgate. Some men . . . have been to see the warship, but were not allowed to go on board. So they intend to send expressly . . . next tide and ask the ship its business, holding you and your men in the meantime to examine you here.'

As he put it the matter sounded so desperate that Duboys must have thought of beacon fires blazing along the coasts next night. For a few moments the three stood in that quiet room where the dusk was deepening, at a loss, not knowing what to say or do. Then Duboys began to try to find out more from Rochester. He however would not stay, but slipped out, to get details, he said. In the heavy silence that fell Duboys heard Mary's voice. 'What shall we do?' she cried. 'What is to become of me?'

The Comptroller came back again; but with no less alarming news. 'My friend here', he said, 'says that there is something going on behind the scenes, and that you had better depart at once for those men of the town are not well disposed.'

Duboys, who had almost lost his nerve, answered tartly that he could not go before the tide, and that, as his arrest would endanger the Princess–for he would be recognized if examined–they had better hide him. 'But', he added, recovering something of his daring and resource, 'as the matter is so desperate it may be best of all to take my Lady down to the boat and get her off in secret . . . for if I fail to escape, my Lady's danger will be as great as if she had made the attempt.'

'No,' the Comptroller answered–'It is impossible, for they are going to double the watch tonight, and, what is more, post men on the church tower, a thing that has never been done before. So all we can do is to see to getting you out of this.'

Duboys would not at once give in; he and the Comptroller–the two men had naturally taken charge of the situation–disputed what should be done. Mary took no part except to repeat, ' "But what is to become of me?", all the time, until at last I said that we must come to some decision, for it was beginning to get dark and once the watch was set I should not be able to go.'

Again Rochester went out. When he came back it was to say that his friend, who knew nothing more than that the Flemish merchant was come for his money, would see Duboys through the watch. But before Duboys went, they must make arrangements for another attempt; this they decided must be put off for ten or twelve days. Then, so they agreed, Rochester should send a servant of his to Duboys in Antwerp with some of the Princess's gear, and word of the precise day on which she would be ready to start as soon as she heard of the arrival of the ships. But this time the attempt should be made from Stansgate, since the Princess in a few days must leave Woodham Walter for Newhall.

The two men were calm enough again, but not so Mary, for the whole time they debated 'my Lady [was] still repeating "But what is to become of me."' Flight is a daunting thing, and her nerve was gone.

All was ready for Duboys's departure, only the Comptroller asked him did he need a letter to the Emperor? 'No,' answered Duboys bitterly. 'I have too good reason for breaking off the undertaking to please me.'

Mary bade him farewell, sent messages to the Queen Regent, and then, with some pathos, said to him, 'You see, it is not our fault now.'

'No,' the Comptroller took it up, 'but his, for not bringing more corn.'

That most unhandsome remark Duboys could not let pass. 'I had corn enough,' he retorted, 'but you ought not to have bought it; that was not in my plan.' He might, one feels, have said very much more.

At last he left, and rode through the woods with Schurtz and Henry, who was to report his safe arrival. It was nearly midnight when they came upon the watch, twenty men under Duboys's friend the bailiff, just outside the town. Schurtz went forward and spoke; from what Duboys, listening to their conversation, could make out, the talk was again only of the corn. Schurtz, Duboys thought, was offering it, in Rochester's name, to the bailiff. Anyway there was no difficulty made, and Duboys may well have reflected how easy it might have been to avoid the watch with the Princess beside him, or even to have passed her through in disguise.

Once at his lodging he found his brother, awake and apparently dressed, for a little while before the bailiff had knocked him up to ask for a view of his merchant's licence to export corn from Flanders. But when he had seen it, he had gone away.

Down they went through the steep streets of the sleeping town to the quay, and on board; all was quiet, there were no lights; the sailors were asleep too. Schurtz, through Henry, advised Duboys to go as soon as the tide served. At two o'clock, just as the light began to grow, Duboys had the boat cast off; it was only when he wakened the crew for this purpose that he heard that his best man, the English-speaking sailor who knew also all the banks and shoals of the river, had last evening gone ashore and had not returned.

That inconvenience, however, must have been but a pin-prick to the unfortunate Fleming, when, passing below the squat, square tower of St. Mary's on the crown of the ridge, he looked up and saw 'no one aloft nor down below on the ground either'. What he may have thought then of the Comptroller's crooked dealing can only have been confirmed when he reached M. Scepperus, riding at anchor between Stansgate and Harwich, just off the long pebble beach of St. Osyth. For Scepperus had not moved from there, and in fact had never been off Stansgate where the men of Maldon were supposed to have reached him.

So the plan, which would have saved Mary three more years of persecution and anxiety, failed. Who can forecast now, what would have happened after those three years, had it succeeded? What would have been the luck of John Dudley's bold scheme, if when Edward died, the rightful heir to the throne had been abroad in Flanders? No one can say. But one thing is certain. In that quiet room in Woodham Walter much that was of great import was decided, and as so much in human history is decided, in haste, and scramblingly.

Meanwhile Duboys, with all his regret, disappointment, and irritation, was tossing in a North Sea gale; when at last he landed at Antwerp, he was ready to try again; he would willingly have waited at his dead master's house for the coming of Rochester's messenger,[10] but he must indeed have known by then that the Comptroller had merely fobbed him off, and that there was to be no second attempt.

For the Emperor and the Queen Dowager there was nothing left to do but openly to deny that there was anything at all in the rumour of Mary's escape, now running everywhere, and privately to scold M. Scepperus, the Queen Dowager declaring roundly that he 'was but a coward, and for fear of one gentleman that came down, durst not go forth with his enterprise'.[11] Rumour indeed was very busy. Some said that the Lady Mary was already in Flanders. The Queen Dowager could, and did, express surprise at this to the English ambassador, who answered politely that there were always plenty of people who would talk at random, and that he himself had not heard the rumour. The Queen said that she would be very glad to see the Princess, of course, but not that way. She only hoped that the English Council would not give her cause to change her mind. Chamberlain replied—Oh no. They had no wish but to treat Mary as the King's near relative. So the pretty conversation ended, and things were where they had been.[12]

But not for Mary. Jehan Scheyfve, the new Imperial ambassador, in blank ignorance of what had been going on under his nose, wrote to the Princess, passing on the Queen Dowager's account of this conversation, and pointing

out that the rumour of her flight was probably spread by the English themselves to give them an excuse for the new severity which she was already
feeling.[13] What for the Queen Dowager was a game of 'saving face' and for
us a rather salt comedy, was for Mary deadly and hopeless earnest. She had
foregone her chance of escape, yet the Council knew that she had planned it.
Now she was left to drink whatever cup Warwick and his friends should
decide to offer her.

Chapter X

THE King and Council had learnt of the plan of escape, whether from the warning of Henry II of France, since March good friends again with England, or from another source; soon people were talking openly at the street corners of London of how M. Scepperus and Jehan Duboys had come 'disguised as seamen to fetch away the Lady Mary'.[1] Promptly the Council moved to prevent such a thing happening again. In a a few days all the ports along the Essex coast near to Newhall were full of soldiers. On July 25th the Council ordered Petre and Lord Chancellor Rich to go to the Lady Mary and bid her either move inland to Oking or to come to Court.

The Council's two messengers arrived, and recited their message. Mary excused herself; she said that she was sick. Change of air, they replied, would do her good. She told them that she had no objection to change of air in itself, but that she would only take it at one of her own houses. For the moment they said no more, and did not mention the knowledge that was so much on their mind—the knowledge that she had nearly given them the slip altogether. But they had not done with her. Rich tried his hand at persuading the Comptroller to persuade his mistress to go to Court. Rochester would not. He knew, he said, that Mary would not hear of it, and he did not intend to waste his breath. Rich rated him, but gained nothing by that.[2]

Then he tried another approach. He left Newhall and returned with his wife—daughter of one of those great merchant houses of London who so often wedded with the new nobility; a sensible, comfortable, kindly soul, as Holbein drew her, with a small firm mouth and a little hairy wart under her chin. They both rode out hunting with the Lady Mary; then they invited her to stay with them. She refused at first but afterwards accepted the invitation, only to be presented with a perfect excuse for putting off the visit by sudden illness in Lord Rich's household.

But already, before the Council's messengers reached her, Mary had felt the first penalty of her failure to take her chance of escape, and a threat of what was to come. The day before she left Woodham Walter for Newhall Boreham she had sent on to the latter house most of her folk, and with them, her almoner and priest, Francis Mallet. At Newhall, before Mary arrived, Mallet, doubtless without a second thought, had celebrated Mass. He had given the Council its chance. Soon after, he was cried at Boreham Cross by the Sheriff of Essex as having broke the Statute.[3] He fled, making for Yorkshire, where Catholics were so many that he would be as safe as a needle in a haystack.

So opened the second great attack on Mary, an attack far more deadly and better directed than the first. Before this, the Council had aimed at the Princess herself, admonishing her, or bidding her servants to admonish her, that there must be no more Mass; and she had turned a deaf ear to it all. But now they were to take the line of penalizing those servants who obeyed her rather than the Statute. For this action her own royal immunity from law did not even need to be contradicted; it was her servants who must obey or suffer.

At the end of November, the next move came. In that month Mallet and another of Mary's chaplains, Alexander Barkley, were summoned before the Council, which, fully expecting trouble from Mary, wrote at the same time to her, asking her 'to suffer the Sheriff in the quietest manner' to serve the summons.[4] But the summons could not be served, for neither Mallet nor Barkley were to be found.

Mary, however, replying to the challenge,[5] fired the first shot in this second 'battle of the promise' as it might be called, for it was the promise made to the Emperor which was again the thing in dispute. In the long wrangle between the King's heir and his Council there are indeed three promises claimed by Mary, and ignored or denied by the Council. The first, the verbal promise lightly given by Somerset, was of no value. Somerset now, though no longer a prisoner, was not much more than one of the petty men creeping between the legs of the new Colossus, John Dudley.

The second promise, that given by Paget to the Emperor during the summer of 1549, when the Council valued the Emperor's alliance above rubies, and far above such small things as promises, was easy to explain away; it was not even necessary to question the Emperor's word. It was enough to say that Paget had spoken irresponsibly, rashly. As for the third – the promise given by the Council to Van der Delft, the Council now found themselves most fortunately able to deny that also. An 'ambassador that dead is' cannot be brought in as witness. They seized their good luck in both hands and replied to Mary in a letter, long, calm, reasonable, almost patronizing in tone. There never had been any promise, they said, that was not temporary and provisional. They read the Princess a long lecture on the soundness of the new religion, and the importance to the realm of her conformity. They concluded with an appeal to her, as though to a friend, to help the Sheriff of Essex to apprehend Mallet and Barkley, or, if she could not bring herself to do this, at least not to shelter them.[6] That was exactly what Scheyfve suspected she was doing – 'I believe Madame', he wrote to the Queen Dowager in the Netherlands, 'that one of her priests is still in her house' – but in letters to Mary he was at pains to declare his conviction of her innocence in the matter. Yet though the chaplains, lurking in some quiet room at Newhall or elsewhere, could not be found, Mary's Mass was threatened by this action of the Council, and it was perhaps this matter which took her up to Court a fortnight before Christmas.

During her visit Edward seems to have brought up the question by saying – ('God knows', cried Mary, 'who were his advisers in this') – that he had heard rumours that she habitually had Mass. Mary did not answer him, but

turned, and called Paulet to come near, to be witness to what she should say;
Paget, her other witness, was, she said in France. Paulet came, the old man
who was to outlive so many there, 'Shebna the scribe' as Knox named him,
who unlike Achitophel, the masterful John Dudley, ruled 'by counsel and
wit', and managed, so he himself said, to preserve his position during these
stormy times, 'by being a willow and not an oak'. With him came Lord
Rich; the two Marquesses, Dorset and Northampton; Lord Wentworth;
Master Thomas and Master Anthony Wingfield. Then, said Mary, 'I declared
openly to the King's Majesty the message I had received from the Council
through the Emperor's ambassador, and the Earl of Wiltshire [Paulet], who
knew more . . . than any other Councillor present, affirmed my statement to
be true.'

Then, perhaps because her courage had broken suddenly as she looked at
the puzzled, troubled, stubborn face of the boy who was called King, she
began to cry. Edward was an excitable child, and easily touched; he also
burst into tears, and told her that he thought no harm of her. So the matter
was dropped, one of the two Marquesses smoothing things over as best he
might with the rather foolish remark that 'the King had no other thought but
to inquire and know all things'.[7]

Some weeks after her return from this visit, Mary received from the Council
letters in answer to some of hers, which Scheyfve, and *a fortiori* Mary herself,
considered insolent. These letters brought up the whole question once more.
She therefore sent back a reply which the ambassador claimed as his own
composition, but which is so like Mary's own in its ringing denunciation of
the Council's perfidy, that it is hard to believe Scheyfve's part in it to have
been more than an arrangement of the arguments. As she told the ambassador,
when he had demurred at a letter of hers as being too sharp in tone, she was in
the habit of writing roughly to the Council, and if she dealt gently with them
they would think she was yielding.[8] No one from this letter of January 27th
1551, could have laboured under that misconception.

In this letter then, once more, and more explicitly than ever, Mary recited
the history of a promise made, so she claimed, to the late Van der Delft, and
it was a promise in writing. 'There were', she affirmed, 'words contained in
letters written as from you all to the late ambassador, about last Whitsuntide
[i.e. May 25th 1550] by one among you whom I could well name.' This
written promise was, she said, the outcome of the refusal of the Imperial
ambassador to accept a verbal promise tendered to him by Paget, and Paulet,
Earl of Wiltshire. There was 'moreover, another promise made to his
Majesty [the Emperor] nearly a year before, by virtue of which I and my
household were given entire freedom to have Mass celebrated'. The Council
had already denied this earlier promise to be binding, letters however were a
different thing.

But it was less the denial of these letters which moved Mary to rage, than
the fact that when she had gone home again the Council denied the truth of
her version of the late audience with the King. Of what had passed there

'those I singled out in my letters' she complained 'have no recollection'. They remembered or affected to remember only the promise which Paget had given. 'God knows', she wrote now with helpless anger and scorn, 'God knows the contrary to be the truth, and you in your own consciences (I say those who were then present) know it also.'[9]

Whatever was the truth, and whoever knew it, it is very hard to come at now. The Council persisted in their denial. Anyone can believe them or believe Mary, and whichever is believed, the other is necessarily a brazen liar. For she, with the utmost precision, called upon her witnesses by name, and they refused to bear witness. And the matter is a tangled one. If the letter written by the mysterious person whom Mary 'could well name', was received by Van der Delft, where was it now? The Dutchman had died in Flanders; why had not the Emperor taken possession of a document so precious? Further, that letter of license had been obtained, according to Mary herself, about Whitsuntide 1550, that is about May 25th. On June 6th, just a fortnight later, Van der Delft had already reached Turnhout. During that fortnight he had seen Mary once; his secretary had seen her twice, and on each occasion she had been ready to take the risk of immediate escape according to a plan already laid. But why escape, when the licence had just been secured that would safeguard her religion? Was it that she so feared John Dudley that even a written promise was not enough? Or was the letter indeed so doubtful in its wording that no trust could be put in it, and it was no more than a straw to catch at when all other help had gone. Again, who was that 'one of you whom I could well name'? Why did she not, when naming Wiltshire, Northampton, Dorset and the rest, name also this one? Was he Somerset whom it was useless to invoke? or Dudley, whom she did not dare to challenge? Yet, whoever it was, it mattered little, for both the named and the unnamed were deaf to her appeal.

The whole Council answered her letter in the usual sense, but this time their reply had a sting in its tail. The King himself, her brother, who had cried to see her tears, added a postscript in his own hand. She had always, even when she feared the worst, counted on his personal indulgence, and believed that what was done against her was done by the Council and not by him. Now the boy wrote—

'Truly sister I will not say more and worse things, because my duty would compel me to use harsher and angrier words. But this I will say with certain intention, that I will see my laws strictly obeyed, and those who break them shall be watched and denounced, even as some are ready to trouble my subjects by their obstinate resistance.'[10] Mary knew the worst now. The King spoke with the voice of John Dudley; and the words he used were open threats.

To Edward she replied stoutly enough, though sadly, protesting her loyalty, claiming the promise, and the acknowledgement of the promise at their last meeting, begging him to wait 'in matters touching the soul' till he was grown, and had heard both sides.[11] But what the King's postscript meant to her can be read in another letter, this time no more than a hastily scrawled

half sheet of paper – written and addressed in her own hand, to a certain
Francisco Moronelli, who had once been a servant to Van der Delft, and was
now in London on some business for his late master's widow. He had gone
to Newhall to see the Princess, but so secretly that the new Imperial ambassador
did not know of it, and Mary had even then snatched at this chance of sending
a message by a man she could trust. So she had already made him promise
that when he was again in Flanders he would go either to M. du Praet, the
Emperor's minister, or to one not so exalted, but a friend, that is to Jehan
Duboys who had dared so much for her, and tell one or other that the Council
had ordered her again to come to Court – always a sinister thing – and that
she was commanded to give up Mass entirely except in her own chamber.

But now worse than this had come on her; now she knew that it was not
only a matter of biding her time till the King came of age, but that he himself
was against her. So she wrote in a panic of fear.

'Francisco, you must make great haste concerning the message, for since
your departure I have received worse and more dangerous letters than ever
before from the King himself.

'Written in haste the 3rd of February.'
And then a postscript, speaking even more clearly of fear and secrecy –

'Francisco, I request you, and command you to burn this note directly after
you have read it. The 3rd of February 1551.'[12]

In her distress, as always before, she was turning to her cousin the Emperor.
Nor did he remain unmoved. It is not likely that Charles bore her any grudge
for her refusal to come away with Duboys, since he had never looked with
any enthusiasm on her plans for escape. Already in September when the first
breath of trouble had reached him, he had bidden Scheyfve go to the Council
with a demand for unconditional permission for the Lady Mary's Mass; 'and
give them plainly to understand that if they decide otherwise we will not
take it in good part nor suffer it to be done', he said.[13]

Now, before Mary had been able to get a personal appeal through to the
Emperor, Scheyfve had gone to the Council again, with the already well
worn demand for a renewal of the original promise to Mary. In answer to this
blunt request the Council first asked for time to refer it to the King. Scheyfve
would have none of that; it was no new matter; the promise had been given
some time ago. At that John Dudley broke across the debate with a deadly
question – 'Had the promise', he asked, 'been made to Scheyfve, that he was
so sure of it?' Scheyfve could not say that it had, only that it was certain, and
that for the promise made to the Emperor, Charles himself could bear
witness. After a wrangling argument, the ambassador, whom the Council
disgustedly considered 'a man much unbroken and rude', left them, insisting
upon 'a resolute answer in three days'.

They sent him his answer by the Lord Treasurer, Paget, Petre, and Hoby;
it was what might have been expected, the same old denial garnished with
the same arguments. But Scheyfve, though of little use as a diplomatist, was
of that dogged type of Dutchman which is hard to convince. After all their

arguments 'he still beat upon the promise without any other proof than his own affirmance', and they could think of no other way of silencing him than a *tu quoque* argument. Master Chamberlain, ambassador to the Queen Dowager of Hungary, had asked to have the English service in Flanders. What was the Emperor's answer to that?[14]

Charles was doing what he could for Mary, more indeed than he had ever done for her mother; but then Mary was a person of greater potential value in the game of Kings than Katherine had been at the time of the divorce; besides, the cordial relations between France and England in these days was a spur to Charles's constitutional caution. But Scheyfve dreaded what might happen to Mary, when in March 1551 she at last decided to come to Court. She had been ill all winter, off and on, with headaches, toothache, and colds; so ill indeed that she could hardly reply to the letters of the Council; but Scheyfve feared that some sinister motive for delay would be attributed to her; he feared all sorts of things for her, that they would 'use her very roughly, keeping her here . . . if she refused to conform . . . taking away her servants especially those she trusted; and forcing her to attend the new services'.[15]

On March 17th she came to London, riding in solemn state, 'with 50 knights and gentlemen in velvet coats afore her, and after her four score gentlemen and ladies, everyone having a pair of beads of black'. The concourse can hardly have consisted entirely of her own household. No doubt gentlemen and their wives had ridden to meet her, just as the common people of London had tramped out six miles or so through the fields to welcome her. So there was much state in her arrival, and the streets of London were thronged to see her,[16] but when she reached the palace she was received only with very ordinary honours by the King's Comptroller.[17]

It must have needed some courage for Mary to dismount there and go into the palace and through chambers and galleries to where the King waited for her with twenty-five of the Council. For she must have felt that in Edward she might find now a stranger and an enemy. What followed was indeed daunting; the King led her into a room apart, the Council followed, but her own people stayed outside. Mary, in the miserable wrangle that began, had to face her adversaries alone.

First they spoke of the promise she claimed in her letters; they denied it. But she countered that by reminding them of what had passed last year when she was at Court. This was the very claim that she had made in her letter, and which her witnesses had not confirmed, but now the King himself spoke, and admitted what she said. Mary turned at once to him; she must have realized that for all that he wrote as a stranger, he had not entirely changed. She spoke to him, complaining that the Council had 'written sourly to her', affirming again that there had been question of the promise. The boy, who perhaps was beginning to fret at Dudley's control as he had fretted at Somerset's, and who at any rate was always kinder to Mary when the sight of her reminded him of their affection, answered that he knew nothing about that, for he had only taken a share in affairs during the last year; neither of them referred to that letter of his which in February had so upset her; perhaps both were glad to forget it.

So Mary went on, now disputing with the Council, now appealing to the King, whose boyish and royal vanity she must have hurt when she said, that 'although he was of great understanding, yet experience would teach him more yet'. He retaliated promptly and with some point, that on the contrary 'she might still have something to learn, and no one was too old for that'.

After this the Council set on her. By Henry's will they said, she must be subject to them. Only in the matter of her marriage, she rapped out. And, talking of her father's will, what of his settlement of religion? They replied, as they had replied before, that they obeyed the will in things not harmful to the King.

Mary turned on them then. She was quite sure, she told them, that 'the late King had never ordered anything in the least prejudicial to the King her brother'. 'It is reasonable to suppose', she said, 'that he alone cared more for the good of his kingdom than all the members of the Council put together.'

Warwick, never a patient man, could not endure such defiance, 'How now, my Lady!' he cried. 'It seems your Grace is trying to show us in a hateful light to the King our Master, without any cause whatever.' Dudley was used to browbeating tongue-tied, frightened countrymen brought in for examination on the charge of disobeying the Statute of religion; he, Northampton, and the Treasurer would bawl at these unfortunates so loudly that the uproar was heard outside. But Mary was not to be cowed by shouting; it was only the necessity for making a decision which shook her, and here she was not shaken. She answered quietly but stubbornly that she had not come here intending to speak so, but they had pressed her hard, and it was the truth. Yet when she had answered Dudley, her courage almost broke. She turned from the crowd of men to her own flesh and blood, to the young King sitting there listening. She told him, suddenly forsaking all her entrenched positions, that, setting aside all promises, it was to his goodness that she trusted. And in the last resort, she said, 'there are two things only, soul and body. My soul I offer to God, and my body to Your Majesty's service. May it please you to take away my life rather than the old religion.'

The boy, hastily, perhaps with shame, protested. He did not want to do anything like that, and there the long, trying audience ended for her.[18] The Council had gained nothing. Mary had lost nothing, and gained the knowledge that Edward had, even now, more affection for her than his letters seemed to show. Yet, though she had got the best of the interview she had much to fear. It was lucky for her that, the very morning she rode to London, Scheyfve had received a letter from the Emperor which he could use to put a shot across the Council's bows.

For the moment the luck of these lords was out. The English ambassador at Brussels, Sir Richard Morison, a garrulous, reckless, self-opinionated man, had placed a stick into Charles's hand by which he might very conveniently beat the Council. Morison had, some time before, asked for the right of hearing the English service. It had been refused. In his exasperation at the refusal he had had the colossal bad taste to serve up to the Emperor an evangelistic sermon on Protestant reform, and Morison's controversial style can be guessed from his despatches, in which the Roman Church is a matter for great mirth, and the Holy Father becomes 'the Hollow Father'.

The Emperor at once informed Scheyfve of Morison's behaviour, adding unpleasantly – 'We believe him to have been sent to us as an ambassador, not as a preacher. His manner was wholly unsuitable.'[19] Armed with such a weapon Scheyfve asked for another audience with the Council. When he had made his usual request that Mary should be undisturbed in her religion, he followed it up with an account of Morison's behaviour, and that with the Emperor's letter, the reading of which, he rejoiced to notice, 'appeared to frighten them sorely'; he evidently enjoyed the spectacle of the dismayed faces about the Council board, as they turned to look at each other. When he had finished, all that Somerset, all that even Dudley himself could say, and they said it two or three times over, was that the words of their ambassador were new to them. Scheyfve followed up his advantage. The Emperor, he reported, declared that if Mary were not well used 'He simply would not stand it', and as ambassador he was instructed to deliver from Charles what young Edward recorded in his Journal as 'a short message . . . of war if I would not suffer his cousin the Princess to use her Mass'.[20]

Whether it was Mary's courage, or this awkward news from abroad that made the Council pause, at any rate, after a few days they allowed the Princess to return to Newhall. All that they did was to send Petre to her before she left. He found her in bed, and asked, meek as a mouse, if she would stay yet a few days longer to please the King; but he added that she might go if she chose. She did so choose, and went freely.[21]

But others were not so fortunate. The Council, if it could not force the King's sister to yield, could make it very uncomfortable for others who took advantage of her disobedience to hear the forbidden service. Sir Anthony Browne, who had to admit that he had heard Mass at Newhall twice or thrice, and once at Romford as the Lady Mary came to town, found himself in the Fleet. Sergeant Morgan, who had seized the opportunity of going to Mass when Mary was in London, was sent to the Tower, as a learned man and therefore a specially bad example.[22] The fact was indeed, as the Council complained, and as the Emperor reluctantly admitted, though not to them, that Mary – frightened yet still doggedly conscientious – would welcome any that came to her Mass.[23] In the country there would be many a squire to ride to Newhall or Woodham Walter on Sundays, many a countryman glad to tramp for miles through the fields to hear again the old service. When she came to London, old friends who would, like Sir Anthony Browne, find it natural to pay her their respects, would make sure to do so at a moment when they might also attend her Mass. That she should permit it was natural and inevitable for Mary, a woman and a devout believer; but to the Emperor it was deplorable strategy, and in letter after letter he warned her that she must not be too unyielding to the Council, must not be provocative, must, if the Council promised to allow her Mass behind locked doors and without strangers present, be content with this. Even if the Mass was taken from her, she must submit; only if they tried to force her to profess the new religion, or 'to commit some such enormity as communicating in both kinds,' might she resist.[24]

The Council had decided to let the Lady Mary's matter alone till Wotton –a favourite of the Emperor's–could replace the injudicious Morison. But in April the arrest of Dr. Mallet in the north parts was the signal for another brisk exchange between Mary and the Council, for she was never one to let her servants suffer without taking a hand in their affairs. She began by a letter to the Council expressing surprise at the news of the priest's arrest.[25] The Council, not unreasonably, retorted that 'howsoever it seem strange to your Grace that he is imprisoned, it may seem more strange to others that he hath escaped thus long'.[26]

Finding herself so answered Mary deserted that position and proceeded to defend another. Mallet, she said, had celebrated Mass, 'but by my command-ment; and I said unto him, that none of my chaplains should be in danger of the law for saying Mass in my house. . . . Wherefore I pray you to discharge him of imprisonment and set him at liberty. If not, ye minister cause not only to him but to others, to think I declared more than was true, which I would not do to gain the whole world . . . and to be plain with you, according to mine old custom, there is not one amongst the whole number of you all that would be more loth to be found untrue of their word than I. And well I am assured that none of you have found it in me.'[27]

So an outspoken downright woman, who could understand no policy but saw all things written clear in terms of right and wrong, addressed a company of the most corrupt, time-serving, and unscrupulous men that ever sat around the Council Board at Whitehall. And yet it was natural that she should speak to them in such terms. For they were to her men that she had danced with, sung with, hunted with. With them from her childhood she had sat at feasts, with them, in the old days, she had gone to church to worship. To her they were as familiar as the parishioners of a country parish to any rector's daughter. And it was her misfortune to see them change, and betray, and cheat, so that she doubted human nature for their sake, knowing that even those like Derby and Shrewsbury, who regretted the old ways, would not dare to open their mouths against what was done; seeing, in the ordinary human way, the new religion, 'the parliament religion', embodied and exemplified in Dudley, rapacious, conscienceless, merciless; in Northampton with his two wives. It was small wonder, honest as she was, and knowing as she did what they were, that she clung to that one thing that stood for everything they stood against– the Mass. She could not give it up, be the pressure what it might.

Though the Emperor's open threats had brought the Council up for a moment, they now came on again. And indeed there was something to be said for them. Mary might fear them, but they feared her not a little. They were at least honest when they told her that her example was dangerous to their settlement. They dreaded that they might have to face active opposition from her; knowing that she had last year tried to escape to the Emperor, they now suspected that she might 'go westward to the Earl of Shrewsbury'[28] and with him might, so they must have thought, raise a power along the Marches where her name would remind men of the old days when as a girl she had been Princess of Wales. So their letters grew more curt, the danger to her servants loomed darker, and the pressure of fear upon Mary herself more urgent than ever.

By the end of June things were so bad that the sage and cautious Emperor fairly lost his temper with Wotton, and rated the new ambassador, even though Wotton was a man for whom he had always had a liking. Dismissing all from his Chamber Charles turned on the Dean.

'Ought it not', he cried, 'to suffice you that ye spill your own souls, but that ye have a mind to force others to loose theirs too? My cousin, the Princess, is evil handled among you; her servants plucked from her, and she still cried to leave Mass, to forsake her religion in which her mother, her grandmother, and all her family, have lived and died.'

Wotton could only reply that the lady was well treated when he left England, and that he had heard of no change; but the Emperor bore on.

'"Yes by Saint Mary," saith he, "of late they handle her evil, and . . . say you hardly to them, I will not suffer her to be evil handled by them. I will not suffer it. Is it not enough that mine aunt, her mother, was evil treated by the King that dead is, but my cousin must be worse ordered by councillors now."'

Wotton, that kindly, witty diplomatist, replied with polite obstinacy that though Mary had 'a King to her father, and hath a King to her brother, she is only a subject and must obey the law'.

'A gentle law I tell you!' retorted the Emperor, and he brought the uncomfortable interview to an end with the dark saying that if Mary had not her Mass he would provide for her a remedy, and added to that a very explicit declaration that his ambassador in England had received orders, if he should be 'restrained from serving of God . . . if the restraint come to-day that he should to-morrow depart'.[29] It was plain speaking, but again it did little more than retard for a time the purpose of the Council which was now set and immovable.

In March Sir Robert Rochester, Mary's Comptroller, had been required to let the Council know the number and names of Mary's chaplains. She had replied–four; Mallet, Hopton, Barker and Ricardes.[30]

In the middle of August three of Mary's gentlemen–the Comptroller, Edward Waldegrave, and Sir Francis Englefield–were summoned to the Council to receive certains orders. They obeyed the summons on August 14th, and received the orders. On the 15th, late in the evening, three indignant and uncomfortable gentlemen dismounted again at the door of Copt Hall in Essex, where Mary was. It is likely that they had not hurried in

that two hours' ride through the summer dusk; at least they took their late
arrival as an excuse for not carrying out their commission that night.

Next day was Sunday, and on that Sunday Mary was to receive the
Sacrament. The bell rang, the priest was vested, the ancient Latin words were
chanted with all their accompaniment of stately and symbolic ritual. The
three gentlemen still reserved the opening of their business with their mistress,
'thinking', as they explained later to the Council, 'that the same would
trouble and disquiet her'. Only after dinner on that August Sunday did they
deliver to Mary the letters they bore, and ask her permission to declare their
message. To this, Mary, who had torn open the letters, promptly replied
'that she knew right well that their commission agreed with such matter
as was contained in her letters, and that they need not rehearse the
same'.

But they pressed, as indeed they must, for permission, and when she gave
it, made their announcement. They had been ordered by the Council to
forbid her chaplains to say Mass, and to see that none of her house should hear
it anywhere. If their mistress were to give them their dismissal, they were not
to obey her, but to stay in the house and see that the orders of the Council
were obeyed.

Flushing and paling with anger Mary listened to them, and when they had
finished she broke out in a right Tudor rage. 'You shall not', she told them,
'declare that same you have in charge to say, neither to my chaplains nor
family, which if you do, besides that you shall not take me hereafter for your
mistress, I will immediately depart out of the house.'

The three unfortunate gentlemen, having unwillingly done so much,
would do no more. They feared indeed that their mistress's anger would
bring on an attack of illness, so, asking her to give them an answer on
Wednesday, they went no further, saying never a word of their commission
either to the chaplains or the household, therein braving the Council's displeasure, whose orders they had so interpreted as to render them useless.[31]
For the Council had in effect bidden them deal with the chaplains and household, not with their mistress.

They can hardly have hoped that Mary's mind would change by Wednesday; if they did, they were disappointed. She was rather 'in further choler
than she was before', and utterly forbade them to make any announcement to
her household. On Saturday they rode again to London, knowing full well
what it was they faced, and to the assembled Council delivered a letter from
Mary, and a report of what they had done and left undone.[32]

In that letter, addressed to the Council, but really appealing over its head
to the King, Mary was at her last ditch, and knew it. She began with a bitter
complaint that 'my servants should move or attempt me in matters touching
my soul, which I think the meanest subject within your realm could evil bear
at their servants' hand'. She had, she declared, 'trusted that your Majesty
would have suffered me, your poor humble sister and bedeswoman, to have
used the accustomed Mass, which the King, your father and mine, with all

his predecessors ever more used; wherein also I have been brought up from my youth, and thereunto my conscience doth not only bind me, which by no means will suffer me to think one thing and do another, but also the promise made to the Emperor . . . was an assurance to me that in so doing I should not offend the law, although they' (the bare disrespectful pronoun is all that she threw to the Council), 'although they seem now to qualify and deny the thing.'

Then, reminding Edward of the kindness that he had shown her at her visit to Court, she made one last appeal. 'Now', she wrote, 'I beseech your Highness to give me leave to write what I think touching your Majesty's letters. Indeed they be signed with your own hand, and nevertheless in my opinion not your Majesty's in effect, that although (our Lord be praised) your Majesty hath far more knowledge and greater gifts than others of your years, yet it is not possible that your Highness can at these years be a judge in matters of religion. And therefore I take it that the matter in your letter proceedeth from such as do wish those things to take place, which be most agreeable to themselves; by whose doings (your Majesty not offended) I intend not to rule my conscience.'

Such an appeal, containing such a snub for a youthful Solomon, was perhaps not likely to succeed; it was sound sense but bad tactics. Mary forgot that the boy was his father's son, and had been fed, from six years old, with the choicest fruits of religious controversy. Edward was now nearly fourteen, and would not any boy of his age have appreciated the sensation of mastering an unruly elder sister? Besides, he was not an average boy, but obstinate, precocious, and beginning now to know what it was to be a King. Inevitably too he believed in the new ways—with his upbringing nothing else was possible to him. If he had shown any wavering, there was Dudley leaning over the King's shoulder, his dark face in harsh contrast to the fair hair, the snub nose, the pink and white complexion of the young, unhappy King. It is likely that Edward frowned over the desperate hardihood of the conclusion of Mary's letter. 'Rather than offend God and my conscience I offer my body at your will, and death shall be more welcome to me than life with a troubled conscience.' But if he frowned, Dudley may well have laughed.

The Council, undeterred by appeal or defiance, proceeded on its way. On Sunday, August 23rd, Rochester, Englefield, and Waldegrave were charged with disobedience in not executing the order given them. They were given one more chance. Each, severally, received the orders which before had been given to them jointly. Rochester and Waldegrave replied that rather than obey they would be imprisoned and punished. Englefield said that 'he could neither find it in his heart or his conscience to do it'. The Council's answer to this was to send them all to the Tower. Having thus one of her chaplains and three of her household under lock and key they turned to deal with Mary. The King wrote a brief letter in which he said that he grieved much that he perceived no amendment in her, and announced the mission of Lord Chancellor Rich and Sir William Petre to her, and the despatch of Sir

Anthony Wingfield, the King's Comptroller, in exchange for the imprisoned
Rochester. The first two were to make perfectly clear to her that the Council
would be obeyed; they were to give her the King's letter, and answer her
own point by point.

They came to Copt Hall on August 28th, and to Mary's presence. She had
been ill off and on all through the spring and summer; it did not make her
more tractable, rather it added a biting tang to all that she said. Besides, she
knew she was beaten.

They presented to her the King's letter, and she went down on her knees
before she would take it into her hands.

'For the honour of the King's Majesty's hand,' she said, wherewith they
were signed, she would kiss the letters, 'and not for any matter contained in
them, for the matter (said she) I take to proceed not from his Majesty but
from you of the Council.' Whereupon she kissed the letters and opened them,
and began to read, but 'secretly to herself', only the commissioners heard
once a gibing comment–'Ah! Good Master Cecil took much pain here!'

Lord Rich, seeing that she had read their letters of credence, would have
begun to speak, but she took him up, begging him to be short–'For (said
she) I am not well at ease, and I will make a short answer.'

Rich, once launched, told her that the King and Council had decided that
she should not 'use the private Mass or any other manner service than such as
by the law . . . is authorised', and if she wished to see the names of all those
who were present at the Council when it had been so decided, they would
show them to her.

She did not thank him for that. 'I care not', she said, 'for any rehearsal of
their names, for', said she, 'I know you to be all of one sort therein.'

They passed on from that point to tell her that they were to charge her
chaplains to say no Mass in future.

She replied that she was the King's humble subject 'but rather than I will
agree to use any other service . . . I will lay my head on a block and suffer
death— ' 'But (said she) I am unworthy to suffer death in so good a quarrel.'
As for her obedience to the King she would, she told them, obey him in
religion as in other things when he was old enough. 'But now,' she said, 'in
these years, although he, good sweet King, has more knowledge than any
other of his years, yet it is not possible that he can be a judge of these things.
For if ships were to be sent to the seas, or any other thing touching the policy
and government of the realm, I am sure you would not think his Highness yet
able to consider what were to be done, and much less (said she) can he in
these years discern what is fittest in matters of divinity. And if my chaplains
do say no Mass I can hear none, no more can my servants. But as for my
servants I know it shall be against their wills, as it shall be against mine, for if
they could come where it were said they would hear it with good will. And
as for my priests they know what they have to do. The pain of your laws is
but imprisonment for a short time, and if they will refuse to say Mass for fear
of that imprisonment they may do therein as they will; but none of your new

service (said she) shall be used in my house; and if any be said in it, I will not tarry in the house.'

When the commissioners could speak again they proceeded to their next point – how out of kindness, and to trouble her as little as possible, the Council had first sent the message by her own servants.

To this – 'It is not the wisest counsel', she scoffed, 'to appoint my servants to control me in my own house. And my servants know my own mind therein well enough; for of all men I can worst endure any of them to move me in such matters. . . . And if they refused to do the message unto me . . . they be (said she) the honester men, for they should have spoken against their consciences.'

The commissioners passed on hastily to the question of the Emperor's promise. They recited to her, as their instructions bade them, the Council's version of the thing, which they certainly must have known by heart by this time.

To that Mary replied in equally accustomed terms. She knew surely that the promise was made; it had been acknowledged by seven of the Council in the King's presence. 'And I have', quoth she, 'the Emperor's hand testifying that this promise was made, which I believe better than you all of the Council; and though you esteem little of the Emperor yet should you show more favour to me for my father's sake, who', here she may well have looked at each one of them with an insulting smile, 'who made the most part of you out of nothing.'

The commissioners, plodding on through their instructions, next informed her that the King had sent someone to take her Comptroller's place, but all the thanks she gave for that was to say 'that she could appoint her own officers, and that she had years sufficient for that purpose; and if we left any such men there, she would go out of her gates, for they two should not dwell in one house. And (quoth she) I am sickly, and yet I will not die willingly, but I will do the best I can to preserve my life; but if I shall chance to die, I will protest openly that you of the Council to be the causes of my death. You give me fair words but your deeds be always ill towards me.'

With this truly feminine tirade she turned her back on them and went off into her own bedchamber, leaving them to do their office with her household. This they did; and her chaplains, 'after some talk', said that they would obey.

The commissioners had done their part and could withdraw. But first Lord Rich was called to the Princess's presence. Mary, 'upon her knees most humbly', gave him a ring to give the King, and a message – how she would obey in all things except in this matter of the Mass and the new service. If the message was gentle, the rider which she added to it was not – 'But yet', said she, 'this shall never be told the King's Majesty.'

The commissioners must have been glad to get to their horses and to be gone from Copt Hall and its railing mistress. But before they got clear away they had to face Mary again. They were told, so they reported to the Council, that she 'sent to us to speak one word at a window'. Hastily and prudently they offered to go up to her, but she would not have it; she preferred the publicity of the window on the courtyard. So, while the servants below might peep and grin, and the horses fidget, she fired her last broadside.

She asked first that her Comptroller might soon return, 'For (said she) sithens his departing I take account myself of my expenses, and learn how many loaves of bread be made of a bushel of wheat, and I wis my father and mother never brought me up with baking and brewing; and to be plain with you I am weary with mine office, and therefore if my lords will send mine officer home they shall do me a pleasure; otherwise if they will send him to prison I beshrew him if he will not go to it merrily, and with a good will.' Then, with a last spurt of undisguised, inexcusable, most undignified, but very human rudeness, as she waved the commissioners farewell, 'And I pray God', she cried, 'to send you to do well in your souls and bodies too, for some of you have but weak bodies.'

The commissioners returned. They retailed, in full, their stormy interview, and surely there have been few such candid reports produced by the victims of an impossible situation. As though they had enjoyed it, they gave to Mary all the honours of the encounter. Perhaps it was malice, perhaps it was humour, or was it mere official exactitude? But at least, whatever Mary said, the Council had won the game. From now on for the next two years the Lady Mary's household had no Mass. At first, for their own sake, she dismissed her chaplains. Later, one or more must have crept back disguised. For she herself had Mass, but now in fear, behind locked doors, and no one knew it except three of her most confidential servants.[33] The Emperor saw too that the game was up. Deserting all claim to the old promise, he now asked, as a favour, the King's indulgence to Mary during his minority.[34] But the Council were in no obliging mood, for they were secure in the revived friendship of France. Poor Master Scheyfve could do nothing with them.

In all this, although it is undeniable that Mary showed a good courage, and all the constancy of Katherine's daughter, yet it looks on the surface as though the Council had a sound case, and dealt not too high-handedly with her. Their argument, that uniformity was a good thing, and her example potent against it, was weighty; she did not deny the beauty of uniformity, but there was the same irreconcilable difference between her and the Lords as that which lay between Catherine de Medici and the Vicomte de Turenne in 1586. 'Le roi ne veut qu'une religion en France', said the Queen Mother. 'Nous le voulons bien aussi, Madame, mais que ce soit la nôtre', Turenne replied. But further, as we have seen, Mary admitted to Mass those that were not of her household, and this was straining her privilege to its limits or beyond, as the Council maintained. Nor, in the case of Mallet and Barkley, had she any legal ground for complaint seeing that the former had celebrated Mass in a house at which she was not present, and the latter in a parish church.

But the legal question was not, for Mary, relevant. The Prayer Book was a poisonous growth, for the soil it sprang from was poisonous. That soil was,

to her, the heretic party which had renounced obedience to the Pope, persecuted her mother, committed sacrilege in church after church; it was the
party of those new gentlemen who now sat in fair stone chambers which had
once been built for monks; round about them the walls were hung with the
embroidered pictures of saints from chapel and sanctuary; they drank their
wine out of jewelled and gilded chalices which had been consecrated to the
use of God. To accept the laws that these men made was to condone their
deeds, and besides that, to sever herself, in their hated company, from loyal
Catholics abroad, from her Spanish kin, from her dead mother, and from all
the faithful departed.

The Council's triumph was so complete that they could afford not to press
it home. In October Waldegrave, having fallen sick, was allowed to leave the
Tower for 'some honest house' so that he could recover.[35] In March 1552 all
three gentlemen were set free to return to their homes.[36] In April, after Mary
had made a fresh and special appeal to the King,[37] they were allowed to go
back to her household.[38]

The Council had done what they set out to do, but it had taken them three
years, and they knew very well that Mary's words were true–that if she and
her servants could have come where Mass was said, they would have heard
it with a good will. Mary stood, and everyone knew it, for all the old order
that was gone, and there were many that longed after it as constantly as she.
She stood too, next to the throne; and only a slip of a boy between her and it.
John Dudley, soon to be Duke of Northumberland, must already have had
long thoughts on the subject.

That same autumn which had seen Mary's surrender saw also the second
and final fall of the Duke of Somerset. Early next year John Dudley made
sure his victory. On January 22nd early, so that not too many should be there
to see it, the Duke, the darling of the Commons, died on the block. Men said
that he could have escaped if he had but jumped down into the crowd that
looked on, only waiting for a signal to help. They talked too of a 'sudden
rumbling a little before he died, as it had been guns shooting, and great
horses coming',[39] but the omen was no help to Somerset. Instead of taking a
gamester's chance of escape he spoke quietly to the crowd–'Friends, have
patience and be content with the King's commands',[40] and so died, a man
'too fine and not fine enough' for the high part he had chosen to play.

After his fall the Reformation went on briskly under the auspices of Dudley, both legally, and beyond the law. The Council under Dudley did not
need to encourage the excited extremists; it was enough to give them their
head, and when they had done what they listed, to legalize the fact. Yet not
all, even of the Protestant party, were pleased at their vagaries. Just before the
second Prayer Book appeared in the autumn of 1552, Cranmer, nettled at the
clamour that rose then against the custom of kneeling at the Sacrament,
denounced these men. The Council, he declared, would not listen to 'these
vainglorious and unquiet spirits which can like nothing but what is after
their own fancy, and cease not to make trouble and disquietness when things

be most quiet and in good order. If such men be heard, although the Book were made every year anew, yet should it not lack faults in their opinion.'[41] But such men as these were the favoured friends and allies of Dudley, and he was still their 'Moses', their 'English Alcibiades', their 'faithful and intrepid soldier of Christ'.

In taking up with the extreme Reformers he had got himself allies after his own heart. They shared his carelessness of precedent, and his daring; they, no more than he, would be restrained from making changes by the fear that they would bring the house about their own ears. But besides this similarity of outlook, in Hooper especially Dudley found a man whose ideas fitted into his own wishes as the kernel into the nut. Hooper believed in Apostolic poverty. Dudley wanted money, and was only too ready to relieve the Church of the temptation of riches.

Chantries had gone, now it was the turn of the Bishoprics. Hooper himself was willing. He accepted, being already Bishop of Gloucester, the see of Worcester, and forthwith alienated the patrimony of his original Bishopric; Ponet did the like, accepting a miserable exchange for his diocese of Winchester. Soon church manors were dropping into courtiers' hands like ripe peaches. Bishoprics were kept vacant as long as possible so that they might be whittled down; Bishop Tunstal of Durham, whose old palatine lordship Warwick coveted, found himself in the Tower for concealment of, as someone said, 'I know not what treason, written to him I know not by whom, and not discovered until what I shall call the party, did reveal it'; while the temporalties of Durham, after a brief sojourn in the King's possession, were made over to Dudley.

So Northumberland and his party enjoyed a year of quiet, troubled only a little by the discontent and restlessness that was in the air, and perhaps by the significant fact that the Lady Mary would not now come to Court; she made seemly excuses but it was clear that she sulked after her defeat, retired and obdurate in her Suffolk and Hertfordshire manors.

If an opportunity was offered her of making clear her opinions, she would not refuse it. So when Bishop Ridley of London paid his duty to her at Hunsdon, and offered a sermon for next Sunday, though she would at first give him no reply, when pressed she was outspoken. 'If', she said, 'there be no remedy but I must make you answer, this shall be your answer: the door of the parish church adjoining shall be open for you if you come; and ye may preach if you list; but neither I, nor any of mine shall hear you.'

'Madam', said Ridley, 'I trust you will not refuse God's word.'

'I cannot tell', Mary answered him, 'I cannot tell what ye call God's word; that is not God's word now, that was God's word in my father's days.'

'God's word', the Bishop told her, 'is one in all times; but hath been better understood and practised in some ages than others.'

Then Mary broke out at him. 'You durst not, for your ears', she cried, 'have avouched that for God's word in my father's days that now you do. And as for your new books, I thank God I never read any of them; I never did, nor ever will do.' She followed that up with a tirade against the Council's doings, and then broke off to ask him–'Was he one of it?' 'No' he told her. 'You might well enough,' she jeered, 'as the Council goeth nowadays.' Ridley had certainly not the better of it then or afterwards, even though, drinking wine in the Hall with Sir Thomas Wharton, he suddenly took the cup from his lips, rebuked himself for having drunk in such a house, and declared that he should rather have shaken the dust of it from his shoes for a testimony against it. The hairs of his hearers stood upright on their heads at the solemn vehemence of the Bishop.[42] But it was at best *l'esprit de l'escalier*. Mary had carried off the honours of the day.

Chapter XI

WITH the beginning of the year 1553 anxieties began to crowd in upon John Dudley, now Duke of Northumberland. The King had caught a chill, and his fever was so high that when Mary came to pay her usual visit after Christmas, he was, for three days, too ill to see her. As she rode down Fleet Street to the palace at Westminster all the great ladies were with her – the Duchesses of Northumberland and Suffolk, the Marchionesses of Northampton and Winchester, the Countesses of Bedford, Shrewsbury and Arundel, and at the gate the husbands of the ladies waited to receive her. Anyone could see the significance of that.[1]

The King did not get better. In March he could not ride to Westminster to open Parliament, so it came to him in Whitehall for his opening.[2] In April he was worse. In May the French ambassadors, hand in glove now with Northumberland, were pressing to have their audience with the King, and to know certainly if his health, as rumour said, was going 'from bad to worse'. But, they obligingly suggested, if he were too ill to see them, they could yet come to the palace and pretend to have seen him.

Northumberland and the Council jumped at the suggestion, and on May 7th the sinister and tragic farce was acted. After a Sunday dinner at Court the Lord Chamberlain announced to the two Frenchmen that the King would see them. They got up, and with due ceremony went off with certain Lords of the Council to the sham audience. When the door was shut behind them the Lords thanked them for their suggestion, talked awhile and then said farewell. The whole affair made it only too clear to the ambassadors that the King was desperately ill; if they had any doubts, the faces of the Councillors would have answered them, and Northumberland, with strange candour, even went so far as to ask them, 'What would you do if you were in my place?'[3]

Did John Dudley ask that question because he had not yet answered it for himself, or because he hoped that their solution would confirm his purpose? Surely the latter, for a fortnight later, on Whitsunday, Lord Guilford Dudley married Jane Grey, daughter of the new Duke of Suffolk and of Frances Brandon, and so grand-daughter of Henry VIII's sister Mary; that is to say Northumberland's second son married the daughter of the next heiress to the throne after Princess Mary and Elizabeth. People also remembered after, even if they did not notice at the time, other significant straws that might have shown them the set of the wind. In May wagons jolted in through the gates of the Tower carrying guns that had been removed from the bulwarks at Gravesend and other small fortifications. Lord Robert Dudley and Lord

KING EDWARD VI
School of Hans Holbein.   Hampton Court Palace.
Reproduced by gracious permission of Her Majesty the Queen.

Warwick, Northumberland's sons both, got licence from the King to retain 150 men.[4] Mr. Secretary Cecil, always a reliable weather-vane, was absent from Council meetings–he was a man who preferred when possible to keep clear of trouble. His friends thought him ill, and sent him recipes for various remedies–let him boil a sow pig with cinnamon, celery, dates, and raisins, or stew a hedgehog in red wine and rose-water.[5] But the cautious and perspicuous Secretary, who saw the Duke of Northumberland set upon Queen-making, had no wish to be cured of a politic indisposition.

While the miserable, innocent lad, who had inherited royalty and disease from his father, rotted away in the palace, John Dudley was very busy preparing for the time that he knew must soon come. Already he had done much. The day that Guilford Dudley married Jane Grey, her sister married the Earl of Pembroke's eldest son, and Guilford's sister the son of the Earl of Huntingdon. So an outsider and a stout supporter were brought at the same moment into the Duke's family circle.

Besides friends, he needed money–needed it desperately. But in April and May commissions had gone throughout England taking tale of 'all the jewels of gold and silver as crosses and candlesticks, censers, chalices, all copes and vestments of cloth of gold, cloth of tissue and cloth of silver' in the churches. In May all these were called in for the King except one chalice for every church and tablecloths for the communion board.[6] What he took, the King sold quickly for cash. Parliament too, loyal and docile, voted the King subsidies. Fines, even the smallest fines, were meticulously collected. Dudley wasted none of all this money on paying the King's debts, or the wages of his servants. It was better employed, to his mind, on buying arms.[7]

But all must be done secretly. It was still pretended that the King walked in the galleries and gardens of the palace, even in the park. The French ambassador, seeing six warships riding at anchor in the river, and hearing of musters–'all this covertly and without stir', might guess and guess again, and think the King perhaps already dead, but when next Sunday he came to Court he found the Council doing its best to look at ease; and heard that the King's fever had left him, and that he should today see the Court 'more splendid and gay than I had usually seen it, with rejoicing of trumpets and other music during dinner'.

Such a show, however, had little effect on the acute Frenchmen, one of whom, Antoine de Noailles, had only lately been sent to England in anticipation of a crisis. They attributed the greater cheerfulness at Court to the fact that the Council, after its long and secret debates of a week ago, from which even the King's secretaries were shut out, had at last come to an agreement. The King might be better, but de Noailles was sure he would not recover, and now the Council was strengthening the watch at night, the gates were opened later and closed earlier, so that the city was shut up while it was still broad daylight.

In the Tower the guards were increased, and the prisoners kept closer, while the number of tall masts in the Thames grew till twenty ships lay there ready; the pretence that they were for a venture going to 'Barbary and the Spice Islands' would not have deceived a child.[8]

The Frenchmen were right when they surmised that the Council had come to a decision. On June 11th Edward sent for Lord Chief Justice Montague the Attorney General, and the Solicitor General. To these shocked men of law he announced that he had determined to leave the Crown by will (his father had set the first precedent of that method), but not to either of his two sisters, nor to his cousin Frances, Duchess of Suffolk. He would leave it to an heir male of Frances born in his lifetime; failing that heir, to her daughter Lady Jane Dudley, the wife of Northumberland's son. Montague's part was to draw up the will. He could only ask for time to deliberate, and retire, appalled.

Next day he was sent for to Ely Place, Northumberland's house, where he found the Council assembled, but without its master. To them the old man declared that to alter the succession would be treason. At that the door burst open and Northumberland strode in, white and shaking with rage. He called Montague a traitor, and shouted that he would fight any man in his shirt in this quarrel. But the Chief Justice would not yield.

Next day Montague had to go again to Court. As he and his colleagues passed through the crowd of assembled Lords they got hard stares in greeting; they might have been strangers. When they came to the King himself, he, 'with sharp words and an angry countenance' rated them for their resistance; and ordered them to do his bidding. It was the end. Montague, being 'a weak old man and without comfort', yielded at last, and drew up, 'with sorrowful heart and weeping eyes', that will which Fuller was to call 'the testament of King Edward and the will of the Duke of Northumberland'. Mary and Elizabeth were declared excluded from the succession; each of them came of a marriage afterwards declared invalid, each of them being unmarried might marry abroad, and so crown a foreigner. The document was signed 'with the King's proper hand, above, beneath, and on every side'.[9] The Councillors too, will they nill they, must put their names to it.

By this time all knew that the King was ill. London was waiting for the poor boy to die, and people talked behind their hands, telling one another strange rumours. Scheyfve, knowing no English, and cold-shouldered by the Council, could only glean these tales from foreign merchants and from spies, and retail them as news to his master. They were sinister enough. Northumberland, some said, was going to make himself King. He was thinking of putting away his wife, said others, and marrying the Lady Mary. When the King died, so went another and far more likely tale, he would seize all her friends, clap them in the Tower, then send horsemen secretly and by night to seize her and bring her to London. Or he would poison her, as he had poisoned the King.[10]

The air was full of fear and apprehension; but all knew one thing for certain – that the King could not live. The Emperor, under pretext of inquiring after Edward's health, had sent three envoys extraordinary to England, men of a very different calibre from that of the middle-class, painstaking, unfortunate Scheyfve. Two were of high birth–Jacques de Marnix Sieur de Thoulouse, and Jean de Montmorency Sieur de Courrières, a scion of the younger branch of that great house. The third, and he was the eyes and ears, the tongue and brain of the embassy, was a protégé of Perrenot de Granvelle, Bishop of Arras, and, like his patron, a man of the Franche Comté. His name was Simon Renard;[11] it was to be a fateful name for Mary.

Meanwhile at Hunsdon, that house of bitter memories, Mary waited, with a sore heart surely for the dying boy, and an anxious head for herself. Yet Northumberland had been very friendly lately. He regularly sent her news of the King's health. He had sent her a gift too–a blazon of her full arms as Princess of England, the arms that she had not borne since she was a girl.[12] But such cordiality, so Mary's friends thought, was dangerous; the Duke was trying to lull her into a false security. They feared either that he would succeed, or that if they warned her, she would show that she had been warned, for she was never good at dissimulation. Yet they must warn her, and fortunately she had learnt caution enough to receive the warning and counsel; and to act as though nothing had happened. It was essential that Dudley should believe that she trusted him, and that he could lay his hand on her at any moment.[13]

It was probably on July 4th that both she and Elizabeth received from Northumberland a summons to London to see their brother. It could mean only one thing. Elizabeth, always a masterly procrastinator, made no move. Mary seems to have obeyed, leaving Hunsdon and moving slowly south as far as Hoddesdon. She reached there on July 6th and on that same evening, at Greenwich, the young King passed to his rest. Northumberland had determined to keep the death a secret, but someone–several persons later were to claim the honour–stole out of Greenwich with the news. Perhaps it was Sir Nicholas Throgmorton who, so he said himself, came in haste to a goldsmith of London and sent him posting off to Hoddesdon.[14] Whoever rode he rode hard; that same night he came to Mary at Hoddesdon, and told her. She stayed only to send word to the new Imperial ambassadors that she was going to Kenninghall, in Norfolk, a manor of her dower lands; the pretext for this move, if pretext were necessary, and it might well be if the news she had was false, was that sickness had broken out in her household.[15] That done, with only two of her women and six gentlemen of her household, she set out through the darkness, riding due north for the Newmarket and Thetford road.[16] It was the longer way, but the safer. To take the road through by Bishops Stortford and Dunmow meant the risk of being intercepted by horsemen from London; but the Newmarket road led straight to Yarmouth, where, if the worst came to the worst, she could take ship for the Netherlands, and for an inglorious and, had she known it, far happier safety than she was to know in England.

She must have struck the road at Royston as it runs through the open rolling country, dead straight, mile after mile. Her first halt, after twenty miles, was at Sawston, just off the road, and there at the house of a loyal Catholic, Master John Huddleston, she rested awhile, and, with the first light of morning, heard Mass. That done, on she went again, but this time she rode in disguise, and behind a servant of Huddleston's.[17] She did not pause again till she came to Hengrave Hall, and when she rode down the long straight avenue to the house, between the triple rows of trees, and over the bridge, she had covered sixty miles.

It was on the evening of July 6th that Edward Tudor died, yet no messenger carried the news from Greenwich to London, except the unknown who sent a warning to Mary. But next day some were allowed to guess. M. Antoine de Noailles was expecting the Duke of Northumberland and Lord Privy Seal to dine with him. Dinner-time came, but the guests were late. Then a gentleman arrived who said that they would be there at two o'clock, but at two o'clock only another message: the Council had business of such import that its members would not be able to leave Greenwich for several days. Knowing as much as he knew, de Noailles could well understand what that meant.[18]

The Council was more reserved towards the three envoys of the Emperor. They, pressing for an audience on July 8th when the King had been two days dead, were told that Edward was in bed, and could not see them – an answer indeed precisely true.

It did not, however, deceive Simon Renard and his companions. They had heard the day before, from some palace spy, that Edward was dead,[19] and if they doubted the truth of the report, there were soon signs that confirmed it. For the Treasurer, the Marquess of Northampton, and the Earl of Shrewsbury rode in from Greenwich to London, and so to the Tower; their pretext was an inspection of that fortress which was the key to London, but when they came away they left behind them, as Constable, Admiral Clinton, a man hand in glove with Northumberland. And there were other things to notice; that day men of the Tower garrison sweated at the work of hauling up the great guns to the top of the White Tower and mounting them there. These things were not usual even at the death of a King. But what the Council had to deal with was not merely the ordinary hiatus between reign and reign, but the forcible wresting of the succession from the normal to the abnormal. Already one of Northumberland's sons had clattered out of London at the head of 300 horse, to lay hands on the Lady Mary wherever she might be, and bring her back a prisoner.[20]

Next day the Council began to take the people into its confidence, and impart the double news of the King's death and the strange accession, but still with great caution. The Captain of the King's Guard announced to his archers that the King was dead, swore them to the Crown, and told them the terms of the King's will. To Greenwich came, by order, the Lord Mayor, half a dozen aldermen, and as many Merchant Staplers and Merchant Adventurers; they were informed of the same.[21]

July 9th was a Sunday, but even the day of rest could be put to good service in this cause. Last week Dr. Hodgskin had omitted the names of the King's sisters from the prayers. This week at Paul's Cross Bishop Ridley went further. Both Mary and her sister he described as bastards, but he preached more especially against Mary, who, he cried, was a papist, and moreover would bring foreigners into the country.[22] At Amersham, under the beech woods of the Chiltern hills, John Knox thundered woe against England if she allied herself with the enemies of the Gospel.[23]

As for the Council, though it went to Court that day, as was the custom, the Court was not now at Greenwich where the dead boy lay, but at Syon House, the Duke of Northumberland's place near Richmond, for there was Jane.

She had come thither from Chelsea, on a sudden summons, and having heard only three days before, to her surprise and dismay, that by Edward's will she was to be Queen. At Syon, banqueted, and courted, with the Lords of the Council kneeling at her feet, and using all the persuasions and arguments they could find, the young thing, not yet seventeen, and (who knows) a little tempted to taste the strange excitements of royalty, had consented to play her part in Northumberland's plan.

Next day from the wharves along Thames side the royal barges were seen to go in state down the river and under the arches of the great Bridge. At the King's Stairs Jane disembarked, was welcomed by the Duke and the Council, and passed into the Tower, her mother bearing up her train for her,[24] that same mother who had in times past 'so sharply taunted, so cruelly threatened, yea presently sometimes with pricks, nips and bobs so out of measure disordered' her daughter–though all in the way of education–that the girl had thought herself to be in hell when she was perforce in her parents' company.

Now Jane was to be Queen; Paulet, Marquess of Winchester and Lord High Treasurer, brought out for her the caskets containing the King's jewels.[25] Perhaps, for all her scholarly highmindedness, she enjoyed turning over the lovely fanciful trinkets; perhaps she put them by with as much scorn as Elizabeth had used towards the jewels of her dead father, which for seven years 'she never looked upon . . . but only once, and that against her will'. Jane, brave and staunch as she was, was yet far other than the gentle Protestant dove of tradition. Her high spirit showed itself on occasion in a schoolgirl pertness, or in downright bad manners. For she could object to a devout Catholic curtseying before the host with–'Why, how can he be there that made us all, and the baker made him?' Or, when Mary sent her a present of 'goodly apparel of tinsel cloth of gold, and velvet laid on with parchment lace of gold', Jane, looking at it with a disapproving eye, would only ask 'What shall we do with it?' 'Marry, wear it', replied a gentlewoman present. 'Nay,' said the provoking chit, 'that were shame, to follow my Lady Mary against God's word, and leave my Lady Elizabeth, which followeth God's word.'[26] Elizabeth, in those days, affected the sober style of dress recommended by the extreme Reformers.

As well as the jewels, the Lord Treasurer brought out the crown itself that she might try it on and see how it would fit. The girl did for a moment hesitate at that, as if she foreboded what must follow, but when she had summoned her courage she put it on her head. Then Winchester told her that there should be another crown for her husband. But here Jane surprised him. She would have none of that; her husband should be a duke, but never King. A domestic storm blew up and raged for some days; Guilford was angry, his mother so furious that she persuaded him to separate from his young wife and retire to Syon.[27] Such resolution and independence Northumberland clearly cannot have foreseen.

By the time she came to the Tower the news of the King's death and of his heir must have been all over London, and that day, at 5 o'clock in the afternoon, at every street corner the heralds proclaimed Queen Jane to a silent crowd which listened coldly while the archers of the guard shouted 'Long live the Queen.'[28]

Northumberland had taken the first step, Now he must make it good, and he was not slow to set about this. The heralds' proclamation-namely that the King's sisters were both bastards, and the elder of them a papist into the bargain-had been printed, and now, damp from the press, it was put up at all the cross-roads of the city, and sent off into the country to be posted in church porches and market squares up and down the kingdom.[29]

As if it were an answer come pat to their proclamation, while the Lords of the Council sat at dinner that day, a messenger brought letters-letters from the Lady Mary herself, claiming her right. 'Astonished and troubled', the Councillors heard the letters read. Mary wrote from Kenninghall; she was still free; her bolt was not yet shot. The Duchesses of Suffolk and Northumberland, whose hearts were most deeply engaged in the perilous business, burst into tears.[30]

But, though the news of Mary's intentions might for a moment take them aback, the Lords of the Council had no real reason to fear. They had London, the treasury, the Tower, the ships, they had 300 horse already hunting for her, and could in a few days put in the field as many thousand men; and at once, to cut off her retreat to the Continent, Northumberland sent half a dozen ships to lie off Yarmouth. Neither they, nor any of her friends in London had the slightest doubt but that in a few days at most Lord Robert Dudley would return to the Tower, and would hand over to the Constable there a small, stubborn, but beaten woman. The Emperor's ambassadors were dismally sure of it; they deplored her action in proclaiming herself Queen; Northumberland might be unpopular and the common people might love her, but such things weighed light against the power of her enemies; and besides, there was her religion.[31] That, they thought, was enough to swamp any ship in such seas.

Mary had sent, besides her letters to the Council, a request to the Emperor's ambassadors. She asked for a messenger to be sent back to her, so that she might keep in touch with them. The ambassadors, as uncomfortable as a cat on hot bricks, dared not do so much as that for fear of suspicion. They did not even care to go for a walk without collecting Spaniards, merchants and other residents, to keep them in countenance.[32]

But next day fresh news came from Norfolk. The Earl of Bath had joined Mary, the Earl of Sussex was on the way to her, Sir Thomas Wharton was with her, Sir John Mordant, Sir Henry Bedingfield and half a dozen other gentlemen, besides 'innumerable companies of the common people'.[33] It was time for the Council to send out a greater force against her, and at once they decided on Suffolk to lead it. But Suffolk was Queen Jane's father, and she, unnerved by the strain of these unprecedented days, burst into tears at the Council table, and begged 'that her father might tarry at home in her company'. Northumberland was their next, and obvious choice. His name was one of fear in Norfolk since the bloody day of Dussindale; and besides that, he was far and away the best soldier in England. But to the Duke himself the choice was far from welcome. In London he had the Council in his grip; if he left them, no one could tell what might happen. 'Well,' he said when they had resolved to send him, 'since ye think it good, I and mine will go, not doubting of your fidelity to the Queen's majesty, whom I leave in your custody.'[34]

Whether his confidence in the Council was as great as he said, or no, he put his whole heart into the preparations for his campaign. If he must go, speed and force were his best weapons. On July 12th it was proclaimed throughout London that there was to be a muster in Tothill fields, pay to be 10d. a day and the purpose 'namely to fetch in Lady Mary'. That same night three carts rumbled out through the gateway of the Tower; they were laden with 'great guns and small; bows, bills and spears . . . and it had been for a great army towards Cambridge'. Early next morning the Duke called for 'all his own harness and saw it made ready'. Throughout the city horses and carts were requisitioned for transport; next day he was to set out, but before setting out he would see the Queen and Council for the last time and try to impress his will upon them.

To the Council he spoke, reminding them that they were to send more men after him to join him at Newmarket. Then, and still more urgently, he called on them not to 'leave us your friends in the briars, and betray us'. After all, he pointed out, he could be the betrayer, just as well as they, 'but now, upon the only trust and faithfulness of your honours . . . we do hazard and jeopard our lives'. Just as he was telling them that 'God's cause, which is the preferment of his word and the fear of papistry's re-entrance, hath been . . . the original ground' of these hazardous doings, the first course of their dinner came up. But while it was laid the Duke went on. He wanted, he said 'no worse god-speed in this journey, than ye would have to yourselves'. One of the Council, nettled by his words, said that if he distrusted any of them, he was mistaken; 'for which of us can wipe his hands clean thereof. . . . Therefore herein your doubt is too far cast. I pray God it be so (quod the Duke): let us go to dinner. And so they sat down.' At parting, Arundel, whom Northumberland had four years ago first used, then discarded and mulcted, wished that he were with him, 'to spend his blood, even at his foot'; and taking my lord's boy Thomas Lovell by the hand said, 'Farewell gentle Thomas, with all my heart.'

On the 14th, having done all he could, Northumberland rode out by way of Shoreditch. The Council had spoken fair; the people showed their feelings openly. As he went he turned in his saddle to one who rode beside him. 'The people press to see us', he said, 'but not one sayeth, God speed us.'[35]

If this were the feeling in London, where many lively wits had taken up with the 'New Learning' and might have been expected to favour Queen Jane, still more was it in quiet country places, when men heard news of the strange doings in London. On June 11th Master Richard Troughton, Constable of a Lincolnshire village near Grantham, stood with John Dove, a neighbour, by 'the common watering place, called hedge-dike, lately scoured for cattle to drink at'. Seeing James Pratt go by, who 'was new come home' he called to him and 'asked how he liked the new-scoured watering place, and he answered, well, and desired God to thank the doers of it, for it was the best deed, said he, that he knew done in that town many years before.'

Having thus dealt with matters of real importance, Pratt asked, what news of King Edward? Richard Troughton discreetly answered – 'None at all', but Pratt took him up, saying that 'the King was dead and that I knew well enough'. Challenged how he knew it for true, Pratt told how Mary had fled before the Duke, the mention of whose name roused all Troughton's ire. He cried out on Northumberland, 'for I feared he would go about to destroy the noble blood of England, wherefore I drew my dagger in the sight of the said John Dove and James Pratt, and wished [it] at the villain's heart, with my hand at it, as hard as I could thrust, suddenly, face to face, body to body, whatever became of my body . . . and prayed God to save the Queen's Majesty and deliver her Grace from him'.[36]

So Richard Troughton, in the magnificent and flamboyant English of his age. And what he said, standing beside the cattle drinking place, must have been repeated in varying terms by countrymen all over England. In East Anglia itself the people went beyond words. From Norfolk and Suffolk, gentlemen, yeomen and common folk came in to Mary at Kenninghall, bringing with them from farms and granges such supplies of bread, beer, fish and flesh, that in the hasty, unorganized muster there was no lack, but cheap meat and drink for all.

But Mary was still in great danger, for her friends were as yet neither sufficiently numerous nor disciplined to stand against the Duke's forces. For greater security she withdrew to the almost royal castle of Framlingham, built by old Norfolk, and his pride; it had only a few months before come into her possession.[37] From there she sent to the Imperial ambassadors a fresh desperate appeal. They contented themselves, however, by reporting her message to the Emperor; 'She saw destruction hanging over her unless she received help from Your Majesty and ourselves.'[38] So the message ran. She received none.

It was little wonder that she was afraid, for Northumberland was said to have 3,000 men, foot and horse, and for their equipment he had had the whole of the Tower armoury to draw on. He had promised the Council to bring Mary back in a few days, captive or dead, 'like a rebel as she was, as he said'.[39] So at Framlingham, set up on its bare green knoll looking over the village, Mary must have waited, with an anxious eye upon the roads that run, dodging the watercourses, by devious ways through the countryside; there were little knots and bunches of men coming along these roads to join her, or sometimes a greater company, and her friends were busy all about, proclaiming her a Queen and mustering what men they could; but it was, so it seemed, a question of time, and no one knew which way the result might go. In many towns, when her people had finished their proclamation and gone away, the perplexed mayor, fearing much the Lords of the Council, would proclaim Queen Jane again, so that with all the rumours, and fears, the confusion and uncertainty, and men arming and riding, the townsmen listened sometimes to three and even four proclamations.[40] But the tide was turning in Mary's favour. Norwich, whose corporation, when summoned on July 11th had refused to open the gates to her messengers, saying that they did not yet know for certain that the King was dead, on July 12th not only proclaimed her, but sent her men and arms.[41]

Then, just about the time when Northumberland was leaving London, came a great stroke of good fortune. Sir Harry Jerningham had gone towards Yarmouth to raise men for her in that direction. There had been easterly gales for the last few days, and as he went he heard that the six ships, sent by Northumberland to intercept any flight to the Continent, had taken shelter in the harbour from the weather. Jerningham, with what men he had, came to Yarmouth. Hearing of his coming, the Captains of the six ships hastily rowed off to their commands. But Jerningham went after them, and out into the harbour in a row-boat, determined to try which way the loyalty of the sailors lay. He was justified. When he had said his say to them, 'the mariners asked Mr. Jerningham what he would have, and whether he would have their captains or no; and he said, "Yea, marry." Said they, "Ye shall have them or else they shall go to the bottom."' The Captains chose the easier course; they said that they would serve Queen Mary, and gladly. So when Jerningham returned to Framlingham he had with him the Captains, their ships' crews, and, an even greater gain, the heavy ordnance from the ships—the first that Mary had to counter that of the Duke, and doubtless a great encouragement to the crowds of simple men that were still thronging to her.

To give these further encouragement, Mary decided to review her troops, and so came on horseback to their camp and rode along the lines. Then helmets were thrown up into the air, harquebuses shot off, and there was such shouting of 'Long live our Good Queen Mary', and 'Death to the traitors', that the Queen's palfrey would do nothing but rear. In the end she was forced to dismount and go the rounds of the camp, with her ladies and her loyal gentlemen, on foot.[42]

Northumberland, after a pause at Ware to let reinforcements catch him up, reached Cambridge on July 16th. He had been sending out parties of horse which sacked and burnt the houses of Mary's known friends; Lord George Howard, returning from one of these forays, came into church that Sunday morning, and handed up to the preacher in the pulpit the very chalice that had been used at Sawston when Mary heard Mass there early in the morning ten days before.[43]

But the muster of nobleman's tenants was not what the Duke had hoped; many of them refused to serve their own lords against Mary. He wrote to the Council 'somewhat sharply' on the subject, 'but a slender answer had he again'. And he was finding even those men he had with him difficult to deal with. Lord George Howard soon fell out with Dudley's eldest son, and galloped off from the camp to Framlingham. Lord Grey, a Protestant, a lusty fighter, and a man of hasty temper, told the Duke that the burning and ravaging of the country 'was no wise course'; the two grew so hot that it came to blows. The Duke had his way and marched on to Bury, burning as he chose; but Grey was not with him; he had gone off to Mary.[44] At Bury Northumberland halted; letters came to him from some of the Council, but it was troops he needed, not letters, and these, besides, were 'letters of discomfort'.[45]

Although he had already 1,000 horse and 3,000 foot, Mary's force also was increasing from day to day while he himself was beginning to reap the harvest of his pride and harsh tyranny, for what could he hope to do with men 'whose feet marched forward whilst their minds moved backwards'. Not yet despondent, however, he sent out 500 horse both to scout and to protect the town, and set himself to try to raise the country folk. He lay in the path of any force that might come out of Buckinghamshire, where Huntingdon's brother had declared for Mary, and determined to prevent junction between the two. Moreover, if England failed him there was still hope of a foreign ally. He sent off a kinsman, one Henry Dudley, post-haste to France to beg there for the help that no one else could give. The price of that help, so much he needed it, he rated high; for he offered Henri II Calais and Guisnes.[46] That same bargain and the name of the man chosen to conclude it we shall find later, in a sinister conjunction.

In London the Council, deprived of Northumberland's presence, was finding its knees weaken. For the first few days, indeed, after the Duke's departure, there seemed little to fear. Men might be coming in to Mary but they were all of the lesser sort, knights or minor nobles at most. But from the point of view of the Council the news did not improve. Three days after Northumberland had marched out, the cautious Renard thought that perhaps, if only Mary could stand the first shock, she might prevail.[47] Then came word of how the ships' crews at Yarmouth had declared for her; at that 'each man began to pluck in his horns'. Nor could the Council even trust its own members. It was suspected that the Lord Warden of the Cinque Ports and the Earl of Pembroke, so recently allied by marriage with Northumberland, were only waiting an opportunity to slip out of the Tower, and to foregather in some private place in London where they might speak their minds, secure from eavesdroppers.[48]

Soon it appeared that they were not the only ones who disliked the air of the Tower. On July 16th, at 7 in the evening, while it was still broad daylight, the gates were suddenly shut, and the keys taken up to Queen Jane. 'The noise in the Tower was that there was a seal lacking', but the truth was that it had been discovered that the Lord Treasurer, the wily old Marquis of Winchester, was missing. This sort of thing would not do, 'and so they did fetch him at 12 of the clock in the night, from his house in London to the Tower'.[49] They had the Treasurer still, but next it was rumoured that Sir Edmund Peckam, Treasurer of the Mint, who had kept the King's privy purse, had got clear away with what money there was in it, and was on his way to Mary. The Council's perturbation grew; the guards of the Tower were increased; it was now not a question of whether, but of when the whole Council would rat.[50]

On July 18th it ratted. At the meeting that day a proclamation was drawn up and approved offering a reward for the arrest of Northumberland – £1,000 in land to any noble, £500 to any knight, £100 to any yeoman bold enough to lay his hand on the Duke's shoulder and demand his surrender.[51]

Next day, Secretary Mason and the Earl of Shrewsbury came to the Imperial ambassadors. It was not quite a week since Mason had visited them with Lord Cobham, but then his business had been to tell the ambassadors, without any polite periphrasis, that by the King's death their mission was ended, and that if they should try to help Mary it would be the worse for them.[52] Now, with very different expressions, Mason and Shrewsbury explained to Renard and his friends that only three or four of the Council had ever consented heartily to Edward's will; the rest had been treated almost as prisoners before they yielded. And, they concluded, today they two and Paget were about to proclaim Queen Mary.[53]

But, though their minds were made up, these converts to Mary's claim still moved warily. They had broken out of the Tower, a dozen or so of them – the Earls of Bedford, Pembroke, Arundel, Shrewsbury and Worcester; Lords Paget, Darcy, and Cobham and others of less importance. They were gathered now at Baynard's Castle, Pembroke's house, but it was afternoon before they took the final step. As the Lord Mayor of London was 'riding in the afternoon about the wood-wharf westward, as he came to Paul's Wharf he met with the Earl of Shrewsbury and Sir John Mason'. There, sitting on their horses by the riverside, they spoke together. When they parted, the Lord Mayor hurried off home, sent out for his aldermen, giving a rendezvous at St. Paul's, and before long himself came to Baynard's Castle.[54]

It was between five and six in the evening that a little knot of riders, with two heralds and three trumpeters, set out from Baynard's Castle to the Cross in Cheap. But before they had gone so far as Paul's Churchyard on the top of the hill, their way was almost blocked by the crowds that came hurrying out to see and hear. At the Cross they drew up, and the trumpeters sounded.

As though the whole town had been waiting, with one rush the streets were full of the men of London, their wives, serving-men and apprentices. Garter King of Arms read out his proclamation in a dead silence, until he spoke a name–'Queen Mary'. Then 'there was such a shout of the people with casting up of caps and crying "God save Queen Mary", that the style of the proclamation could not be heard'.[55]

From the Cross, the Lords of the Council moved off to St. Paul's where the choir waited. There *Te Deum* was sung with the organs blowing, while the bells in the steeple rocked and clashed and were soon answered by bells from every part of the city. Down below, the town went mad. Men with money in their purses flung it broadcast among the people; money showered down from the windows of merchants' houses into the crowded streets. Respectable elderly men, tearing off their coats, joined in the dances that were soon making May Day of the town. Others ran through the city shouting to all the news of the proclamation. In Leadenhall Street a friend of Northumberland's heard the news and tried to persuade the people not to credit it; he was on horseback, or he would not have escaped with his life. When night fell there was no darkness, for bonfires had been built and lit; folk lugged out trestles and table-tops, set them for a banquet, and stayed eating, and drinking the Queen's health round about the blaze, while all through the night the bells of every steeple in London kept up their mad din.[56]

Through the crowds, messengers, booted and spurred, pushed their way, and then rode out under the old gates into the country, bearing their news. At about 9 o'clock, in the dusk and the firelight, the Earl of Arundel and Lord Paget with 30 horse set out to ride post to the Queen. As they passed the banqueters, the citizens of London, their mouths crammed with good things, called out to them, asking if they did not rejoice at this good news, 'at which all thanked God, and said–God save Queen Mary'.[57]

These lords were the bearers of a letter from the Council over the writing of which the authors must have sweated. Yet the result of their labour could hardly be convincing. The most that they could do was to cover over the late actions of the Council with a flimsy veil of excuse. 'We', they declared, 'having always (God we take to witness) remained your Highness's true and humble subjects in our hearts . . . seeing hitherto no possibility to utter our determination here without great destruction and bloodshed both of ourselves and others till this time, have this day proclaimed in your city of London Your Majesty . . .' and so on. Finally, their dread of destruction and bloodshed having evaporated with the danger of it, they vowed themselves entirely hers 'to the effusion of our blood'.[58]

While the city feasted, with songs, shouting, and the clash of bells, silence had fallen on the Tower, Suffolk, when he heard what was being done, had come out of the gates, bidding his men leave their weapons and follow him. 'I am but one man', he said, and so led them up the slopes to Tower Hill, and there looking down over the river and the shipping and the walls of the old fortress, he proclaimed Queen Mary. Back again in the Tower he went to the chamber where his daughter sat at supper, under the royal canopy. With his own hand he tore the hangings down, saying that such things were not for her. Lady Throgmorton had gone out that afternoon to stand godmother, as proxy for Queen Jane, to a child of one of the Royal Guard; when she returned, she found every sign of royalty gone from the empty chambers which she had left crowded and splendid so few hours ago. When she asked for Queen Jane they told her that both Guilford and his wife were prisoners.[59] They, poor lad and lass, had soon finished their brief playing at Kings and Queens. Mr. Secretary Cecil aptly wrote the epitaph of the short reign when, on one of Jane's letters patent signed with her name–'Jane the Queen', he later added the endorsement–'Jana non Regina'.

Through the country the news ran like wildfire. At Northampton, when Sir Thomas Tresham read the proclamation, the crowd carried him with them, whether he would or not. At Grantham, worthy Master Richard Troughton rode in from South Witham to give the Mayor and aldermen the benefit of his advice as to how to draw up a proclamation. 'And so', he says, 'we went to the market cross, in the hearing of the country people, and solemnly with the noise of shawmes 4 several times blowen with distinction', silence was commanded, and the Queen proclaimed, 'And immediately after . . . praying God save the Queen, I cast up my hat, and then all the people saying God save the Queen cast up their caps and hats. And when the people were quieted I began to sing "*Te Deum Laudamus*" and so we did sing it solemnly to th'end.'[60]

Late that same night that Mary was proclaimed, the news of it came to the Duke at Cambridge whither he had returned from Bury. It left him thunderstruck. Next morning he did the only thing he could–he called for four trumpeters and a herald, and, when they could not be found, went himself into the market place with the Marquis of Northampton and the Mayor, proclaimed Mary, waved his white Captain General's truncheon and shouted 'Long live the Queen', 'casting up his cap after as if he had been joyful of it', and tore down with his own hands the proclamation of Queen Jane. Within an hour another messenger rode into Cambridge bringing letters from the Council, bidding the Duke's army disperse, and warning him to come no nearer than ten miles of London.[61]

Later in the day the Mayor plucked up courage enough to arrest the great Northumberland, but when the Duke objected that the Council's letters had bidden that each should go his way, and that therefore his arrest was contrary to the Council's will, he was set free again. But he did nothing with those few hours of liberty. His son Warwick indeed spent the night booted and ready to ride with the first light, but before either he or his father had got away, in rode Arundel and Paget, and came to the Duke in his chamber.

Northumberland, stunnned yet with the suddenness and completeness of the landslide that had ruined all his plans, fell on his knees, asking them 'to be good to him for the love of God. . . . "And consider (saith he) I have done nothing but by the consents of you all, and the whole Council."

' "My lord" quoth he, (Arundel), "I am sent hither by the Queen's Majesty and in her name I do arrest you."

' "And I obey it my lord (quoth he), I beseech you my lord of Arundel (quod the Duke) use mercy towards me, knowing the case as it is."

' "My lord (quod the earl) you should have sought for mercy sooner. I must do according to my commandment." '

Northumberland was a prisoner, and for the next two hours began to learn the maddening inactivity of imprisonment, as he walked up and down in the room looking out on the street, where free men went by about their business. After a while he saw Arundel pass, and called out to him from the window—

' "My lord of Arundel! My lord! I pray you a word with you."

' "What would you have, my lord?" said he.

' "I beseech your lordship, (quod he) for the love of God let me have Cox, one of my chamber to wait on me."

' "You shall have Tom your boy," quod the Earl', who had, in London, so short a time ago, said farewell to that same Tom, 'with all my heart'.

' "Alas, my lord," quod the Duke, "what stead can a boy do me? I pray you let me have Cox." '[62]

Yesterday morning Northumberland had been the father-in-law of the Queen. Today he must beg for a single gentleman to serve him. Arundel, for all his old grudge, was not unmerciful. Both Tom and Cox were sent.

If his fellows, little as they liked him, were ready to oblige him in small things, the common people were not so. They had no pity for a beaten man whom they had always hated. The Queen had ordered that all prisoners should pass through London in peace, but when Arundel brought in the Duke, they would not be quiet. Arundel, pausing at Bishopsgate, had made his prisoner take off his hat and scarlet cloak, and from there to the Tower he rode bareheaded through streets lined with 'men in harness afore every man's door', and full of an angry crowd, which in spite of rebuke, threw stones and shouted at him for a traitor and a heretic; one of his younger sons who rode behind him broke down under the strain of it, and wept as he rode.[63] So they came to the gate of the Tower.

Besides Jane and Guilford, Suffolk was already safe under lock and key there, and the idlers who hung about, watching alternately the river and the gate, had enough to see during the next few days. For not only Northumberland was brought in, but his three sons, and his brother Sir Andrew Dudley, the Marquis of Northampton, the Earl of Huntingdon, Lord Hastings, Sir John Gates Captain of the King's Guard, his brother Henry, and Sir Thomas Palmer. Two ecclesiastics also joined the prisoners. Dr. Sandys had preached before the Duke at Cambridge against Mary; Bishop Ridley had, at Paul's Cross, denounced her as a bastard. Sandys was brought in from Cambridge; Ridley from Ipswich; he said that he had been on his way to ask pardon.[64]

Meanwhile Queen Mary, after those first messengers from the Council, had received a stream of loyal subjects, though some of these, considered to have come too tardily from the late rebel army, were handed over to the

Sheriff as prisoners. On the day after their proclamation, the Council, tender of their Queen's safety, had appointed a guard of 500 to attend on her. Her army by now amounted, some said, to 35 or 40 thousand, and since all who could brought in jewels or plate, this huge force was costing her nothing.[65] A cheap accession, de Noailles, with suppressed bitterness, considered it. A miracle Reginald Pole thought it; and others, among them the Queen herself, were with him.

The first thing Mary did, it was said, after she heard of the proclamation in London, was to order the crucifix to be set up openly in the chapel of Framlingham.[66] But surely in her own chapel she must have done so before. That she had it set up now in the parish church would be nearer the truth, and the restoration must have meant to her more than all the crowding, the cheering, the new pomp – more even than the affection of the country people, since what that restoration meant was for her at the heart of everything – was indeed that for which she was Queen. From now on she believed, and in the teeth of all difficulties, and through dark and darkening days she held to the belief, that by God's grace alone she had come to the throne, and in order that His work should be done by her. No one who knew her ever had doubted what her line of action would be, should she some time have the power to do as she chose; her worst enemies could not say that she had ever concealed or compromised her beliefs. But from now on, her accession – the suddenness, the ease, the unlikeliness of it all – was never to be out of her mind. For it was a clear and shining sign from God, so that it would be a sin for her to doubt, from henceforth, that she was His chosen instrument to restore the Church.

From Framlingham she moved, just before the end of the month, to Newhall, a place for her of many memories. There, representatives of the City of London found her, and presented a purse of crimson velvet, very heavy and jingling, for it contained £500 in half sovereigns.[67] On August 3rd she left Wanstead in Essex, with over 700 gentlemen in velvet suits going before her, and her ladies after. Elizabeth, with 1000 horse, with spears, bows, and guns, and all her gentlemen in green 'gauded with white velvet satin taffety', had come out to join her, and now turned back again to London.[68]

It was 7 o'clock in the evening of August 3rd when Mary rode into the city. She had on 'a gown of purple velvet, French fashion . . . her kirtle all thick set with goldsmith's work and great pearl . . . with a rich baldrick of gold pearl and stones about her neck, and a rich billement of stones and great pearl on her head', and she rode on a palfrey whose gold-embroidered trappings came down to the ground, her train being borne up by Sir Anthony Browne, who carried it over his shoulder. At Aldgate Bar the Lord Mayor greeted her, kissing the sceptre 'in token of loyalty and homage', before he gave it into her hands. She thanked him, graciously remembering the city to have been always good to her. The people, excited and overwrought, wept for joy at the gentleness of her words, voice, and smile. The Queen passed on, Elizabeth following her, then the Duchess of Norfolk and the Marchioness of Exeter, through streets fresh gravelled, and hung with cloths and tapestries, the city companies standing armed, trumpets blowing and guns firing 'like great thunder'. The children of Christ's Hospital stood ready with an oration, '100 poor little children . . . all dressed in blue with red caps'.[69]

When she reached the Tower the Constable and Lieutenant greeted her, and then there was 'such a peal of guns both small and great, and so long and so thick that hath not been heard'. In the gateway she paused, because three men knelt there. Two of them she must have known well, though it was long since she had seen them–for they were the Duke of Norfolk, and Stephen Gardiner lately Bishop of Winchester. The third was a young man; Edward Courtenay, son of her old friend the Marquis of Exeter, who since his father's execution had grown to manhood in a prisoner's narrow world. She stooped to each one of the three kissing him, and saying to all 'These are my prisoners.' Then she passed on under the arch, into the royal fortress, palace, prison of the Tower.[70]

QUEEN MARY I
By Anthonis Mor.   Prado, Madrid.

Chapter XII

THIS first Queen to bear rule in England since the ill-starred Matilda, was now a woman of thirty-seven, a small creature, thin and slightly built, with reddish hair, and a complexion which had once been her chief beauty, and which still, in spite of the lines that marked her face gave her something of a look of youth.[1] During her father's lifetime she had been said to resemble him, especially in her mouth; the likeness showed itself too in her laugh and way of speaking. She had, a strange thing in one so small and thin, a loud and deep voice, almost like a man's; her eyes were grey and so short-sighted that to read she must hold the page close to her face. Yet those who spoke with her and met her look found it keen and searching; that at least is what an ambassador thought at the beginning of her reign; perhaps it was only an honestly frank and fearless look that he misread, for a keen and searching intellect Mary certainly had not. Yet the royal dignity which he saw in her was genuine enough. Mary, like all her house, was as perfectly convinced of her royalty as if that very cadet family had sat on the English throne for centuries. After her father and John Dudley she never feared a man, but spoke out, lost her temper, and chid what she considered presumption, with regal freedom.

With this conviction, however, there went in her an utter simplicity of character. Had she been a citizen's wife she might have been described as an active little body, for she enjoyed exercise, rode for her health, and at least when she was younger, walked two or three miles most days; even indoors she did not often sit down. Her walk, so an observer noticed, lacked the 'grandity' which so many admired in Elizabeth's deportment; perhaps that was as much as to say that she bustled about.

Her chief interests too were those of a very ordinary woman – namely, people, clothes, and babies. When she was Queen, staying out in the country at the Archbishop's palace at Croydon, she would go out in the summer evenings with two or three of her ladies, would call at the cottages like any squire's wife, and sit down to talk while the goodman ate his supper. She would never, in these visits, allow any word of respect to distinguish her from her ladies, so that the wife only knew that some of the great folk from the palace had been talking to her. But in the talk Mary would hear of wrongs done by her own officers – of a cart requisitioned and not paid for, or a man taken from his harvesting to ride an errand – and when she got back the injustice would be put right. Such small matters were the things that she could understand and deal with; she had lived almost all her life in small country manors, in close touch with the neighbourhood, hearing the talk of servants and husbandmen; she remembered it now, and took care that, except for such short distances as that between Westminister and Croydon, she did not move her residence at harvest time, when every man was busy in the fields and all the horses and carts were needed.[2]

Children had always been dear to her; even Elizabeth, child of her mother's and her own arch-enemy, had, while she was still a child, a warm corner in Mary's heart. Far more had Mary loved the little brother, the clever pretty boy, but apart from these two, any child was a thing of importance to her. She was godmother to upwards of a score of babies born to people in her household; she gave them presents, saw to their schooling, and always took an interest in them.

She was indeed cut out by nature and inclination for the intimate personal relationships of a private life. In such a life she might have been happy. As it was, her women loved her and respected her, and yet they sometimes treated her as one who needed instruction in the ways of the world. Once, and it was not two years before her death, 'Queen Mary, being in the gallery, ready to go to the Chapel, within the traverse, the Lord William Howard, Lord Chamberlain, being with her, he taking his leave; without the traverse stood the maids of honour, expecting to wait on the Queen to the Chapel–Mistress Frances Neville, standing next to the traverse, the Lord Chamberlain passing by, a merry gentleman, took her by the chin, saying "My pretty . . . how dost thou?" Which the Queen saw and heard, the traverse being drawn. The Queen gone forth, finding her farthingale at her foot loose, made sign to Mistress Neville to pin it, which, kneeling down, she did. The Queen then took her by the chin as he had done, saying "God-a-mercy my pretty . . .". She hearing the Queen say so, blushed as she seemed to be astonished, replying–"Madam what says your Majesty?" The Queen answered–"What is the matter? Have I said or done more than the Lord Chamberlain did? And may I not be as bold with thee as he?" She replied–"My Lord Chamberlain is an idle gentleman, and we respect not what he saith or doth, but your Majesty, from whom I think I never heard any such word, doth amaze me, either in jest or earnest, to be called so by you. A . . . is a wicked misliving woman."'

There is humour, but there is a pathos too, in this story of the middle-aged, married woman instructed and rebuked by a chit of a girl. And the rebuke was accepted with a childlike simplicity. 'Thou must forgive me,' said the Queen, 'for I meant no harm.'[3]

Simplicity and sincerity were fundamental in her character. She had been forced, in the unhappy past, to learn to be discreet, to hold her tongue, even on occasion to deceive by concealment. But she never learnt to lie; and for the most part her way was, as she often wrote–'to be plain with you'. She was unwaveringly loyal to people and things she loved; she was stubborn because she had little or no imagination, an anxious, exact honesty of intention, and a great hatred of decisions.

Religion continued with her to the end, for it was a basic need of her heart. Reason had in her little to do with it. She thanked God she had never read Protestant books of divinity. She knew her way to God; she was convinced that that way was the only one, and could not conceive that others might reach the same communion by a different road; it was blindness in her, but it was a blindness shared by almost all her contemporaries. And, to speak of her private and personal experience of religion, apart from all controversy, and as she herself had known it, in lonely watchings, in secret, fearful celebrations of the Mass, and now once again in all the pomp of the old ritual – that personal experience was most surely a living and lasting thing with her. For long it had been her one passion. When her marriage brought another absorbing devotion that invaded and almost broke her heart, can any doubt but that while she was buffeted by waves of sorrow such as even she had not known before, her sheet-anchor still held firm upon the ground of God?

But a Queen needs other qualities than those of a private woman, and Mary needed, and for her misfortune lacked, all those gifts of intuition, judgement and political aptitude that Elizabeth had in such full measure. Conscience with her took the place of judgement, and, applied to policy, conscience is a deceivable and deceiving guide unless it is enlightened by a quick and sensitive imagination. What she *ought* to do Mary always knew, or thought she knew. What was wisest to do she had no way of being sure, but, confused and harassed, struggled on, longing for guidance but unable to trust her natural advisers. The shifts, treacheries, and self-seeking of the Councillors disgusted her. She despised the men and could not use them for her ends; she despised them, and yet she was deceived by them, for they took her measure as quickly as an unruly fourth form takes the measure of an inexperienced or incompetent master. A subtle and keen politician like Renard, the new Imperial ambassador, felt for her an uneasy pity mingled with scorn. 'I know the Queen,' he wrote to Granvelle, 'so easy to get round, so simple, so little experienced in worldly matters, and such a novice in all things. . . . To tell you, between ourselves, what I think of her – I believe that if God does not preserve her, she will be lost.' Van der Delft, Jehan Duboys, even her admirer Chapuys would have agreed with him.

Not that she was a coward. Her resistance to her father, and to her brother's Council, her resolve at Edward's death to raise her banner and defy Northumberland – all these things had shown her courage, and her behaviour during Wyatt's rebellion was to give yet another proof. When it was a matter of physical danger, she was a lion. When it was a matter of judgement and policy, she was a sheep, or, as disastrously, a mule. And such a woman had been cast up 'upon the high shore of this world' at a time when problems were to be solved that even the most perspicuous found dark and impenetrable as thunderclouds. Well might Renard prophesy disaster, and yet of all men he was the one who did most to bring it on her.

If this was the Queen, what were the men who were to be her instruments and ministers? It cannot be said that she was fortunate in them, even though among their number were men that Elizabeth was to use with such harmony and success that it is yet debated whether the triumphant policy of her reign was the Queen's or theirs. From these men Mary was divided by a gulf as wide as the miles between Rome and Geneva. Yet she was forced to use them; Northumberland's Protestant friends, if they had not appeared glaringly in the late sedition, must be continued in office, since the new Queen dared not alienate such a large band; but she could never really trust them.

Besides the definitely Protestant party in the Council there were such men as Derby, Shrewsbury, and Arundel who had acquiesced, unwillingly perhaps, but still without open protest, in the late changes of religion, and in Northumberland's plot. Of such men she was to make her ministers, and of Paulet, Marquis of Winchester, that old man of the sea, determined and able to adjust himself and remain in the front rank; his cold heavy-lidded eyes still look inscrutably out of his portrait, as, vulture-like in face, leaning forward a little on his staff, the old man considers the world and its chances. And there was Paget, a man of no gentle blood, 'neither on the father's nor on the mother's side', but able, comfortably devoid of scruples, intent on a greater stake than Paulet played for, since Paget wished not only to be in the front rank, but to direct the policy of the State from beside the Queen's Chair. These were the men the Queen must use. She might add to them her own old servants, but these, though honest were entirely inexpert, and could be of little help to her in the business of government.

For her Chancellor she had to her hand a better man. Gardiner, who had been Bishop of Winchester till Edward's Council imprisoned him as too able and too staunch a supporter of the old ways, had also been Henry VIII's trusted servant and adviser. 'Wily Winchester', 'Stephen Stockfish', had held many offices; he was a man of affairs, with a lawyer's rather than a churchman's training and bent. It is true that to Mary's way of thinking he had not a clean slate, for he had helped to forward her mother's divorce and the separation of England from Rome. But apart from his firm stand in Edward's reign he had, during the latter years of Henry VIII been identified with the policy of conservative recoil summed up in the Act of Six Articles, and to such a pass had things since come, that Mary and others looked back at those days as a golden age, while a preacher of the opposite persuasion, warming to his subject, waxed so indignant against the dead King as to denounce him as a papist. Henry could truthfully be called many names, but hardly that.

Gardiner was undeniably an able man; Henry VIII did not choose fools. Equally undeniably he was an honest, though not a spiritually minded man, for his changes of front had conviction behind them, and when he could not reasonably change his opinions, he was ready to suffer for them. He had, what is invaluable in a statesman, a sound practical sense, with a grasp of the realities of the situation, and the Englishman's eye for what will work. In more important things he understood his fellow countrymen, knew what they confusedly wanted, knew even better what they simply would not stand. Both in his conservatism, which, rather than any deep religious conviction, made him set his face against the Protestant party, and in his distrust of foreign influence, he was a sound adviser, and it would have been well for Mary if she had listened to him and seen things with his eyes.

But Gardiner, though statesmanlike in his views, and in private life a witty, warm-hearted, humourous man, a writer of the liveliest and aptest letters, must have been a difficult person to work with. Henry had been able to use him; it had been the King's custom on occasion to 'whet' him, as Gardiner said, that is to give him a taste of the royal tongue. Gardiner bore it with a stubborn good humour that Henry liked, and as a reward was allowed 'in a good honest manner [to] follow mine own inclination, [rather] than to take pains to speak as though butter should not melt in my mouth'.[4] But though a good lieutenant to a man like Henry, Gardiner was not well fitted to be chief adviser to an unapt, inexperienced mistress. For one thing, there never was such an unpopular man; it is hard to find any who spoke a good word for him, while his numerous enemies were eloquent in his dispraise. He had been a most unpopular ambassador in France. Soon he was at loggerheads with the greater part of the Council. A quick-witted man himself, he did not suffer fools gladly, but would listen with unconcealed impatience to some blundering or pompous speaker, snatching off his cap to ruffle that tuft of hair that always stood up on his head, and which people nicknamed 'his grace', and breaking in at last with a half angry, half laughing mockery.[5]

As early as July 27th—that is to say even before Mary came to London, he was demanding from the Earl of Pembroke and the Marchioness of Northampton restitution of lands and rents seized by them from the diocese of Winchester at the time when Church possessions were a lucky dip into which the nobility might plunge its hands. The present owners might have no shadow of right behind them, but Simon Renard, another man who could not stand Gardiner at any price, deplored the action as precipitate.[6] It certainly was remarkably prompt, seeing that Gardiner was still a prisoner in the Tower.

To the handicap of his hot and hasty temper, untamed by five years' imprisonment, with its monotony, its continual walking up and down 'for the good of my stomach', there was added another impediment to his success —the growing enmity between himself and William Paget. They had been good friends at Cambridge, had acted in the same college theatricals, and since those days had preserved the friendship, so that Gardiner, if ruffled or depressed, would write to Paget, in order, as he said, 'to make purgation' of the trouble.[7] But not a week after Gardiner's appointment as Chancellor, they were at odds. It was for Mary a disastrous quarrel, since Paget now only took thought to find a tool to undermine the Chancellor's position. Soon he was to find one ready to his hand, and that tool, the Spanish marriage, all but toppled over the throne as well.

With all his faults it is not impossible, however, that Gardiner might have steered the ship of state, weather-beaten and strained in all her timbers as she was, to some port of comparative peace, had it not been for the Queen herself. But though Mary made him Chancellor, he was not, even at the outset, in her full confidence, and he never contrived to gain that trust, which, if given fully, might have enabled him to carry out his policy in the teeth of the Lords of the Council.

Disastrously for Mary, but perhaps inevitably, the man who had most influence over her during that first year of her reign that shaped the rest, was no Englishman, but the Emperor's ambassador, Simon Renard. He it was who, muffled in a cloak, passed by confidential servants through postern doors giving on the river, and up privy stairs to the Queen's presence, dropped in Mary's mind the seeds of the Emperor's suggestions. She trusted him, because she trusted her cousin; for long she had had no one else to trust.

The work that lay before the Queen and Council might have daunted the strongest heart. An empty treasury and bonds to Antwerp merchants already overdue; a hungry and discontented folk; the whole legacy of the late upheavals in religion; the settlement of the late rebellion–these were the problems at home. Farther afield there was Scotland angry and dangerous; Ireland, stirred up to the pitch of rebellion by the adroit mischief-making of France; Calais and Guisnes, flimsily defended and always a source of apprehension when domestic troubles weakened England. In addition to these, there was the choice that England must make between friendship with France and friendship with Spain, if she needed support from a foreign power.

Temporarily, but promptly, because the business was one of manageable dimension, Calais and Guisnes were dealt with. On July 31st the good soldier and captain, Lord Grey, though so lately in arms against the Queen, was given power to have the drums beat through London to muster men for service in the Pale.[8] It was, however, treachery, rather than open attack from France that had been feared, and of this fear Lord William Howard the Governor of Calais, very soon ridded the Queen and Council. For on July 24th that truculent and indiscreet gentleman had received a letter from the Constable of France. The Constable, who had of course known of Northumberland's plot, but had not yet received news of its disaster, wrote offering the Governor of Calais French assistance, in case any prince (by which he meant the Emperor) should try, while fishing in troubled waters, to bring up Calais on the hook. ' Timeo Danaos et dona ferentes', Howard may have muttered if he had Latin. When he answered the letter he returned the Constable no thanks for his altruism but tersely informed him of the course of events in England. Then, after noting the Frenchman's offer to come to Calais with an army, the Governor replied that Calais had been committed to him not to hand over to the French King or to any other, but to defend. 'But' he concluded, 'since you have given me such notice, have no doubt I will so provide for you that if you wish to try any enterprise against this town in peace or war . . . by God's grace I will do so much that you and yours will repent of it. And so, Monsieur, I pray God give you a long life.'[9]

That undiplomatic answer made clear to both Henri II of France and the English Council, on which side Howard stood. In England some of the Lords were at pains to excuse the manner of it to the French ambassador, in private calling Howard a fool, in public accounting for the crudity of his letter by the difficulties of the French language.[10] The Queen, on the contrary, as one might have expected, declared roundly that he had spoken 'like an honest man'.[11]

After the question of Calais, the settlement of the late rebellion was the most straightforward business before the Council, though, until the Queen's intentions were known, the Emperor suffered acute anxiety on the subject. 'For God's sake', he wrote to his ambassadors, 'let her moderate the lust of vengeance that probably burns in her supporters.'[12] So far as Mary herself was concerned, the advice was superfluous. Renard and Charles were to find the Queen only too ready to pardon.

It was certainly true, as Renard said, that to punish impartially all the leaders would have left the Queen without any Council at all, and that, in the case of many of the Lords clemency was forced upon her. But there were many who could have expected no mercy. Such men as Northampton, Hastings, the two Gates brothers and Palmer, had been deeply dipped in treason; still more obviously marked for the block were Northumberland and his sons, Suffolk, and the young usurpers themselves, Guilford Dudley and Queen Jane. Yet already on July 31st Suffolk had the Queen's pardon and came out of the Tower. Northumberland's sons, with the exception of Guilford, were, after trial and condemnation, set free; so were Northampton, Hastings and Sir Andrew Dudley, the Duke's brother; so was that Henry Dudley who had carried to France the Duke's offer to trade Calais and Guisnes for French help. There were fines in plenty, and deprivations of office, but for a rebellion which had actually set the crown on a usurper's head, and a price upon her own, the Queen exacted the lives of three, and only three men – Northumberland, Sir John Gates, and Sir Thomas Palmer.

But what is more surprising than this, being indeed unprecedented, was the Queen's refusal to lift a finger against Lady Jane Grey. In her grandfather's time royal blood alone, without a suspicion of treason, had been fatal to the young Earl of Warwick; in her father's time royal blood without overt treason had brought the Marquis of Exeter and Lord Montague to the block, and kept the former's innocent son a prisoner for all his young years. Now, when Simon Renard saw the Queen in the middle of August, Mary told him, as though she expected to be scolded for her clemency, that she had not yet pardoned anyone, but that, as for Lady Jane Grey 'she could not be induced to consent that she should die'. Jane had written to her a long and dignified confession and exculpation, and the Queen quoted it to Renard. 'Three days before they went to fetch her at Syon House to take her to the Tower and make her entry into the town as usurping Queen she knew nothing of it, nor was she ever a party to, nor did she ever give her consent to the Duke's intrigues and plots.' 'My conscience', said Mary, 'will not permit me to have her put to death.'[13]

Renard, who had in his pocket the Emperor's injunctions recommending mercy, must have found them a positive embarrassment. Indeed, when he had mentioned the Emperor's advice, Mary's reply had been to ask promptly – 'Would the Emperor like me to pardon the Duke of Northumberland?'

And now she would not put out of the way the woman more dangerous than Northumberland; the woman who possessed not only royal blood, but such title to the crown as Edward's will could confer. This was indeed to have too much of a good thing. Renard began to dread the effects of her clemency as much as Charles had feared those of a policy of revenge.

The Emperor, he hastened to say, did not want anyone in particular to be pardoned. Sometimes it was necessary to be cruel, and he raked out of the bottom of his mind a classical example to enforce that; the son of Maximus, he reminded the Queen, had not been spared, innocent though he was.

Mary apologetically defending herself, told him, with great simplicity, more of her astonishing intentions. She promised that she would take every possible precaution *before setting Lady Jane free*. Elizabeth, when she came to the throne, was to keep Jane's sister a captive for years, merely because she married without permission. Mary, not a month after Jane's nine days reign, contemplated setting the enemy free. Renard may well have groaned within himself at such statecraft. But for Mary the thing was no more than plain justice. Jane was the girl who had lived for a while in her household; to whom she had given trinkets; she had written to Mary explaining the innocence of her intentions; Mary believed her; why should she be kept in prison?[14]

As to Northumberland, though the Queen was so ready to contemplate pardon, there could be no question. He must die. On August 18th he came before his peers in Westminster Hall, doing reverence to the Court three times before he took his stand, but getting from his judges in return at most a slight touch of the cap.[15] There was a grim and biting comedy in the solemn scene, for as he himself maintained, the Court had been with him in all his treasons. Palmer, at his trial next day, urged the same thing, but urged it with the fury of a man trapped. The judges were traitors too, he shouted, 'and have deserved punishment as much as me and more'.[16]

No excuse for Northumberland would serve. He might have exclaimed with Shakespeare's Crouchback –

> There is no creature loves me,
> And if I die no man shall pity me.

He had ruled all 'by stout courage and proudness of stomach' and now that he was fallen, no man spoke for him. Mary showed more pity for him than most. She insisted on sending him a priest 'to comfort him', and though the recantation of his Protestant views which followed was of immense value to the Government, Renard, at any rate, found nothing politic in her motive, but only a womanly and Christian pity. Lady Jane Grey, indomitable herself, thought scorn of Northumberland. She was in Master Partridge's house in the Tower, treated more like a guest than a prisoner; if a chance friend of her host dropped in to dinner both men would apologize for their intrusion when they found that the Lady Jane that day intended to dine downstairs. Jane, however, was gracious, and the talk at table animated. It turned, as was natural, upon the Duke's recantation; the guest wondered if he hoped by it to obtain pardon. 'Pardon!' broke out the girl furiously, 'Pardon! Woe worth him! He hath brought me and all our stock in most miserable calamity by his exceeding ambition. . . . Who is judge that he should hope for pardon whose life is odious to all men!'[17]

On August 21st, in the presence of the Common Council of the city, Northumberland and his fellow traitors heard Mass, and confessed that 'they had erred from the true Catholic faith 15 years'.[18] The words, it was hoped, would sink into the minds of the city fathers, but there was no question of mercy for the Duke. At about 8 o'clock next morning, in a gown of pale grey, 'crane coloured' damask, he came to his execution. He leaned a while on the Eastern rail of the scaffold speaking to the people and looking his last on the morning. Then he knelt, prayed, and recited the Creed in Latin; the scarf was bound round his eyes and he laid himself down, but because the scarf slipped he had to rise up again, and in that minute, says one who watched, fascinated, 'surely [he] figured to himself the terrible dreadfulness of death'. Laying himself down again he struck his hands together once, 'as who should say, This must be, and cast himself upon the said beam'. The executioner, a man lame in one leg and wearing a white apron like a butcher, smote off his head.[19]

The execution of Sir Thomas Palmer and Sir John Gates followed, but there was no more bloodshed. In November, Lord Guilford Dudley, Lady Jane Grey, and Lords John and Ambrose Dudley were arraigned at the Guildhall and condemned to death. So was Archbishop Cranmer, who would not, however, have been imprisoned at all had not he followed up his part in the plot by an action that forced the hand of the Government against him. But, the sentences passed, the prisoners returned to the Tower. A few weeks later they were all, 'on suggestion that divers of them be and have been evil at ease in their bodies for want of air, "allowed" liberty of walking within the garden of the Tower'.[20]

We have, in following the history of the prisoners of the late rebellion, run ahead through the first five months of the reign, and must now return to the days immediately following Mary's accession. As the confederates of Northumberland went in to the Tower or the Fleet, other prisoners came out, the dispossessed and imprisoned Bishops, Bonner, Heath, Gardiner, Day and Tunstal, with the Duke of Norfolk and Edward Courtenay. In some cases the very room that one Bishop had learned to know so minutely well, that every stone, every shadow had grown familiar, was immediately filled by an ecclesiastic of the opposite persuasion, while the late tenants were seen 'coming in great joy and magnificence about the town, mounted on mules and little pompous horses, dressed in great gowns of black camlet over which were beautiful surplices, their heads being covered with satin hoods like the monks'.[21]

They and many orthodox Catholics were doubtless confident that now—

> Jack shall have Jill
> Nought shall go ill,
> The man shall have his mare again
> And all shall be well.

No one of either party could have any doubt what the Queen's religion had always been, was, and would be. The wave of popular enthusiasm that brought her to the throne had made no terms. Foxe indeed claims that the Queen gave her word to the Suffolk men, as the price of their support, that she would alter nothing in religion, but the statement is incredible unless the reader judges Mary capable of a solemn and unforced lie. It may be, however, that she expressed herself to the Suffolk men with the same gentleness that, as we shall see, she used to the Londoners during the first month of her reign, and that they read their own interpretation into the words. Most Protestants saw as clearly as Sir Peter Carew, who, far off in Devonshire, proclaimed her as Queen, 'albeit he knew very well that there was like to come great alteration in religion' if she came to the throne.[22] At Framlingham Protestants and Catholics had flocked to her standard, simply because Dudley was hated, and she, a Tudor, was loved.

But there was one Catholic who feared rather than hoped. This was the Emperor Charles. Just as he had dreaded impolitic reprisals against the rebels, so he dreaded, and with far more reason, rash procedure in religious reaction. He wrote explicitly to his ambassadors, giving them instructions as to the advice meet for the Queen. The utmost that he would have allowed her was to have Mass in her chamber, admitting, of course, whom she would. It was to go back in fact to her practice of three years ago. 'Thus', he urged, 'she may gradually bring about a better state of things. . . . Not only must her chief care be for the kingdom's welfare but she must manage to make all her people understand that this is her only object. Let her be in all things what she ought to be, a good Englishwoman.'[23] The advice was unexceptionable, and it would have been well for Mary if it had been the last that the Emperor gave her. But she herself was always half Spaniard, and Charles was soon to do his best to nullify the counsel he had given.

At present the ambassadors were a strictly moderating influence, conveying advice of the old statesman, their master, most patient, most persistent of men, to a novice, a woman, and as Charles had cause to know, an enthusiast and a bungler. But Mary's conscience was a nervous horse to ride. Already she was fretting, fearing that it would be wrong to let Edward go to his grave without the solemn hallowing of the old ritual. She appealed to the Imperial ambassadors, as though they, coming from a Catholic country, alone possessed a source of pure, untainted counsel.

The ambassadors, with the Emperor's injunctions in mind, replied by letter, firmly. They had heard in London that for her to give the late King Catholic burial would be to alarm all the tenderest feelings of the Protestant party. Although, they said, her scrupulosity and resolve to allow no wordly considerations to deflect her from the path of religion, and the true service of God was 'a state of mind . . . most holy, and in which it is necessary to persevere to the end for salvation's sake' yet here, for peace and quiet's sake, she must not persevere in it.[24] The upshot of the matter was that the Queen accepted a compromise suggested by Renard. The late King was buried in Westminster

Abbey, 'with small ceremony', the Imperial ambassador thought, but still with banners, singing children, horses 'trapped with velvet down to the ground' and the body carried in a chariot covered in cloth of gold. Over the dead boy, Archbishop Cranmer read the English funeral service. But in the ancient chapel of the White Tower the Queen and her ladies listened to the Requiem Mass of the old church.[25] Everyone knew that it was so, and knew also that she heard Mass every day. So she had done for years, and in the teeth of danger.

She did not, however, at this time, wish to force others. At Newhall, when she had told Renard her intentions as to Edward's funeral, she had gone on, in a rambling way, from that to the whole question of religion. Renard thought her confused remarks worth recording for the Emperor's perusal; and so they were, for Mary was letting him see straight into her mind. She told him first, and this she said she would tell the Council, that religion had been changed since her father's death simply because the Protector would have it so. Then she said that she wished to force no one to go to Mass, but meant to see that those who wanted to go should be free to do so, and soon she would make public proclamation of her intentions. She spoke of the Council; they would not object, she said, and she let Renard see that little she cared if they did, for already she had begun to take the measure of the Lords, and was already disgusted with their divisions, with their accusations, counter-accusations, and excuses for their late treason. She showed him too that she was quite sure of the loyalty of the great mass of the people, on whose shoulders she had been borne to the throne; she believed that many of these had been misled, or frightened into the new ways; but she hoped with confidence that all would return, because such was the merciful will of God.

From all this two things must have been clear to Renard, as they are clear to us. She believed firmly that English Protestantism was no more than the temporary aberration of a few, and she intended to use no compulsion against those who differed from her in religion.[26]

That startling intention she solemnly announced to the Council on August 12th in a declaration which she bade them publish, a declaration 'uttered unto them by the Queen's own mouth . . . which was that, albeit her Grace's conscience is stayed in matters of religion, yet she meaneth graciously not to compel or constrain other men's consciences, otherwise than God shall (she trusteth) put into their hearts a persuasion of the truth that she is in, through the opening of his word unto them by godly, virtuous, and learned preachers'.[27]

Such were Mary's words, spoken at what must have been one of her first Council meetings. She spoke deliberately and solemnly, and she was a woman accustomed to say what she meant. It was a policy as strange and unprecedented as the mercy accorded to rebels, but in those first days of her reign, when, because it was the work of God, nothing she hoped seemed impossible, she felt as little fear, and as little of the hate that fear breeds, for the Protestants, as she had felt for Northumberland and his tools.

In hoping for reconciliation she totally mistook the temper of the Protestant

party. Did she totally mistake its numbers? Just how widespread was Protestantism? How deeply was it rooted and grounded in the hearts even of those
who had acquiesced in the religious changes?

These were the questions that perplexed many minds at the time, and
received many answers. Each side–Catholic and Protestant–was frequently
appalled, to the pitch of despair, by the numerical strength of the enemy, and
it is hard for us now to judge the validity of their fears. London was, by nearly
all foreign observers, judged to be riddled with heresy, yet when the Queen
first came to the city an Italian saw how the little images of the Virgin or of
Saints, which had been kept carefully hidden away, were set up again in many
and many a window.[28] Nor must it be forgotten that many of the most
earnest, or at least most vocal, Protestants were not Englishmen at all, but
French, Dutch, even Polish refugees. These, and the effects of their influence,
were to be found largely in the Eastern Counties where trade kept people in
touch with the Netherlands and Germany; or in Kent and Sussex which lay
across the main routes between France and London. The North and North-
West were, and for years yet continued, almost solid for Catholicism, but, as
Professor Pollard says 'it was not there that sixteenth century governments
were made or marred'. The South-West, which had risen in 1549 against the
Prayer Book, was soon to be an anxiety to the Catholic Queen, under one of
the new generation of Protestants; but the trouble was not religion, it was the
Queen's marriage.

Mary hoped, when she spoke to the Council on August 12th that it only
needed persuasion to turn the hearts of the opponents of the old ways. But
already that history of violence and disorder had begun which was to contradict all her hopes and force her to use methods the opposite of what she
intended. On August 11th a priest, an old man, impatient perhaps with the
impatience of age that dare not be content to wait, had celebrated Mass at
St. Bartholomew's. Though this was still clean against the law, it was obviously not against the Queen's intentions, but when he had finished, the people
set on him and he nearly lost his life.

That was on a Friday. On Sunday at Paul's Cross Gilbert Bourne, Bishop
Bonner's chaplain, preached; from the same pulpit last week a Protestant
had been free to preach. Below, in the churchyard, among the graves, was a
crowd largely composed of young folks, apprentices, citizens' wives, and
maid-servants. In the galleries facing the preacher were the greater personages
–the Lord Mayor, Bishop Bonner, Lord Courtenay and his mother among
them. Bourne must, during the past few days, have seen the welcome that the
Bishop of London got from the people; on his way from the Marshalsea
prison everyone had cried out welcome to him until he 'came to St. Paul's
and knelt on the steps and said his prayers, and then all the people rang the
bells for joy'. It was therefore not unnatural that his chaplain should remind
the congregation of the years of imprisonment the old Bishop had suffered,
for a sermon delivered in this same place. But at the Cross, whether by acci-
dent or arrangement, was no such crowd as that which had welcomed the old

Bishop. A murmuring arose; someone cried out that the Bishop had preached an abomination; others 'made a hallowing . . . "thou lyest", and others shouted "Pull him out! Pull him out!"' meaning the unlucky Bourne. Then began 'a great uproar and shouting at his sermon, as it were like mad people . . . as hurly burly and casting up of caps'. Some of those near the preacher, not content with making a noise, began to climb up the pulpit. Bourne stepped back and found beside him Bradford and John Rogers, both well-known Protestant preachers, who cried out above the din, 'For Christ's sake and for the love of Christ to be quiet again.' But even while they spoke some-one threw a dagger which hit a side-post of the pulpit with such force that it 'rebounded back a great way'. At last, but not without difficulty, Rogers and Bradford got Bourne from the pulpit and into the school-house. From there Courtenay, the Marchioness of Exeter, and Bonner hurried him through the Cathedral to safety. Meanwhile the Lord Mayor and aldermen went about the churchyard trying to break up the crowd and send folk to their houses, but for long they would not go, still crying 'Kill him! Kill him!' Such was the first challenge of the London crowd to the Queen's religion.[29]

Nor was this hooligan behaviour the only sign that there was a tussle before her. Before she had come to London several preachers, 'Scotsmen in particular', had preached what Renard considered 'scandalous things' in an effort to rouse up the people, 'going so far as to say that men should see Antichrist come to life, and popery in the land'. This, the attack of the com-missioned officers of the Protestant army, had not slackened. Before the middle of August the Queen herself complained to Renard that there were preachers who 'used scandalous and seditious propositions against religion and against her person'.[30]

Over the heads of the attacking force came also, like a flight of arrows, the first of those paper darts which were to fly so thickly in a few months more. A leaflet was scattered about the city: it lay on doorsteps, it blew about among the filth and litter of the streets; anyone might read it, but it was addressed to 'Nobles and gentlemen favouring the word of God! Take counsel together', it urged, 'and join with all your power and your following. Withdraw your-selves from our virtuous Queen Mary because Rochester, Englefield, Weston, and Hastings, hardened and detestable papists all, follow the opinions of the said Queen. . . . But Winchester, the great devil, must be exorcised and ex-terminated with his disciples . . . before he can poison the people and wax strong in his religion.'[31]

Against such attacks the Queen and her Council must take action. They did so promptly, yet not with undue severity, considering the importance of the weekly sermon at Paul's, and the greatness of the uproar there; considering also that the Queen was not yet crowned, that Northumberland was still alive, and that some people were even beginning to say it would be better to have him back than to have changes in religion.

The Lord Mayor and aldermen were first called up to appear before the Council in the Tower. They were then given orders to call up the common

council of the city 'wherein to charge every householder within their liber-
ties to keep his children, apprentices, and other servants in such order and awe
as they follow their work of week days and keep their parish churches of
holyday'. Thus the young and headstrong, apprentices, servants, and poor
men whose heads were ringing with such war-cries as that lately posted up on
placards about the town—'*vox populi*—*vox dei*'—such people should be kept
from the heady wine of religious controversy.

Seditious preachers were dealt with too; every alderman was bidden to
send word to all parishes in his ward that no person should preach 'or make
any open or solemn reading of Scripture, or let any other preach in his pulpit,
except those specially licensed by the Queen'.

The Lord Mayor was given till Wednesday to make up his mind as to
whether he could keep the city quiet—if he felt unable to do so he must then
yield up the sword of his office to the Queen. But the Lord Mayor and
aldermen preferred to obey the orders they had to arrest five or six of
the authors of the riot 'as nigh as they can', and were active in the business.
Three men were committed on August 16th, and Bradford, Veron, and
Becon next day as seditious preachers, while Rogers was ordered to keep his
house.[32]

Two days later a proclamation was published. It was still mild in tone, but
less so than the Queen's first personal declaration to the Council. Mary was
already beginning to realize, as she confessed to Renard, that the re-establishment of her religion would be a difficult thing to accomplish. But, she said,
her conscience would not let her rest without trying. She had told Renard
on the 16th, and the proclamation repeated it in statelier words, that 'she had
so far no better way than to leave each one free as to the religion he would
follow; if some desired to abide by the settlement of the late King her father,
let them do so; if some held to the old, and others to the new, they should not
be interfered with or constrained to follow any other course until the coming
Parliament' should decide things by law. As to her own doings, the proclamation declared with some dignity that the Queen 'cannot now hide that
religion, which God and the world knoweth she hath ever possessed from
her infancy hitherto, which, as her majesty is minded to observe and maintain for herself by God's grace, during her time, so doth her highness much
desire, and would be glad the same were of all her subjects quietly and
charitably embraced'.[33]

The wish, pathetic in its impossibility of fulfilment, reads like Mary's own
contribution to the proclamation. So too does the exhortation to her subjects
to leave 'those new-found devilish terms of papist or heretic, and such like,
and, applying their whole care, study, and travail to live in the fear of God,
exercising their conversations in such charitable and godly doing, as their
lives may indeed express that great hunger and thirst of God's word, which,
by rash talk and words, many have pretended'. Such words might well be
spoken by a simple and devout woman, her eyes fixed, in the woman's way,
upon individuals, her mind full of dreams of a world in which men and

women lived together in charity. But these were 'dreams out of the ivory gate and visions before midnight'.

Finally, deserting the ideal for the real, the proclamation dealt with immediate things, again prohibiting unlicensed preaching, because 'it is well known that sedition and false rumours have been nourished and maintained in this realm by the subtlety and malice of some evil disposed persons which take upon them, without sufficient authority, to preach and to interpret the word of God after their own brain'. As well as unlicensed preaching, 'the playing of interludes, and printing of false-bound books, ballads, rhymes, and other lewd treatises in the English tongue, concerning doctrine in matters now in question', were forbidden. In all this the Queen and Council did no more, did indeed precisely the same in the Catholic sense as had been done in the Protestant during the reign of Edward.

So, for the moment the matter stood. Next Sunday, with the Marquis of Winchester, the Earl of Bedford, the Earl of Pembroke, and Lords Rich and Wentworth to hear and to see, Watson, Gardiner's chaplain, preached at Paul's Cross by the Queen's order. In addition to the group of great nobles of the Council, Sir Harry Jerningham, Captain of the Queen's guard, attended the sermon with 200 of his men, and lest that should not be enough, the city companies stood all the service through in their liveries and hoods, to watch order. The sermon, dealing with the 'obedience of subjects and what erroneous sects are reigning in this realm by false preachers and teachers . . . was quietly ended without any tumult', and was, so it was hoped 'to the godly edifying of the audience'.[34] But the congregation must have been largely composed of keepers of order.

These measures, and perhaps also the Duke of Northumberland's recantation, just now joyfully published by the Council, were as a bucket of cold water upon popular Protestant excitement. There was a lull in the disturbances. Vespers were sung publicly at St. Paul's; there was no commotion. Bonner celebrated Mass there with the organ playing; all was quiet. There was Mass at 'St. Nicholas Colabey goodly sung in Latin, and tapers set on the altar, and a cross', all this 'not by commandment but of the people's devotion'; no one wagged a finger. The first attack of the Protestant party had fallen back defeated. The Catholics, illegally as far as Parliamentary laws went, but legally according to the proclamation – and law-making by proclamation had become a commonplace in Edward's reign – celebrated their services in London, Worcester, Kingston, Oxford and Cambridge, even in Canterbury; doubtless also in many other parish churches all over England. A feeling was abroad that the tide had turned; it showed itself in a rumour which even Gardiner, newly made Chancellor, believed, that Archbishop Cranmer, Primate of England, Henry's Archbishop, Edward's Archbishop, had offered to sing Mass before the Queen. Even on September 6th Bishop Bonner was writing, with cheerful jocularity, of Cranmer's submissive behaviour.[35]

Before another week was out London was buzzing with excitement over a declaration by the same Archbishop. In this he denied utterly ever having made the rumoured surrender, and offered an open challenge in his own name and that of the Italian Protestant Peter Martyr, to defend the Communion service of the English Prayer Book, and to show 'that the Mass in many things has no foundation of Christ, the Apostles, or the Primitive Church, but is manifest contrary to the same, and contains many horrid blasphemies'.

A little more than a year ago Cranmer had been disgusted with the '[vain]-glorious and unquiet spirits which can like nothing but what is after their own fancy, and cease not to make trouble and disquietness when things be most quiet and in good order'. These men, questioning and debating, when the Second Prayer Book was making, as to whether a Christian man should sit, stand, or kneel at the Sacrament, had roused to wrath the temperate Archbishop. These men, of whom were John Knox and his friends, believed that nothing should be done which was not commanded in the Bible, a doctrine which Cranmer had declared with heat was 'untrue, and not only untrue, but also seditious and perilous to be heard of any subjects, as a thing breaking the bridle of obedience and loosing them from the bond of all princes' laws'.[36] Now, Cranmer, and others like him, who would have adjusted the doctrine of the Church of England to a delicate philosophical balance between extremes, must make common cause with such extremists because of a common fear which for the time united them. Above all Protestant differences loomed the shadow of the Mass, a symbol for them, as much as for their opponents, containing as it did an affirmation of the mediatory office of the priest, and a ritual, which, to their craving for simplicity, was repulsive, blasphemous and ludicrous. Against the Mass, all Protestants must fight.

Here then, neither from legionary nor centurion, but from a great proconsul, came a challenge which the Queen and her Council must accept or refuse. They accepted it, but in justice to them it must be admitted that the quarrel was none of their seeking. It was the Protestant party, which by the violence of the rabble, by sermons from their preachers, and now by a formal declaration from the Primate of the Church showed that they would not allow any return, even though coupled with toleration, to the old ways of the Church. The Queen had said, the Parliament might say, that there should be Mass. But the Protestant party had delivered its ultimatum–No Mass. This was not the passive resistance recommended by a few men such as Pilkington. It was open war.

Yet the Queen and Council, who had shown such a definite unwillingness to proscribe traitors, had till now used much moderation against these adversaries also. Cranmer, who had been a partaker in Northumberland's treason, had not, it is true, received any cordial welcome from the Queen when he came to Court in August. But till the middle of September he was free and safe. About the end of August he had been summoned before a commission, but no questions were asked of his acts or beliefs–he was only ordered to

provide an inventory of his goods. It is possible that the intention of the
Government was to retire him on a pension.[37] Only after his challenge did he
find himself in prison.

Bishop Hooper and Coverdale Bishop of Exeter, had already been summoned to London by the Council and on their appearance had been lodged
in the Fleet, on no charge of heresy but on one of debt to the Crown. It was not
unnatural, that all the tinder being so dry, the Council thought such a firebrand
as Hooper best out of the way. Yet they seem also to have wished that he,
and many others like him, would remove their troublesome persons out of
the realm, following the example of many Protestants who had already fled
abroad. Hooper was not arrested, but summoned to come to the Council, and
thus given an opportunity of escape which his friends urged him to take;
Rogers was for five months not imprisoned but only confined to his house;
Latimer received his summons to the Council by a pursuivant who candidly
confessed that he was bidden not to tarry for him; even Foxe deduces from
this that the intention of the Council was that the Bishop should escape,
though for that intention he does not give the devil his due. It was perhaps
by chance, that on the day of the Queen's coronation, the Tower itself was
left open and unguarded, so that any of the prisoners could have made off;
but not all the opportunities of escape thrust at prominent Protestants can
have been accidental.[38] Many took the chance; of the Bishops, Bale, Scory
and perhaps Ponet had fled, and as early as August Protestant preachers were
recommending from the pulpit a general exodus.[39]

It was the same with the foreign Protestants. Hardly had the gate of the
Tower closed behind Cranmer, than his friend Peter Martyr, who had perhaps been the chief mover in that defiant challenge which had put the Archbishop there, was asking for his passports; they were granted him without
difficulty. A colony of Lutheran weavers, settled by Somerset at Glastonbury,
left England without hindrance; Laski, the Pole, with his foreign congregation, chose to go, and went freely. The Mayors of Dover and Rye were
ordered to let all Frenchmen pass out of the country unless individuals were
excepted.[40] Gardiner, indeed, made it almost a game, the rules of which he
explained to Renard. He would begin, he said, by summoning the undesired
alien to come to the Chancellor's house. If that did not dislodge him, the
next step was to let him know, if he were a Frenchman, that the King of
France, if a Netherlander, that the Emperor, was about to demand his extra-
dition. This last, said Gardiner, never failed.[41] There is no room for doubt that
the Government in these early days much preferred the room to the company
of the Protestant leaders.

But the first two months of Mary's reign must have left her puzzled, hurt,
and disappointed. She had ridden into London with people weeping for joy
about her. Now she was preparing for her coronation, and already there were
fears that as she rode through London this time there might be a tumult or
attack.[42] In the Council, and among her own ladies, she was finding troubles
enough. Already her old servants and the faithful Catholics in the Council

were offended because so many traitors sat with them at the Council Board. Derby, who had brought fifteen thousand men to help the Queen, said to Scheyfve that trouble might well come from this discontent. For himself, he said, it did not matter, he did not need office, but others, lesser men he meant, might be driven into opposition by such treatment.[43] Even the Queen's confidential ladies were not to be trusted, but were making a pretty penny out of bribes from suitors to the Queen.[44]

Nor were the ex-traitors grateful to have escaped with whole skins. Fines had taken the place of executions; fines were of much more use to the empty exchequer; but when the money had been paid, a resentful traitor remained, and while the axe lay unused folk began to forget their awe of Kings, till, said Renard they 'have come to judge [the Queen's actions] so freely that they go so far as to laugh at them'.[45]

It must have been with a heavy heart and growing misgivings that Mary prepared for her coronation, though even now she had only to make it known that she was determined to pay Edward VI's and even her father's debts, to win sudden popularity among the horde of old servitors, officers, captains, and soldiers who had forgotten even to hope for their arrears; she had only to declare that she would remit the third part of a subsidy still unpaid, to have people shouting 'Long live the Queen–Long may she prosper!'

But as well as such troubles and uncertainties Mary was beset by scruples that must be kept secret from almost all. For her, to be anointed with chrism hallowed in England, was to fear that she was not anointed at all. So she sent a message secretly to Granvelle, asking him to let her have some from Flanders.[46] Then, a greater difficulty yet–she and the whole kingdom and every Bishop in it were under the ban of the Pope. She sent with the utmost secrecy to Rome, asking that she and they should be absolved.

She feared also that something might be introduced into the coronation service which would prohibit her from restoring the old ways; therefore she intended, she told Renard, herself to add words to the old form, so that whereas she should have sworn to rule by 'the laws of England', she would now swear to 'the just and licit laws'.[47]

To add to her anxieties there was even talk in the Council, most sinister it seemed to the Queen, of summoning Parliament first, and putting off her coronation till this had sat, so that, as Gardiner argued, Parliament should make her title sure, by repealing both the Act which had bastardized her, and the will of Edward VI. That was what he said, but the Queen smelt danger in the fact that it was the Protestants in the Council who backed him up. She feared that the object of the suggestion was rather to leave her with a title dependent on the sanction of Parliament, and to bridle her so that she could not change the religion of Edward's settlement. On these terms she would have none of the idea, and she got her way; but she must have realized on what shifting sands her feet were set.[48]

Yet, in spite of all, the coronation went off well. Even 'hot Gospellers' liked a show, and London had been dressing itself for the ceremony for three weeks beforehand. On September 25th the Queen moved from St. James's – the quiet hunting lodge between the deer park and the open country – to Whitehall, and thence came by barge to the Tower, with all the crafts of London, and the Mayor and aldermen, in barges gay with coloured streamers, and on deck minstrels making their music louder and louder, like canaries, against the din of the guns.[49]

Three days later she came again from the Tower, this time riding through the streets to her crowning in a 'chariot of tissue, drawn with 6 horses, all betrapped with red velvet. She sat in a gown of blue velvet, furred with powdered ermine, having on her head a caul of cloth of tinsel beset with pearl and stone and about the same . . . a round circle of gold, much like a hooped garland . . . the said caul and circle being so massy and ponderous that she was fain to bear up her head with her hands.'[50] But the crown itself was to prove far heavier.

All the way there were crowds and pageants. The Florentines, an ingenious people with a long experience of shows, had produced a notable edifice on the top of which stood the figure of an angel all in green, which by a mechanical device lifted a trumpet to its lips whenever a trumpeter within the covered car blew a blast, so that the angel itself seemed to blow the instrument, 'to the great marvelling of ignorant persons'.[51] At Ludgate, newly repaired, painted, and richly hung, there were minstrels playing and singing. At Paul's Churchyard the Queen 'stood long' looking at the pageant there, 'make all of rosemary with all her arms and a crown in the midst'; [52] and there also, seated under a vine, his playing children with him, was an old friend of hers, John Heywood, one of the old-fashioned Catholics, relative by marriage of Sir Thomas More, a witty man and writer of merry plays against Friars and monks. So she moved on over strawed grass and flowers to the palace of Whitehall.

Next day was the coronation itself. She passed to the Abbey down a railed way carpeted with blue. Inside, on a high stage, she received the orb, and two sceptres as both King and Queen, was girt with the sword, and had the spurs bound on her heels.

These would have been strange ceremonies for any woman – they were stranger still for a woman like Mary, who, a few days before, had both shocked and touched her Council's feelings by falling on her knees before them, and speaking to them, very earnest and troubled, of the duties of Kings and Queens, and how she was determined to acquit herself in the task God had been pleased to lay before her, to his greater glory and service, to the public good, and all her subjects' benefit. She had, she told them, entrusted her affairs and person to them, so now she would adjure them to do their duty, as by their oaths they were bound to do. Especially she appealed to Gardiner, her Chancellor, reminding him that he had on his conscience the administration of justice.[53] It was not an ordinary thing for a sovereign of England to kneel before the Council, to show human fear of the burden of royalty, and to beg for their help because she and they were there to serve God together. But it was not ordinary that the crown of England should be on the head of a woman, and a woman painstaking, honest, and above all things conscientious, but woefully and consciously unable to grapple with the problems before her; a woman who, though she was prepared to be stubborn on certain occasions, fully agreed with the general verdict that a female had no skill in matters of state and needed the help and guidance of men, of a Council, better still of a husband.

The coronation ceremonies, beginning at ten in the morning, lasted till well on in the afternoon; at the end the Queen went to her dinner in Westminster Hall, carrying the sceptre in one hand and nervously twirling and turning the orb in the other as she walked. With all the old state and ceremony the banquet was served; the Champion rode up and down the Hall challenging any to question her right; about the Queen stood the great nobles, her officers, splendid in glowing colour, or gleaming in cloth of gold and silver, or sombre in that black velvet which was so dear to Renaissance taste. The candles were already lit, and the October dusk had come before the Queen left Westminster Hall and went down to her barge on the darkening river.[54]

Four days later, after the ancient Mass of the Holy Ghost had been sung at St. Margaret's, the Queen and Council, with 'all the trumpeters a-blowing before all' went to open her first Parliament—the Parliament which for her was to be, or so she hoped, the means by which many old wrongs should be righted. If it was a packed Parliament, that was no more than might be expected after any Tudor election, but probably there was on this occasion as little need of manipulation as there could be, for when the summons went out the country was still carried on a high tide of loyal enthusiasm, because the lawful succession had not been broken. But in addition to that, moderate men, or old-fashioned men, all through the country, though they had conformed to the religious prescriptions of the Protestants, looked forward now with equanimity or mild approval, if no more than that, to a return to the orderly ceremony of their younger days; to a service book that was not declared to be inspired by God in one year, and to need radical alteration three years later; above all to a settlement of religion which should act as a sedative upon the too lively brains and tongues of the restless, discontented poor commons. The elected members doubtless expected, most of them, that their work would be to set back the clock to the last days of Henry VIII, who had taught them that it was perfectly possible to be rigidly orthodox in belief and yet to keep the gates fast barred against the Pope. Confident of this, the country gentlemen mounted their horses and rode out from under their half-timbered gatehouses, through the pale reaped fields towards London. Even those whose houses and lands not long ago had belonged to tonsured monks, can have had few qualms.

At the opening of Parliament they found that the Queen's plans reached much farther than they had expected; that she was in fact determined on 'going as far as the Pope's authority'. It was a surprise to them. Even Renard had only known it for a month, and he had learnt it with no small dismay, for this, he well knew, would rouse to a fever of apprehension every possessor of Church lands.[55] Emphatically the ambassadors wrote home that the Pope must be made to reflect how 'the question of Papal authority is odious', and not in England only, and that patience and caution in this matter were essential. The Imperial ambassadors were not the only ones to advise Mary of the danger of her intended course; the English ambassador in Venice spoke for many when he urged the Council 'to warn the Queen not to be too fervent a Papist'.[56]

How far did Mary's wisest counsellor agree with her in this rash venture? What did Gardiner think of the measure which was, to Mary's loyal, uncompromising mind, the obvious necessity, the only means by which England could be restored to itself after a period of madness, and be again the country of her childhood?

Gardiner in the old days had written urgently in the opposite sense; the tract expounding his arguments, his *De Vera Obedientia* was soon to be seized on with malicious joy by a Protestant enemy abroad, and served up for England to digest with a *sauce piquante* of question and comment, to show how 'my Lord Doctor Doubleface' had changed his front. It was a legitimate weapon to use, and one not easy to parry; yet, on the other hand, no statesman is worth his salt if he dare not learn from experience, and change his mind. '*De Vera Obedientia*' had been written eighteen years ago; Gardiner, in common with others of his generation, had seen harvested some of the fruits of Henry's experiment, and was inclined to judge accordingly the tree on which they grew. It is very possible, though he may have doubted the wisdom of Mary's eagerness and deplored her tactics, though he may have spoken the truth when he declared that in this 'the Queen went before him',[57] that on the whole he concurred with her belief that the English Church must be no longer cut off from the Catholic Church abroad.

In his speech at the opening of Parliament the Chancellor declared to the Houses the Queen's intention of submission to the Pope. But that was, for the moment, all. No action was yet taken to effect it. The Queen apologized for this to Reginald Pole in a letter, telling him that she dared not yet show 'the intent of her heart in this matter'.[58]

The first work of Parliament was one of mercy. All the offences newly erected into treason and felonies, by laws passed in her father's and her brother's reign, were reduced to their old moderate proportions. Nothing was to be treason, but what had been made so by the old Statute of Edward III; nothing felony but what Henry VIII had found so when he came to the throne. The recent extension of the Statute of Praemunire went the same way; clergy as well as laity might breathe more freely in this new reign. In the second session the same conservatism was manifest. The Queen's title was vindicated from 'the corrupt and unlawful sentence' which had divorced her father and mother, and from the subsequent laws, which, as Parliament

said, had confirmed 'the illegitimation of your most noble person, as if it
were possible'.

But in the Bill reversing the divorce decree, one very important omission
had been made. The Commons ignored entirely the Pope's Bull which had
given judgement in the case. The result was that they left the Queen, though
unwilling, still Head of the Church. She had tried to shake the mantle of that
dignity from her shoulders, and the Lords had been willing to reduce her
title by annulling all legislation dating back to one year before the Statute
which had bastardized her; this would have tacitly annulled the Acts which
dealt with religion and the Pope's authority. But the Commons were too
wide-awake, or too obstinate, and among them the core of the resistance
was to be found in the holders of abbey lands. The agitation amounted almost
to a plot; it was made a matter for bargaining with the Queen; she should
have the divorce repealed only if she would forego the restitution of Papal
supremacy.

The Queen was disappointed, and also troubled in her conscience. Renard,
patient, astute, entirely practical, tried to persuade her that the wisest course
was to wait until the next session of Parliament to make a second attempt.
At that, she said that he must prepare for her a written argument for the persuasion of Parliament. Eight arguments he promised her, and wrote of the
effort to his master with a wry smile. 'I realise, sire,' he said, 'that she will
want me to play the part of a counsellor in matters theological, which I have
never studied nor professed, and on obscure and knotty points that would
require a better head than mine. However, as I see that people over here are
no sharper than other folk, I am waxing bolder in my efforts to obey her
orders.'[59]

Apart from this reservation of their cherished Royal Supremacy, Parliament gave the Queen what she wanted, though it was only after a week's
'marvellous dispute' that the Acts of Edward's reign dealing with the Prayer
Book, the sacraments, and married priests, were repealed. It was also enacted
that, after December 20th next, no other service should be used in England
other than those which had been in use in the last year of Henry VIII. It was
to this that the Commons looked back, as to a golden age, ignoring the years
of Henry's reign which lay before his attack on the Church, and abandoning,
as doubtless Mary herself did by this time, her brief dream of toleration with
persuasion.

But the restoration of even such a measure of stability was to be no easy
thing. Thick and threefold came the troubles in London and in the country.
The great disputation of the Doctors of 'the new sort and the old', arranged
to take place in October, in a forlorn hope of securing some sort of accord,
had broken down into a mere wrangle. The Queen had given permission that
all might speak freely, and the dispute was open to the public, the nobles
standing near, the people farther off. But this conference, arranged with the
same motives as Catherine de Medici's Colloquy of Poissy, was also as fruitless. Weston, the prolocutor, 'that had some impediment in his speech but

was otherwise a bold man' complained, not without reason, that they had
spent two days quarrelling 'over one only doctor, and one only word', so that
it is little wonder, that though 'there came much people . . . they were never
the wiser'. No agreement was reached, and nothing had been gained in
charity or mutual understanding.[60]

Besides these argumentative encounters, there were fresh instances of
violence against those professing the old ways. A merchant of London, a man
of substance, attacked a preacher who had declared that the new religion
meant the damnation of souls. Another preacher was heckled and hustled
for a sermon on the Real Presence. In the country there were stirrings too.
Loyal Norfolk produced a petition signed by 100 persons; its bearer was
pilloried. Kent sent up another petition. Leicestershire, where Suffolk's lands
lay, was restless.[61] Part of the unrest was religious, but some of the offenders
got themselves into trouble for pulling down the hedge of an enclosure.
Everywhere there was grumbling and discontent, hard for any, then or now,
to diagnose whether as a result of high prices or of the restored Mass. England
was ill at ease, turning in a sort of half sleep, and thrashing out at anything,
first this, then that, not knowing clearly what it was that galled.

On the day that Parliament rose, a dead dog with a shaven crown and a
rope round its neck was slung through the windows of the Queen's presence
chamber.[62] It was the first thing which stirred the Queen's temper to open
resentment, but in its brutal and insulting jocularity it was something harder
for her to bear than anything that had gone before. She told Parliament
before dissolution that she would be forced to use methods other than
clemency. This was the first note of warning, and it was to be dreadfully
fulfilled. But it is just to the Queen to remember that till now clemency had
most undoubtedly been used.

So Mary's first Parliament closed, but the disagreement between Queen
and the Commons on the subject of the Papal Supremacy was not the only
nor the worst unhealed quarrel between them. This, if not inflamed by
another, might have been accommodated. But the Commons by this time
knew that the Queen was determined upon a foreign, upon a Spanish marriage. That was to introduce poison into the relations of Queen and people.

A shower of pamphlets also began to descend, or rather to blow across the
Channel. Besides the *rechauffé* of Gardiner's tract, there were 'An Admonition
to the Bishops of Winchester, London and others', 'Whether the Christian
faith may be kept secret in the heart without confession thereof openly to the
world' and 'The Communication between the Lord Chancellor and Judge
Hales'. The latter indeed arose from a sad tale. Judge Hales, that upright and
inflexible man, had been the only Justice to refuse to sign King Edward's
will. But since the Queen's accession he had continued, with strict legality,
to enforce King Edward's laws against the old religion. He was sent for,
examined by Gardiner, and imprisoned. He recanted, then tried to commit
suicide and failed. He was set free; he tried again to kill himself and succeeded. It was a real stricture upon the Government that a man so loyal and

so just should have been driven to such an act. But from Gardiner's point of view, Hales's very qualities made him worth attempting as a convert.

This is by the way. The noticeable thing about these tracts is, first, that they all appeared before the end of October, while still no blood had been shed, no compulsion put upon those who still clung to the English service. Disturbers of the peace, or active adversaries of the Queen's religion might find themselves in prison, but that was all. Secondly the matter of these pamphlets was no restrained logical argument or demonstration, but stuff hot and hot, denunciation, mockery, abuse. So, Gardiner was 'now Lord Chancellor and common cut-throat of England', though up to now no throats had been cut. The fire-breathing productions were indeed, as has been said, part of a 'systematic plan of attack . . . conducted by an able and resolute adversary'. The Protestant party was the adversary, which, to the Queen's appeal for peace, answered with Jehu, 'What hast thou to do with peace?'

Chapter XIII

I N order to look at the question of 'the Queen's marriage' with the eyes
of the sixteenth century, we of today must forget our own knowledge
of two great reigns. Our historical experience of Queens must exclude
both Elizabeth and Victoria, and remember only the unfortunate
Matilda. If, in 1553, a man looked from English history to the history of
other nations, there was, apart from the recent fame of Isabella of Spain,
only the occasional spectacle of a widowed Queen-Mother, struggling against
factious nobles for the sake of her son. Till the last few years there had been
no queens regnant. Yet the phenomenon, so strange and disconcerting,
became, after the middle of the century, suddenly common. In England at
the death of Edward VI there were seven heirs to the throne; but all of them
were women. One of these had already, in 1553, been, for ten years of
minority, Queen of Scots. Two had been simultaneously proclaimed Queen
of England; of these one now held the crown. To her a half-sister was to
succeed, who would show what a Queen could be.

At the moment, however, no one expected a woman to rule for herself.
Everyone took it as a matter of course that the new Queen of England would
marry. Only Cardinal Pole and the aged Friar Peto believed and said openly
that the Queen ought to remain a virgin and leave the future with God. Pole,
warned by the Pope, did not express his opinion to Mary herself, but Peto
wrote urging it, and reinforcing his counsel with arguments both theological
and practical.[1] No other counsellor gave her such advice; all urged marriage
on her, and for two reasons – because it needed a stronger hand than hers to
hold steady the rudder of the ship of state, and because there might spring
from her marriage a male heir to set at rest all doubts as to the future.

The first of these arguments, grounded as it was both upon the universal
estimation of women and upon the character of the Queen, was hard to
answer. Mary was no woman to play the Lords of the Council one against
the other; not even a woman to choose one wise man among them, and, relying entirely on his advice, to throw into the scales in his favour all the weight
of her royal prestige. For the first her incapacity and honesty alike unfitted
her; for the second it was again a question of incapacity, for Mary found it
well nigh impossible finally to make up her mind to any course. She would
believe her mind made up, but a tactful and persistent pleader would set her
doubting, hesitating, reconsidering. Besides all this, it is hardly possible to
imagine the harassed delicate woman, who in the first fortnight of her reign
found such a mass of business to transact that she said she did not know where
to begin, for long bearing alone the burden of that crushing weight.

Apart from the woman's need of a helpmate, the second argument in favour of her marriage – that an heir might be born – was far less cogent than the first. Mary was thirty-seven, an age for those days almost ludicrously past the usual age for a first marriage. She had also for years been constantly in ill health. Every autumn she was liable to bouts of illness; she had lost many teeth; she suffered from indigestion, and from racking headaches. Mental strain, and certainly she had had enough of that, was perhaps responsible, rather than physical defect, for the amenorrhoea from which she suffered, and from which she found relief in hysterical crying fits.[2] When, in the summer of 1549 the Council first forbade her to use the Mass, she spoke to them in a letter of 'the short time she had to live'.[3] The expression may be partly accounted for by agitation and unhappiness, but it would have come strangely from the pen of an ordinarily healthy woman of thirty-three.

Was it likely that such a woman, whose mother moreover had in her youth and prime borne only one child to survive infancy; whose father in six marriages begot only herself, with her frail constitution, her sister, and a boy who had died at sixteen, riddled with disease – was it likely that she, at close on forty years old, should bear a healthy child? It was almost unthinkable, and had others besides Pole counselled her not to marry, Mary might have been spared much sorrow. But the advice of her counsellors told with Mary in the same direction as a fear, and a hope which swayed the Queen herself. The fear was that the Protestant Elizabeth, heir to the throne both by Henry's will and universal estimation, would succeed her; and Elizabeth was always, for Mary, the daughter of Anne Boleyn. The hope was that as God had wrought a miracle to set her on the throne, he would as miraculously perfect his work by giving her a son to make safe the restoration of the old Church.

At the outset of her reign Mary had, in the fullness of her heart, received Elizabeth with affection. But the question of the Mass had broken the brief concord. The Queen, whose conscience would not suffer her to leave her half-sister in danger of damnation, would have Elizabeth to her chamber and argue and expound for hours at a time. When that took no effect she began to show her displeasure.[4] Elizabeth was not slow to apprehend either the Queen's altered demeanour or its reason. She begged for a private audience. It was granted, and they met in a gallery with a half-door between them, and behind each, her ladies. Elizabeth fell on her knees, shed tears, asked for more instruction, pleaded with truth that she had been taught from childhood the new religion only.[5] The Queen relented. Elizabeth shortly after experienced a conversion, and though she complained of stomach-ache, appeared at Mass for the first time on September 8th, though she would not, for some weeks yet, wear the jewels that her sister now showered on her.[6]

She gained little by her suppleness. There was, though Mary, conscientious woman, could not acknowledge it, ineradicable hate and injury between them. There may well have been jealousy too. If the Queen, confused and discouraged in the task to which she had set hand and heart, did not feel jealousy for the girl of twenty, poised, confident, subtle, 'a creature full of beguilement' as Renard warned his master, she was more than human. Elizabeth too had a knowledge of life beyond that of her elder sister whose reputation had never been blown upon; even if the girl's relations with Seymour had been regrettable, even if they had been scandalous, yet they had given her experience, and a good woman can regret things which she ought not.

Besides, there was the unbridgeable difference between their standards. This girl, brought up, as she confessed, in the new belief, had now, after a few weeks, and under pressure of mere argument, thrown them all overboard. It is not likely that Mary expected from Elizabeth or anyone else such loyalty to the newfangled notions, as she herself had given to the old; but the discrepancy was too glaring. If she realized the difference in temper which made it possible, the difference between their aims, and between the things which each counted of prime importance, it cannot have improved her opinion of Elizabeth. It must have seemed to her monstrous that any woman should use a profession of religion as a counter in a game, making it a thing of convenience, while keeping, untouched and apart, her own private beliefs, at which anyone might guess and guess again. So Mary roundly declared that the surrender was hypocrisy, and pointed to Elizabeth's friends and household—heretics all. It would, she said—giving bitterness a mask of duty—be too heavy a burden on her conscience to let this girl succeed—a heretic, illegitimate, and only too much resembling her mother. Sometimes she would go so far as to say that she could see, in Elizabeth's features, a likeness to Mark Smeaton, the musician, who had been a very handsome man; the girl in fact was no half-sister of hers.[7]

It was the boiling up of all the misery and bitterness of the past, and it did Mary herself more harm than it did Elizabeth. For Mary, though she might hate her half-sister, could never bring herself to deal with her any way but gently; in danger it was always to the Queen that Elizabeth, with a just confidence, turned for help. But though she would not injure, Mary could not trust the girl, who besides being Anne Boleyn's daughter, was now the hope of all the enemies of Mary's religion and her Spanish kin. The Queen well knew that the French ambassador, the bold gamester de Noailles, intended to play Elizabeth as a card against all her Catholic and Spanish aims. She could not help but suspect, even though it might be unjustly, that Elizabeth would naturally lend herself to his game. Mary, with her strong loyalties, her loves and hates, must needs believe that the girl she hated, hated her. She could understand neither Elizabeth's colder, harder temper, nor that incomparably patient, amazingly cautious brain of hers. Neither trusting nor dealing decisively with Elizabeth, she laid up for herself a harvest of trouble. Had she unequivocally acknowledged her sister as her heir, in default of issue, the assurance of that succession might have contented for a time not only that extreme Protestant party which was to wreck all her plans, but also many moderate men whose chief grudge against her was to be the fear of a foreign King. There is some evidence that Protestants believed that the Queen's life would not last long; Peter Martyr, writing in November 1553 to Calvin, after forecasting trouble to come in England 'if Winchester . . . shall begin to rage according to his passion', hinted darkly that, even if it were so, 'it is the judgement of almost all men, that this calamity will not be of long continuance; who, in proportion to their wisdom, have no light reasons for entertaining an opinion to that effect'.[8] This sounds like a reference to the Queen's delicate health; if so, Protestants, and indeed all England, might have been content to wait for the accession of an English heir.

Renard saw the danger, and warned the Queen fairly that she must either make convincing pretence of affection, or shut Elizabeth in the Tower. Mary would not do the latter. After a long lecture from Renard she made up her mind to dissemble as well as she could. Elizabeth had asked for leave to withdraw from Court. The Queen had at first refused, but now consented, and said farewell with proper courtesy, even making a parting gift of a costly hood of sables. It was left to Renard to speak certain 'reasonable words' to the girl, warning her against putting trust in French promises. Paget and Arundel went further, and used what was almost a threat. If she intrigued with heretics they told her, or with Frenchmen, she would be sorry for it.[9] After this, Elizabeth, twenty years old, but already mistress of herself, cautious, secret, inscrutable, rode off, followed by her green and white liveried household, to keep Christmas at Ashridge.

The accession of Mary, daughter of hated Spain, had been a sad blow to the plans and hopes of Antoine de Noailles. Through the critical days of Jane's short reign, de Noailles's letters had shown, without dissimulation, to which of the two Queens he wished success. 'There is still danger that Madame Mary will bring many to her allegiance.' . . . 'The Duke has missed the chief move in this game; that is to seize Dame Mary'–such phrases spoke plainly of his sympathies.[10] When her accession was secure, there was, of course, a change of tune. With all the ports closed and messengers stopped and searched on the roads, discretion was necessary, and Mary suddenly became 'the virtuous and Christian princess who should restore the Catholic religion; . . . she who by right of nature and other disposals should have the crown'.[11] But these were only words. For close on twenty years now Spain had fought France, across the Pyrenees, in Italy, along the ever-debatable ground of the French northeast frontier. With apprehension de Noailles and his master watched the Queen, half Spanish by birth, three-quarters Spanish by sympathy, and feared the worst.

They were right in so doing, but for a time yet, hope mingled with their fear. All, as they saw clearly, depended on the Queen's marriage, and that was not yet decided. The subject had come up at once; everyone was now urging Mary to marry. The only discord in the chorus arose when it came to the point of naming a bridegroom. Seven names were put forward, but of these only two, or three if Reginald Pole is counted, were ever treated seriously. The King of Denmark, the Prince of Piedmont, the King of the Romans– these were possible but never probable husbands. Even Don Luiz of Portugal, so often before proposed as Mary's partner, and so much to be commended in that 'his countenance was not that of a Portuguese'—even Don Luiz was not much more than a red herring across a hot scent. Round the other two names, controversy, intrigue, and surmise were to rage for close on six months. For one of these suggested bridegrooms was an Englishman, the other an alien; one, of the blood royal of England, pricked on and coached with all the ingenuity that de Noailles and the Venetian ambassador could command, was desired of almost all his countrymen, and faithfully supported both by the judgement and affection of the Lord Chancellor. The suit of the other was in the hands of Simon Renard, one man against many, but that man subtle, patient, and vigilant as the old serpent himself. One was Edward Courtenay, son of the late Marquis of Exeter; the other was Philip, son of the Emperor Charles.

Courtenay was, of necessity, an unknown quantity at the beginning of the reign. For fifteen years a prisoner in the Tower, men knew only the nobility and tragedy of his house. When the prisoner came out, all could see that he was a handsome, well-made young man. The Court found also that he had studied much during his captivity, spoke several languages and was able to take his part on several instruments in that informal music-making that was an ordinary recreation of gentlemen; even his opponent Renard admitted that 'there was such a civility in him which must be deemed natural rather than acquired by the habit of society'.[12] Renard forgot, however, that though the society in the Tower was circumscribed, it was also select, and comprised the head of one of the oldest noble houses in England, and the deposed Bishop of one of the oldest sees.

But if Courtenay was a young man of some charm, of more than presentable appearance, and of as much culture as his contemporaries, there were certain lessons which no growing lad could learn in the Tower. He had never, poor boy, ridden anything more than the ponies of his childhood; to ride 'the great horse' in the lists or at the ring, with the whole crowd of onlookers made up of men and women equally accustomed to judge horseflesh and horsemanship, was beyond him. He had not yet learnt to handle the long bow, a weapon for which even yet Englishmen had an affection, half sentimental, half practical; and he was to spend pleasant hours with the wife of a kinsman as his instructor; pleasant hours in which they had jokes together about a bow of hers that he was strong enough or clumsy enough to break.[13]

But still worse than his ignorance in such things was the lack of that self-control which a man never his own master cannot learn. He was plunged suddenly into the gaiety and new splendour of the Court, and now, after the sombre colours and unadorned simplicity which had been the fashion at Edward's Court, the ladies were coming out gay as butterflies in summer;[14] and the Queen, with her passionate starved love of finery, the gayest of all.

This splendour, his high birth, his higher prospects, all went to his head. He found himself courted by many who counted on his future greatness; he could not resist giving himself airs, and it was even said that he allowed some, anticipating time to come, to speak to him on their knees.[15] This, silly as it was, and dangerous as it would have been in the days of Mary's father, was not, however, the worst. It would have been well for him if he had confined his foolishness to the Court, but, free at last, after so many years, to range at will, he tried now to pack all the experience of those years into a few months. There was talk of his going about the city to women of ill fame;[16] other young men might do as much, but not a young man who wished to recommend himself to such a woman as Mary, who, her whole youth embittered by the results of what she must consider her father's unbridled lust, had, with rigid obedience to her mother's advice, schooled herself to a nun-like renunciation of the flesh.

Even such delinquencies might have been overlooked, and even by Mary, because she was a very human woman, if only Courtenay had had the address and self-confidence that experience can give a man of ordinary gifts. But by training Courtenay had it not; by temperament he was never anything more than a very commonplace young man, easily persuaded or pushed in this direction or that, lovable enough, with a well-made body apt for sport, and enough physical courage; but more frivolous than dangerous, more vain than ambitious, and without that spark of magnanimity which alone could have made him anything but what he was–a tool in the hands of abler men.

Such was the man who, on the very day that Mary was proclaimed in London was spoken of as her future bridegroom; whom the English people desired and expected her to marry; whom some even thought she had married, when the rumour went round that the Queen had long been the wife of one of the prisoners in the Tower.[17]

But if the Londoners and de Noailles had cast Courtenay for the part of husband, others had different plans. Mary was still at Framlingham when the Emperor wrote to his son on the subject of her marriage. Although, he said, the English would not, at first, consent to the Queen marrying an alien, yet discretion and tact might enable her to revive the idea of a marriage with Charles himself, whom, as he said, without undue modesty but with some truth, the English had always liked, and preferred to any other foreigner. But, he concluded, he was considering putting forward Philip as his substitute.[18] Such was the first ventilation of that scheme which was to wreck alike Mary's life and reign, and which was to bring such a harvest of tares to the Emperor and his son. The letter itself contains in brief that monstrous blunder of Charles, the wise, the practical statesman. Together with an exact appreciation of the facts, it shows an equal blindness to their import and consequences. It was perfectly true that the English would detest the idea of a foreign marriage; it was perfectly true that of all foreign sovereigns, they had the friendliest feeling for himself. But to realize this, and not to realize the profound difference which in English eyes lay between the Emperor, and a Spaniard such as Philip, was indeed a strange instance of political stupidity. It is stranger yet when one remembers that it was for the sake of the Netherlands, first and last, that Charles devised and carried through this match. Spain could reap little profit from a close alliance with a small and distant power, but for the

Netherlands English friendship had always been important and soon would be essential. When Charles himself had gone, and the eastern Habsburg lands had passed with Imperial Germany to his brother and his brother's sons, the Netherlands would desperately need a near ally to secure them against the constant nibbling of France. Born at Ghent, brought up by a Netherlander in the Netherlands, among that people so bound to England by the necessities of trade, so closely related by blood, and so much like the English in its practical, shopkeeping bent, Charles understood, and was understood by England. Yet he shut the eyes of his understanding to the one great argument against his plan, and pressed on an unwilling nation his son Philip, a man in training, language, and temperament Spanish to the core.

It was at Newhall on July 29th that Renard first approached the subject. He had not yet taken the measure of the woman with whom he had to deal; he therefore mentioned the question of a marriage with extreme caution. It was, so he said, essential that she should marry, and the Emperor, as her nearest living kinsman, would be happy to advise her in her choice. Mary only thanked him then, but a little later she came back to the subject with a question that must have given the perspicuous Renard more than a hint of what was in her mind. In the uncertain days that followed Edward's death, the Emperor had instructed his ambassadors to recommend Mary to the forbearance of the Council, and to assure them that the Emperor had no wish to marry her to a foreigner. Now she asked if this was the truth. She wanted to know what the Emperor really meant; she wanted his advice.[19] Renard, used to dealing with crafty and oblique men of affairs, did not at once realize how truly this simple, plain-speaking woman meant what she said. She wanted the advice of the Emperor.

Indeed in this business of the marriage Mary herself was the strongest ally that Renard had. In every audience and every letter she betrayed first that her preference was for a foreigner; soon that her preference was for a Spaniard. Nor was this strange. Now was harvested the crop for which Henry VIII had sown the seed, in the years when he had gone about to break his daughter's will. In those days of her greatest misery it was to Spain, and to the Emperor as to her Spanish cousin, that all Mary's loyalty, gratitude, and affection had gone out. England was a country run mad, where men blasphemed against God and the Saints, and against the Vicar of God; where her mother had died, certainly in wretchedness and perhaps by poison; where for her nearest kin she had a father whom she had hardly seen for years, who only took notice of her existence to humiliate and bully her, and a half-sister whom she rated a bastard. Spain was the country of her mother's youth, the champion of Christendom against the Turks, and for her the one source of help and kindliness. Such things as these a woman of Mary's temper, tenacious and obstinate, could not forget. For all her conscientious determination to rule her country well, for all her pride in her inheritance, she was yet more than half Spanish in thought and feeling, and distrusted, as well she might, the English nobility. It was a calamity for her, yet it was a calamity which she had not earned. Not she herself but her father was to blame for the fact that his heiress was an alien in England. In the old days, after she had submitted to Henry and was again at Court, Chapuys had found her a useful ally, and had used her almost as a spy. She sent him word of French intrigue; she even told him the informal message she had overheard the King give to a Privy Councillor for the French ambassador.[20] That was in the past. Now she was Queen of England, but, so the Venetian ambassador reported, she despised the English and boasted her Spanish blood.[21] Even allowing for exaggeration here, and some venom, Mary was far different from that half-sister of hers who proudly declared herself 'mere English'.

It was for this reason that Renard, passing secretly in the dusk through back doors, coming to the Queen when the Court was empty, closeted with her for long private interviews, was to be the counsellor on whom, more than on any other, Mary was to lean. Onlookers guessed something of his importance, and of his mission, but not all. When all the rest of the congratulatory embassies, which had greeted the Queen's victory, had gone home, the Imperial ambassadors remained; they were therefore, by common consent, credited with some special mission.[22] This was true in Renard's case, but what detained the rest of the embassy was not their master's orders. The truth was that the Queen would not let them go. Everything, she told them distractedly, was in such trouble and uncertainty that she 'did not know how to make herself safe and order her affairs; still less did she dare to speak of them to any', so they reported to Charles, 'but to ourselves'.[23]

Very soon Renard must have felt that he knew the Queen pretty well. In one way she was difficult to deal with; she was no natural conspirator. When she came to London and stayed, as all Kings stayed, in the Tower till her coronation, she wished to see him privately, and sent word that he should come. Renard replied that he could not pass through all the gates and guards of the Tower; Newhall had been a different matter. Could he not, she sent a message, pass in disguised in a cloak?[24] In a cloak! He reported the episode to the Emperor with, one may guess, an exasperated laugh. But apart from this, his task was all too easy. He had, all ready to build on, her distrust of English treachery, and he began to hope that in spite of all the talk there was of the Courtenay marriage the Queen did not want it. He found in her besides, something that went strangely with her simplicity. 'I have noticed', he said, 'that she is great hearted, proud, magnanimous.'[25] That Tudor pride, of which the Lords of the Council in Edward's reign had had experience, Renard made his ally. A young man, her own subject, and a Plantagenet only through the female line, would not, he was confident, be to her mind as a husband. He had as yet no instructions from the Emperor, but he determined that when she went to Windsor, and he might see her more freely, he would, on his own responsibility, drop a word in season of Prince Philip and so 'as if of myself, try to put her into a marrying humour'.[26]

Throughout August, when matters more grim were afoot, such as the trial and execution of traitors, the business of wooing went forward but little. The

Emperor, however, was preparing the way. He ascertained from Philip that he was not irrevocably committed to the Portuguese match, but was ready to obey his father in all things. 'I think it best', wrote that life-long martyr to duty, 'to leave it all to your Majesty to dispose as seems fitting.'[27] Yet, even with his way clear in this direction, the Emperor felt a belated misgiving. The disturbance which the reintroduction of the Mass had caused in England made him doubt if it were safe to bring up so soon the thorny question of a foreign marriage. One thing, however, he was determined not to suffer; no other should foul the stream above his drinking place. The ambassadors of the King of the Romans, who came to ask his help in negotiating a match between the Queen of England and the Archduke Ferdinand, were sternly warned off. It was the suspicion of just this sort of marriage, they were told, that the Emperor was striving to dispel in England. Renard was instructed that if they persisted and the matter was opened, he was to inform the Queen, but tactfully, that this was not a suitable marriage for her.[28]

Something too might be done to prevent Courtenay running off with the prize. The Queen, so Granvelle wrote to Renard, could be put on her guard against the fellow. She should know how he was getting himself talked about. And the French were singling him out in a marked manner; Henri II had even, it was said, sent to him, as to the Queen, letters of credence recommending his two special envoys, while these envoys, inviting to dinner the Lords of the Council, had included the young man, pretending that they thought him a Privy Councillor. But, added Granvelle, with the caution of his long experience, 'be careful not to say too much, for if she took it into her head [to marry him] nothing would stop her, if she is like other women; and she would always bear you a grudge'.[29]

But, though slowly, things were going well. In the middle of August, when Renard mentioned a foreign marriage to her, he found it easy to read, in her laugh and the look she gave him, that the subject was agreeable;[30] already they shared an understanding to which other people were not admitted.

Yet at the beginning of September, the Emperor and his servant were still playing with the utmost caution. The Council was suspicious of this bugbear of foreign marriage, though whether the candidate was to be the Archduke Ferdinand, King of the Romans, Prince Philip, or another they did not yet know. De Noailles was almost equally nervous. He believed, but wrongly, that Renard and his colleagues had already suggested Philip's name to the Queen, and under his anxious gaze Courtenay's chances wavered up and down. The young man was made Earl of Devon on September 3rd; his mother, old friend of the Queen's as she was, had the Queen's ear, and much opportunity for persuasion, since it was she who usually slept in Mary's chamber; in confidential talks in the night one woman might do much to influence another. Courtenay also had on his side Mary's old and dear friend, Susan Clarencieux, her lady in waiting. He called her 'mother', as he called Gardiner 'father' for the great affection that had grown up between them in the strange small world of the Tower.[31] Besides all this, Renard, de Noailles, the Queen herself must have known that the common people wanted Courtenay.

On September 7th, de Noailles, almost but not quite sure that Philip was already offered to Mary with most favourable terms, wrote home urging that something must be done to strengthen French influence. Let the King write a friendly letter, praising the Queen's work for religion. Let the Queen Catherine send Mary gifts of 'ribbands, collars, sleeves and other fal-lals since she takes more pleasure in clothes than almost any woman alive'. Let the Queen send too a timely gift of a portrait, for Mary had just had one painted and was anxious to show it off.[32] Nor was de Noailles content with such methods, but himself became marvellously busy. The very day he warned the King that Philip was the likely bridegroom he sent privately to one of Courtenay's closest friends. The next night this gentleman was admitted by the back door into the garden of de Noailles's lodging, and, probably over some of the Frenchman's good wine, was told to warn Courtenay that he must be thinking betimes of how to prevent the match. It would be well for him to make friends of as many about the Queen's person as possible, as many as might be of people at large, and more especially of those who were to sit in the next Parliament, so that a petition might come thence to the Queen, asking her to choose an Englishman; among Englishmen she could choose none but Courtenay himself. Besides all this, de Noailles did his best to alarm the very cautious Venetian ambassador.[33]

He even went to see the Chancellor, a man he vehemently disliked, so as to talk to him of the danger of a Spanish marriage. Very sound sense it was too, which he declared to Gardiner, and profoundly must the latter, as anxious even as the Frenchman, have agreed with him. Granted that the Queen needed a husband to support her and give her children, for either purpose, de Noailles argued, Philip would be a bad choice, since he clearly could not stay in England. 'Perhaps', said this enemy of Mary, speaking more in her interest than those she counted friends, 'perhaps she would not see him a fortnight in all her life.' As for peace, the peace that the Queen said she desired, 'it was a perpetual war against the King [of France] that the Emperor wished her to espouse rather than his son'.[34]

Meanwhile, in the midst of all this ferment was the Queen, more agitated than any. As she sat with her women at embroidery, as they dressed and un-dressed her, or in walks in the garden, they all were talking of nothing but this one thing–her marriage.[35] But the Queen's agitation was caused chiefly by considerations which did not trouble the heads of Councillors and ambas-sadors. For them the question was who should be King of England. For her it was a question of the man who was to be her husband. She was very sure that it was a matter for herself to decide; she wished to keep it a matter private between herself and her cousin Charles, and since secrecy was necessary, she would be secret. But she did not like pretence, and was a bad dissembler, so that she had to beg the Emperor's ambassadors to make no mention of marriage at a public audience, 'because she could not feel sure of being able to keep an even countenance' and to pretend that this was the first she had heard of it from them.[36]

She was in fact, in a flutter of excitement, and longing to hear the name that the Emperor would suggest. But already she had suspicions which were fast becoming hopes. Prince Philip had sent over his major-domo and Don Inigo de Mendoza to congratulate her on her accession. Nervously, and like a shy girl clinging to her mother's presence as protection against a proposal, Mary actually brought the Council from London to Richmond so that the two Spaniards could not mention marriage to her [37]

Four days later, on September 8th, Philip's name was, for the first time, mentioned between her and Renard; but even now, so cautious a hunter was the ambassador, so simple a quarry the Queen, it was she herself who spoke it. Renard began the conversation by sounding her on the subject of Courtenay. He told her how the common rumour was that he should be her husband. The Queen at once gave the information he wanted as to that, by telling him that she had not seen Courtenay more than once since she had set him free, and that she did not want to marry anyone that she could think of in England. Had the Emperor, she asked, suggested no one?

Renard, doubtless concealing his delight, told her, 'No,' and that it would be difficult to find a husband of middle age, as she desired. There were of course the Archduke of Austria, the Prince of Piedmont, the heirs of Florence and Ferrara, and the Dauphin of France. But if twenty-seven or twenty-eight years old were too young for her, there was no one of middle age, and among the elder princes, said Renard, there was not one who was not either too old or too ill for matrimony.

The crafty hunter had set his snare, and baited it with those significant words – twenty-seven or twenty-eight years old. Prince Philip was in his twenty-seventh year. Mary was very easy to catch. 'At that she said straight out that his Highness was married.' Renard replied that he did not think the contract was concluded. Woman-like, Mary ignored him, and insisted on speaking of Philip as though he were not only betrothed but married. She was sorry to hear, she said, that Philip had married so near a relation as the Princess of Portugal. Then she hurried on. All the other possible bridegrooms were too young; she was old enough to be the mother of any of them. 'Besides,' she continued, giving herself more entirely into Renard's hand, 'His Highness would wish to live in Spain, and the Emperor must know how much Englishmen hate the idea of having as King a man who has other realms in his hands.' Renard, able now to discuss Philip, said that he had mentioned the Prince, 'because of the great sense, judgment, experience, and moderation that shone forth in him, and because he was already an old married man with a son . . . of six or seven years old'.

Mary, who was listening doubtless, but also following out her own thoughts, and they were not the thoughts of a statesman, interrupted the eulogy. She had not, she told him, ever known that thing which was called love; she had never harboured voluptuous thoughts; she had never thought of marriage till God set her on the throne. And then, mingling policy with this intimate revelation of herself, she told him that she would never dare raise the subject of a Spanish marriage with her Council. The Emperor would have to see to that.[38]

The whole interview, with its comedy and its pathos, reveals Mary to the reader, as she must have revealed herself to Renard. She was no hard bargainer with a relish for barefaced lies like her father; no practitioner in exquisite and airy diplomatic strategy like her sister. She was a woman who confessed with an honest simplicity to an ignorance passing that of many a girl of half her age. Our knowledge of the pain that was to come to her from love and marriage makes that confession a tragic thing.

The more rumours that went about of the possibility of this Spanish match, the more open became the disapproval of her Council for such an idea. Gardiner had from the start made it clear to the Queen what his advice would be. He talked to her of Courtenay and his merits; the young man was of the blood royal, stood nearest of all male scions to the throne, was well conditioned and beloved. Now not Gardiner alone, but three of her old servants, Rochester, Waldegrave and Englefield, men who had been her advisers and friends through dark days, and whom she had seen suffer for their loyalty, were urging her to marry Courtenay. Yet even in these she would not confide, putting them off with the reply that Courtenay was very young and quite untried, and that she would decide nothing till the meeting of Parliament.[39]

On September 13th, Granvelle wrote telling Renard that Prince Philip was prepared to marry anyone whom the Emperor chose. Just a week later the Emperor sent his instructions. Philip was to be proposed, if the Queen thought the English would not object, or if their objection might be safely overruled. As everything showed that the English people would object to Philip, it was for the Queen, guided by Renard, to decide whether their preferences should be ignored.[40] It was for her to disentangle and dissect the causes of the uneasy stirrings of discontent whose manifestations were clear—tumults at Masses; insults to priests; seditious papers here, there, and everywhere. The causes, however, were harder to diagnose. Was all this turmoil due, at bottom, to the unease of a people whose temper was soured and irritated by financial disorder and economic change? Or was it so many had grown to love the new Prayer Book and the new ways that they wanted no reaction? Or was it the fast spreading rumour that the Queen was to marry Spain which was the goad that pricked them to audible mutterings of discontent? These things would have been hard enough for anyone to decide; they were far beyond the grasp of the Queen; she had chosen that only aliens should advise her, and they, though clear-sighted enough, were not impartial. Renard held on to the goal which was the Emperor's—the alliance of England that should give the Netherlands security. And this, it has been pointed out,[41] was the one reason for the match never mentioned to Mary.

At the beginning of October Renard judged that nothing more could be done without some of the Council knowing that the match was definitely proposed. The Queen had told him that Paget was in favour of a foreign marriage, and Renard knew also that Paget had old scores to pay off against the Council that had sacrificed him, when, in Edward's reign, he had been ill advised enough to promise to the Emperor, either with or without their consent, that Mary should have her Mass. Nor was it only a question of enmity; Paget, a self-made man, had suffered confiscation and financial loss; such men may often be bought. But Renard must go to work with caution, for Paget, with his broad, bland face, cold eyes, and the thick beard that covered his mouth, was a much more difficult subject to handle than the simple Queen.

The conversations began, and Renard made his tentative suggestion. He had then to endure from Paget a good many shrewd pricks, such as a fleeting reference to Philip's instantaneous unpopularity in the Netherlands on his first visit there; a regret that Philip could speak no tongue but Spanish; and a commendation of Don Luiz of Portugal as suitable in age, appearance and circumstances. Then, with promises of secrecy, Paget hurried away to a meeting of the Council. But next day Renard found that the interview had not been wasted. When, early in the morning, before people were about, he knocked at the back door of Paget's garden and was admittted by the owner himself, he found that Paget had come round so far as to be ready with advice. Let the Emperor, he said, write private letters to seven of the Council–to two nobles, Arundel and Shrewsbury; to two Bishops, Gardiner and the old, dearly loved Tunstal, Bishop of Durham, whom Mary and the whole Council must trust; to two new men–that is Paget himself and Mr. Secretary Petre; and to one old servant of the Queen's–Rochester; for, said Paget, these governed the Council.[42] Renard may have been grateful for the advice, but in itself it was a secondary thing. The chief gain was that he now knew that he had an ally, and Paget was a useful ally since he could work upon other members of the Council. But perhaps more valuable than his help, there was the part he might play with regard to the Queen. If she began to scruple at the match, to realize the fast gathering volume of protest and discontent among Englishmen, high and low, here was an Englishman ready to persuade her that all would be well.

Paget went to work at once. He had just been made Knight of the Garter, and that very day dined with M. de Noailles, 'with his great order round his neck'. De Noailles, who was a gentleman by birth, made game, in his letters home, of Paget's gold chain and of his complacency; but the Englishman had the best of the joke, for he left de Noailles convinced that the whole Council was so set against the Spanish match that it was hardly to be feared. This chimed in with what the Venetian ambassador had told the Frenchman, for he believed that the whole affair 'had gone up in smoke'.[43] Next day de Noailles's hopes soared higher yet, for he heard that Courtenay had spent the afternoon, from one o'clock till six, in his mother's chamber, which adjoined that of the Queen, and that for these five hours no one had been present but the Queen, the young man, and his mother. The tale was not true, but de Noailles believed it.[44]

There were, however, other interviews, unreported but authentic, and of these the Frenchman did not know. The very day that Paget, pompous in his new order, sat at de Noailles's table, Renard had an audience with the Queen. It was public, but when the ambassador came close to make his reverence, while a girl near by sang to a lute, he was able to whisper in the Queen's ear that he had credentials from the Emperor to deliver, and a private message to give. As they stood a little apart talking together, Renard was even able to put into her hand, without any seeing, the letter he spoke of. She concealed it quickly, and told him he should come to her at five or six next evening.[45]

At the appointed time he came, by boat, to the gallery of the palace that opened on the river. He was brought to the Queen, and, in that audience, at last made an official proposal. The Emperor, he told her, offered Philip for her husband.

Mary had received the proposal she had so openly angled for. Now, the need of diplomacy being over, she could let her instincts guide her, and her instincts bade her draw back. First of all there was a political excuse. She thanked Renard, but did not know, she said, how the English people would take the match, seeing what manner of men they were; nor whether the Council would consent. Then it was a personal doubt. She knew little of Philip. She had heard that he was not so wise as the Emperor had been when he was young. If he wanted passion and sensual pleasures he was not for her, for she was – she shied at the exact figure – ' of that age Your Majesty knows of and she has never given way to thoughts of love'. Again that insistence on the last, as if Renard were no ambassador, but a friend and a confessor ! And she had not yet done. For now she told him that to whom she gave herself, him would she love and obey, and she would do nothing against his will. But if Philip should wish to encroach on the government, she could not allow it, and if he tried to put his own Spaniards in office, the people would not stand it. This matter of marriage, she said, was of such importance that she must consult the Council – because it was for all her life. But she could not break the matter to them; the Emperor must do it. Then, with another sudden turn, she told him that she was as free as she had been on the day of her birth; she had never even taken a fancy to any man. So she rambled on, and though Renard knew now that he had little to fear of the Queen's refusal, he might, if he had cared at all for the woman, have been afraid what marriage might do to such a one as she confessed herself.

But it was as an ambassador that he hastened to answer her. To her entreaty that he would tell her the truth of Philip's character he replied that it was 'too wonderful to be human'. Descending to detail, he assured her that he was 'a prince of so stable and settled character that he was no longer young'. Combined in him were the safe virtues of a husband of fifty, and the ability of a young man to beget children whom he would live long enough to protect throughout their minority. As for the other doubts, he brushed them away like mere cobwebs; all could be avoided by the provisions of the treaty of marriage.[46]

He may have thought at the time that she was sufficiently reassured, but on the following Saturday he received a scribbled note from the Queen.

'Sir,

'If it were not too much trouble for you, and if you were to find it convenient to do so without the knowledge of your colleagues, I would willingly speak with you in private this evening, as you four are to come to-morrow. Nevertheless I remit my request to your prudence, and discretion. Written in haste, as it well appears, this morning, 13th October. Your good friend.

MARY.'[47]

In answer to this appeal, whose apologetic tone, the tone that a pupil might use to a respected tutor, shows what a hold the ambassador had on her, Renard went, and found that the Queen was doubting yet. First of all she told him that Paget had recommended the match to her. Then she tried to account for her summons by saying, that now some of the Council were in favour of her marriage, she wished to hear from Renard what conditions were offered. But all this time, jumping from one subject to another, she was only beating about the bush. Suddenly she stretched out her hand and took Renard's hand in hers. Then she adjured him solemnly to tell her whether all that he had said about Philip was true, whether he was indeed of even temper, balanced judgement, and well conditioned.

Renard replied that, if his word was enough, he would pledge it that Philip had qualities as virtuous as any prince in the world.

The Queen, tightening her hold on his hand said, 'It is well', and for a while no more.

Then back she came again, fearing she knew not what, truth-telling herself, but knowing how false men's tongues could be. She asked him, was he speaking for truth's sake, or was he moved by a subject's feelings; by love or fear?

He replied that he gave his life hostage if what he said were not true.

Even then, all she could do was to murmur that she wished Philip could pass through England so that she might see him.[48]

Next time Renard saw her he soon learnt that others had been at work. For Gardiner, her Chancellor, coming to her with Waldegrave and Englefield, had made definite proposals of Courtenay. He had even gone so far as to warn her against a Spanish marriage, telling her that 'England would never abide a foreigner, that Courtenay was the only possible marriage for her in England; and that, as for Prince Philip the country would not accept him willingly'. Englefield then took his cue; he said that Philip had a kingdom of his own, and would not want to leave it; he added also that Philip's subjects did not speak too well of him. Next it was Waldegrave's turn – he told her that if she married Philip it would mean war with France.[49]

To them the Queen had shown no signs of yielding; she had retailed some of Renard's arguments, and bidden them lay aside private considerations, and so dismissed them unanswered. But Renard could see that the combined attack had shaken her. He did not play for safety but put fortune to the touch. He begged her to tell him if she were going to follow their advice, and so would not, after all, wish to marry Philip.

That brought the Queen up again, like a ship into the wind. She had no liking for Courtenay, she said. She had not made up her mind. Wotton wrote from France that the French were doing all they could to prevent the Spanish marriage. So she wavered between one side and the other. Then, seizing on an excuse for deferring decision, she asked again for the conditions which the Emperor would offer. If she might have them she would keep them secret. Then, hastily, 'I do not mean, by this,' she said, 'that you are to write to His Majesty that I have given my word, for I do not mean to give it until I feel sure of being able to abide by it . . . for I do not wish to be thought inconsistent.'

Renard must have feared, as the Venetian ambassador had hoped, that the whole affair was going up in smoke. He tried a well-worn expedient. Stiffly he replied that he would ask for the conditions, but was amazed to see her defer so to the Council as to allow them to command her affections and urge her to marry a vassal for whom she had no liking.

The shaft hit.

'They have no such authority', she retorted, 'in matters that touch me so nearly.' She added that she did not believe what they said about Philip.[50]

Renard had won back her wavering will. She began to tell him what he should ask the Emperor to remember in framing the articles. The ambassador may well have plumed himself on his own skill when he left her, but, knowing her as he did by now, he cannot even yet have felt secure. He must have been relieved when, after a great supper given by the Queen, his two fellow ambassadors departed to return to the Emperor. He could work more surely alone.

It was a few days after their departure that he was granted audience both by the Queen and Council. At this audience he was to make public the suit of Philip. But first he saw the Queen, who, if she had been agitated before, was now half hysterical, and on the verge of tears.

She had, she told him, wept for close on two hours that very day, praying to God to guide her to a right decision. And now, she checked Renard, he need not say more. She had chosen him before this for her second father-confessor, and now she felt that she could no longer keep back her word, for she believed she would agree to the Emperor's proposal. She felt she must follow the Emperor's advice. She wanted to speak privately to him about Courtenay. She could not say more now or she would burst into tears, but she would give him public audience.

So the poor, distracted, flustered woman gave her word at last, qualified by those two words–'I believe', of which qualification Renard remarked to his master, doubtless with an indulgent smile, 'Your Majesty will understand what that means.'[51]

Yet the words did mean something. They meant that, though Mary thought herself resolved, she had not yet got rid of an obstinate misgiving, a dread that she was making a mistake. On the one hand her heart told her that Philip, of that very house of Spain from which she sprang, and to which her loyalty was given, Philip was the husband whom she could love. And Renard had said that the marriage was also politically wise. But on the other hand there was Gardiner, there were her old friends and servants and the Lords of the Council, all but Paget, Arundel, and perhaps Norfolk; there was that great Leviathan, the unwieldy body of the English people, from the throat of which came groans and mutterings and even articulate ejaculations against the marriage. No wonder she hesitated, swayed this way and that, for she had no political instinct to direct her. She had honest purpose, rooted prejudice, old loyalties; she had her belief in God's guidance. But now, at the last resort, weary of balancing arguments, she decided, as many truly religious but injudicious people have decided, to empty her mind of thought, and to wait for inspiration. She meant most honestly well. But if ever an honest soul thus remits the arduous effort of reason, the abdication may deliver the ship not to any breath of God's will, but to those dark under-currents of desire, the strength and set of which impartial reason should detect and discount.

On the evening of Sunday, October 29th, she sent again for Renard. He found her in her chamber alone, except for Dame Clarencieux. In the room also, with the lamp burning before it, was the Holy Sacrament.

Mary told him that since the Emperor's letters came she had not slept, but, waking, had wept and prayed for guidance, calling especially upon that Holy Sacrament which was to her more even than the memorial of Christ – was a thing tangible, visible, comprehended within the four walls of the room, yet the vehicle for the whole immeasurable Being of God. And still, she said, she prayed this Sacrament to come to her aid.

Turning from the ambassador, she knelt, and began to repeat the ancient hymn – *Veni Creator Spiritus*. 'And', says Renard, no fool, and no saint, but moved nevertheless, 'we did the same.'

The Queen stood up again and spoke to him. She had, she said, considered all; she had talked with Arundel, Paget, and Petre. She was sure, she went on, of the Emperor's kindness; he would now be doubly her father, and he would see to it that the Prince was a good husband to her.

So it had come at last to the final word. Mary could bear to question no more. She told Renard that she believed she was inspired by God, who had done so many miracles for her, to give her word, there in the presence of the Sacrament, to be Prince Philip's wife. She said, and it was true, that, her mind once made up, she would never change. She promised that she would love her husband perfectly.[52] That was truer than she could know, but perhaps the woman who had never loved guessed what capacity for loving there was in her.

That same night, Renard, descending to a level upon which he felt more at home, wrote to Philip that the Queen had given her promise, and advised him to practise his French and Latin.[53]

Chapter XIV

THE Queen's word once passed, all Mary's honesty, all the Tudor obstinacy that grew with resistance, combined in the keeping of it. And nothing less than all this would have sufficed against the mountainous wave of opposition that gathered itself together and rose up against the marriage, even before it was officially announced. .

The six persons selected to receive letters from the Emperor had received them, but, with Gardiner, Rochester, even Pembroke, it did not mean that because the Emperor addressed them by such melting terms as, 'Right Reverend Father in God', 'Dear and well beloved', or 'My Cousin', their resistance was at an end. By Gardiner's advice young Courtenay was busy canvassing his friends. Three times had he gone to Englefield to ask him, ill with fever and full of domestic troubles as he was (for his wife had just left him), whether he could not come to Court. Both Courtenay and his mother had been to see the Earl of Pembroke, who, uncertain of character but a great power in the West, was well worth winning. It was decided too, that Parliament should take a hand, and petition the Queen not to marry a foreigner.[1]

Till that petition could be delivered, the only man in England of sufficient weight and consequence to do anything against the match was Gardiner himself. Of him, Renard, who was bold enough, and now hopeful enough, to take the bull by the horns, asked an audience, and got it. But when in the audience he asked Gardiner's opinion of the Spanish match, he got that too, with far more candour than he had expected. For Gardiner, tongue-tied before the Queen by some scruple, or cowardice, or miscalculation, now spoke out. He deployed before Renard such a battery of arguments that the ambassador was for once taken aback. There was against the match, Gardiner said, not only the English hatred of foreigners, not only the known pride and harshness of the Spanish character, England's certain dislike of which 'would only be imitating Your Majesty's [the Emperor's] subjects, who could never learn to bear them in Flanders'. Even if Philip really intended to fall in with English ways and customs the people would never believe it, but would fear the worst from him, and with the people, Gardiner said most truly, 'fearing and believing were the same'. Greater than all these, but entering into, and intensifying each, was the reaction of France to the marriage; and France, in Ireland and in Scotland and Calais, had only too many opportunities of damaging England as an ally of Spain.

There was yet another thing – and here Gardiner spoke as an Englishman, a churchman and a conservative. He believed, he said, that the re-establishment of religion was of greater importance than any marriage. But a peaceful settlement of religion would be impossible if there was to be a Spanish bridegroom. Already the French were doing what they could to inflame the fears of the Protestant party, telling them that Philip would be sure to use force to bring England back into line with the Catholic nations. Such belief would both harden their resistance, and set alight just that element of panic that would spread as quickly as sparks in the stubble. In all this there was sound sense and clear vision. But Gardiner's next words showed that he had the longer sight of the European statesman. For though, as he said, perhaps with a smile, he was not so much a politician as many thought him, yet he had had time in prison to ponder these matters. England was always the Emperor's ally at heart; Charles would do better to depend on that than try to bind the country too closely to him. And for England the friendship of the Netherlands was worth more than any problematical possession of that country by a child of Mary and Philip.[2]

So Gardiner relieved his mind of the fears, and no doubt of the indignation which the growing certainty of the Spanish marriage had wakened in his mind. But though he spoke plainly to the ambassador, with the Queen he maintained his unfortunate reticence. He saw her after this interview, but he repeated nothing of all that he had told Renard, saying only, when the Queen told him that she had decided on a foreign marriage—'And what will the people say? How will they stomach a foreigner who will promise things that he will not keep?' 'If you', retorted Mary, 'prefer the will of the people to my wishes, you break your promise.' Gardiner was silenced.[3]

The opposition, however, believed that it had still one hope of influencing the Queen's mind. It still remained for Parliament to petition her to marry an Englishman. But the difficulty was to present the petition, for the Queen refused to grant private audiences; she was either genuinely ill, or used this as a convenient pretext, for she knew that the petition was under way.[4]

At last, however, on November 16th, a deputation waited on her. The Speaker and some of the Commons were there; Paget, Arundel, and some Lords. Paget at least must have been smiling in his beard, knowing all that he knew of the matter. It was said, that after so many postponements, when at last the summons came to the deputation, it was so unexpected that the Speaker could not find his address; if this were true it was perhaps in fumbling for his forgotten periods that he lengthened it out so tediously that the Queen, who could not anyway have found it pleasant hearing, had to sit down before he had finished.

Then she answered him, speaking for herself—taking the part, so Paget gibed at Gardiner, of her own Chancellor. She was after all a Tudor; the question was of her marriage; it was hardly likely she would meekly listen to criticism from the commons. But besides this a woman who had for so long suffered agonies of indecision, and had at last made up her mind, would not receive with gratitude contrary advice which came too late. So she treated them to a bit of royal and feminine petulance. She was, she told them, offended at the suggestion that she should marry a subject, and as for their interference at all, 'she found it very strange'. Parliament was not accustomed to speak so to the King of England. Waxing hotter, she stormed at them, declaring that if they forced her to marry any not to her liking it would be to procure her death, 'for I will not live three months, and I will bear no children, and so, Mr. Speaker, you will defeat your own ends'. All this was unreasonable enough, but what came next was worse. For she told the deputation that all her affairs were conducted by divine dispensation, and that she would pray to God to guide her in the choice of a husband, suitable to the kingdom, and agreeable to herself.[5] The deputation retired; it had its answer.

What little trust the Queen yet reposed in Gardiner, she now chose to revoke, for to him she traced all the opposition that angered and half scared her, but could not move her obstinacy now she had at last decided. She openly reproached him for setting the Speaker on her, informed him she did not want him to make any mistake, and therefore would tell him that she would never marry Courtenay. Gardiner – perhaps his years in prison had broken him – burst into tears, said that he had only mentioned the considerations urged by the Speaker, and excused himself by his fondness for Courtenay. 'Is it suitable', the Queen snapped at him, 'that I should be forced to marry a man because a Bishop has made friends of him in prison?' Gardiner could only say that he gave it up.[6]

He must have realized that the matter was as good as settled, though he cannot have known that it was already only a question of which portrait of Philip was to be sent to the Queen – not the Lucas Cranach because 'that, being on wood, and large, would be difficult to carry; but the one by Titian', so Granvelle thought, only the Queen must be told that the original of the portrait had 'filled out and grown more beard than he had when it was painted', and that the picture must be put in a proper light, and looked at from a distance, 'as all Titian's paintings have to be looked at'.[7]

Yet the formal acceptance of the marriage articles was yet to come, and Renard was too wary to take for granted that till this was concluded, his work was finished. The articles which he received he carefully doctored, so that the proem and conclusion no longer spoke of the affair as settled. Then he presented them.

At last, early in the afternoon of December 7th, he was sent for to the palace. The whole Council was to meet, so that all the nobles of that unwieldy body should hear what was proposed and sanction or reject the match. The debate continued for close on three hours; from time to time Renard, waiting outside, heard that there were some who even now tried to wreck the project, though most accepted it. At last, when the candles were lit and the winter darkness very blue outside the casements, the Chancellor, Lord Arundel, Thirlby, Bishop of Norwich, the Comptroller, and some others came out and announced to him that, except for very trifling alterations, the articles had been accepted as they stood.[8]

Renard had succeeded. His hand had gentled and guided the Queen; when necessary he had given her a prick of the spur, reminding her, did she at all incline her ear to the Council's objections, that she was 'a Queen and

Sovereign lady'. He, making the most of her distrust of all Englishmen, had won the prize he had set out to win. Yet, able though he was, one may suspect that, if Charles his master had not had the wisdom of the old serpent, all would have been in vain. For it was Charles who kept Reginald Pole fretting at Dillingen and at Brussels till the marriage was made–Pole, Mary's cousin, the representative of the great old Catholic houses, the one Englishman of birth and standing who had never surrendered to the new ways. The Emperor had cause to know something of the power of Pole's name and reputation since, in the old days, he had himself considered the possibility of sending him to England in order to bear a part in Chapuys's great scheme of an Imperial invasion. He may also have remembered that only five years ago the Western rebels had demanded that Pole should return and take a high place in the young King's Council.[9] What influence Pole might have had over Mary was later to be seen, and what he thought of the marriage may be inferred from his remark that he was forbidden to return to England because the Emperor could 'not bring himself to believe that I would help him to put my country into the hands of a foreigner'.[10]

What Gardiner had said to Renard of the reaction of France to the marriage was only too true. At Melun, a few days before Christmas, Dr. Nicholas Wotton, Mary's ambassador, waited on the French King. Henri had a very bad cold, but that did not account for such a mood of depression as that which Wotton reported to the Council. 'Whatsoever words the King used to me, his countenance was very sad, yea and his words few, and not pronounced with such assurance and alacrity as he used to do, but some times staying in his tale and repeating his words again, as though his mind was somewhat troubled.' What the trouble was Wotton did not need to guess, for Henri spoke of it. It was the fear of the Spanish marriage.

Talking to Wotton as one man to another Henri prognosticated gloomily that though the Queen might truly desire peace now, yet when she was married that would change, for 'a husband may do much with his wife'. 'Like as that is true,' Wotton objected, 'so I take it again that a wife of wit and discretion may do as much with her husband.' The King, however, was not convinced; perhaps he agreed with the Constable that Wotton the ecclesiastic, 'being not of that vocation himself', was no reliable authority upon the subject of matrimony.[11]

If Henri was gloomy with Wotton, when he wrote to de Noailles he was venomous. Already what Gardiner feared had come to pass. Henri looked upon Mary as an enemy. Courtenay was still his main hope, no longer as a bridegroom for the Queen; but rather as a lever to dislodge her from the throne. 'If it seems that Courtenay is inclined and has the means to be trouble-some', the King wrote, de Noailles should 'sous main' promise him French help, so that, as Henri concluded, 'if the said Courtenay has good enough heart and wit, it will be easy with the help and backing of other discontented men, to make this Queen poorer and more unfortunate than ever she was before, and serve her right, since she so soon forgets herself'.[12]

Courtenay then, was to be the trump card in the game which Henri took up again after so short an interval of time. Lady Jane Grey should have served to prevent any accession of the Spanish Tudor; she had failed. Courtenay should have married Mary; he had failed. Yet there was still hope that he might supplant her. And, for the moment, it seemed that perhaps Courtenay would lend himself to such a plan. He had taken offence at the evident failure of his courtship before ever the marriage was formally announced, before even the Parliament protest had been made. De Noailles heard that he had a plan of slipping off to Greenwich with some of his friends, on pretext of riding the late King's great horses there. But while he was at Greenwich, Paget and Arundel were to be attacked and murdered by other friends of his, while in the darkness of that same night Courtenay should take ship for France.[13] It was the plan of a gang of lads. De Noailles, whose head was stronger and cooler than Courtenay's, restrained him. Both the ambassador and his master knew that the young man's flight to France 'would be, when all is said, to take away the means of attaining what he desires'.[14]

There was another item in the programme, which Henri and his ambassador proposed to follow, as there was another possible aspirant to the crown, whose fractional claim added to that of Courtenay would so nearly make an integer. The majority, even now, looked rather to Elizabeth as Henry's daughter, than to Courtenay. It could only strengthen the young man's title if he were to marry her and her claim, and since he might not have the Queen, have instead her half-sister. But if de Noailles thought that he could entice Elizabeth into a plot, he was mistaken in the red-headed, pale young woman, whose reputation among her teachers was that of a pupil with great wit and 'a marvellous meek stomach'. De Noailles was vastly pleased with the ability which she showed in avoiding a suggested match with that Spanish pensioner, the Prince of Piedmont. He did not, however, realize, that with regard to his own suggestions, she used exactly the same policy of *fainéant*, so that she managed to keep herself uncommitted and uncompromised through all the conspiracies of the reign. Her discretion was more than unfathomed; its depths were not even suspected.

Yet even if one of the possible Pretenders to the Crown was a shuttle-witted irresolute youth, and the other a young woman too astute to commit herself in any direction, Mary's throne was far from secure. England was indeed an arsenal packed with open kegs of gunpowder. Ruinous poverty and its consequent bitterness among the poor; greed and treachery among the rich; these were things for which Mary was not to blame. Nor was it her fault that the unsettling changes in religion had shaken the whole fabric of contemporary thought, so that men were asking strange questions and shirking no answer, however dangerous. She had, however, deliberately, by her foregone decision to bring England back to the Catholic Church, challenged the Protestant party, and the members of this party were largely men of a temperament, daring, positive, and reckless–ill enemies to make. Accustomed to question everything in heaven and earth, they had been a divided and quarrelsome army when in possession of the Promised Land. Now they were driven to bay by an enemy so bitterly hated that their differences were, for the moment, thrust upon one side. By sermons, pamphlets, declarations, ballads, plays, as by rioting and violence, their irreconcilable spleen had been already shown. Such men were only waiting for an opportunity to make trouble. Give them allies, at home or abroad, and they would stick at nothing.

Mary herself, by her insensate action in forcing a foreign match, had provided them with allies both at home and abroad. France was now her enemy, and as Gardiner had pointed out, France had heaven-sent opportunities for making trouble in Scotland, Ireland and Calais. In England, though many – probably the vast majority of Englishmen – welcomed a return to the Mass and to the familiar decorum of the past, yet, in the question of a Spanish marriage, they were as resolved as any Protestant. The cry that a foreigner should never be King of England was a shibboleth that men of whatever Church could well pronounce.

On Christmas Eve, at a village in Cornwall, two men, John Cowlyn and a person called Jackman, came to the house of a certain John Combe. When, Cowlyn asked his host, had he come from church? 'An hour agone', Combe told him, and then added – 'I have heard and seen this day that thing I have not seen in four years before, for I have, thanked be God, heard Mass and received holy bread and holy water'. Whether his two neighbours had only come to him to make mischief, or whether they had already drunk too much of the mulled ale of Christmas, they were in a quarrelsome mood. 'I would all priests were hanged', cried Cowlyn. 'God forbid,' retorted the conservative Combe, 'for the Queen's grace hath granted it.' Then said Cowlyn – 'The Queen, a vengeance take her !' 'Amen !' said Jackman. 'I may say it well,' Cowlyn justified himself, 'for before New Year's Day outlandish men wilt come upon our hands, for there be some at Plymouth already.' Jackman put in – 'Before twelve months you shall see all houses of religion up again, with the Pope's laws.' The conversation, seditious enough in all conscience, concluded with a yet bolder flight. 'We ought not', said Cowlyn, 'to have a woman to bear the sword.' Jackman said – 'If a woman bear the sword my Lady Elizabeth ought to have it first.'[15]

It would be hard to find anything more comprehensive of the elements of the unrest and discontent that were to poison Mary's reign, than this talk of sheep-skin or russet-coated country folk – first the Mass, the monasteries, the Pope – that is to say every grudge at the reaction in religion; then, Spaniards 'upon our hands' – this to stir up all, even those who, like John Combe, thanked God that the parish church was again become as they remembered it; and, lastly, flat sedition against the Queen herself, a forecasting of John Knox's denunciation of the monstrous regiment of women, and, inconsistent but none the less dangerous, the counter-claim, put forward by malcontents, of Elizabeth, the English, the Protestant heir.

A man with such a keen nose for rumour as Simon Renard, was not likely

to be altogether in ignorance of what was being said about the marriage, and
what was actually intended against it. He might not know that the Mayor
and aldermen of Plymouth had sent an astonishing message to de Noailles;
they asked to put their town under the protection of France, and for a French
garrison to make that protection real, a proposition which showed to what
height the tide of panic was already rising. He might not know either that a
certain English gentleman had promised Henri II to bring over to the coast of
France eight or nine warships of the Queen's navy.[16] But he did know, and
could guess the significance of the constant bickering and sparring that went
on in Antwerp between Spaniards and young gentlemen, who in a foreign
land were very full of their Englishry. He knew that the obliging Paget was
adamant when it came to a question of disinheriting Elizabeth, and was
actually advising the very thing which the French plotted secretly to do,
namely to marry Elizabeth to Courtenay.[17] He knew too how Londoners, in
the streets, on Thames-side wharves, and at Paul's, were muttering that
Netherlanders would be welcome, but never Spaniards, while heretics even
went 'so far as to say that they would rather die than suffer Spaniards to rule
this country'.[18]

Already a frenzy of fear and hate had seized upon the English countryman.
Rumours ran like wildfire. In distant counties these rumours had time to
grow to monstrous proportions before the news that bred them was able to
catch them up. Gentlemen dreaded Spanish pride, and in imagination saw
Spaniards filling all the profitable offices in England : Protestants remembered
the Inquisition in Flanders; merchantmen thought of the tales they had heard
of Spanish soldiers in the towns of Italy; yeomen and simple countrymen
dreaded armed invasion, fire, sword and rapine. When, in the middle of
January, the Government ordered that the advantages of the marriage should
be explained to the people from every pulpit in England, it was too late.

Short of dropping the whole marriage project, what could be done to
placate English feeling was done. Though the articles of the treaty of marriage
had been framed with the most anxious and indulgent care for the prejudices
of England, so that except for Philip's possible personal influence over his
wife, no loophole was allowed for his entry into English politics, yet Renard
knew well that even this was not enough. So did Charles. He wrote to his
son full instructions both for himself and for his suite. The latter must
consist of persons of a suitable age to realize their responsibility – no young hot-
heads to take offence at trifles, and Philip himself should at once send some
ring or jewel of value, which Charles justly remarked, 'will be eagerly
looked for'. When he came to England he must make himself at once, and all
the time, agreeable to the Queen and to the English.[19] Charles, doubting the
instinct of that strange, elderly young man his son, was doing his best to
supply its place with instruction.

But altogether, as Renard recognized, the match would be as hazardous as
it was great, and he began to be afraid, not that the marriage would be
rejected, but that Philip would be in danger when he came. It was cold

comfort for a prospective bridegroom to receive an urgent message from his bride, bidding him be sure to bring with him his own physicians and cooks.[20] But it was too late now to shelve the matter. The Emperor's envoys with instructions to conclude the treaty, arrived at Dover two days after Christmas; three of them were, after the Emperor's ordinary use, Netherlanders; Count Egmont was their leader. The commissioners waited a few days to recover from their sea-sickness, and then in state, and receiving organized and magnificent hospitality, they made their way to London. There they landed at Tower Wharf to the sound of many guns, and were escorted by Lord Courtenay to Durham House. But the Londoners showed no signs of welcome; only a silent, sullen crowd watched them covertly. The day before, when their servants had ridden in through the snow, the schoolboys had pelted them with snowballs.[21] London streets were soon to see more deadly missiles flying.

For the moment, however, the marriage treaty went smoothly on. The two parties were within the prohibited degrees of relationship, but a dispensation had been procured from the Pope, who, as a recognition of this accommodation received from Philip a present of a couple of mules 'to carry him from his palace to his vineyard'. These mules had been the subject of ambassadorial letters, for Don Juan Manrique de Lara had elicited from the Pope the information that mules 'light in colour and on no account black' were what he admired, and warned the Prince that one mule only 'would really be no better than nothing at all'.[22]

The strained relations between the Queen and her Council were also improving; for the Queen, having got her way, remembered that she was English. On the one hand she refused to treat personally any further in the matter of her marriage, saying to Renard that it was not seemly she should. But besides this, she told him, pointing to the ring which had been put on her finger at her coronation, that she had married her country first, and that the Council would protect its interests.[23] On the other hand the stubborn resistance of the Councillors was breaking down–perhaps the gold chains so urgently requested by Renard in letters to the Emperor had some part in that–and the marriage was now becoming a matter for arch jesting at Court. As the Queen sat in her chair after dinner on Twelfth Night, Lord William Howard, a plain, often a loose, talker was near. The Queen sat silent and full of thought. Howard went to her and whispered a few words, then turning to those round about he asked–Would they like to hear what he had said? The Queen tried to stop him, but of course he would out with it. He had said that he wished His Highness was present in that place, and he pointed to the seat at the Queen's right hand, so that he might drive thought and care away. Mary, blushing but unwilling to let the subject drop, asked why he said that. Howard saucily retorted that he knew very well she was not angry at what he said, but really liked it. At that, so Renard told the Emperor, 'Her Majesty and the whole company laughed.'[24]

Those days were probably the happiest of Mary's adult life. She had, as she

told Renard over and over, never known love. Now she was waiting for it,
ready to surrender herself to her heredity. Her father had gone this way and
that seeking love, or the nearest he knew to it. So had her great-grandfather,
Edward IV. Her mother had been a devoted wife, faithful, patient, and gentle.
Her father's sister, Mary Tudor, as soon as she was free from the crown of
France, had married, in secret and dangerously, where her heart had been.
Henry's other sister, Margaret of Scotland, had been almost as vehement and
changeable in her affections as her brother. It was not likely that Mary, the
child of such a house, would be a tepid lover. For years, giving scrupulous
obedience to her mother's charge, she had put away all thoughts of love from
her, but now she could hold out her hands to them, welcome them in, and
hug them to her. She must marry because she was a Queen, but now she
could dream of Philip because a woman's duty is to her husband. She must
hope for England's sake, to bear a child; but if a child came he would be more
to his mother than the heir of England. So she sat and sunned herself, in spite
of all perplexities, in the thought of her happiness to come, and many of her
Court must have found her ridiculous, though some may have seen her as
tragic–a woman of thirty-eight, looking forward to her marriage with the
simplicity of any girl, but with a woman's capacity for passion and for pain.

That fool's paradise which Mary had made for herself was soon violated
and laid waste. The articles of the marriage treaty were signed on January
12th. On January 16th the Council bade one of its Clerks write a letter to Sir
Thomas Dennys ordering him to send up to London a Devon gentleman,
Sir Peter Carew of Mohun's Ottery.[25] The summons precipitated the outbreak of what should have been a fourfold rising, it also anticipated the plans
of the conspirators by six precious weeks; so at least de Noailles said, and he,
of all men, should have known.[26]

The plot was an ambitious one. Armed risings in Devon, Leicestershire, Kent, and Wales were to be led by Carew, the Duke of Suffolk, Sir
Thomas Wyatt, and Sir James Crofts respectively. Courtenay was to be the
figurehead of the Devon rising; two horses, a roan and a white, were left in
the stables of the Bell at Andover for his use in the wild race that he should
have ridden into the West.[27] And if he put himself at the head of the Western
rebels, to what other prize could he have aspired but the crown itself?

In addition to all this a certain William Thomas had a plot of his own to
assassinate the Queen. He had held conversations with Sir Nicholas Arnold in
London on the subject, asking him–a rhetorical question doubtless–'Whether
were it not a good device to have all these perils that we have talked of, taken
away with very little bloodshed, that is to say, by killing of the Queen? I think
John Fitz William might be persuaded to do it; because he seems by his
countenance to be so manly a man, that he will not refuse any peril that might
come to his person to deliver his whole native country from so many and so
great dangers as be now offered thereunto, if he might be made to understand
them.' Fitz William, manly but thick-headed, accepted the part cast for him,
and told Wyatt of it. But Wyatt was not a man to deal in assassination. Even

the Attorney General at his trial absolved him from this–the plan that 'the Queen should have been slain as she did walk'. 'I do not burden you', he said, 'to consent to this; for this much I must say, you disliked it.' Wyatt, in his answer, gave evidence of how much he had disliked it. 'I made a cudgel', he told his judges, 'with a whole [? hole] brent in it and a whole iron . . . and sought John Fitz William a whole day and could not find him. The next day I sent the cudgel by my man and bade him bob him well, for the knave is but a spy, and to utter it he durst not.'[28] Yet for all Wyatt's disapproval, Thomas was in touch with all the conspirators, and was actually at Mohun's Ottery with Carew at the end of December.

Such was the English side of the conspiracy. The share of France, for France was in it at least as deep as she had been in Northumberland's devices, would, apart from de Noailles's assiduous activity as a go-between and counsellor to the conspirators, depend upon the success of the rising. The French King was very ready to welcome any seditious captain, who might like to bring his ship over to France, and de Noailles recommended that persons of quality should be stationed at the great Norman and Breton ports, so as to get in touch with the rebels as soon as they had done the dirty work.[29] But that work they must first do for themselves. Meanwhile the ambassador and the conspirators were as thick as thieves. De Noailles knew that Carew, when summoned by the Council, 'would take good care not to come'. He knew, that on the alarm caused by the summons, Sir James Crofts determined to leave London while yet he could. When news came that Sir Peter Carew had vanished, and that therefore the rising in the West was hanging fire, de Noailles wrote to his master news straight from the horse's mouth. 'I know', he said, 'that the man I told you of '–it must have been Wyatt–'is not a whit abashed by this; he goes away to-night to the place you know of. The others left three days ago, determined to do their duty.'[30] And it was de Noailles who, with perfect exactitude, prophesied that there would be trouble for the Queen about Candlemas Day. On that day Wyatt was at Deptford in his march on London.

A trifle, so it was rumoured, had let the cat out of the bag, and led to the forestalling of the whole elaborate plan. Courtenay gave an order to a tailor for the trimming of a coat of mail. Even if that were no more than a rumour, certainly the French ambassador and many others believed that it was 'that young fool of a Lord Courtenay' who had confessed to the Chancellor, or allowed the Chancellor to worm out of him all that he knew of the plot.[31] The Government acted promptly. When news came of the disappearance of Sir Peter Carew, Pembroke was sent off to Wales, the Lord Warden of the Cinque Ports to Kent, Bedford to the West country. No one seems to have expected trouble in the Midlands; no one could have guessed that Suffolk, pardoned and set free by the Queen, his daughter reprieved but still in the Tower, would make any move.

It is with Peter Carew and the West that we must first concern ourselves, because, though no rising took place there, the suspicions of the Council were first directed thither. Peter Carew it was who had acted a signal part in

suppressing the Western revolt in Edward's reign. Yet, Protestant in sympathy as he was, he had, like many another Protestant, declared openly for
Mary when it was a choice between her and Northumberland. Now the
Spanish marriage had done with him what it did with many another, pricking him out of patience and driving him into open resistance. And he was,
though not one of the great landowners of Devon, a man made to lead. Of
middle stature, but broad shouldered and strong, with black hair, a beard
'thick and great' and a dark, ruddy complexion, he had been in his boyhood
so ungovernably wild that his father, taking him from school, had for a while
collared and leashed him together with a hound to tame him to obedience.
That parent, one of the stern, even the savage school of educationalists, had
soon after allowed the boy to leave home in the company of a French gentleman only slightly acquainted with the family. Once in France Peter Carew
disappeared. For several years nothing was heard of him, until one of the elder
Carews, travelling abroad, heard his own surname spoken, and answered
from a crowd of lackeys and horse-boys. He made inquiries, and found that
his young kinsman, deserted by the French gentleman, had sunk to this
position. From that time Peter was again brought up as a gentleman, but not
as a stay-at-home. From France he went, like so many adventurous fellows, to
Italy, where there was always a chance to sell a good sword. There he served
with credit under that great Captain, the Prince of Orange, who, when
Carew wished to return, gave him letters of recommendation to King Henry.
At the English Court he became a great favourite. Perfect in the French tongue,
and speaking Italian well, he had seen men and countries; he had even been
so far afield as Turkey. Besides all this he had the ordinary accomplishments
of a gentleman; could ride with the best, and sing; the King took pleasure in
singing duets with him. Nor was he only globe-trotter, soldier, and courtier.
In the arts of government and war, in the science of mathematics, he read all
he could lay hands on in the three tongues at his command, and in these
subjects 'sharp was his understanding, pithy were his arguments, and deep
was his judgment'.[32] Such a man might well catch the eye of a king; still
more of his own untravelled neighbours. A generation later he would have
been one of many; in his own day Peter Carew was a rare and splendid bird.

Since the Members of Parliament had come home, just before Christmas,
with news that the Queen was to marry the Prince of Spain, the South-West
was full of a great ferment. Gentlemen rode about the stony, narrow lanes,
or sent their servants to ask of a neighbour, if he would 'assent to the landing
of the King of Spain or not?' while on the alehouse bench country folk were
telling each other that Philip was to land in Devon, 'with a great navy and a
great puissance'. The belief in Devon that this county was singled out for a
landing was perhaps justified; for it had been suggested by the Council that
the Prince might be pleased to land at Plymouth in order to escape as soon
as possible from the misery of sea-sickness. The Devon men, however,
unaware of such a human failing in their ogre, felt themselves in imminent
danger. Many an indignant gentleman must, like Sir Ralph Hopton, have

inquired of his labourers, how would they like it when Spanish soldiers outraged their wives before their faces, and have received the answer which he
did from 'one Pypit his workman', that 'he would rather cut off the Prince
of Spain's head himself'.[33]

Peter Carew, his uncle Gawain Carew, a Mr. Gibbs, and some other gentlemen, liked the prospect of Philip's arrival as little as did 'Pypit'. When the
news of the marriage treaty first came, Carew would have had a letter written
to the Queen warning her of what was being said in Devon, and telling her
'that if the King of Spain should land there it would be a great destruction to
the country'. But that letter, which was never sent, was not by any means the
extent of his efforts. Throughout the early part of January he was very busy
in and out of Exeter. One day a servant of his would be seen leading through
the streets six horses laden with armour and hand-guns. Another day a man
of the city, riding along with a lackey of Carew's, would hear that last Friday
night after the gates were shut, Sir Peter 'went over the walls of the said city
in his boots, and from thence unto John Christopher's house at Stoke, and for
that his boots grieved him, he cut them upon the way'. The same lackey had
carried secret letters from his master to his mistress, hidden in the sole of his
shoe or the lapel of his coat, bidding her make ready all those arms and the
'harness' (armour) which Sir Peter had in Exeter, so that it might be carried
out 'in hand-baskets by parcels'.[34] For all this quiet stir had its purpose, and
that purpose was the surprise and seizure of the city of Exeter.

Upon these plans the summons of the Council burst most rudely. Sir Peter
Carew and his uncle wrote protesting their complete innocence. Sir Peter gave
out that he was at once setting off for London to obey the Council's summons.
But instead, he disappeared. Fresh orders came from the Council. Sir Gawain
Carew, Sir Arthur Champernown, and Mr. William Gibbs were arrested.
Nothing was heard of Sir Peter Carew. Only some time after, a certain John
Fursman, who, on January 28th, had ridden from Dorchester to Weymouth,
reported what he had seen and heard that day. For, that evening, as he came
down to the great sweep of the bay, he had been surprised, late as it was, to
see two small fishing boats at sea about two leagues out. At supper, chatting
with his host and a neighbour, Edmund Knoplock, he asked what boats they
might have been. One, so Knoplock told him, was a bark of herrings, but 'in
the other boat was passed three gentlemen, one being a little man, the other
of mean [i.e. middle] stature, and the third a more longer young man'.
Knoplock had been standing near when the three climbed into the boat; he
saw that one wore a gold chain about his neck, and heard another say as the
boat pushed off—'The King of Spain will come shortly and he shall be well
barked at as ever man was.'[35] There is no doubt but that the man of middle
stature was Sir Peter Carew. He had military experience enough to know well
when a venture was hopeless. Cutting his losses he was now on the way to
France.

Others were less discreet. Three days before Carew sailed out of Weymouth
into the twilight, the Queen sent a messenger to the Duke of Suffolk, now

apparently so much in the Queen's confidence that it was even thought she
intended, at the first suspicion of a plot, to put him in command of her troops.
The messenger, who reached him early in the morning, bade the Duke come
at once to the Queen.

'Marry,' quoth he, 'I was coming to her Grace. Ye may see I am booted
and spurred ready to ride, and I will but break my fast and go.'[36] He gave the
messenger money; bade someone else give him drink, and sent him off. But
when the man had gone, Suffolk called his servant John Bowyer, told him to
go to his house in London to fetch 100 marks which were there, and also to
find Lord Thomas and Lord John Grey, and bid them be gone from the city
by six in the evening, and ride for Leicester where they should meet him.
Then, taking horse, he left Sheen, but not by the road to London.[37]

He was gone for a while, 'no man knoweth whither'. His sons too,
vanished from London as he had bidden, and rode north-east; they stopped
only at Sir Thomas Wroth's house, at nine o'clock that night, and even there
did not so much as dismount, but talked to Wroth and a friend at the door,
sitting on their horses. They borrowed a horse and a man to guide them
through Enfield Chase, and then went on again 'towards St. Alban's way',
through Dunstable and Brickhill to Stony Stratford, where at last they drew
rein and ate and baited the horses. On again they rode, hoping to catch the
Duke at Towcester; they missed him, and went farther, finally coming up
with him at Lutterworth in 'one Johnson's house'. Next day, at Bradgate, in
the heart of the Duke's own lands, it was published among their men 'that
they would go against the Spaniards with all their power'.[38]

But Suffolk's bolt was soon shot. On Tuesday evening when they reached
Leicester, and the Duke rode about the walls, the gates were all shut. Protestant
and turbulent as the city was, it would have none of him. One hope was left.
A man of his was in touch with Protestants in Coventry; they spoke boldly
of sending the Duke money and of opening the gates. Suffolk, arming himself and all his servants, rode off at once to Coventry; but here again the gates
were shut, and within the town the Mayor proclaimed Suffolk a traitor. Worse
than this was to come. He heard now that Huntingdon was after him with a
force of fifty horse.

No attempt was made to break into Coventry and reach friends in the
town. The shiftless, trustless, yet well-meaning nobleman had no more
determination in treason than in loyalty. He rode off with all his folk to his
own house of Astley, 'and there every man put off his harness'; the one word
now was flight. His young sons were borrowing frieze coats from the servants
for disguise, and dividing their money, while everyone took up what they
might of weapons, horses or cash, and so scattered.[39] The Duke threw himself upon the mercy of one of the keepers of his park, a man called Underwood,
who hid him in a large hollow tree 'standing about 2 bow-shots south-westward from the church'. There, for a few miserable days, Suffolk remained
undiscovered, only to be betrayed; some said by the keeper, others that it was
by a dog that sniffed obstinately at the tree.[40]

Carew fled to France; Suffolk's part in the rebellion was a mere flash in the pan; Crofts did not even get so far as attempting to raise the Welshmen; Kent was therefore left to bear the brunt of the action. Sir Thomas Wyatt, son of the poet, was to lead the revolt there. In his wild youth Wyatt had been in trouble with the Council, along with Surrey, his father's literary disciple. They were charged both with eating meat in Lent, and going about London streets at night taking shots at citizens' windows with cross-bows, though the object of this, said Surrey, with something of undergraduate humour, was to awaken the victims to a sense of sin.[41] But since those days Wyatt had seen soldiering at Boulogne, where his 'natural disposition to war' was commended and he was one of those who had come out boldly for Mary at Edward's death.

At the first hint of alarm he must have gone down from London to Allington, where the new house that his father had built stood beside the towers of an older castle, in whose moat the ducks swam, regardless of the coming of the Spaniards. In the very parlour where his father may have written those songs which still sing themselves, without any music of the lutes which he tuned to them, Thomas Wyatt the younger sat beside his fire on Monday, January 22nd, as any idle gentleman might, that cold and blustery weather. But Wyatt was not idle. He had already sent out men this way and that, calling his neighbours to come and speak with him. Sir Anthony Norton was the first of these to arrive. What, asked Wyatt, now the Spaniards were coming into England, would he 'do in defence thereof'? Norton, perhaps, had talked big when action had not been imminent, but now he drew back. He could do nothing, he said, seeing that his house lay so near both to Mr. Southwell's and Lord Abergavenny's. 'Well,' cried Wyatt, 'if such as ye are will not consider your fate, I can do no more but as one may do. If the worst come I can go into other parts where I shall be heartily welcome and joyously received.'

Upon an awkward pause entered three more Kentish gentlemen. These were less cautious than Norton, and began earnestly to discuss recruits and chances. Mr. Southwell, they said, would have been a great gain, could he have been persuaded to join, so much 'hath he the love and hearts of men in the parts of his lordship'. Sir Thomas Cheyne, Lord Warden of the Cinque Ports, whom the Queen had just sent down into Kent, would, they thought, find none of his men to follow him. Lord Cobham, said one, was sending three sons. But to that 'answer was made that such sending'—that is, when the sender kept himself free to take the other side—'was the casting away of the Duke [of Northumberland]'. And, said the objectors, 'our lives are as dear to us as my lord's are unto him. . . . Wherefore, said they, let him go himself and set his foot by ours.' After this the group drew together and began to talk in whispers, leaving Sir Anthony Norton free to withdraw or join them. He chose the prudent course, and after drinking a cup of wine in the hall, mounted his horse and rode away from a very dangerous house.[42]

Wyatt was not to be turned by the defection of a few. These must have been busy days for him, with servants riding hard on messages to friends, neighbours, and kinsmen. For the rising was to be in the hands of such–Harper from Chart, Cuthbert Vaughan from Great Chart, Knevetts from Chedington, Mantells from Horton Monachorum, Iseleys from Reade and Staplehurst, all these were friends, if not relations.

On January 23rd, in the cold and dark of the morning two hours before dawn, a young man stopped at the smith's house at Ightham in the Kent Weald, and asked for his horse to be shod. It was William Iseley, son of Sir Henry Iseley, and while Cotman the smith worked, and the young man stood at the fire, they began to talk.

The Spaniards, said Iseley, 'are coming into the realm with harness and hand-guns . . . for this realm shall be brought into such bondage as it was never before'. What Cotman answered he did not afterwards confess. Perhaps he was wise enough to hold his tongue as he bent over the hissing shoe. But the young man had not done. When he swung into his saddle at the smithy door his last words were a challenge. 'Smith,' he cried, so that all the street could hear, 'if thou beest a good fellow, stir and encourage all the neighbours to rise against these strangers.' But the smith was still cautious. 'Why', said he, 'these be marvellous words, for we shall all be hanged if we stir.' 'No,' quoth Iseley, 'ye shall have help enough, for people are already up in Devon and Cornwall, Hampshire, and other counties', and so rode off again into the darkness.[43]

This was on Tuesday. Thursday was, and still is, market day at Maidstone. But at that Thursday market the sale of butter, eggs, cheese, salt meat, late apples and pot-herbs, was interrupted by the clanging of the church bell, and then by a roll of drums. While people crowded and jostled together to see and hear, Sir Thomas Wyatt of Allington, and Sir Henry Iseley–men as well known to all there as Maidstone Market Cross itself–read out a proclamation, and afterwards set it up to be read. Queen Mary, Wyatt told them, would marry a stranger. Yet, notwithstanding, 'we seek no harm to the Queen, but better counsel and counsellors . . . for herein lyeth the health and wealth of us all. For trial hereof and manifest proof of this intended purpose; lo, now even at hand Spaniards be now already arrived at Dover, at one passage to the number of a hundred, passing upward to London, in companies of ten, four and six, with harness, harquebuses, and morions, with match light, the foremost company whereof be already at Rochester.'[44]

At that news the hearers must have felt as if, waking, they had found their nightmare true. They had heard rumours of the arrival of Egmont and his fellows; now they learnt that these inoffensive and rather sea-sick Flemings were in reality Spaniards marching secretly in small companies upon London. No wonder if many a man of them hurried home and took down from the wall of his house-place a sword, or a bill, and turned out into the early dusk of February to defend England against such a threat. No wonder, when a gentleman, who had ridden all night from London, came clattering into Maidstone, crying that all England was up to drive away Spaniards, no wonder that the countrymen – yeomen, labourers, squires, believed and followed Wyatt.

While most of these simple folk who left their homes for ever, went out only to defend England against an alien master, there were some who aimed, as Sir Robert Southwell thought Wyatt himself aimed, 'at some mark nearer home than Spain, except he deceiveth me'. One of these, a rich man and a friend, came to Wyatt, to make sure if this was so, if we may believe Master John Proctor, the conservative schoolmaster of Penshurst. ' "Sir," quod he, "they say I love potage well; I will sell all my spoons and all the plate in my house, rather than your purpose shall quail, and sup my potage with my mouth. I trust", quod he, "you will restore the right religion again." ' But Wyatt – even Master Proctor was forced to admit it – knew that this was not common ground for the men who followed him. ' "Whist!" said he, "you may not so much as name religion, for that will draw from us the hearts of many." '[45] He knew well that it was not that cry, but the fear of the Spaniard that would certainly rouse Kent and might open the gates of London.

Wyatt wasted no time. With the men that he could gather he moved that day to Rochester, and on the way thither met Sir George Harper, a man who was to prove a double-dyed traitor, but now most welcome. Together they entered the town, fortified the east side, and broke down the bridge to the west. Wyatt had done well, and his luck still held. There were ships in the river below Gravesend, which the Queen had had made ready for the escort of her bridegroom. Wynter, an able Captain, was in command, and he with his officers and their crew came over to Wyatt, bringing not only their own arms but the great guns from the ships.[46] It seemed at the time a gain of tremendous importance. Not only would the guns help to secure Wyatt's forces in Rochester, but, when he had made wheeled carriages for them, they were to go along with him. The guns proved more useful for prestige than for service, and in the end, it was by his delay over one of them, when its carriage broke down, that Wyatt threw away his last faint chance of success.

For the moment, however, if, as many thought, Wyatt had friends in London and allies in France, he might well be hopeful. Speed was the essential thing. He must gather his Kentish bands before Abergavenny, Southwell and the Lord Warden could rally the loyal gentlemen of Kent; before the Queen could send forces from London. The Iseleys and Knevetts were, he knew, busy about Tonbridge, collecting arms, chiefly by means of breaking into enemies' houses; on January 27th Wyatt wrote urging them to join him. Another danger had also to be provided against. When a herald came from the Queen, Wyatt met him at the gate of Rochester and refused him entry; he could not afford to lose any of his men, lured away by promise of pardon. The herald tried to push his way into the gate, but failed after a scuffle. In the end the message – a general pardon for all who laid down their arms within twenty-four hours – was heard by Wyatt only and the few people with him.[47]

The loyalists had been taken by surprise, and small wonder, for February was no month for a rising, and Wyatt's plan had never intended it for such.

Moreover, Lord Abergavenny was unable to trust his men, and dare do nothing against Wyatt's proclamation at Maidstone – not even so much as one stout-hearted gentleman did at Milton. For there a certain Christopher Roper, 'a man of good worship', stood up in the market-place when Wyatt's proclamation was read, and called him and his men traitors. He was taken, and at once brought to Wyatt at Rochester, and charged with his words. 'This tongue', replied the stubborn fellow, 'spake it, and doth now avow it.'[48]

But Abergavenny, though he could do nothing to prevent Wyatt's proclamation, with its trumpets and its drums, was by no means idle. On January 26th he was in London, bringing news of the occupation of Rochester. On the 27th he was back again at Malling with Sir Robert Southwell, having orders to join the Queen's forces at Gravesend. On Saturday, which was Malling market day, while the people stood about 'to a very great number in the manner of a ring', the Sheriff read the royal proclamation against Wyatt, and then gave it over to one of Abergavenny's servants, a gentleman named Barham to repeat. He did so, and afterwards, carried away by the excitement of the moment, he added 'of his own head', – 'You may not so much as lift a finger against your King or Queen.' 'I know', said Wyatt, when he heard of it – 'I know that Barham well, but yet I never took him to have so wide a throat; if I live I may happen to make him crow a higher note in another place.'[49]

Next day Abergavenny intended to fall back on Gravesend, presumably in the hope of joining any royal force marching from London. But something which happened in the night changed his plans. Wyatt's friends the Iseleys and Knevetts, who had been profitably employed round about Tunbridge, and were just got back from Penshurst, 'where they had Sir Henry Sidney his armoury', now received Wyatt's urgent request that they should join him. They had five hundred men of the Weald with them, and they were ready to obey, but Abergavenny lay at Malling, and they decided to give him a wide berth and march by the longer road to Rochester, through Wrotham; this would also allow them to search Sir George Clerk's house for arms. That same night Abergavenny's camp was wakened by an alarm. 'Treason, treason, we are betrayed!' was the shout. But the scare was caused only by the arrival of a messenger with news of the Iseleys' and Knevetts' intentions.[50]

Now, however little he trusted his men, Abergavenny must attack, or allow two forces of the enemy to combine. Next morning, he and the loyal Kentish men moved out, through familiar lanes, and against men they had met at market, at the hunt, at church. Near Wrotham Heath they heard clearly the sound of the rebels' drums beating before them. Abergavenny, turning aside, drew up his men at Burrough Green; he counted that the enemy must pass this way to Sir George Clerk's house. But though he waited, no one came; the Iseleys and their men, warned in time, had 'shrunk as secretly as they could by a bye way'. Abergavenny pursued. At last he caught sight of them as they moved up Wrotham Hill, their ensign displayed and altogether 'seeming to be in great ruff'. Sending on his horse, Abergavenny caught them at the top of the hill in a field called Blacksoll field.

The skirmish did not last long. Iseleys' yeomen shot off their bows, and there was 'a fierce brag shown by some of the horsemen'; then the whole force broke and fled into the bare winter woods, 'in such sort' as a Kentish gentleman said who saw the rout, 'that they shall never meet again until Domesday'.[51] Iseley lay hidden in the undergrowth all night, then fled westwards into Hampshire. The two Knevetts, leaping from their horses, crept into the wood; when clear of pursuit they set to work 'to rip their boots from their legs and run away in . . . their hose'.[52]

Anthony Knevett brought the news to Wyatt at Rochester. It was a shrewd blow. Not only had Wyatt lost his hope of reinforcements of 500 good men, with the arms that they had collected, but also Abergavenny was now free to join the Queen's forces which had arrived from Gravesend.

These, under the command of the old Duke of Norfolk, whose armour and authority must have sat strangely upon him after so many quiet years in the Tower, consisted chiefly of 200 men of the guard under Sir Henry Jerningham, the same Norfolk squire who had done such good work for the Queen last summer, and 600 of the city bands, all in white coats, divided into six companies of 100, each with its own Captain. It was not a large force—Norfolk thought it scurvy. Not more than 300 Kentish men had met him there, though there were certain gentlemen waiting for him—notably Lord Cobham, cousin of Wyatt's, whose two sons, in the old provident way, had gone out with the rebels, while he kept the family balance true between loyalty and treason. But of Norfolk's brother, Lord William Howard, the Admiral, not a word; of Sir Thomas Cheyne, Warden of the Cinque Ports not a word; and Lord Abergavenny, only the news that he had turned aside to safeguard Clerk's house from the Iseleys' band.[53]

The Duke began by sending a herald into Rochester with an offer of pardon. This time Wyatt allowed the man to do his office and the offer seemed to have an effect. For, though the only reply from Wyatt's folk was that they had need of no pardon, there came stealing into the Duke's camp in the small hours of the next morning, a deserter from the rebels, Sir George Harper, who probably brought Norfolk his first news of Abergavenny's successful skirmish, and who asked and got the Duke's promise of pardon. By candlelight Norfolk sat down and wrote the news to the Council.[54]

Next day, he set off for Rochester without waiting, as he had first intended, for the coming of the Admiral. He felt not too hopeful of forcing Rochester bridge. 'Howbeit', he told the Council, 'we shall do what we can.'[55]

He did not intend a direct attack on Rochester. If Wyatt would not come out he would play for time, sending in proclamations and messages encouraging desertion, until Lord Abergavenny and Southwell, joining with the missing Sir Thomas Cheyne, could come up on the other side of the town. But if Wyatt would cross the Strood bridge to him, then he would fight. From this determination he was not to be moved by a letter which he received that morning. Lord Cobham, who, after great expressions of loyalty, had gone back to Cooling, now wrote warning the Duke that Wyatt expected the Guards and Londoners in Norfolk's army to desert to him, and advising him in round terms not to trust Sir George Harper.[56] Norfolk, perhaps justifiably, refused to be scared. He sent word to Cobham to meet him on the way with 100 men, and set off through the wind and rain of that tempestuous winter day, in weather 'so terrible that no man could stir by water, or yet well by land'.[57]

On Spitell Hill, where the road from Gravesend drops down to the bridge head, the Duke drew up his forces, and went forward with Sir Henry Jerningham to see to the placing of his guns. But, as the first gun was fired to challenge the town, he heard the White Coats on the hill behind him begin to shout—'We are all Englishmen, we are all Englishmen! A Wyatt! A Wyatt!' and down the hill they came against the Duke, led by a certain Alexander Brett, one of the Captains. Sir George Harper had done his work.

If Norfolk had been a younger man he might have turned the guns on them, though even that, with Wyatt on his other hand, would have served him little. As it was he did nothing, but set spurs to his horse, and with Jerningham and a few loyal men, galloped off to safety.

Wyatt came out of the gate, and to him went Harper, 'footing it afore the other Captains with his sword drawn. "I promised you a good turn," said he, "and say not now but I have paid it!"' In the excitement and confusion that followed, Wyatt rode over the bridge, calling upon all the Londoners to follow him, but, with that touch of fine leadership which makes the rebellion such a tragic waste, crying also—'So many as will depart, good leave have they.' All the London bands and a good part of the Guard chose to stay; a few only took themselves off, and 'you should have seen', said one who did see, 'some of the guard come home, their coats turned, and all ruined, without arrows or string to their bows, or sword, in very strange wise'.[58] They left the road to London open behind their heels.

But for Wyatt the question was, what should he do next? Abergavenny and Southwell, though far outnumbered, lay at Malling and Maidstone respectively. Should he turn first on them? At a council of war there was debate on it; but the London Whitecoats clamoured for a march on the city. 'London', they said, 'longed sore for their coming.' Wyatt may well have believed them. If these bands were anything to go by, London was his.

So it was decided. He paused only to storm Cooling castle, which Lord Cobham held without too great determination, and then for the Kentish men it was 'Hey for London Town.' They may well have hoped that already the worst was over. They had routed the royal forces, and now, when they reached Blackheath, that fatal field for rebels, they were met by fresh messengers from the Queen, no mere heralds these, but gentlemen of the Privy Council: Sir Edward Hastings, Master of the Queen's Horse, and Sir Thomas Cornwallis. These brought a very placatory message. If Wyatt and his friends were in arms only against strangers, and for fear of the Spanish marriage, the Queen would appoint persons to confer with him on this matter.

Said Wyatt, thinking doubtless that the game was in his hands—'I yield

thereto, but for my surety I will rather be trusted than trust', and asked, as
that surety, the custody of the Tower, 'and her Grace in the Tower', the
removal of three or four Councillors, and appointment of others to be chosen
by him. No wonder that 'upon this lewd answer, long and stout conference
was between them', and nothing agreed.[59] That night Wyatt camped about
Blackheath and Greenwich.

London had already begun to feel itself a besieged city. It was a week since
the first alarm of the rising had reached it, and the small boys and idlers must
have grown used to the novelty of harnessed men 'keeping the city', and of a
couple of aldermen 'perusing the gate guard' every evening.[60] To the
Council, sitting anxiously and long at Westminster, ill news was coming in
by every post from Kent. Mud-splashed messengers handed in letters with
such breathless superscriptions as –

> 'To the Queen's Most
> Excellent Majesty.
> hast hast
> post
> hast
> with all diligence possible
> for thy life
> for thy life.'[61]

And those letters were seized and opened in haste, not with a knife slipped
neatly under the seal to detach it, but rather rashed open, in dread of the
contents, so that the seals tore holes in the paper, holes that still in the scholastic quiet of the Public Record Office, bear witness to the fears and confusion
of those scrambling days.

Yet, faced as the Council was with such a crisis, when it had made a few
dispositions, had appointed Pembroke and Clinton to command the Queen's
forces, and Lord William Howard to the defence of the city, it fell to quarrelling. Accusations and counter-accusations were flung across the council board;
it was Paget's fault for pushing the Spanish marriage; it was Gardiners' fault
for pressing on with the changes in religion. Rumours were busy too.
Courtenay was at the back of the plot. The Lady Elizabeth was in it, she was
moving away from London, she was gathering troops, her household now
ate in a week what ordinarily lasted a month.[62] With more justice the Council
believed that the French ambassador was deep in the plot. 'Little Nicholas',
one of his messengers, had been stopped, and his letters opened; 'Thanks be
to God,' wrote de Noailles to his master, 'things are going well.' Gardiner
confessed that such a breach of diplomatic privilege was unusual, but thought
it excusable when a man was so 'het' with a crisis as he.[63]

In the midst of the turmoil the Imperial ambassadors began to fear for their
safety; even Renard was asking what would happen to him if the Londoners
rose. At last Egmont and his colleagues slipped away by night, taking whatever small ships they found ready in the river, and leaving their horses to

follow. They had an escort of the Queen's Guard, but when the strangers were safely embarked, these men relieved their suppressed feelings by shouting insulting remarks and firing off their harquebuses as a valediction. And now Wyatt had reached Southwark.

But Renard stayed, and the Queen, perplexed almost to despair, not daring to trust more than a handful about her, and none in the city, the Queen stayed too. In the debates of the Council there was indeed much question as to whether and where she should go, at first with hardly a doubt that go she must. Courtenay's faction suggested Calais; it was a suggestion suspect both from its source and from its content; none of her friends seriously dreamt of her going overseas; had she gone she would certainly not have returned. But others, more level headed, or more careful of her crown, suggested other alternatives. There was Windsor, a strong castle and clear of the city; there was the Tower itself, the royal fortress of London, whither at the first news of trouble arms and stores had been sent. Or she might, some said, leaving the seditious capital, throw herself on the loyalty of the Catholic country folk. But while they debated Mary found her suspicions confirmed by the fact that they did not, for all their promises, provide her with a single man in addition to the two hundred archers of her guard.[64] She suspected them of she knew not what–she suspected them all.

Yet, daunted and dismayed as she was, on the day that Wyatt's demands came from Blackheath, she had taken all her dogged courage in her hands, and having given notice to the Mayor and aldermen, rode down to the Guild-hall to speak to the citizens of London, some of whom, as de Noailles knew, were actually talking of handing her over to Wyatt,[65] and whose bands had gone over to the enemy. She had with her the Chancellor of England, Lords of the Council, and ladies of her household. There, standing under a cloth of estate, she spoke to the city companies, in her strong deep voice, royally and wittily as she was a Tudor, simply as she was a simple woman.

'I am come to you in mine own person', she said, 'to tell you that which already you see and know; that is how traitorously and rebelliously a number of Kentishmen have assembled themselves against both us and you. Their pretence (as they said at the first) was for a marriage determined for us; to the which end to all the articles thereof ye have been made privy. But since, we have caused certain of our Privy Council to go again unto them . . . and it appeared then unto our said Council that the matter of the marriage seemed to be but a Spanish cloak to cover their pretended purpose against our religion.' With that she told them Wyatt's insolent terms.

'Now, loving subjects,' she continued, 'what I am, ye right well know. I am your Queen, to whom at my coronation when I was wedded to the realm and laws of the same . . . you promised your allegiance and obedience unto me. . . . My father as ye all know, possessed the same regal state which now rightly descended unto me, and to him always ye showed yourselves most faithful and loving subjects; and therefore I doubt not but ye will show your-selves likewise to me. . . . And I say to you, on the word of a prince, I cannot tell how naturally the mother loveth the child, for I was never the mother of any, but certainly if a prince and governor may as naturally and earnestly love her subjects as the mother doth love the child, then assure yourselves that I, being your lady and mistress, do as earnestly and tenderly love and favour you.'

Then she came to the great matter – the foreign husband.

'I am not', she told them, 'so bent to my will, neither so precise nor affectionate, that rather for mine own pleasure I would choose where I lust, or that I am so desirous as needs I would have one.' And she promised them if this marriage should not seem advisable to 'all the nobility and commons in the high court of Parliament . . . then I will abstain from marriage while I live'.

She was telling the truth; or as near as she could now get to it, and it was what she had told Renard – 'that she would never take another husband' than Philip. She did not tell the Londoners, as she told Renard, that she considered herself already Philip's wife, and Renard was not told, or did not report to the Emperor the full force of the Queen's promise, but only that 'if the reasons in favour of it [the marriage] had not been understood, they might be repeated in Parliament'.[66] Yet I think that even now if she could have been convinced that honest, loyal, and Catholic Englishmen hated the match, she might have lived unmarried. The trouble was, that in her eyes resistance to the marriage was inextricably confused with treachery, rebellion, and heresy.

But the Londoners did not yet know this, and when she went on to ask them if they would defend her against these rebels – 'for if you do', she said, 'I am minded to live and die with you, and strain every nerve in your cause, for this time your fortunes, goods, honour, personal safety, wives and children are in the balance' – they rose to her.

She had touched the feelings of her listeners – their old affection for her father, their self interest, their liking for a stout courage; they answered her with cheers, shouting, and throwing up of caps. When it was over, the Queen withdrew, drank a cup of wine with the Lord Mayor, and then, riding to the Crane in the Vintry, took her barge and returned to Westminster, a small, tight-lipped woman, never afraid of men, but only of decisions.[66]

That same day came a gleam of comfort to the loyal but anxious citizens of London. It was proclaimed throughout the city that the Earl of Huntingdon had taken the Duke of Suffolk and two of his sons, and was bringing them back to London.

But still Wyatt came on. That night he was at Deptford Strand, and lay there all next day. On Friday night he left Deptford and came towards Southwark. Messengers brought news of his movements. The Lords of the Council were wakened. Between two and three o'clock in the morning they came to the Queen's bedchamber in the palace at Westminster. She must, they told her, get up, take boat, and escape while yet she might.

But Mary would not. Instead she had Simon Renard sent for. Yesterday, with Wyatt at Deptford, there had again been fresh talk of her leaving London, and the Chancellor himself had advised her to go to Windsor. But, when she had asked Renard's advice, he had given her a flat 'No'. 'No, if she valued her crown.' If needs must, he told her, go to the Tower, but if once she left London, Elizabeth would be queen and religion down. That was the strongest argument he could have used. So now she sent for him again.

He came to that strange agitated Council meeting beside the great curtained royal bed. The Council was disputing the question. Renard could only repeat what he had said yesterday.

The Queen, shaken as always by argument, and not daring to trust any man who was English-born, spoke at last, clinging to what she felt her duty, if only it were humanly possible to do it. She would stay, she said, if Pembroke and Clinton, the Captains of her army, would be true men to her. And so she would send them a message, asking them if they would be true, and upon their answer she would act. The messenger was sent, and returned. The two lords begged her to stay, 'assuring her that God would give her the victory'.[67] She believed them, and she stayed.

That day all the streets of London were full of men in harness, for most householders, as well as the Mayor and aldermen, went armed about their daily business. In Westminster Hall the lawyers pleaded their cases with armour under their robes, and the Lord Mayor's servants were armed as they waited on him at dinner, At home all the women were busy making white coats for their men to wear.[68]

Then, in the afternoon, the boom of the Tower guns broke upon the uneasy murmur of the city. The watchers there had seen Wyatt's flags moving through the trees and the few houses on the Southwark shore. At the south end of London Bridge Lord William Howard bade them cut loose the drawbridge; the gates of the city were slammed to, and the bolts shot, but not before galloping posts rode off with orders to break down the Thames bridges for fifteen miles above London. Mayor and Sheriffs turned out, bidding all close up their shops, and shutter their windows. 'Then should ye have seen taking in wares of the stalls in most hasty manner; there was running up and down in every place to weapons and harness. Aged men were astonied, many women wept for fear, children and maids ran into their houses shutting the doors for fear',[69] and there they must stay in the stuffy twilight of the shuttered rooms while the men of the house watched armed before the door.

That was a strange night in London. Not for more than a hundred years had rebels come so close to her gates. At Whitehall the pensioners were ordered to watch in armour in the Court-'so', says the lively Edward Underhill, the ruffling 'hot gospeller' who found the darkest spot was under the candle, and the safest place for a Protestant, the Queen's own household-'so, being all armed we came up into the chamber of presence with our pole-axes in our hands, wherewith the ladies were very fearful, some lamenting, crying, wringing their hands, said "Alas, there is some great mischief toward; we shall be destroyed to-night. What a sight is this to see the Queen's chamber full of armed men, the like was never heard of." '[70]

If the Court was so like a garrison, the city too was ready for war. Underhill, turned summarily away from the palace by the chief usher – 'That heretic shall not watch here'–went off, with a saucy word of thanks, to his comfort-able bed at home. He reached Ludgate but found it shut. He cried out to the guard to open. ' "Who?" quoth one. "What?" quoth another, and much laughing they made.' But, though they treated the crisis with the incurable levity of the Englishman, they kept the gate shut. Underhill had to trudge off to Newgate, where a friend of his was on gate watch, before he could get into the city.[71]

But Wyatt made no attack, and the Queen forbade that the guns of the Tower should be fired upon the houses of Southwark, so for three days there was an uneasy pause. Wyatt, having drawn a trench and set his guns against the bridge-head, waited. Lord William Howard, with a day and night watch of three hundred, kept the bridge, and he also waited.

Probably Wyatt hoped, probably he succeeded in getting into touch with friends in the city. But he had indeed arrived just two days too late. De Noailles was sure that had he been able to reach the city on the morning of February 1st, he might have marched in unopposed and received the Queen, a prisoner, at the Londoners' hands. But her speech, made the very same day, spoiled all that.[72] Yet even now there was a chance that London would let him enter. He did nothing to imperil that chance. Food he found in plenty in the suburbs, but not a thing must be taken without payment, and there must be no looting. Certain gentlemen, more out of hand than Wyatt's yeomen and shop-keepers, found their way to Winchester House and there 'made havoc'. After they had done, there was not a lock left on the doors nor a book in the library left undamaged 'so that men might have gone up to the knees in leaves of books cut out and thrown under foot'–so said Master John Stow who loved books and who saw, noted, and deplored the damage.[73] But this was the only instance of looting. For the rest, it was 'a strange matter what pains he took, himself coming on foot amongst' the people. He knew that London would judge him by his behaviour at Southwark, and that if the city feared a sack it would certainly keep its gates shut. That he did know this, and had the power to keep his men in hand, shows what a leader there was in this poet's son, whose wild youthful pranks and whose lawlessness cannot obscure those other qualities which he shared with happier men, who lived to see a happier reign. For he knew and loved, as Drake knew and loved his Englishmen, and he could command them. It was said, that when a price had been put upon his head he took care to wear his name written in his cap, so that each man should have the power to sell him.[74]

But he could not stay for ever at Southwark. For one thing a threat had been conveyed to the Southwark people, that the guns of the Tower would retaliate for the death of a waterman who had been killed by a shot from Wyatt's side of the river. For another, Abergavenny, having at last heard that 'my Lord Warden was forthcoming', had joined that dilatory gentleman, and having collected loyal forces from Kent was coming on towards London.

So, on Shrove Tuesday morning Wyatt shouted a last challenge to the guard at the head of London Bridge. 'Twice', he cried, 'have I knocked and not been suffered to enter. If I knock a third time I will come in by God's grace.'[75] Then the rebel army marched out of their comfortable quarters in Southwark, moving through the deep mud of the winter roads south-westward in the hope of finding a bridge across the Thames.

It was not till four o'clock that afternoon that they reached Kingston. Thirty feet of the bridge had been broken down, though the piles still stood in the swollen river. To make matters worse, a guard had been posted on the farther shore. Even when his guns dispersed these, Wyatt seemed little better off, but he was not daunted. He had with him, among all the inland men of the Weald, Wynter's sailors from the Queen's ships. Some of these volunteered to swim over; they came back, in some barges which lay moored on the other side. In these Wyatt, and enough men to form a guard, crossed over to the Middlesex shore. Then, with ladders, planks, and ropes, the bridge was rigged again securely enough to bear both men and guns. But such a work took time. It had been dark for hours when, at ten o'clock, his tired men went over the bridge, dragging the rumbling great gun-carriages after them.[76]

They were tired, they were hungry, they were benighted, and their last hope lay in speed. Even now, many men believed, Wyatt had accomplices in London who would have been glad to open a gate for him. When the Council informed Sir Thomas Cheyne that Wyatt was likely to cross at Kingston, he replied in an agitated letter–'I would not wish he should do it in any wise,' he wrote, 'for then he trusteth on some others to join with him, or else he durst as well be hanged', since, in the march round London, Wyatt was cutting himself off from Kent.[77] It was not only his enemies who believed that haste would profit him. His friends insisted on the dangers of delay, because, they said, 'by that means the hour was broken by appointment'. But apart from the slow pace of his tired men, Wyatt made other delay. The carriage of one of the great guns broke down. He would stay till it was mended. Brett, the traitor White-coat captain, Cuthbert Vaughan, the late King's bear-ward, and Dr. Ponet, erstwhile Bishop of Winchester, all tried to persuade him to leave it behind in the mud, and make what haste he could to come to London; but he would not. Delay and waning hopes began now to work upon his forces. Ponet 'at the very place where the gun did break', took leave. He promised to 'pray unto God for their good success' but preferring to await the answer to prayer in a safe place, made off without stop or stay to Germany.[78] Another deserter was Sir George Harper, that rat, who slipped off, hoping to make his peace.

At last, with a force of weary, muddy, rain-soaked, and hungry men, who had toiled through the darkness, the late dawn, and most of the forenoon, at eleven in the morning of Ash Wednesday, Wyatt found himself at Knightsbridge. He should have reached the city early in the morning, before it was light. Now it was too late, for London was awake and all astir. Those friends of his, who in the sleepy small hours might have taken a risk and opened to him one of the northern gates, dared not do it now that their neighbours were coming out.

And Londoners had been early on foot that strange morning. At dusk in the evening before, a trumpeter had gone through the city bidding all, horse and foot, to be outside the walls, at St. James's Palace, by six next morning. But in the middle of the night came a breathless scout with news that Wyatt was already at Brentford. At four o'clock drums went about through the dark streets and the citizens roused up to dress and arm hastily by rushlight and candlelight.[79]

When at last Wyatt came along Knightsbridge, Pembroke had already drawn up his horsemen and guns 'on the hill in the highway above the new bridge over against St. James's'; that is on the open slope where now Bond Street runs up towards Oxford Street. His foot were lower down, nearer to Charing Cross, 'at the lane turning down by the brick wall from Islington ward', and a few more horsemen were posted at about the position of Trafalgar Square. The Queen, after a fresh rumour had got about to the effect that she was going to the Tower, had now sent a message from Whitehall to the city 'that she would tarry there to see the uttermost'.[80]

When Wyatt had posted his guns on a hill beyond St. James's Palace 'almost over against the Park corner', he moved on. He had intended to pass along the northern suburbs of the city to Holborn and so to Newgate; perhaps Underhill's friend or some other Protestant malcontent had promised to open the gate. But Pembroke's force made this impossible without fighting. So, after a few encouraging words to his men, Wyatt came, on foot as they were, but in bravery of velvet and steel, booted and spurred 'down the old lane . . . hard by the Court gate of St. James's'. Pembroke made no movement till the enemy was almost past, then Clinton, and Musgrave who led the light horse, charged down on their 'tail', cutting it off. There was a scuffle, some shooting from the guns on both sides, but nothing more. Pembroke did not press on. Wyatt did not turn back, but made for Charing Cross, where he met and easily scattered a small force of horsemen. But for all that the whole attack was in reality breaking up. The rearguard was lost; in the fight at Charing Cross the Knevetts and young Cobham left the main force and made for Westminster; the Marquess of Winchester's men were between Wyatt and Ludgate; and Ludgate was shut. Yet with desperate courage he pushed his way up Fleet Street, his naked sword held by the point, and his men crying, 'Queen Mary hath granted our requests and given us pardon. The Queen hath pardoned us', so that the Treasurer's men let them go by in the narrow road without a blow struck. Meanwhile the Court and the city were smitten with panic. It was said that when fighting was afoot at Charing Cross the shrieks of women came, with the boom of cannon on St. James's field, to the leads of the White Tower where the prisoners, the Marquess of Northampton, Sir Nicholas Poyns and others, craned their necks and strained their ears to learn how the day went. At Whitehall the panic was not all from the women. While Sir Richard Southwell with 500 men had charge of 'the back side as the woodyard and that way' (that is to say the part of the palace which stood between what is now Scotland Yard and the river) old Sir John Gage, Lord

Chamberlain, was in command on the other side, and had drawn up his men outside the gate. But when Knevett and Thomas Cobham, with that company of rebels who had left Wyatt at Charing Cross, broke suddenly though the gatehouse, Gage, three of the Queen's judges, and all their men, bolted back so hurriedly that the poor old man tripped and fell in the mud. As best they could they bundled him in and slammed the gate behind them, while the rebels began to shoot arrows into the yard, and one casualty at least–the nose of a Lincoln's Inn lawyer–was recorded.

Inside the palace no one knew exactly what had happened in the 'great hurliburli' outside. Men of the guard were pushing their way into the Hall; the pensioners were trying to keep them out. Someone, on a rumour that Pembroke had gone over to Wyatt cried, 'Treason! Treason!' As the confused mob of shouting men jostled in, the women began to scream and to rush about through the painted and tapestried rooms and galleries trying to bar doors and shutters against they knew not what danger.

Up into the gallery above the gatehouse where the Queen sat the rout came trampling with shouts of 'All is lost! Away! A barge, a barge!'

But Mary would not move, no, not 'one foot'. Where, she asked, was Lord Pembroke? They told her–'On the field.'

'Well, then,' said she, at her gallantest, 'Fall to prayer, and I warrant you we shall hear better news anon, for my Lord will not deceive me, I know well.' Then, surely remembering how that was the very thing she did not know, since there was not one who had not deceived her–'If he would,' she added, 'God will not, in whom my chief trust is, who will not deceive me.'

Her hardihood stopped the panic. The crowd sobered, and ebbed away. Soon the pensioners were asking that the gates might be opened so that they could strike a blow at the Queen's enemies. Sir Richard Southwell brought their request to the Queen. She gave her permission, but sent them a message begging 'that you will not go forth of her sight for her only trust is in you ... this day'. So the gates were flung open once more and the pensioners passed out, and for the next hour, marched up and down, waiting valiantly for an attack that never came.

Meanwhile, Wyatt had reached Ludgate. Some said that a few minutes before his coming the gate was opened, and that it was only when John Harris, 'a merchant tailor in Watling Street', seeing Wyatt's banners down the hill, cried out in warning–'I know that these be Wyatt's ancients', that they shut the gate; and even then some there were angry with Harris, perhaps some of those 'hollow hearts' that rejoiced at Wyatt's approach. At any rate, the gates were shut when he came; and when he knocked, saying that 'Here was Wyatt whom the Queen had granted their requests', he was answered by the voice of William Howard–'Avaunt, traitor. Thou shall not come in here.'

It was the end. Wyatt himself, as he said, 'had kept touch', but his friends had failed him. For a few minutes he sat on a bench outside the Belle Sauvage inn, then, a beaten man, but free yet, he turned and went back down the Strand and Fleet Street.

It was near Charing Cross that fighting began again, as some of Pembroke's men, coming inwards, met Wyatt and his weary fellows tramping out. Not many blows were struck. A herald, Clarencieux or Norroy, it matters little, cried to Wyatt to yield, rather than 'be the death of all these your soldiers. Perchance ye may find the Queen merciful.' Wyatt, shaken by the plea, hesitated, then, to his honour, took the chance. 'Well, if I shall needs yield', he said, 'I will yield me to a gentleman', and did so to Sir Maurice Berkeley, who bade him 'leap up behind him'. Others took up both young Cobham and Knevett, who must somewhere have rejoined their friends, and so, only a few minutes after the messenger who announced his capture at the palace, Wyatt was brought thither, passing below the window where the Queen sat watching. His men yielded for the most part without fighting, though one stout-hearted, desperate fellow, a pikeman, set his back to the wall of St. James's, and kept seventeen horsemen at bay for long enough, till at last he was cut down.

The rebellion was over. The prisoners, one by one and in batches, were brought to the gates of the Tower, where already Lord Cobham and the deserter Harper were lodged. They were greeted there with ungenerous taunts by men who had hardly recovered from a bad scare. Knevett was seized by the collar, Alexander Brett, the London Captain 'by the bosom', and reproached for going over to the Queen's enemies. Young Thomas Cobham was greeted with – 'Alas, Master Cobham, what wind headed you to work such treason?' 'Oh sir,' cried he, 'I was seduced.' Cuthbert Vaughan, reputed to be the handsomest man of all the rebels, was not so craven. Sir John Bridges, Lieutenant of the Tower, cried out on him, with threats, for a traitor. 'I pray God, Sir,' said Vaughan bitterly, 'to send you charity.' He was, he added, no traitor, 'and as for death, I do not much care. I am already determined to die.' He was one of the few leaders taken in arms who were to be allowed to live.

Wyatt himself had the sharpest taunts. Sir John Bridges, calling him traitor, laid one hand on the prisoner's collar, the other on his own dagger. 'And if it was not (saith he) that the law must justly pass on thee, I would strike thee with my dagger.' Wyatt, 'looking grievously and with a grim look' upon the Lieutenant, after a scornful silence, answered contemptuously, 'It is no mastery now', and passed in, after so many crowded, harassed days of planning and marching, of hopes and fears, now over for good and all, into the quiet and passivity of prison.[80]

Chapter XV

WYATT's rebellion, a fortnight of danger, confusion, and crisis, was over. But the Queen's anxieties were not. In the examinations and investigations that were to fill the spring and early summer, Mary had presented to her, not as arguments but as concrete facts, all that could be urged against the Spanish match: the confused but vehement refusal, even to the pitch of armed treason, of yeomen, ploughmen, craftsmen and country gentlemen, to have a Spaniard as King: the irreconcilable resistance of Protestants, ready to seize upon any pretext for making trouble: the dangers of rival claimants: and, behind all, France, adroitly conniving, under a transparent veil of friendship, at every plot that might damage or hamper the power that had chosen the Spanish alliance. Nor was this all. Mary had faced an armed enemy bravely. It had needed resolution, but the issue was simple, and she had had behind her, united by the common danger, her Council and the Londoners. Now, with the danger, that temporary cohesion had passed. She was to discover that the Council was so infiltrated with discontents, rivalries, and disloyalties, that there was not one of the Lords, who whole-heartedly, and in everything, would stand by her in her declared intentions; and that there were many who, while willing enough that the rising should serve as a warning to the Queen, did not wish the punishment of rebellion to be an exemplar for the dissuasion of future rebels.

From all this mass of evidence Mary might have deduced the one clear fact – that the Spanish marriage had been a flame to set all the tinder in England ablaze. She chose instead to argue that it was the only means of smothering the conflagration. Only Spanish orthodoxy, she believed, was sufficiently untainted to rid England of heresy; only the power of Spain was enough to defend her against France and that other enemy at England's back door – Scotland. More legitimately she reasoned that to bear a child would rid her from the fear of rival claimants, and that a husband would relieve her of the intolerable burden of suspicion and bewilderment under which she laboured in public business, and would stand between her and treacherous or quarrel-some councillors. But apart from argument, she was, after all, a Tudor, and no Tudor suffered gladly the hand of the people on the bridle; still less when the matter in question was a marriage, and the hand had been armed in steel. A lesser woman would not have dared pursue the marriage; a greater would have realized the folly of it. Mary with her obstinate courage and her short-sighted judgement, held on.

It is, however, only justice to her to remember that the advantages which Renard had hymned to her, were not so chimerical in the eyes of the sixteenth century as they seem to us. Besides the support of a husband, the close protective alliance of Spain, the son to succeed her and confirm her work, he promised to that son a mighty inheritance – England and the Low Countries for certain; if Philip's son, Don Carlos, died, then Spain, Naples and the Indies as well. Even the first was magnificent; even the second was not an impossibility to the generation that was familiar with Charles the Emperor, that lord of many kingdoms, whose progress behind his ill-assorted and restive team was, if uncomfortable and full of risk, at least a matter for general admiration. Nor had the England which still quartered the French lilies in her arms drifted so from the days of the Hundred Years War that the union of two countries seemed altogether absurd, while the Netherlands were far closer to her in feeling and in interest than the kingdom of France.

The first necessity, however, before the Queen could welcome her betrothed, was to punish the rebels and thereby make his arrival safe. She must now bare the sword and give her rebellious people a sharp and memorable lesson. She had come to the throne with hardly any bloodshed; believing in the love and loyalty of her people, she had thought it needless to punish the misguided folk who had followed the Duke; the great lords who had been the real traitors had likewise gone scot-free. But now her own commons and country gentlemen, the same who had gathered to cheer her in the old days before she was Queen, and who like Wyatt himself had stood by her against Northumberland, were traitors taken in arms against her. Small wonder that she was for a while angry, with a dark, unhappy anger. Gardiner in sermons, and Renard in private audiences were urging her to severity, and their advice chimed in with her mood. Severity was also a political necessity, for the danger had been sharp and close. For a time the Queen, brooding over treachery, did nothing to stay the course of justice, and if any asked for pardon for his friend or kinsman, she saw in the plea only fresh evidence of treason.[1]

Three days after Wyatt's surrender the trials began. The Lord Mayor, sitting in the Old Bailey, tried eighty-two persons in one day, and the same day the trials of thirty-two more were despatched at Westminster. These were the lesser fry, taken in arms, and now kept in prisons, or when room there fell short, in churches throughout the city. There was no need to linger over their cases. Nor were their deaths long delayed, for the next ten days citizens of London saw nothing but gibbets and hanged men as they went about their daily business. In twenty or thirty different places in the city the sinister raw new gallows cast their shadows across the housewife's shopping basket; a man was hanged one day, and left all night; next morning his carcase was taken down to make room for another.[2] Nor were these in London the only gibbets. Some of the condemned were sent down into Kent, that people there might not miss the lesson of seeing a neighbour hanged for rebellion.

But though for some of the common prisoners execution was swift, to others hope came on the heels of despair. The hangings went on till February 22nd. That day the prisons were cleared; the poor fellows formed up tied two and two, with halters about their necks, and so driven in dismal companies, 'to the number of 400 or more' to the palace at Westminster. There, the Queen stood at an open window in the gallery by the gatehouse. They saw her, and went down on their knees in the February mud, crying for mercy. They got it; she pardoned them out of hand.

After pardon, they were led on through the palace to Westminster Hall, followed by an excited crowd, and under that ancient roof their bonds were untied. Then there was throwing up of caps and slinging off of halters; the latter, as interesting souvenirs, were quickly picked up by the Londoners, some of whom were lucky enough to collect no less than three or four apiece.[3] Down in Kent too the executions were slackening. Sir Robert Southwell wrote to the Council for leave to set free upon surety some husbandmen and artificers, since these men, he wrote, with a perverse ingenuity of spelling hard to equal, were not 'ringle dores'.[4]

Beside the unknown, unremembered victims of Wyatt's unhappy venture, there were other prisoners, of greater note, who could yet be as summarily dispatched, because they lay already under sentence of death. Lady Jane Grey and Lord Guilford Dudley, whose residence in the Tower might have been terminated at any time by the Queen's pardon, could now expect no other path to freedom than that cleared by the axe. Jane's father, pardoned and treated with perfect confidence by the Queen, had taken arms against her for a second time. All the excuse the choleric, hasty, unstable man could give was that he had been offended at the small esteem shown him by the Council, and alarmed at the arrest of Warner, late Lieutenant of the Tower, so that he had yielded to the persuasive tongues of Carew and Sir James Crofts; and he protested to the Mayor of Leicester his loyalty to the Queen, 'the mercy-fullest prince that ever reigned'.

For his ill-advised, rash action, not only he, but his daughter and son-in-law must suffer, although the rising had been in no way connected with such title as Jane Grey had to the succession. Till now she and her husband had lived in the Tower, separated, for it was too dangerous to allow the chance of a child of this marriage, but in pleasant enough captivity. Now she must die, not for her faith or for any great cause, but simply as the victim of her father's instability and ingratitude. But she would die, nobly and fearlessly, all the uncharity and pertness in her transmuted into pure, still courage.

Before she died they made her watch from the window in Partridge's house while her young husband went out to execution, and then, after what must have seemed hours, she saw the slow, jolting cart come back, in which lay his body, headless and the head itself, wrapped separately in a cloth. After that she had not long to wait before they led her to the scaffold 'upon the green over against the White Tower'.

She came with a book of prayers in her hand, which if it is the same that still exists in the Harleian collection, had been used, when other means were denied, for communication among the unhappy family, since on the blank pages are written three notes, one from Lord Guilford Dudley to the Duke of Suffolk, another from Lady Jane Grey to her father, the third a few words from her giving the book to Sir John Bridges, Lieutenant of the Tower. In just the same way, the night before she died, she wrote, in a Greek Testament, a letter to her sister Katherine.[5]

Behind her came her maids who 'wonderfully wept', but she was calm. Upon the scaffold she asked permission to speak to the people. It was given. She confessed the legal guilt of 'the thing done against the Queen's majesty', but washed her hands of the blame of it, 'as innocent before God, and you good people, to-day.' Then after a few words more, protesting her faith, she made an appeal to the silent crowd, poignant in its simplicity, courage and helplessness. 'Good people,' she said, 'I pray you, so long as I am alive, to pray for me.' Her Protestantism forbade her to wish for prayers any longer than that.

After this, and a psalm said in English, she took off her gloves and kerchief, and handed them to Mistress Tilney, her waiting maid, and the book to the Lieutenant's brother. Next, her outer gown with its standing collar must be taken off. The executioner stepped forward to help her, but she shrank away from such a strange attendant, and turned to her own women for help. When they had done this and given her a clean kerchief to put about her eyes, they could do no more for her, but must hand her over to the executioner.

He, having begged and got her pardon, asked her to stand where the straw was strewn on the scaffold. As she moved that way, she saw the block. 'I pray you despatch me quickly', she said, and kneeled down; but then, with a qualm of fear, asked hurriedly, 'Will you take it off me before I lay me down?' 'No', he promised her.

She tied the handkerchief about her eyes, and then, shut alone into the dark, for the first time lost her nerve, and, feeling blindly round with her hands for the block, cried out–'What shall I do? Where is it?' One standing by guided her to it. She lay down, calm again, and said only–'Lord into thy hands I commend my spirit.' The executioner had heaved up his axe, and now it fell.[6]

The Duke of Suffolk was the next great victim. His defence was haughty, for he challenged Arundel, his judge, to say if it were treason 'for a peer of the realm, as he was, to raise his power and make proclamation, only to avoid strangers out of the realm'. Arundel had no answer. Then Suffolk turned to the serjeants-at-law standing by and asked them 'whether it were or no; but they would say nothing'. The court charged him next with resisting, with his 200 men, Huntingdon, who as the Queen's lieutenant represented her person. He replied that he did not know Huntingdon for such; then with a spurt of the old rancour that was between them–'I met him indeed with but 50 men or thereabouts, and would not have shrunken from him if I had had fewer.'[7] The admission that he had resisted was judged sufficient. He was condemned, and returned to the Tower under his guard, not as he had come out in the morning to his trial, 'very stoutly and cheerfully enough, but . . . with a countenance very heavy and pensive, desiring all men to pray for him'.[8] Six days later he was executed on Tower Hill, a man 'of nature to his friends gentle and corteuous, more easy indeed to be led than was thought expedient, of stomach nevertheless stout and hardy, hasty and soon kindled, but pacified straight again . . . upright and plain in his private dealings',[9] but in his public life false, changeable, and ungrateful.

The trials of the greater rebels continued. Lord Thomas and Lord John Grey, Suffolk's brothers, men judged by de Noailles to be of much more wit and worth than the Duke himself, were perhaps (Thomas was certainly) more guilty of treason than their elder. There were also Sir James Crofts, William Thomas, Sir Nicholas Throgmorton; there was Sir Thomas Wyatt himself. His trial took place in the middle of March, but it was not until April 11th that he came to the block, for the Council found that brave soldier as he was, he had not the deadly passive courage a prisoner needs; both before and after his trial he confessed much and incriminated many – of these latter the chief were – Sir James Crofts; Lord Courtenay; Elizabeth; the King of France.

Always, throughout the investigations, the hand of France was visible. Those of de Noailles's letters which the Chancellor's men had seized, proved, so Gardiner told Renard, that the French had known the whole of the plot and the names of the conspirators for two months before the outbreak. The letters which reached France in safety prove that he was right. Even when the rebellion was over, de Noailles did not cease frankly to express his reviving hopes. On February 12th he wrote to the Constable of France a letter full of sour reflections upon Mary and her Council. 'Whatever success', he concluded, 'the said lady has had in the past days, I do not think she is yet out of the wood, but rather I can see that the discontent of her people grows, and I think that a better opportunity will come for putting in practice the same design.'[10]

This intention to make trouble in the future was perfectly appreciated by the English Council. The suggested attack on Calais which once more was to have accompanied the grand plan of the rising, had been abandoned with the failure of the English part of the plot.[11] Scotland, labouring under the disabilities of a child Queen, and a woman for Regent, could be of little danger, but Shrewsbury was sent up to the Border to look to the security of the North and of Berwick specially.

There was another weapon in the hand of France, a newly found one, in the crowd of young Englishmen, participants in the late plot who, like Carew, escaped to France; and whose presence there was to be the subject of constant and heated remonstrance from England. Henri II stoutly denied that he had seen them or knew where in wide France they were, but the diplomatic lie carried no conviction. It was known in England that the two young Killigrews, who had fled from Devon, had somehow got a ship and had taken to sea; for the next two years they were to lead an up and down existence as gentlemen pirates in the Channel.[12] Sir Peter Carew was heard of, busily buying up harquebuses, and the Queen and her Council thought that they could guess from whom the ship, and from whom the money for firearms came. Two of the Earl of Devon's family were there–another Edward and John Courtenay. When Cardinal Pole came to France on his business of peacemaker between Henri and Charles, he found that his young nephew Thomas Stafford–son of his sister Ursula–expected to be allowed to use his house as a convenient rendezvous for a number of discontented, idle, and talkative young Englishmen, each of whom like young Stafford, was saying that–'as for a Spanish rule in England he could not find it in his heart to abide it!' Pole forbade him the house, and ordered him to leave the French Court, but when the saucy young pup replied that his uncle had the right to do the first but not the second, it was Pole who left France. His sensitive honour would not allow him to stay, lest he should, in England, be suspected of disloyalty. When the French, thinking him a very fit person to have grudges against England, reminded him of all the wrongs of his house, he only replied that 'he never forgot he was an Englishman'.[13]

For months the diplomatic exchanges on this subject of the refugees varied from tart to openly quarrelsome. In answer to English complaints, the French ambassador could always find stuff for counter-complaints in such matters as the seizure of his letters in the rebellion, the capture of some French merchant vessels by Flemings in British waters; he had also the *tu quoque* argument to use, in that certain undesirable French subjects had taken refuge in England; the keen point of this reproach was soon blunted by the fact that one of these, a man called Berteville, was to be of the greatest use to de Noailles and the discontented Englishmen, as a go-between in the next great conspiracy; but this did not mean that the ambassador surrendered the use of the argument.

Now and again in her encounters with de Noailles, the Queen, never one to dissimulate, and harassed beyond endurance by the treachery that she was learning to recognize all about her, would lose her temper, and reply to the Frenchman that 'as he complained so often it was reason that she should complain too'. She then proceeded to enumerate all her complaints against his master, but in particular the shelter given to Carew, repeating over and over, as de Noailles reported, 'how you, Sire, had chosen not to observe treaties, and telling me all the time with what integrity and sincerity a prince ought to keep his word, and how for a thousand deaths she would not break hers'. Then, as if realizing that this was not the correct language of diplomacy, she said that because she was a woman, she might more freely speak her mind.[14] Once indeed she was so enraged against de Noailles and his master that all the ambassador had to report of an audience was that she had swept past him without a word, 'and I assure you, Monseigneur,' he wrote to the Constable, 'she did this with such a wrathful countenance that there was no womanly gentleness to be seen in it'.[15]

Sometimes it was de Noailles that lost his temper. He, like many others who had less reason, could not get on with Gardiner, and when the Chancellor, speaking to him one day, 'fortuned . . . to look upon a book lying open upon a window of the gallery as they passed', the Frenchman broke out with such heat that Gardiner, who had as sharp a tongue as any, 'was forced to tell him

in plain words that it was not the part of an Ambassador to use such language;
whereupon some warm expressions passed on both sides'.[16]

But disloyal Councillors, traitors taken in arms, and foreign enemies, were
not the only persons Mary must fear. Whatever confessions might be ex-
torted from prisoners, it was inevitable that she should suspect two persons –
those two who would have profited if the designs of the least scrupulous
among the conspirators had succeeded, and the Queen had been deposed and
murdered. Those two were Courtenay and Elizabeth. However innocent
they might be, or however little the prisoners should betray of their complicity, they must lie under suspicion.

On the very day that Lady Jane Grey died, Courtenay was brought to the
Tower; one cannot help wondering what were his thoughts as he returned to
that familiar place. When it came to procuring evidence sufficient to bring
the young man to trial, difficulties began to appear. There had been of course
plenty of talk. All the conspirators had heard Courtenay mentioned as one of
the foci of the plot. The Duke of Suffolk admitted that he had once said 'at
his table over his supper, that he would undertake . . . [at] need, only with
100 gentlemen, to set the crown upon Courtenay's head'.[17] It was discovered,
or rather it was said, that the earl had a cypher cut upon the body of a guitar,
which he used when he corresponded with Carew.[18] When he was arrested,
various strange suits of clothes were found in his house, which could only be,
so it was thought, for use as disguise.[19] All these things seemed sinister and
suggestive, but beyond such things nothing could be found. He had done
nothing. He had not ridden down into Devonshire. He had not tried to
escape. Even if, on the day that Wyatt marched up the Strand, the young
man had first refused to serve under Pembroke, claiming to be as good a man
as he, and then distinguished himself by running away, this was not treason.
As to the plan, divulged in so many confessions, that the Earl of Devon and
Princess Elizabeth should be married, Paget, some months before, had seriously and frankly suggested to him that same marriage, and he had declined
it as not good enough for a man of his unblemished lineage.[20]

If it was hard at the time, it is harder now to gauge the extent of his complicity. Certainly not even the Chancellor's influence could have saved him
if there had been clear proof against him. The truth probably is what de
Noailles believed; that the young man had been willing enough to listen to
the plot for his advancement, but that when he discovered that his doings
were being reported to the Lords of the Council by spies in his own household, he was so scared that the conspirators could get nothing more out of
him. Courtenay, vain, irresolute, inexperienced, was just the man to dabble in
conspiracy until it came to the point when he must be prepared to play the
game in earnest, and face, as a harsh reality, the terrible penalties of treason.

Wyatt had been kept alive for a month after his trial and condemnation;
at the mental and perhaps physical horror of that time we can only guess. It
was hoped that he might yet confess something which would incriminate
either Courtenay or Princess Elizabeth, or both. Just what he did confess is

obscure. Lord Chandos said that he had admitted the guilt of both.[21] It was reported that he was given a last interview with Courtenay in the Tower over the Watergate, when he was actually on his way to execution, and that he had fallen on his knees, begging the Earl 'to confess the truth of himself'.[22] Yet, on the scaffold, he denied that either Elizabeth or the Earl had been involved. De Noailles thought that he had incriminated them on a promise of pardon, and that when he found that the promise was to be broken he did his best to clear their names. This is possible, for his bearing on Tower Hill was not so unmoved as that of some other leaders of the insurrection, and, unless he was a man broken with his experiences of the past month, it seems from the account of his behaviour that he may have been shaken, to the last minute, by a torturing hope of mercy.

Courtenay was a man, and the last flourish of the White Rose; Elizabeth, though a woman, was the daughter of Henry VIII. She was as dangerous a figure-head for a conspiracy as Courtenay, and it was infinitely more dangerous to put her out of the way. More and more as time went on, Mary was to realize the peril that lay for her in the existence of the young woman whom she could consider as nothing better than a bastard. She was to see the Council divided and disabled by bitter quarrels and disloyalties on Elizabeth's behalf; she was to see France determined to use her as a tool in one conspiracy after another; she was to see Elizabeth stand in the way of her own and her beloved husband's plans for the future of England. Yet it was Mary herself who saved the girl from death, and who prevented her marriage to a foreigner. Partly from a scruple of conscience, partly from jealousy, Mary preserved her to be 'England's Elizabeth'.

During the first days of the revolt the Council had sent to summon Elizabeth to London lest 'any sudden tumult should arise where you now be'.[23] But Elizabeth had not obeyed, and to confirm the Council's worst fears, news came that she was moving away from Ashridge; that chimed in only too well with the information which they received that the conspirators had urged her to go to Donnington. Further confirmation followed. A copy of the very letter which Elizabeth had written to the Queen was found in the rifled post bag of 'Little Nicholas', de Noailles's courier, on its way to the French king.[24] What more natural than to suppose that Elizabeth herself had provided the French ambassador with the copy?

The Council, now that the rebellion was over, sent another summons to Elizabeth; this time it was peremptory. Elizabeth replied that she was too ill to come. More than one of the Lords of the Council had had personal experience of diplomatic illness; they sent to Ashridge two of the Queen's own physicians and three of the Privy Council—Lord William Howard, Sir Edward Hastings, and Sir Thomas Cornwallis. The physicians went first to see the Princess. They returned to the Lords, and reported that she was fit to travel. Only then did the Privy Councillors wait upon her and give her the Queen's command. No further evasion was possible. Elizabeth protested that she feared the journey would endanger her life; asked for delay; then yielded.[25] By very easy stages, never more than eight miles a day, she was brought to London, and was carried through the streets in her litter; the curtains were drawn back so that everyone should see her pass; a white-faced girl, dressed all in white, 'proud, haughty, and defiant',[26] so Renard saw her. The Queen refused to receive her, and she was lodged in a part of the palace from which none could go out except they passed the guard. There she remained for a little more than a month, examined by the Council, but still not allowed to see the Queen.

On Saturday, March 17th, she heard that she was to go at once to the Tower. It was the Marquis of Winchester and the Earl of Sussex who brought her the news. She was for a moment aghast, and no wonder; so many young and royal heads had rolled in the straw of the scaffold there. Then she begged them to allow her to see the Queen. They refused. She asked to be allowed to write her sister a letter. Upon that the lords disagreed; Sussex was not unwilling; Winchester said no. In the end it was Sussex who had his way.

So, in some room in the palace by the river, Elizabeth sat down to write to the Queen, for the order which sent her to the Tower, came, she maintained, from the Chancellor; it was none of the Queen's doing.[27] But besides any hope she may have had in her half-sister's clemency, there was another object in her mind as she bent over the paper, slowly filling the page with her elegant clear writing. Mere delay, another day's grace, would be a gain perhaps of incalculable value. It was easier to get into the Tower than to get out. Perhaps tomorrow the Queen would send for her. And meanwhile, as she wrote, the tide was turning; soon it would be impossible for the waiting barge to shoot London Bridge. So she wrote on, playing for time. But if the letter still to be seen at the Public Record Office is the very one she wrote that day with the lords waiting behind her, signs of the strain that the manœuvre cost her are visible upon it. The first page is of almost faultless precision; turn over, and in the last ten lines the corrections and alterations come thick.

'If anyone', she wrote, 'did try this old saying that a King's word was more than another man's oath, I must humbly beseech your Majesty to verify it in me, and to remember your last promise and my last demand, that I be not condemned without answer and due proof which it seems I now am.' The Council, she complained, had not believed in that innocence which now she swore, 'and I therefore humbly beseech your Majesty to let me answer afore yourself, and not suffer me to trust to your Councillors; yea, and that afore I go to the Tower, if it is possible, if not afore I be further condemned. . . . I have heard in my time of many cast away for want of coming to the presence of their prince, and in late days I heard my lord of Somerset say that if his brother had been suffered to speak with him, he had never suffered.' Then, after protests of innocence and loyalty, she concluded—'As for the traitor Wyatt, he might peradventure write me a letter, but on my faith I never received any from him; and as for the copy of my letter sent to the French King, I pray God confound me eternally if ever I sent him word, message, token, or letter by any means, and to this my truth I will stand to my death.'

The letter finished high up on the second page, but there was danger in the blank space; some enemy might forge a damning admission there. Carefully she scored long diagonal lines across the paper, leaving only a small space at the foot. That space she filled with a last appeal. 'I humbly crave but one word of answer from yourself,' and at last, at the very bottom, signed herself 'Your Highness' most faithful subject that hath been from the beginning and will be to my end.

ELIZABETH.'[28]

The letter was written, folded and addressed. The tide had risen, and she had won her day's grace. But it was only a day and nothing more. Next morning was Palm Sunday, and while children in the country were bringing their pussy willows to church, Winchester and Sussex came again for Elizabeth and brought her through the Queen's garden to the Thames. She looked up as she passed below the window of the Queen's apartments, hoping still for the chance of seeing her, but no one looked out. The Queen, 'this pious morn', was walking in a procession.

They went by barge down the Thames, leaden under heavy clouds and pock-marked with rain, and so to the watergate of the Tower, since called 'Traitor's Gate'. The river ran so high that to get out there Elizabeth would have had to step ankle deep in water. She refused to move. Winchester came back to ask what was amiss, and when she told him, replied tersely that 'she should not choose'. He had the grace to offer her his cloak, but she refused it. When finally they got her ashore, she saw, drawn up in the narrow ward, the armed guard of the Tower. 'What,' she cried, 'are all these harnessed men for me'. 'No Madame'. 'Yes,' cried Elizabeth, desperately playing the card that was to serve her so often in less grave encounters, 'I know it is so; it needed not for me, being, alas! but a weak woman.'

Before the two lords left her, Sussex, all along more kindly or more far-sighted than Winchester, gave her a gleam of hope, for he told her that many of the Council were sorry for her trouble. "'And as for me," saith he, casting his hands abroad ... "sorry I am that ever have lived to see this day."' When he left her, he would not allow the door to be locked on her, since, he said, she was a king's daughter, and the Queen's sister.[29]

Whether the Queen had given the order or not, the manner of its execution was not easy to bear. The Lords of the Council, she declared, would never have dared to do such a thing in her father's time; 'she only wished he might come to life again for a month'.[30] Meanwhile, Renard, watching the dilatory methods of the Council, realizing their divisions, tracing, in this sign and that, the sympathy which individuals among them had for one or other of the prisoners, must have gnawed his nails with impatience. Gardiner, though he said openly that there would be no peace while Elizabeth lived,[31] was secretly doing all he could for Courtenay; with disgust Renard heard that already, by March 14th, the young man had been moved to more comfortable rooms in the Tower.[32] On the other hand, the ambassador must have known how the faction that opposed the Chancellor, and which included Sussex and Paget, were as tender of Elizabeth's safety. No wonder he grew angry; the Emperor's instructions, though secret, had been explicit. The trials of the two great persons, Elizabeth and Courtenay, should proceed briskly; if the Council would only agree to it, they should be as briskly executed.[33] Renard, seeing little hope of any such agreement in the Council, did his best to instil into the Queen a much needed understanding of the principles of good government. He thought that a study of Thucydides might provide her, in its examples of just severity, with the guidance she needed. He therefore presented her with a French translation of the historian.[34]

But it needed more than the precepts and experience of antiquity to bolster up the Queen's wavering determination. On Palm Sunday as she was in her oratory after vespers, Paget and a number of the Council came to her and persuaded her—though against her will, because she saw in the persuasions symptoms of a new plot—to pardon six Kentish gentlemen. So Renard reported the episode.[35]

Mary may have told Renard, to whom she always behaved as a docile pupil to a revered but stern master, that it was against her will, but in fact her small appetite for vengeance was sated. On Good Friday the Comptroller, Southwell, and Secretary Petre came to her, and asked and got pardon for eight more of the greater rebels, including the Marquis of Northampton, Lord Cobham, and his son. It was, so the Queen excused herself to Renard, knowing well that excuse was necessary, an old custom in England to pardon prisoners on Good Friday. Who, knowing how deep religion went with her, can doubt that she obeyed the ancient, gentle custom with a spring of gladness in her heart?

But to Renard the news was the last straw. He did not conceal his disapproval. It was a pity, he said bitterly, that she had not waited to know if these men were guilty or no. The Queen hastily tried to soothe him. The Chancellor had taken surety for them, she told him, and Northampton, who had nothing but what he wore on his back, would, she was sure, be faithful.

Renard was not placated. He drew out of his armoury the sharpest arrow he knew. He doubted, he told her, if, with all these men pardoned, and Elizabeth and Courtenay still alive, Philip would be safe in England. The shot went home. The Queen, 'with tears in her eyes', answered 'that she would rather never have been born than that any harm should happen to him'.[36]

The poor harassed conscientious woman was indeed torn between her fears, her scruples, and counsels from this side and that. The case of Elizabeth she found especially hard to decide. The day after Wyatt's execution, two London apprentices were pilloried for spreading the news that he had cleared Elizabeth in his last speech. But a few days later the Queen told Renard that there was not enough evidence to convict her sister. It was to the Queen's credit that she should so decide, for certainly she deeply distrusted the girl. 'She is what I have always thought her',[37] she had told Renard at the start

KING PHILIP II OF SPAIN

By Titian (1553). Museo Nazionale, Naples.

of the investigations into Wyatt's treason; but whatever the Queen thought, Elizabeth got justice at her hands. Soon the princess was allowed to pass from the four rooms of her lodging in the Tower, to walk in the gallery near by, then in the Lieutenant's garden. There, though forbidden to speak to any of the other prisoners, as they were forbidden even to look from their windows while she was walking, the sadness of that fatal place was lightened for her by the talk of a child, a girl, who, on occasion, brought her some tiny keys that she might unlock the gates and go free. Even to other prisoners there was some softening of the grimness of captivity and the fear of death, for a little lad, a jailer's son, was allowed to bring posies of flowers to them, until it was suspected that he carried messages between Courtenay and the Princess.[38]

In May it was observed that the Queen's rancour was passing; she spoke of Elizabeth as her sister, and, significant trifle, Elizabeth's portrait was restored to its place beside that of the Queen.[39] In the same month, the captivity of the Princess in the Tower came to an end. She heard suddenly that Sir Henry Bedingfield, a Norfolk gentleman, was to remove her to some place in the country. Her momentary alarm at the news was unnecessary. She began her journey, it is true, in a broken, worn litter, guarded by Bedingfield with his 100 fellows, in blue coats and armed with guns, pikes, and bows. But her passage through the country was as much a triumph as Mary's had been in the days of her adversity; country people by the way showered on her an embarrassing profusion of cakes, biscuits, and flowers; Eton College boys crowded out to welcome her, and at Woburn, a 'plain husbandman' who turned out to be 'a very protestant' took up his stand outside the town so as to see her grace pass and got more than he wanted, for he was taken up to point the way.[40]

So they came to Woodstock, where Elizabeth was to suffer, not too patiently, the frets and pricks of an honourable captivity. She got some sport, it is likely, out of her solemn, solid jailer Sir Henry Bedingfield, whose 'Norfolk understanding' was, as he confessed, not very nimble. Elizabeth would sulk, or storm, or jeer at him for his exact obedience to orders, and he reported her painstakingly to the Council–'Her Grace saith she is sure your Lordships will smile in your sleeve when you know this my scrupulousness'. Or she would at times merely tease him, trailing the conscientious man after her, one sunny afternoon in summer, through one garden to another, and at last to the orchard, because, elsewhere, she would find 'noe shadowe'. But through it all the obstinate and cautious country squire refused to be put out of his way; he did his duty with a stolid thoroughness, and for all Foxe's high-coloured stories, with adequate respect. And if the captivity was irksome to the girl, it was for Sir Henry no bed of roses, but a service, as he said, 'from whence to receive the discharge . . . were the joyfullest tidings that ever came to me, as our Lord Almighty knoweth, to whom all secrets be hidden'.[41] The sentiment of the words is clear though the expression is a little obscure.

Meanwhile Henry's other daughter was suffering, not from the emptiness and boredom of captivity, but from press of business, from the clash of personalities, from the thronging, and to her, quite insoluble problems of tangled and difficult days. Already, a few short weeks after the breakdown of Wyatt's rebellion, popular discontent, neither cowed by his failure, nor conciliated by the Queen's courage, was making itself heard. It was audible first in such rumours as that which went about the streets during the trials, men saying to each other that 'too much noble blood had been shed already for the Spaniards'. Even the London children took their part in the debate, for two hundred or so of them devised a game in which one brat was Wyatt, and another the Prince of Spain, and the rest English or Spaniards. The Spanish side was routed and the Prince of Spain so nearly 'hanged by the neck till he was dead', that he would carry the marks, said de Noailles, for many a day. Yet to make the game any fun at all there must have been some at least ready to play Spaniard.

More serious than children's games, was a happening which showed beyond question which way feeling in London was turning with regard to the captured rebels. Not a week after Wyatt's death, Sir Nicholas Throgmorton came to his trial. All day long the Court sat – Throgmorton fighting for his life through the hours. At last at about five o'clock the jury gave their verdict – 'Not guilty'. As the prisoner walked back to the Tower, the crowds in the streets shouted and threw up their caps.[42] It was the first acquittal in the trials. Others might be pardoned, such as Wynter, Cuthbert Vaughan, Sir James Crofts; but here it was not pardon, it was not the Queen's mercy, it was the judgment of citizens of London. The jury suffered for it to the tune of six months' imprisonment and a heavy fine, but they had had their great hour. The rebuff so upset the Queen that she was ill for three days; she was ready enough to be merciful, but as little as any of her family did she relish independence in the commons, especially when it concerned a gross and open rebellion. As if to underline the event, someone stole away Wyatt's head from the pole at St. James's, a daring and impudent act.[43]

Things were indeed going badly. The Queen, who for weeks had gone about in fear of an attack on her person, so that the Presence Chamber was crowded with extra guards, and the night silence broken by the challenges of their rounds, now dreaded a fresh rising.[44] It was said that artillery was brought into the Tower and other fortresses, that arms had been taken from the Tower to St. James's; that no lord, however high in rank, might come into the presence attended by more than one person. People were whispering that before St. John's day 'there will be more than 50,000 men of these commons in arms to resist this prince'.[45]

To add to all other anxieties, there were constant difficulties in the restoration of the old ceremonies of the church. Some of these ceremonies, which gave opportunity for stately show or pleasant conviviality, were not unwelcome even to the London apprentices. Few could be offended when the Mayor and Aldermen went in procession to the sermon at Paul's Cross, all 'in their violet cloaks furred, as they used every Sunday in King Henry VIII's time'. The procession of the Fraternity of Clerks was allowed to pass in peace, with its surplices, copes of cloth of gold, garlands, standards, streamers, the canopy borne over the sacrament, and twelve staff torches burning; nor would any, even the most Protestant among the fraternity, cavil when at the Guildhall all 'did put off their copes and so to dinner every man'.[46] It was pleasant enough too, in the month of May, to join in the Rogation-week processions and to follow the sweet voices and music of the Chapel Royal through the fields beyond the Tower.

But there were plenty of violent spirits ready to raise objections to the restoration of the ordinary Mass and Latin service in parish churches, and even the Mayor and Aldermen had to be cautioned because, in the matter of this restoration, they 'had yet very slackly set forth' the orders for it. Individual citizens went beyond slackness. At a procession on Corpus Christi day, a joiner, armed with a knife, attacked the priest and tried to tear the Host from his hand. During a sermon at Paul's Cross a gun was fired at the preacher; the shot 'yt the wall and yt was a pellet of tyne', so Master Henry Machyn recorded, and he probably stayed behind to see.[47]

Less violent but more ingenious was that 'voice in the wall', which was London's nine days' wonder in March. This voice, known as 'the white bird', or 'the spirit in the wall', made a strange whistling noise that certain in the crowd would interpret as denunciation of the old ceremonies and of the Spanish marriage. But it was discovered that the 'bird that spake in the wall' was only a young serving maiden named Elizabeth Croft, who, put up to the device by a servant of the Knevetts, had 'lain whistling in a strange whistle made for that purpose', while it was her accomplices in the crowd who declared that the notes expressed certain seditious words, against the Queen, the Prince of Spain, Mass, confession and the like.[48]

If, during all these trying days, the Queen had had beside her a loyal and united Council, even if there had been one party in that Council which she could have unreservedly trusted, she would not have been so completely bewildered and daunted by all her anxieties. But the Council was divided into two jarring factions and those factions themselves fell apart and re-formed themselves into different combinations over certain questions, so that there was none on whom the Queen could depend as her own. Obsessed by their own interests and quarrels, and snarling at each other like ill-tempered dogs, when it came to action, they would often ignore, or evade, the Queen's orders, and concentrate all their energies on circumventing each other. She, resolute and undaunted as she could be in a business she understood, was now all at sea. and powerless to rule her advisers. How powerless can be imagined from her excuse, given in answer to one of Renard's reproachful exhortations – 'She spent her days', she said, 'in shouting at her Council, but all with no result.'[49] Well might the harassed and bewildered Queen wish, as she told Renard, that Philip were with her already to take these matters in hand.[50]

The two ringleaders of this strife were the Chancellor and Paget. Behind the one were ranged the Great Chamberlain, Sir John Gage, and the old Catholic servants of Mary – Rochester, Waldegrave, Englefield; all those who

had wished, with a return to the old ways, to keep the monarchy English
by marrying Courtenay and the Queen. On the other hand, Paget, the one
Englishman who had consistently supported the Spanish marriage, was
backed by a mixed crowd of lords – most of whom, it is to be feared, were
moved either by no less selfish motives than his own, or by their dislike of
Gardiner. Of these, Pembroke and Sir John Mason were tinged with Protestantism, but Catholics such as Sussex, Sir Edward Hastings, and Cornwallis
were with them.

For help Mary turned as she had turned all along, to the one adviser whom
she really trusted – Simon Renard. He had plenty of advice ready for her. He
told her that she must, at all costs, reconcile the two parties in the Council.
She must learn to dissemble with those whose loyalty she suspected, so that
she seemed to trust them. She must make new friends, and reward those who
had served her well against Wyatt. She must also, so he told her, give up
interfering in private affairs, a prohibition which doubtless distressed Mary,
who, generally out of her depth in business of state, liked to use her power in
personal affairs which she could understand; so she would pardon a prisoner
at his wife's request, and after, as she did for Cobham's son and his wife, try
to patch up an unhappy marriage. All this advice Renard enforced with his
most dire threat. If she did not do so, the Prince would not be safe.

Mary was always vulnerable to that argument. Now she protested 'that
she had neither rest nor sleep for the anxiety she took for the security of His
Highness' coming'. In the last few days, she said, the Council had been more
amiable; they had, she said, 'prayed her to have no fear about the state of her
affairs'; the Chancellor had spoken to her like an honest man, Arundel had
assured her of his good will; so had Paget and Petre. She must, she added
pathetically, 'believe them, or never trust anybody'.[51]

Renard had one more recommendation to make. He had already discussed it with the Chancellor and Petre, and separately with Paget. All
agreed with him that there were too many in the Council; and no wonder,
for it included not only the bulk of Edward VI's Councillors, not only all
those loyal and long-tried servants of Mary such as Rochester, but also many
country gentlemen who had come with tenants and servants from their quiet
countryside to put her on the throne, like Sir Edward Hasting, that man 'of
many worthy parts, somewhat given to melancholy and much addicted to
chess'.[52]

If the Queen was right in diagnosing the slight improvement in their
tempers it was only temporary. Parliament had just opened, and Gardiner's
policy was soon to present Paget with such an opportunity for making
trouble that it would have needed a much honester man than he to have let
it slip. All the old disputes, and some new ones too, now boiled up again.

When first, in the Council, and in those informal, momentous talks with
Renard, the business of the coming Parliament had been discussed, two important bills only had been contemplated; one to accept the marriage treaty,
the other to confirm the possession of Church lands to their lay owners.

But whereas Renard, looking across Europe, saw the moves of that Imperial game which straddled the Continent, Gardiner, with his eyes bent upon his native land, saw the anarchy which was disabling the Church of England, and was convinced that no peace could be in the Kingdom till order was restored to the Church, and the quickly seeding tares of heresy rooted out. Now he determined that there had been long enough delay; the time to act was come.

Besides the publication of certain Articles directing the Bishops to take disciplinary measures for the restoration of order, good behaviour, and decency in Church, he wished to bring before Parliament a bill for the discontinuance of the title of 'Supreme Head of the Church'. At that, there was immediate outcry. All the 'detainers' on the Council, nervously conscious of their possession of Church lands, dreaded that this was only the thin edge of the wedge. Renard realized the danger that lay in their fear. Little he cared what title the Queen went by, so long as Prince Philip might safely come to England, and he used all his authority with the Queen against the measure. After a great deal of friction Gardiner dropped his bill, which he was very possibly entirely justified in desiring. He had once been a convinced exponent of the doctrine of Royal Supremacy, but since those days he had seen much water run under the bridge. Henry VIII was perhaps an astonishing type to find at the Head of the Church of God; but it was harder still to get used to the idea of a child or a woman filling that same office. In addition to the theoretical, the practical dangers had become abundantly clear, and Gardiner was a practical statesman.

On April 2nd, the splendour of velvet, gold and jewels, and after the ancient Mass of the Holy Spirit, the Queen opened her second Parliament. The Chancellor began by announcing, though only of grace, the Queen's contract of marriage, in which, said Gardiner, making the best of a bad business, she must have as free choice as any of her subjects. He then proceeded to the business before them, inviting them to confirm the marriage treaty, and adding to the invitation, as a significant rider, that no part in the government should fall into the Prince's hands; he was to be the Queen's consort, no more. They should next, in order to secure the Prince's person, make any act against him to be treason. Thirdly, they should empower the Queen to dispose of the Crown by will, as her father had done, and as she had prevented her brother from doing. So much for a beginning. Other projects of the Chancellor were to appear later.

The confirmation of the marriage articles went through without a hitch; Renard's list of those to whom money, those to whom gold chains should be given, had been carefully perused by the Emperor, and though Renard fretted at the Emperor's preference for promised pensions, rather than cash down, yet any who had a pension in prospect knew that he was expected to earn it. When, however, the confirmation had gone through, the Chancellor introduced more controversial measures. A bill restoring the lands of the old Bishopric of Durham was brought in; it passed, but only after such an outcry

by the 'heretics' among the Commons, that Renard feared, so he said, for
the Queen's person. The measure for allowing the Queen to bequeath the
Crown by will was defeated.

And by this time the members of the Council were almost in a state of war.
Gardiner's party, the Catholic servants of Mary as Princess, grudged at the
suggested reduction of the Council. They, like the labourers of the parable,
had borne the burden and heat of the day, and now saw that they were not
even to receive a penny. They did, however, manage to 'prime' the Queen
against Paget, whose loyalty she had already begun to suspect. Mary, never
a good hand at concealment, let her feelings become visible; Paget, taking
offence, was driven into a reckless opposition. In Parliament he did all he
could against that bill which, while it was doubtless drawn up by the Chancellor, expressed the Queen's anxious wishes – the bill making treason any
act against the Prince of Spain, Paget failed in this, but Gardiner, whose
arbitrary behaviour during this Parliament explains much of the enmity by
which he was always surrounded, soon gave him another chance. When
Renard and the Queen were speaking together, a note was brought to the
ambassador from Lord Paget, a hasty note, full of phrases of urgency and
alarm.

'Behold,' Paget wrote, 'he you wot of [Gardiner] comes to me since
dinner with a sudden and strange proposal, namely that since matters against
Madame Elizabeth do not take the train which was wished, there should be
an act brought into Parliament to disinherit her. . . . Sir, for the love of God
persuade the Queen to dissolve Parliament instantly, and to send those who
have been chosen for the government of the countries, into their districts,
for the times begin to be hot, men's humours are getting inflamed, warmed,
fevered. . . . By God, Sir, I am at my wits' end to know what to do.'[53] Paget's
warning was timely, but the trouble among the members was very likely of
his own making.

What prevented the introduction of this bill, or what alternatively persuaded the Queen to let Parliament continue for another fortnight, we do
not know. But in that fortnight Paget again showed what Mary and Gardiner must have considered the cloven hoof. For a bill which the Chancellor
had introduced as part of his great plan of campaign, and by which heresy
was once more to be punishable by death, was passed by the Commons, but
was then thrown out by the Lords owing to Paget's efforts. The result of this
even Renard, who disliked the Chancellor and was generally indulgent
towards Paget, thought must be 'confusion in the Council and Government',
for the 'heretics' had shown themselves not merely irreconcilably opposed to
doctrinal change, but seditious, violent, and unruly.

At last on May 5th the Queen dissolved Parliament, and was, to Renard's
surprise, heartily cheered by her faithful Commons, and sought out by the
Lords with individual promises of fidelity. A strange people, the English, he
must have thought, and added, very likely, the reflection, which he passed on
to his master – '*N'est croyable l'inconstance de ceulx pas deça*'.[54]

The protestations of the Lords though they cheered Mary greatly, left Renard's spirits low. After the departure of Parliament the lords of the Council were still at each other's throats. Paget, having done his worst, talked of asking leave to go to the baths in Cornwall; he was suffering, he said, from pains in his legs. He seemed at first not to dare to approach the Queen with his request. It was true that he begged, and got, the Queen's pardon, though not till she had rebuked him for the past, and cautioned him for the future.[55] But Paget's penitence and withdrawal seemed to the Chancellor and his friends no better than part of a plot, laid by him, with Arundel, Pembroke, Cobham and the other 'heretic peers'. Gardiner himself feared almost anything – chiefly perhaps a warrant from the opposite party which should lodge him in the Tower. The Queen had actually to forbid the Lieutenant of the Tower to receive the Chancellor as a prisoner unless he should be shown her ring as a sign, 'which', de Noailles remarks for the instruction of his master, 'they call here a *toque*'.[56]

Paget was becoming the villain of the piece, though it is hard to see what he thought he could gain by his behaviour. Some even assured the Queen that only if she imprisoned him would there be peace; they added that Arundel had better be locked up too, for he was fortifying his castles in Sussex. Even Thirlby, the wise and sober-minded Bishop of Norwich, recalled home on the suggestion of the Emperor himself, that he might be a moderating and restraining influence in the Council, had nothing to say for Paget. In King Henry's time, the Bishop remarked, he would have been in prison by now.[57]

No one knew what trouble might be brewing. The Queen was 'so perplexed that she knew not which way to take'. Posters and broadsheets warned Londoners that it was time for them to 'take up arms for the kingdom's liberty'.[58] Abroad, France was said to be moving pontoons and guns in the direction of Calais, while in many a Norman town lounged and quarrelled the English refugees. With such discontent at home and danger abroad, neither Renard nor Gardiner would take the risk of advising the imprisonment of such an influential man as Paget. On May 22nd he came to the Queen, and asked leave to go away into the country. But Mary's patience was out. In a royal rage she turned on him, retailed to his face one by one every shift and change of all his doings since first he had served her father, till the present time. She was not, she told him, going to put up with his plottings. She knew that he was useful so long as he was honest, but he was dangerous when he played a thieves' game. If he behaved well, so much the better for him; if ill, he should pay for it.

Paget was so taken aback that he burst into tears, and professed a penitence which the Queen must accept, though she found it hard to believe in, especially when she heard, two days later, that he was hob-nobbing at home with Sir Philip Hoby, one of the most suspected men among the political 'heretics'.[59] And after all, though Mary in hot blood might speak confidently, when her anger cooled she was what she had always been, a woman knowing neither whom to trust, nor how to use men without trusting.

Paget would creep back into favour as others had done, and always the Queen would be surrounded with double dealing that she suspected but could not circumvent.

At last, however, on May 24th, her business in London was done and she might set out for Windsor. London was left behind with its summer heat, and stench, and dust; its mocking Protestant rabble; the long wrangles of the Council; and for a while Mary could forget both the disobedience of her own subjects and the insolence of the French Ambassador. Before her were the sweet airs of the country, the glades of Windsor, flowering hedges, hay harvest and the first wild roses. And before her, separated only by a few more weeks, lay marriage with that bridegroom from her mother's country who should be her counsel and support, taking upon his man's shoulders the burden that she found too heavy to bear.

Chapter XVI

ND yet, who knows with what stifled misgivings she rode through the pleasant countryside. She could not have forgotten that she was nine years older than her betrothed; and Philip had shown himself a laggard lover. On March 6th Count Egmont, having arrived with powers to conclude the betrothal by the binding '*verba de presenti*', had been brought by Pembroke and the Admiral, at about half-past one o'clock in the afternoon, to a chamber in the palace where waited the Queen and her Council. In the same room, and giving it, to Mary, the sanctity of a church, was the consecrated Host. Before the ratifications of the Queen and Prince were exchanged, Mary went down on her knees in the midst, and, as in the presence of God, declared that 'she had consented to marry, not out of any carnal affection or desire, nor for any motive whatsoever but for her kingdom's honour and prosperity, and that her firm resolve was to keep the marriage oath which she had made to the Crown'. The Councillors standing round, men of that strange age, with the morals of pirates and the susceptibility of poets, heard her with tears in their eyes.

After her oath, the betrothal followed, and after that the Queen knelt once more, and now begged all her lords to pray with her 'that God might give her grace to accomplish the treaty she had sworn to favour her marriage'. She had taken oath, and now prayed for strength against that power, as yet unknown to her, the persuasive compulsion of an absorbing passion.

In all this she was acting and speaking solemnly, both as Queen and as Christian soul. But when Egmont presented her with a ring sent by the Emperor, she suddenly became again the woman of small, ordinary vanities, and went all round the company showing them the new jewel. She was delighted with it, yet it came, not from Philip, but from the Emperor; and Philip, though now her betrothed husband, had as yet written her no word,[1] and this in spite of a message, conveyed in a letter of Renard's as early as February 19th, to the effect that she would have liked to write 'with her own hand ... but ... it was not for a lady to begin'.

More than a month later, there was still no personal letter from him. It was the Emperor's envoy, Hurtado de Mendoza, who then brought a portrait of the prince, and other gifts. Mendoza had, however, the courtier's wit to glide over an unpleasantness. He was on his way to Portugal, and the Queen remarked to him, so he reported, that it 'was a good time to go to Spain. "A better time to come from Spain to England," said I, at which her Majesty laughed till she spluttered'.[2] But sly pleasantries, though they might make her laugh, could not altogether blind her to the fact that even yet Philip had not written. Mary had declared at her betrothal that she could not be the first to write, but by April 20th, when still she had no word, she wrote her first letter, excusing herself on the ground that Renard was just sending off a courier, and that she had news to give him—namely the confirmation by Parliament of the marriage treaty.[3] She had been beaten in the game of indifference, as she always would be beaten by Philip.

The Emperor, had she known it, was hardly less anxious. More than once, especially during and just after Wyatt's rebellion, bad news was suppressed, or a serious situation made light of in letters to the Prince, lest they should cool his very moderate enthusiasm for the marriage, and retard his dilatory preparations.[4]

Meanwhile the solemn embassy, which was to escort the Prince from Spain, had set off, with the Earl of Bedford at the head of it. Sir John Mason and forty young and comely English gentlemen followed in April, very proud of their fine outfits, which included, as a compliment to the house of Burgundy, Frisian sailor suits—breeches, jacket and coat.[4] At home too, preparations were beginning. The Admiral and 'all his captains were dressed in white and green velvet and satin taffeta and sarcenet, the trumpeters also in green and white, and all the mariners' in the same, that is to say in the Tudor colours.[5] The Queen was having clothes made for Philip—a suit of gold and a suit of silver tissue; in fact long ago before the marriage had been publicly announced, de Noailles had heard to his disgust that an urgent order had been given to certain embroiderers, to work the hangings of a bed, adorned with the arms and devices of Spain and England.[6] London had begun to make itself ready for the arrival; the gibbets were taken down, the Cross in Cheap was scaffolded round, covered with canvas and then gilded. Measures were taken for the comfort and protection of the Spaniards who would come with Philip; rates of exchange were fixed; English nobles instructed that they must admonish their servants not to misuse the Spaniards; honest wine merchants were ordered to be ready to provide wine, at reasonable prices, for the many foreign ambassadors, 'who drink only wine', expected to attend the marriage.[7]

At last, at Valladolid, on May 11th, Philip made up his mind that it was time to send someone to visit the Queen with 'a letter in his own hand ... and a great diamond set in a rose' which his father had once given to his mother. The Marquis of Las Navas, 'an ancient gentleman about the year of 50 or better', was to be the envoy, and with him he was to return part of the English deputation. Philip bade them farewell courteously in Latin, a language in which he was probably more proficient than they, for one of them confessed that he himself was able to reply to the Prince's word 'but rudely'.[8]

Yet it was not till an evening in early June that Las Navas arrived at Plymouth, and was received by 'great shot of ordnance'. Howard and all his captains were rowed out to the harbour mouth to meet and bring him in to the town and his lodging, 'and so', Howard reported, surely with a grin in his beard, 'left him, for I understand he had been a very sick man at sea'.[9]

But even yet, if Philip sent a ring, the Emperor went far beyond him, sending not only jewels, but 'those most beautiful tapestries representing the Tunis expedition'.[10] And Philip, though he had at last shown himself aware of his bride's existence, and though in April the Emperor was urging that the sooner he arrived in England the better for his prestige–Philip did not come.

It was not only Mary who felt the delay. Renard was on thorns, and his patron Granvelle openly indignant. 'I am not surprised', the old Bishop wrote, 'that this lingering makes people angry in England and gives the Queen pain, for we feel it in precisely the same way here.'[11] Complaints began to make themselves heard on every side. The Flemish admiral instructed to meet Philip, wrote that his ships were victualled for a fortnight only–and heaven only knew when Philip might come. Tempers were fraying too. He dared hardly land his men at any English port, for the English sailors picked quarrels, jostled them, and jeered at the Emperor's ships for 'muscle-shells'. It was perhaps no wonder that the English were so quarrelsome. At the end of June the captains of the English ships left their stations without orders and sailed for Plymouth, 'saying that they would serve no longer without pay unless they received better stores, for the meat that had been sent stank, and the beer was sour, and whereas it had been promised that they were only to serve for one month, they had already served three.'[12]

At the beginning of July the Queen was in despair. She told Renard that she felt the delay because it encouraged the heretics, but no woman, least of all Mary, could have ignored the personal slight, since it was one to which her age made her very vulnerable.

But at last, on July 12th, when the '100 sail of tall ships' that were to carry the Prince to his bridal had been lying in Corunna harbour for a full month, Philip, in the afternoon of the day, came on board the *Espiritu Santo*. The ship, a huge Biscayan merchantman, was decked with long painted pennants, trailing from masts, shrouds and stays; at the main flew the banner of Spain, thirty yards long and made of crimson damask embroidered in gold: the whole great hull was hanged with fine scarlet cloth, save at the forecastle where there was crimson brocade with a device of golden flames; the last an unhappy similitude some might think. On July 13th, and it was a Friday too, the whole fleet set sail, and for a day and a night laboured in a head wind and heavy sea. After that the weather cleared, luckily for Philip, who was 'wont to be very sick upon the sea'.[13]

The news that the Prince had left Corunna was brought to the Queen just after the middle of July, and as it happened, on that very day the younger de Noailles, who had lately come to England, and who always got on better with the Queen than did his brother Antoine, came to her asking an audience. He got it, and he found a happy woman. His business too was pleasant–no matter of refugees, detained merchant ships, or intercepted letters–but the christening of a new-born child. The elder Noailles' lady had just given birth to a son, and the shrewd fellow had sent his brother to take the opportunity of paying a pretty compliment to the Queen, begging that she, 'who had re-established in this realm the sacraments of the Catholic Church, should grant me the honour of having him baptised, surrendering to her the choice of the godparents'.

This was just such a business as Mary loved, and one that she could understand. She threw herself into it with enthusiasm. On this happy day, and when it was a question of a little child, she forgot all the encounters she had had with the French ambassador. She would, she told François de Noailles, have carried the boy to the font herself, had she been in London, and not even now setting off to Winchester for her marriage. But she would certainly choose godparents, and she set herself to it, suggesting this name, rejecting that, changing her mind, considering, reflecting, and in the midst of it all asking the questions that any woman would, of the birth of the child, and what name he was to be given. At last, after giving, as Antoine de Noailles said, 'more patience and time than I would have asked in four good audiences', she chose the Earl of Arundel and the Chancellor as godfathers, and appointed the Countess of Surrey to act as her own proxy.[14] But who can doubt that while she, poor soul, was so eagerly considering the question, thoughts flitted through her mind of the time which she hoped would come, when another, a royal child, should be born, and should need godparents and a name.

Renard also was happy. On the day he heard that the Prince's ship had been sighted off the Needles, that is to say on July 19th, he wrote off at once to the Emperor, to give him the news. It was a decorous letter in the ambassador's usual precise style, but in a postscript his exultation and relief broke through the dry crust of convention. 'Sire,' he wrote, 'a year ago this very day the Queen was proclaimed Queen of England.'[15]

Such exultation cannot have been in Philip's heart when he heard the hail of the man on the foretop announcing that England was in sight. It was not only that his bride was a delicate woman nine years older than himself, whom he might, with a very acid humour, refer to as 'our dear and well beloved aunt', when he wrote to his friend Ruy Gomez announcing his betrothal.[16] Such a marriage was, for a king's son, all in the day's work. But, quite apart from the wife, the kingdom towards which he was going gave little promise either of comfort or of easy profit. His position there, hedged in by every ingenuity that a profoundly mistrustful and wily Council could devise, was to be that of a mere consort. His acts, if he interfered in the Government, were to be invalid; those of the Queen remained totally unaffected by her marriage. No forts were to be garrisoned by his troops, no officials were to be appointed by him; no English money should be sent out of the country, no Spanish soldiers should he bring in. Even the number of his Spanish friends and servants was to be small; he must instead be served by clumsy, suspicious, touchy English lords. Above all he had sworn, with all the solemnity possible, that his quarrels should not be the quarrels of England – that is, that England should not be drawn by him into the old, hard-wearing war with France. He was in fact barred from all advantages which had been his aim in seeking the marriage.

. To the best of his ability indeed Philip had taken what precautions he could against the bonds of the treaty which were devised so straitly to fetter him. Long ago, on the first Sunday of the year, he had made a solemn declaration before witnesses – that though he would authorize his commissioners to swear in his name to the clauses of the marriage contract, he had done this only 'that his marriage with the said Queen . . . might take place, but by no means in order to bind himself or his heirs to keep the articles'. Therefore, so he announced, they had no power to bind him. 'This he swore by Our Lord, by St. Mary, and by the sign of the Cross as it stands here – on which he bodily laid his right hand.'[17] So ran the strange document drawn up by a notary, for use, one must suppose, at the Last Assize.

But quite apart from the shackles of the treaty, events in England during the last few months had made it very clear that Philip was going to no bed of roses. Even the meticulous observation of the treaty would not, it seemed, suffice. His father, well grounded in all the arts of ruling; Granvelle, the old, tried man of affairs; Renard, cautious and keen observer of English peculiarities, all bestowed on the young man quantities of good advice. He must above all be affable, show himself to the people, take the nobles with him to hunt. He had, they all remembered, a bad reputation in Flanders, where, a few years before, he had been thoroughly unpopular because of his stiff and silent pride. All the more eagerly now his mentors strove to impress on him the need of amiability. He was to have the advantage, in this assault upon the hearts of the chilly islanders, of a plentiful supply of money for distribution to the greatest, gold chains to less important persons, jewels and trinkets to the ladies, especially those dearest to the Queen; Mistress Strelly, Mistress Russell, and Susan Clarencieux.[18] For weeks, Paget, the Chancellor, and others had been preparing lists of those to receive Spanish gifts, and Renard, in a fever of apprehension, had been exhorting the Emperor not to give offence by presents insultingly small.[19] Pembroke, Arundel, Derby and Shrewsbury were to receive pensions of 2,000 English Crowns; pensions of 1,000 were to go to Lord Dacre, the High Treasurer, the Comptroller, Petre, the Lord Warden – and so on. All this would certainly help to endear Philip to the recipients. In smaller matters, he received no less store of advice. Since he might have no Spanish soldiers, he should dress some of these in the livery of lacqueys, and so let them land unsuspected, their harquebuses coming on with the baggage in chests. And, since he knew no English, he must have an interpreter, but it would also be well to learn a few words of greeting.[20]

To the suite which followed him, and which had been chosen with the utmost care, instructions were equally profuse. Trouble, the Emperor knew, came more often from insolent servants than from their masters; the Spaniards who were admitted into England, must, one and all, be ready to endure anything at the hands of the English. Above all, no wives and ladies must come from Spain. No Spanish gentleman was to be allowed to bring his wife with him; 'even soldiers would be likely to get on better with the English'. Yet, when all had been provided for, the Emperor's thoughts came back to the

chief source of anxiety–Philip himself. 'Duke,' the father broke out, in a
revealing postscript to a letter to the Duke of Alva, who was to accompany
the prince–'Duke, for the love of God see to it that my son behaves in the
right manner; for otherwise I tell you I would rather never have taken the
matter in hand at all.'[21]

So, towards an unfriendly shore and an uncertain prize, came Philip,
Prince of Spain. The Queen had for months been poring over his pictured
face, which still lives in Titian's and Mor's portraits, more clearly than it
interested descriptions of contemporaries. Yet these descriptions are of service.
All agreed, that though small and slight, Philip was comely enough. His
height, wrote Master John Elder, little Lord Darnley's tutor, was just that
of 'John Hulme, my lord Jedwardine's kinsman'; but his exactitude is no
help now. A fine, broad brow, large blue eyes, fair complexion, 'a yellow
head and yellow beard . . . which make him look like a Fleming', these and
the heavy Habsburg chin are all to be seen in his portraits. The portraits give
too, a hint of his bearing, for, said Elder, 'his pace is princely, and gait so
straight and upright, as he looseth no inch of his height'.[22]

The erect carriage and his natural stateliness remained even after he had
learned the habit of affability. That habit was painfully acquired and must
have been irksome to him, for he was by nature unbending and reserved.
It was noted that, though he would listen attentively, he would not look at
the speaker; for the most part his eyes were lowered; if he raised them it was
to glance aside.[23] And this unkingly shyness was perhaps responsible for a
failing which the Venetian Badoer noticed. The King, he said, would not,
when talking to any man of rank, go beyond generalities to those searching
personal questions that are the courtesy of royalty. Sometimes he would
indulge his solitary humour by rising very early and riding out with a few
friends to some place where he could be quiet and alone. For the rest he
was sober in diet, but preferred solid dishes, and cared for neither fruit
nor fish.[24]

The passive docility with which he accepted the marriage chosen for him
was strange in a man of his age; stranger still was the self-control which enabled him to lay aside in England the 'Spanish gravity' which had displeased
the Flemings, and to act the part of an accessible prince. These qualities are
not often to be found in a young man, but it has been shrewdly questioned
if Philip was ever young. It is true that after his long self-discipline in England,
he had a youth's fling in Flanders; enemies reported him as wallowing in
gross sensuality; certainly he would on occasion, even in the midst of grave
affairs, neglect everything to go out masked by night, to meet who knows
what indiscreet adventures and wild merriment.

Only a strong, an iron sense of duty could have driven Philip to play a part
he so much disliked as that which was forced upon him in England. But this
sense of duty, proceeding as it did from a religion profound and scrupulous,
made the English marriage seem his Heaven-appointed part in the great task
of restoring Catholic unity, and exalting the Habsburg house. He undertook

it, ready to endure discomforts, slights and dangers, with that controlled equanimity which, as a Venetian observed, was so rare among Spaniards; perhaps he inherited this from that resolute mother who, at his birth, when urged to cry out lest repression should injure her, replied, 'Silence! Die I may but wail I will not.'

The same sense of duty kept him, throughout his life, hard at work. He must, to satisfy his conscience, oversee everything. 'I have seen', Soranzo said, 'a bill of not more than 20 ducats-worth of goods signed by him.' Laboriously he plodded through document after document, correcting, like a schoolmaster, and with a distorted sense of proportion, even mistakes of spelling. Once, many years later, a Spanish agent in France sent to the King a letter in which Marie de Luxemburg described the death of Henri III, as '*d'un coup de pissetolle dans la tayte*'. Philip, King of Spain, Naples, and the Indies, found time to underline the word *pissetolle* and to write in the margin 'Perhaps some sort of knife, and by *tayte* I do not see that anything but head can be meant, which is not *tayte* but *tête* or *teyte* as you know'.[25]

This was Philip: narrow, conscientious, slow; who though capable of the follies and physical self-indulgence of a young man, had never youth in his heart; who yet could inspire deep and lasting affection in the four women to whom he was successively husband. Later, he was to be a delightful and loving father to his daughters, writing copious letters to them on subjects ranging from yellow jonquils at Aranjuez to an *auto-da-fé*, but concerned mainly with such matters as children and fathers everywhere are interested in: 'the bird is not a heron but something quite different; as I wrote to you it is very small, and herons are big birds'. The foxes in the park, the deer that are shedding their horns early, the little girls' prowess with their cross-bows, all these things the King had time to remember, and care enough to ask specially that the two of them should send him their exact height in silk ribbons so that he could see how they grew.[26]

Yet, because of his obtuse imagination, he could be cruel. He was cruel to Mary, he was cruel in Flanders, so that his name is still, in Protestant countries, synonymous almost with monster. Monster he was not, but a resolute, stupid, conscientious man, saddled with a task too great for his powers, and in the doing of it directing himself by rigid principle, as careless of his own ease as he was of the sufferings of others.

On Thursday, July 19th, the Spanish ships were met by the Flemish and English fleets at the Needles, those gleaming white bastions that stand at the gateway to the sheltered Solent, in summer lying like a great lake between green and wooded lands. Through thunder of guns from mainland and Wight, Philip, following now Lord William Howard, who had gone about to lead the way in, came into Southampton Water. He did not land that night, but next day, and was brought in a barge by the Admiral and a group of nobles. At the quay where the Queen's own minstrels made melody to welcome him, more English lords waited, amongst them Sir Anthony Browne, appointed Master of the Horse to the Prince, very fine in black velvet worked all over with gold, and holding by the rein a white horse, harnessed and housed in crimson velvet, a gift from the Queen to her bridegroom. Mounted on this the Prince went first to Mass to give thanks for safe landing; and only when that was done, to his lodging. There, in rooms beautified for the occasion by hangings of damask where the monogram of the Queen's father gleamed in woven letters of gold, Philip sat down to dine, and at once began his task of conciliation. His clothes, he said, were not fine enough for one about to marry so great a Queen. The bardings of the horse she had just sent him might serve perhaps instead. After dinner he asked for a cup of ale, and, telling the Spaniards present that they must forget Spanish ways and learn to live as Englishmen, he drank it down.[27] In every trifling thing, and trifles weigh heavy, he did what he could to make himself agreeable. On his way to church, when a shower of rain caught him, he borrowed a cloak from a passing Englishman. The first time he received the Chancellor he kept his hat on; someone told him that this was not the English custom; after that Philip's hat came off at audiences.[28] While he received the English lords without ceremony, and was waited on by Englishmen, only the Duke of Alva was allowed to serve him at table; the unfortunate Spanish soldiers on board the ships were not even allowed to land; when the fleet had been hastily re-victualled it was ordered to push on for the Netherlands.

On July 23rd, in a persistent downpour of English summer rain that had fallen from Friday onwards, 'without ceasing so much as an hour', Philip set out for Winchester where the Queen waited for him, his black velvet and white satin, his diamonds and his gold embroideries all muffled up in a cloak of red felt that still was not thick enough to keep him dry. On the way, there was a frequent exchange of compliments and gifts between himself and his bride. The Chancellor had come to Southampton with a diamond ring from the Queen; Ruy Gomez rode to Winchester to carry to her another from Philip – 'a rather smaller one'. Other jewellery had been sent to her earlier, and a bale of tapestries, but these went direct to London, as there was nowhere in Winchester for them to hang; so the Queen could only inquire what they were like. As Philip went down the dripping lanes, he met young gentlemen leading hackneys by the rein – more gifts from the Queen; or pages in crimson brocade and gold sashes, and nobles in black velvet or crimson damask who placed themselves at his command. At last in the persistent deluge he reached St. Cross Hospital outside Winchester, where he changed his wet clothes for a suit of black and white velvet worked over with gold bugles, and then went on to the Cathedral, where there was such a crowd of folk eager to get a glimpse of him that many were nearly stifled.[29]

Not till after supper, and in the dusk, when already the torches were lit, did Philip pay his first visit to the Queen. Led through a garden where flowers, fountains, and pleached arbours reminded the Spaniards of the pleasant gardens in books of chivalry, they came to the foot of a small privy stair that led up to a gallery – that apartment so fashionable in sixteenth-century houses, with its double lines of windows, and its suitability for dancing, games, or the

THE PRINCESS ELIZABETH, AFTERWARDS QUEEN
Anonymous, Flemish School.   Windsor Castle.
Reproduced by gracious permission of Her Majesty the Queen.

walking to and fro which was so necessary in ill-warmed and draughty rooms.

In this long gallery Mary waited for him. She was dressed in a gown of black velvet, a petticoat of frosted silver, a head-tire of black velvet lined with gold–the sombre colour and rich materials so dear to the taste of the age– while in the candlelight the jewels in her girdle and collar flashed as she moved. For she could not sit still. Any moment Philip might be here, and they would see each other. So, as she waited, she moved restlessly up and down.

A sound of footsteps on the private stair, and at the door stood a small, fair, upright man in black and white and gold. Philip at last. She came quickly towards him, kissed her own hand and took his.

He, equally polite, kissed her on the mouth, 'English fashion', and then, she leading him by the hand, they crossed the room to the canopy of state, and sat down, to talk a while together, she speaking French, he Spanish. One would give much to know what they said.

After a little while the English Councillors and the Spaniards whom Philip had brought were called near. The Spaniards kissed the Queen's hand; the English were presented to Philip; Lord William Howard always 'a great talker and jester' cracked a few broad jokes. Then Philip asked to be presented to the Queen's ladies, and when this was done, insisted on kissing each one of them, hat in hand, 'so as not to break the custom of the country, which is a good one'.

Before he left, bettering the Emperor's counsel, he asked the Queen to teach him some English words of farewell to use to her Council as he went out. She taught him to say–'Good night my lords all'–a formula which he duly repeated.

Next day, after staying late in bed, and receiving from the Queen two more magnificent suits–one of gold-threaded brocade, with pearl and diamond buttons, the other of crimson brocade, Philip rose, dined in state, and went in public to the Queen between two lines of the guard, to the Hall where she waited for him with all the minstrels playing.

It was, however, at a second meeting, after supper that night, that he produced the trump card with which the shrewd Emperor had provided him. He had come unannounced, with a few gentlemen, through the gardens, and found the Queen alone except for some old ladies. To her he announced 'the privilege of Naples', that is the cession of the Kingship of Naples made by the Emperor in his favour, so that the Queen of England should wed, not a Prince, but a King. It was a pretty stroke of diplomacy. Mary, delighted, led Philip and his gentlemen into a hall behind her lodging, and there, to an assembly of Councillors, ladies and gentlemen, de Figueroa, the old man with his white beard, solemnly read the Emperor's donation. It was then decided that the gift should be proclaimed by the heralds in the Cathedral.

So, next day, the pompous, splendid ritual of royal marriage was preceded by the sound of trumpets, and the heralds' voices proclaiming in Latin, French, and English, the titles of the two high contracting parties–'Philip and Mary

19

by the Grace of God King and Queen of England, France, Naples, Jerusalem, and Ireland, Defenders of the Faith, Princes of Spain and Sicily, Archdukes of Austria, Dukes of Milan, Burgundy and Brabant, Counts of Hapsburg, Flanders and Tyrol.' But when it came to the marriage ceremony, the Queen's ring was the plain gold circle of custom, 'because', she said, 'maids were so married in old times', and through the hour-long Mass the Queen's eyes never moved from the sacrament. These things–the wedding of a man and a maid, and the presence of God at their union, were the realities for Mary that day.

After the wedding came the usual banquet with music, and the heralds' proclamation, and the shouts of largesse. The King and Queen ate from gold plates and dishes under a canopy held by four English lords; Philip would not dream of letting his Spaniards share the honour. Dancing came after, the King and Queen standing up together in a German dance, and knights from Spain leading out the fair ladies and 'most beautiful nimphes' of England. Meanwhile, the Spaniards decided that the English ladies were mostly elderly, or that even if young, tall and slender, they were not beautiful–'though some are better than the rest';[30] the English plumed themselves on the fact, patent to them at least, that 'me lord Braye, Mr. Carew and others danced far more featly than the strangers';[31] and Master Edward Underhill devised how to send to London that 'great pasty of a red deer in a great charger, very delicately baked', which was his share of the leavings after dinner. Other pensioners, daunted by its weight and size had refused it; but Underhill never lacked confidence. The pasty went safely up to London to his wife and her brother, 'who cheered therewith many of their friends'.[32] At last, when darkness had come, the Bishops, after the old custom of England, blessed the marriage-bed, and the ill-matched, sad, mistaken nuptial was accomplished.

For a few days the Queen and her husband remained at Winchester, the Queen, after the English convention, not appearing in public. The Spaniards occupied their time in seeing the sights of Winchester; notably the Round Table with the names of King Arthur's Knights written about it; and in making the acquaintance of the Queen's ladies, who in the antechamber, were always ready for 'dancing or talking with whoever cared to keep them company'. The days ended early too, for another of the English ways which the foreigners found it wiser to copy, was to go to bed betimes, rather than to return home in the dark at the risk of being robbed.

On Saturday the Duchess of Alva arrived, and had an audience with the Queen. In the Chamber of Presence there was but a single chair–that upon the dais. Mary led the Duchess thither, and herself sat, according to her habit, the habit of all English ladies of the time, which she had not lost in one year of sovereignty–upon a cushion on the floor. The Duchess naturally refused the chair, and a very pretty comedy of courtesy began. Two velvet brocade stools were hastily brought in, but when the Queen sat on one, down went the Duchess on the floor; if that was the English fashion, she would observe it. But that brought the Queen from the stool to a cushion beside the Duchess. Politeness was at last satisfied; they both rose up again, and sat each upon a stool. With Las Navas to interpret the Queen's French into the Castilian which she understood but did not speak, they settled down to conversation. The subject was true English; they talked about the weather.[33]

Just now and for a time Mary was happy. She had been married three weeks when she wrote to the Emperor in the stately style proper to a Queen, thanking him for sparing his son to her in the midst of war. Yet, in spite of the formal phrases it is the letter of a woman already fallen deep in love. Her marriage, she told the elderly cousin to whom she had once been betrothed, and who was now her father-in-law–'renders me happier than I can say, as I daily discover in the King my husband so many virtues and perfections that I constantly pray God to grant me grace to please him, and behave in all things as befits one who is so deeply bounden to him'.[34] Whether that 'he' or 'him' were God or her husband, perhaps even Mary hardly knew. Her state of mind indeed was obvious to all. All the affection, all the passion that her starved and thwarted youth had been unable to spend, she now threw at the feet of this restrained, courteous young husband. Philip himself told his friend Ruy Gomez (and one fears it was with a smile), that when they were alone she 'almost talked love-talk to him'.[35] Certainly his behaviour to her was outwardly as faultless as was his meticulous tact in dealing with the English, so that one of his own Spaniards could believe that the King and Queen were 'more in love than words can say'.[36]

But, in addition to this great happiness, Mary had the joyful relief of seeing that the English courtiers did not find her husband the ogre that rumour had reported him. And if they were taking kindly to this one Spaniard, she must have been glad to see about the court other Spaniards, and to hear spoken by that dearly loved nation the very words that she had heard her mother speak.

She had more trivial pleasures besides, but such as she wholeheartedly enjoyed. There were her own wedding-gowns to wear, and a perpetual changing from one to another; there were suits to devise for Philip; there was a gift of dresses and coifs from the Princess of Portugal to be opened; some time after the arrival of these Renard, amused at the Queen's simplicity, remarked that 'she has not yet finished looking at them and gloating over them'.[37]

Philip's lot was harder. Mary might be 'a dear thing', but Ruy Gomez, with a young man's cruel candour, must add that she was 'older than we have been told', and trying to look on the brighter side–'I believe if she dressed in our fashions she would not look so old and flabby'.[38]

Gomez's sympathies were entirely with his master, the young bridegroom. 'To speak frankly with you,' he wrote to a friend, 'it would take God himself to drink this cup, and the best one can say is that the King realizes fully that the marriage was made for no fleshly consideration, but in order to cure the disorders of this country and preserve the Low Countries.' Even the young Spaniard who thought the King so much in love did not see Mary through rose-tinted spectacles. To him the Queen was 'not at all beautiful, small, and rather flabby than fat . . . of white complexion, and fair, and has no eyebrows'. 'She is', he added, 'a perfect saint and dresses badly.'[39]

From Winchester to Basing, from Basing to Windsor the royal household moved, splendid in the midst of the splendour of ripe corn and summer woods. At Windsor, Philip was stalled as Garter Knight, and there was hunting in the forest. So they drew towards London. On August 11th they came to Richmond, and from there on the 17th passed down the river in painted, gilded, tapestried barges to the Chancellor's house in Southwark where they banqueted, and killed a buck or two in the little park, on the way to Southwark Place. Next day, 'all on horseback, two and two', but with only a handful of Spaniards among the procession, they crossed London Bridge, where all the houses were painted white and yellow, into the city, through staring and not unfriendly crowds, past shows and pageants. There was Orpheus taming beasts, 'a great arbour or tree' representing the common descent of Mary and Philip from Edward III in the manner of a Jesse window, Gog and Magog, and other delights. Only one regrettable incident marked the progress through London, and that was trivial, and perhaps due to a mistake. In the turret above Gracechurch Street conduit, figures of the Nine Worthies, among whom Edward VI and Henry VIII had somehow found a place, stood in all the glory of a new coat of paint. In the old King's hand was a book, and '*Verbum Dei*' was painted on the back of it. Gardiner's quick eye caught sight of it, and his ready wit interpreted a slur upon 'the Queen's Catholic proceedings'. The painter was sent for, and well scolded, he soon put the matter to rights by painting out the book, and giving the King a pair of inoffensive gloves to hold instead.[40]

Even when they were settled in London, gaieties were not over; indeed they continued all winter. One Sunday there would be dancing, with 'a masking in cloth of gold and silver apparelled in mariners' garments', this devised by the Admiral. Or there would be a display of the pretty, skilful, 'cane game' of the Spaniards, in which the players rode at targets or threw canes at each other, all to the music of 'drums made of Ketylles' and trumpets, and at which the rival bands wore livery of different colours, green and silver, white and gold, yellow and silver, purple and silver, black and silver. The English populace, watching the strange sport, enjoyed the beauty of the players' habits, but frankly laughed at the game;[41] they preferred the rough and tumble, the strenuous risks of the tilt-yard.

Still, for the Queen, all went well. She was reported to be 'fatter and of a better colour', and she wrote to the Emperor such accounts of her husband that he was delighted and, it seems, a little surprised, although, as he said, 'lovers were scant indifferent judges'.[42] To the ambassador he hoped that Philip would 'order himself with such *douceur* and gentle demeanour as no good man should have occasion to mislike God's appointment of his coming into the realm', and he began to hope that it would be so. Philip's behaviour was indeed so exemplary that his father, while thanking God for it, remarked, with a tinge of acid in the words, that he must have much changed.[43]

Meanwhile, life for Philip himself was far from being a mere round of gaieties. Nor was he, like Mary, living in a fool's paradise of love. He did not,

indeed he could not, forget the difficulties that faced him, and he would not
forget the task of which his marriage was only part. In carrying out this task,
less even than Renard, did he consider the Queen herself. Renard, who had
made the marriage with as little regard for the two persons concerned as a
chess player has for his pieces, was now touched by the Queen's total surrender
to her belated happiness, and, to his credit, took her feelings into consideration when discussing the question of Philip's departure from England. But in
Philip, dutiful as he was, always at hand to help her from her horse, attentive,
someone said, as a son – the comparison must have been sour on the tongue – in
Philip there is no trace of any real sympathy for the woman who was his wife.
All his attention and care were concentrated upon the task he had set before
him, that of acquiring control of England.

   To accomplish his purpose it was essential that there should be as little
friction as possible between himself and his English subjects. But from the
beginning there had been trouble, and whether English or Spaniards were
more to blame it is hard to say. When Philip arrived he found, that in addition
to the household he had brought with him, an entire English household had
been appointed. Regardless of expense, he decided to retain both. But the
Spaniards, in spite of solemn and frequent warnings, were soon grumbling
that they were only allowed to kick their heels in the antechamber, without
ever doing their Prince service. 'We might as well', they said, 'go and serve
his Majesty (the Emperor) in this war, as hang about doing nothing and paying 25 times the proper price for everything.'[44] This last complaint of theirs
was probably justified. Pilgrims, foreign visitors, tourists, these are made to
be preyed upon in every age. But in London not only did Spaniards find that
it was hard to get lodgings at any price, but they were shouted after, even by
women and children, called 'Spanish knaves', and told that they need not have
brought so much luggage with them, for they would not stay in England
long.[45] There were scuffles in the streets; a servant of my Lord Privy Seal
picked a quarrel with two Spaniards in broad daylight, but, seeing that he
was not getting the best of it, 'pulled out a pistol from under his cloak, aimed
it at one of them, and then, when he was 7 or 8 houses away, fired it into the
air to show what a brave fellow he was'.[46] There were other clashes, and
rumours and fears of far more. Nothing of a serious nature did happen, but
Spaniards spent one wretched Sunday expecting a massacre, and believed,
that but for the prayers offered for them in Spain, they had already been dead
men.[47] There was certainly always the possibility, especially when the Court
was not in London, of the two nations flying at each other's throats.

   Englishmen were complaining every bit as much as the Spaniards. Philip's
English household said that it was the Spaniards and not they who served the
King, and that they were never admitted to his privy chamber. Acquaintance
had not ripened between the two sets of gentlemen, who held so little communication together that one of those who had been to Spain to fetch Philip,
remarked, that 'far from being able to learn Spanish, he would be forgetting
what little he had learned on his journey'.[48] If there was coolness at Court,

there was open disgust in the city, and the Emperor admitted that the Londoners had one just cause for resentment in the swarm of Spanish artisans who had followed the King in the hope of profit. Londoners were saying that there were 'so many Spaniards in London, that a man should have met for one Englishman, above four Spaniards'.[49]

Yet, in spite of all this feeling on each side, an impartial observer, the Duke of Savoy's ambassador, could declare that Spaniards, though not liked, were treated not so very ill, and that the irritation was already, by the beginning of September, dying down. 'Things have never', he said, 'been really as bad as they were painted to me when I first arrived here. The worst ill treatment is directed against purses, and I bear my share of that.'[50] A Spanish gentleman, who was certainly not enjoying his stay in England, hit off the strained, uncomfortable, but not desperate state of things when he said that 'we Spaniards move among the English as if they were animals, trying not to notice them, and they do the same to us'.[51]

Apart from this inevitable difficulty, Philip's problems were the problems that Mary had struggled to solve, and had struggled in vain; these, and two of his own, not yet acknowledged, but always in his mind. The division of the Council that made all effective action impossible; the religious disorder that was so closely linked with sedition and foreign intrigue; the question of Elizabeth and Courtenay–such were the problems which, with the emptiness of the exchequer, had been, and remained the main difficulties of the reign. But Philip looked beyond these to the object for which he endured the English marriage, and to the means by which he must attain that object. He must, as soon as he could, secure his position in England by coronation. This done he could the more easily drag England into that war against France, in which he had so solemnly sworn he would never involve her. If there were any doubt that such already was his purpose, Renard's words, written not ten days after Philip's landing, are sufficient proof. He was wondering, the ambassador wrote to the Emperor, whether it would be well, seeing the strained relations between English and Spaniard, for Philip to pass on to the Low Countries at once with an English force of 500 light horse and 2,000 foot. This, he said, would not only give idle and discontented young gentlemen something to do, but would at once bring England into the war.[52] It was for this that Philip had married the Queen of England, though the woman, Mary Tudor, did not yet realize it.

The King wasted no time in setting to work. Not three weeks after his arrival he was discussing with Gardiner and Heath the question of the moment–Reginald Pole's return; he had of course already discussed it with his father's ambassadors. Philip thought it wiser that Pole should not yet return; Pole stayed where he was. At the beginning of September Philip was transacting business with the Council so as to get used to English ways. And Paget, desperately anxious to reinstate himself, was, in conversations with the Emperor, giving advice that fell in with Philip's dearest hopes. Let the King, he said, with a manageable Council to help him, take over the Government.

This, 'given the Queen's gentle character and inexperience', was, Paget thought, the best that could happen. She, of course, would have to attend Council meetings, so that King and Queen should seem to act as one, and from her must apparently come any such startling changes as a reduction of the Council. But when a matter had been decided by a sort of private committee, she should be told of it, and persuaded to introduce it, as if of her own will.[53]

With Paget at his elbow making such suggestions, and a wife as deeply devoted to him as Mary, all seemed to be falling out as Philip wished. The Queen, however much she might desire and sincerely intend to keep the vows of that first marriage, the marriage to her kingdom, of which she had so often spoken before her marriage to Philip, was only too willing to lay down the burden of affairs, to let her husband face and manage the Council, for her, to let him guide her and make her decisions. She knew him as royal, prudent, pious, unshakeably Catholic. She was ready to believe that as he and she were one, so might Spain and England become one, and Philip be wise for both.

Philip had at once realized the perennial divisions of the Council. On the one side the Chancellor and Mary's old friends; on the other stood Paget and the nobles of doubtful orthodoxy. Philip tried to reconcile, then chose between them. There was little doubt which way his choice would fall. Gardiner, he well knew, had resisted hotly the idea of a Spanish match. Paget, who had helped Renard to make this marriage, was the man for him. Things even went so far that there was, late in the autumn, a suggestion, carried across the Channel to the Emperor by Paget himself, that the Council should be drastically reduced, by deducting from it the High Treasurer, the Comptroller, Waldegrave, Englefield, the Lord Warden, Sir Richard Southwell, and Secretary Bourne—in fact the greater part of the Chancellor's party. The scheme fell through, but the knowledge that it had existed was quite enough to enrage both the Chancellor, and those who should, by it, have suffered amputation from the Council.[54]

Before this time, however, it was clear enough that Paget's period of eclipse was passing, and that instead the Chancellor's light was dimmed. The great question of the moment was the return of Cardinal Pole. Gardiner, always believing that the return to orthodoxy and order in the Church was one of the first necessities for England, was ready for it. He gave it as his opinion that when the hot weather was over, and English tempers cooled by the first autumn frosts, it would be safe and also advisable to let the Cardinal return. Pole, besides being a Cardinal, was an English noble of royal blood, and would have more weight in the business of reform than any other. Not that Gardiner would have had Pole come in without full powers from the Pope to confirm in their possession those 'detainers' of abbey lands; but, given this, let him come at once.

Paget and his party, however, were more fearful in their prognostications of trouble in the country, should the Cardinal arrive as Papal Legate, even should he have come with full powers, and they had some grounds for their

fears. In Sussex there was railing against the Queen's religion; in Essex refusal
to attend the Latin services; in Suffolk a conspiracy, a small, foolish rising, and
a riotous crowd that tried to set fire to a church when Mass was being sung;
in Kent there were seditious letters; in London folks were saying that
Edward VI was still alive; and everywhere 'seditious new sayings' and tales
were whispered about the King and Queen, books full of strange and dangerous promptings to disobedience printed abroad, were smuggled in, and now
passed secretly from hand to hand; there were ballads and rhymes sung in the
streets at night, making a mockery of the Mass; there was railing against
Spaniards. Even at Court men were talking. That cheerfully incorrigible
Protestant Edward Underhill composed a ballad mocking at Papists, and as a
consequence went into retirement in Newgate prison for a time with his
Bible, his nightgown and his lute.[55] Well might Philip fear that the slightest
disturbance would wake all the dogs who slept round about with one eye
open; well might he fear, knowing what he knew of the Cardinal's uncompromising rectitude, that Pole, in a matter of conscience, would shrink from
no disturbance.

Reginald Pole, Cardinal of England, was now a man of fifty-three, and had
not set foot on English soil for close on twenty years. In early manhood a
favoured plant watered by the benevolence of Henry VIII, he had studied at
Padua, and in Paris, keeping clear as best he could of the earlier stages of the
King's divorce business. But, when he returned to England, Henry brought
him to a stand with the offer of the Bishopric of Winchester, or the Arch-
bishopric of York. It was quite clearly his price. He was given a little time to
reflect, and his family, knowing his way, and apprehensive of his answer, were
earnest to persuade him, till he promised them 'to do some violence' to his
conscience. Yet, when he came to his audience in Henry's own Privy Chamber,
his answer was to exhort the King not to ruin his own soul. Bystanders saw
the King's features convulsed with rage, and his hand go to the dagger at his
side. But, controlling himself, he said no more than–'I will consider what you
have said and you shall have my answer.' When the young man had gone,
the King, turning to the lords there, told them that he had nearly struck him,
but, said he–'There was so much simplicity in his manner that it cheated my
indignation, and I could not think he meaned me any ill.'[56] The story, if true,
reflects credit on both men, and certainly there is nothing in Reginald Pole's
life to make it unlikely.

The gentle but courageous scholar left England soon after, to live years of
'learned leisure' among the vineyards and olive gardens, and beside the lovely
lakes of Italy, in touch with a number of men, high-minded and scholarly as
himself, who, in their tastes and ideals, belonged to the earlier, happier, more
liberal days of the reform movement. Books and gardens Pole and his friends
loved; years later in England the Cardinal remembered the trees in the
Farnese gardens, and grieved as much that the Orsini had cut them down as if
he had planted them himself; as he said, 'you know that in the matter of trees
I am not free from fleshly affection'.[57] But going deeper than such tastes

religion was his life; pure, temperate, charitable, kindly, he longed for the
Kingdom of God upon earth. Though Pole was not, by temperament, a man
to go out readily to make clear the way for its coming, there was a moment
when, at the accession of Paul III, it seemed that he and his friends might, in
their 'Consilium de Emendenda Ecclesia', provide a programme of reform
which the Papacy itself should make effective. But their work came too late,
and neither Pole nor Contarini but the fiery Caraffa was the man of the future
age.

In appearance, this son of the valiant Countess of Salisbury had the look at
once of an aristocrat and a scholar. Fair-haired in youth, and with a fair beard,
his long oval face, his kindly, cheerful eyes, his slim figure, were those of a
patrician. But though healthy, he was never strong, and suffered so much
from indigestion that he was not able to endure the prescribed fasts. His habits
were those of a scholar rather than a nobleman, for he preferred to live simply,
would often do without the help of a servant when he got up or went to
bed, and, though dainty, was sparing at table.[58] He had a reputation for quiet
wit, but it would be unfair to him to quote his recorded jokes, for such small
beer goes very flat with time; and as a letter writer he was generally intoler-
ably prolix and artificial. This was the man–an English gentleman of most
ancient blood, a scholar, a Prince of the Church, whose life was governed by
the creed that he confessed–who asked to return to his native country to help
in the work that he, the Queen, and King Philip, were all determined to
accomplish–the restoration of England to the Catholic fold. Yet, for close on
a year and a half after Mary's accession, he must wait till the politic caution
of the Emperor and of his son was assured that Pole's arrival in England
would do nothing to thwart their schemes.

It had been, at first, not only the precarious religious equilibrium in England
which decided the Emperor to refuse his permission to the Cardinal. It was also
a question of what part Pole might play in the matter of the Queen's marriage.
Many years ago, as his mother and Katherine sat together over their needlework, they had talked of the Countess's young brother, Warwick, judicially
murdered at the demand of Queen Katherine's father, so that the Tudor house
should have one less rival to fear. That death Katherine never forgot, nor that
her marriage had been made in blood. But another marriage might wipe out
the guilt, and she had looked forward to the time when the small Princess
Mary should be the bride of one of the Countess's sons, and so restore the
Crown to the ancient Plantagenet house. When, many years later, Mary came
to the throne, both were still unmarried; she, and the one surviving son of
her mother's friend. Pole's minor orders were no bar. The marriage might
still be made. It was therefore little wonder that the Emperor, with his
double preoccupation of preserving the delicate balance of peace, and of
introducing Philip as the Queen's bridegroom, should dread the arrival of
such a man in England. Pole would certainly, on the one hand, support the
Queen in the most rigid interpretation of her duty, and on the other, who
could guess to what his own ambition or the persuasions of other men might

not lead him? So the Emperor had reflected, and when one remembers with
what unreserved trust and affection Mary was to greet the Cardinal, how
quickly that trust and affection ripened into a deep and close friendship, and
how the Queen was to put her conscience and judgment under Pole's guidance, one is inclined to think that the Emperor was wise in his generation. If
Pole had been in England and at the Queen's side when she was agonizing
over her decision as to the marriage, she would surely have listened to him,
with as much respect as she listened to Ambassador Renard. There is no
telling what would then have happened. He might have persuaded her to
remain single. She might have been persuaded to marry him. Pole therefore
got as far as Dillingen on his way home, but for many months he got no
farther, for the Emperor, the Pope, even Mary herself under the influence of
Renard, combined in telling him that he must not yet enter England.

From Pole's answer to her letters, Mary must have learned, even in these
early days, and even if she had not yet known it, what manner of man was
the Cardinal of England, and how much alike were his mind and conscience
to hers. For Pole argued, as she herself must have argued, that the whole of
her life was a refutation of this worldly policy of delay. In danger she had not
dissembled; why should she now in triumph? The matter was not one for
policy but for faith, he said.[59] The Queen, agreeing with him, yet daring to
obey neither what her conscience told her nor this counsellor as rigorous as
conscience, could only reply that, though she regretted delay, she could not
yet openly show 'the intent of her heart in this matter'. She must wait till
Parliament met, and hope that the mercy of God would work a miracle upon
this intractable material.

But Pole saw the whole English situation from far off, and to him it seemed
quite simple. He did indeed condescend to argue the policy of the case with
the Emperor. There was, he said, danger in delay. The Queen's claims rested
on the Pope's dispensation for Katherine's marriage. No one in England could
really object to the Pope's yoke which there had always been light. Every
rebellion in the last twenty years showed that the people really desired to
return to the Church, and if the nobles, gorged with their monastery lands,
feared it, Pole would welcome the Emperor as a mediator between them and
the Pope.[60]

So he reasoned with the astute politician; yet such argument was for Pole
but answering a fool according to his folly. To Mary he spoke very differently.
Gentle as he was, he had no mercy on her. For one thing, her last letter to him
had been in Latin, and a pathetic and very human bitterness mingled with his
rebuke. Why, he complained, had she written to him in Latin? Did she
suppose that in his long years of exile he had forgotten his native tongue?
But he would answer her in Latin, since she willed it, and since she had asked
for his advice he would give it; and he gave it in two stinging letters. The
responsibility would be wholly hers if she did not at once return to the Ship of
Saint Peter. It was impudent and sacrilegious to say that matters of religion
must be cleverly handled, and left till the throne was safely established. Shall

the throne be safe, he asked, without God's help? And will God grant his help
to schismatics and heretics assembled in Parliament? Northumberland's
government went down before the wrath of God. Mary, a virgin, pious,
beloved of the Lord and trusting in him, was set up by God's hand alone.
Therefore let her not now, he cried, be scared by those counsellors who
prophesy tumults. Why did God support her in her defiance of Henry VIII?
In order that being crowned Queen she might set policy before religion, and
tremble at shadows?[61]

Every word must have gone straight to Mary's heart. No wonder that
Renard after hearing the Queen talk about Pole, reported that–'judging by
what she told me, she has more regard and deference for the Cardinal than for
all her Council put together'.[62] Pole had given her the advice of one who
thought and acted according to the most rigorous decisions of conscience.
She herself was another such soul, though, pulled this way and that by fears,
by contrary advice, by sheer bewilderment, she stumbled in the way. It was
perhaps a crazy measure to apply to policy, this measure that he and she had
in common; but it was, and is, a measure neither mean nor low.

From Dillingen, Pole had come to Brussels, and there had again been held
up by the adverse wind of the Emperor's decision. To occupy the Cardinal's
time, and keep him out of mischief, Charles let him go into France that summer
of 1554 to try his hand at peace-making in the dispute between himself and
Henri II. But Pole, no diplomatist, and easily discouraged by contact with
ideals less lofty than his own, did not long persevere in that hopeless task.
Before very long he was back again in Brussels, and again showing a vigorous
though dignified disapproval of the delay that was endangering so many souls
in England. For the return of England to the Church was for him primarily a
'business of souls'. All England still lay under an interdict, and those who died
unabsolved died in peril of damnation.

Yet Pole realized well enough the reasons why he had been so long refused
permission to return to his home. When the Queen and Philip were safely
married, one of these was removed, and the Cardinal returned to the attack
in a letter to the new King. With eloquent and convincing sincerity he appealed,
rather he demanded, leave to return. Like Peter, he said, he stood at the gate
of the house and knocked. The maid had come down and opened to Peter,
but Mary had not opened to Pole. The Apostle stood with him, waiting, and
a greater than the Apostle, Christ himself. So Pole spoke to Philip.[63] To the
envoys who came to sound him on his intentions with regard to Church
lands, he gave no sign of the willingness to compromise which was now the
prime condition of his return. It stuck in the throats of Philip, the Emperor,
and the wily Granvelle, that by too rigid an adherence to principle Pole
might rouse to a fury of fear those 'detainers' of Church lands who feared
that a Legate in England unless well shackled down by precise engagements,
might try to exact the restitution of their lands.

But to a man like Pole, it seemed better, even wiser, to risk failure in his
holy task rather than to stain his cause by any sacrifice of principle. He could

not, therefore, bring himself to undertake that those who possessed Church lands should, before absolution, receive a free and unconditional promise of undisturbed possession. To trade absolution and such a promise for their submission, was obnoxious to him. Would Peter, would Christ, have struck a bargain in such a business?

It is perhaps the saddest of all sad things in history to see goodness defeat itself and honesty tie its own hands. Pole had to deal with the Emperor, a man well meaning and passably conscientious indeed, but absorbed in the cares of the world; with Granvelle, priest by profession, but by preference a statesman; with Philip, devout, but utterly convinced that the Kingdom of God was identical with the Habsburg supremacy; with the nobles and gentlemen of England, their consciences calloused by violence, treachery and greed. To such, Pole's wisdom was foolishness. 'You have rejected Christ', the Cardinal told Philip. 'Not rejected. Only restrained', might Philip, the Emperor, Granvelle have replied, and with them many thousands of cautious, sensible Christians, both then and now.

All through the autumn the negotiations lasted, for they were many-sided. Philip, who had charged himself with the whole business, must, with the help of his father, deal with the Pope, the Cardinal, the Council, and Parliament. The Pope must give the Cardinal full powers not only '*componendi et transigendi*' but also '*cedendi et remittendi*', and must surrender all right to hear appeals in the matter of Church lands. The Cardinal must promise to put into practice these same powers without reservation. The Protestants of the Council must be cajoled, bribed, persuaded into welcoming the return of their fellow noble. Parliament, when it met, must be gentled into consent.

It was all done at last, but it took many journeys by Paget, by Renard, by a host of lesser messengers. Pole yielded, with what mental reservations only his friends knew. The Pope granted the necessary powers, but before that was known for certain, either the King or Queen gave their personal promise to the English Council that he should do so. That same day a messenger clattered off to the coast to bring news to Pole that the ban upon his return was removed.

On November 12th Mary and Philip opened Parliament, but as it was only five days since the Pope had promised to endue Pole with full powers, the brief had not arrived. It was Philip who dealt with this situation, as it is likely he had dealt with the last doubts of the Council. Summoning to the Palace a certain number of lords and commons, he met them in the Queen's presence, and, supported by his Spanish priests and friars, so ably did he deal with them that, as he reported to his father, they agreed 'since it was for the service of God, that I should take the matter into my own hands'.[64] It is likely that Mary was only too glad he should do so, and that just now she herself troubled little about the Council and Parliament. Philip was there to help her for one thing, and for another her mind dwelt upon two great and shining hopes. She was sure now that she was pregnant; and the Cardinal's coming would, she believed, re-establish the Church of her childhood in England.

Things did indeed seem to be brightening after a stormy time. The very hope of an heir was having a composing effect upon the kingdom. As Mason said when the Emperor confidently prophesied a man-child: 'be it man, be it woman, welcome shall it be; for by that shall we at least come to some certainty to whom God shall appoint, by succession, the government of our estate, being that thing yet so uncertain to us, as it maketh all good men to tremble to think the Queen's Highness must die; with whom, dying without fruit, the realm were as good also to die'.[65] Mary's other hope, the reconciliation of England to the Pope, was very near accomplishment now, for Parliament and the Council had consented to Pole's arrival.

Travelling slowly, for even in a litter Pole's delicate health could only endure short stages, the Cardinal came to Calais. There the bells rang to greet him, Lord Wentworth came out and met him; the wind was fair; he set sail the same day. So at last, shortly after noon on November 24th, Pole passed once more, as he must have often passed in his youth, under the echoing arches of London Bridge; not now as a young man, half scholar, half courtier, but as a prince of the Church, before whom went a cross, two silver pillars and two silver poleaxes; to escort whom had come out the Bishops of Durham and Ely, Lord Paget, Lord Montague, and the Earl of Shrewsbury with his household, all in blue doublets and red hose, scarlet caps and blue feathers. At the steel-yard Pole was met by the Chancellor, at the Court gate by the King himself, who brought him through crowds of watching gentlemen, servants and guards, to where the Queen stood among her ladies at the top of the stairs. She kissed and welcomed him as a kinsman, but it was as Legate that, in the great Hall, he stood on her left hand, while Philip stood on her right.[66]

After formalities of introduction, Pole left for the quiet of Lambeth, beside the river and among its fields; as he rested there a messenger followed him from Court. It was Lord Montague, to tell the Cardinal from the Queen that at the voice of his salutation the babe had quickened and leapt in her womb.[67] Perhaps that moment, and that day were the happiest of all Mary's life. Certainly she was to know none happier in the future.

The first part of the Legate's task–the reconciliation of England with the Church Catholic–was accomplished in the next few days. A sermon by the Legate; a 'supplication' voted in Parliament, whose members declared themselves 'very sorry and repentant of the schism and disobedience committed in this realm'; and then 'in the Great Chamber of the Court at Westminster', while all were on their knees–except the Queen, who alone in that assembly had been faithful–Gardiner, in a great silence, gave the absolution which the Legate had empowered him to give, and the three Estates, solemnized and exalted for the moment, replied with a repeated cry of 'Amen'.[68]

England was once again a Catholic country. On the first Sunday in Advent, with the King and Queen attending, and a huge concourse of people thronging the streets and packing the Cathedral, the Cardinal Legate celebrated High Mass in Saint Paul's, and the Chancellor, speaking for the people of England, renounced and repented his and their past sins.

Only one dissentient voice had made itself heard. When the vote of the Commons was taken upon the supplication and submission to the Pope, Sir Ralph Bagnall refused his voice, because, he said, he 'was sworn to the contrary to King Henry VIII, which was a worthy Prince, and laboured twenty-five years before he could abolish (the Pope) . . . and to say I will agree to it, I will not'.[69] Sir Ralph Bagnall, like 'Dapers the dicer, Morgone of Salisbury Court, buskine Palmer, lusty Yong',[70] had been a friend of Edward Underhill before the 'hot gospeller' turned serious-minded. Such a man was a strange champion for the independence of the Church in England, but he was none the less dangerous for that.

Chapter XVII

A WAVE of sincere emotion had caught Lords and Commons, lifted them for a moment out of the world of greed and gain, and brought them to their knees in the face of the eternal values. Many a man among them may, like John Elder, have remembered with remorse 'how lasciviously I lived in England these twenty years, and the most part thereof have followed the same track of liberty and voluptuous living as a great number have done'.[1] But the wave drew back again, leaving them stranded among all the hopes and anxieties of selfish interests. The Pope had absolved them from sin. But would he leave them in undisturbed enjoyment of the fruits of sin? A messenger was sent off to ride post to Rome with a warning from the Parliament of England, that nothing would it do until it had his confirmation of possession for those who held Church lands.

That confirmation received, Lords and Commons turned their attention to the legislation that was required of them. Quickly, if not quite smoothly, bills passed both houses restoring the old acts against heretics, forbidding the assembly of worshippers in secret conventicles, repealing all the religious and ecclesiastical changes made by Henry VIII's Parliaments from the twentieth year of his reign onwards, abrogating also the Royal Supremacy which was of an older date than that, and devising punishments for sedition.

But there were two matters which it was not safe to let even this sober and Catholic House of Commons snuff over. Philip, convinced that his taking behaviour towards Englishmen deserved recognition, had hoped that this Parliament would consent to his coronation. Once crowned, whether the Queen bore a child or no, he would have some definite and assured position in the country's constitution. But though a bill went through appointing him regent, should Mary die in childbirth and a child survive, it was yet judged by the Council to be too risky a thing even to suggest placing a crown upon the Spaniard's head, and, with the crown, investing him with all the inherent and traditional powers and sanctity of a King.[2] Philip, with as good a grace as he could show, shelved the question for a better opportunity.

The Chancellor was another man disappointed of his object. He, for just the same reasons that were to move the counsellors of Queen Elizabeth to demand the life of Mary Queen of Scots, had declared that there would be no peace until the Queen's half-sister was dead. Now he had given up that desperate plan for another. If she must live, let her be legally bastardized.[3] It was just such a measure as a statesman trained in the school of Henry VIII might have imagined as easy to compass; but though Gardiner did not always realize it, times were changed. Instead of a King who knew his own mind, not to mention the mind of God, and who feared no man, there was a

289

conscientious woman, whose judgment, in matters of policy, wavered like steel between magnets, with the conflicting advice of her counsellors; instead of a nobility and Council awed and all but cowed by a ruthless and daring severity, there was a Council divided and insubordinate, a nobility restless and surly. Apart from all else the Protestant party, militant and dangerous, would not suffer the title of the Protestant hope to be touched. So Gardiner's bill was never formally put to the Houses, and Elizabeth remained heir to the throne.

On January 18th Parliament was dissolved. Two days later, at Philip's request, the prisoners yet remaining in the Tower under sentence for complicity in Wyatt's rebellion were set free; Sir James Crofts, Gawain Carew, Throgmorton, the comely Cuthbert Vaughan, the double traitor Harper, all returned to the world of men. Down in Kent Sir Thomas Wyatt's widow received from the Queen certain of her husband's lands in trust for their son George.

It was not to be long before a greater than any of these, no condemned prisoner, but a prisoner under suspicion, was received again into royal favour. At the end of April, through wild, windy weather, Elizabeth was brought to Hampton Court by Sir Henry Bedingfield, in some doubt as to what would be her welcome. She need not have feared. The Queen might never be able to ering herself to trust the daughter of Anne Boleyn, but she was not a woman to take revenge in cold blood on one whom she had spared in anger. As for Philip, it was to his entire advantage to make a friend of this young woman, an unknown quantity to all, save that she was certainly Mary's heir. Already astute Italians and disillusioned Spaniards counted her the trump card that Philip must hold in his hand, lest the Queen should die in childbirth and the child with her, and his personal safety depend upon the possession of such a hostage. Besides, both Philip's and their own prophetic sight went further than this; if Mary died would it not be well for Philip to offer himself as the husband of another Queen of England.[4]

For a fortnight, however, Elizabeth was allowed no sight of the Queen, and Bedingfield's men still kept guard before her doors. Yet the French, who were generally good authorities upon the subject of Elizabeth, reported that Philip went to see her three days after her arrival, and so little malice did the Queen bear her that she sent a message to her before his visit, bidding her wear her richest gown.[5] At last, after Elizabeth had received, and parried, the exhortations of the Chancellor and some of the Council to submit herself to the Queen –a submission which would have been a tacit acknowledgment of guilt– suddenly, at ten o'clock of a May night, word came that she should go to the Queen. Sir Henry Bedingfield and Mary's old friend and Mistress of the Robes, Susan Clarencieux, had come to fetch her, and so with her ladies, her gentleman usher, and grooms carrying torches, the Princess was brought through the dark, sweet-smelling garden, to the foot of a little stair. There her people must stop, while she, with Bedingfield and Mistress Clarencieux, went up to the Queen's bedchamber.

In that room, with its coloured arras hangings, and the great curtained bed, the Queen waited. Elizabeth went down on her knees and at once, without waiting for an accusation, declared her innocence.

'You will not confess your offence,' Mary answered her, 'but stand stoutly in your truth: I pray God it may so fall out.'

'If it doth not, I request neither favour nor pardon at Your Majesty's hands,' Elizabeth protested.

'Well,' said the Queen, 'you stiffly still persevere in your truth.' And then, rather sourly, 'Belike you will not confess but that you have been wrongfully punished.'

With a flicker of demure wit Elizabeth replied—'I must not say so, if it please Your Majesty, to you.'

'Why then,' said the Queen, it may be with the shadow of an answering smile, 'belike you will to others.'

'No, if it please Your Majesty. I have borne the burden, and must bear it. I humbly beseech Your Majesty to think me ever to be your true subject, not only from the beginning hitherto, but for ever, as long as life lasteth.'

Her profession was accepted. The Queen, always ready to believe the best, spoke to her 'a few comfortable words' and afterwards something in Spanish, but what she said, and whether it were spoken to Philip who, according to one account, was hidden there behind the hangings, neither we, nor Master Foxe, but only, as he said, 'God knoweth'.[6]

After that meeting Elizabeth was soon free of the Court, and a little while later, went away with her household into the country.

Another, whose name had so often been coupled with hers—Edward Courtenay—had, a little time before, been set free from Fotheringhay, summoned to Court, and then sent off with letters for the Emperor upon those travels, which Gardiner predicted might be terminated at any time once the Queen's child was born, but which were only to end with the early close of the young man's sad, frustrated life.

After the dissolution of Parliament Lords and Commons rode off home along the foul winter roads, to the care of their estates, to their hunting and coursing. They left to the Bishops the business of combating those heresies, which as they themselves stated in the preamble of the bill restoring the death penalty, 'had much increased of late'. It is from the next month, from February 1555, that the persecution begins which, almost four centuries later, still endows Mary Tudor with her terrible nickname. Till this date the reign had been marked by a startling clemency and forbearance. Coming to the throne in the teeth of a dangerous conspiracy, the Queen had spared all but three of those actually in arms against her. The great blunder of the Spanish marriage had been answered by a rebellion that had battered upon the gates of London itself. Punishment for this had been exemplary, but far from savage. There was no question as to the guilt of, for instance, Crofts and Vaughan, yet they were pardoned. The two great personages whose lives were a danger

20

to Mary's throne, her sister and Courtenay, were both alive and free. It was not thus that Mary's father had dealt, either with rebels or with possible pretenders to the Crown; nor was Elizabeth herself to be so trusting.

With regard to religion, and that was the thing nearest to the Queen's heart, Mary had at first shown herself equally forbearing. At the very outset of her reign she had solemnly declared that she wished for nothing else but the restoration of the old Church and peace for all. Many Protestants, it is true, had been put in prison. Married priests, after some delay, had been deprived. But the Chancellor's attempt, in Mary's second Parliament, to revive the old heresy laws, seems to have received no special support from the Queen.

Now there was to be a change of policy. The first Protestant to suffer was a Canon of St. Paul's, John Rogers. During the same month, February 1555, two country parsons, Saunders and Taylor, and Hooper Bishop of Gloucester, were burned alive. In March another Bishop, Ferrar of St. Davids, followed. During the summer two more noted preachers, Cardmaker and Bradford, were among the martyrs. In the autumn Oxford scholars witnessed the spectacle of two Bishops, Ridley and Latimer, chained to the stake and burned in the town ditch among the first drifts of the falling leaves. They, with the Archbishop of Canterbury, Thomas Cranmer, that rider of un-broken horses, ex-tutor, royal Chaplain, master of the English tongue, had, in the early summer of 1554 defended their faith at a disputation in Oxford, and received condemnation. In that disputation had been voiced the convic-tions that strengthened such a man as Latimer, though he might be 'so fearful that he would creep into a mouse-hole', to face the heretic's death. These men and many others assuredly died soberly, rationally, courageously, for a high ideal, an ideal which, if it could have been shorn of its unfortunate associations, their persecutors would not have found unlovely.

Before entering upon the history of those terrible three years, during which close on three hundred men and women were burned on grounds of a differ-ence of religion, it is only just to Mary and to her councillors first to examine what were the motives that influenced them to take this line, so different from that foreshadowed at the beginning of the reign; and, secondly, to assess, if possible, the individual responsibility for beginning and carrying out the dreadful and fruitless policy.

To modern minds, accustomed by the passage of time to a variety of creeds, the penalty of death, and a terrible death, for difference in a matter of dogma, is offensive. Yet in the middle of the sixteenth century none on either side, except a few speculative souls, felt any qualms at the application, in principle, of such a penalty. The reply to the challenge of heresy was the same from either party – 'Burn the heretic'. What Catholic sovereigns did to Protestants, Protestants did to Anabaptists. Calvin himself advisedly and deliberately declared that it was the duty of the Christian to destroy preachers of false gods, 'so that we spare not kin nor blood nor life of any, and forget all humanity when the matter is to combat for his glory'. And Calvin was a man whose theories were convictions, which convictions he was not afraid to put into practice. In Protestant Geneva there was little opportunity indeed for burning heretics, but when the need arose, he did not shrink. Servetus, with whom his difference was purely theological, found no mercy in him.

And there was at that time more than a little excuse for the application of such a desperate expedient. By the middle years of the century it seemed as though Protestantism, like a bursting grenade, would split itself into shivers, losing in its disruption all trace of its original form. As it has been said–'It was against a rising flood of denial and scepticism that Calvin and the Pope, alike, stiffened every muscle and hardened their hearts. Neither Calvin nor the Pope was wholly unjustified in thinking that what was at stake was Christianity itself.'[7]

The right wing, if we may call it so, of the Protestant party was moved by a burning desire to return to that which it considered the purity of Christian doctrine and practice, retaining every fundamental doctrine and paring away only the crusted interpretations of the last ten centuries or so. John Bradford, to save whom Bishops and noblemen strove so hard, put the case for this section of Protestant opinion. 'Only transubstantiation,' he said, 'which was had on my own confession, was the thing on which my Lord Chancellor proceeded. Will you condemn to the devil any man that believeth truly the twelve articles of the faith, wherein I take the unity of Christ's Church to consist, all though in some points he believe not the definitions of that which you call the Church?'[8]

The appeal might have succeeded, indeed would hardly have been necessary in those early days of the reform movement before the Church was a walled city under siege, when her citizens were free to wander out of her gates at will, and without much danger of rebuke to pluck flowers and branches from that very stock which later was to be declared poisonously heretical. In those days 'the little old man', Lefèvre of Etaples, was speaking openly of communion in both kinds; Erasmus was flicking at the belief in relics, pardons, and indulgences with the lash of his nimble wit; Colet was dismissing much of the scholastic writings as stuff 'which more rather may be called blotterature than literature'.

But now, because, as inevitably happens in every struggle, each party judged its opponent by the worst and most dangerous, not by the best and most moderate men of that side, such independence could not be allowed. Even Protestant writers, Protestant leaders, admitted how far many Protestants had strayed from the common and fundamental truths of Christianity, held both by Catholics and by the moderates of their own side. 'There were now', says Strype, speaking of the year 1556, 'abundance of sects and dangerous doctrines; whose maintainers shrouded themselves under the professors of the gospel. Some denied the divinity of Christ; some denied his manhood; others denied the godhead of the Holy Ghost, original sin, the descent of Christ into Hell . . . the baptism of infants. Some condemned the use of all indifferent things in religion.' There were 'schismatical spirits'[9] who had imbibed the principles of Pelagianism, Arianism, and Anabaptism.

Faced with a crop of heresies old and new, sober and moderate Protestants
were aghast. Though in the heat of their polemical fury such writers as John
Foxe should willingly accept all such 'schismatical spirits' as members of the
same army of martyrs, Protestant prisoners themselves could fall out so
sorely that the two parties refused to communicate together at Christmas-
time.[10]

If Protestants were distressed by the strange religious company in which
they had to fight their battle againt the Mass, old-fashioned Catholics hardly
knew whether to hate or to despise their adversaries. 'Remember,' said
Weston, answering Latimer at Oxford, 'Remember who were the beginners
of your doctrine: a few flying apostates, running out of Germany for fear of
the faggot. Remember what they were who have set forth your doctrine in
this realm; fling-brains and light heads, never constant in one thing, as might
be seen in turning the table one day west, one day east, one that way, another
this way, when like a sort of apes they could not tell which way to turn their
tails. They say they will be like apostles and have no churches. A hovel is good
enough for them. They get them a tankard and one saith, I drink and am
thankful: The more joy of thee, saith another. A runagate Scot [made such
an heresy that Christ was not God, and matched it in the last Communion
Book, so well was that accepted].'[11]

This was what, in Edward's and Mary's reign, Protestant doctrines had
seemed, to the Catholic, to mean. But in Mary's reign they wore also another
habit, which made them equally obnoxious to those who cared more for
peace and order than for theological truth. As Sir Thomas More had said
– 'Heresies breed disorders, and fear of these have been the causes that princes
and peoples have been constrained to punish heretics by terrible death, whereas more easy ways had been taken with them.' Such people as made no stir
about their Protestantism might, it seems, go safe the whole reign through,
provided some enemy did not inform against them and force the hand of
complaisant Justices of the Peace or Bishops. Dr. Walter Haddon, well known
for 'a good Protestant' who had yet welcomed Mary to the throne in a Latin
poem, was not molested. Strype put this down to Mary's gratification at his
verses, but a peaceful and inoffensive life is a more likely reason for his
immunity. Even Edward Underhill, after one sojourn in prison, had no more
troubles, and he declared that there were others 'preserved still in London,
that in all the time of the persecution never bowed their heads to Baal, for
there was no such place to shift in in this realm as London notwithstanding
the great spyal and search; nor no better place to shift of Easter-time in (when
all must communicate) than Queen Mary's Court, in the room that I did'.
So Underhill stayed, having got old Daunce, the bricklayer preacher, to wall
up his Bible and Protestant books 'in a brick wall by the chimney-side in my
shamber', to be retrieved, providentially untouched of mould or of mice,
when Elizabeth was Queen. But Underhill had a short way with that danger
which came from informing enemies. He let two neighbours know, without
any ambiguity, what would happen to them if they laid information against

him. 'I will', he warned them, 'go further with you than Peter did, who strake off but the ear of Malchus, but I will surely strike off head and all.'[12]

There were, of course, loyal and peaceable Protestants; these were ignorant, simple-minded folk and saintly scholars who were ready to die for their beliefs, but from the first day of the reign to the last the Protestant cause was inexplicably confused, both in fact and in estimation, with disobedience, sedition, disloyalty, and foreign intrigue. Years after, William Cecil was to state explicitly that those who were burned, 'never at their death denied their lawful Queen, nor maintained any of her open and foreign enemies, nor procured any rebellion or civil war, nor did sow any sedition in corners'.[13] It was a bold denial, but it was, so I believe, a lie. Every one of the charges from which Cecil so brusquely discharged the Protestant parties, can be seen to be justified at some period of the reign.

Three days after Mary's arrival in London, in July 1553, John Rogers, in the pulpit at Paul's Cross threw down the gage, 'confirming such true doctrine as he and others had taught in King Edward's days, exhorting the people constantly to remain in the same, and to beware of all pestilent popery, idolatry, and superstition'.[14] That challenge had been repeated by the Archbishop in the next month and, when the Queen had prohibited any but licensed preaching, by many an unlicensed Protestant preacher. Such protests might be wrung from the speaker by an overwhelming sense of duty to witness to the truth, but they were, for all that, after the Queen's proclamation, illegal, and what was worse, inflammatory. The verbal challenge of the preachers, from country parson to Archbishop, was reinforced by every form of violence from arson to rebellion. The earlier attacks on the Queen's preachers had been followed up by rioting all over the South and East of England. A priest in Kent had his nose cut off. A church in Suffolk was set on fire while Mass was being sung.[15]

Both in the first months of the persecution, and after, there were burned many who can only be described as a danger to the social order. Many of Foxe's martyrs came to their end for offensive ribaldry or for wanton and unjustifiable violence. When Foxe includes in his 'Acts and Monuments' the story of such a man as Thomas Flower, he reveals the fact that in his eyes two qualifications were enough to put a man's name under the heading of 'God's saints'; one that he hated the old ways; the other that he contrived, for no matter what crime, to be put to death during Queen Mary's reign.

This Thomas Flower, alias Branch, had been monk and priest, but had later married and practised as a physician. On Easter Sunday, 1555, leaving his wife in their lodging at Lambeth, very early that spring morning he had himself rowed across the river, and then wandered restlessly about. At St. Paul's, his half-crazy mind full of warring and uncontrolled impulses, he listened to the long-ago familiar Mass. From there, home again; but he could not rest. Suddenly he made up his mind what to do. Dressed in a serving-man's coat, with a wood knife in his belt, he passed once more over the river to St. Margaret's in Westminster. There, at the administration of the Sacrament to the people, Branch pulled out his knife, leapt on the priest crying – 'What doest thou give them?' – and struck him again and again, so that the consecrated host was splashed with the celebrant's blood. At that moment Branch believed that he was led by the spirit of God, but afterwards, in Newgate, the unfortunate religious hysteric decided that 'his act was evil and naught'.[16] It is such cases as that of Branch which makes the reader of Foxe's book wonder on what accusation many more of his heroes were arrested. Their theology was, for Foxe, the only thing that mattered. But was that, in the eyes of the government, their only crime?

Much indeed of Protestantism carried a seditious heart under its cloak of religion. Wyatt was said by some to have acknowledged that the change of religion was at the root of his treason. Whether that is true or no, it is beyond question that Ponet, lately Bishop of Winchester, and a man of note among the Protestants, would have been taken in arms against his sovereign in that same rebellion had it not been for his very timely retreat. Meanwhile Goodman, the Protestant pamphleteer, was declaring of the rebels 'that none but papists or traitors can justly accuse them of treason or disobedience'.[17]

The result of the policy of persecution was not the peace that had been hoped, but a fiercer outburst of recrimination, violence, and treasonous publications. Protestants in London still met by stealth, sometimes in a house in Blackfriars, sometimes in a clothmaker's loft; sometimes they were rowed out into the dark river to ships at anchor there, sometimes they crept out by night into fields or churchyards, there to hold their services and make their contributions to the sustenance of their friends who had fled abroad. In those secret meetings they would use the words of the English Prayer Book which had so lately been the only legal form of prayer, but to it they added an intercession not so justifiable, namely, that God would 'turn the heart of Queen Mary from idolatry – or shorten her days'. Protestants indeed hardly made a secret of the latter hope. In 1556 one Bartlett Green, a man, says Foxe 'of a meek humble, discreet, and most gentle behaviour to all' was asked, in a letter from one of his friends in exile, whether it was true, as rumour had it abroad, that the Queen was dead. Green's reply, which to Foxe's surprise, some of the Council thought to be 'very heinous words' was this – 'The Queen is not yet dead.'[17]

By no means the least irritating and damaging part of the attack upon the government was the paper warfare at which Protestants became so adept. Long before the persecution began, while yet Mary waited and hoped for the birth of the child she so longed for, someone nailed on the Palace gate a writing – 'Will you be such fools, oh! noble Englishmen, as to believe that our Queen is pregnant; and of what should she be, but of a monkey or a dog?'[18] From hand to hand and mouth to mouth passed verses against that common butt, the Spaniard; rousing verses with all the swing and gusto of the age in them, and fit to make the hairs of true Englishmen prick with horror at the bloodthirsty intentions of the strangers – –

Spare neither man, woman or child,
Hang and head them, burn them with fire,
What if Christ were both meek and mild
Satan our Lord will give us hire.
Now all shaven crowns to the standard.
Make room! pull down for the Spaniard![1]

Such things as these, and many a 'scandalous bill' against the King and
Queen were the work of anonymous authors. But there was much that was
not anonymous, which proceeded from the leaders of the Protestant Church
now in exile at Geneva, at Basle, at Strasbourg. These men, as Maitland has
pointed out, allowed, even encouraged to escape from England, now occupied their safe if monotonous leisure in a strange land directing against the
Queen, her Bishops and her Catholic sympathizers salvo after salvo of black-
letter pamphlets of such a character that they could only, on the one hand,
embitter the feelings of those attacked, on the other inflame the passions of
those to whom they appealed.

In the late summer or early autumn of 1554 Bonner, the stout-hearted,
vigorous old Bishop of London, issued a number of Articles in connexion
with a visitation of his diocese. These, as quoted by Strype, consisted largely
of the ordinary questions that an earnest Bishop should ask of his clergy:
whether by their lives they have given good example to the laity, whether
they are given to overmuch haunting of ale-houses and taverns, whether they
have exhorted the people to loyalty and charity. Nine of the Articles, but only
nine, dealt with such debatable questions as married priests, use of the English
service, refusal of the laity to attend Mass.

A 'Declaration' in answer to these articles was composed by Bishop Bale,
somehow brought into England, and distributed, either in MS. or print. Bale
warns his readers that the articles were not so innocent as one might imagine.
'This limme of the devil and working tool of Satan,' he declared, 'bloody
Bonner, seeketh here to deprive you of faith, true doctrine, and God's
religion.' It is true that the reaction in religion towards which Bonner's
questions were directed, was for the Protestants 'a fall to Antichrist' as Taylor
put it, but that can hardly excuse the language of this champion of Christ.
'What is thy idolatrous mass and lowsy Latin service, thou sosbelly swill-
bowl, but the very draf of Antichrist and dregs of the devil?' he asks. 'I think
there are not greater devils than you be,' he says to the old Catholic Bishops,
'neither yet more manifest adversaries to truth of God. . . . Be ashamed of thy
blasphemous doings thou most beastly bellygod and dampnable dung hill
with thy Golden pillows before thee.'[20] Such exhortations from one Christian
to another, from one priest to another, were, it has been shown, the stock in
trade of the Protestant party abroad, and also practically their monopoly.
In these early days of the controversy such violence and unseemly coarseness
was so largely confined to that party, that all which Strype could find to complain of in the replies of their opponents was that Bonner went so far as to
called Cranmer 'dolt', and, 'a man of prostituted conscience'.

While Bale attacked the Bishops, Knox, Goodman and Ponet set themselves to prove (and to ram home their proof with vituperation and abuse), either that the Queen was no Queen, or that she was a wicked Queen and that it was the duty of every one of the 'best part' to disobey, resist, and rise against her.

For Knox it was 'more than a monster in nature that a woman should reign and have empire above men'. Besides that, this woman was 'a wicked woman, yea a traitoress and bastard'. Add to the last the 'monstrous cruelty' of 'that horrible monster Jezebel of England', and, on these three counts any honest Protestant might decide that she had no right to the crown, and hope, with Knox, that 'God shall kindle the hearts of such as sometimes did favour her, with deadly hatred against her, that they may execute his judgments'.[21]

Goodman's shot, however, carried yet further. 'Knox', as Maitland has said, 'was the best man to tell the people why they should not obey Queen Mary, but Goodman the best tutor for those who wished conscientiously to obey nobody',[22] and in the Protestant ranks there were more than a few of these. When Goodman reasoned of the common people 'How they are charged to see the Laws of God kept, and the transgression of the same punished, if their rulers do neglect them. And that they may lawfully punish their Magistrates as private persons transgressing the Lord's precepts', there were Protestants ready and eager to accept the burden of the duty laid upon them.

The Protestant party in fact included many who hoped to make the cause they fought for, to quote Maitland again, that of 'liberty against law, of the poor against the rich, of the laity against the clergy, of the people against their rulers'.[23] In February 1555 there was discovered a plot, at first considered serious, but later discounted as no more than a scare. But, genuine or no, there is something to be learned from the heads of that proclamation, which, it was believed, should have been published by certain gentlemen with the intention of rousing the commons. For this 'placard' declared, so Renard reported, that 'the people will no longer suffer that their fields and pastures should be closed but open to the common folk, also to proclaim, in the neighbourhood where Courtenay is, a King Edward, Courtenay himself. . . . Also to proclaim in another part that good Englishmen will take arms against the Spaniards and strangers; also in those parts most stubborn in religion, to proclaim the new religion against the acts of Parliament and the Pope's authority. . . . Counting that all these points will have great power of persuasion, as indeed', the ambassador concluded ruefully, 'they have.'[24]

Men like Elizabeth's Archbishop, Parker, who lived through the dangerous years of Mary's reign, did not, even long after, belittle the peril of that time. Parker, looking back, told Lord Keeper Bacon that in those days there were certain books 'that went then about London, being printed and spread abroad, and their authors ministers of good estimation . . . at which *exhorrui cum ista legerem*'. Well may he have shuddered as he read them, for, said he, 'if such principles be spread unto men's heads, as now they be framed, and referred to the judgment of subjects to discuss what is tyranny, and to discern whether his prince, his landlord, his master, is a tyrant-by his own fancy and collection supposed; what Lord of the Council shall ride quietly minded in the streets among such desperate beasts? What minister shall be sure in his bed-chamber?'[25]

It was this huge and growing force of disorder and rebellion that Mary, her husband, her Council, and her Bishops, had to face. It was the same which Charles V in the Netherlands, Henry II in France must also face. The alarm and apprehension of all these rulers was extreme, but no harder to understand than the panic which the ruling and propertied classes of the rest of Europe suffered after the French revolution in the eighteenth century and the Russian Revolution in the twentieth. To stem the rising tide which threatened their dykes and breakwaters, and whose high-water mark they could in no wise prophesy, the Catholic sovereigns of the middle of the sixteenth century, all over Europe, fell back upon the same remedy, the old and barbarous method of burning heretics. If it is realized what were, to the eyes of Queen and Council, the political, social, and moral implications of Protestantism, that ghastly and mistaken policy appears, not justifiable indeed, but, given the reality of the danger and the potency of fear, almost inevitable.

Yet ghastly and mistaken the policy certainly was, for the conscience of the age gradually sickened at it, and the idea of religious toleration, partial and often only temporary in intention, took hold of men's minds. Elizabeth, when her turn came, would not ground her duel against Roman Catholic conspirators upon a difference of religion, but upon the question of allegiance. The peace that de l'Hôpital in France had tried and failed to secure by toleration of the Huguenots, the war-weary Politiques at last came to rate above any blessing that might follow unity in religion. William of Orange with his keener vision could see so far as to realize that toleration was not only expedient, not only inevitable, but was also right.

Setting aside, however, the question of justification for the persecution in England during Mary's reign, upon whose shoulders must the blame rest for its inception, and for its continuance?

Gardiner, besides being the butt of much of Foxe's abuse and accusation, was, by Paget to Renard, and by Renard to the Emperor, credited with originating the policy of persecution. To judge from Renard's letters of April 1554–February 1555, Gardiner had indeed a complete policy for the restoration of the old ways. Not only was the church to be disciplined by its Bishops, not only was it to be linked again with the Church abroad, but, to check disorders, example should be made of great and leading heretics. Already in the spring of 1554, and before the disputation with Hooper, Ridley, and Latimer at Oxford was concluded, he was talking of 'the three . . . bishops, whom he means to have burnt unless they will recant'.[26] Paget, always in these days his bitter enemy, and only to be reconciled when the Chancellor was a dying man, warned Renard again and again that Gardiner was all for violence and haste in restoring the Catholic Church; 'he would like', Paget said, 'to use blood and fire'.[27]

It is not at all unlikely. Gardiner, looking back across the empty gulf of his imprisonment in the Tower, must have recalled with peculiar vividness the last years of Henry VIII's reign, when he, devoted and affectionate servant, had been the King's right hand. In those days, 'the old man' as Henry called himself, looking round on divisions which, like cracks after an earthquake, showed dangerously in the fabric of the Church, had determined to bind and underpin the shaken building. The means he had devised were those set forth in the Act of the Six Articles, fixing, once and for all, so Henry intended, what his subjects should believe. The penalty of open disagreement was the usual and traditional – that of burning. Great was the outcry against it among the Protestants when the King was dead and Edward his son reigned in his stead; far less had been the resistance while the Whip of Six Strings was held in the hand of the old and merciless King. During the eight years in which the Act was on the Statute Book, even Foxe could only discover twenty-six victims. Henry's remedy, in fact, must have seemed, as Gardiner looked back, exactly to have fitted the case; peace, or at least quiet, had been obtained, and many irreconcilables had removed themselves into exile for safety.

The policy of 'blood and fire' once initiated, and Gardiner having, in Strype's unexpected phrase, 'broken the ice of burning and taken off the heads of the captains as it were, of the Protestants', the Chancellor left to others the business of trial and condemnation. And, wiser than others, he soon saw that as that policy had not at first succeeded, so it would never. Even Foxe, who certainly cannot be numbered among the Chancellor's few friends, admitted that once he realized this, he did nothing to perpetuate the policy. 'Gardiner,' said he, 'seeing that his device disappointed, and that cruelty in this case would not serve his expectation, gave over the matter as utterly discouraged, and from that day [the day of the first trials] meddled no more in such kinds of condemnations.'[28] If then we accept Foxe's word that the 'device' was Gardiner's, we must on the same authority allow that the continuance of the policy was not his work.

Renard, at the beginning of the persecution, included the Bishops with Gardiner in his condemnation, and especially the Bishop of London, for being 'so hot and hasty in religion, and such friends to the Pope, burning heretics from day to day'. [29] Yet, out of the mouth of Foxe himself comes ample proof that many a Bishop, and Bonner as much as any, tried long and earnestly to find some means of balking a resolute martyr. Bonner, it has been shown, would labour for weeks to reclaim a recalcitrant heretic, as he did with the ruffling, sharp-witted Hawkes; the picture of 'Butcherly Bonner' that one may bring away from a reading of Hawkes's case is a picture of the Bishop of London, sitting under the vine in his garden on a summer evening, and arguing doggedly with the prisoner, while the old Bishop of Chester, deprived for marriage, but penitent, comes across the grass bringing a present of a dish of apples and a flagon of wine.[30] A stubborn, warm-hearted, somewhat hot-tempered and very outspoken old man, Bonner went into battle determined to make the heretic yield. He did sometimes lose his temper, yet it must be admitted that he had generally ample provocation, and through all rebuffs, taunts, and defeats he honestly and obstinately strove to recall the prisoner from beliefs which he was convinced were unreasonable, dangerous, and repulsive. The stigma attached to his name is not that he was the instigator of the persecution – he was only one of the instruments of its application – but that his contribution to the horrible total of martyrs was large. As Bishop of London, however, he had to deal not only with the city itself, a hot-bed of heresy according to every foreign ambassador, but also with Hertfordshire and Essex, the latter almost as full of Netherlandish heresy as of Netherlandish trade.

As for the Bishops in general, they cannot, in justice, bear the whole blame even of carrying out the law as it stood. Some of this must go to the laymen who informed against or who arrested the victims. Three of the Essex Justices, Brown, Tyrrell, and Lord Rich were notorious for their energy. Indeed, in the first six months of the persecution it was the Bishops and not the Justices who were, in the matter of applying the heresy laws, rebuked for sloth by the Crown.[31]

If Gardiner were only the initiator, and the Bishops only the instruments of the policy, what of the responsibility of the Cardinal of England? All Pole's record, and all his reputation, argue against the charge. Years ago, when he had been among the likely candidates for the Papal chair, one consideration which told against him was that he had spared heretics during his legation at Viterbo. Though Paul IV's suspicions must weigh light in the balance against any man, yet it is perhaps worth remembering that Pole and several friends of his among the Curia were suspected of heresy in 1557 and Pole himself was ignominiously recalled from England on that charge.

When after his return home he first preached to an English congregation, mercy was all his text. Englishmen, he said, have in the last reign been allowed less freedom than the subjects of the Turks, who at least freely worship as they will.[32] The words were a strange preface to the persecution which was to follow, but it is hard to believe them insincere. In those first days indeed Pole had not learnt the new brood of Englishmen which had grown up during his twenty years of exile. Later he was to speak of those who differed from him in religion with more harshness. 'For be you assured', he told the Londoners a year and a half or so after, 'there is no kind of man so pernicious to the Commonwealth as they be; there are no thieves, no murderers, no adulterers, no kind of treason to be compared with theirs; who, as it were undermining the chief foundations of all commonwealth, which is religion, make the entry to all kinds of vices . . . as we have had no small experience since religion was changed.'[33]

Yet though his words were strong, he kept his reputation for leniency, even with his opponents. He was known to have rebuked Bonner for precipitately bringing heretics to punishment. It was noticed that he preferred to order that the dead carcases of Bucer and Phagius should be dug up and burned, than that living heretics should go to the stake; this perhaps because, Foxe suggests, he was 'loth to be so cruel as the other'.[34] It is indeed hard to believe that the gentle and scholarly Cardinal, with his old predisposition towards a liberal and reforming policy, could have been enthusiastic for persecution.

On the other hand, had he taken a definite stand against it, his immense influence over the Queen, the prestige of his name in the Council, his position as Legate, would have ensured that at least his protest was heard. But he made no protest. When Paul IV accused him of heresy he justified himself by pointing to the heretics whom he was extirpating in England.

If we exclude from examination the responsibility of the Council, though the attitude of this body must have at least been acquiescent, two persons are left to bear the blame of the policy—Philip and Mary. Philip's later reputation in Flanders makes him seem a likely scapegoat indeed. The man who said that he had rather 'not rule at all than reign over heretics' was unlikely to suffer personal doubts as to the righteousness and efficacy of the punishment. He has been, however, very definitely absolved by modern writers, even by those who would have been glad to cleanse Mary's name from the old dark stain.

It has been argued in Philip's favour that either he had no influence over the course of events, or that he had influence, and used it definitely against the policy. One of his biographers has gone so far in this second direction as to claim that he was responsible for five months' pause in the persecution, which broke out again after he had left England;[35] but this is by no means borne out by the figures of the persecution; fifty-four persons were burned during the last seven months of his stay in England, i.e. February to September 1555, thirty-seven during the next seven months.

Yet, apart from this, the case for Philip is not so strong as it might seem. Enough perhaps has been said to show how far he concerned himself with English affairs, and what his influence counted for, nor are the examples quoted the only ones. Philip's own letters to his father are sufficient proof, that though he had by no means all that he hoped for in England, he had certainly much part in what should have been his wife's business; the gist of the letters is almost always what he has done in this matter, or what should he do in that? Further, against the one statement of the Venetian ambassador on June 11th 1555 that Philip had as yet refrained from interference in the business of the Council,[36] must be set an equally explicit statement by Michiel in 1557, that Philip's authority in England was as great as if he were its native King, although Michiel thought that he did not use it.[37] Others, not granting Philip a complete alibi, but asserting that his influence was for mercy, argue from the Emperor's warnings of the necessity of caution in religious matters that Philip himself was in favour of caution. Renard's manifesto to the King,[38] written at the time of the first executions, that is in February 1555, is quoted as proof that Philip must have sympathized with the ambassador's acute anxiety, and agreed with him that the policy of persecution was unwise. Similarly, the sermon preached before the King during this month by his own chaplain, Alphonso a Castro, denouncing the wickedness and foolishness of burning men for religion, is taken as voicing Philip's own views on the subject.

But there is another interpretation of these facts. Why, indeed should Renard write so urgently, so persuasively, so solemnly to Philip, if Philip was in agreement with him? Does not the very existence of the letter suggest that Renard thought it necessary to put these considerations before the King? And why, to hark back to the argument of Philip's impotence in English government, why write at all to a man who had no power to decide?

That letter of Renard's was surely written by the Ambassador to Philip because Philip had power, and because his views in this matter were not Renard's and not the Emperor's. Renard was Charles's and Granvelle's man, not Philip's; he was neither chosen by Philip, nor, when Philip had power to choose his men, did he remain an ambassador, but was before long shelved and even treated with rancour by the son of his late master. There is therefore no necessity at all for believing that Charles' ambassador and Philip spoke with the same voice.

Further, all Renard's objections were voiced in the early days of the persecution, and their ground was one–the fear of disturbance. When there was no disturbance, the ambassador's protests sank and died. If, then, Renard's letter to Philip was needed to persuade the King to put caution before what he considered his duty as a Christian ruler, and if Philip partially yielded to the emphatic warning of his father's trusted servant, what more likely than that the sermon of Alphonso the Friar was a device imagined by Renard himself for disassociating the King from the policy of which the ambassador dreaded such dire results. Certainly, after this first appearance of disapproval, Philip did not, any more than the ambassador, give any sign of an attempt to check or modify the application of the policy.[39]

But what was Mary's part in the miserable business? In the next century Fuller was to acquit her of most of the blame. 'She had been a worthy princess if as little cruelty had been done under her as by her.' Such an acquittal by a writer who drew his predispositions from some who could remember her reign, has its value. Nearer still in time came that preacher who, forty-five years after her death, could refer to her as 'a good woman, as they say, but an ill prince', but the latter only because she 'put her own and her people's neck under the Spanish yoke'.

Yet it is not this tradition, but that of Foxe which has persisted. For the eighteenth and nineteenth centuries she was the Jezebel that Knox called her, her Tyrian purple stained darker yet with the blood of God's elect. Of later and more critical historians some do nothing to lighten the burden of her guilt. Even Professor Pollard, who acknowledges her, and justly, 'the most honest of Tudor rulers', and who admits her naturally clement spirit, lays upon her the greater part of the responsibility of the persecution.

Apart from the general consideration that she was Queen and therefore ultimately responsible for any policy, the charges against her rest upon three

particular pieces of evidence. The first is that note, which the Venetian
ambassador who translated and sent his version home, headed as 'The Opinion
of the Queen of England which she wrote with her own hand.'[40] It was
given, he added, to Cardinal Pole at the time when the heresy laws were
passing through Parliament. In this expression of her 'opinion' as to how best
the Church should be reformed, after speaking of her hope that preachers
would be able, 'by their piety and doctrine, to smother' heresy, the Queen
wrote:

'Touching the punishment of heretics we thinketh it ought to be done
without rashness, not leaving meanwhile to do justice to such, as by learning
would seek to deceive the simple.' This is the English version. That which the
Venetian sent home appears re-translated into English in the Venetian
Calendar. The words here are slightly different. 'Touching the punishment of
heretics', the sentence runs, 'it would be well to inflict punishment at this
beginning without much cruelty or passion, but without omitting to do . . .
justice on those who choose by their false doctrine to deceive simple persons.'
There is some difference between punishing 'without rashness' and 'without
much cruelty or passion'. Yet there the writing stands bearing witness against
a woman kind-hearted, unrevengeful, whose reign as yet had seen no bloodshed except that which necessarily followed the rebellion of Wyatt. It has
been argued from this document that she was the instigator of the policy.
It is at least as legitimate to construe it as her surrender to advice which she had
resisted or doubted. But at the least, in this document she certainly consented
to the policy.

A second piece of evidence against her is that letter sent to Bishop Bonner and
probably also to the rest of the Bishops in her name and Philip's on May 24th
1555. This letter rebuked Bonner for delay in dealing with those heretics who
had been handed over to him for examination. Let him, so the royal order
ran, see that this was done 'so as . . . both God's glory may be better advanced
and the commonwealth more quietly governed'.[41]

But at that date Mary had been already for several weeks at Hampton
Court, and almost daily expecting the birth of her child. Since May 9th, so the
Venetian ambassador said, she had lived in an even greater privacy than before,
hardly ever leaving her room. From this month, right up to the beginning of
August, except for occasional appearances at a window, she was seen by
hardly any except the crowd of women who came to attend the birth, and
she took no part in the business of State. It is at least open to doubt whether
she, her mind absorbed in the anticipation of that hope which meant all to
her, could be responsible for this order. If Philip attended Council meetings
for her, who more likely than he for the author of it; perhaps he again,
certainly the Council, and only very improbably Mary, were also responsible
for those letters which were sent out at about this time urging the justice to
organize the apprehension of heretics, directing them to be present at executions, and thanking them for their zeal.

The third specific charge against Mary is founded upon that letter of

direction sent in August 1558, three months before her death, to the Sheriff of
Hampshire rebuking him for staying the execution of a heretic who had recanted at the first touch of the flame, and bidding him see the business carried
out. I make no attempt to clear her memory upon this charge; though already
she was a very sick woman it was not till the end of the month that those long
periods of insensibility are known to have begun, periods in which she lay as
if dead. She may have presided at the Council meeting and ordered, or consented to the letter. By this time, sunk deep in misery, and quite without hope,
she may in her despair have forgotten to show to another that pity which she
herself required.

Apart from this, the terrible persecution of her reign, the panic reply of a
social and political order threatened by a force which seemed determined on
nothing short of anarchy, was understandable if not excusable. It was easy
for Mary to convince herself, by all that was worst in the Protestant party,
that their doctrine was evil, as the fruits of it were, to her mind, evil.

These men, whose past and present history read to her as a perpetual flux
of belief, a loosening of all the bonds that held society together, these men
seemed to her to mock at and defy God himself. Worst still, they were instant
to corrupt, as she saw it, the simple, ignorant people of England, who in
their hearts, she was sure, still loved the old ways, and for whom the return
to the fold, that December of 1554, had been like the return of a traveller, long
absent from home in savage and dangerous places, to the remembered lights
and rejoicing of the Christmas Feast. It was for this reason, that to Cranmer
and the other leaders and teachers of the New Learning, she was implacable.
They had chosen by their false doctrine to deceive simple persons.

The months passed, and the fires were lit and re-lit, and more and more men
and women went voluntarily to death, impelled by a lofty and pure sense of
duty, or by a potent hysteria, part scruple, part angry hatred, which for us is
hard to understand. If the Queen had misgivings, and we shall see that such
misgivings she had, these were the arguments with which she must have
answered them. But she had, I think, other arguments at hand too. Philip was
beside her, the husband to whom she had given herself with single-minded
devotion. For him she prayed in words which Pole wrote for her, speaking
to God of her husband as 'a man who, more than all other, in his own acts
and guidance of mine reproduces thy image, thy image whom thou didst
send into the world in holiness and justice'.[42] If this man, so idolized, believed
in persecution, how could she stand against him? For, if mercy pulled her one
way, obedience pulled her the other. In this manner, by the very nature of the
case, her conscience must be surrendered to others. This heresy in England,
this offence against God as she believed it, had come by the refusal of men to
believe what their fathers and mothers, what their pastors and masters, what
Holy Church told them was the truth. How then could she, fighting God's
battle against the evils that had come of that disobedience, exempt, even if she
wished, her conscience from control? This policy, initiated by that 'most
politic Gardiner' in order to check the alarming disorders of the time, accepted

by a Council, scared, as men of property may always be scared, by attacks on the established state of things, and because scared, merciless–this policy was accepted not only by her husband, but also by the Pope's own Legate. And Pole, besides being Papal Legate, was of all Englishmen most akin to her, not only in blood but in spirit. Both, finding themselves exiles, bewildered and a little daunted, in a world that had values far other than theirs, were seeking 'a better city, that is, an heavenly'. Mary, who needed always to be persuaded, though once persuaded she would be obstinacy itself, could not think to look beyond these two men, sent by God to be her guides. Afterwards, in the sad days when Philip had all but shattered his own image in her heart, it was to the Cardinal alone that she turned, 'saying freely', as the Venetian heard with a kind of pitying wonder, 'that in government affairs, most especially in cases of conscience and offence against God (about which she shows herself beyond measure sensitive) she refers herself to the Cardinal, protesting that should errors be committed they will be visited on him'.[43]

So the policy of persecution was conceived, and carried out. Who led in it, and who followed after, we do not know. It had never been so thoroughly tested before. Never had the duty and wisdom of religious persecution been doubted; never had it, in England, been put into practice upon a large scale. But now the thing became, not a principle taken for granted and rarely applied, but a fact in the experience of gentle and simple alike. Women at their marketing, men at their daily trade, the cobbler at his bench, the plough-man trudging the furrow–all learnt to know the awful smell of burning human flesh, the flesh of a neighbour, of a man or woman as familiar as the parish pump. Mingling with the steam of washing day, or with the reek of autumn bonfires, or polluting the sweetness of June, that stench of human burning became a matter of everyday experience. Such an experience, even in a cruel age, left behind it a memory and a disgust. As de Tavannes said after the midnight butchery of Saint Bartholomew–'*Le coup fini, le sang blessa les consciences.*'

Chapter XVIII

I N this kingdom the Queen's lying-in is the foundation of everything',
said Renard, and added, with gloomy foreboding, that if she did not
bear a child affairs would be in such a bad way that 'a pen would hardly
write them'.[1] That was at the end of June 1555, when it was becoming
necessary to face the possibility that the Queen was not, after all, pregnant.
Between that time and the day at the beginning of the previous April when
Mary had gone to Hampton Court to make ready for her lying-in, lay two
months of hope, anxiety, and growing fear.

When she removed to Hampton Court it was supposed that during the
next few weeks 'this young master should come into the world'. There she
began a life of retirement, seen sometimes indeed by her subjects, as when on
St. George's day she looked out of a window upon the procession of the
Garter Knights and the crowds that watched them, but for the most part withdrawn in her own apartments among the crowd of noble- and gentlewomen come in from all over the country to assist at her delivery. Besides
these there were the women who should nurse the child and others who
should rock the child; in the Queen's chamber the cradle already stood,
'very sumptuously and gorgeously trimmed', with a Latin verse and its
English translation inlaid upon it.[2]

For a month the Court, and beyond the Court the whole of England
waited, their expectation based less on the likelihood of a middle-aged and
delicate woman bearing a child, than upon the very telling argument of past
events; for this was Mary, the Queen who might well say 'Deposuit potentes
de sede et exaltavit humiles'. Such at any rate was the foundation of Mary's own
belief.

If some doubted, they held their tongues, or told their doubts only to such
safe listeners as the French ambassador, who retailed these remarks with satisfaction in his letters home. Some assured de Noailles that the Queen could not
bear a living child. Someone else, who had received a bribe of 200 crowns of
French gold, reported that the Queen's own doctor said she ate so little that it
could not keep the child alive. Some declared 'It is only a tumour, as often
happens to women.'[3]

But such doubts and speculations were not spoken aloud. Everything, on
the contrary, was done to reassure Mary. 'To comfort the Queen and give her
heart and courage, three most beautiful infants were brought for her Majesty
to see; they having been born a few days previously at one birth, of a woman
of low stature and great age like the Queen, who after delivery found herself
strong and out of danger.'[4] And Mary was not required to bear triplets but
only a single heir. With the greatest confidence, and according to the usual

procedure, letters were written announcing the birth of a 'fil'–with room
left in the line to add the longed for 's', or the less gratifying but still satisfactory 'lle'.[5]

Then, at daybreak on the last day of April, word came to London, though
none knew how, that the Queen had been delivered of a son some time after
midnight. Even magistrates and royal officers believed and spread the news,
and soon shopkeepers had barred their shutters for holiday; men had run to
the churches to ring the bells; crowds coming to church found the old,
stately processions going about the aisles with lights and singing; and one
parson, exalted by loyal enthusiasm, 'took upon him to describe the proportion of the child, how fair, how beautiful, how great a prince it was, as the
like had not been seen'. Outside, folk set up trestles and laid on wine and
food; some, though it was daylight, lit bonfires.[6] During the morning the
rejoicings lasted, and for a few hours London rejoiced in the future; there
was to be another Tudor King to rule over England. Had it indeed been so,
no one can guess what England today would have been, for all that Henry VIII
had done might have been again undone. But in the afternoon it became
known that the rumour was a lie. Messengers from Hampton Court went
about contradicting it; there were yet, they said, no signs of delivery. As
Mason remarked, when the rumour, which had reached Brussels two days
later, was in like wise exploded, 'We were merry for a time, and are now
returned to our accustomed hope and expectation'.[7]

At Hampton Court the Queen waited, still confidently hoping. Yet, after
the first week of May, as if she dreaded people's eyes and tongues, she kept
herself even more private than before, and hardly left her chamber. A fortnight later ambassadors were still calculating, doctors and midwives still
prognosticating. 'Her Majesty's belly having greatly declined, a sign as they
say of the nearer approach of the term,' it was expected that either the birth
would take place at the next change of the moon, that is on May 23rd, 'or
after the full moon and its occultation on the 4th or 5th of June'.[8] It did not
take place on May 23rd. They must still wait.

Doubters picked up scraps of disconcerting gossip from the Court, as it
filtered through from the women about the Queen to the outer world. De
Noailles heard from 'the man of the 200 crowns' who, it appears, was a great
friend of two of the Queen's great friends, 'that is to say one of the best midwives in the town, and an old lady who has been with her more than 20
years', that the Queen, 'though pale and peaked', was not pregnant at all,
but that 'the said midwife, more to comfort her with words than anything,
tells her from day to day that she has miscalculated her pregnancy by two
months'. Mary no longer took her daily walks, nor moved here and there
about the room in her usual active way, but sat for hours upon cushions on
the floor, her knees drawn up to her chin, evidently ill, but not, some now
said, because she carried a child, since she could not then have sat in such a
position without pain, or without smothering the child.[9]

Yet no one, knowing how passionately the Queen longed for a child, dared tell her any of their doubts, and this passionate longing was left to work upon her, probably producing the very symptoms which she so much desired to appear, since this condition of pseudo-eyesis can be subconsciously induced by the mere desire of a woman to bear a child. The symptom of amenorrhea had been present before; if it appeared again at this time what more natural than to suppose that it was a symptom of pregnancy? She had always been subject to digestive disorders; sickness now might be interpreted as morning sickness; even that 'swelling of the paps and emission of milk' which the Venetian ambassador reported[10] is not, apparently, a physiological impossibility. So Mary, as honest a woman as any, had deluded herself with a hope that gradually dwindled and became overlaid with a torturing dread of disappointment. Yet she could not give up the belief that this great, this crowning mercy, without which all the rest must be in vain, should yet be granted her. Through the dreary drenched summer she waited, shut away in rooms heavily scented to drown the growing stench of a palace long over-crowded; craving for one thing only—to be as the wives of husbandmen, butchers, scavengers—to bear a child.

At the beginning of June prayers and processions had been instituted for the Queen's delivery, and Mary could be seen at a window every morning watching them go round about the court, looking, thought the Venetian ambassador, very well.[10]

People by now were talking louder. Rumours came to Englishmen in Italy that the Queen had been, a month ago, delivered of 'a mole or mass of flesh' and was still at death's door. Mason in Brussels wished that the Queen would only come abroad and go to Mass as usual. Having all ready as she had, he said, 'could be none inconvenience though she should travail within one day after her being abroad. This long keeping in with a multitude of women, the time of the year being so hot,' might cause sickness, he thought, and certainly was causing rumours.[11] Soon, in Sussex, there were reports that the Queen was dead, and a man appeared who called himself Edward Courtenay. People were saying that if the Queen could have found a suitable child she would have had it smuggled in to Hampton Court and announced the birth of a prince. Years after, a certain Isabel Malt, of Horn Alley, Aldersgate Street, declared to Master John Foxe that on Whitsunday of this year, that is June 11th 1555, Lord North and another great lord came, tempting her 'with many fair offers' to give them the child she had just borne, and with it, her promise to swear, if asked, that she had never borne any such child. Women came after them, of whom 'one, they said, should have been the rocker'. But, as the humble mother would not give up her child, the boy grew up in his own station, as—it is the one indisputable fact which Foxe vouched for in his tale—Timothy Malt.[12]

Fantastic as it might be, it was such a story as this of which Bishop Ponet was to make use, against a forlorn, disappointed, humiliated woman, 'When Pharaoh the tyrant commanded the midwives of the Egyptians to kill the male children that should be born of Israelite wives, think ye he did only command them? No, without doubt–ye may be sure he commanded them not only upon threatened pains but also promised them largely; and perchance as largely as these do, that being desirous of children procure the midwives to say they be with child, when their belly is puffed up with the dropsy or mole, and having bleared the common people's eyes with processioning, Te Deum singing, and bonfire banketting, use all ceremonies and crying out whilst another bird's egg is laid in the nest.'¹³ Renard listened with growing alarm to rumours such as these, and watching, saw 'the faces of men . . . strange, and more dissembling than ever before; they in whom we trusted are those we fear most, and doubt their faith and loyalty!'¹⁴ In that long period of suspense all that he had achieved seemed in danger of wreck. There was, in sum, 'little intercourse between the nations (English and Spanish), of justice and policy none, of daring malignancy more than ever'.¹⁵

In spite of all rumours and doubts, the Queen would not yet give up hope. She knew, poor soul, she must have known for months, that Philip was fretting to be gone; that only the hope of this child had kept him with her; she must have begun to fear that if there were to be no child, once gone, he might never return. So with desperate urgency she bade the Council write to Sir John Mason and order him to contradict any statement that she was not pregnant. The letter was written, but English merchants in Antwerp said that private letters came from members of the Council which told Mason that they did this by the Queen's orders, and not because they believed what she said.¹⁶

Almost at the end of July the doctors and women were promising the Queen that she was certainly carrying a child, but that the birth would not take place till August or even September. Then, not ten days later, Mary surrendered to the truth. The Court moved at last to Oatlands. It was 'not merely to give opportunity for the cleaning of Hampton Court where they have remained so long, and of which the place has great need', not merely an excuse for sending back to their houses 'the flock of noble ladies' who had come for the delivery, and who could not be put up in the smaller house at Oatlands. It was a tacit yet public admission that the Queen had given up hope. Processions and prayers for the Queen's delivery ceased, and once more Mary took up her ordinary life again, giving audiences, doing business, and going to Mass, with what a sore heart no one knew but herself. To a woman of hers, Mistress Frideswide Strelly, the only one who had never pretended to believe her with child, the Queen spoke once of those who had let her so long believe a lie. 'Ah, Strelly, Strelly,' she said, 'I see they be all flatterers, and none ever true to me but thou.'¹⁷ It was the cry of a deeply wounded, of a beaten woman.

She must have known already how, both as Queen of England and as the wife of Philip, this long-drawn-out miserable tragedy of her false pregnancy had undone her. She had no excuse now for keeping the King in England. Afterwards, in all the stubbornness of her nature, she was to summon him with reiterated urgency to return, in order that their marriage might be fruitful. Now, defeated and humbled to the dust, she surrendered, after one last, desperate resistance, to the arguments of her husband. Having convinced her,

so it seems, that he would always love her most dearly, Philip got her consent
to his departure. He was to leave at the end of the month. He was only, it was
said, to be away for a fortnight, to see the Emperor and return; all his household would remain in England waiting for him; but people were whispering
that, once away, he would go from the Netherlands to Spain, and once in
Spain, when would he come back?

On August 26th, through streets crowded by Londoners, and countrymen
come in for the great Bartholomew Fair, the Queen, refusing at the last
moment to lose Philip's company even for a few hours, and go leisurely by
river, passed through London in an open litter with her husband on one hand
and the Cardinal on the other. London, after so many weeks, so many strange
tales, went half crazy with joy at the sight of her. That 'stormy people,
unsad, and ever untrue, aye indiscreet and changing as a vane', shouted and
cheered as she passed along; they would have cheered Princess Elizabeth too,
and perhaps more tumultuously, but she had been sent by water, and did not
go through the city. The Queen and her husband took barge only at the Tower
Wharf, and so, dropping down the river, reached Greenwich Palace. It was
dark when they landed at the long bridge, where they were met by the Chancellor, already a very sick man, and by other members of the Council who
waited for them in the light of many torches.[18]

Three days later, Philip left her. She came with him as far as she might
through chambers and long galleries, to the head of the stairs, letting the
watching courtiers see no more than 'a sort of stately sorrow'. Only when
the Spaniards who went with him kissed her hand, and when the King himself kissed every one of her ladies, as he had learnt to do on his first evening
with her at Winchester, her composure was shaken. At last he took his leave
of her and went down to the barge. She turned back into the palace that was
now empty for her, and at a window overlooking the river, believing herself
unseen, gave way at last to a flood of tears, and so stood, weeping, and watching the neat figure among the crowd below. She watched while he went up
into the barge; and while the sailors cast off; she saw him stand on the after-
deck; as the boat passed below the window, he waved his cap to her. She
watched still while the barge drew quickly away along that sickle-shaped
reach of the river between its green banks–she watched until she could not
see him any longer.[19]

It was, and perhaps she knew it, the end of her happiness. Less fortunate
than her own unfortunate mother, it was a short time only that Mary had to
look back upon. Far away lay her sunny childhood. Between that, and what
had seemed the miraculous day of her accession, lay years of misery, humiliation, and anxiety. God's kingdom in England had been quite overset; she
alone in those years had been loyal to the truth as she knew it. Then came
the death of young Edward, her own midnight flight, her return in triumph,
her crowning. She had been sure then that she was ordained to bring England
back to God, and for a little while it had seemed easy. For a little while only.
But while difficulties gathered round her there was always one hope yet to

look forward to: the husband, Catholic, and of that Spanish blood so dear to her because her mother's, who should assist her in her great task of restoring England to God's church. Philip had come, and it had not been merely that a King had married a Queen, not even that she had beside her one of her nearest kin. She had learnt suddenly a thing she had not known before, passionate love for a man. Overwhelmed by happiness, what wonder if she counted on one more miracle yet, and a greater one than all; that she should bear a child to be King of England and to keep it Catholic. But she had not borne a child, and now Philip had gone. He had said a fortnight, or a month, or six weeks, but as she stood at the window at Greenwich, watching the barge through her tears, she must have known better than to believe him.

The long agony of her waiting had begun. Philip had gone to Gravesend, and thence to Canterbury. As though to make the parting more cruel, she heard that he was delayed at Canterbury, waiting for a fair wind; he might as well have spent the time with her at Greenwich. All that she could do to bridge the widening space between them she did. There were gentlemen waiting all day in the Palace Yard at Greenwich, booted and spurred, and posts riding every hour through the Kentish lanes bearing letters between the Queen and King. It was not till September 4th that Philip went on to Dover and crossed in the *Barge de Boulogne*, a fair crossing of two and a half hours as he wrote with his own hand to the Queen.

Four days later he came to Brussels. It was not yet dark, but a procession of 400 torches met him to welcome and bring him in. It was the first of many gaieties in which he was to take part. A man of thirty, he had spent more than a year of marriage with a woman nearly ten years older than himself, a year of rigid self-discipline, of a ceaseless and apparently convincing simulation of love. Marrying for reasons of state, he had been unfortunate enough to find as his wife a woman neither attractive nor indifferent. It is to his credit that he had for a year contrived to make the Queen happy, and to make her believe, even for a little while, in his equal affection. 'Never apart or out of sight' of each other, they had been to the amazement of outsiders, and Philip might well consider that he had done his duty by his wife; he may have been sorry for her; he may even have had some kindness for her; but the strain had been too great for him not to suffer from reaction. Although we need not believe Protestant accounts of his promiscuous depravity, yet the tales of his presence at this or that marriage feast lasting into the small hours; of play and masking through the streets in any weather, were it rain, wind, or snow; of the beautiful Mme d'Aler[20]–all this, and much more that was only hinted at by discreet letter writers, may well have been true; and yet it would be unjust on these grounds to say that Philip was worse than many a young man of that age or of any other. What was most blameworthy in his conduct was not unfaithfulness to his wife, but the calculating, callous use he was to make of his knowledge of her love, in an attempt to wring what political advantage he might from the disappointing and fruitless match.

No one yet told the Queen of Philip's frivolities, but the days were dark enough for her without that knowledge. As much as she could she hid her grief, but Queens have a scanty privacy, and Mary was known all over Europe to be 'extraordinarily in love'[21] with her husband; that love was indeed a factor to be reckoned with in European diplomacy, and its manifestations something to be noticed and reported by ambassadors to their masters. As the distance between husband and wife lengthened, Philip's letters became more infrequent. When Michiel, the Venetian ambassador, had an audience on September 12th, the Queen told him 'very passionately with the tears in her eyes, that for a week she had had no letters from him'. Michiel, courtier-like prophesied the King's quick return, saw how that pleased the Queen and went on to develop the theme. He had in other ways a successful audience, for the Queen began to talk about some coloured silk which some months before he had been asked, in her name, to procure from Italy. Now, after speaking of it to Michiel, she turned to Lord Montague and Princess Elizabeth who were both present, and told them all about it in English.[22] Thus Michiel reported, and the Signory must have read how an unhappy Queen tried for a few moments to forget her pain in that flimsy but unfailing comfort of women, the subject of clothes.

She sought also a less trivial solace in work. Desperately she threw herself into the business of state, seeking, not to forget, but to serve Philip. At prayer the whole of most mornings, at the Council board every afternoon, sitting up far into the night to write long laborious letters to her husband, informing him, since she must needs feel that that was his chief interest, of every detail of public business, she laboured to quench her sorrow, to do her duty as a queen, and to keep in touch with him. Yet still, with a woman's fond extravagance, she would send an English gentleman across the Channel merely to deliver to him a ring and to wish him health, long life, and speedy return. Another messenger went off, carrying some of the King's favourite game pasties, and no doubt both ring and pies had been the object of meticulous and loving attention.[23] When, for the sake of economy, the fleet which escorted the King was dismissed, the Queen raged at the Council, ordered it to be recommissioned, and kept it for long, ready at any moment to fetch the King back from Calais.

If she needed occupation, there was, in all conscience, enough business to occupy her, for on October 2nd Parliament began to sit, a Parliament recruited from among gentlemen and noble families, which was therefore to prove itself one of the most outspoken and intractable that she had to face. But a Parliament there must be, for the Exchequer was empty, loans taken up abroad were falling due, officers of the royal household had hardly been paid since the day of Edward's death, and, it was even said that the Queen could not pay for making or mending of her shoes.

It was this poverty that was the chief subject in the Chancellor's speech. Gardiner put the case strongly. No gold in the royal coffers when she came to the throne, but a fine inheritance of debts, from both her father and her brother; compulsory expenses since her accession both before and after her marriage–(everyone must have remembered the cost of meeting Wyatt's rebellion, and the expensive splendour of the marriage)–but, Gardiner put in, the Queen had not been extravagant and Philip had laid down, piece for piece, more Spanish gold than she had spent English. Yet she had had to borrow to pay the old debts, while at the same time voluntarily foregoing the tax and subsidy granted to Edward. Nor had she filled the exchequer with the revenues of many proscribed rebels, but had in her clemency given back to them both lives and lands. He asked therefore for a subsidy, and also for two-fifteenths.[24]

But the Commons were in no generous mood. They had come up to London full of dark suspicion, and ready to find, in any and every measure, the slot of Spain. If they were asked for money, they at once concluded, what Englishmen had suspected all along, that this money was destined to fill the pockets of Philip's Spanish soldiers, or to be otherwise spent in Philip's wars. It only hardened their resistance to the money bill, when they learned that the Queen, while asking them to minister liberally to her needs, was intent upon the restoration to the Church of all that was left of the monastic spoils of her father and brother. But, looming larger even than the financial question in the mind of the Commons, there was another project which they rightly believed the Queen to intend–Philip's coronation. Again, as in the last Parliament, this project was never divulged, but the Commons knew of it, or guessed, and that was as bad. With such preoccupations there was certain to be a stormy session.

Before it had well begun the Queen lost the best statesman, the best political strategist that she had. De Noailles, when he went to see Gardiner in August, had found him not only unusually friendly–so that the Chancellor would show his old enemy the repairs being done to his house–but also desperately ill. In October, when the French ambassador saw him again, both the friendliness and the illness had increased. At the end of a long audience Gardiner insisted on seeing the Frenchman out; when de Noailles tried to prevent him making the effort, Gardiner insisted, saying that he wished people to know that he was not dead yet, and so led the Frenchman out through three rooms full of staring people; but so weak was he that de Noailles had to hold him up by the arm.[25]

Yet he had been able, with indomitable energy of spirit, to make his speech to Parliament with so much of his old wit and pungency of phrase, that many, listening, admired. But it was almost his last effort. Before Parliament had well started to worry and tear to pieces the bills presented to it, on November 12th, Stephen Gardiner, the witty, irascible, sharp-spoken man, so well hated by almost all, after having made his peace with his old friend and long-time enemy Paget, died at York Place in the middle of the night.

It was not only that the Queen had lost in him the one man who, knowing his Englishmen, and knowing too all the moves and gambits in the delicate game of statesmanship, could alone have gentled the Commons into a friendly mood. The vacancy of the Chancellorship meant jealousy in the Council on the subject of the new appointment, and it meant too a difference between Mary and her husband, for Paget had set his heart on having the seals, Philip wanted him to have them, but the Queen did not.[26] Eventually, after she had kept them some time in her bedroom, she gave them to Heath, Archbishop of York, compensating Paget by giving him the Privy Seal.

Heath, however, was no adequate substitute for Gardiner. The Queen had gained her subsidy indeed, but, as de Noailles confided to his friend and colleague in Scotland 'there are many other acts which will certainly not manage to pass as the Queen wishes, as they aim at things hateful to them (the Commons), and the death of the Chancellor will increase the difficulty. But, said the Frenchman, 'I for my part am not very sorry, as I hope that our master's affairs must go the better for it.'[27]

Mary, left to face Parliament with neither Gardiner nor Philip to help her, could do little with it. She had wished for a bill giving her power to dispose of the royal domain without consent of Parliament, a bill which in de Noailles' opinion, aimed at a bequest of the crown; and why should the Queen wish for power to bequeath the crown unless she meant to bequeath it to Philip? De Noailles's suspicion was to be the bugbear of Englishmen from now until the end of the reign. The bill was naturally defeated, though Mary's supposed intention was probably no more than a figment of the Commons' excited imagination.

But important as these bills were, in them the Queen's heart was not engaged. It was, and deeply, in that other project, guessed at, talked of, dreaded, and perhaps the cause of all the ill-tempered intractability of the Commons. For they, no less than de Noailles, believed that the coronation of Philip was designed as the first step towards letting 'the absolute rule of the realm fall into the hands of the King'.

Caring for Philip as she did, it was not surprising if Mary intended thus to give him that thing which, after an heir to the Netherlands and England, he most desired, hoping so to bring back his waning affection. It was said that Philip himself had written a letter which must have struck straight to her heart, for in it he told her that though he wished to gratify her desire for his return, it was not in accord with his dignity that he should come back to England, to be again no more than an uncrowned consort.[28] If he wrote such a letter, and if, as de Noailles believed, the Queen was hearing of the 'many little visits he pays over there to ladies who are younger than she',[29] then Mary was wretched indeed, for it was beyond her power to give him the crown he coveted. Not a week after Parliament met, Gardiner had openly renounced, on behalf of the Queen, that intention which had never been openly avowed. They must not, he told the Commons, be disturbed by false reports, for 'nothing would be said about the King's authority, or about His Majesty's person'. Mary had to report failure to Philip, at least for the present, but suggested, if Badoer in Brussels heard a true tale, that when the Commons had gone off to their homes she would persuade a number of the greater lords to contrive his coronation without parliamentary authority. Philip, according to Badoer, already 'the Prudent', bade her not to attempt this unless she were sure of success.[30]

Apart from the subsidy, the Queen succeeded in only one of all her aims, and in this succeeded by no more than a narrow margin. In the early spring, shortly after the Cardinal's arrival and the reconciliation of England to the Papal obedience, she had decided that it was her duty to restore all those first fruits and tenths of benefices which, since the breach with Rome, had been paid to the Crown instead of to the Pope. In her eyes, as in the Cardinal's, such restoration was the only right course, but politically the act was dangerous. Every holder of old abbey lands, hearing of it, would dread that the next thing would be an enforced compliance with such an example; that, even if the Queen herself used no compulsion, the Pope, whose hankerings after restitution were partly known, partly guessed, would be encouraged to apply to England a singularly ill-timed bull of excommunication published at about this time, against holders of Church lands in other countries. What most English 'detainers' thought of that, was spoken for them by the Earl of Bedford, who, standing by the fire in the Council chamber when the matter was being talked of, suddenly wrenched the rosary from his belt and slung the broken string into the flames, 'swearing deeply that he loved his sweet abbey of Woburn more than any fatherly counsel or commands that could come from Rome'.[31]

But Mary, when she was convinced of a duty, was not a woman to turn back, either for fear or favour. Towards the end of March 1556 she had sent for four of the Council, and had announced to them her intention of restitution, taking the wind out of the sails of all their prudent arguments by declaring that even if, 'considering the state of the kingdom, and the dignity thereof, my crown imperial cannot be honourably maintained and furnished without the possessions aforesaid; yet notwithstanding, I set more by the salvation of my soul than by ten kingdoms'.

The Council, finding no answer to that, had retreated upon another line of defence. What had been taken by consent of Parliament, could be given away only by that same consent. Therefore Mary, in this autumn Parliament, after having asked her subjects for a generous subsidy, must also ask their consent to increase the poverty of the Crown. It was on all counts a risky endeavour, and she knew it.

She was, as usual with her in the autumn, far from well, but, hearing that this bill of hers was likely to be resisted, she sent for three score of the Commons to the palace. They came, one short November afternoon, about ten weeks after Gardiner's death, and the Queen, with 'her usual gravity and dignity' told them her mind. She had, she said, been preserved to the succession simply to re-establish religion; if they needed proof of that, it lay in her past dangers and her deliverance. Religion had been restored by Parliament, but this was no use if her conscience was still burdened with the tenths and first fruits, and with those cures of souls that used to depend on the abbeys, and impropriated rectories, the restoration of which, she told them, would benefit all. 'You have', said she, 'shown that you care for my person; but that is no good if you care nothing for my soul.'[32] What they answered her then we do not know, but back in the less rarefied air of St. Stephens, the Commons proceeded to haggle. It was clearly foolishness to restore the tenths and first fruits to the Pope, since at the outset of the Reformation the clergy themselves had complained of these payments as intolerable; the Commons certainly would have none of that. The Queen, yielding on this point, suggested, with a transparent honesty and pathetic confidence in human nature, that the revenue in dispute should be surrendered to the laity, for them in turn to surrender to the Church. At last, after many debates and more parliamentary juggling, the Bill passed, and the Queen was allowed to surrender £60,000 a year to be used by the Legate for the augmentation of small livings.

It had taken, to pass this bill, 'so much anger', as de Noailles said, 'and so many promises', that the Queen might have known that she would get little else out of this surly and grudging Parliament. Less than a week later a bill came to the Commons from the Lords which was devised to recall all that irregular army of Englishmen abroad, who had, since their flight, given the government every trouble that they could imagine and devise. The flood of pamphlets from Strasburg, Geneva, or Basle; the sinister appearances at the French court or upon the French coast of young English gentlemen in the pay and favour of the French King – these would cease, if, with a promise of the restoration of confiscated goods, a threat to confiscate goods not yet impounded, every Englishman without a licence to travel was summoned to return home. The bill would mean, in fact, the collapse of that complicated and efficient machine of political propaganda and attack which the Protestant party had built up on the Continent.

But this measure, which would have destroyed at a stroke the freedom of action of the Protestant party abroad, was one which their friends at home could not accept. The Lords passed it, but when it came to the Commons there was trouble. In the House Sir George Howard and Sir Edward Hastings, the latter a faithful servant of the Queen, almost came to blows. When the Queen's party tried the manœuvre of putting off the division till an opportunity when the House might be empty of the opposition, Sir Anthony Kingston and two or three of his friends held the door, swearing that they would allow none to pass out, till a division had been taken. It was taken then and there, and the bill defeated, and as a natural result of such a setback for the Queen, 'audacity and discontent gained ground daily'.

Mary, though kindly, had a hasty temper on occasions, and lately it had been tried, not only by an intractable Parliament, but by a fresh outburst of seditious writings. She gave no sign of caring for the defeat of the bill, but soon after she sent suddenly for the Lords and Commons. They came, through the frozen streets, to Whitehall, and there the Queen dissolved Parliament, and with the same promptitude shut up Sir Anthony Kingston and two or three of the worst malcontents in the Tower.

The Queen, as Michiel told the Doge, was eager to be done with Parliament and London. She had interests far nearer her heart than the management of refractory Commons. She turned with relief from the compromises and crooked ways of statecraft to the task for which she believed herself sent – the restoration of God's Church to that state which she remembered in her young and happy days. It was this task, little as she could accomplish, and that little always under the shadow of impermanence, that was to be her chief comfort in the dark days ahead.

Of the old ways, many had been revived. Processions of priests, school-children, and city companies: dirges, masses 'for all crystyn solles': rood lofts with the images of the Crucifix between the Virgin and St. John – all these things could be restored without much difficulty. And all these things must have brought some comfort to Mary's sore heart, for she was a woman to whom observance – the visible, the remembered ways – meant much. On Holy Thursday 1556, the Queen held her Maundy, as it had not been held for many a long year.[33] She was at Greenwich, and around the great hall benches were set, and in front of the benches, stools for forty-one old and poor women to put their feet on, forty-one being the number of the Queen's years. After two of the household, the under-almoner and grand almoner, had each of them washed the right foot of each of these old women in came the Queen with a long linen apron over her gown, which was of purple cloth lined with marten's fur, and the sleeves so wide that they touched the ground as she moved. Besides the apron she had a long towel laid stole-wise across her neck. As she came to the first old woman the Queen went down upon her knees, and while her ladies stood around, each with a long apron and a towel like the Queen, and each bearing in one hand a silver ewer and in the other a bunch of sweet-smelling and medicinal herbs to purify the air. Mary, kneeling all the while, washed carefully, dried, crossed, and then fervently kissed the old withered feet,'as if she were embracing something very precious'. So she did to each woman, shuffling from one to another, for greater devotion, upon the knees of that voluminous gown of finest cloth. When the washing was done, alms were given. The Queen went round the hall six times (as Pole's secretary who watched, reported it to a friend in Italy), giving at successive journeys, a wooden platter with 'great pieces of salted fish and two large loaves, a wooden bowl of wine or rather I think hippocras', a piece of cloth 'of royal weave', a pair of shoes and stockings, a leather purse bulged out with forty-one pennies, and last of all the aprons and towels that had been used. A final gift, to the oldest and poorest of the women, was the gown itself that the Queen had worn, and one would like to know its history in that poor hovel to which it was taken. Such was the Queen's Maundy, and one can well imagine with what trembling hope, what fears, what penitence, what confidence of belief, the Queen fulfilled the old, prescribed forms that April day.

A greater thing than the restoration of ceremonies, and one very much in the Queen's mind, was the re-establishment of monastic houses. Already in the spring of 1555 English friars were returning from Flanders, whither they had fled to keep their vows. Now sixteen Benedictine monks, who had not fled, voluntarily resumed their habits. The Queen, when they came before her, wept at the sight of that long ago familiar black gown and the new-shaved tonsures; now at last, she must have thought, 'time would run back and fetch the age of gold'. These monks were, in the autumn of 1556, established at the old abbey of Westminster, after Canterbury the holiest place in England for Englishmen. But it was perhaps on the house of Friars Observant at Greenwich that Mary's interest centred most. Her birthplace, Greenwich had often been her home during the early years of her life, and after, in the troubled days that followed her mother's repudiation. Now it had become her favourite residence, and from the palace she could watch with closest attention and great thankfulness the newly returned, barefooted friars as they went about their business.

To St. Bartholomew's Hospital at Smithfield, next year at Easter-time, returned the Black Friars; in June the Savoy hospital was refounded, in the winter the Carthusians came home to Sheen, and in the house of Syon across the river, the nuns were back again. Yet in all not a dozen of the great company of abbeys were, even for a short while, re-tenanted by religious; to set up more was impossible, for, except the Queen, and here and there one like the Oxford gentleman who voluntarily restored Church lands, none in England cared to contribute to this revival of the past.

Yet in the work of restoration Mary had beside her one strangely like to herself in aims and ideals. There was little resemblance in the externals, either of appearance or temperament, between the small, vehement, outspoken, quick-tempered Queen, and my lord Cardinal with his lean frame, his quiet eyes, the 'taciturnità' that his friends teased him for, and his scholastic habit of mind. But they were alike in this–both, devoid of artifice and self-seeking, judged everything throughout the changes and chances of this mortal life not by temporal standards, but *sub specie aeternitatis*, and with simple literal sincerity, endeavoured to fit their actions to the polity of that other world that was to them the only abiding reality. More and more, as Philip's absence lengthened, the Queen came to lean upon the Cardinal. He lived in the Palace. Though he was not of the Council, all important questions were referred to him, and to him the Queen submitted the whole direction of her conscience. She, with her vigorous, obstinate, yet vacillating temper, had always needed a man to lean on. Philip had come and gone. Pole, her kins-man, born of a stock of more ancient royalty than her own, had now, though so lately only a memory of her childhood, become a friend, dearer and more revered than any other. Like an elder brother he watched over her, re-ported to Philip her health and doings, advised, controlled, directed her. Such as believe in the Providence of God may think that he was sent to be her support through a time of lonely wretchedness otherwise all but un-endurable.

Pole himself had a hard task before him. Not only were there many gaps

in the ranks of the clergy, where married priests, or others not rightly ordained, had been deprived, but the Cardinal, as well as the Queen, considered
that it was necessary not only to purge the Church of its erring members, but
to educate, to enlighten, to uplift those that remained, and to restore, as soon
as might be, the old and hallowed ways of the past. If Mary, with her limited
imagination, yearned especially over the tangible signs of a Catholic England,
Pole's eyes looked further. He saw, as men like Colet, Lefèvre, Erasmus, had
seen, before the dust of controversy rose and darkened men's vision, the
urgent need of the time (but when indeed is the need not urgent?) for that
reform which is the reform of every man's life, according to the plain precepts of Christ, and showing itself in simple practical efforts to do and to be
good. First prayer, then penance, then works of mercy – that was the way that
Pole pointed out to the Londoners. He did not expect over much of them.
For when he had spoken of the ruined abbey Churches – 'notwithstanding',
he added, 'my meaning is not, that this, being a noble act and grateful to God
and profitable to the realm, that you should forthwith take in hand the
building of these, which I know you are not able to do; and if you were able,
and had such a gay mind to restore the ruins of churches, yet there be other
churches that are now first to be holpen, and those be your parish churches'
which, though not cast down by authority, yet 'have been suffered to fall
down of themselves, and in like manner spoiled as the monasteries were. And
to this I exhort you forthwith to set your hand; which you may in no wise
fail to do, except you will have your people wax brutish and wild, and your
commonwealth without foundation.' But the duty of church-building as of
almsgiving, that had once loomed so large upon passionate, greedy, fearful,
and yet believing minds in the Middle Ages, was now out of vogue. Two
Italian cities, the Cardinal told the Londoners, gave more alms in a month
than the whole kingdom of England in a year.[34]

It was this hardness of heart, which with irreverence, spiritual arrogance,
and resentment of authority – fruits of a period of bitter controversy – Pole
saw as the worst sin of the laity. But, to lead common men into better ways,
better priests were needed. In Edward VI's day, there had been a great shortage of candidates for ordination, and so there was still. Even when a parish
had a priest, parishioners grudged him that reverence which had traditionally
been given to the office, Protestants despising men of conservative feeling,
Catholics equally scornful of married priests. Against this declension of the
priesthood Pole directed most of his energies. Having called a synod, which
met in November 1555, he proceeded to the reform of the clergy 'according
to the old antiquity of the church', with such effect that, as Mason wrote to
Devonshire, with an acid humour – 'the more part of the priests of England
would be content he were in Rome again'.[35] For Pole's plan of campaign,
besides providing a new translation of the New Testament, and books of
homilies of Catholic instruction, and banning anew heretical books, besides
the restoration of Catholic ceremonies and furniture in churches, was
directed against such 'fearful evils' as non-residence, alienation of Church

lands, carelessness of Bishops with regard to candidates for ordination, and in general against the self-indulgence, luxury, or avarice, which made priests ill examples of any teaching they might give. So, nearly twenty years later, Pole launched in England that programme of reform which had been laid before Paul III. But when the synod had been prorogued in the early spring of 1556, and the Bishops dispatched to make Visitations in their dioceses, they did not meet again. One prorogation after another put off the re-assembly of the synod from month to month, and finally *sine die*. When Pole was deprived of his legatine authority he lost the power to convoke a synod of all England, although, as Archbishop, in his own province and diocese he persevered in the *Reformatio Angliae*.[36]

Another work, the complement of this, but far more painful, was still going on. 'The great multitude of briars and brambles . . . cast into the fire', in Pole's phrase, that is the number of heretics burned, still mounted up, and yet the enthusiasm and devotion of that obstinate party in no wise lessened, rather it increased. In the spring of 1556 the government, after seeming to be on the verge of a great victory, suffered a notable reverse. Archbishop Cranmer, condemned at last in Rome, was to suffer death at Oxford. But first the priest and Archbishop must endure the long and harrowing ceremony of degradation. Dressed for this in rough canvas travesties of the deacon's, priest's, bishop's, and archbishop's vestments, he must stand while these were one by one stripped from him, while all imaginary trace of the tonsure was obliterated by the barber's shears, his fingers scraped of any hallowing of the sacred oil. After this he was removed, not to the easy confinement at Christchurch, where he had passed the last months, but to Bocardo, the prison on the town wall beside the Saxon tower of Saint Michael's. There, more and more explicit written submissions were desired of him, and to the number of six he wrote them, one after another, accepting among many other things the papal supremacy, and recanting the doctrine of the sacrament which he had so long preached. 'Exceedingly offended I against Henry and Katherine in that divorce, whereof I was the cause and author, which was the seed plot of the calamities of the realm. Hence the violent death of good men, hence the schism of the whole kingdom, hence heretics, hence the slaughter of so many souls and bodies. . . . I am worse than Saul and the thief, I am the most wicked wretch that earth has ever borne. I have sinned against heaven which through me stands empty of so many inhabitants. . . . I have sinned against earth, depriving men of the supersubstantial food. Of them that perished for lack of it I am the slayer; and the souls of the dead I have defrauded of this daily, celebrious sacrifice.'[37]

That passage, with its sombre eloquence, explains Mary's implacable hatred of Cranmer. Not only was he the man of all men who had made possible the repudiation of her mother, showing Henry a way when he was ready to give up in despair; he was also the hireling shepherd who had led his flock to the wolves. She had prophesied that he would never stand to his faith, and she was right. But it was not only physical fear that wrought on him. His subtle and balanced mind apprehended the force and implication of every argument with far more exactitude than was possible for intellects of coarser fibre, and he found, when pressed by the natural fear of a horrible death, that his hold upon his old opinions was slipping. Maybe he did not even know to what extent fear had loosened his grasp, to what extent the arguments of his judges had made him suspect the validity of those dogmas he had professed.

But the knowledge, that in spite of all repeated and amplified recantations, he was to be burned, must have enlightened him as to this, while it removed that pressure of hope to which he had, half consciously, yielded. In the church of St. Mary the Virgin at Oxford, while Bishops, and doctors of the University waited for the final solemn recantation of a man who was to die within the hour, he broke out first with a prayer–the most moving of all he ever wrote, for in it a soul cried aloud, and it was a soul articulate in its agony.

' O Father of Heaven,' he prayed, 'O Son of God, Redeemer of the world, O Holy Ghost proceeding from them both, Three Persons and one God, have mercy upon me, most wretched caitiff and miserable sinner. I have offended both Heaven and earth more than I am able to express. . . . What then shall I do? Shall I despair? God forbid. O good God, Thou art merciful, and refusest none that come to thee for succour. . . . God was not made man for our small offences. Thou didst not give thy Son unto death for our little and small sins only, but for all and the greatest sins of the world, so that the sinner return to Thee in his heart; as I do here at this present!'

Next, having repeated the Lord's Prayer, he exhorted the people to loyalty and obedience, and made confession of the Christian faith, all this according to the expected form. 'And now,' the degraded Archbishop said, 'I come to the great thing that so much troubleth my conscience, more than anything that I ever did,' But when the packed congregation of priests and doctors listened for his explicit and final recantation, they got other fare. For what he repented of and recanted was that recantation itself which, he said, with a simplicity akin to the finest courage, he had made 'for fear of death, and to save my life if it might be'.[38]

This Samson, as Professor Gairdner has called him, having lost alike hope and honour, had plucked down the house upon his enemies' heads. 'Thou wilt drag with thee innumerable souls to hell!' a Friar shouted at him, as he went from the excited confusion of Saint Mary's to the stake. Cranmer's former recantations might be published, but compared with this they would weigh light as puff balls against a bloom of iron.

The failure of the Queen's pregnancy, the example of the Archbishop, the poverty of the Crown, the unpopularity of the Spaniards, all these things emboldened the Protestant and discontented. The Privy Council found it necessary to order that there should be a good force of officers at executions to thwart 'such as shall misuse themselves either by comforting, aiding, or praising the offender', and to forbid that apprentices or servants should be allowed by their masters to be at large at the time of these executions. For popular sympathy was quickening to an alarming degree. When twenty-two heretics were sent to London for execution, they were met at Stratford le Bow by companies of Protestant sympathizers. As they approached London the crowd grew, till close on a thousand people thronged about the prisoners at the gates of Fulham Palace.[39]

If there was mounting excitement in Protestant ranks, Catholics, and among them the Queen herself, felt a growing misgiving at this apparently fruitless burning of men and women. When, in April 1556, Mary sent Paget to Brussels that he might use all his subtlety in persuading Philip to return, she charged her envoy with another matter also. He was to go to the Emperor, and ask his advice in the matter of heresy—for Charles, in Germany and the Netherlands, had been applying the same policy of rigorous suppressions as had been in force in England since the revival of the heresy laws. In England, Paget was to say, the remedy had not brought that cure which had been hoped of it. The Queen therefore wished to know what should now be done.[40]

What Charles replied, Badoer, the Venetian, could not discover. The Frisian Viglius, president of the Council in Brussels, had the same doubts as the Queen of England. In eighteen months, he said, the total of Lutherans and Anabaptists burned, hanged, and drowned was 1,300, and he believed that 'for the avoidance of greater cruelty, the execrable intentions of these sectaries must be tolerated as much as possible, they being too great in number, to stamp out by such methods.[41] But when Charles, a few months before, had surrendered the rule of the Netherlands to Philip, he bequeathed to his son the duty of persecution, and it is not likely that the uneasy scruples of Mary got any sympathy from him, now it had been proved that burning heretics in England did not cause rebellion. Still less was she likely to get any understanding from Philip, who was later to lose the Netherlands because he would not listen to the advice and reiterated appeals of his aunt, Mary of Hungary, and remit the rigour of the Inquisition there.

As autumn passed into winter, and winter into spring, Mary's hope of her husband's return must have changed into a gnawing dread. Daily she heard of the departure of this or that Spaniard, and missed, from about the court, faces that had grown familiar to her since the day of her marriage. Philip's Guard and most of his household were ordered to leave for Brussels, and though Philip might write and explain that this meant nothing but that he would need them when the Emperor withdrew with his household, it was not hard to put a different construction upon the order. People in England were saying of the departing Spaniards, that they left 'with a mind not to revisit England for a very long time', and Mary might well fear that that was their master's mind too. When Pole read to her a passage from one of Philip's letters in which he begged the Cardinal to prevent the Queen from injuring her health by too much application to business—'her health which is of greater consequence to me than anything else', she broke down.[42] Such a message might mean much or little.

In December she heard that Philip was ill of a fever. At once she sent her own chamberlain to convey her sympathy and to bring back news. The messenger brought word of the King's recovery but 'lest the Queen, who is easily upset, should take it too much to heart'[43] he suppressed, as he had promised, the information that Philip had been out twice masking 'in this horrible weather'.

The remainder of Philip's suite, his confessor and his chapel furniture were sent for. Mary began to believe that even if he kept his promise to come after Epiphany he would then be on his way to Spain, and once in Spain it might be years before he came again. Her misery was so palpable that some thought she would, in order to bring her husband back, 'do some crazy thing in this Parliament for him'.[44] What that thing was, everyone knew. Badoer, the Venetian ambassador in Brussels, heard from the messenger whom the unhappy woman had sent to Philip, that she implored forgiveness for doing nothing towards his coronation, telling him, as if with a cry of despair, 'that when she looks round and carefully considers the men about her, she scarcely sees one who has not done her an injury, or who would fail to do so again if he had the chance, and that since she became Queen the miseries and dangers she had undergone have been and still are so great,' that the thing was impossible 'without endangering her crown; but that she hoped in a short time to comfort his Majesty with that which he seems to desire'.[45]

All this time both she and the Council were corresponding with the absent King. Minutes of the Council meetings were sent to him, and returned, carefully annotated by Philip. The Queen asked his advice as to appointments; but here it was the same as in the matter of the coronation, Mary could do little to please him if in his absence the Council chose to resist his desires.

So Christmas came, a sad one for Mary, though merry enough for Philip, for the towns of the Netherlands were among the gayest and most splendid of the age; there was, said an Italian, 'a constant succession of gay assemblies, nuptials and dances; while music, singing, and cheerful sounds prevailed in every street'. In January the Emperor completed that formal renunciation to his son of all his titles and possessions except the Empire and Burgundy. In October he had resigned the Netherlands; now it was Spain and Sicily. He gave into Philip's hand his will, and the gold matrix of the seal with which it had been sealed, bidding him break this. So, divested of his great dominions, he dismissed all but Philip, and then, so it was said, 'took out from a little coffer certain small papers . . . and after reading them, tore them up[46]'.

Charles had laid down his burdens. Philip shouldered them, and if it was unlikely that the King of Naples should soon revisit England, it was still more unlikely that the ruler of Spain, Naples, Sicily and the rest, would find the time to do it for many a long day.

Mary fought against the realization of this, but Philip's delays, broken promises and excuses drove her into brief, miserable rages that faded into moods of complete self-abasement, in which she begged humbly as much for his forgiveness as for his return. Her enemies told a tale of how she had flown at Philip's picture and scratched the unmoved face with her nails.[47] Even so soon as October she had said to one of her women that 'if so be as the King should not return, after I have done all to bring him back, I will take care to live the rest of my days without the company of men, as I did before my marriage'.[48]

Throughout the winter and spring her demands for his return varied between peremptory and abject. After Christmas she sent first Mason then Paget to plead, to argue, almost to threaten Philip. Paget, who had brought her husband to her, she did not trust–no, not one yard–but she had a very lively respect for his ability. And he, having her favour to win back, must have used all his wiles, but it would not do. Though the King sent back word that if he did not come next month 'he was not a king to be trusted', the month passed, and many more months, and still he did not come. So torn between anger and pain, Mary spent the days; and in the long sleepless nights, turning over the past in her mind while the owls swung and hooted outside, she would decide sometimes, and tell her women, that she regretted her marriage, and would not, had she again the choice, choose as she had done. Yet she could never shake herself free for long from the uncontrollable desire for Philip's return.

As though she were doomed to lose him, everything he asked of her as the price of his return was impossible. He had asked to be crowned. She had not dared to contrive it. He had asked that she should threaten to declare war on France so as to bring Henri II into a mood for peace; there was nothing the Council dreaded more than a war with France on Spain's behalf. Now Philip wished her to deal with the question of Elizabeth's succession in such a way that she should not remain a potential enemy. The Queen, following Gardiner in this, would have been glad to have the young woman legally declared the bastard that she had always held her. Philip had another plan. Elizabeth should marry that bridegroom already suggested for her, the Duke of Savoy. Savoy, dependent upon the Habsburgs even for his bread and butter, and for any hope of recovering his lost principality, would be a faithful and docile ally through whom Spain might manage England. Now, while the Queen lived, and while Elizabeth was still no more than the heir presumptive, was the time to make sure of the match. But Elizabeth refused, and there was no hope that either Parliament or the Council would consent. Between them all the Queen was helpless; and Philip was cruel.

Chapter XIX

'THIS royal throne of kings, this sceptred isle . . . this England,' was, in Mary's unhappy reign, less like to the securely moated house of Shakespeare's imagination than to a ship driving upon a lee shore. The long-drawn-out war between the Emperor and France was that perilous coast; the Queen had blundered into danger by the Spanish marriage; after that, French intrigue, French enmity, had combined with her own Spanish bent to drive England ever closer to the reefs of war.

That war, which Henri of France and Philip of Spain inherited from their fathers, had been at the back, when it was not at the front of every political situation in Europe since the accession of Charles V to the Imperial dignity. At first it was fought out, by the choice of François I, in Italy, but Henri II had transferred the seat of war to the north-eastern border of France, a battleground more vital to both parties. There the struggle had dragged on during the years between the death of François I and Charles's retirement to the cloister of Juste. There Philip inherited it. From thence it was to slide eastward into Germany as the Imperial branch of the Habsburg house took it from his hands.

English policy with regard to this rivalry of France and the Habsburgs had, in the time of Henry VIII and Wolsey, taken the form of coquettish advances to both of the great opponents, followed by sudden coy withdrawals. '*Souvent femme varie*', but not so often as the English alliance, given now on one side, now on the other. Later, Elizabeth's policy was to show less startling variations, but, with its non-committal discretions, to be almost as unaccountable. Only Edward VI and Mary surrendered the advantages of the Jack on the middle of the European see-saw. In Edward's reign the Council had suffered from such an overmastering craving for an anti-Catholic alliance, that England had necessarily inclined to a close alliance with the German Protestant Princes, and consequently with the French, who were always to be found by the side of any opponent of the Emperor. Now Mary, reacting naturally but unwisely against that policy, had preferred the close, and as she hoped, the protective alliance of Spain, to the more hazardous advantages of neutrality. Her choice was perhaps inevitable but it was disastrous.

That is not to say that the rocks upon which England was driving were invisible to the English Council, or even to Mary herself, or that no steps were taken to avoid danger. On the one hand the stipulations of the marriage treaty were devised to prevent England being involved in the war; on the other hand one effort after another was made to bring about a peace between the combatants. In English eyes peace was necessary, not only nor mainly because of the growing thundercloud that darkened in the east, where the

Turk was making ready for his great advance, but also by reason of an empty exchequer and for the sake of what were known as the 'Queen's proceedings', that is the restoration of the old ways in religion. If, said Mason in one of his pithy, witty letters to the Council - if the Queen might have peace for three or four years, 'the new and tender branch newly grafted, being subject yet to shaking and every little wagging of the wind, should be so fastened and grown into the whole tree as no danger of any blast were afterwards to be feared. The people which be yet diversely drawn, some by opinions and some by other means, may in that time grow into one conformity, and your empty coffers have something in them, to be able to strive with such storms as by any malicious enemy might fall into the realm.'[1]

That was written in the summer of 1554, before the arrival of Philip in England, and in those days, the Queen herself desired peace as ardently and whole-heartedly as any. She was ready, and said so repeatedly, to mediate between the two rivals. It was not only her Englishmen at home who were urging on her this task, which, indeed, her pious mind believed to have been divinely appointed for her. Pole, still unable to obtain the Emperor's leave to come to England, wrote in the same sense. Pole had been, and still was, officially engaged on the Pope's behalf in the same business of peace-making. When, at the end of June 1554, fighting actually began again, and the Emperor must put on his armour and buckskin jerkin, gear which he found three fingers tighter than it had been, Pole thought it was time to make a fresh effort. He spoke to the Bishop of Arras of peace, as Mason himself had spoken a month before, but neither of them got much satisfaction. The Bishop, questioned by Mason as to whether the Emperor indeed wanted peace, had replied, 'Yes, a good peace.' 'How', countered Mason, 'can a peace be made if not treated, and how can it be treated unless consent be given and arrangements made?' To Pole Arras' answer was even more bellicose-'A good peace', he said, 'could only be made by a good war.' Pole replied, speaking in a language that was strange to Granvelle, and to many statesmen since, that war was never good.

But though the Cardinal might condemn all war, and the Queen declare to de Noailles that peace was her desire, and that 'as for the friendships between my brother (of France) and me, I sing and I always will sing the same ditty, and I will show, not by words but by deeds that I love truth',[2] nothing could be done while neither of the combatants would make the first move. In January 1555, however, during the usual winter lull, Pole, having heard of hopeful signs in France, approached the Emperor again, and this time with more success. In March it was announced that Charles would send Commissioners to meet those of the King of France. But the Emperor, procrastinating as usual, eked out delays with every excuse he could devise. As usual he laid all the blame upon his health, but others suspected he was waiting till the Queen's delivery put Philip in an unassailable position in England.

So it was not till May 20th that these Commissioners were gathered together, the French at Ardres, the Imperialists at Gravelines, the English at

Calais. Wooden huts had been provided and set up by the English-one for
each body of commissioners, and one for the meeting-place. It had been decided to open the session after dinner on Ascension Day, in order to begin so
good a work in a propitious hour. The time was kept, but from the start the
prospect of a fruitful issue was small. 'Peace! either truce or peace', said
Henri II when questioned. 'My ministers will not depart from what is reasonable', but at the word 'peace' he made a certain movement with his body and
eyes that indicated he had little hope.[3] And it was right. From the beginning,
the Spaniards in their sombre mourning clothes (the Emperor's mother had
recently died) and the Frenchmen in all the colours of the spring, had been
spoiling for a quarrel. Pole on the first day had made them embrace each
other, and then, to sweeten discourse, the English had brought in 'a handsome
collation', but such well-intentioned devices could not reconcile jarring
interests. On June 7th the meeting broke up, having achieved nothing.

The conference had done England perhaps more harm than good, for it
had convinced the French that the Queen was no impartial mediator. De
Noailles, whose temper was easily lost, flew out at one audience, declaring
to the Queen that she never heard but one side-the Imperial. His master, he
said, had offered strict reciprocity-'If the Emperor will give up, the lord
King will give up; ... if he will keep, will keep, or if he promises for the
future, will on his side also promise.'[4]

Mary too was ready to lose her temper over the question. When the de
Noailles brothers suggested a new conference she told them they must bear
well in mind that in the end she would not fail to show her affection and
obligation to Philip, 'giving it almost openly to be understood that she would
cease to be neutral'.[5] But she still, it was believed, wanted peace, and Henri
still gave out that he would rather have her mediation than that of any other.
She was indeed in this, as in so many other matters, swayed by sudden but
short gusts of temper. When in October Pole spoke to her of peace she told
him 'very sharply' that it was not to be spoken or thought of, but soon she
changed her mind and bade him to continue the already revived negotiation.[6]

But at the beginning of the next year (1556) much to the disgust of both
the Queen and the Cardinal, the two irreconcilables came together, without
any mediator, and patched up a truce, the Truce, it was called, of Vaucelles.
It was a sad rebuff for the would-be peace-makers, and recriminations in
England went the complete round. Pole's hard-working emissary, the Abbot
of San Saluto, blamed the Legate for negligence and timidity; Pole blamed
the Queen for not allowing him to speak openly; the Queen blamed her
Council, and in particular Arundel and Paget, for exaggerating the exhaustion
of France, thus leading her to believe that an appeal for mediation must be
made to her. Though Philip celebrated the proclamation of the truce with a
joust, in which he and Ruy Gomez maintained 'that the ladies of Brussels
were prettier than those of Mechlin', the Queen could feel little but chagrin
at the affront to her well-meant efforts.

There was worse to come. No one, least of all the parties to the truce, expected it to last. There were delays and evasions in the declaration of it, accusation and counter-accusation about the non-observance of it; it was impossible to hope that it would be the prelude to a final peace. Both France and Philip must therefore prepare for war, and both, in doing this, would concentrate their attention upon England; Philip straining every nerve to drag the Kingdom after him into the war, Henri using any means so to undermine Mary's throne that her intervention should be either impossible, or at the least negligible. There was not a doubt in Henri's mind, apparently, that, in the long run, Philip's influence would prevail, and that he would reap the reward for the English marriage.

He may have been right; by this time he probably was, but it was largely due to his own actions, and those of his ambassador in London, that his prognostications were so completely fulfilled. In justice to Mary it must be remembered that the attitude of France towards her had been consistently inimical. From the beginning of her reign, and before, Henri had feared the worst. After her marriage he gave Mary up as a soul lost to Spain. Intermittently, and when it suited his book, he might make an effort to appear friendly; for the most part he did not make the effort, but, openly received Mary's escaped rebels, and covertly egging on likely conspirators, he did his utmost to weaken her hold upon England, and make her alliance a worthless gain to Philip.

In this he had Antoine de Noailles' eager service. The work was to the ambassador a labour of love, for his hatred of the present rulers of England amounted to a passion. His personal relations with the Queen varied between concealed and open hostility; Gardiner he had disliked even more; Philip was, in the nature of things, anathema. Through all his dispatches runs the same train of personal bitterness. 'I shall never be easy till I have my revenge',[7] he wrote to the Constable, after the seizure of his letters during Wyatt's rebellion. He was true to his word, and it is permissible to guess that, with another ambassador in England, French and English relations might have been easier.

Throughout Mary's reign France had been, as we have seen, the refuge for all the English gentlemen who wished to hibernate in the south during the winter of their discontent, just as Geneva, Strasburg, or Basle was the bourne of religious refugees. Although the young men were not of any immediate use to the King of France, once Wyatt's rebellion had failed, yet it was as de Noailles urged, 'very necessary to keep them for that enterprise since there are few left apt to carry it out'. So Henri would grant pensions to a few, and give audience to one or other in strict privacy and at midnight, and blandly evade the repeated and emphatic appeals of the English ambassador or Queen Mary herself, to hand the men over or expel them from France. Sometimes in answer to their appeals the King would protest that it was the very warmth of his friendship for the Queen that made any English gentleman welcome in France. Sometimes he would wear a mask of innocent ignorance. When Wotton first tackled him on the subject of that rumour about Carew, namely that 'a great milord, for so they call him here', had 'come hither to require succour and aid'.... 'I have not seen him,' quoth the King, 'nor know him not. Marry I remember I have heard speak in times past of one of the name, that was Master of the Horse in England.' 'Yes, Sire,' answered Wotton patiently, 'there was one such indeed, but this is not he.'[8]

But though Henri might keep the refugees in France until there was a chance of employing them against England, he would be lavish to them only in promises. As time went on the members of that unruly gang found their leisure very heavy on their hands, and their purses very light in their pockets. They had little to do but hang about the narrow streets of Norman towns so like, with their plaster and carved wooden beams, to the town at home, just as the Norman orchards and little valleys and chalk downlands of the coast were like to the English countryside. They were cut off from the duties and pastimes of their own homes, they lacked money for drinking or gaming. No wonder tempers were frayed, and there were fights and quarrels among them, while that 'tragi-comedy' as old Wotton called it, was played out, and foolish youngsters learnt wisdom in a hard school. Some learnt not wisdom but treachery, and, like Sir William Pickering, who had already been employed in a like capacity in Edward's reign, offered to spy on the others. Wotton believed that many would, if they had hope of pardon, 'return home with their hearts', and de Noailles agreed with him, prophesying that they would come back 'one after the other; for I have never known an Englishman who wanted to die out of his country'.[9]

In the late summer of 1554 Sir Peter Carew deserted to Italy, where he may have met Sir John Cheke, who was not enjoying his stay there. Cheke disliked Italy, for there, said he, it was—'Courtesans in honour, haunting of evil houses noble, breaking of marriage a sport, murder in a gentleman magnanimity, robbery finesse if clean conveyed'. Italians, he declared, were 'in speech cautious, in deed scarce, more liking in asking than in giving'. His comfort in this uncomfortable sojourn he carried in himself—the voracious appetite for knowledge that he shared with so many men of his day. The long idle hours of his exile in Padua he intended to spend in learning Italian, and then 'philosophically to course over civil law!'[10]

Carew on the other hand went, as man of the world rather than scholar, to Venice, much to the alarm of poor Peter Vannes, the Queen's ambassador there. Vannes, a man of unusually timid and anxious disposition, was at a loss what to do and evidently feared the worst. That, the Venetian ambassador in Brussels told Sir John Mason, was a mistake. Venice, of all towns in Europe was the best place for Carew, for in 'that noble city he may learn obedience and quiet'. So cultivated Venetians, with serene pride and some homesickness, were wont to recommend Venice as a civilizing, sedative dose for young, half-barbarous northerners.

Peter Carew's exile was to last little over two years. In the spring of 1556, Lady Carew, who had worked for him early and late with the Council, using what they acknowledged was the importunity of 'a good and loving wife', obtained his pardon from Philip in the Netherlands. Hearing this, he and

Cheke set out to visit Paget who was in Antwerp, but on the way between Mechlin and Antwerp, as if to provide a suitably bizarre conclusion for this last of Carew's adventures, the two were ambushed, seized, taken to Ghent, and then brought blindfold to the coast and put into a fishing boat; and so, in momentary fear of death by drowning, stabbing, or shooting, taken out to sea. Only when the ringing of a bell came to them through the darkness did they begin to hope, for Carew recognized the note as that of the Tower bell.[11] This was the end of his wanderings, for soon afterwards he was set free, on payment of a fine, and, with kind words from the Queen, went off to live the life of a country gentleman, till a sovereign more to his wilful taste sat upon the throne.

Just at the time that Carew came home, a fresh batch of malcontents was crossing the Channel outward bound. Another plot was toward, and it was to the suspicions engendered by this that Carew and Cheke probably owed their last adventure.

In the middle of March 1556, a blazing comet stood in the sky. Night after night it shone, and the Londoners, peering up at it from their narrow roads between the steep roofs, watched it with misgiving. To increase their fears, a gang of a dozen ruffians went about the city, publishing everywhere that the Day of Judgment was at hand. The Venetian ambassador, writing home, gave news of the comet, the activities of the gang, and of their arrest in the same letter. The fellows, he said, had intended to start fires in various parts of the city, and in the confusion and panic which would follow, to loot what they might.

Such was his first news. A week later he reported that the business was greater and more dangerous than any attack upon the property of Londoners. It was a new plot against the Government. By March 28th the gates of the Tower shut upon a company of gentlemen, mostly young, and some of good family—John Throgmorton, Henry Peckham, John Daniel, William Rossey, John Dethick, and a few more. Throgmorton was one of the two chiefs of the conspiracy. The other, the same Henry Dudley who, at the bidding of Northumberland, had tried to buy French support at the price of Calais, was in France, with other of the conspirators.[12]

Fear of Philip's coronation supplied the motive for this new plot, as the dread of the Spanish bridegroom had been the breeding-ground of Wyatt's treason. It was a fear that moved gentle and simple alike. Parliament had been driven almost to panic by it. In streets and lanes the common people were talking of it with no less dread. So a certain William Crowe, a bricklayer, arrested and examined when the Council was casting its net for traitors great or small, confessed to his examiners. He was, he said, returning one night across Finsbury Fields from making the tunnel to a privy, when he met a man with a crab-tree staff who gave him a drink out of a little bottle of muscatel or malmsey. After that 'this examinate said that the Earl of Pembroke should go fetch the crown from the Earl of Shrewsbury to crown the king withal . . . but this examinate and 500 more would spend their lives in keeping the crown in Englishmen's hands, and that strangers should never have it. Item, this examinate saith that he . . . told the said man that if there were a painter that would make a flag, there would be 500, yea and 500 more that would die in this quarrel that no stranger should have the crown.'[13]

But if this fear of a crowned alien was the main cause of the new conspiracy, there was also, as in Wyatt's, a strong, though again not a predominantly Protestant flavour among the conspirators. When these were prisoners together in the Tower two of them enlivened the tedium of the hours by acting a ribald play against the Mass. Another, John Daniel, in one of his many and voluminous confessions, informed the Council that one of his companions, Edward Horsey by name, would recite to him a rhythm jingle beginning:

'Goodman priest now beware your pallate . . . and brought out a rhyme thereof of fire and faggot, and helmet and sallet, which I cannot', wrote Daniel virtuously, 'so perfectly say as he said it'.[14] It was not surprising that those who were examining the prisoners thought it worth while to ask one of them whether he and the others had talked of a rebellion 'whereby God's word might prosper and be set up again, to banish Spaniards and popery'.[15]

But while the causes that led both Wyatt and Dudley into treason were much the same, the conspiracies were as different as the men engaged were different. Wyatt's rebellion had been the work of a company of landed gentlemen leading their tenants. Wyatt had risen and had called up the Kentish men counting upon the countenance and support of France, if he succeeded, but relying more upon the dogged, obedient courage of the commons. The plot was certainly treason, but the rebels used such temperate behaviour and showed such gallantry, that the rebellion takes its place among the tragic and honourable risings of English history, along with Kett's and the Peasants' Revolt.

In 1556 the conspirators, though mostly gentlemen, were of a different type. It has been suggested that the plot was the work of those who had formed the determined and embittered opposition to the government in the late Parliament.[16] But as well as these there were among the conspirators soldiers cashiered or out of employ, or royal officers unpaid or discharged, and it is impossible not to suspect that an underlying motive for treason was to be found, in many cases, in their hopes of the profits that rebellion might bring. If so it was unfortunate for Mary that her own poverty should raise up enemies against her.

Of John Throgmorton, one of the two heads of a conspiracy, little is known. He was a man about twenty-eight years of age, probably a relation, but not a brother, of that Nicholas Throgmorton who had claimed to be the man who sent Mary word of Edward's death. He had been brought up in the household of Lord Thomas Howard; he had travelled in Europe.[17] That is all we know of him, that, and the fact he was a brave man, the only brave man among a pack of cravens.

Henry Dudley the other leader, and, unlike Throgmorton, a survivor of the plot, was a distant cousin of that great Lucifer, the late Duke of Northumberland, and had been Captain of the Guard at Guisnes in King Edward's reign; Guisnes and Calais were then a gathering-place for Protestants; they remained so in Mary's reign, but many of the Protestants by then had become traitors. Dudley had been given command of a ship by the Queen, and had been removed from this on suspicion, during or just after Wyatt's rebellion.[18] Mary had once paid his debts, but he was, for all that, a discontented, disappointed man, who went about grumbling that 'there was no account made of him than was of those that knew nothing what service meant'.[19]

Another man of importance among the conspirators was that Sir Anthony Kingston who had spent some time in the Tower for his part in procuring the rejection of the bill which would have recalled, on pain of confiscation, all Englishmen from abroad. Richard Uvedale was a Hampshire gentleman in command of the castle of Yarmouth in the Isle of Wight. John Dethick had been in charge of Wisbech castle; one of the two Ashtons who had escaped abroad must have been an ex-soldier, for he was said to be 'skilled in service'; John Daniel was another; so was Fernando Lygons, for after the execution of most of his companions he turns up, having probably received the reward of an informer, in command of a troop on the Scots Border.

Others of the conspirators were young Henry Peckham, brother of Sir Edmund Peckham, a respected official of the Mint; Edmund Rossey, Keeper of the Star Chamber; 'Mr. Heneage' of the Queen's Chapel Royal. Besides these there were lesser men, like Bedell, and worse men, like Hinnes, the latter a thorough bad lot who knew how to make skeleton keys, and who, a year before had been hired, so one of his fellows said, with a dozen or so other ruffians to attempt to kill the King and Queen at a Cane Game.[20]

These men found a meeting-place much to their taste in the house of one Arundel, also an old soldier, a man who had served abroad in French pay, and who, returning two years before to England, had brought with him 'good and profitable proposals' from Henri II himself to his 'especial friends' there;[21] what those proposals, and what those friends we can well imagine. It is very possible that this Arundel kept the tavern called by his name; if so it must have been a handy meeting-place for those who wished to discuss Henri II's proposals, and a snug nest for the hatching of a plot.

Here then was devised the second dangerous conspiracy of Mary's reign. That there were many parts to the plot is certain; exactly in what they consisted is more difficult to determine, since they rest upon the testimony of men terrified by the fear of torture and death, and frantically informing against each other. Nor can these testimonies be tried by the touchstone of fact, since the plans of the conspirators were never put into practice. So far as it is possible to judge, however, from such evidence, the Exchequer was to be robbed, the Tower seized, the Queen killed; there was to be a rising in the west; the English gentlemen harbouring in France were to land in the Wight, led, if he could be persuaded to it, by the exiled Earl of Devon; finally he and Elizabeth were to be married and crowned.

Renard heard that Henri II had not only listened to a suggestion that Mary should be poisoned, but had actually 'relished the scheme'.[22] Throgmorton, in his trial, was accused of having said, when he and Dethick had taken oath on the Bible not to reveal the plot–'If any of us be accused by any man, let us revile him, and stand earnestly against him. But I trust it shall never come out, for I had rather my dagger were in her heart (thereby meaning the Queen) and all her Council.'[23] Those were desperate words, but though they may have prejudiced the prisoner's judges against him, they do not prove a plan to kill Mary. So, if there were such a plan, and it is far from unlikely, seeing what reckless and ruffianly fellows were engaged, nothing more is known of its details beyond that one brief assertion of Renard's, that poison was to be the means, and a wild brag of John Dethick's, that 'he would not doubt with 300 men to take the Queen out of any house she had'.[24] But here again a capture does not necessarily include murder.

The man responsible for the betrayal of the Tower to the conspirators was a certain 'Mr. Chamberlain', an 'assured friend of Henry Dudley; an honest man. Look, what he hath promised, he will perform it', so Dudley told one of his fellow plotters.[25] He was perhaps that very groom porter of the Tower who had embraced Alexander Brett, the London train-band Captain, on his way to execution, and received from him a last message for Sir Thomas Wyatt.

The rising in the west was to be led by Sir Anthony Kingston. The Queen and her Council had hoped that his imprisonment would be a lesson to him, but he had not taken it to heart. No sooner was he free than he went off to the house of Christopher Ashton, and there, in a long private talk, he boasted –'They have put me in the Tower for their pleasure, but so shall they never do more.'[26] Kingston was probably that gentleman darkly alluded to by the conspirators as being 'able to bring a great part of Wales at his tail', whose men, 'with stakes sharpened at both ends, and pikes', would be able to stand against horsemen, 'his ordnance being such of the longest of the French King had, and such pieces that would fetch further than any in this realm, that should be drawn with twenty men and more, so shadowed with men that their enemies should not know where the ordnance were'.[27] Kingston's own account of his dealings with the conspirators can hardly be believed. He did indeed acknowledge that at Christmastide last he had entertained at his house both Dudley and Ashton. Ashton had broken a coin with his teeth, and had given one half of it to Kingston, bidding him to keep it, and when he should receive the other at the hand of a servant, to credit the man's message.[28] But when it came to treasonable designs, Kingston, according to his own account, was deaf as an adder to all their charming, and quite incredibly discreet for such a man. One morning as he and Dudley were walking together in the garden, Dudley asked his host, 'How he liked the world?' To whom he answered, 'Well.' And then Dudley said, 'so did not he, and said he would go abroad'. Sir Anthony, not liking the talk, so he said, broke it off and went into breakfast.

But if Kingston were, as is practically certain, one of the leaders in the conspiracy, and if the plot was already taking shape in the winter of 1555, which is highly probable, his violent opposition to the Queen's bill for recalling the exiles from abroad is easy to understand. For the conspirators intended that all those young gentlemen overseas should indeed return, but in arms and with the help of France. So, on the Fleet bridge one day two men paused, as any acquaintance might, to pass the time of day, and the latest bit of news. But these were Hinnes and Bedell, two of the conspirators. 'God speed, Captain,' said Hinnes. 'What will ye say,' asked Bedell, 'and ye see our English gentlemen land in the west part?' 'Think ye so?' replied Hinnes. 'Such a thing I hear,' saith he, 'but as for my part I care not; I will be sure to serve my country truly.' 'And how?' 'In such sort that there shall no *stranger* come a-land.' Said this examinate (Hinnes), 'It is well said.' It was well said and neatly, for the innocent words had an implication not so harmless.[29]

For this invasion Bedell was busy preparing. He, so one of the conspirators told another, 'daily doth convey men out of Southampton'. He was collecting also 'harness, shirts of mail and other for a hundred men', besides 'so many shovels, spades and poles for ships as came to £6 or thereabouts'. With these on board, he invited Hinnes to go out fishing with him. Hinnes, however, so he told his questioners, considering such a cargo 'no fit tools to catch fish withal', refused.[30]

But for this part of the plan French help was necessary, and the conspirators had early set about obtaining it. Henry Dudley, knowing France, and having already been in touch with the French King on behalf of his great cousin Northumberland, was obviously the man for this. In the first talk concerning the conspiracy, which took place at Christopher Ashton's house at Fyfield, he and Dudley 'did devise how they might know what aid they might have at the French King's hands, so they did write what help they would have of him, or else not to meddle'. The answer, which came through the French ambassador, 'granted Dudley's full request', whereupon the conspirators might proceed.[31] Dudley accordingly set about sounding likely fellows for the desperate game. When John Daniel came to London in company with Lord Grey, a message reached him from Henry Dudley–'Would he go to him at Acton?' He did, and lodged in the same house. In the middle of the night, in came Dudley, put on Daniel's dressing-gown and slippers, and sitting down on his bed, proceeded to talk. 'Here', he said, 'is the French King's ambassador, who seeth what estate I live in, and how my living is gone and mine office taken from me'. The French King's ambassador, moved, so it seemed, by pity, had offered, if Dudley would go over to serve the French King, sufficient pay for himself and his men. In fine the question was, would Daniel go with him? Daniel was uncertain. He asked a week's grace, as he had the possibility of marriage with a widow and wished to inspect her. The lady proving less attractive than Dudley's offer, he later consented, and heard more of what was behind it.[32] If his frenzied confessions in the Tower were true he was never anything but unwilling. After one treasonable talk he slunk off alone into the garden, and there in an arbour knelt down to pray for enlightenment as to how to extricate himself. Sir John Harington, a very likely man to find in such company, came along and caught him. 'What man! You are well occupied on your knees so soon after dinner!' and so passed on, leaving Daniel overwhelmed with shame 'that any man should see me on my knees'.[33] John Daniel had either a copious imagination, or else a very retentive memory.

For some years a certain Frenchman named Berteville who had fled out of France for some crime had been living in London under the name of Fountain. It is possible that he was taking pay as a spy from the English Council; he was certainly in the employ of de Noailles, but the creature kept the last rags of his honour by avoiding the oath of allegiance to Queen Mary. By the end of January 1556 if no sooner, the conspirators were in touch with this man, and soon after this matters began to move. By means of Henry Peckham they got hold of a copy of the will of Henry VIII with the intention of proving thereby that 'the Queen usurpeth the crown and hath broken her father's will by marriage with an alien'.[34]

The next business to be carried through took Dudley and Throgmorton down into Hampshire. For Dudley thought it necessary to go over to France and see the French King in person, and preparations must be made for the attack upon the Isle of Wight. So on February 2nd these two gentlemen arrived at Chilling, the house of Richard Uvedale, Captain of the Castle at Yarmouth in the Isle of Wight. The master was that day away from home, having gone 'on hunting with Sir Richard Cotton', but 'a young ploughboy called Valentine' was sent off to tell him that guests had come, and he returned. They were fatal guests for him, and it would have been well for him had he not received them.

What they told him at first seemed harmless enough. Throgmorton said that Dudley wished to get out of England for debt—Uvedale was ready to help, and sent off to Yarmouth to fetch a boat that would put him across. But there was more. The next thing Uvedale heard was that Dudley was to go to the French King, to gather a band of men, mostly from among the English in France, and, returning, land at Portsmouth and drive away the Spaniards. 'And thou wilt do like a good fellow and help me,' said Dudley, 'and see what thou canst do there . . . provide so that the ordnance there may be pegged up against I come, and by God's blood I will drive out this Spaniard or I will die for it.'[35] So they made known to Uvedale the heart of the mad scheme.

The dangerous guests stayed some days at Chilling, waiting both for the boat Uvedale promised and for Dudley's gear to arrive. Their host noticed they were busy over letters, many of these in cypher; and, he himself, so he said, left them mostly to themselves and went off hunting; sometimes they came with him, but even then, as they rode home, or waited at the coverts, their talk was in French, and of traitorous matters. One day when the Captain of Yarmouth came back from a good day's sport, pleased with the kill, he found that Dudley's luggage had arrived–fine new clothes less fit for an escaping debtor than for a man going to Court. There was a cloak of black velvet furred with wolverines, a pair of velvet hosen and a velvet hat. There was also a buff jerkin.[36] On February 8th Dudley crossed over to France in the ship of a certain Master John Peers.

The visit of Dudley's to France, and presumably to the French Court, did not last long. He must have come back shortly after, for the preparations of the conspirators were by no means completed and one important matter must be seen to. This plot needed, as Wyatt's had not, a good supply of money, for the force that was to attack from France was both needy and greedy. Just at this time there lay at the Exchequer, in locked chests, £50,000, the proceeds of the Queen's hard-won subsidy. The plan was to steal one chest or more; to hide the spoil 'in some secret place, as under the water by the Bridge, or on the further side, amongst the sedges' of the Southwark shore, or, as John Throgmorton advised, in Master Rossey's own garden which lay upon the river side. For being there with Rossey one day, Throgmorton asked whose were the windows that looked out on it, and 'hearing them to be Rossey's own, said, "All the world could not devise a meeter place for our barge to receive the money. But in anywise," said he, "make up the broken pales at the end of your garden next the bridge." ' At that same meeting Rossey offered to put the gold on board the barge. 'That is well. Let that be your part,' said Throgmorton, and then, being a man careful of detail, 'And in any wise,' said he, 'remember to speak for rushes to cover the boards that we must go on.'[37]

But that money, which some said was to be taken to the Isle of Wight, others over the Channel to France, was not to be the only means of paying the soldiers who were to pull down the Crown. The conspirators aimed at no less a thing than setting up a Mint of their own. It was for this further purpose that John Dethick went to William Hinnes, and asked him if, having his skill in alchemy, he could turn 'ealdergylders' into gold. That, Hinnes objected, was felony and treason. No, Dethick answered him, for it is not an English coin. 'Though it be neither treason nor felony,' said Hinnes, who was a complete and experienced rogue, 'we cannot coin so close but the hammers must be heard' which 'may soon bring us both shame and rebuke.' 'How say ye,' answered Dethick, 'if there shall be a place appointed on the other side of the sea, whereas ye may knock and do what ye list at your pleasure?' 'Where call ye that place?' inquired Hinnes. 'There is a castle hard adjoining the sea in which ye work.' 'Whose is it?' Hinnes insisted. 'Captain Tybald's.' 'Will he be so constant?' 'Yes,' answered Dethick, 'and shall be a doer therein himself.'

Such was all apparently that Hinnes should have been told, but he, as Dethick complained, had a 'curst brain', and guessed so much that he had to be told all, though Dethick tried to make things safe by a threat of what would happen to Hinnes if he informed. 'Think you to escape?' he cried.

'No, no! There be who ye know not that shall with a dag or dagger soon dispatch you out of the way.'[38]

On March 10th Dudley was again at Chilling, and again Uvedale provided him with a boat for France. When he came again it would be in arms, with the English exiles at his back. Uvedale had promised that there should be no resistance in the Isle of Wight. So Dudley crossed over to make the final preparation for the intended invasion.

The plans of the conspirators were almost complete. A few days before Dudley's departure Throgmorton, Dethick and Bedell were let into the Receipt of the Exchequer by Rossey who was Keeper of the Star Chamber. There, doubtless working in haste, and quietly, they weighted one of the chests in which lay the Queen's last subsidy, and in whispers debated how they would break the locks and carry the treasure to the river.

In three weeks they and their fellows were in the Tower and the conspiracy was forestalled.

From that time till early July, when the last executions took place, they endured the horrors of imprisonment, examination and trial. The record of those examinations, preserved among the State Papers, makes ugly and painful reading, with only the courage of John Throgmorton to ennoble a sordid business.

He, while John Daniel and Rossey made jests upon the Mass, looked beyond the modern, to the austerities of the ancient world, reciting to his fellows a story of the Romans and 'commending much an old man that was taken by the *Athenenses* [*sic*] whom the Romans would have redeemed with a great number of young men . . . but this old man would in no wise agree thereto, but received his death at the *Athenenses*' hands very patiently, considering his old years, and also what profit these young men should be to the Romans'. At the ending of this tale Throgmorton, 'lamented much that these Romans were not Christened men, commending much the zeal that this Roman had to his country.'[39] His first thought when he came into the Tower had been of loyalty, and of the oath that he and Dethick had sworn to each other. Dethick was in a room below him, and he managed to prise up a board, and speak to him, giving him a warning, and a reminder of what he must face, 'For look,' he said, 'how many thou doest accuse, so many dost thou wilfully murder,' and he pressed Dethick to promise to stand firm even in the face of torture. Dethick at last consented, and Throgmorton drank his thin Tower porridge to him, in token of the bond.[40]

Yet it was Throgmorton alone who endured the rack without betrayal of his friends, though 'I do assure you it is a terrible pain', he told his fellow prisoners. Others of them might be allowed to sham agony, and be let off with little hurt, but not so Throgmorton. Nor had he even assurance that, once condemned, he should not suffer torture again. He tried to persuade his companions that this at least he need not fear, but they had no comfort for him; the Lords of the Council, they said, might do what they would.

Whatever was done, his spirit was unbroken. On April 23rd Dean Feckenham of St. Paul's came to tell him that he must prepare for death, but afterwards insinuated a hope that he might have his life, if he would give his friends cause to ask for it; that is if he would betray the plot. When the prisoner replied that he would die rather than reveal anything, the Dean left him, refusing absolution and sacrament as to an impenitent soul.[41] The condemned traitor let the priests go, his notions of right, though warped, being truer to line than those of Feckenham. He turned for heartening to his fellows in the Tower. 'My masters I pray you to pray for me,' he said, 'for I shall not long be with you, for I cannot live without I should be the death of a number of gentlemen.'[42]

While Throgmorton held his tongue and faced death, the rest of the conspirators implored pardon and produced ever fresh and fuller confessions. 'Pity me, pity me, for God's sake,' Daniel scrawled, in a place where he 'could not well see his hands', and where he lay wretchedly among newts and spiders.[43] Others of the crew were worse employed, listening to the talk of their fellows and reporting it to the Lords of the Council. One, by the handwriting it may have been Lygons, set apart in a cell by himself, whiled away the interminable hours of the prisoner's day by writing a list of remembrances –questions that the Lords of the Council should put to this one or that of his late associates–awkward questions which might extract a useful confession. Then, since time went so slow, he added a list of remembrances for himself– 'Item–to speak for a table to write upon. Item to declare my own danger in this case that it be not otherwise used.' On the back of the sheet he wrote one more remembrance that was not needed, for surely the thing would not out of his head; yet the poor creature must needs write it down–'Item–I hear that the servants say that the world did mislike me for that I should accuse Throgmorton, for if I had held mine own he had not gone to the rack.'[44]

The first executions took place on April 28th, Throgmorton and Uvedale leading the way. They were not over till the beginning of July, and between those dates the Council, thoroughly scared, laid hands on men of quality and common folk alike. Five young knights, among them William Courtenay, cousin of the Earl of Devon, were arrested, on account, so it was thought, of their wild talk at Throgmorton's execution.[45] Kingston himself was taken in his bed, and sent towards London under arrest, but had the good fortune to die on the way. The Earl of Bath went down to keep order in the west, suspect now for Kingston's sake; the eastern counties were also under suspicion for their known Protestant bent. The Admiral was sent to Portsmouth; inquiries were set on foot in the Isle of Wight; a ship put out to cruise off the west of France and give news of anything stirring there.

Everywhere there seemed to be danger. The Queen, so men were saying, wore armour, dared but sleep three hours or so at night, and was guarded by harnessed men.[46] It was certainly true that her guard was doubled, and that she appeared not at all in public. That, and the increasingly sombre tone at Court gave Clinton, one of whose servants had been executed after the plot, cause for a good grumble, when he came back from a mission in France.

Drawing the French ambassador aside to a window, he remarked how different was the French from the English Court, adding as de Noailles reported, that the English 'could neither see their King nor their Queen . . . and that he would rather be a poor gentleman in your kingdom than an admiral where he is'.[47]

Whether or not Mary wore armour, it is likely that her nights were sleepless for her state was wretched indeed. The Dudley and Throgmorton plot was to her as the writing on the Babylonian palace wall. It had revealed the power of discontent at home, the presence of traitors among her household and officers; the inextinguishable enmity of France. The exiled Courtenay expressed what many must have been thinking of this revelation of the state of England, in a letter written to his good friend Mason. 'To tell you the truth,' he said, 'those that profess to be most wise and understand the world best, yea and those not of the inferior sort, seemeth to judge that our country is far out of frame. Saying that if so many as hath been of late and now be punished, be punished without fault, then wanteth justice, and on the other side, if they be offenders, then say they that the realm is ill governed where so many are ill contented.'[48] It was shrewdly argued, and not unhappily put.

But the conspiracy, besides disclosing the weakness of Mary's position, necessarily reminded the Queen and her Council of those same two dangerous persons who had been, throughout her reign, the focal points of all discontent. At Hatfield, living in a household predominantly Protestant, and therefore disaffected, practising her Italian with a man gravely suspected of the authorship of a treasonable pamphlet, waited Elizabeth. She, so young men were telling one another, was 'a jolly liberal dame, and nothing like so unthankful as her sister, and she taketh this liberality of her mother, who was one of the most bountiful women in all her time and since.'[49] One of the conspirators was reported to have said that the object of Kingston and his friends was 'to send the Queen's Highness over to the King, and to make the Lady Elizabeth queen, and to marry the Earl of Devonshire to the said Lady Elizabeth'. Elizabeth was young, she was healthy; married to an Englishman she would bear English sons. The King wished to marry her abroad; the Queen wished Parliament to bastardize her; but more and more, so the astute Venetian saw, men's eyes were turning to her[50] and wise Councillors realized that to move against her either way would be dangerous. But, since she was a woman, and as a woman, unmeet to rule men, she must be married. So once again there was a name on the tip of many tongues, the name of the Earl of Devon.

In May several of Elizabeth's servants were examined. Sir John Saint Loe and Mistress Ashley utterly denied knowledge of the conspiracy. The Italian master had to give fuller answers. Asked when he came to London, and what he did there, he replied first that he 'could not remember it well', but afterwards produced an account of a day full of frivolous details and pleasant innocent meetings. For he had been to a milliner's shop, to a hosier's, to a bookbinders', 'to a friend of mine called Mrs. Watson' in March Lane, 'to look how she did'; he had spent the night in the house of Mistress Burnell.

He had gone next day to buy lute strings 'for my lady's grace my mistress' lute'. But never by day or night had he been to the French or Venetian ambassadors' houses. Even when all this was told he must add a postscript, remembering also that he must inform the Lords of the Council that he had bought black lace to edge a cloak, sarcenet in Cheap, points, 2 pairs of gloves, and 2 dozen buttons.[51]

The same apparent guilelessness that was in the man, was also in the mistress. Elizabeth wrote, protesting, in elegant scholastic periods, her innocence and loyalty. Boxes of seditious pamphlets might be unearthed at houses where she had lived, but no word of her own writing was there to condemn her. Even if the Council had intercepted a certain letter that had come in February from the Constable of France to de Noailles in London, they could not have been quite sure of her complicity. 'Above all,' wrote the great Montmorency, 'see that Madame Elizabeth makes no move of any sort or kind to undertake the thing you wrote of, for that would ruin all.'[52] The words have a sinister sound. Yet it may well be that de Noailles, like many an unfortunate ambassador that was to come after him, had over-estimated the complaisance of Elizabeth. At least she had left no tracks.

The Queen, however little she liked her half-sister, was not unkind. When Elizabeth's three servants had been arrested, she sent Sir Edward Hastings and Englefield with a reassuring message and a ring. The removal of Elizabeth to the house of the unwilling Sir Thomas Pope, and the reorganization of her household followed the inquiry; but that was all.[53]

The Earl of Devon, whose inherited royalty had dogged his steps with sorrow from his boyhood, was more certainly innocent of any complicity with the conspirators, and was also more deeply injured by the almost inevitable burden of suspicion which fell upon him. A year before, just after Easter, the young man had been dispatched to honourable exile on the Continent. The pretext was that he should travel for his improvement; no such ill fate for a young man, could he only have broken free from the webs of diplomacy, the fears, hopes, and suspicions that were spun about him wherever he moved. But that he could never do. Directly he landed at Antwerp he was told that he must, without pausing to admire that great mart of the world, proceed to Brussels to report himself to the Emperor, or it would be looked on as suspicious. Yet though he was unenterprising, there was something obstinate and contrary about the young man. He did not arrive in Brussels for another week.[54] Once there the other side of his character showed, for he would not move on to Milan or Naples to broaden his experience, although Gardiner's impatient remark that 'his being at Brussels was but very dull', was passed on to him by a friend, who added 'and I think no less'.[55]

But at Brussels Courtenay remained, lonely, and discontented. 'I would spend a hundred pounds,' he wrote to Abergavenny, 'to have your company here a month, for I lack such company. But sure I trust one day to see you in England again with your broad dagger on your back.'[56] Writing to another friend he spoke of Sir Thomas Tresham, 'wishing as you do, if my chance had been such as I had remained in England, that we might have been there this summer together practising with our crossbows among the deer.'[57] To his mother, old and dear friend as she was to the Queen, he was discreet. 'I like my being here well enough, saving that my purse waxeth too light.'[58]

But there was another cause, besides a young man's homesickness and a temporary shortness of funds that made him ill content in Brussels. From the first he had felt the Emperor's suspicion chill the air about him. By the end of the summer, he had more tangible grievances. His servants had several times been attacked in the streets; one day as he rode through Brussels there was a scuffle; some Spaniards had come to blows with his people. He reproved the peace-breakers, but it was no use. A crowd gathered, threatening and angry. Courtenay with his men had to fight their way back through the streets to his lodging. After that he sulked, like Achilles in his tent; when Granvelle sent him an invitation to dinner the answer was that he was out.[59]

If he felt himself unwelcome in Brussels, there were others only too willing to receive him. The Duke of Ferrara, close ally of France, was making 'the greatest and most particular offers' of hospitality to him. To what extent Courtenay accepted the invitation, the Emperor did not know, but he had his suspicions. When the young man applied for leave to return to England before travelling farther afield, it was refused in Brussels though it had been granted by the Queen at home.[60] Finally at the end of November Courtenay set off for Italy; and, perhaps because he despaired of peace within the radius of the Emperor's influence, perhaps pricked out of his sluggish yet uncertain ease by his own youth and the spirit of the age, he talked of going farther. 'After having seen and well acquainted myself with the state and princes of Christendom, and the manner of their courts,' he wrote to Lady Barkeley, he intended 'to depart further to the Great Turk's Court, at Constantinople, and peradventure beyond.'[61]

It was not to be so. No flash of adventure was to lighten his shadowed life. He was at Venice when news of the Dudley and Throgmorton plot reached him, and he soon heard that one of his own servants had been arrested. Again suspicion centred on him. The English refugees in France were talking of him saying 'that one should shortly come into France that should make them all glad' and 'that the Vidame had sent unto my Lord Courtenay, that if it should please him to come into France he would provide for him 30,000 crowns, and any other thing that he had before should be at his command-ment'. But if they reported Courtenay's answer correctly, the young man showed caution, and also a flash of that pride that was his inheritance from a line of kings; for 'my lord Courtenay sent the Vidame word again that he thanked him much ... but my Lord Courtenay said that it was not for him to enter any King's realm upon any subject's promise'.[62] Yet, though he did not go into France, and though Throgmorton in his confessions might declare that the Earl of Devon was 'not yet privy to the matter', there was the fact that the conspirators looked to him; and there were rumours that Henry Killigrew had gone into Italy to fetch him, or that he was afraid for his life to return to England; or that Ferrara was trying to persuade him to serve France against England.[63] Mason adjured him to let people at home know where he was, since 'this corrupt world breedeth strange rumours daily', and only when the executions had ceased and what Mason called the 'hurly burly' settled down did the authorities at home declare that both Elizabeth and the young Earl had 'too much wisdom truth and respect to duty and honesty . . . to be party to any such matters'.[64]

Such matters did not much longer concern Lord Courtenay. For a couple of months more, he remained in Venice, living very much retired, so as to avoid the almost unavoidable suspicions that clung to him like burrs. But at the beginning of September, as he flew his hawk from an exposed and shelterless island six miles from Venice, a tempest of wind and rain caught him; drenched to the skin, he was forced to return, not in the gondola in which he had gone out, but in a slower, more seaworthy boat, and once home, with a young man's carelessness, would change none of his clothes. About a fortnight later, already very sick, travelling 'by certain wagons called *coches*, very shaking and uneasy to my judgement', as Peter Vannes wrote, he came to Padua, arriving on a Saturday night. Once there he grew worse; two of the best physicians of the town visited him, but except for them, and good Peter Vannes, he lay alone, refusing to be visited by his friends. On September 17th, unable to receive the sacrament for his swollen tongue and clenched teeth, he died. [65]

Even after death suspicion followed him. A sealed casket containing his letters was abstracted from his effects by the order of the Venetian Signory. Later, when Vannes demanded it, it was sent secretly in a wrapper, from Padua to Venice. There a carpenter, sworn to silence, was bidden to open the casket, but in such a way that it should seem untouched. From the letters inside, certain papers, marked by the Council of Ten with a + were kept out; the rest, wrapped again in a linen cover, were laid once more in the casket, resealed, and handed over to Vannes.[66] What those marked papers were, which the Signory would not willingly let the Queen of England read, the Venetians alone knew; the Venetians, and perhaps the King of France.

Chapter XX

OURTENAY's death relieved the Queen of one of her many anxieties. She was heard to say, so it was reported, that God had shown his justice. The French muttered 'that there was more in it of human help than divine',[1] but probably they were as unjust to her as she to Courtenay. On the one hand everything goes to show that the young man had resisted all invitations both of the French King and of the English exiles; on the other, though an Albanian divulged a highly coloured tale of how Ruy Gomez had paid him to shoot Courtenay at a window,[2] Courtenay did not die that way, and the only ground for the accusation against Mary seems to have been the undeniable fact that Courtenay's death was a relief to her.

But though the fear of what Courtenay might intend, or what others might intend for him, need trouble her no longer, and though in the autumn the Queen could bring herself, in spite of her suspicions, to recall Elizabeth to court, there was little else to cheer her. A divided and insubordinate Council: an empty exchequer and a very grudging response to forced loans: a discontented people: cruel and scurrilous libels, pictures of herself 'almost naked, wrinkled and uncomely, suckling Spaniards at her breast, and round about, the legend–'Maria Ruina Angliae,'–[3] such were her troubles at home.

For fear of assassination she lived now in a seclusion strange for royalty; all the guard had been called up, and the palace was full of armed men, but in the Queen's chamber there were only five women trusted enough to be with the Queen at night. And those nights were long; for it was said that Mary slept only for three or four hours, 'the rest of the time she spends in tears, regrets, and writing of letters to bring back her husband, and in rages against her subjects, for she is utterly confounded by the faithlessness of those whom she most trusted, seeing that the greater part of these miserable creatures [the conspirators] are kith and kin or favoured servants of the greatest men of the kingdom, even of Lords of the Council. . . . She says in private that she now trusts none but Lord Montague and her Grand Esquire, two young men who are not of the sort to rescue her from the dangers into which she has fallen.'[4]

That private sorrow, Philip's absence, which the French ambassador put first among Mary's griefs, was perhaps the worst that she had to bear, for not only did she suffer the pain of separation, but her pride must have smarted at his manifest indifference, and she had learnt by now what it was to be jealous, and to know that she had cause. Yet, though the Queen might rage against her husband in private, might try miserably to snatch at her abandoned dignity and declare that Philip might come if he chose but she would never seek him as she had done, his absence was fretting her into an illness. She looked ten years older, said a woman, de Noailles' wife.[5] The sharp eyes of the Venetian ambassador noted that her face was thinner, and he listened to, and recorded for the information of the Signory, her confession that her need for Philip's presence was wearing her away, and that for the last few nights she had hardly slept.[6] Unhappy as she was, it is to be hoped that she did not know of the persistent and widespread rumour which prophesied that before long Philip would be asking the Pope to dissolve his marriage.[7]

Without this, her public cares were almost unbearably heavy. One of the most long standing, and most sordid of these, was the poverty of the Crown. When she succeeded to the throne Mary succeeded also to an empty exchequer and a plenitude of debts. The inadequacy of the royal revenue, which must be made to cover all expenses, both private and public, to pay for the Queen's shoes, ships, and sealing-wax, the wages of her soldiers, and her losses at cards –had been recognized by sympathetic observers as long ago as the days of the last Lancastrian King. Henry VII, by extreme parsimony and a policy of peace, had filled the Exchequer again. Henry VIII, with superb abandon, had flung the money about in handfuls, but before the bottom of the chest was reached, he had discovered a new source of wealth. Abbey rents, abbey gold and silver plate, abbey jewels, had poured in for some years–but for longer than that they had poured out again into the capacious pockets of an insatiably greedy new nobility, until at the end of Edward VI's reign the Crown had parted with almost all of its gains.

What was left of these spoils, Mary had obstinately and against opposition given back, putting it into the hands of Cardinal Pole, for application to the many necessities of the Church. There remained to her, then, apart from the revenue of the royal demesne and the proceeds of justice, three chief means of acquiring money, as distinct from loans which must be repaid at least in theory; that is to say, confiscation of traitors' lands, debasement of the coinage, and Parliamentary grants.

The first was used with great moderation throughout the reign–it was indeed difficult for the Queen to keep, for any long time, a rebel's lands, since that rebel was sure to have about the Court, or even in the Council, a relative who would plead for their restoration, and Mary was easily persuaded to a personal kindness. So Wyatt's widow and son got manors back a year after the rebellion, and Peter Carew's wife was allowed to send money out to him in Italy even before his pardon. That very bill which should have recalled the dangerous crowd of English exiles, on a threat of confiscation of goods and lands, tells its own story of forbearance.

The second, and most legitimate, source of revenue lay in the hands of Parliament, but any sympathy which the Commons might have had for the Queen's poverty was mitigated by their suspicions as to the destination of any grant they made. They did not remember the cartloads of Spanish gold that had been led, with ostentatious rumbling, through the streets of the city at the time of Philip's arrival. They forgot the money which had come into the country with Philip's Spanish suite, and which had remained, for the most part, in the hands of English landladies and shopkeepers. They were not supposed to know of the handsome bribes in cash, gold chains, and pensions with which Philip paid for the dubious support of the greater lords of the Council. Even if they knew and considered these things, they counted them little as against their estimation of Philip's intentions. They and the country at large were sure from the outset that that intention was to use England's wealth and manhood for his own ends, and for all Philip's wary walking, he could not live the suspicion down. The Queen, as needs she must, came in for half at least of their distrust. If, to supplement the grudging supplies of the Commons, she asked a loan, and loans became more and more frequent as the reign drew on, it was argued that she wished the money either to give to Philip, or to pay mercenaries to hold the peace while Philip was crowned, or to use in some obscure way to induce the Commons to enter that war with France in which they were determined England should have no part. In some way or other the cloven hoof was discerned in the request. How much truth there was in these fears is impossible to say; but it was certain that at the end of 1556 Mary had 'accommodated her consort' with 100,000 crowns, and perhaps with more. The Commons, harbouring such suspicions, and worked upon also by de Noailles, doled out therefore only grudging and insufficient supplies.[8]

The sole legitimate remedy left was retrenchment, and this had not soon enough been seriously taken in hand. 'The Lord,' wrote Mason in March 1555 to his old colleague Petre–'The Lord put some good man in mind, whom the Queen can be content to believe, to advise her to take the measure of her realm, and to proportionate her receipts and expenses together, and to bring her charges to the rate as they were in her grandfather's time and in the beginning of her father's. Good Lord! how often have I heard this matter spoken of and wished for. . . . They have peace. They had such ways to bring in money as they never had, and yet remain they needy and most miserable. . . . They see the sore and seek not to amend it; unless it may be thought an amendment to hold away poor men's duties which other courts are specially careful to pay for the sake of their honour.'[9]

Except that he ignored the necessary difference in the Queen's 'charges' caused by the depreciation of the currency, Mason's remarks were sound. It was indeed necessary that receipts and expenses should be proportionate, and, strangely enough, what the experienced Gardiner had not taken in hand, the scholar and recluse, Cardinal Pole, steadfastly set about.[10] Yet how economize if not by that very 'holding away of poor men's duties', that Mason deplored, the cessation of pensions, the reduction of guards, household officers and the like? And what more tempting form of economy than to let officials wait for their pay–as indeed Henry and Edward had let them wait? So it was done. Archers, gentlemen pensioners and the like were 'broken'. Others, still kept in employ, were left unpaid–just as the cobblers who made and mended the Queen's shoes, and the bakers and butchers who supplied her table.[11] Unfortunately this means of economy caused much discontent. A poor man has no friends. A poor Queen fared worse, for her poverty made her enemies.

The insufficient supply from Parliament had to be supplemented by loans. Early in the reign the Queen managed to borrow from the Emperor; fifty cases of ducats, 'packed, sealed, matted and corded', marked with a broad arrow, and numbered 1 to 50 were sent off by Sir Thomas Gresham.[12] Charles had lent willingly, since in those days it seemed possible that loans to England would prove profitable. When she could borrow no more from the Emperor, the Queen turned to the great Antwerp bankers, while the London Merchant Adventurers were ordered to stand surety for her. Again, as in Edward VI's reign, the names of Jasper Schetz and Anthony Fugger appear in the Council registers, and Sir Thomas Gresham, dining with this or that one among those masters of kings, would, over the spiced wine, bargain for a reduction in the rate of interest, beating it down to the moderate figure of 12 or 14 per cent, and then go away and see to the packing of the money –hidden securely in bags of pepper.

But when the term of the Antwerp loans fell due, the Queen must pay or renew. To pay meant another loan. In the summer of 1555, the Merchant Adventurers put up £12,000 for the payment of the foreign loans, to the great admiration, so Gresham reported, of the Antwerp Bourse, which was not used to such financial probity in Princes.[13] After that loan, however, the Queen was to demand many others, from the Merchant Adventurers, from the Staplers, from the city; lastly, to spread the discontent yet more widely, from gentlemen all over the country. And this first general loan, demanded in the early autumn of 1556, was made yet more unpopular by the order that the payments were to be made, not into the hands of the High Treasurer, but of the Queen's private officer, the Comptroller. Unwilling lenders smelt, in this, proof of a most obnoxious purpose.[14] That particular cause of suspicion was not repeated, but the loan was, and that no more than a year later,[15] for by this time, added to all the accumulated weight of debt, there were the charges of war.

Yet, for all the grumbling, Mary's reign was a period of at least moderate rectitude in finance. The coins that she issued–perhaps it was significant that she returned to the old, full-face representation of the sovereign's head, with the ship on the reverse–were also of the old standard of purity and weight. Her poverty, however, prevented her from recalling the debased money by means of which Henry VIII, Somerset and Northumberland had attempted to balance their budgets. So bad money continued, as Gresham foretold, to drive out the good. Twice the Queen refused money which she might have had from Parliament–once at the outset of her reign when she remitted a subsidy which had been granted to Edward, and again in the Parliament of 1555 when she, of her own will, withdrew her request for one-fifteenth. In spite also of de Noailles' scoffing, a serious attempt was made to pay off the accumulations of debt, and had the Queen been able to practise economy to the end of her reign things would not have looked so ill. But the disastrous war, into which at last she stumbled in Philip's wake, sent up the expenses again, and though the loss of Calais pricked the Commons into a sudden angry generosity, the burden was too great. It was well for England that Elizabeth, with an inspired parsimony as rigid as her grandfather's, but veiled with the glitter of romance, should take over the task of economy, and through long years of a delicately balanced peace, allow the crippled finances of the country to recover.

Peace, above all things, was what England needed, but peace in Europe was unlikely to last long. Not more than six months after the proclamation of the Truce of Vaucelles, Soranzo, the Venetian, was telling the King of France that 'it greatly surprises everyone that the Pope should wish for peace, that your Majesty should do everything to avoid breaking the truce, that the Catholic King should say the like, and that at the same time, in every direction, there should be so many armies marching'.[16] We in our time can share in his dolorous surprise.

In this Pope of whom Soranzo spoke, a new and dangerous personality had stepped out upon the European stage. With his voluble, eccentric, irresponsible pronouncements, his fiery temper, his bellicose Italian nationalism, Paul IV appeared like a blazing portent in the southern sky. Ardent, uncontrolled, with the intolerance and impetuosity of a very young man, this octogenarian Pope was no scholarly, cultured, indifferent de' Medici, or della Rovere, but a Neapolitan, a fanatic, a man, in spite of his years, belonging to the new and terrible line of religious reformers and persecutors. People said, when they heard of his wild words and actions, that he was in his second childhood, and they comforted themselves with the thought of his great age, 'one blessing among so many mischiefs'. 'God amend him or shorten his days', said Mason; but the malign old man would not be so obliging as to die.

At the moment it was by his national, rather than his religious enthusiasms that the peace of Europe was endangered. France, Spain, England, Germany, all these were for him nations of barbarians, and he hated them all; Italy, he muttered fiercely into the Venetian ambassador's ear, should be for the Italians. But Spain he hated most, as the oppressor of Naples, and France he would use to break the Spanish power there and in Milan.

He had not been Pope six months when he was raking up memories of the sack of Rome; six months later he had confiscated the lands of a great Imperialist–Marc' Antonio Colonna, and so threatening was his attitude that some of the Colonna women slipped out of the gates of Rome one midnight in disguise, pretending to be gentlemen going out for their pleasure.[17] To the Venetian ambassador the Pope raged against the Emperor and his son; the father was quite out of his mind, he said, when he abdicated; both were equally bad Christians, for in Lent good joints of meat went into their Courts; and the Spaniards all were 'no better than renegade Jews'.[18] The truce, which was then almost made at Vaucelles, worked upon him so strongly that he reached a pitch almost hysterical in his denunciations. One day de Sarria, the Spanish ambassador, was stopped at the gates of Rome. He had the guard there disarmed and so passed out to his hunting. The Pope was furious. When de Sarria's brother presented an explanatory memorial to the Pope as he sat at dinner, Paul no sooner saw whence it came, than he dashed it down on the table with the spectacles he had just put on, crying, 'God's life! he shall not come. We will give him the punishment he deserves. We will have his head cut off, his head cut off!'[19] To widen the breach, he decided on a defiant gesture. Into the Chapel where the Pope and Cardinals sat in congregation, came the Count of Montorio, the Pope's nephew, resplendent in cloth of gold. There and then the Pope, who had given no warning of his intention, invested him with the confiscated Colonna lands, thus virtually shaking his first in the face of that power to which he contemptuously referred as 'Philip, late Charles.'[20]

Not even Paul IV, however, was mad enough to provoke the Emperor without providing himself with allies. He had done his best to prevent the conclusion of the Truce of Vaucelles; now, in June 1556, another nephew, Cardinal Caraffa, came on a mission to France. Caraffa, who possessed qualifications strange for a Cardinal, had for eighteen years served as a mercenary soldier in the Emperor's own armies, but, discontented with his service, had left it. Now he came to France on no peaceful mission, but charged with the work of concluding a league against the Emperor and his son, and bringing with him such valuable works of art and antiquity as were fit to tickle the palate of any Renaissance king,[21]—even of the austere and athletic Henri II. Either the lovely things he brought, or the Pope's arguments and offers prevailed. The league was concluded; it was to include also Switzerland, Ferrara, and the Turk.

With the assurance of French support, Paul continued his provocations against the Spanish power in Italy; he also made rapid and obvious preparations for war. Philip, in command now of his first war, since Charles had retired to Juste, moved slowly and unwillingly. But just about the time that the Earl of Devon went out in his gondola, hawk on fist, to that unfortunate day's sport that caused his death, the Duke of Alva marched against the States of the Church. And Henri II had said that he would regard an attack on the Pope, France's ally, as an attack on France.

With growing anxiety and discouragement Mary must have listened to news of the Pope's wild sallies against her husband, and of the outbreak of war. Even when Alva came near to Rome, and there was talk about another sack, she could have found little comfort in the Spaniard's successes. For one thing, neither she nor Philip himself could regard with equanimity a war against the head of Christendom; for another, any war gave Philip too many excuses for further delay in returning, for yet another, this war against the Pope and France in Italy was sure to develop into a war against France in Picardy, and for England war in Picardy meant danger to Calais.

For some time there had been two parties in France competing for influence over the King. On one side stood the Constable, the great Montmorency, that experienced statesman, 'one of the doublest and dissemblingest gentlemen that is in the world; for there is no more assurance of his word than to hold an eel by the tail'. On the other there was the great house of Guise, just now gathering its forces for its splendid and fatal flight towards the sun. Montmorency generally wanted peace. In 1555 he was specially anxious for it as his son was a prisoner, and under his influence the Truce of Vaucelles was made. But the Guise wanted war; and small wonder, when the head of their house, Duke François, was one of the best captains of his age. Diane de Poitiers the middle-aged, massive solemn mistress of the sombre King, counselled it too. So when trouble blew up between the Pope and King Philip, Henri was pushed into his one Italian venture. On November 16th 1556, the Guise set out for Italy.

No one supposed, however, that the war would be confined to that ancient battle-ground. When the Constable's nephew, d'Andelot, went into Picardy, ostensibly on a routine business of changing the garrisons, Philip took it as a threat against the Picard border, and England at once grew alarmed for the safety of Calais. Yet Henri did not want, had never wanted, a war with England. All his and de Noailles' cossetting and encouraging of English rebels had been done in the hope of so crippling Mary's power that she could not move to help her husband. But in the end the French were to overreach themselves.

While Henri was belatedly striving to keep England out of the war, Philip was as bent on bringing her in. If Mary could not bear him a child, if she dared not crown him, if she would not, without the consent of Parliament, give Elizabeth to his friend and dependent the Duke of Savoy, there was only this one thing left. Philip's determination to have it was proportionate to his resentment at the other disappointments.

Without his presence, however, nothing would be done. The Queen might threaten to the French ambassador that she would help her husband, but when that news had struck fear into Henri II's heart, the next post brought word that the Council would not support her, but would only mutter, with glum faces, warnings 'of the little trust that could be placed in her subjects'.[22] England itself had griefs against France: English ships had been captured and plundered at sea, all but unconcealed help had been given to rebels, and, worst of all, the Queen of Scotland, who was also the heir presumptive to the English crown, had been married to the Dauphin of France. But against these motives for war, Englishmen, even the great bulk of Catholic Englishmen, set the exhaustion of the exchequer, their hatred of the Spanish connexion, and the knowledge that if they went to war on Philip's side, and were victorious, it would not be England that would profit.

Philip's personal influence, and more bribery, might, however, do much. So, resolute as ever in pursuit of that aim, in the service of which personal pride and ambition were indistinguishable from a selfless devotion to duty, Philip came to England.

In the past two years Mary had had only too many promises from her husband that he would return, in a month, or before Christmas, or after Easter. Poor though the crown was, and deep in debt, she had fitted out ship after ship and kept them ready for his return. But this time the news of his coming was true. When she knew that, she was in a transport of joy. Gone was all her anger, and with it her dignity. On the eve of his arrival, when the Queen expected him 'howerlie', a ship was ordered to lie in Calais roads, ready in everything, 'so as at his arrival there His Majesty be not forced for want there-of to stay one hour longer than he would'.²³ On March 20th 1557, he came to her at Greenwich, and at once, and without effort, had her again his humble servant.

Philip cannot have come over in sanguine mood, though he had the Queen's promise, and may have hoped something from his pensioners in the Council. He admitted, however, to Granvelle, that he 'found more difficulty than he had thought'.²⁴ Though Pole, the mainstay of the peace-party, avoided contact with a power at war with the Pope by withdrawing to Lambeth when Philip arrived, the Catholics in the Council were still deter-mined on non-intervention; it was, strangely enough, only to the Protestant nobles that the hazards and profits of war made any appeal.

The Queen, ready to 'try to force not only men but also the elements themselves to conform to her will', if thereby she might prevent Philip leaving her, used all means to put pressure on the Council. She tried persua-sion, she discoursed to them on the balance of power in Europe, she tried threats. Philip went so far as to offer to open to English ships the jealously guarded Peru trade.²⁵ They would have none of it. All they would agree to was, that if Flanders was attacked they would keep the old treaty of 1546, and send out the covenanted 5,000 foot and 500 horse to defend it.²⁶ Well might the King of France confide that England would not dare to break with him, and the whole question of support 'would resolve itself into money'.

But at the beginning of May even the cautious Philip was able to say that things had 'taken a turn for the better, though still so uncertain that it will take us all our time to put them in order and get the English to declare war without waiting any longer'.²⁷ This 'turn for the better' in Philip's affairs was the result of the latest efforts of the Pope and the King of France to damage Mary as the wife and ally of Spain.

In May 1557, Paul IV revoked the Legation of Cardinal Pole. The revoca-tion, at first thought to be no more significant than the general recall received by all legates in King Philip's dominions, was soon found to be of a different and more sinister nature. Pole was to return to answer 'some religious suspicions', that is to say the Pope was using Pole's known liberal tendencies as a handle against him.

Then was seen the peculiar spectacle, on the one hand of a Pope revoking, on a charge of heresy, at the risk of irreparably damaging the recovery of Catholicism in England, the Cardinal who had at least lent his name to the bloody repression of heretics; on the other of a Queen who had led back her subjects, will they nill they, to the Roman obedience, now holding up the Papal nuncio at Calais so that the actual letters of recall should not be received, and therefore not disobeyed,²⁸ and at the same time protesting to the Pope that, if there were charges to be laid against Pole for heresy, 'she would, in

observance of the laws and privileges of her realm, refer them to the cogniz-
ance and decision of her own ecclesiastical courts'.[29]

Meanwhile in Rome, Sir Edward Carne, Mary's ambassador, protested
appealed, argued against Pole's recall. The Queen, on a hint from the Pope,
humbled herself to ask as a favour the restoration of Pole's Legation.[30] Paul's
only reply was to declare, with the impudent malice of a bad child, that he
was inspired by the Spirit to make Cardinal of England, in Pole's place, 'the
Confessor of the Queen . . . a very old man, a barefooted friar who led a good
life and was well lettered', that is to say Friar William Peto. Cardinal Caraffa,
backing up his uncle's policy, sent congratulations to Sir Edward Carne on
this proof that the Queen of England had not forfeited the Pope's favour in
spite of her unfortunate connexion with Philip. Sir Edward replied tartly,
'There was not', he said, 'the slightest cause for congratulation at this, as they
had made a blockhead Cardinal and Legate.'[31] When the Pope very disingenu-
ously told Carne that 'he hoped he had done what was agreeable to her
Majesty . . . and beneficial to the whole Kingdom', Carne was hardly less
outspoken. Peto, he replied, was a good man doubtless, but no good Legate,
'for he was an old dotard who could not bear any fatigue, but merely stay in
his cell reciting orisons'. Nor did Carne see how it could please the Queen to
have the Legateship taken from a near and dear kinsman; the Pope called Peto
her confessor – but he had only once, and that before she was seven years old,
heard her confession. As for the change being for the good of England, that it
could not be, seeing that Peto, a poor man and of humble birth, would get no
respect there.[32] Paul, shifting his ground with bewildering inconsequence
replied to all this that he could not help it; he must have Pole's counsel at
Rome.[33] Carne had the last word. The Pope, he said, could do as he pleased
but he himself dared not announce the refusal of her request to his mistress.[34]

Throughout that year and the next the debate dragged on. Friar Peto
refused the offered dignity, and Sir Edward Carne was instructed, should the
Pope give a flat denial of the Queen's repeated request, to protest, and leave
Rome.[35] Neither side would yield. A solution was only made possible by the
death of Peto, and when he died there was no question of appointing another
cardinal in England.

Henri II of France had found a weapon to use against England in that
same Thomas Stafford who had been such a trial to his uncle, Cardinal Pole,
by reason of his treasonable talk. Of the house of Buckingham, and of royal
blood on both sides, he had, since leaving England in 1554, wandered over
Europe, seeing Poland, and Germany, but coming to rest in that haven of
discontented Englishmen, France. There, disporting the leopards and lilies of
England, without any heraldic difference to indicate that his was a cadet
branch, he was made much of by Henri II, allowed midnight audiences, and
given presents of money – after Henri's usual manner with potential disturbers
of Queen Mary's peace.

Since the end of January 1557 Wotton, the old and kindly ambassador, so
suspect in Renard's eyes for his half-humorous sympathy with the young

scoundrels of English refugees, had been writing home warnings of a great plot brewing. At first he knew nothing precise. Then in April a spy brought to him the plan of a port, unnamed; but he thought that it looked like Scarborough, and warned the Council of the possibility of invasion.[36]

On Easter day two ships sailed from France; in both there were French soldiers bound for Scotland, but one of them, the *Fleur de Lys*, carried also Thomas Stafford and forty Englishmen. Off Scarborough these passengers disembarked; then the ships sailed on, taking no part in what came after.[37] Stafford seized the town, and issued a proclamation which should have brought all the country in to him, for it played on all the night fears of Englishmen. Twelve castles were, he said, to be handed over to the Spanish King Philip on the day of his coronation; the Queen was half-Spanish and as she loved Spaniards so she hated English; Spaniards were pouching English money; Spaniards said that they would rather live with Turk, Jews, and Moors, than with the English; lest this statement should be misunderstood, the proclamation interpreted it to mean that they intended, as they used those people badly, 'to use us worse'. Therefore he, Thomas Stafford of that House of Buckingham which had always stood by the Commons against tyrants, was come to save England from 'the most devilish device of Mary, unrightful and unworthy Queen of England, who, both by will of her father . . . and by the laws of this noble realm of England hath forfeit the Crown for a marriage with a stranger'.[38] So ran Stafford's appeal.

The rising, no less foolish and hare-brained than the petulant revolt of Essex against Elizabeth, was also no less disastrous for its promoters. The Earl of Westmorland, raising the local militia, took prisoner, without bloodshed, the small company of fools. Twenty-seven Yorkshiremen were hanged at home. Stafford and some few others were taken up to London, and there executed. The silly, boyish affair was over.

But it had done its work, though that work lay not in the intentions of its authors. Henri II, of course, disclaimed all responsibility for it. When news of the disaster had reached France, he spoke of it to Soranzo. 'You must have heard', said he, 'what that fool, Thomas Stafford, has done in England. Before he left he came to me here in this very room where we are now, and as I leaned on the balcony, he told me of these plans of his, begging me to give him help and counsel.' But Henri, so he said, had refused utterly, and 'I bade him beware, as I already saw him without his head if he persisted in these ideas of his'.[39] That was true prophecy, but no one doubted what would have been the French King's line if Stafford could have raised the north, and if some friend had done for him that which Lord Stanley had done at Bosworth for Mary's grandfather, when, as the tale went, he had culled the crown of England from a hawthorn bush and put it on the first Tudor's head. There were, according to Henri's own confession, 3,000 French troops in Scotland, and with Yorkshire in a new King Thomas' hands, the back door into England would have been easy to force.

In England there was much alarm at the invasion. Beacons were freshly piled on the hills, and watchers were appointed to them. But there was anger too. Now at last in the Council the persuasions of the King and Queen found willing listeners. The impudence of the scheme, and the remembrance of all the other cockatrices' eggs that had been hatched in France were too much for cautious English neutrality. On May Day, when the still countrified Londoners were bringing into town their green budded branches, the Council met and decided that 5,000 foot and 1,000 horse should be raised for four months, 3,000 foot for Calais, and 6,000 men for the fleet. The truce, it was still maintained, would not be broken; the old treaty with the Low Countries was being fulfilled, nothing more.[40] But that pretencê was thin.

Throughout May preparations went on. The subsidy was coming in; the Queen was selling Crown lands – all was to go to Philip for the war. Captains along the south coast were bidden to guard well such places as Poole, Southampton, and the Isle of Wight, while the Admiral had his orders to keep the Channel with his ships.[41]

At last, on June 7th, according to magnanimous custom of this realm, never to go to war without first giving notice', a man dressed in plain black cloth, who had landed at Boulogne as a servant of the English ambassador, came to the door of the French King's Council Chamber in the abbey of Saint Remy at Rheims, and asked for the Constable. He was a herald of England, Norroy King of Arms. Such an arrival, so sudden and so closely disguised, was oversetting. The Constable swore that the man deserved to be hanged for coming into France without any signs of his quality.[42] But it was not only the strangeness of his coming that disturbed the French. 'This country', wrote Soranzo from Rheims, 'holds no other war in account but that with England,' for 'though the English are not of that strength and courage that they were once upon a time, when they were the better of this nation' yet now the French could not help 'calling to their mind their ancient courage' and dreading the issue.[43] So, when the King came back from hunting, and consented to receive the message which he knew the herald must bring, he did it with a very ill grace.

Henri sat, surrounded by his lords, under a cloth of estate. In came Norroy, his tabard, embroidered with the leopards and lilies, over his arm. Shaken perhaps by the Constable's reception, he began abruptly with his message. Henri interrupted him. 'Who sent you;' 'The Queen of England my mistress.' 'Where is the patent?' snapped the King. It was handed over, and a secretary read out what was written – a declaration of war in the name of Mary Queen of England.

Henri accepted the defiance; said that he trusted in God to help him; declared, with a display of petulant bad manners, 'that as the herald came in the name of a woman it was unnecessary for him to listen to anything further, though he would have done so if his adversary had been a man'; and broke off the audience. Then, said Soranzo, 'taking us into a chamber he said to us laughing, "Consider how I stand when a woman sends to defy me to war. But I doubt not God will assist me." ' Yet all this, perhaps, was only to carry off his chagrin with an air, for the acute Venetian surmised that Henri had interrupted the herald because he did not wish to have to justify himself against the Queen's accusations in the matter of the help given to English rebels.[44]

That summer, which must have been an anxious one for Mary, may also have been a little happy, for Philip was with her. With her he had come to Windsor for the Feast of Saint George, and she had watched him, from a window overlooking the garden, as he walked in the procession of the Knights. On Ascension Day she had gone with him to Westminster in state, round about the cloisters, ancient even in those days, and so into the church for Mass. In June there had been days of hunting.

But with the declaration of war, Philip's work in England was done, and at the beginning of July he went away. As if she knew that this was to be their last parting, Mary came down with him to Dover, and to the very strand itself. When he had gone it was all over. Her only comfort was that she could now feel that she was working with and for him, and that her men were fighting by his side. For war had begun.

Chapter XXI

IT opened well enough for England. The fleet 'haled over with the coast of France' now to east, now to west, putting French ships to flight, sometimes taking a prize 'laden with malmsey and muscadine', sometimes making a landing in France and burning a village. But the heart of the war lay ashore. With Pembroke in command, the English force set sail after Philip, 5,000 foot, among them 500 men in blue from the city of London. They were to have their share in a striking victory. The French town of St. Quentin was besieged. The Constable tried, and failed, to throw in the supplies that Coligny so desperately needed, and, to make matters infinitely worse, let himself be caught. His force was wiped out and the way was open to Paris. But Philip was not the man to risk such a stroke as that, fatal as it must be to one or other of the opponents; perhaps François de Guise was the only captain of the day who would have risked it. Philip therefore stopped before St. Quentin, laid siege, battered the walls, and on August 27th took it. English gentlemen, thinking some profit due to themselves, but innocent of the ways of mercenary troops, were shocked at what followed the almost bloodless assault, for 'the Swartzritters, being masters of the King's whole army, used such force, as well to Spaniards, Italians, and other nations as unto us, that there was none who could enjoy nothing but themselves. The town was by then set on fire, and a great piece of it burnt. Divers were brent in cellars and were killed immediately; women and children gave such pitiful cries that it would grieve any Christian heart.'[1]

It was a resounding triumph for Philip, and in London *Te Deum* and procession, bonfire and banqueting, celebrated the news. A fortnight after there were more rejoicings, this time for the peace that was made between the Pope and the King, and a week later, still more for another victory. But the tide was on the turn. The Guise, summoned in haste from Italy, and riding as though Satan was behind him, had come home to France, and now commanded the French armies. He advanced, and as he advanced Philip withdrew. The victories were past, and Englishmen were soon to taste the sourest of all their defeats.

In Calais and the Pale, England had, since the fourteenth century, possessed 120 square miles of French territory, a trophy of much national pride, and, it was thought, of vast importance as giving a door upon Europe for England's trade, and also as securing command of the Channel.[2] From Gravelines to Wissant, and stretching nine miles inland, lay a country, high on the west, but low and marshy, with many pools and flashes, in the east. Good roads crossed it, a system of canals drained it, and a series of forts defended it. Hammes, Guisnes, and Newnham Bridge were the chief of these, with Calais itself on the harbour, formed by the estuary of the river, and Rysbank on the dunes opposite.

At no time during Mary's reign had the English government been able to feel at ease in their minds on the subject of Calais. The declared enmity of France would have been enough to cause them anxiety, but this was not the only source of danger. They feared treachery almost more than they feared attack, and very likely they were right to do so. There is evidence to show that even before Mary's reign Calais was a refuge for Protestants. Henry VIII had been so alarmed by the heretical opinions of the garrison that in 1540 he appointed a commission to inquire into these and ordered that the Captain of Rysbank should be sent home under arrest.[3] When in 1555 Gardiner stayed at Calais during the fruitless peace negotiations of that summer, a quarrel blazed up between him and the Deputy Wentworth, because the Chancellor had tried to exercise his episcopal authority over one of Wentworth's gentlemen,[4] and Gardiner declared that Calais was so full of heretics that if Wentworth were not removed the town 'would not be English one year together'.[5] It was no wonder that there should be many Protestants in Calais, for Wentworth himself was such, and came of a family whose connexions were all of that colour of thought. It is perhaps of some significance that such dangerous persons as Sir Andrew Dudley, Henry Dudley, Alexander Brett, and Sir John Pickering had all held commands at one or other castle in the Pale during King Edward's reign.

After the death of Edward, Henry Dudley's name continued to occur, time after time, in sinister conjunction with the French on one side and Calais on the other. While Northumberland gambled for the crown in England, it was Henry Dudley whom he sent over to the French King, promising him, as the price of aid, Ireland, Calais, and Guisnes. An attempt on Calais does not seem to have been any part of the plot of 1556, but after that time there were frequent alarms, and in most of these Dudley's name appeared.

His career in France, since the day that he landed from Richard Uvedale's boat, had not been one of unmixed success. Very fine at first in his velvet hat and fur-lined cloak he 'bore men in hand that Her Majesty has done him divers great wrongs, and . . . would be called here Monsieur de Lisle',[6] a title which his great kinsman Northumberland had borne. The affectation made Wotton laugh, though he admitted that the rest of the business was no laughing matter. But, when the plot of 1556 had utterly miscarried, Dudley and the other refugees began to experience the waning of royal favour and to feel the pinch of poverty, as no fresh gifts came from the King of France, and pensions were left unpaid. Peter Killigrew, a Devon man and born sailor, took to Channel piracy, and did well enough at it for a time. One of the Ashtons and doubtless other refugees joined him. Their less fortunate friends thereupon tried to borrow from them; Dudley, 'making great moan of his poverty', did the same.[7]

But in the autumn of 1556 Dudley was doing what he could to restore himself to a position of importance with the French King. Wotton had a warning that a dangerous person called 'Chesnes' – 'he who by subtlety took Marano from the King of Bohemia fourteen years ago' – had gone to Boulogne with the intention of entering Calais in disguise and 'practising' secretly with some of the garrison. Nor was that all; Wotton also heard that Dudley had told the King that the forts of the Pale had food enough for no more than twenty days, and had volunteered to get them for France; to support this attempt, Wotton believed, men were actually mustering at Rouen.[8] All that winter the alarm lasted, and many were the items of information about Dudley reported home by the ambassador. Dudley had told the King that Guisnes needed a garrison of 2,000 and had only one of 300 men. The King had given Dudley 2,000 crowns and a letter to a rich gentlewoman recommending him to her as a husband. An Englishman had lately been asked by a Frenchman whether Dudley's brother were not Captain of Hammes. Yes, he was told. 'Why then,' said he, 'he may do the French King a pleasure.' Late in November Henri was sending into Picardy a supply of files which would cut great chains noiselessly, instruments for sapping walls, and a bridge to cast over a wide ditch.[9]

The Council was convinced that the danger to Calais was immediate. Dudley, they told King Philip, was trying to tamper with men of the garrisons of Guisnes and Hammes. Some soldiers had promised to betray one or both. The French too were increasing their forces near the Pale; they gave out that they only intended building a fort near Ardres, but the conjunction of events was suspicious. The Council acted promptly. At the beginning of December Pembroke was sent over as Governor with a force of 300, to be distributed throughout the garrisons of the Pale; and the dissaffected men were gradually and unostentatiously withdrawn.[10] Whether the danger had been real or not the Council certainly believed in it. Early next year a certain informer called Lent, who might, however, said Wotton, 'be a very false liar', told him that the French had nearly had Guisnes, for the force which attempted Meguy had really been sent against Guisnes, and if Dudley had gone thither when he was told, things would have happened. There was much talk of a Frenchman in Calais named Touteville who had committed suicide immediately after Pembroke's arrival. He had been in touch with one Devisat, who had taught the late Duke of Somerset's children French. It was said, and Wotton thought it possible, that these two had a plan to set fire to the powder stored in Calais. But nothing certain could be known of all this, since Touteville was dead and Devisat had got out of Calais over the wall.[11]

For a while the reinforcements, and the wakefulness of the English, had dispersed any trouble that might have been intended from France. But in May 1557, when war had been resolved on, the possibility of French attack and of French intrigue against the Pale must again be reckoned with. The Council of Calais faced it with misgivings. There was, they sent word to the Council of State, great lack of 'munition and other habiliments of war. . . as this bearer Mr. Highfield master of your ordnance here can declare more amply'.[12] Nor was the garrison sufficient, they considered, for a sudden attack, and that, from the concentration of the French fleet at Harfleur, was what they feared. At Guisnes there was the same shortage. A week after the declaration of war, Lord Grey, the Captain there, had only 300 men, not nearly enough for safety, and only 100 above the peace strength of the garrison.[13]

Yet, if the registers of the Privy Council for that summer do not merely record good resolutions never fulfilled, much was done. Three hundred men were actually dispatched by the end of May; Pembroke was to go out again; a scheme was drawn up of works to be carried out that summer and next, a new wall, new sluices, new ditches, traverse walls and the like. In July the Council was arranging for the crossing of 200 foot and 50 horse, and 100 'hapquebutters'.[14]

All they could do, however, in the wretched state of the Queen's finances, was not enough, and if there was disloyalty, treachery, or disaffection within the Pale, was indeed useless. A sinister entry in the minutes of the Council for the end of July, records the order that the Deputy of Calais was to send four men home, well guarded, in the next ship.[15] They were bound for the Tower. Early in August the Council was rebuking the Mayor and Aldermen of Calais; they had elected a mayor 'most unmeet' although 'the placing of a meet man in that room is of much importance at this present time'.[16] After that date there is silence from Calais until just before the catastrophe.

It was on December 15th that the Venetian, Michiel, ambassador now in France, heard 'very confidentially' that the Duc de Guise had sent 5,000 Germans by water to Pontoise, and the rest of his foot, 4,000 Swiss and 9,000 or 10,000 French to Amiens, Abbeville and Montreuil. The Guise himself was to follow with the cavalry to Amiens.[17]

The object of this most secret expedition was – Calais. For Gilles de Noailles, passing through Calais on his way home after the outbreak of war, had noted the weakness of its old-fashioned defences, the high proud walls and towers that had defied the siege engines of the past, but could not face cannon as could the crouching, earth-filled ramparts of the new military science. What de Noailles said, Marshal Strozzi, a professional soldier, had corroborated, for on last St. Martin's night, he had, daringly, and at great risk, reconnoitred the defences.[18] So now, at that time of year when the spirits of comfort-loving English soldiers were known to be at their lowest ebb, the Guise, late in the season though it was, and bitter the weather, finding his army to be '*preste et gaillarde*', decided on the adventure.[19]

But, because the success of that adventure depended upon surprise, its aim was masked by complicated and deceptive manœuvres. The Duc de Nevers had made one of the first feints – a pretence of marching on Luxembourg; when he had laid a false scent he halted, and sent troops by forced marches to join Guise at Compiègne.[20] The Guise himself had marched by 'the upper road towards New Hesdin' as if he were making eastward and not towards Calais. When all the forces united they would, according to one estimate, total 30,000 foot.[21]

It was just a week after Michiel got his news of the expedition that the

English commanders heard from Flanders of the movements of the French,
but as yet, though they suspected, they did not know for certain that Calais
was to be the object of the attack. [22] Four days later, that is on the day after
Christmas, between nine and ten in the morning, Wentworth sat down to
write his suspicions to the Queen. They were stronger now.

The Guise was at Compiègne; he had in fact expected to be there sooner,
but had been delayed because his unpaid Swiss had refused to move. He gave
out that his destination was Ardres, but Wentworth believed that his force,
and the five great ships of war in St. John's harbour near Boulogne, were
meant for something more than the revictualling of that fort. As he wrote,
in came a letter written by a man who had been at Abbeville on the 23rd, and
who had seen there most sinister preparations – just before dusk a long procession of carts laden with powder and shot, thirty battering and field guns,
ladders and planks, many horsemen, many Germans, Swiss and French, and
these, significant fact, receiving their wages.[23] That was often a necessary
preliminary to an action.

Next day Wentworth and Grey were writing again, surely one of the most
despondent letters ever penned by any commanders, and surely too composed
by Wentworth, and not by that tough, indomitable fighter, Grey; the voice
is Jacob's voice, even though Esau put his hand to the document. For Calais
the best the two commanders could say was, that if the enemy attacked they
would abandon the town, and try to keep the turnpike – that is the turning
gate across the quay side, for along the latter help could come to the castle.
But, they complained, there was great want of food. Hammes fort might have
been well enough, but the frost was making the marshes good going for the
enemy. Newnham Bridge had no food except the Captain's store. The
Rysbank, opposite Calais, had no food and 'by the shore side may the enemy
come in a night to it'.[24]

On the last night of the old year the alarm of the enemy's approach came
from the north-west corner of the Pale, that is from Sangatte, or Sandgate;
the Guise arriving there had paused to make hasty entrenchments. But
François de Guise was not, like King Philip, a man to lengthen out a campaign.
Early next morning, when in England folk were celebrating the eighth of the
Twelve Days of Christmas by giving and receiving of presents, six ensigns of
foot and some horse of the French 'showed in great bravery coming down the
hill from the chalk pits to the causeway leading to Newnham Bridge'.[25]
There was a skirmish, then a hot attack, as the English were driven back to
the bridge. Worse still for the defenders, French bands were reported on all
the roads between Sandgate and Guisnes. During the day Froyton church was
taken, though the little bulwark there, and that of Nesle between Froyton and
'Senter Caes' bulwark, still held their own. So ended that day's fighting, and
the English watchmen, staring out through the dark night, guessed, by the
enemy's camp fires, that no movement was being made that night.

But next day there were fresh disasters. All the High Country, that is the
western part of the Pale and its forts, was lost; Froyton and Nesle bulwarks

were surrounded, and fell; the garrisons, in Wentworth's phrase, escaping
'right manfully through the marshes'.

To save Newnham Bridge Wentworth opened the sluices and let in the
tidal water to flood the parts there about, so that as he wrote exultingly, the
retreating French who expected to be 'up to the girdle-stead, as they had
been when they came to the attack, this time, for all their haste, went up to
the breast. And if they had tarried a little longer I had put in so much water,
as I think would have put them head over ears, and . . . at the next tide I will
take in more.' Yet, in spite of this, late at night the causeway was won, and
worse still there were movements along the dunes towards Rysbank. Wentworth, finishing this day's letter home, forecast an attack on that fort, and
from thence an attack on Calais itself. He feared, so he told the Council, that
this was his last letter out, for he expected soon to be cut off.[26]

Now, in Calais, things went from bad to worse. On January 3rd the French
guns had been in place against the Rysbank and Newnham Bridge for three
hours before daybreak, and the winter sun had not long been above the
horizon when both forts fell. French horse swept round the town to the south,
and soon the whole of the Low Country was in their hands, and of all the
forts in the Pale only Hammes, Guisnes, and Calais and the tiny Boots
Bulwark,* were yet unconquered. And now, from the dunes beside Rysbank
the French guns opened fire across the Calais river upon the wall between
the water gate and the prison.

Wentworth, who had already 'taken in a confused number of countrymen',
tried to organize them to work at the defences. But he found these fellows
difficult to handle, indeed 'the women did more labour about the ramparts
than the said countrymen, which for lack of order in time did absent themselves in houses and other secret places'.

All next day the battery went on, and the English replied as well as they
could, though Highfield, Master of the Ordnance, complained that his pieces
had no cover, that he was short of ammunition, and that, for lack of labourers,
he could not remove sixty guns from the farther ramparts and concentrate
them along one side, which, defended by the sea as it was, had been counted
till now impregnable. The outlook was black indeed, and Wentworth was a
man easily discouraged. Yet during that day's confused noise and hurry he
spoke to his Master of Ordnance, 'Although there comes no succour,' said he,
'I will never yield, nor stand to answer the loss of such a town.' When dusk
fell and the bombardment ceased the defenders must labour to fill up the
breach by the water gate, 'with timber, wool, and other matter'.

But on January 5th, the French changed their tactics. No longer did they
batter the town wall and the fortified turnpike. They turned their guns instead
against the old castle of Calais, 'which, being a high and weak wall without
ramparts', was ready within the day for an assault. Long that evening did the
Council of Calais sit in debate, while the guns thundered from over the

---

* This last was never taken. It lay to the eastern side of the Pale, and after England had lost
Calais, King Philip helped himself to it.

harbour and the walls splintered and shook. At last it was decided that the castle should be blown up by gunpowder, 'which one Saulle took upon him to do; notwithstanding', says Highfield, 'I said openly that if the castle were abandoned, it should be the loss of the town.'

Next morning, being Twelfth Day, the *Jour des Rois*, at about eight in the morning, when the low tide allowed the attacking force to wade, waist deep, across Calais river, the French came on to the breach which gaped in the castle wall. The English garrison took to their heels and fled across the bridge to the town; Saulle lit his powder train, it flared up and he was frightfully burnt, but the flame was trodden out and the train scattered by the enemy, and he had failed.

Without a blow Calais castle had fallen, and, if something were not done, the French would be over the bridge and within the town walls. A small band of men, under Sir Anthony Aucher, Marshal of Calais, who had already done good service at Newnham Bridge, held the bridge between town and castle; they did more indeed, for, driving the French back they came to the castle gate and all but forced their way in. Had they done so, the castle might have fallen once again to its old masters, for the Guise himself had been forced to withdraw before the rising tide cut him off from the Rysbank. But Aucher's sally, gallant though it was, and so nearly successful, ended in disaster. The French, after a hot scuffle, beat off the attack and shut the gate; the Marshal himself, his son, Calais Pursuivant and a dozen men fell in the fighting.

All that now remained to do was to break down the bridge and hold the town, admittedly the strongest part of the defences. But though the first was done, Wentworth, an inert fighter, had no more spirit left in him. 'Within an hour' after the fall of the castle he sent out a herald to ask for an exchange of hostages. Next day he surrendered.

The unfortunate folk of Calais were herded into the Churches of Our Lady and St. Nicholas, upon whose high altars, by order of the Duc de Guise, they must lay 'a great and sorrowful offertory', their gold, silver and jewels, while in the town outside the French soldiers sacked their houses. All day, without meat or drink they stayed there, and all night. Next morning, merchant and serving-man and baker's wife, each with no more than a groat in their pockets, went out of the gates of Calais and were brought, kindly enough and courteously, across the Channel to the English coast. So much for Calais. Now for Guisnes.

It was on January 4th that Grey wrote to the Queen that he was cut off from Calais and, for men and victuals, from England too. As for the succour of Calais he said – 'there resteth now none other way . . . but a power of men out of England, or from the King's Majesty or from both, without delay, able to distress and keep them from victuals coming to them as well by sea or by land'. Turning to Guisnes itself, he promised what he would do when attacked, that is to say – draw in all his men from the town to the castle and hold that. 'I have', he concluded his letter, 'as good provision of victuals as I could by any means out of the country, with which (God willing) to defend and keep this place as long as any man, having no better provision of furniture and victuals than I have. . . .' And he signed and dated the letter, 'At your Highness's castle of Guisnes, most assured English even to the death'.[27] It was a letter far different from Wentworth's despondent reports and forecastings, and in it Grey promised no more than he was to perform.

Just a fortnight after the first alarm had come to Calais, on Thursday January 13th, the French arrived before Guisnes.[28] After 'a hot and stout skirmish' Grey did as he had said, withdrew from the town to the castle, setting fire to houses of the town.

Just before the siege began, fifty Spanish soldiers, under Mondragone, one of Philip's best Captains, and a number of Burgundians, had come in; these with some English, the whole force numbering 450 men, were told off to garrison the 'Mary' Bulwark, a round tower isolated from the castle, new, brick-built, surrounded by a deep water-filled ditch, and thought to be impregnable. If it proved to be otherwise its defenders would have little hope for their lives, since Grey had rammed up the gate of the castle behind them, leaving open only the small postern.

Having withdrawn into the castle and posted his men, Grey might have sat down to wait for attack, but that was not his way. The French had entered the town, glad no doubt to be under cover after their chilly nights on the dunes of Calais, and 'thinking to find quiet lodging in these vacant houses'. But they got no quiet that night, for out came Grey in a sally, and killed several, set fire to more houses, and would have made prisoner the Guise himself 'had he not left his cloak behind him, of the which cloak one of our gentlemen had hold of'.

It took the besiegers the next four days to bring up and place their heavy cannon, for the defenders 'kept them such play with great ordnance and often sallies that they hardly could cast their trenches or plant batteries'. Yet the work went on, the Guise labouring at it among his men; at last by Monday it was done, and now, with the cannon placed and defended, the real assault began upon the Mary Bulwark. The Guise, 'thinking by gaining the stronger to come more easily by the weaker' concentrated upon that outwork a terrific battery.

Of that bombardment we have two accounts, one, by Lord Grey's son, who was in the castle, the other by Thomas Churchyard who was in the Bulwark itself. Both men, in their tale of those terrible days, used all the stops of the magnificent instrument, the English of their day, now stately, now intimate, often humorous, always lusty, apt, and vivid.

Two French batteries were in place by daybreak; the bombardment began at 11 a.m. It was deadly. It not only dismounted the English counterbattery 'but also clean cut away the hoop of brick of the whole fore front . . . wherewith, the filling being but of late digged earth, the sand did croomble away'. After such a battery, assault must come. A 'forlorn hope' of 50 crossed the ditch, 'which was full now of the ruin of the wall, came to the breach, and with as little pain ran up the same, the climb was so easy'. After a few pistol shots, and 'pushes of pike' they retired to report. Next came the real attack by 'a band or two of Gascons. . . . Up they come. Then a little more earnestly we leaned to our tackling, our flankers walked, our pikes, our culvers, our pots of wild fire were lent them, the harquebuses saluted them, so as jolly Mr. Gascon was sent down with more haste than he came up, with god-speed, and so ended Monday's work,' with the early darkness. It was well for those in the Bulwark that it was so, for the bastion was such a ruin that if they had not had night to dig a great new trench and rampart they must have abandoned the Bulwark there and then.

Next day the merciless bombardment began again. After an hour and a half the breach was 'so bare (it moulded away like a hillock of sand) that we', says Churchyard, 'were forced to fight on our knees'. The garrison, wearied out with last night's labour and alarms, must face, 'all that dangerous day', one assault after another by constant reinforcements of unwearied men. New batteries also were so placed that they should destroy the English 'flankers', that is the flanking batteries in the castle commanding the Mary Bulwark. So it went on till 'the very dark night' but even then there was no rest for the defenders, since the ruin of the long bombardment forced them 'of new to become mould-warps'. Too busy to rest, though men might fall asleep fighting, the defenders of the bulwark laboured. But the Castle was awake too; 'we that were not in the Castle might hear the great business and stir through the whole body and heart' of the fortress.

At 'pype of day' the French guns opened again upon both Bulwark and Castle. Grey himself had a narrow escape as he sat on a bench with Sir Henry Palmer and Sir Lewis Dives at a high part of the castle ward whence he might watch the battle and whence 'a quoit might be thrown into the Mary Bulwark'. A shot broke up the bench, but none of the three was hurt. It was still the Bulwark that bore the brunt of the attack. This day's battery drove through 'the rampire and a new countermure of earth' built in the breach, and about one o'clock, those in the castle 'might descry the trench before the breach to be stuffed with ensigns'. The assault was ready. Soon they came on, eight or nine ensigns of Swiss and three of the Gascons. 'Without stay the Gascons fly into the ditch, the breach they run up, our harquebusery receiveth them, they two for one requite us. The top of our vanmure, or rather trench, they approach, the pike is offered, to handy blows it comes; then the Switzer with a stately leisure steps into the ditch, close together marcheth up the breach; the fight warmeth, the breaches all covered with the enemy.' So they went at it ding-dong for an hour, fiery Gascons, the steady professional Swiss, redoubtable Spaniards, and the slipshod English soldiers, who so loved their ease, but, when stirred, were as good fighters as any.

At first harquebus men on Webb's Tower did good service against the swarming attack, but soon the French guns were trained upon the Tower and brought it down. After this came on a fresh assault, met at the breach by two hundred of Grey's small reserve. But with all the English 'flanker's gone except for two whose gunners had been bidden 'not to disclose them but upon extremity', and with ammunition exhausted in the Bulwark, the defenders must fight with only pike and bill. The odds were too great, and 'the easiness of the fight thus alluring the enemy, unappointed companies flew into the breach'. Here was extremity indeed. Lord Grey sent word to the hidden guns 'that they should no longer spare'. They did not. Shooting into the mass of men, 'what havoc they made it is not hard to guess. . . . Three or four bouts of these salutations began to clear well the breach; the ditch grew the fuller.' Again it was only the darkness that stopped the fighting, and both sides might lie down to lick their wounds for, 'as we', said Arthur Grey, 'went not scot free, so surely no small number of their carcases took up their lodging that night in the ditch.'

In the darkness Lord Grey himself came into the half-ruined Bulwark to hearten the men there. The dead were buried, the wounded carried away and the needs of defence seen to, as far as it could be done, though 'some (needs) yet that were great could not be helped, as corn, powder, fire works, yea and pikes began to fail us'. But Grey's spirit did not fail. He only withdrew from the bulwark when hurt in the foot by a scabbardless sword that was lying about, and then went off, telling the little garrison to do 'no less valiantly the next day, assuring them that one or two more banquets as this last given, would cool their courages for any more assaults'.

During the night, however, the French also were busy; the noise they made kept the bulwark waking and watching. At last by the flames of some cressets, the English could see that the enemy was at work making a bridge to cross the ditch; empty casks 'fastened together and sawed boards laid thereon' it proved to be in the morning light.

The forenoon was spent by the French in a bombardment by which the last flanking batteries of the castle were destroyed and the gunners killed. There was now no hope for the Mary Bulwark. Hurriedly conferring together, Grey, Dives, Palmer and Mondragone decided to make in the Bulwark a 'fricoisie', that is 'a charge for a Mortar . . . of stones, bullets, nails and pieces of old iron closed together with grease and gunpowder', to withdraw all but a few men, 'and then to have blowen it up whole'. This heroic remedy was begun, but the assault came on again 'with greater fury and force than yet at any time'. For another half-hour the defenders hung on, then d'Andelot broke in through the breach, 'which my Lord [Grey] seeing, and from the castle, he leapt to the top of the rampier, wishing of God that some shot would suddenly take him'. From that desperate position someone dragged him down by the scarf, and before he got again to his feet a cannon-ball grazed in its flight the place from whence he had fallen.

Meanwhile a desperate and bloody fight was raging in the bulwark. Grey, himself again, shouted to Lewis Dives and others to follow him to the gate, meditating who knows what mad sally. But in the castle 'the maze was such', said Arthur Grey, 'that, beside the said Lewis, myself, and Brickwell, with half a dozen armed corslets, not a man did follow'.

Yet it was well for the small remnant of the defenders of the Bulwark that these few came to the gate. For the former had now abandoned the outwork, leaping down into the dyke behind, 'and so scramble for their lives, and creep up into a hole of a brick wall', apparently between the Bulwark and the castle gate, a sort of bolt-hole which Grey had made for this very purpose. After them now came the French, but fell back before the pikes of the little crowd of fugitives and shot from the castle wall. Yet, unless Churchyard and his companions could get into the castle there was little hope for them, 'and the cry and the noise was so great and terrible on all sides' that they could not be heard, shout as they might. At last Sir Lewis Dives heard Churchyard's voice and answered. 'Then', says Churchyard, 'I plied the matter so sore, for life, that, with much ado' the wicket was opened, Grey himself holding it, and they slipped in. Crowding after them again came the French, 'pelly melly with us if a cannon shot had not made place while the gate was a-shutting'.

The defenders of the outwork had reached a place of very precarious safety. At the sight of the downfall of the Mary Bulwark that great, new, and impregnable work, the men from the Garden and Wetherby Bulwarks, and from the base court, fled into the castle , so that only the keep and the body of the castle remained in English hands. The end was at hand. But 'my lord, having received all his, caused the gates to be rammed up'.

It was dark by now, and through the dark a trumpet could be heard from beyond the ditch, and a voice, calling upon Lord Grey. It was the Guise's messenger sent with an offer of parley. At that word all the men at the walls of the castle came flocking in, clamouring that he should 'harken to the message and . . . have consideration of their lives'. He did not refuse, but drove them back to their posts again. Then the trumpeter was told that the offer was accepted.

The Guise demanded the exchange of two hostages from either side. From Guisnes Lewis Dives and Arthur Grey 'were put out' and were brought up by d'Andelot 'over the late unfortunate bulwark, being come upon which, naked and new slain carcases, some of them yet sprawling and groaning under our feet, were only the earth we trod on'.

No more was done that night, but next day Grey went out to meet the Duc de Guise. Both the Guise and the whole French army might well have believed that terms had but to be formulated and accepted. It was not so. For an hour the two Commanders debated ; the Guise considered Grey's demands nothing more than 'a stout brag', and no wonder, for the Captain of the ruined castle insisted that the men should leave with ensigns displayed. That was refused, and back went Grey into Guisnes.

His own heart was stout, but he had to reckon with his garrison. When he returned and it was known that he had refused to surrender, soldiers again crowded in on him from the walls, in an uglier mood than yesterday, some threatening to throw him over the wall, some clamouring that he should have pity on them. Grey tried to stiffen them to his own desperate courage. Said he :

'We have begun as becomed us; we have yet held on as duty doth bind us; let us end then as honesty, duty, and fame doth will us. . . . We may yet dearly enough sell our skins ere we lose them. Let us march out with our ensigns displayed, or else here within die under them displayed.'

It was the great, the unsubstantial plea of honour that he urged, but the soldiers thought as little of honour as did Shakespeare's fat knight himself. They 'in a mutiny flatly answered that they for his vainglory would not sell their lives'.

At that, and as if to drive home the lesson, there was a cry from the walls. One of the French hostages came running, to warn Lord Grey that the Switzers were advancing to the attack, though the truce still held. The same honourable scruple that bade him give his warning was in the Guise also; he beat off with his truncheon those who were preparing to set fire to the gate.

At last Grey yielded. By the new terms of surrender he, Sir Henry Palmer, Sir Lewis Dives, and all the captains became prisoners. The castle and everything it contained was yielded. But the soldiers marched out with their arms, and every man with a crown in his purse.

So Grey and his fellows went off into captivity, Palmer, a wounded man, to die a prisoner, Lewis Dives to buy his liberty for 1,500 crowns, Grey to find, because of a well meant but maladroit message from the Queen, his reputation and therefore his ransom increased to an enormous sum. For, by a herald who later came into France, Mary sent word to Grey 'that she considered herself no less well served by him than she had been ill-served by Lord Wentworth, and that she exhorted him to be of good cheer'. Henri II laughed when he told this to the Venetian ambassador. 'Look ye,' said he, 'what a proceeding is this! When was a crowned head ever known to send to proclaim to the enemy the esteem in which his captive subjects are held.'[29] It was indeed unlucky praise for Grey, since on the strength of it Strozzi, whose prisoner he was, at once put up his ransom from 7,000 to 17,000 crowns, and he did not at last get free for less than 24,000 crowns.[30]

Chapter XXII

'CALAIS was lost,' said Thomas Churchyard, 'I cannot tell how.' It was lost, said another Englishman, by 'negligence of the Council at home, conspiracy of traitors elsewhere, force . . . of enemies, helped by the rage of the most terrible of tempests of contrary winds and weather'.[1] As usual after a disaster, accusations were flung about from all sides. King Philip, who declared later that he would have relieved Calais the day after it surrendered, accused Grey and Wentworth of having refused his offered troops; it is very possible that his accusation was true, and that at some time or another Spanish troops had been refused, for in many English minds there was a rooted suspicion that Philip wanted not so much to help, as to help himself to Calais. Yet Grey and Wentworth both denied the charge and retorted that they had sent out letter after letter to the King asking for succour.[2]

Henri II to whom the news of the great victory came in the dusk of an evening when he was dancing at a wedding, had his own theories as to the reasons for the success of the Guise. Calais had not, he said, a sufficient garrison, but if what men there were had been led by captains of experience and ability, the fortress would have held out till the relief from Flanders and England had arrived. The entry of these reliefs, said Henri, the Guise could not have prevented; and this was probably true, for his lines about Calais were long and there had been no time for entrenching on any considerable scale. In Henri's estimation the victory was won by the narrowest margin of time. If Calais had held out but one day longer he thought that François de Guise would have been driven to withdraw, even without the arrival of a relieving force, by those very gales which defeated the English efforts to send troops, but which, had they caught the French army outside Calais, would have been equally disastrous for the attack.[3]

In England, perhaps to salve wounded pride, treachery was the commonest explanation of the loss. Wentworth and several of his officers, including John Highfield, Master of the Ordnance, were indicted on a charge of selling Calais to the French. The trial did not take place till 1559, and then Wentworth and two others were acquitted, the verdict on Highfield being that he was guilty of negligence. But the acquittal of Wentworth does not prove his innocence, for at that time old scores against noted Protestants were very likely to be smudged off the slate.

Even if Wentworth were innocent of treachery, he was at best but a tepid fighter, and a man of little judgement or resolution. What Mary thought of him was plain, and plainly expressed in a letter which Michiel in France either saw, or heard quoted. For Wentworth was in command of a great fortress and 'being in such a place', said Mary, 'she marvelled at his standing in fear of his own shadow, openly reproaching him with cowardice.'[4] Yet inaction was perhaps his worst fault. Serious the Deputy must have known his position to be during the siege; from his letters it would seem that he thought it desperate; yet, this being so, it is hard to understand why, when he had let in water about Newnham Bridge, he did not go further, as he promised, and flood the whole country about Calais. Henri II certainly thought he was to blame in this, and that the reason for his negligence was that he feared to spoil next year's harvest on lands belonging to himself and others;[5] Highfield, who had a motive for trying to shift the blame from his own shoulders, said that Wentworth considered the flooding of the whole land was unnecessary, 'without more appearance of besieging, because the sea, being entered in, should hinder the pastures of the cattle, and also the brewing of the beer'.[6] On January 2nd, the Deputy told the Council that he must soon let in the salt water, beer or no beer.[7] Yet he did not do it, and Calais waited, as if paralysed, for the attack.

Yet, even if Wentworth were a true man, there may have been treachery in others. There had been so much talk of betrayal, so many sinister rumours about Henry Dudley and others, that perhaps there was fire amongst all the smoke. Nothing definite seems to have come out about any plot, but many still clung to the idea that a plot there had been. Savoy, questioning Highfield as to the reasons for the fall of the town, was told that 'the cause was not only the weakness of the Castle, and the lack of men, but also I thought that there was some treason, for as I heard, there were some that escaped out of the town, and the Frenchmen told me that they had intelligence of all our estate within the town'. Highfield himself was later arrested by Savoy on 'strong suspicion that there had been an understanding between him and the French'.[8]

This belief in treachery was strengthened by the siege of Guisnes. What could be done against the French by a man of gallantry and resolution was shown here. A minor fortress had held out for a week against a terrific bombardment and constant assaults by an army vastly superior in numbers. It was said that eight or nine thousand cannon-balls were fired against the Mary Bulwark alone. The Bulwark, always the 'windy corner' of the fighting, had been garrisoned by Burgundians, a few Spaniards, and Englishmen. The old Burgundian Captain, bedridden with gout, 'would not be let from his charge, but in his bed ended his life in the Bulwark'. When the small remnant escaped, there were, out of the 400 who had held the outwork, an English, a Burgundian, and a Spanish officer, and 27 men.[9]

Grey and his men did what they could to wipe out the slur that Calais left upon the English name, for the defence of Guisnes vindicated the courage of Englishmen. Let them be well led, and by a man who knew neither disloyalty nor fear, and they would fight to the death. Henri II himself told Michiel that the English 'let themselves be cut to pieces by the battery'; if, he said, the garrison had been entirely Spanish and English, Guisnes would not have surrendered, for it was the Flemings and Walloons who forced Grey to yield by refusing to fight.[10]

Whatever blame attaches to the defenders of Calais, certainly the Council at home was to blame for negligence, the unintentional muddled negligence of an unwieldy body, divided and quarrelsome, perpetually and increasingly short of money for the needs of government. Over-confident in the old reputation of Calais, they put off till too late such decisive and adequate measures as might have safeguarded the town and sent the Guise off after some other game. Even as late as December 29th they answered Wentworth's appeal of the 27th by a promise that the Earl of Rutland should come over and a couple of officers 'of good knowledge and service'; but no word of reinforcements. The Queen and her Council only promised to keep the Channel open and to send food.[11] Two days later, deceived, as Wentworth had been, by news of the Duc de Guise's appearance at New Hesdin, they cancelled even Rutland's commission.[12]

On January 2nd, however, the government wakened to a real alarm, and after that it was scurry and bustle and one order on another. First certain noblemen and gentlemen 'were ordered to raise 50 foot apiece and have them at Calais by Friday or Saturday next'.[13] The next thing was that these were to wait at Dover.[14] Two days later London was raising men for the Queen's navy.[15] On January 7th, the very day that Calais surrendered, the Queen was urging gentlemen of every shire to raise men to succour Calais, 'the principal member and chief jewel of our realm', which troops were to wear 'white coats with red crosses after the old accustomed manner of this realm'.[16] On January 9th the Vice-Admiral was ordered out to attempt to clear the narrow seas of those French ships that were standing off Calais to prevent relief arriving.[17] If he could do this he was to throw reinforcements into the town. A fishing boat of Rye was to carry letters to the governors of Philip's castles nearest Calais. Letters were to be shot in to Wentworth on cross-bow bolts.[18] All was hurry – letter followed letter and order, order.

It was not till January 10th that the 'heavy news came to England ... that the French had won Calais, the which was the heaviest tidings that ever was heard of'.[91] And that same day a great gale blew up the Channel beating the English ships, dismasting and driving them ashore, quenching all hope of relieving Guisnes. It was as if 'the same was done by necromancy and that the Devil was raised up and become French', so an Englishman said, but added cautiously, 'The truth whereof is known to God.'[20]

At the news of the attack the Queen had rallied all her courage, and even when Calais had fallen there was yet a hope that Guisnes might be saved. Sitting long at the Council table, signing letter after letter, Mary did her best, now that it was too late, to redeem the disaster. Though on January 13th 'our ships that were set towards the seas for the keeping of the passage and safe wafting over of our army ... have been so shaken and spoiled of their tackle, some of them also being dispersed abroad and others driven on shore', yet the men of that army which should have been 'wafted over' must be ready to start at an hour's warning.[21] In the third week of January she was calling up men from London, from the home and eastern counties, and from Kent, for the relief of Guisnes, and Philip had promised to clear the narrow seas for them.[22] A few days later she was scolding old Sir Thomas Cheyne because he mustered so few men in Kent, and these quite unprovided of their white cloth coats;[23] these same white coats, just such a detail as would catch Mary's interest, crop up in nearly every letter. Not till the end of the month were the levies disbanded, though nothing could have been done with such forces, being, as Cheyne complained, 'very simple men', and fit only for an emergency.[24]

Though Calais and the Pale were lost, the war went on; not only across the Channel but also for England along the Scots Border. Scotland had, as the ally of France, come into the war late in the summer of 1557. All that autumn there was the usual Border raiding–'manful service at the water side' by Henry Percy; Leonard Dacre riding night after moonlight night on the same sort of business. Philip refused to declare war upon the Scots, though, as the Council complained with much bitterness, England had incurred this Scots war by their declaration, on his behalf, of war against France.[25] Yet Scotland, even when fed with French troops, was no very dangerous enemy. The Queen Mother, Mary of Guise, might want war, but the greater part of the Scots nobles did not. When Huntley gave his voice for continuing the fighting he was asked 'would he be a Scot or a Frenchman?'[26] In October the Regent's army broke up and went home for that winter. Next year, though there was more fighting, it was a drain upon the exchequer indeed, but no pressing danger.

For a few months after the fall of Calais a French invasion on the south seemed much more imminent. The scare ran right along the south coast. The Lord Warden told the Queen that he had never seen Kent so unready and undefended. When Lord Montague inspected Sussex in May he declared that the county was in great danger, since 'for five or six miles from the sea coast there is only plain downs, without stick of woods', and the inhabitants were so conscious of their indefensible position that they were actually leaving their homes when he arrived.[27]

The Isle of Wight and the west were, however, considered to be the most vulnerable spots. The island could be defended by the fleet, but the long coast line beyond must look to itself. Elaborate instructions were given to the Earl of Bedford, appointed Lieutenant of the three westernmost counties. He was to see to the building of beacons, and these were to be watched night and day by men 'who do know and understand the meaning of their charge'. Besides that, he had orders to call the local gentlemen up and take muster of the tenantry, provide for the defence of places likely to be attacked, arrange for posts to ride inland with news of invasion, and if the worst happened, to retreat to a strong town, breaking bridges, cutting branches and throwing down trees behind them.[28]

In July news came which suddenly not only restored something of confidence but even gave hope of the recovery of Calais. The French made a sudden attack on Dunkirk, and had taken it. But with the English and Flemish fleets supporting him, Egmont had caught the French army, under the

25

Captain of Calais, before Gravelines, and broke it, while the fleets bombarded it from the sea. Doubtless it gave Clinton pleasure to report that 'especially the bands of Calais went to wrack, so as very few returned home'.[29] As a consequence of this victory Dunkirk was retaken. Now was the chance, while the French were shaken and reduced in number, to make an attempt to regain Calais also. One of the Vice-Admirals produced a plan. He was rewarded by a pension, but the plan was never put into practice.[30]

Yet for all that, Englishmen did not give up hope. Even in Elizabeth's reign it was thought worth while to draw up lists of 'such persons dwelling in Callyce and Hames, as be well affected to the English nation. . . . In Calis Mistress Burton, at the three heads. In Calis, at the balance, the wife is sure. In Calis, Sergeant Marian, the sergeant of the haven . . . a sure and trustie friend . . .'[31] and so on. But now Philip, for whose sake, as all Englishmen knew, Calais was lost, did not do over much for its recovery. The negotiations which closed the war were not terminated during Mary's lifetime, but before her death it was already plain to many observers that the King of Spain would not make the restoration of Calais a *sine qua non* in the settlement.

It is Foxe who related that anecdote of Mary which is known by everyone who has been taught English history. What Foxe heard was on the authority of 'Master Rice', and a Master Rice had been in Mary's household when she was Princess. Rice told Foxe that he, with Dame Clarencieux, 'being most familiar and most bold about her', noticing the Queen's 'much sighing', asked her if she were sorrowing for the King who had left her. 'Not that only,' said she, 'but when I am dead and opened you shall find Calais lying in my heart.'[32]

Those words, hackneyed now almost to nullity, caught the imagination of Foxe, as they have caught popular imagination ever since. Even the writer of the *Book of Martyrs*, even those readers of his who execrated the 'Bloody Mary' of Protestant tradition, felt a prick of sympathy for the woman who spoke them.

And no wonder, for in them Mary betrayed a grief within a grief. Spain had failed her; by now, obstinate as she was, and faithful to her loyalties, she must have known it. But this was not the worst—she had failed England. When Calais was lost that loss and the shame of it must have thrown the Spanish Tudor back upon her inheritance of English blood which she had too long forgotten. Now at the last she remembered what she had once before known at her miraculous accession, that England was not only the England of greedy courtiers and false great lords of the Council, but of the thousands of simple folk who had used to love her. The humiliation of defeat taught her to remember that England had as proud a past as Spain, and to know that she herself was an Englishwoman.

Her realization of this came too late. All through her reign her Spanish affections had set her upon a course right athwart that of the England of her adult life. Hatred of the Spanish alien in England, jealousy of the Spaniard waxing rich as Croesus in the marvellous Indies—these two passions were growing and strengthening in Englishmen, fostered by every device that the Protestant party would imagine, and Mary would have had to change her very nature in order to sympathize with such emotions.

After her marriage the divergence between her and her subjects increased. The Queen, so the Venetian Surian said, wished nothing but to please King Philip, and Philip had very clear notions as to what rôle England was to play in the Habsburg scheme of things; he had hoped that the Queen would provide an heir, to found a new Habsburg dynasty; Mary had failed to do that; but the kingdom might still supply him with money, and a sort of out-work for the defence of the Netherlands. It was no part of his scheme that England should compete for the trade of Spain. While Mary lived he stifled as far as he might the first stirrings of that great outburst of adventurous commercial enterprise which filled the reign of Elizabeth with a record of greed, daring, and noble self-sacrifice.

Already in Mary's lifetime there were signs of what was to come. Venetian ambassadors praised the seamanship of those English sailors who could leave and enter the port of Calais in any weather, and Venetians knew a good seaman when they saw one.[33] After the loss of Calais the course of the war at sea was not inglorious. The English fleet, once recovered from the storm, held the Channel. There were raids and burnings along the French coast; not great victories in themselves, but leaving no doubt as to who was master of the Narrow Sea. There were such engagements as that of the *Mary Rose* and a French warship. The *Mary Rose* had a crew of twenty-two men and a few boys; the Frenchman was said to have two hundred. For two hours the English ship, without any help from two small vessels in her company, engaged the Frenchman, actually boarding her once, and if, said Henry Machyn proudly, 'if the *Mary Rose* had enough men to hold her, they would have brought the Frenchman off'.[34]

Already also there were signs that England, not exhausted by wars, and not burdened by scattered possessions, was seeking outlets for that abundant energy which made the kingdom so hard to govern. English seamen, who had grown up with tales of the New World in their ears, were ready now to emulate the great adventurers of Spain and Portugal. English merchants began to find their markets cramped. But, since the Pope had divided the newly discovered lands between Spain and Portugal, and since both these powers (and Philip spoke for both) were jealous of trespassers, English merchants were thwarted in their appetite for novelty. In 1556 some merchants fitted out ships which should have tapped the source of the King of Portugal's trade in Guinea. They were warned off by Philip; they protested, and pleaded. Philip was unmoved. Loss or no loss, their ships should not sail.[35]

In another direction English trade had already taken the initiative. In the summer of 1553, while Edward VI was yet alive. Sir Hugh Willoughby sailed in the *Bona Speranza* with Richard Chancellor in the *Edward Bonaventura*, on that voyage 'intended for the discovery of Cathay' which brought Willoughby to his death, and England into touch with Russia. It was May when they went down the river past Greenwich; 'the greater ships are towed down with boats, and oars, and the mariners being all apparelled in watchet or sky-coloured cloth rowed amaine. .... And being come near to Greenwich ... presently upon the news thereof the Courtiers came running out, and the common people flocked together, standing very thick upon the shore; the Privy Council, they looked out at the windows of the Court, and the rest ran up to the tops of the towers.' So with shooting of guns and cheering of the sailors, 'insomuch that the tops of the hills sounded therewith, the valleys and the waters gave an Echo', the ships went down the river. 'But alas, the good King Edward (in respect of whom principally all this was prepared), he only by reason of his sickness was absent from this show.'[36]

Edward's sister was on the throne when Richard Chancellor's ship returned. Sir Hugh Willoughby was lost; he and his men were found afterwards, frozen to death in a Lapland bay. But Chancellor had 'held on his course towards that unknown part of the world, and sailed so far that he came at last to the place where he found no night at all, but a continual light and brightness of the Sun shining clearly upon the huge and mighty sea'.[37] So, reaching the White Sea at last he landed at the mouth of the Dwina and learned that the shore he touched was that of Russia or Muscovy.

In 1555 Chancellor sailed again on a second voyage charged with a mission to the Tsar, and instructions to treat for the establishment of trade relations with Russia. He did this, saw Moscow, and next year in July, set out for home, with four ships, two of them being those lost in Willoughby's expedition, and now recovered. But this time Chancellor's luck was out. Willoughby's two ships were never heard of again; the *Edward Bonaventura* foundered in Pitsligo Bay and with her went down her Captain and most of the crew.

But one of the few survivors was an ambassador from Muscovy, a man whose name, Osep Napea, was no stranger than his garb to the staring country folk who saw him ride towards London at the end of February 1557, escorted by eighty merchants in gold chains, members presumably of the new Muscovy Company, once the Merchant Adventurers, who had brought him all the way from Scotland. A foxhunt was arranged in his honour. Then Viscount Montague met him and his escort with three hundred horsemen. Outside London four merchants presented him with a richly trapped horse; he was welcomed by the Lord Mayor, and so rode to his lodging in Fenchurch Street, where stood the 'bed of estate with furniture and hangings', which had been lent to the Merchant Adventurers, for their guest, out of the Wardrobe of the Tower. But if the Russian's escort of Englishmen was pompous, and the Queen's gifts to him magnificent—cloth of gold raised with crimson velvet, purple velvet, damask purfled, and crimson damask—certainly the ambassador himself was worthy of such display, for the gown he wore was 'of tissue embroidered with pearls and jewels' and even his night-cap was set with pearls and stones.[38]

But this north-eastern commercial venture, innocent as it seemed, and remote from any Spanish interests, was looked upon with suspicion by some

Spaniards at least. The Russian ambassador had taken his leave of both Queen and King in 1557; Philip was resplendent in his velvet Garter robes; the Muscovite did reverence 'in the manner of his country, which is to bend his body like the cordeliers, and touch the ground with his right hand'; all had been diplomatic politeness.[39] But next year, in March, Fresneda, Philip's confessor, and a man much in his confidence, was writing a warning to the King. The English, Fresneda thought, had an ulterior motive in these Russian expeditions. He only hoped that 'these voyages may not be the cause of trouble between Spain and England, for it is easily to be understood that the object of them is to go thence to the Spanish Indies'.[40] Englishmen in fact would learn, from the Russians, of that yet undiscovered North-Eastern passage to Cathay, which seemed so possible to contemporary geographers.

Whether that suspicion was justified or no, it is undeniable that what signs there were of the future of English expansion at sea were mostly to be found in those quarters where there was most enmity to the Queen and her Spanish policy. Long ago, while Edward VI was still alive, Northumberland with the French ambassador had straitly questioned Sebastian Cabot as to Peru, 'I,' Cabot reported to the Emperor, 'told them that it was a rich country in silver and gold . . . [and] I got out of both of them that they wished to fit out a fleet for the Amazon river. . . . On board there would be 4,000 soldiers, not counting seamen.' Their plan was to build a fort at the mouth of the river, and from thence work upwards in pinnaces, conquering the country from the Spaniards.[41] Such a plan, in its daring and its scope, was worthy of John Dudley.

During Mary's reign it was such men as Peter Killigrew, the Horseys, the Tremaynes, and other out-at-elbows refugees trying to mend their fortunes by indiscriminate piracy, who anticipated by a few years, and in the confined waters of the Channel, the methods of Elizabethan seamen. Killigrew, taken at sea in a French ship, the *Sacret*, came to the Tower and to the question for his evil practices; he might have fared much worse than he did had not war broken out within the next nine months; but then such men as he were too valuable to waste, and the ex-pirate, ex-refugee, all but ex-rebel, appears as Captain of her Majesty's ship *Gerfalcon*.[42]

But, in one of Killigrew's confessions there occurs a remark significant indeed. He and his friends intended, he said, to go a voyage to 'pirrow or gynney' without any merchandise but to take prizes, 'they cared not of whom'.[43] Now Peru was the Emperor's, and Guinea was the preserve of the King of Portugal. This was to try a higher flight than Channel piracy.

But if, in England, the sap was stirring, and spring on the way, with the Queen it was not so. The future was not for her, and the past held nothing but failure. Apart from Philip, one thing always she had hoped for, above all others – the restoration of the Catholic Church in England. She must have known by now that it was doomed to go down at her death. The burning of heretics went grimly on, but there were always more heretics ready to be burned. People looked on with a growing disgust; the church of that Queen who had married a Spaniard began to seem to many an alien un-English church; after Calais was lost her subjects had less respect than ever for her and for it; and 'not a third of the usual number' of people, it was said, went to mass.[44]

Another disappointment darkened for her the first days of summer. In January, after the loss of Calais, she had announced to the King that she was with child;[45] she had delayed the news until then, so that there might be no doubt this time. Count Feria had been sent over at once, ostensibly to express Philip's delight at the happy news; more probably to discover whether it could possibly be true. It was not true. On May 1st the Spaniard informed his master that the symptoms had again been delusive.[46]

All through that spring and early summer the Queen had been ailing; and Feria noted that his master's interests suffered when she could not attend to them.[47] Philip grew more interested in her than he had been for some time, for those disorders, natural enough for an expectant mother, must, if there were no state of pregnancy, carry a more serious interpretation. His plans had for some time run beyond the end of Mary's life, and he now became acutely anxious to settle the future before all power in England passed out of his hands. Several times already he had suggested, or rather urged Savoy as a suitable husband for Elizabeth, who must, unless Mary of Scotland were to succeed, be looked upon as the heir of England; and Mary of Scotland, the bride of the French Dauphin, was the last person in the world whom Philip would have chosen to see upon the throne of England.

Elizabeth, in Philip's eyes, was different. She was, it is true, suspected, and on very good grounds, of being a concealed Protestant; she had also a reputation of wit and guile. But, properly married, she might serve Philip's turn well enough, and Savoy, a pensioner of Spain, dependent on Philip for any hope he had of recovering his patrimony from the grasp of the French, was a very proper bridegroom.

In June 1556, Henri II had told Soranzo that the Emperor intended to take Elizabeth to Spain and perhaps marry her to Don Carlos.[48] In December his news was that Madame Elizabeth had been sent for to Court and told that she was to marry Savoy. But Elizabeth refused. She wanted no husband; her sorrows were such that she wanted nothing but death; and she wept so bitterly that the Queen's eyes filled with tears.[49] Mary thereupon sent her away from Court and the matter dropped. But it was raised again when Philip came to England next year. In a roundabout way the Venetians heard that the Duchess of Lorraine, who came to England with Philip, was to take Elizabeth back with her for the marriage. But whether it were the Queen, the Council, Elizabeth herself, or all three who resisted the project, it again fell through.

Probably all three resisted; almost certainly Mary did. For, soon after the war started, Philip, more and more anxious to safeguard the future, made another attempt, this time trying to force the Queen to have the marriage celebrated without troubling Parliament for their leave. What is known of this wretched business, and wretched it was for Mary, seeing that her repeated refusal was alienating what little there was left of Philip's affection, is to be learnt from a letter of hers, answering one of his.[50] That letter, with its hurried apologies, its reiterated promises, explanations, and excuses, is the measure of Mary's unhappiness and abasement.

'I have received', she wrote, 'Your Highness's letters of the 18th of this month, and thank you most humbly for them, especially since you write . . . that you have taken mine in good part, for I assure you that I did mean well in them, and seeing that Your Highness did the same, I will say nothing now except, seeing that you hold that I should examine my conscience to know if it is in conformity with the truth or no, to supplicate your Highness most humbly to name and appoint what persons you judge fit to speak with me about this affair, and I will hear them with a very true and sincere heart, whoever they may be. Notwithstanding, in my last letter I promised to Your Highness that I would agree to this marriage . . . if I should have the consent of the kingdom, and this I will do, but without that consent I fear that in the end neither Your Highness nor the kingdom will be the better for it. For once before, you remember, by my own request I heard Your Highness' friars, but then Alphonso propounded to me questions so dark that my poor understanding could not comprehend them; as for one, he asked me–who was king when Adam lived; and told me that I was constrained by one of the articles of my Credo to make this marriage. But he explained nothing of those things which are too hard for me to understand, so that, in so short a time it is impossible for me to regulate my conscience. But one thing I promise to Your Highness upon my faith to you, that what men soever it shall please you to appoint to me, they shall not find me stubborn, nor I hope, unreasonable.

'But, since Your Highness writes in those letters, that if Parliament set itself against this thing, you will lay the blame upon me, I beseech you in all humility, to put off the business till your return, and then you shall be judge if I am blameworthy or no. For otherwise Your Highness will be angry against me, and that will be worse than death for me, for already I have begun to taste your anger all too often, to my great sorrow. And to be plain with you, according to my simple judgement, and under Your Highness' correction, seeing that the Duke of Savoy is just now away at the war, and certain of the Council and nobility of this realm with Your Highness, I cannot see in what way the affair could be well managed, nor to my mind (even if my conscience were as clear about it as yours), could it come to the end you desire without your presence here.

'Wherefore, my lord, in as humble sort as I may, I, your most true and obedient wife–(which indeed I confess that I ought to be, and to my thinking more than all other wives, having such a husband as Your Highness–not that I am speaking of the multitude of your kingdoms, for that is not the chief thing in my eyes), I beg Your Majesty that we two should pray to God and put our whole trust in him, that we may live and come together again; and that very God who has the thoughts of the hearts of princes in his hand, will,

I make no doubt, so enlighten us, that the outcome shall be his glory and your contentation. But I beg Your Highness nevertheless to pardon my assurance of God's mercy. For, though I have not deserved, nevertheless I have had experience of it, and that beyond the expectation of all the world, in whom I have the same hope that I have always had.'

Philip's motive in all this is simple and obvious. The Queen's refusal is harder to understand. Did she really consider the consent of Englishmen necessary? Or was she trying to use this business of the marriage to bring Philip once again to her? Probably both of these. But one of the many inter-lineations in the letter gives a clue to yet another motive. Most of the corrections are designed to soften and lower its tone–as the original, 'to ask Your Highness' permission', is altered to, 'beg most humbly'. But there is another in which Mary's stubborn, and alas! embittered spirit speaks, and that is an addition which Strype, who copied the letter, did not reproduce. After the words–'I will say nothing now except, seeing that you hold that I should examine my conscience to know if it is in conformity with the truth or no, to supplicate Your Highness most humbly to name and appoint what persons you judge fit to speak with me about this affair,' Mary added, 'for that which my conscience holds, it has held for this four and twenty years'. It was twenty-four years since Elizabeth was born. But what was this that Mary in her conscience had held since the year of Elizabeth's birth?

The Venetians, whose secret service was excellent, learned something of what had gone on at an interview between Philip's confessor de Fresneda, and Mary, which must have taken place soon after this letter was written. Fresneda had been sent 'to persuade her for the safety and quiet of the Kingdom and religion, lest Elizabeth, feeling herself spurned, should . . . take an anti-Spanish husband, to give her hope of the succession'. But the Queen refused, 'obstinately maintaining that she (Elizabeth) was neither her sister nor the daughter of . . . King Henry, nor would she hear of favouring her, as she was born of an infamous woman, who had so greatly outraged the Queen her mother, and herself'.[51] This then was 'what Mary's conscience had held for four and twenty years'. And now, in the last months of her life, when the Queen saw everything break and fall away under her hand–her hope of issue gone, Philip's love gone. Calais gone, Catholic England gone–now all that hoarded bitterness of her kind but not easy temper rose and filled her. Even the argument that a Catholic husband for Elizabeth would safeguard the restored religion in England failed to move her. She would not acknowledge Elizabeth as her successor, see her married, perhaps even see her bear the child which had been denied to the Queen herself. She would not let Philip, with the cold humanity of statesmanship, prepare to set Elizabeth on the throne in her place. Yet, had Mary dreamed that as an alternative he would contem-plate more than this, proposing to set Elizabeth in her place as his wife, surely she would have hurried the young woman into no matter what other marriage. She did not know or guess it, and with a tragic and very human weakness, she let her jealousy of Elizabeth take hold of her. Ill, utterly defeated and forlorn, in this she forgot even that 'assurance of God's mercy', which, like many another she had not deserved but had experienced.

Yet, though he could not persuade, Philip could still punish her with his displeasure. In April 1558 an ambassador arrived from the King of Sweden to propose his son as bridegroom for Elizabeth. Mary, hearing this, and knowing how very contrary to Philip's plans such a marriage would be, grew almost distracted. She thought Feria was reporting unfavourably to Philip on her conduct of affairs, she thought that Philip 'would blame her for not having concluded that (marriage) of a year ago'. 'After Madame Elizabeth had replied that she had no wish to marry,' Feria reported to Philip, 'she calmed down, but she is still in a terrible taking about it.'[52]

The summer drew on, a very sickly summer, and the Queen was a very sick woman. She could not sleep; her old accustomed 'melancholy', that 'superfluity of black bile' as her doctors called it, returned. In June she was 'worse than usual'. In August she was ill again. In September she had a high temperature, an unusual symptom for her, but the doctors affirmed that her ordinary trouble would, mysteriously, be the better for it. Just what her disease was, no one seemed exactly to know. Neither Feria nor d'Assonleville gave it a name; Foxe doubtfully says 'a dropsy' which might mean almost anything, though perhaps a tumour had been the cause of her late hope of pregnancy. It has also been suggested that the 'fever' abroad in England that summer was a serious form of influenza, and that the Queen contracted this;[53] but if so this would account only for the last few weeks of her illness.

At all events, in the third week of October the news from England was so serious that Philip decided to send Feria once more with one of his own physicians. It was not, however, in order to preserve the Queen's life that the Count was to hurry across the Channel. His mission was, at this last moment, to press Mary once more to do what she had so often refused, that is to give Elizabeth in marriage to a Spanish nominee, and with promise of succession.[54]

There were others as interested as the King in that last question. The Council, London, all England was shaken with excitement. Most men looked to Elizabeth. But some, so Philip's ambassador, d'Assonleville, heard, began to believe that the Netherlandish alliance would still be necessary and thought of a Spanish husband for her; others favoured an English bridegroom, the Earl of Westmorland, or Arundel; others spoke of a Danish or Swedish prince; Elizabeth herself was believed to be considering 'a Scottish lord, her kinsman, a handsome and noble youth, son of a sister of Henry VIII, who was married in Scotland'; that is perhaps, more correctly, the grandson of Margaret Tudor, Henry Darnley, thirteen years old now but always a big boy for his age.[55]

The first week of November saw some alleviation in the Queen's condition. The attacks of her illness ceased for a few days, and she had intervals of quiet. At once the Council seized their opportunity. Weighty were the reasons they put before her why she should now nominate Elizabeth as her heir, and at last

Mary surrendered. On November 8th, the Master of the Rolls and the new Comptroller, Boxall, were bidden to go to Hatfield; they were to tell Elizabeth that the Queen was very glad she should succeed to the Crown, and they were to ask her to make two promises – one to maintain the old religion, the other, to pay the Queen's debts.[56]

The arguments which the Council urged upon Mary are not recorded, but they are easy to imagine. Yet it was probable that Mary herself was not much to be moved by any reasoning which the Councillors could have imagined – she was drifting beyond arguments into that state of peaceful carelessness that comes sometimes when death had been accepted by the body, and the human mind and soul know that they have no more business in the world.

She had now only to wait for death. Three years ago, when she believed that she was to bear a child, she had made her will; those bequests, saving that there was no child to whom she might leave the Crown, should stand. There was money to poor scholars at Oxford and Cambridge, an endowment for a hospital for disabled soldiers, the first of such, had it ever been founded; bequests to her re-founded monasteries; to Philip a prayer that he would accept 'and keep for a memory of me, one jewel' that 'table diamond' which the Emperor had sent her at her betrothal; then, as if she could not stop giving to him, a list of several more, among them Philip's first Christmas present to her.[57]

To this will she had, at the end of October 1558, added a codicil, which did little more than acknowledge the mistake she had made – 'as I then thought myself to be with child' – and call upon her successor to fulfil the terms of the will.[58] When she had done that she had done all that was possible.

On November 9th, the day after her surrender to the importunities of the Council, Feria arrived. He was primed with secret instructions for the Queen, for Pole and for Figueroa, who had remained in England to watch his master's interests; he brought also a letter to Mary. No doubt it was full of the same business as those secret instructions, but she, though pleased to receive it, had, mercifully, slipped too far into the mists of sickness to be able to read it, though the sight of Feria reminded her of fears that could no longer touch her, and she told him that if the King made peace without getting Calais back for England 'it would cost her her head'.[59]

But now for long periods she was unconscious; once she spoke regretting a wedding that she would not see; Jane Dormer, one of her maids, and dear to her, was betrothed to Feria; Mary had delayed their marriage, always hoping that Philip would return; now she was sorry she had done so.[60] Another time when she drifted out of unconsciousness, she saw that her women were crying. The Queen 'comforted those of them that grieved about her; she told them what good dreams she had, seeing many little children like Angels play before her, singing pleasing notes'.[61] Music and little children – she had loved both during her life, and now, instead of anxieties, sorrows, and uncertainties, her dreams were full of these.

On November 17th she heard Mass very early in the morning, as she heard it every day, and was able to make the responses. At six o'clock, before the daylight came, she died.[61] On the evening of the same day, at Lambeth, died her cousin, Reginald Pole, the Cardinal of England, so like to her, as people said, in mind and temper, so like, as he himself had told her, in the fortune of their lives.

Perhaps no other reign in English history has seen such a great endeavour made, and so utterly defeated. All that Mary did was undone, all she intended utterly unfulfilled. But, as her body, without its inhabiting soul, lay stiff and still in the empty palace of St. James, deaf to the clatter of horses' hoofs as the last hastily departing courtiers rode up the hill to take the Edgware Road, her soul surely had come into peace. For, mistaken often, almost always misguided in her public office, with much blindness, some rancour, some jealousy, some stupid cruelty to answer for, she had yet trodden, lifelong and manfully, the way that other sinners know. If her enemies could have brought her, as Pharisees brought another woman, to Christ, in the temple at Jerusalem, He might again have stooped down, written in the dust, and then, looking up, dismissed them with the same unanswerable word.

Note on Authorities

OF THE contemporary authorities from which this life of Mary Tudor has been drawn, the largest in extent is that vast ocean–the various *Calendars of State Papers* published by order of the Master of the Rolls. Among these Calendars the widest in its scope is the magnificent collection of documents called *Letters and Papers, Foreign and Domestic, Henry VIII*, in which ambassadors' reports, Thomas Cromwell's memoranda, depositions of prisoners, lists of the King's Christmas presents, copies of the King's love-letters, are mingled with the letters of all sorts of men, English and foreign, gentle and simple, at home or abroad. Yet, huge as is the variety contained, and adequately full as are the transcriptions and abridgements, it would be pleasant, had a student several lives, to go from these to the originals, and to discover those trivial things crowded out of the *Letters and Papers*, as for instance that in 1539 those who examined Sir Anthony Browne thought it worth while to ask him 'Why he should have such affection to the said Lady Mary.' To which he 'saith that he was only moved thereunto for the love he beareth to the King, for never received love messages, tokens, or recommendations from her, nor hath sent her any'.

More specialized than this massive work are the *Calendars of State Papers, Venetian and Spanish*. The Venetian intelligence service was always excellent, Venetian ambassadors generally impartial and discerning; Navagero, ambassador to the Papacy during the pontificate of Paul IV, added to these qualities a zest for reproducing the half-crazy vehemence of the Pope's conduct and conversation, that goes beyond the limits of a diplomatist's duty, and re-creates for the reader that strange, feverish, intractable old man. Unfortunately for the student of English affairs in Mary's reign, after the departure of Michiel from London in October 1557, no other Venetian ambassador was accredited to England. During the last year, therefore, of Mary's life, we are deprived of this valuable witness.

In the *Calendar of State Papers, Spanish*, our luck is even worse. The successive Spanish ambassadors during the reign of Henry VIII and Edward VI were naturally keenly interested in Mary; their letters provide information which often no one else could have acquired, since whatever the Spanish or rather the Imperial ambassador in England, he was, after the beginning of the divorce proceedings against Katherine of Aragon, in Mary's confidence. Most unfortunately, however, the publication of this Calendar was interrupted.* It is a copious source until December 1553, but from that date until after the end of Mary's reign nothing more is printed. The stream, however, runs underground, if one may be allowed such a figure of speech, for another year.

* See Foreword, p. XIII.

Those who choose may tap it in Dr. Royall Tyler's *Transcripts* at the Public Record Office, which carry on the story till the arrival of Philip in England and are invaluable for these first months of Mary's reign. After that date the reports of Spanish envoys sent over by Philip must be sought in such foreign collections as those of Weiss, Gachard, and Kervyn de Lettenhove.

No collection of documents drawn from French ambassadorial sources has been published in England, though during the period covered these of course appear in the *Letters and Papers, Henry VIII*. For Edward's and for Mary's reign they must be sought in French editions. Odet de Selve's *Correspondance*, covering the period between 1546 and 1549, has been edited by Lefèvre-Pontalis. The letters of the de Noailles brothers exist in the small eighteenth-century edition of Vertot. This source again ceases abruptly in 1557 with the English declaration of war, but apart from this, Vertot published by no means all of the documents existing in the Bibliothèque Nationale. Transcripts of these made by M. Baschet, and included among the *Transcripts* at the Public Record Office, must be used to fill in the gaps.

Letters and Papers, Henry VIII included, as we have seen, documents of both Domestic and Foreign interest. But after 1547 these two classes were separated by the editors, and the foreign and domestic papers published separately. Nor is this separation the only change. Instead of the twenty-one broad-shouldered volumes of the *Letters and Papers*, many of them in two, some in three parts, there is, for the Foreign papers of the succeeding years, one volume each of the reigns of Edward VI and Mary, and for the Domestic, a single volume which covers the whole period from 1547 to 1580. Naturally therefore, not only is the material calendared far less varied – the editor indeed confining himself to the *State Papers, Domestic*, at the Public Record Office, but even these documents are allowed only the briefest summary.

It is necessary therefore to go to the MS. State Papers, preserved at the Public Record Office to get any idea of the contents of the documents calendared. No one who does this will regret the necessity, though a student coming new to the handwritings of the second quarter of the sixteenth century, may at first despair at the sight of some of the pages. Clerks, taking down with scurrying pen the confessions of prisoners in the Tower, had some excuse for handwriting which is bad even for a bad period; but why, one is inclined to ask with some bitterness, why did Sir John Mason, that witty and informed letter writer, always use inferior ink that paled and sank into the paper? And why did he always, apparently, write with a broken quill? Reading through these volumes, a student becomes as familiar with some handwritings as with that of many a friend. There is Cuthbert Tunstal's exquisite adorned signature, Elizabeth's elegant Italianate hand; Mary's, Italian too, but very different from her sister's, being always bold, square, and uncompromising.

Among these Papers the greatest connected series of documents is that which concerns the Dudley and Throgmorton Plot, in this a contrast to Wyatt's rebellion, the history of which is represented by a few documents only. There are here not only depositions of the chief conspirators, but also of simple men; of a bricklayer; of some sailors – how they went for a walk, came to a farm, asked to buy ale, and were given some, and then directed on their way, past a pond and down a lane. The answers of the chief prisoners, however, make anything but pleasant reading, and the confessions of all but John Throgmorton are copious and repeated and shamelessly unreserved.

To return to the printed authorities: there are, besides the great collections of documents two other smaller but still official sources. The *Acts of the Privy Council* are complete and published for the period. In the *3rd and 4th Reports of the Deputy Keeper of the Public Records* contents of the 'Baga de Secretis' are published. The 'Baga' themselves, white sheepskin bags, tied up with thongs, are to be seen in the Public Record Office; they contain the very parchments, indictments, Commission of Oyer and Terminer, etc., used in the treason trials of four hundred years ago.

In addition to these systematic and official collections of documents there are many which are partial, such as that of Tytler – *England under Edward VI and Mary*; but Tytler certainly had as good an eye and thumb as Jack Horner, so that the collection, though not large, is both varied and interesting. There are, besides, such books as Ellis's *Original Letters*, the *Miscellaneous State Papers* (Hardewick), and Hearne's *Sylloge Epistolarum*, the last of which contains in full letters of Mary only summarized in *Letters and Papers, Henry VIII*.

Special collections of letters may be also mentioned here. Stephen Gardiner, one of the wittiest and pleasantest letter writers, is always good reading and full of rapid and terse illustrative anecdote, for he was a man who could not tell a friend of unreasonable demand by the Council, without adding that this 'was like the balowing the priest made in the north for bringing the ducks again that were lost, for he said the parishioners must bring them again, see them or see them not'. Unfortunately for the student of Mary's reign, Gardiner's letters are almost all of dates previous to her accession and in subject unconnected with her, but they are nevertheless invaluable as demonstrating the conservative theory of the Bishop. Of another calibre are those letters of Sir Henry Bedingfield published by the Norfolk Archaeological Society, which gives the official but often laughable account of Elizabeth's detention at Woodstock.

The sixteenth century saw the last of the chroniclers; but it also saw the first of the Diarists. In this royalty led the way, for Edward VI kept a diary in which he mingled matters of State with records of his games and his illnesses. Master Henry Machyn, an undertaker, followed this new fashion; he had always one eye on the funerals of the week, but was by no means oblivious to more dangerous doings in London. Indeed he stands between the diarists and the last chroniclers. Then there is Wriothesley, who belonged entirely to the chroniclers; he came of a family of heralds, and was cousin to Lord Chancellor Wriothesley; there is also the writer of the *Chronicle of Queen Jane and Queen Mary*, probably Rowland Lee, an official in the Mint, with friends in the Tower who could give him much information; and there is the keeper of the Grey Friars' Chronicle which continues after the dissolution; and writing some time after the events, yet an accurate observer and a keen antiquarian by nature, there is Master John Stow, the merchant tailor who, 'tall of stature, lean of body and face, his eyes small and chrystalline', had watched and remembered so much of the past. On a different footing from all these is that lively, scandalous hotch-potch of gossip and rumour *The Chronicle of King Henry VIII of England*, the work probably of a Spanish inn-keeper and interpreter.

For special events and crises there are several accounts by men who either participated in the action or who looked on. De Guaras, a Spanish merchant, resident in London, wrote an account of Mary's accession. John Proctor, a Kentish man and schoolmaster of Tonbridge, set down what he believed to be the truth about Wyatt's rebellion, so as to vindicate the name of Kent from the indiscriminate charge of treason, since people would talk 'as though very few of Kent were free from Wyatt's conspiracy'.

In the sixteenth century the memoir, that form so foreign to the medieval literary habit, began to come to its own. Earliest of these, and greatest in its simplicity and power, is the *Life of Cardinal Wolsey* by George Cavendish, which does not so much describe, as suddenly throw open a small casement upon the sights and sounds of four hundred years ago, so that the reader hears the clattering of the men at arms' pikes as they lead a prisoner to execution, or watches a man leaning against a tree by the archery butts at Hampton Court, so deep in thought that he does not see the King who comes up behind and claps him on the shoulder. Arthur Grey, son of that Lord Grey of Wilton who defended Guisnes so well, and himself a participator in the defence, wrote, probably during the next five years or so, an account of his father's life, culminating in that piece of magnificently vigorous prose which describes the siege. More of the same siege can be learned from another Englishman, Thomas Churchyard, in Arber's *English Garner*, and there is an interesting French account of the fall of Calais in *Archives curieuses de l'histoire de France*.

Long after the death of Mary, Jane Dormer, once her young maid, now the old Countess de Feria, had an English steward by name Henry Clifford. In 1643, thirty years after the death of the Countess, Clifford published a life of his mistress. He was himself an old man by that time and his work looks across the years of a full century to the childhood of Jane. But it must have been founded on what he had himself heard from his mistress, that noble old lady to whom Englishmen in Spain would while she lived pay their respects, and bring her news of the new England she did not know.

But there is another body of information, dense and intractable as a tropical forest—the letters, controversial writings and the histories of the makers of the Reformation. Into that forest I have ventured but a little way, fearing to be lost, and I have relied chiefly on the accounts which others have brought back from it – upon Professor Gairdner, Canon Dixon, S. R. Maitland, P. S. Allen and others. Yet, though the heart faints, some of that tract must be penetrated. Strype's *Ecclesiastical Memorials* are a part of the wood, but cleared of undergrowth. Foxe is primeval forest, closely packed, richly various, and untamed. Nicholls's edited *Narratives of the . . . Reformation* are, as it were, scattered spinneys and easier far to penetrate.

For the background of the period, there are a number of descriptions of contemporary England, from Leland to Harrison: the Venetians contribute perhaps the most reliable foreign version, a Frenchman, Etienne Perlin, one of the most amusing, with his careful hints on manners and pronunciation; 'ou es ou goud ad Paul's' was, so he said, the correct English words to use, should you wish to ask your way to St. Paul's. John Stow, describing, recording, comparing, with inexhaustible patience, the records of London, his own memories, and the present London in which he wrote, is in a class by himself. Again, not to be numbered among any formal descriptions of place or period, but none the less revealing, are the *Household Books of Princess Mary*; many dead people, dealing with the small material things of every day, come to life in these purely utilitarian pages.

List of Authorities

MSS.

Baga de Secretis. In the Public Record Office.
Baschet. Transcripts.
State Papers. Domestic. In the Public Record Office.
Tyler, R. Transcripts. In the Public Record Office.

PRINTED AUTHORITIES

Contemporary

A Collection of Ordinances and Regulations for the Government of the Royal Household. Society of Antiquaries. 1790.
Acts of the Privy Council, 1542. Ed. J. R. Dasent, 1890–1907.
Ambassades de Messieurs de Noailles en Angleterre. Pub. Vertot à Leyde, 1763.
Antiquarian Repertory, a Miscellany . . . 1807–9.
Arber, *English Garner*. Vol. VI, 1903, from ed. of 1877–96.
Archives curieuses de l'histoire de France. 1e serie. Paris. 1855.
Baxter, Richard, *Reliquiae Baxterianae*. London. 1696.
Beccatelli, I., *Life of Cardinal Pole*. Trans. B. Pye. 1766.
Bedingfield, *Papers*. Ed. C. R. Manning. Norfolk and Norwich Archaeological Soc., Vol. IV. 1855.
Calendar of State Papers. Venetian. 1502–1557.
Calendar of State Papers. Spanish. 1485–1553.
Calendar of State Papers. Foreign. Edward VI and Mary. Ed. Turnbull. 2 vols. 1861.
Calendar of State Papers. Domestic. Vol. I. Ed. Lemon.
Cavendish, G., *Life of Wolsey*. Temple Classics. 1899.
Chronicle of Calais. Camden Soc., 35. 1846. Ed. Nichols.
Chronicle of Queen Jane and Two Years of Queen Mary. Camden Soc., 48. 1850.
Chronicle of King Henry VIII of England. Ed. M. A. S. Hume. 1899.
Chronicle of the Greyfriars. Camden Soc. 1852.
Clifford, Henry, *Life of Jane Dormer*. Ed. J. Stevenson. 1887.
A Complete Collection of State Trials. Vol. I. W. Cobbett, T. B. Howell, etc. 1816.
Correspondance politique de MM. de Castillon and de Marillac. Ed. Kaulek. 1885.
Correspondance politique d'Odet de Selve. 1546–9. Pub. Lefèvre-Pontalis. 1888.
Dormer, Jane, *Life of*, v. Clifford, Henry.
Edward VI, Literary Remains. Ed. J. G. Nichols. Roxburghe Club. 1857.
Ellis, H., *Original Letters, illustrative of English History*. 1824, 1827, 1846.
Florio, M. A., *Istoria de la vita e de la morte de l'illustrissima signora Giovanna Graia*. 1607.
Foxe, J., *Acts and monuments*. Ed. Cattley and Townsend. London. 1837–41.
Fuller, J., *History of the Worthies of England*. Ed. J. G. Nichols. 1811.
Furnivall, F. J., ed. *Early English Poems and Treatises on Manners and Meals in Olden Times*. E.E.T.S., O.S. and 32. 1867.
Gachard, *Correspondance de Philippe II sur les affaires des Pays Bas*. Brussels. 1848–79.

Gachard, *Lettres de Philippe II à ses filles* . . .

Gachard, *Voyages des Souverains des Pays Bas*. Collection des chroniques belges inédites.

Gardiner, S., *Letters*. Ed. J. A. Muller. 1933.

Grafton, R., *Chronicle*. Ed. H. Ellis. 1809.

Granvelle, *Papiers d'État du Cardinal de Granvelle*. Pub. Weiss. Collection des documents inédits sur l'histoire de France.

Grey, A., *A Commentary on the Services and charges of William Lord Grey of Wilton*. Camden Soc., 40. 1847. Also in Holinshed.

Guaras, de, *Accession of Queen Mary*. Trans. and ed. Garnett. London. 1892.

Hakluyt Soc., *Early Voyages and Travels to Russia and Persia*. Ed. Morgan and Coote. 1886.

Hardwicke, *Miscellaneous State Papers*, 1501–1726. Vol. I. Ed. H. Yorke, Earl of Hardwicke. 1778.

Harrison, *Description of England*. Ed. Furnivall. New Shakespeare Society. 1877.

Haweis, J. O. W., *Sketches of the Reformation and Elizabethan Age taken from the Contemporary Pulpit*. London. 1844.

Hearne, *Sylloge Epistolarum*. In T. Livius, *Vita Henrici Quinti*. Oxford. 1716.

Holinshed, *Chronicles of England*. London. 1577.

Hooker, *Life and Times of Sir Peter Carew*. Ed. John Maclean. 1857.

Hume, M.A.S., v. *Chronicle of Henry VIII*.

Italian Relation . . . *of Ireland and England about the year 1500*. Camden Soc. Trans. C. A. Sneyd.

Legend of Sir Nicholas Throckmorton. Ed. J. G. Nichols. London. 1874.

Leland, J. *De rebus britannicis collectanea*. Ed. T. Hearne. 1715.

Lettenhove, Kervyn de, *Relations politiques des Pays Bas et de l'Angleterre sous le règne de Philippe II*. Bruxelles. 1882.

Letters and Papers, Foreign and Domestic of the reign of Henry VIII. Ed. Brewer, Gairdner and Brodie. 1862–1932.

Lodge, E., *Illustrations of British History, Biography and Manners*. London. 2nd ed. 1838.

Machyn, Henry, *Diary*. Camden Soc., 42. 1848.

Madden, F., *Privy Purse Expenses of the Princess Mary*. 1831.

Narratives of the Days of the Reformation. Ed. J. C. Nichols. Camden Soc. 1859.

Nichols, J., *Illustrations of Manners and Expenses in Ancient Times in England*. London. 1797.

Norden, John, *Speculi Britanniae Pars*. Essex, 1594. Camden Soc., 9. 1840.

Perlin, E., *Description des royaumes d'Angleterre et d'Écosse* in *Antiquarian Repertory*.

Pollini, G., *L'Historia ecclesiastica della revoluzione d'Inghilterra*. 1594.

Proctor, *History of Wyatt's Rebellion*. In *Antiquarian Repertory*, III.

Reports of the Deputy Keeper of the Public Records.

Shelton, John, *Works*. var. ed.

State Papers. London. 1830–1852. 11 vols.

State Trials, v. *Complete Collection of State Trials*.

Stow, J., *Annales*. London. 1601.

Stow, J., *Survey of London*. Ed. Kingsford. 1908.

Stubbes, Philip, *Anatomy of the Abuses in England*. New Shakespeare Society. Series VI, no. 4. London. 1887.

Tanner, J. R., *Tudor Constitutional Documents*. . . . 2nd ed. Cambridge. 1940.

Tytler, P. F., *England under the Reigns of Edward VI and Mary*. 1839.

Verney Papers. Camden Soc., 56. 1853.

Vertot, v. *Ambassades de . . . de Noailles.*
Weiss, v. Granvelle.
Wriothesley, *Chronicle of England during the reigns of the Tudors.* Camden Soc. N.S. 1875 and 1877.

Later Works

Allen, J. W., *History of Political Thought in the Sixteenth Century.*
Archaeologia. Pub. Soc. of Antiquities. London.
Baschet, A., *La Diplomatie venitienne. Les princes de l'Europe au 16ᵉ siècle.* Paris. 1862.
Blomefield, F., *Topographical History of Norfolk.*
Brewer, J. S., *The Reign of Henry VIII.* London. 1884.
Burgon, *Life of Sir Thomas Gresham.* London. 1839.
Burnet, C., *History of the Reformation.* Ed. Pocock. 1865.
Byrne, M. St. C., *The English Home.*
Chambers, R. W., *Sir Thomas More.*
Chester, J. L., *Life of John Rogers.*
Crisp, F., *Mediaeval Gardens.* London. 1924.
Dillon, C., *Calais and the Pale.* In *Archaeologia.* Vol. 53, ii. 1893.
Dixon, R. W., *History of the Church of England from the abolition of the Roman jurisdiction.* London. 1878–1902.
Dodds, M. H. and R., *The Pilgrimage of Grace . . . and the Exeter Conspiracy. . .* Cambridge. 1915.
Forneron, H., *Histoire de Philippe II.* 1881–2.
Foster Watson, *Vives and the Renaissance Education of Women.*
Friedmann, P., *Anne Boleyn, a chapter in English History, 1527–1536.* 1884.
Gairdner, James, *History of the English Church in the Sixteenth Century, from the Accession of Henry VIII to the death of Mary.* London. 1902.
Garner and Stratton, *Domestic Architecture of the Tudor Period.*
Garrett, C. H., *Marian Exiles.* The Cambridge University Press. 1938.
Harbison, E. H., *Rival Ambassadors at the Court of Queen Mary.* Princetown University Press, U.S.A. 1940.
Hartley, D., and Elliot, M., *Life and work of the people of England.* Vol. II. 1925.
Howard, G., *Lady Jane Grey and her times.* 1822.
Hughes, P., *The Reformation in England.* Vol. I. 'The King's Proceedings.' London. 1950.
Hume, Martin, *English Historical Review,* VII, 1892. The visit of Philip II, 1554.
Janelle, *Obedience in Church and State.* Cambridge. 1930.
Jones, P. v. B., *The Household of a Tudor Nobleman.* University of Illinois, Studies . . . Vol. 7. 1917.
Law, E., *History of Hampton Court Palace.* 1885–91.
Maitland, S. R., *Essays on Subjects connected with the Reformation.* 1899.
Mattingly, Garrett, *Catherine of Aragon.* 1942.
Muller, J. A., *Stephen Gardiner and the Tudor Reaction.* 1926.
Neale, J. E., *Queen Elizabeth.* 1934.
Pollard, A. F., *Henry VIII.* 1913.
Pollard, A. F., *Thomas Cranmer and the English Reformation, 1489–1556.* 1926.
Pollard, A. F., *England under Protector Somerset.* 1900.
Rae, James, *Deaths of the Kings of England.*
Rowse, A. L., *Tudor Cornwall.* London. 1941.

Schenk, W., *Reginald Pole, Cardinal of England*. London. 1950.

Smith, H. Maynard, *Henry VIII and the Reformation*. London. 1948.

Smyth, C. H. E., *Cranmer and the Reformation under Edward VI*. 1926.

Stone, J. M., *The History of Mary I, Queen of England*. 1901.

Strype, *Ecclesiastical Memorials relating Chiefly to Religion under King Henry VIII, King Edward VI, and Queen Mary I*. Oxford. 1822.

Tawney, R. H., *Religion and the Rise of Capitalism*.

White, Beatrice, *Mary Tudor*. 1935.

Notes

The following abbreviations have been used:
Acts of the P.C.=Acts of the Privy Council.
Ambass.=Ambassades de MM. de Noailles, Vertot.
Antiq. Rep.=Antiquarian Repertory.
Cal. Dom.=Calendar of State Papers – Domestic.
For. Cal.=Calendar of State Papers – Foreign.
H.O.=A Collection of Ordinances and Regulations for the Government of the Royal Household.
L. and P.=Letters and Papers of the Reign of Henry VIII.
Span. Cal.=Calendar of State Papers–Spanish.
S.P. Dom.=State Papers–Domestic.
Tyler=Tyler, R., Transcripts.
Ven. Cal.=Calendar of State Papers–Venetian.

INTRODUCTORY (pp. 1–19)

1. *Antiq. Rep.*, II, pp. 278–9. Receyt of the Ladie Kateryne. . . .
2. ibid., p. 313.
3. ibid., p. 316.
4. ibid.
5. Law, E., *History of Hampton Court Palace*, I, p. 174.
6. ibid., p. 182.
7. *State Papers*, Henry VIII, Part V, p. 482, no: DCXLII. Wallop–Henry VIII. November 17th 1540.
8. *Archaeologia*, XXV, 1834, pp. 311–13.
9. *Antiq. Rep.*, loc. cit.
10. Crisp, *Mediaeval Gardens*, I, p. 61, quoting G. Markham, 'The English Husbandman', 1613.
11. Law, op. cit., App. G, p. 370, 1.
12. ibid., App. H, p. 372.
13. *Acts of the P.C.*, N.S. II, pp. 146, 174.
14. Law, op. cit., ibid.
15. ibid., pp. 74–5.
16. Skelton, J., *Colin Clout*.
17. Law, op. cit., p. 63.
18. Furnivall, *Manners and Meals* . . . , p. 179.
19. *Antiq. Rep.*, II, pp. 191, 196.
20. Stow, *Survey of London*, ed. Kingsford, I, pp. 88–9.
21. Jones, *Household of a Tudor Nobleman*, p. 10.
22. ibid., p. 58.
23. *H.O.*, pp. 153–4, cap. 52–3.

24. *H. O.*, p. 149, cap. 38.
25. *Antiq. Rep.*, II, p. 184 et seq.
26. Nichols, J., *Manners and Expenses . . .* , p. 12.
27. Leland, *Collectanea*, VI, pp. 8–10.
28. Furnivall, op. cit., p. 141.
29. Leland, op. cit., p. 25.
30. *H.O.*, pp. 154–5, cap. 55.
31. ibid., pp. 151–2, 155–6.
32. ibid., cap. 58.
33. ibid., pp. 156–7, caps. 63, 65.
34. *Antiq. Rep.*, II, p. 184. Cf. *H.O.*, p. 121.
35. Furnivall, op. cit., pp. 69–70, 176, 181–2.
36. *H.O.*, p. 48.
37. Perlin, *Antiq. Rep.*, IV, pp. 501–14.
38. Harrison, *Description of England*, Pt. I, Book II, p. 234.
39. Stubbes, *Anatomy of Abuses*, p. 149.
40. *Reliquiae Baxteriana*, p. 2.
41. Jones, *Household of a Tudor Nobleman*, p. 110.
42. *Italian Relation of England*, pp. 30–1.
43. Stow, *Survey*, I, pp. 142, 177.
44. ibid., p. 345.
45. *Italian Relation of England*, pp. 10–11.
46. *L. and P.*, X, 674.
47. Machyn, pp. 1, 2, 3, 6, etc.
48. Stow, *Survey*, I, p. 330.
49. ibid., pp. 88–9.
50. Ellis, *Letters*, II, 2, p. 253.
51. Strype, *Ecclesiastical Memorials*, I, 1, p. 135.
52. *Literary Remains of Edward VI*, I, pp. clxxii–clxxiii.
53. ibid., pp. clii–cliii.
54. Stow, *Survey*, I, pp. 93–5.
55. ibid., p. 101.
56. Norden, . . . *Essex*. Intro., p. xii.
57. Perlin, *Antiq. Rep.*, IV, pp. 501–14.
58. Machyn, p. 99.
59. ibid., pp. 143–4.
60. *Ven. Cal.*, IV, App. 171, p. 1672.
61. *Italian Relation . . .* , p. 20.
62. *Ven. Cal.*, loc. cit.
63. Perlin, *Antiq. Rep.* IV, pp. 501–14.
64. *Ven. Cal.* loc. cit.
65. Strype, *Ecc. Mem.*, II, ii, p. 135.
66. *Ven. Cal.* loc. cit.

CHAPTER I (pp. 20–30)

1. *L. and P.* II, 1, 1573; cf. II, 2, p. 1470.
2. *L. and P.* II, 2, 3871. Passamonte–Queen Katherine, January 6th 1518.
3. *Jane Dormer*, pp. 73–4.

4. *Ven. Cal.*, II, 1287. Giustinian's Report, September 10th 1519.

5. *L. and P.*, II, 2, 3976. Giustinian–the Doge, February 18th 1518.

6. ibid., 4480. Notarial attestation; cf. 4481. Giustinian–the Doge, October 5th 1518.

7. ibid., III, 1, 895. Council–Wolsey, July 2nd 1520. cf. ibid., 896 and 970.

8. *Span. Cal.*, Suppl. to I and II, p. 74. Lachaulx–Charles V, March 10th 1522; ibid., p. 364, de Courrières–same, June 29th 1524.

9. ibid., IV, 1, 1240. Wolsey–Tunstal, March 6th 1525.

10. ibid., 1421. Tunstal–King, June 16th 1525.

11. Foster Watson, *Vives and the Renaissance Education of Women*, p. 141.

12. ibid., pp. 131 and 133.

13. Tytler, II, pp. 494–5. Hoby–Cecil, November 30th 1557.

14. *L. and P.*, IV, 1, 1519. Katherine–Mary [July 27th or 28th 1525].

15. Madden, *P.P. Exs.*, pp. xxv–xxix.

16. *L. and P.*, II, 2, 1476–7. King's Book of Payments, January 1517.

17. Madden, loc. cit.

18. *L. and P.*, IV, 1, 1577. Household Expenses of the Princess Mary, August 1525.

19. ibid., 1691. Inventory of Stuff belonging to the Princess's Household, 1525.

20. ibid., 1785. Bishop of Exeter–Wolsey, November 27th 1525.

21. Madden, *P.P. Exs.*, pp. xli–xlii.

22. *L. and P.*, IV, 2, 2705. Clerk–Wolsey, December 12th 1526.

23. ibid., 3028. Lee–Wolsey, April 8th 1527.

24. ibid., 3105. Dodieu. Relation.

25. ibid., pp. ccviii–ccxi.

CHAPTER II (pp. 31–43)

1. Hughes, *Reformation in England*, I, pp. 157 and n., 161.

2. *L. and P.*, IV, Introduction, pp. cccxxxiv–cccxxxv. Cf. Hughes, *Reformation in England*, p. 234 and n. 3.

3. *L. and P.*, V, 238. Chapuys–Charles V, May 14th 1531.

4. *Span. Cal.*, IV, 1, 224, p. 351. Same–same, December 6th 1529.

5. *L. and P.*, V, 361. Same–same, July 31st 1531.

6. *Span. Cal.*, IV, 1, 182, p. 279. Same–same, October 8th 1529.

7. ibid., IV, 2, 968, p. 476. Same–same, June 28th 1532.

8. *L. and P.*, V, 750. *P.P. Exs. of Henry VIII*, June 1530.

9. *Span. Cal.*, IV, 1, 373, p. 633. Chapuys–Charles V, July 11th 1530.

10. ibid., IV, 2, p. 1003. Same–same, October 1st 1532.

11. ibid.

12. *L. and P.*, V, 238. Same–same, May 14th 1531.

13. ibid., 171. Same–same, April 2nd 1531.

14. Friedmann, *Anne Boleyn*, I, p. 190. Chapuys–Granvelle, February 23rd 1533.

15. *Span. Cal.*, IV, 2, cont., 1061, p. 643. Chapuys–Charles V, April 15th 1533.

16. ibid., 1062, p. 646. Same–same, April 27th 1533.

17. *Span. Cal.*, loc. cit.

18. *Chronicle of Henry VIII*, pp. 12–13.

19. Wriothesley, I, pp. 21–22.

20. *L. and P.*, VI, 563.

21. *Chronicle of Henry VIII*, p. 14.

22. *State Papers*, I, ii, p. 407. Mountjoy–Henry VIII, July 3rd 1533.

23. British Museum MS. Otho, C, x, p. 199. Report of Mountjoy, July 4th 1533. *State Papers*, I, ii, pp. 402–4.

24. *L. and P.*, IV, 2, 4990. Vives – – 1528.

25. *Span. Cal.*, IV, 2, cont., 1058, p. 630. Chapuys–Charles V, March 31st 1533.

26. *L. and P.*, VI, 849, 1009, and 1041. Hussey–Cromwell, July 17th, August 21st and 28th 1533.

CHAPTER III (pp. 44–57)

1. *Span. Cal.*, IV, 2, 1127, p. 795. Chapuys–Charles V, September 7–15th 1533.

2. *L. and P.*, VI, 1139. Hussey–[the Council], September 20th 1533.

3. ibid., 1199. Rotulus Maresc' dominae Mariae, October 25th Henry VIII.

4. ibid., 1207. Mary–[Henry VIII, October 2nd], 1533. Cf. *Span. Cal.*, IV, 2, 1133 and 1137. Chapuys–Charles V, October 10th and 16th.

5. ibid., 1186.

6. *State Papers*, I, ii, pp. 408–9. Mountjoy–Cromwell, October 10th 1533.

7. *Span. Cal.*, IV, 2, 1144, pp. 839–40. Chapuys–Charles V, November 3rd 1533.

8. ibid.

9. *L. and P.*, VI, 1126. Katherine–Mary.

10. *Span. Cal.*, IV, 2, 1161. Chapuys–Charles V, December 6th 1533. Cf. *State Papers*, I, ii, p. 415.

11. *Span. Cal.*, IV, 2, 1164, p. 894. Chapuys–Charles V, December 23rd 1533.

12. *L. and P.*, VII, 214. Same–same, February 21st 1534.

13. ibid., VI, 1193. Articles against Mary Baynton.

14. *State Papers*, I, ii, pp. 415–18. Suffolk, etc.–Henry VIII, December 19th 1533.

15. *Span. Cal.*, IV, 2, 1165, pp. 898–9. Chapuys–Charles V, December 27th 1533.

16. ibid., V, 1, 4, p. 15. Chapuys, January 17th 1534.

17. ibid., IV, 2, 1165, pp. 898–9. Same – Charles V, December 27th 1533. Cf. ibid., V, 1, p. 1.

18. *L. and P.*, VII, App. 13. Castillon–Francis I, March 16th 1534.

19. ibid., 497. Stonore–Cromwell.

20. ibid., 1. Articles devised by the Council.

21. *Span. Cal.*, V, 1, 4. Chapuys–Charles V, January 17th 1534.

22. ibid., 10. Same–same, February 11th 1534.

23. ibid., 19. Same–same, February 26th 1534.

24. Strype, *Ecc. Mem.*, I, i, pp. 483–4.

25. Gardiner, *Letters*, p. 130.

26. Friedmann, I, p. 231 and n.

27. *Span. Cal.*, V, 1, 32. Chapuys–Charles V, March 30th 1534.

28. *L. and P.*, VII, 214. Same – same, February 21st 1534.

29. *Span. Cal.*, loc. cit.

30. ibid., V, 1, 45. Chapuys–Charles V, April 22nd 1534.

31. ibid.

32. ibid., 57. Same–same, May 14th 1534.

33. ibid., 86. Same–same, August 29th.

34. ibid.

35. *L. and P.*, VII, 1129. Buttes–Cromwell, September 2nd 1534.

36. *L. and P.*, VIII, 263. Chapuys–Charles V, February 25th 1535.
37. ibid., VII, 1129 ut sup.
38. *Span. Cal.*, v, 1, 102. Chapuys–Charles V, October 24th 1534.
39. ibid.
40. ibid., 111. Same–same, November 18th 1534.
41. ibid., 118. Same–same, December 19th 1534.
42. *L. and P.*, VIII, 200. Katherine–Chapuys [February 12th 1534]. Cf. *Span. Cal.*, v, 1, 134.
43. *L. and P.*, VIII, 263. Chapuys–Charles V, February 25th 1535.
44. Hearne, *Sylloge Epistolarum*, p. 107. Katherine–Cromwell. Cf. *L. and P.*, VII, 1126 and VIII, 328.

CHAPTER IV (pp. 58–68)

1. *L. and P.*, IX, 74.
2. *Jane Dormer*, pp. 19–22.
3. *Span. Cal.*, IV, 2, 1073. Chapuys–Charles V, May 18th 1533.
4. *L. and P.*, VIII, 263. Same–same, February 25th 1535.
5. ibid., 48. Same–same, January 14th 1535.
6. ibid., VII, 1206. Same–same, September 30th 1534. Cf. ibid., VIII, i, and Mattingly, pp. 278–90.
7. Mattingly, pp. 291 and 299–302. *Span. Cal.*, v, i, 218.
8. *L. and P.*, IX, 71. Mary–the Queen of Hungary, August 12th 1535. Cf. *Span. Cal.*, v, 1, 194.
9. *Span. Cal.*, loc. cit.
10. *L. and P.*, VII, 1060. Instructions for Nassau. Cf. ibid., p. 1483.
11. ibid., 1209. Henry VIII – –.
12. ibid., 1392. Decisions of the Emperor's Council, November 4th and 1391. Answer of James V.
13. ibid., VIII, 819. Chapuys–Charles V, February 9th 1535.
14. ibid.
15. ibid., 174. Gontier–Chabot, February 5th 1535.
16. ibid., 18. Charles V–Chapuys, January 5th 1535. Cf. *Span. Cal.*, v, 1, 126.
17. *State Papers*, VII, pp. 530–2. Hackett–Cromwell, December 23rd 1533 (spelling modernized).
18. *Span. Cal.*, v, 1, 138. Chapuys–Charles V, March 4th 1535.
19. *L. and P.*, VIII, 501. Same–same, April 5th 1535.
20. ibid., IX, 566. [Bishop of Tarbes–Bailly of Troyes, October 1535.]
21. ibid., VIII, 502. Chapuys–[Granvelle], April 5th 1535.
22. *Span. Cal.*, v, 1, 150. Chapuys–Charles V, April 17th 1535.
23. ibid., 231. Ortiz–Granvelle, November 22nd 1535.
24. ibid., 183. Chapuys–Charles V, July 25th 1535. *L. and P.*, XI, 484. Cromwell–Chapuys.
25. *L. and P.*, IX, 566 ut sup.
26. *Span. Cal.*, v, 1, 245. Charles V–Chapuys, December 29th 1535.
27. ibid., v, 2, 3. Chapuys–Charles V, January 9th 1536.
28. Strype, *Ecc. Mem.*, I, 1, p. 372.
29. *Span. Cal.*, v, 2, 9, and 37. Chapuys–Charles V, January 21st and March 10th 1536.

CHAPTER V (pp. 69–83)

1. *Span. Cal.*, v, 2, 9. Chapuys–Charles V, January 21st 1536.
2. *L. and P.*, VII, 1193. Same–same, September 27th 1534.
3. ibid., IV, 2, 4537. Henry VIII–Anne Boleyn.
4. Friedmann, I, p. 134.
5. *Jane Dormer*, pp. 80–1.
6. *Span. Cal.*, v, 2, 9. Chapuys–Charles V, January 21st 1536.
7. *L. and P.*, x, 307. Same–same.
8. *Jane Dormer*, pp. 79–80.
9. *Span. Cal.*, loc. cit.
10. ibid.
11. ibid.
12. *L. and P.*, x, 199. Chapuys–Charles V, January 29th 1536. Cf. *Span. Cal.*, v, 2, 13.
13. *Span. Cal.*, v, 2, 21. Chapuys–Charles V, February 17th 1536.
14. *L. and P.*, x, 307 ut sup. Cf. *Span. Cal.*, loc. cit.
15. ibid.
16. *L. and P.*, x, 670. Pate–Henry VIII, April 14th 1536.
17. ibid., 308. Chapuys–Granvelle, February 17th 1536.
18. ibid., 726. Henry VIII–Pate, April 25th 1536.
19. *Span. Cal.*, v, 2, 43. Chapuys–Charles V, April 1st 1536.
20. *Jane Dormer*, p. 41.
21. *Span. Cal.*, v, 2, 43 ut sup.
22. ibid., 55. Same–same, May 19th 1536.
23. *L. and P.*, x, 720. Chapuys–Granvelle, April 24th 1536.
24. ibid., 797 and 798. Kingston–Cromwell, May 1536.
25. *Chronicle of Henry VIII*, pp. 56–7.
26. Wriothesley, I, Intro., p. xxvii. *Span. Cal.*, v, 2, 55.
27. *Chronicle of Henry VIII*, p. 70.
28. ibid., p. 65.
29. *Span. Cal.*, v, 2, 55. Chapuys–Charles V, May 19th 1536.
30. ibid.
31. *L. and P.*, x, 1212. Bishop of Faenza–[M. Ambrogio?], June 26th 1536.
32. ibid., 968. Hearne, p. 140. Mary–Cromwell, May 26th 1536.
33. *L. and P.*, x, 991. Hearne, pp. 146–7. Mary–Cromwell, May 30th [1536].
34. *L. and P.*, x, 1022. Hearne, p. 147. Mary–[Henry VIII], June 1st 1536.
35. *L. and P.*, x, 1079. Hearne, p. 148. Mary–[Cromwell], June 7th 1536.
36. *Span. Cal.*, v, 2, 61, pp. 137–9. Chapuys–Charles V, June 6th 1536.
37. *L. and P.*, x, 1109. Hearne, pp. 124–5. Mary–Henry VIII, June 10th 1536.
38. *L. and P.*, x, 1108. Hearne, p. 125. Mary–Cromwell, June 10th 1536.
39. *L. and P.*, x, 1133. Hearne, pp. 127–8. Mary–Henry VIII, June 14th 1536.
40. *L. and P.*, x, 1129. Hearne, pp. 126–7. Mary–Cromwell, June 13th 1536.
41. *Span. Cal.*, v, 2, 70, p. 182. Chapuys–Charles V, July 1st 1536. Cf. *L. and P.*, XI, 7.
42. ibid.
43. ibid.
44. ibid.
45. ibid.
46. *L. and P.*, XI, 9. Chapuys–Granvelle, July 1st 1536.

47. Hearne, pp. 137-8. [Cromwell–Mary, June 1536.]

48. *Span. Cal.*, v, 2, 70. *L. and P.*, xi, p. 7 ut sup.

49. Hearne, pp. 142-3. *L. and P.*, x, 1137. Confession of . . . the Lady Mary.

50. *Span. Cal.*, v. 2, 48. Chapuys–Charles V, May 2nd 1536.

51. ibid., 70 ut sup.

52. *L. and P.*, VII, 1036. Examination of Lady Anne Hussey, August 3rd 1534 [*sic*], see ibid., x, Intro., p. xxxix.

53. ibid., xi, 1406. George Throckmorton's confession, [December 1536].

54. *L. and P.*, xiv, 1, 190.

55. Hearne, pp. 144-6. Mary–Cromwell, [June 23rd 1536].

56. *Span. Cal.*, v, 2, 70 ut sup.

CHAPTER VI (pp. 84-96)

1. Wriothesley, I, p. 51. *Span. Cal.*, v, 2, 71. Chapuys–Charles V, July 8th 1536. Cf. ibid., p. 72. Same–Granvelle, July 8th.

2. Hearne, p. 129. Mary–my Lord [Cromwell], July 1st 1536. *L. and P.*, xi, p. 6.

3. ibid., 148. Chapuys–Granvelle, July 23rd 1536.

4. Hearne, pp. 144-6. *L. and P.*, x, 1186. Mary–Cromwell, [June 23rd 1536].

5. Wriothesley, I, pp. 59-60.

6. *L. and P.*, xi, 860. – – du Bellay, October 24th 1536. *Chronicle of Henry VIII*, p. 73.

7. Hearne, pp. 135-6. Mary–my Lord – –, December 8th 1536.

8. *Span. Cal.*, v, 2, 72. Chapuys–Granvelle, July 8th 1536.

9. ibid., 104. Chapuys–Charles V, October 7th 1536. Cf. ibid., 105. Chapuys–Cifuentes.

10. *L. and P.*, xi, 220. Same–Granvelle, August 3rd 1536.

11. ibid., xii, 1, 1267. May 23rd. Hussey–Lady Lisle. Cf. Madden, *P.P. Exs.*, p. 30, June 1537.

12. Wriothesley, I, p. 57.

13. *L. and P.*, xii, 2, 1060. Remembrance of Interment [of Jane Seymour].

14. ibid., xiii, 2, 830. Depositions. 1538.

15. Strype, *Ecc. Mem.*, II, ii, pp. 50-6.

16. Wriothesley, I, pp. 82-3.

17. *Chronicle of the Greyfriars*, Pref., pp. xv–xvi.

18. *Narr. of the Reformation*, pp. 35-9.

19. *L. and P.*, xvi, 1089 and 1183. Marillac–Francis I, August 12th and September 16th.

20. ibid., xiv, 1, 980. [Worth]–Lord Lisle, May 18th 1539.

21. ibid., xiii, 1, 1104. Bransetur–Pate, May 31st 1538.

22. ibid., xiv, 1, 37. Chapuys–Charles V, January 9th 1539.

23. ibid., xiii, 2, 702. Cf. *L. and P.*, xiii, 2, 827 and 3rd Report of the Deputy Keeper of the Public Records, App. II, p. 255. Charges against Lord Montague.

24. Ellis, *Letters*, II, 2, p. 114. Southampton and Ely–Cromwell.

25. *Chronicle of Henry VIII*, pp. 90-1.

26. *L. and P.*, xvi, 314 and 523. *Span. Cal.*, vi, 1, 143 and 151. Chapuys–Mary of Hungary, December 5th 1540 and February 6th 1541.

27. *L. and P.*, xvi, 1331. Privy Council–Cranmer, etc., November 11th 1541. Cf. ibid., 1332. Marillac–Francis I, November 8th 1541.

28. ibid., xiv, 2, 99. Pole–Contarini, August 29th 1539.

29. *L. and P.*, xiv, 2, 744. Marillac–Montmorency, December 17th 1539. Cf. ibid., 737. Wriothesley–Cromwell, [December 24th 1539].

30. ibid., 744 ut sup.

31. ibid., xx, 2, 764. Privy Council–Gardiner, November 10th 1545.

32. *Span. Cal.*, VIII, 204. Van der Delft–Charles V, February 27th 1546.

33. *L. and P.*, XVII, 371. Marillac–Francis I, June 3rd 1542.

34. Strype, *Ecc. Mem.*, II, i, p. 206.

35. Hearne, pp. 108–9.

36. *Span. Cal.*, VIII, 51. Chapuys–Charles V, May 9th 1545.

CHAPTER VII (pp. 97–112)

1. Madden, *P.P. Exs.*, December 1536–December 1544.

2. *L. and P.*, XXI, 1, 802. Prince Edward–Queen Katherine, May 12th 1546.

3. Madden, *P.P. Exs.*, pp. 85 and 88.

4. ibid., pp. 175–201.

5. *L. and P.*, XVI, 1186. Francis I– Marillac, September 17th 1541.

6. ibid., XVII, 261. Marillac–Francis I, April 22nd 1542. Cf. ibid., Add., I, 2, 1294. Lady Kingston–Wriothesley.

7. Madden, *P.P. Exs.*

8. *Jane Dormer*, p. 80.

9. *L. and P.*, XI, 203. Lady Bryan–Cromwell, 1536.

10. Hearne, pp. 149–51. Wriothesley–my Lord – –, December 17th [? 1537].

11. Ellis, *Letters*, 3, 3, p. 210. Richard Cromwell–Thomas Cromwell.

12. *State Papers*, I, pp. 586–7. Audley–Cromwell, September 8th [1538].

13. *L. and P.*, XX, ii, 732. Gardiner–Paget, November 5th 1545.

14. *Jane Dormer*, pp. 59–60.

15. Strype, *Ecc. Mem.*, II, i, p. 13.

16. *Acts of the P.C.*, N.S., II, p. 29.

17. *Lit. Rem. Edward VI*, I, p. cclxxviii. *Chronicle of Henry VIII*, p. 153.

18. *Acts of the P.C.*, loc. cit., pp. 29–30.

19. Tytler, I, p. 168. Wightman–Cecil, May 10th 1549.

20. Ellis, *Letters*, I, 2, p. 149. Mary–Admiral Seymour, June 4th [1547].

21. Tytler, I, pp. 111–13. Fowler–Admiral Seymour, July 19th 1548.

22. Strype, *Ecc. Mem.*, II, i, p. 198.

23. *Lit. Rem. Edward VI*, I, pp. cxv–cxvi.

24. *Jane Dormer*, pp. 60–1.

25. ibid., pp. 61–2.

26. *Lit. Rem. Edward VI*, II, pp. 311 and 317.

27. ibid., I, p. lxxiv.

28. Haweis, p. 45.

29. Gardiner, *Letters*, 125, p. 345. Gardiner–Cranmer, [June 1547]. Spelling modernized.

30. Maitland, *Essays on . . . the Reformation*, XIII, p. 206.

31. Gardiner, *Letters*, 124, p. 308. Gardiner–Cranmer, [June 1547].

32. Strype, *Ecc. Mem.*, II, i, p. 53.

33. Foxe, VI, pp. 28–30. Somerset–Gardiner, [May 27th] 1547.

34. Haweis, p. 86. Cf. Hughes, *Reformation in England*, I, pp. 95, n., 99–100.

35. *Narr. of the Reformation*, pp. 270–1. Cf. Hughes, loc. cit., pp. 83–5.
36. Gardiner, *Letters*, 124, p. 315 ut sup.
37. Haweis, pp. 87–8.
38. *Acts of the P.C.*, N.S., II, App., p. 521.
39. Arber, *English Garner*, ed. Pollard, VI, pp. 161–9.
40. Strype, *Ecc. Mem.*, II, i, pp. 97–8.
41. ibid., pp. 126–7.
42. ibid., pp. 369–70.
43. *Ven. Cal.*, V, p. 934. Soranzo's Report. August 18th 1554.
44. Haweis, pp. 58–9.
45. Strype, *Ecc. Mem.*, II, ii, p. 19.
46. ibid., II, i, pp. 141–2.
47. ibid., pp. 527–30.
48. Gardiner, *Letters*, 79. Gardiner–Paget, 1545.
49. J. W. Allen, *Political Thought in the Sixteenth Century*, p. 211.
50. Haweis, p. 269.
51. Strype, *Ecc. Mem.*, II, i, p. 139 .
52. R. H. Tawney, *Religion and the Rise of Capitalism*, p. 143.
53. Stow, *Survey*, I, p. 128.
54. Strype, *Ecc. Mem.*, II, i, pp. 128–30.
55. Tytler, I, p. 113. Hales–Somerset, July 22nd 1548.
56. Gardiner, *Letters*, 64. Gardiner–Edmunds, May 15th [1543].

CHAPTER VIII (pp. 113–129)

1. Dixon, IV, pp. 178–9.
2. ibid.
3. Cf. Foxe, V, p. 731. *Articles of the Rebels.*
4. Strype, *Ecc. Mem.*, II, i, p. 319.
5. Tawney, loc. cit., p. 148. *Span. Cal.*, XII, p. 15. Egmont–Philip, January 7th 1554.
6. Quoted by R. W. Chambers, in *Thomas More*, p. 143.
7. Tytler, I, p. 364. Hooper–Cecil, April 17th 1551.
8. Strype, *Ecc. Mem.*, II, ii, p. 425. Somerset–Hoby, September 1st 1549.
9. ibid.
10. ibid., pp. 429–37. Paget–Somerset, July 7th 1549.
11. Greyfriars, p. 61.
12. Rowse, *Tudor Cornwall*, pp. 268, 271–2.
13. *S.P. Dom.*, 10, 8, No. 30. Council–Mary, July 18th 1549.
14. *Span. Cal.*, IX, pp. 406–8. Van der Delft–Charles V, July 19th 1549.
15. Tytler, I, p. 185. Smith–Cecil, July 19th 1549.
16. Brit. Mus. Add. MSS., 27402.
17. *Ven. Cal.*, VI, 2, 884. Michiel's Report, May 13th 1557.
18. *Span. Cal.*, IX, p. 330. Charles V–Van der Delft, January 25th 1549.
19. ibid., pp. 350–1. Van der Delft–Charles V, March 30th 1549.
20. *Span. Cal.*, IX, p. 360. Mary–Charles V, April 3rd 1549.
21. ibid., p. 375. Charles V–Van der Delft, May 10th 1549.
22. ibid., p. 386. Same–same, June 8th 1549.
23. ibid., p. 382. Van der Delft–Charles V, May 28th 1549.

24. Tytler, I, p. 51. Mary–Lady Somerset, April 24th 1547.
25. *Acts of the P.C.*, N.S., II, pp. 291–2. Cf. *Span. Cal.*, IX, pp. 393–4. Van der Delft–Charles V, June 13th 1549.
26. *Span. Cal.*, loc. cit.
27. ibid., p. 388. Mary–Charles V, June 12th 1549.
28. ibid., pp. 393–4. Van der Delft–Charles V, June 13th 1549.
29. ibid., pp. 397–8. Same–same, July 3rd 1549.
30. Foxe, 6, pp. 7–8. Mary–the Council, June 22nd 1549.
31. ibid., pp. 10–11. Mary–Somerset, June 27th 1549.
32. ibid.
33. *Span. Cal.*, IX, pp. 406–8. Van der Delft–Charles V, July 19th 1549.
34. ibid.
35. ibid., p. 430. Same–same, August 13th 1549.
36. *S.P. Dom.*, 10, 8, Nos. 51–3. King Edward–Mary, August 1549.
37. *Span. Cal.*, IX, p. 447. Van der Delft–Charles V, September 15th 1549.
38. ibid., p. 449. Charles V–Dubois, September 17th 1549.
39. Tytler, I, p. 241. Cranmer, etc–the Council, October 11th 1549.
40. Greyfriars, p. 64.
41. *Span. Cal.*, X, pp. 5–6. Van der Delft–Charles V, January 14th 1550.
42. ibid., IX, pp. 445–6. Same–same, September 1549.
43. ibid., p. 449. Charles V–Dubois, September 17th 1549.
44. ibid., X, pp. 5–6 ut sup.
45. Howard, *Lady Jane Grey*, p. 213.
46. *Ven. Cal.*, V, 934. Soranzo's Report ut sup.
47. Baschet, *Transcripts*, 3, 22, pp. 15–17. Relation des plusieurs particularités.
48. Dixon, 3, p. 533.
49. *S.P. Dom.*, 10, 9, No. 57. King Edward–the Bishops, December 25th 1549.
50. Stow, *Survey*, I, pp. 143–4.
51. *Span. Cal.*, IX, p. 450 ut sup.
52. ibid., p. 469. Van der Delft–Charles V, November 7th 1549.
53. ibid., p. 489. Same–same, December 19th 1549.
54. ibid., X, pp. 5–6 ut sup.
55. ibid., IX, p. 450 ut sup.
56. ibid., p. 382. Van der Delft–Charles V, May 28th 1549.
57. ibid., X, p. 17. Same–same. January 31st 1550.
58. ibid., pp. 40–1. Same–same, March 8th 1550.
59. *Acts of the P.C.*, N.S., III, p. 14.

CHAPTER IX (pp. 130–143)

1. *Span. Cal.*, X, pp. 80–6. Van der Delft–Charles V, May 2nd 1550. This letter contains the account of the interview.
2. ibid., p. 47. Same–same, March 17th 1550.
3. ibid., pp. 94–6. Same–same, June 6th 1550.
4. ibid.
5. ibid., p. 117. Charles V–Mary of Hungary, June 25th 1550.
6. ibid., p. 107. Mary of Hungary–Scheyfve, June 13th 1550; and ibid., p. 111. Charles V–Mary of Hungary, June 21st 1550.

7. *Span. Cal.*, x, pp. 135–6. d'Eecke–Mary of Hungary, July 17th 1550.
8. ibid., p. III ut sup.
9. ibid., pp. 124–37. 'Report of Jehan Duboys . . .'. [Middle of July] 1550. The whole of the account of Mary's abortive escape is drawn from this report, in which Duboys gives an account of the transaction with a wealth of self-justificatory detail.
10. ibid.
11. *Lit. Rem. of Edward VI*, II, p. 291.
12. *Span. Cal.*, x, pp. 148–9. Mary of Hungary–Scheyfve, August 3rd 1550.
13. ibid., pp. 150–2. Scheyfve–Charles V, August 3rd 1550.

CHAPTER X (pp. 144–161)

1. *Span. Cal.*, x, pp. 150–2. Scheyfve–Charles V, August 3rd 1550.
2. ibid. Cf. *Lit. Rem. of Edward VI*, II, pp. 286–91.
3. *Span. Cal.*, loc. cit.
4. *Acts of the P.C.*, N.S., III, p. 171.
5. Foxe, 6, pp. 13–14. Mary–the Council, December 4th 1550.
6. ibid., pp. 14–18. The Council–Mary, December 25th 1550.
7. *Span. Cal.*, x, pp. 410–11. Scheyfve–Mary of Hungary, December 15th 1550.
8. ibid., pp. 205–9. Mary–the Council, enclosed in letter of Scheyfve, January 27th 1551.
9. ibid.
10. ibid., pp. 209–12. King Edward–Mary.
11. ibid., pp. 212–13. Foxe, 6, p. 12. Mary–King Edward, February 3rd 1550–1.
12. *Span. Cal.*, x, p. 219. Mary–Moronelli, February 3rd 1551.
13. ibid., pp. 172–3. Charles–Scheyfve, September 4th 1550.
14. *For. Cal.*, *Edward VI*, 294. The Council–Morysine. Cf. *Span. Cal.*, x, pp. 230–7. Scheyfve–Mary of Hungary.
15. ibid., pp. 251–61. Scheyfve–Charles V, April 6th 1551.
16. Machyn, pp. 4–5.
17. *Span. Cal.*, x, p. 264. Scheyfve, Advices, April 9th 1551.
18. ibid., pp. 251–61 ut sup.
19. ibid., pp. 237–41. Charles V–Scheyfve, March 7th 1551.
20. ibid., pp. 251–61 ut sup.
21. ibid.
22. *Acts of the P.C.*, N.S., III, p. 239. *Greyfriars*, p. 69.
23. *Span. Cal.*, x, pp. 247–8. Charles V–Scheyfve, March 17th 1551.
24. ibid., pp. 284–5. Scheyfve–Charles V, April 26th 1551.
25. ibid., p. 287. Mary–the Council, May 2nd 1551. Cf. Foxe, 6, pp. 18.
26. *Span. Cal.*, loc. cit. The Council–Mary, May 6th 1551.
27. Foxe, 6, p. 19. Mary–the Council, May 11th 1551.
28. *Acts of the P.C.*, N.S., III, p. 264.
29. *For. Cal. Edward VI*, 393. Wotton–the Council, June 30th. *Span. Cal.*, x, pp. 311–16. Charles V–Scheyfve, June 29th 1551.
30. *Acts of the P.C.*, N.S., III, p. 240.
31. ibid., pp. 333, 337.
32. The account of the transactions between Mary and the Council taking place

between August 15th and August 20th 1551, is contained in the *Acts of the P.C.*, N.S., III, pp. 336–52. Cf. Foxe, 6, p. 23; and *Span. Cal.*, x, pp. 356–64.

33. Guaras, p. 100.
34. *Span. Cal.*, x, pp. 349–56. Charles V–Scheyfve, September 3rd 1551.
35. *Acts of the P.C.*, N.S. III, p. 395.
36. ibid., p. 508.
37. Howard, *Lady Jane Grey*, pp. 141–2. Mary–King Edward, April 4th 1552.
38. *Acts of the P.C.*, N.S., IV, p. 20.
39. Machyn, p. 14.
40. Guaras, p. 84.
41. Smyth, *Cranmer and the English Reformation*, pp. 263–4.
42. Foxe, 6, pp. 354–5.

CHAPTER XI (pp. 162–178)

1. *Span. Cal.*, XI, pp. 8–9. Scheyfve–Charles V, February 17th 1553.
2. Wriothesley, II, pp. 81–2.
3. *Ambass.*, II, pp. 3–7. Noailles–Henri II, May 7th 1552.
4. Strype, *Ecc. Mem.*, II, ii, p. 111.
5. Tytler, II, pp. 169–71. Audley–Cecil, May 9th 1553.
6. Wriothesley, II, p. 84. *Greyfriars*, pp. 77–8.
7. *Span. Cal.*, XI, p. 35. Scheyfve–Charles V, April 28th 1553.
8. *Ambass.*, II, pp. 31–4. Noailles–the Constable, June 16th. Cf. ibid., pp. 46–9. Same–Henri II.
9. Tytler, II, pp. 165–8.
10. *Span. Cal.*, XI, pp. 49–50. Scheyfve–Charles V, June 11th 1553.
11. ibid., p. 59. Letters of Credence to de Courrières, etc., June 23rd 1553.
12. ibid., p. 35. Scheyfve–Charles V, April 28th 1553.
13. *Ven. Cal.*, v, 934. Soranzo's Report ut sup.
14. *Chronicle of Queen Jane*, p. 1 n.
15. *Span. Cal.*, XI, pp. 72–6. Embassy–Charles V, July 7th. Cf. ibid., pp. 82–3. Same–same, July 11th.
16. *Ven. Cal.*, loc. cit.
17. Fuller, *Worthies*, I, p. 177 (sub. Huddlestone). Cf. Foxe, 8, p. 591; and Guaras, pp. 89–90.
18. *Ambass.*, II, pp. 50–3. Noailles–Henri II, July 7th 1553.
19. *Span. Cal.*, XI, pp. 77–80. Embassy–Charles V, July 10th. ibid., pp. 72–6 ut sup.
20. ibid., Cf. Machyn, pp. 35–6.
21. *Span. Cal.*, loc. cit.
22. *Greyfriars*, p. 78.
23. Strype, *Ecc. Mem.*, III, i, pp. 19–20.
24. *Span. Cal.*, XI, pp. 106–9. Advices from England, July 20th 1553.
25. Stone, *Mary I, Queen of England.* App. C, quoting Pollini, *L'Historia Ecclesiastica della revoluzione d'Inghilterra*, p. 355.
26. Foxe, 8, pp. 700 and 603.
27. Stone, loc. cit.
28. *Span. Cal.*, XI, pp. 77–80. Embassy–Charles V, July 10th 1553.
29. *Greyfriars*, p. 79.
30. *Span. Cal.*, XI, pp. 82–3. Embassy–Charles V, July 11th 1553.

31. *Span. Cal.*, XI, pp. 72–6. Embassy–Charles V, July 7th 1553.

32. ibid., pp. 82–3. Same–same, July 11th 1553. *Ambass.*, II, pp. 57–61. Noailles –Henri II, July 13th 1553.

33. *Chron. of Queen Jane*, p. 5. Wriothesley, II, p. 87.

34. *Chron. of Queen Jane*, loc. cit.

35. ibid., pp. 6–8. *Greyfriars*, p. 80. Wriothesley, II, p. 87.

36. Howard, *Lady Jane Grey*, p. 307.

37. Hawes and Loder, *History of Framlingham. Woodbridge.* 1798.

38. *Span. Cal.*, XI, pp. 88–9. Embassy–Charles V, July 14th 1553.

39. Guaras, pp. 91–2.

40. ibid., pp. 89–90.

41. *Chron. of Queen Jane*, pp. 8–9.

42. Guaras, p. 92.

43. Foxe, 8, p. 591, who says that the chalice was brought into church at Bury, but Northumberland was not there on a Sunday. I therefore suppose that the episode took place on the day he arrived at Cambridge.

44. *Span. Cal.*, XI, pp. 106–9. Advices from England. *Ambass.*, II, pp. 73–5. Noailles –Henri II, July 18th 1553.

45. *Chron. of Queen Jane*, p. 9.

46. *For. Cal., Mary,* 556 and 558. Wotton–Queen Mary, November 12th and November 17th 1553. Cf. *Span. Cal.*, XI, pp. 123–4. Embassy–Charles V, July 29th 1553.

47. *Span. Cal.*, XI, pp. 91–3. Embassy–Charles V, July 16th 1553.

48. *Chron. of Queen Jane*, p. 9.

49. ibid.

50. *Span. Cal.*, XI, pp. 91–3. Embassy–Charles V, July 16th. *Ambass.*, II, pp. 71–3. July 14th.

51. *Acts of the P.C.*, N.S., IV, p. 296.

52. *Span. Cal.*, XI, pp. 83–7. Renard etc.–Charles V, July 12th 1553.

53. *Span. Cal.*, XI, pp. 94–7. Same–same, July 19th.

54. Stow, *Survey*, I, p. 67. Wriothesley, II, pp. 88–9.

55. *Span. Cal.*, loc. cit. Machyn, p. 37. Guaras, pp. 95–7. *Chron. of Queen Jane*, pp. 11–13. Wriothesley, II, pp. 88–9.

56. *Span. Cal.*, XI, pp. 106–9. Advices from England, July 20th 1553.

57. Wriothesley, loc. cit.

58. Ellis, *Letters*, II, 2, p. 243. The Council–Queen Mary, July 1553.

59. *Narr. of the Reformation*, p. 152. *Span. Cal.*, XI, pp. 111–16. Embassy–Charles V, July 22nd 1553.

60. *Chron. of Queen Jane*, App., pp. 112–13.

61. Guaras, pp. 97–8. Wriothesley, II, p. 90.

62. *Chron. of Queen Jane*, pp. 10–11.

63. Guaras, pp. 98–100. *Span. Cal.*, loc. cit. and pp. 119–21. Wriothesley, II, pp. 90–1. *Greyfriars*, pp. 80–1.

64. Machyn, pp. 37–8. Cf. ut sup. Strype, *Ecc. Mem.* III, 1, pp. 24 and 27. *Greyfriars*, p. 81.

65. Stow, *Annales*, p. 1035. *Ambass.*, II, pp. 93–4. Noailles–de Gye, July 29th 1553.

66. Guaras, p. 97.

67. Wriothesley, II, pp. 91–2.

68. Machyn, pp. 37–8. *Chron. of Queen Jane*, p. 13. Wriothesley, II, p. 92.

69. Wriothesley, II, pp. 93–5. *Greyfriars*, pp. 81–2. *Chron. of Queen Jane*, p. 14. Machyn, pp. 38–9. *Span. Cal.*, XI, pp. 150–2. Embassy–Charles V, August 6th 1553.

70. *Greyfriars. Chron. of Queen Jane*, loc. cit.

CHAPTER XII (pp. 179–202)

1. The description of Mary is drawn from the following sources. *Correspondance Politique de MM. de Castillon et de Marillac*, 368. Marillac – Francis I, October 1541. *Ven. Cal.*, v, 934. Soranzo's Report, 1554. Cf. Baschet, *Diplomatie venitienne*, p. 128. *Ven. Cal.*, VI, 2, 884. Michiel's Report, 1557. Madden, *P.P. Exs.*, Introduction, quoting Puttenham, *Art of English Poesie*.

2. *Jane Dormer*, pp. 64–6.

3. Stone, pp. 485–6. No source is given for this story, and the word which the Lord Chamberlain used is omitted.

4. *Span. Cal.*, XI, pp. 227–9. Renard–Granvelle, September 9th 1553.

5. *L. and P.*, XV, 223. *Narr. of the Reformation*, p. 180. *Troubles of Thomas Mountain*.

6. *Span. Cal.*, XI, pp. 119–21. Embassy–Charles V, July 27th 1553.

7. Gardiner, *Letters*, p. 87. Gardiner–Paget.

8. Grey, . . . *Services* . . . , App., p. 40. Baschet, *Trans.*, 3, 20. Noailles–the Constable, August 3rd 1553.

9. *Ambass.*, II, pp. 85–8. The Constable–Howard, July 24th. Howard–the Constable, July 26th 1553.

10. ibid., pp. 105–7. Noailles–the Constable, August 7th 1553.

11. *Span. Cal.*, XI, pp. 129–35. The Embassy–Charles V, August 2nd 1553.

12. ibid., pp. 122–3. Charles V–the Embassy, July 29th 1553.

13. ibid., pp. 166–73. The Embassy–Charles V, August 16th 1553.

14. ibid.

15. Guaras, p. 102.

16. *Span. Cal.*, XI, pp. 183–93. The Embassy–Charles V, August 27th 1553.

17. *Chron. of Queen Jane*, pp. 25–6.

18. Wriothesley, II, p. 100.

19. *Chron. of Queen Jane*, pp. 18–23. Guaras, pp. 108–9. *Antiq. Rep.*, IV, pp. 507–9. Perlin, *Description of England*.

20. *Acts of the P.C.*, N.S., IV, p. 379.

21. *Antiq. Rep.*, loc. cit. Perlin.

22. Hooker, *Life of Sir P. Carew*, p. 54.

23. *Span. Cal.*, XI, pp. 109–11. Charles V–the Embassy, July 22nd 1553.

24. ibid., pp. 117–19. The Embassy–Queen Mary, July 24th 1553.

25. *Greyfriars*, pp. 82–3. Machyn, p. 40. *Span. Cal.*, XI, pp. 155–7. The Embassy–Charles V, August 8th 1553.

26. *Span. Cal.*, XI, pp. 129–35. The Embassy–Charles V, August 2nd 1553.

27. *Acts of the P.C.*, N.S., IV, pp. 317–18.

28. M. A. Florio, *Historia de la vita . . . de . . . Giovannia Graia*, p. 38.

29. Stow, *Annales*, pp. 1036–7. Machyn, p. 41. Wriothesley, II, pp. 97–98.

30. *Span. Cal.*, XI, pp. 166–73. The Embassy–Charles V, August 16th 1553.

31. ibid.

32. *Acts of the P.C.*, N. S., IV, pp. 317–18, 319 and 321.

33. *S.P. Dom.*, II, I, No. 7. Proclamation by the Queen. *Span. Cal.*, XI, pp. 157–9.

34. Wriothesley, II, p. 100.

35. Dixon, *History of the Church of England in the Sixteenth Century*, IV, p. 38 n.

36. Smyth, *Cranmer and the English Reformation*, pp. 263–4.

37. Dixon, loc. cit., IV, pp. 37–43.

38. Muller, *Gardiner and the Tudor Reaction*, pp. 232–3 and n.

39. Garrett, *Marian Exiles*, p. 2.

40. *Acts of the P.C.*, N.S., IV, p. 349.

41. *Span. Cal.*, XI, pp. 214–21. The Embassy–Charles V, September 9th 1553.

42. ibid., pp. 251–5. Same–same, September 23rd. *Ven. Cal.*, V, p. 813. Report to the Pope, [October 21st] 1553.

43. *Span. Cal.*, XI, pp. 166–73 ut sup. ibid., pp. 251–5. Same–same, September 23rd 1553.

44. ibid., pp. 183–93. The Embassy–Charles V, August 27th 1553.

45. ibid., pp. 238–42. Same–same, September 19th 1553.

46. ibid., pp. 214–21. The Embassy–Charles V, September 9th 1553.

47. ibid., pp. 239–42 ut sup.

48. ibid.

49. Wriothesley, II, p. 103. Machyn, p. 45.

50. *Chron. of Queen Jane*, p. 28.

51. Stow, *Annales*, p. 1042.

52. *Greyfriars*, p. 84.

53. *Span. Cal.*, XI, pp. 259–61. The Embassy–Charles V, September 30th 1553.

54. *Chron. of Queen Jane*, pp. 31–2. Machyn, pp. 45–6. *Span. Cal.*, XI, pp. 261–4. Renard–Prince Philip, October 3rd 1553.

55. *Span. Cal.*, XI, pp. 214–21. The Embassy–Charles V, September 9th 1553.

56. ibid.

57. Gardiner, *Letters*, Intro., p. xxxii.

58. *Ven. Cal.*, V, 807. Queen Mary–Pole, October 8th 1553.

59. *Span. Cal.*, XI, pp. 294–300. Renard–Charles V, October 15th 1553.

60. Dixon, IV, pp. 90–1.

61. Strype, *Ecc. Mem.*, III, 1, pp. 79–80. *Acts of the P.C.*, N.S., IV, pp. 373–5. Cf. ibid., pp. 340 and 368.

62. *Span. Cal.*, XI, pp. 414–19. Renard–Charles V, December 8th 1553.

CHAPTER XIII (pp. 203–219)

1. *Span. Cal.*, XII, p. 122. Renard–Charles V, February 20th 1554. *Ven. Cal.*, V, 856. Pole–di Monte, February 10th 1554.

2. ibid., VI, 2, 884, p. 1056. Michiel's Report, May 13th 1557.

3. Foxe, 6, p. 8.

4. Baschet, *Trans.*, 3, 20. Noailles–the Constable, September 7th 1553.

5. *Span. Cal.*, XI, pp. 214–21. The Embassy–Charles V, September 9th 1553.

6. Baschet, *Trans.*, 3, 20. Noailles–the Queen of Scots, September 24th 1553.

7. *Jane Dormer*, pp. 79–80.

8. Gorham, G. and C., *Gleanings of a few scattered ears during the period of the Reformation in England*, p. 305. No. XCVII. Martyr–Calvin, November 3rd 1553.

9. *Span. Cal.*, XI, pp. 414–19. Renard–Charles V, December 8th 1553.

10. Baschet, *Trans.*, 3, 20. Noailles–Vendôme, July 13th 1553. *Ambass.*, II, pp. 57–61. Same–Henri II.

11. *Ambass.*, II, pp. 83–4. Same–same.

12. *Span. Cal.*, XI, pp. 111–16. The Embassy–Charles V, July 22nd 1553.

13. *S.P. Dom.*, 11, 5, No. 13. Courtenay–Lady Barkley, May 8th 1555.

14. *Ambass.*, II, pp. 103–5. Noailles–Henry II, August 7th 1553.

15. *Span. Cal.*, XI, pp. 238–42. The Embassy–Charles V, September 19th 1553.
16. *Ambass.*, II, pp. 219–23. Noailles – Henri II, October 17th 1553.
17. *Span. Cal.*, XI, pp. 111–16 ut sup.
18. ibid., pp. 126–7. Charles V–Prince Philip, July 30th 1553.
19. ibid., pp. 129–35. The Embassy–Charles V, August 2nd 1553.
20. ibid., VI, 2, 90 and 94. Chapuys–Mary of Hungary, January 1st and January 15th 1553.
21. *Ven. Cal.*, V, p. 934. Soranzo's Report, 1554. Cf. Baschet, *Trans.*, 3, p. 21. Noailles–the Queen of Scots, December 24th 1553.
22. Baschet, *Trans.*, 3, 20. Same–same, October 18th 1553.
23. *Span. Cal.*, XI, pp. 251–5. The Embassy–Charles V, September 23rd 1553.
24. ibid., pp. 153–4. Renard–Granvelle, August 7th 1553.
25. ibid.
26. ibid.
27. *Span. Cal.*, XI, pp. 177–8. Prince Philip–Charles V, [August 22nd 1553].
28. ibid., pp. 163–4. Charles V–the Embassy, August 14th 1553.
29. ibid., pp. 164–5. Granvelle–Renard, August 14th 1553. ibid., p. 195. The Embassy–Queen Mary, [late August 1553].
30. ibid., pp. 165–6. Renard–Granvelle, August 15th 1553.
31. ibid., pp. 238–42. The Embassy–Charles V, September 19th 1553.
32. *Ambass.*, II, pp. 142–8. Noailles–Henri II, September 7th 1553.
33. ibid., pp. 174–82. Negotiations of de Noailles, September 6–25th 1553.
34. ibid.
35. *Span. Cal.*, XI, pp. 212–14. Renard–Granvelle, September 8th 1553.
36. ibid., pp. 199–207. Report of Scheyfve's secretary in letter of The Embassy–Charles V, September 4th 1553.
37. ibid., The Embassy–Charles V.
38. ibid., pp. 212–14 ut sup.
39. ibid., pp. 233–7. The Embassy–Charles V, September 14th 1553.
40. ibid., pp. 230–1. Granvelle–Renard, September 13th 1553. ibid., pp. 243–8. Charles V–Renard, September 20th.
41. Muller, *Gardiner and the Tudor Reaction*, p. 236. Cf. Harbison, p. 59.
42. *Span. Cal.*, XI, pp. 265–72. Renard–Charles V, October 5th 1553.
43. Baschet, *Trans.*, 3, 20. Noailles–Henri II, October 7th 1553.
44. *Ambass.*, II, pp. 217–18. Same–same, October 8th 1553.
45. *Span. Cal.*, XI, pp. 288–93. The Embassy–Charles V, October 12th 1553.
46. ibid.
47. ibid., p. 293. Queen Mary–Renard, October 13th 1553.
48. ibid., pp. 294–300. Renard–Charles V, October 15th 1553.
49. ibid., pp. 312–15. Same–same, October 23rd 1553.
50. ibid.
51. ibid., pp. 319–24. Same–same, October 28th 1553.
52. ibid., pp. 327–30. Same–same, October 31st 1553.
53. ibid., p. 326. Renard–Prince Philip, October 29th 1553.

CHAPTER XIV (pp. 220–247)

1. *Span. Cal.*, XI, pp. 332–6. Renard–Charles V, November 4th 1553.
2. ibid., pp. 337–45. Same–same, November 6th 1553.

3. *Span. Cal.*, XI, pp. 337–45. Renard–Charles V, November 6th 1553.

4. *Ambass.*, II, pp. 233–8. Noailles–Henri II, November 4th 1553. ibid., pp. 253–7. Same–same, November 14th.

5. *Span. Cal.*, XI, pp. 363–6. Renard–Charles V, November 17th 1553.

6. ibid., pp. 370–3. Same–same, November 20th 1553.

7. ibid., pp. 354–5. Granvelle–Renard, November 13th 1553. ibid., p. 367. Mary of Hungary–same, November 19th.

8. ibid., pp. 414–19. Renard–Charles V, December 8th 1553.

9. Schenk, *Reginald Pole*, pp. 64–5, 83.

10. *Ven. Cal.*, V, 820, n. Pole–the Pope, [? October 27th] 1553.

11. Tytler, II, pp. 262–72. Wotton–the Council, December 23rd 1553. *Span. Cal.*, XI, pp. 466–74. Renard–Charles V.

12. Baschet, *Trans.*, 3, 21. Henri II–Noailles, November 23rd 1553.

13. *Ambass.*, II, pp. 258–62. Noailles–Henri II, November 17th.

14. Baschet, *Trans.*, loc. cit.

15. *S.P. Dom.*, 11, 2, No. 2. Sir J. Arundel–Earl of Arundel, January 13th 1554.

16. *Ambass.*, II, pp. 334–43. Noailles–Henri II, December 23rd 1553. Baschet, *Trans.*, 3, 21. Constable–Noailles, December 30th 1553.

17. *Span. Cal.*, XI, pp. 393–7. Renard–Charles V, November 28th 1553.

18. ibid.

19. ibid., pp. 403–7. Charles V–Prince Philip, November 30th to December 16th 1553.

20. *Span. Cal.*, XII, p. 111. de Molina–Renard, February 17th 1554.

21. ibid., XI, pp. 460–1. Egmont, etc.–Charles V, December 27th 1553. *Chron. of Queen Jane*, p. 34.

22. *Span. Cal.*, XII, p. 8. de Lara–Prince Philip, January 6th 1554.

23. ibid., p. 11. Ambassadors–Charles V, January 7th 1554.

24. ibid., p. 14.

25. *Acts of the P.C.*, N.S., IV, p. 385.

26. *Ambass.*, III, pp. 43–6. Noailles–Henri II. January 23rd and January 26th 1554.

27. *S.P. Dom.*, 11, 2, No. 18. St. Leger–Earl of Arundel, January 26th [1554].

28. T. B. Howell, *Cobbett's Complete Collection of State Trials*, I, pp. 861 et seq.

29. Baschet, *Trans.*, 3, 21. Noailles–the Constable, January 12th 1554.

30. ibid. Noailles–Henri II, January 12th. ibid., Noailles–d'Oysel, January 22nd 1554.

31. Strype, *Ecc. Mem.*, III, 1, p. 151. Baschet, loc. cit.

32. Hooker, *Life of Sir P. Carew*, pp. 5, 6–9, 10, 38–40, and 110–15.

33. *S.P. Dom.*, 11, 2, 33. Deposition of Christopher Mompesson, [? January 1554].

34. Hooker, *Life of Sir P. Carew*, App. E, No. 5.

35. ibid., No. 10.

36. *Chron. of Queen Jane*, p. 37.

37. *S.P. Dom.*, 11, 3, No. 19. Deposition of John Bowyer.

38. ibid., Cf. ibid., 2, No. 25. Lord Rich, etc.–the Council, January 29th 1554.

39. ibid.

40. *Chron. of Queen Jane*, App. VI, pp. 124–5. *Span. Cal.*, XII, p. 85. Renard–Charles V, February 8th 1554.

41. *Acts of the P.C.*, N.S., I, pp. 104–5.

42. *S.P. Dom.*, 11, 3, No. 18, i. Deposition of Sir Anthony Norton.

43. Tytler, II, p. 278. *S.P. Dom.*, 11, 2, No. 10, I. Deposition of Cotman, January 23rd 1554.

44. *Antiq. Rep.*, III, pp. 72–3. Proctor, *History of Wyatt's Rebellion*.

45. *Antiq. Rep.*, III, pp. 69–71.

46. *Ambass.*, III, pp. 46–9. Noailles–Henri II, January 28th 1554.

47. *Antiq. Rep.*, Proctor, p. 75.

48. ibid., p. 71.

49. ibid., p. 79.

50. ibid., p. 80.

51. *S.P. Dom.*, 11, 2, No. 31. Dodge–the Council, January 28th 1554.

52. *Antiq. Rep.*, ut sup., pp. 80–2.

53. *S.P. Dom.*, 11, 2, No. 21. Norfolk–the Council, January 28th 1554.

54. ibid.

55. ibid., No. 23. Same–same, January 29th 1554.

56. ibid., No. 23, i. Cobham–Norfolk, January 29th 1554. Enclosed in above.

57. ibid., No. 23 ut sup.

58. *Chron. of Queen Jane*, pp. 37–9.

59. *Antiq. Rep.*, ut sup., p. 90.

60. *Chron of Queen Jane*, p. 40. Wriothesley, II, p. 107.

61. *S.P. Dom.*, 11, 2, No. 28. Cobham–Queen Mary, January 30th 1554.

62. *Papiers d'État de . . . Granvelle*, IV, pp. 207–9. *Span. Cal.*, XII, p. 77. Renard–Charles V, February 8th 1553.

63. *S.P. Dom.*, 11, 2, No. 20. Gardiner–Petre, January 28th 1554. Gardiner, *Letters*, p. 158. *Span. Cal.*, XII, p. 65 n.

64. *Ven. Cal.*, V, 854. Pole–di Monte, February 8th 1554. Tyler, *Abstracts*. Renard–Charles V, January 29th.

65. *Ambass.*, III, pp. 52–4. Noailles–Henri II, February 3rd 1554.

66. Foxe, VI, pp. 414–15. Wriothesley, II, pp. 108–9. Machyn, p. 53. *Span. Cal.*, XII, p. 79. Renard–Charles V, February 5th 1554. Harbison, *Rival Ambassadors*, pp. 132–3.

67. *Span. Cal.*, XII, p. 86. Renard–Charles V, February 8th 1554.

68. *Chron. of Queen Jane*, pp. 40–1. Wriothesley, II, p. 109.

69. *Chron. of Queen Jane*, p. 43.

70. *Narr. of Ref.*, p. 161. *Autobiography of Underhill*. Cf. Machyn, p. 53.

71. *Narr. of Ref.*, p. 164.

72. *Ambass.*, III, pp. 52–4. Noailles–Henri II, February 3rd 1554.

73. Stow, *Annales*, pp. 1046–7.

74. *Chron. of Queen Jane*, p. 45.

75. ibid., pp. 45–8.

76. *Antiq. Rep.*, Proctor, ut sup., p. 99.

77. *S.P. Dom.*, 11, 3, No. 11. Cheyne–the Council, February 7th [1554].

78. Stow, *Annales*, pp. 1047–8.

79. *Chron. of Queen Jane*, pp. 45–8.

80. ibid., p. 48. The following account of events in London is drawn from Proctor, *Antiq. Rep.*, III, pp. 99–102. Wriothesley, II, pp. 110–11. *Chron. of Queen Jane*, pp. 48–52. *Greyfriars Chron.*, pp. 86–8. Edward Underhill's *Narrative* in *Narratives of the Reformation*, pp. 161–8. Stow, *Annales*, pp. 1048–52.

CHAPTER XV (pp. 248–266)

1. *Span. Cal.*, XII, p. 168. Renard–Charles V, March 22nd 1554.

2. ibid., p. 106. Same–same, February 17th 1554. Wriothesley, II, pp. 111–12.

3. Machyn, p. 57. Wriothesley, II, pp. 112–13.

4. *S.P. Dom.*, 11, 3, No. 32. Southwell–the Council, February 24th 1554.

5. *Chron. of Queen Jane*, p. 57 n.

6. *Ambass.*, III, pp. 125–7. Parolles de Mme. Jehane Gray. *Chron. of Queen Jane*, 55–9.

7. Stow, *Annales*, p. 1053. *Chron. of Queen Jane*, pp. 60–1.

8. ibid., p. 60.

9. Holinshed, II, p. 1734.

10. Baschet, *Trans.*, 3, 21. Noailles–the Constable, February 12th 1554.

11. *Span. Cal.*, XII, p. 124. Renard–Charles V, February 24th 1554.

12. *For. Cal.*, 170. Crayer–Lord Grey, March 24th 1554.

13. *Ven. Cal.*, V, 871 and 872. Pole–di Monte, Same–Morone, April 4th 1554.
Span. Cal., XII, p. 223. Renard–Charles V, April 22nd 1554.

14. *Ambass.*, III, pp. 195–203. Noailles–Henri II, May 8th 1554.

15. ibid., pp. 131–7. Same–the Constable, [1554].

16. *For. Cal.*, 211. The Council–Wotton, May 29th 1554.

17. *Chron. of Queen Jane*, pp. 60–1.

18. *Span. Cal.*, XII, p. 139. Egmont and Renard–Charles V, March 8th 1554.

19. ibid., p. 96. Renard–same, February 12th 1554.

20. *Span. Cal.*, XI, pp. 288–93. Renard–Charles V, October 12th 1553.

21. *Chron. of Queen Jane*, p. 72.

22. ibid.

23. Hearne, *Sylloge*, pp. 154–5. Queen Mary–Princess Elizabeth, January 26th 1554.

24. *S.P. Dom.*, 11, 2, No. 20. Gardiner–Petre, January 28th 1554. Gardiner, *Letters*, 158.

25. Tytler, II, pp. 426–8. Lord Admiral, etc–Queen Mary, February 11th 1553.

26. *Span. Cal.*, XII, p. 125. Renard–Charles V, February 24th 1554.

27. ibid., p. 167. Same–same, March 22nd 1554.

28. *S.P. Dom.*, 11, 4, No. 2. Princess Elizabeth–Queen Mary, March 16th 1554.

29. *Chron. of Queen Jane*, pp. 70–1.

30. *Span. Cal.*, XII, loc. cit.

31. Strype, *Ecc. Mem.*, III, 1, pp. 128–9. *Span. Cal.*, XII, p. 200.

32. *Span. Cal.*, XII, p. 151. Renard–Charles V, March 14th 1554.

33. ibid., p. 112. Charles V's Instructions to d'Egmont. February 18th 1554.

34. ibid., p. 168. Renard–Charles V, March 22nd 1554.

35. ibid., pp. 167–8.

36. ibid., pp. 175–6. Renard–Charles V, March 27th 1554.

37. ibid., p. 140. Egmont and Renard–same, March 8th 1554.

38. Foxe, VIII, p. 613.

39. *Ambass.*, III, pp. 203–7. Noailles's Report, May 8th 1554.

40. *Bedingfield Papers*, pp. 149–54.

41. ibid., p. 222.

42. *Span. Cal.*, XII, p. 221. Renard–Charles V, April 22nd 1554.

43. ibid.

44. *Ambass.*, III, pp. 95–103. Instructions for la Marque, March 4th 1554.

45. ibid., pp. 183–6. Noailles–Henri II, April 29th 1554; and pp. 211–16. Same–same, May 13th.

46. Machyn, pp. 62–3.

47. ibid., p. 65.

48. Stow, *Annales*, p. 1056.

49. *Span. Cal.*, XII, p. 22. Renard–Charles V, April 22nd 1554.

50. ibid., p. 157. Same–same, March 15th 1554.

51. ibid., pp. 197–8. Same–same, April 3rd 1554.

52. *D.N.B.* sub Hastings, Edward.

53. Tytler, II, pp. 381–3. Paget–Renard [April 1554]. Cf. *Span. Cal.*, XII, pp. 219–20. April 19th (?).

54. *Span. Cal.*, XII, p. 262. de Courrières and Renard–Charles V, May 25th 1554.

55. ibid., pp. 239, 251. Renard–Charles V, May 6th and May 13th 1554.

56. *Ambass.*, III, pp. 218–22. Noailles–Henri II, May 18th 1554.

57. *Span. Cal.*, XII, pp. 251, 259. Renard–Charles V, May 13th, and Renard and de Courrières–same, May 22nd to May 25th 1554.

58. ibid., p. 259.

59. ibid.

CHAPTER XVI (pp. 267–288)

1. *Span. Cal.*, XII, p. 142. Egmont and Renard–Charles V, March 8th 1554. ibid., p. 121. Renard–Prince Philip, February 19th 1554.

2. ibid., p. 162. Mendoza–Granvelle, March 19th 1554.

3. Hearne, *Sylloge*, p. 156. Queen Mary–Prince Philip, April 20th 1554.

4. e.g. *Span. Cal.*, XII, pp. 96–7, 98. Renard–Charles V, February 12th and 14th. pp. 170–1, Granvelle–Mary of Hungary, March 22nd 1554.

5. ibid., p. 178. Mendoza–Granvelle, March 29th 1554. Strype, *Ecc. Mem.*, III, i, p. 186.

6. *Ambass.*, II, pp. 275–80. Noailles–Henri II, December 1st 1554.

7. Strype, *Ecc. Mem.*, III, ii, pp. 215–16. *Acts of the P.C.*, N.S., v, p. 40.

8. *For. Cal.*, p. 207. Dudley–the Council, May 17th 1554.

9. *S.P. Dom.*, 11, 4, No. 11. Howard–the Council, June 9th 1554.

10. *Ven. Cal.*, v, 898. Damula–the Doge, June 17th 1554.

11. *Span. Cal.*, XII, p. 304. Granvelle–Renard, July 3rd 1554.

12. ibid., pp. 271, 294. Renard–Charles V, June 9th, and de Cappelle–d'Eecke, June 29th 1554.

13. Tytler, II, pp. 410–11. Bedford, etc.–the Council, June 5th 1554.

14. *Ambass.*, III, pp. 280–2. Noailles–the Constable, July 23rd 1554.

15. *Span. Cal.*, XII, p. 314. Renard–Charles V, July 19th 1554.

16. ibid., p. 247. Prince Philip–Gomez, May 11th 1554.

17. ibid., p. 4. 'A writing *ad cautelam* . . .' January 4th 1554.

18. ibid., pp. 143–4. Egmont and Renard–Charles V, March 8th 1554.

19. ibid., p. 48. Charles V–the Ambassadors, January 24th 1554.

20. ibid., pp. 295–6. 'Notes for Prince Philip's guidance . . .' (?) June 1554.

21. ibid., p. 214. Charles V–Prince Philip, April 9th 1554. p. 185. Same–Alva, April 1st 1554.

22. *Chron. of Queen Jane*, App. x, pp. 165–6, John Elder, 'Copie of a letter sent into Scotland'.

23. Baschet, *Diplomatie venitienne*, Ch. v.

24. ibid.

25. Gachard, *Correspondance de Philippe II* . . . , I, p. xlix, n.

26. Gachard, *Lettres de Philippe II à ses filles* . . . , pp. 137, 148–9, and 158.

27. *Ambass.*, III, pp. 284–8. Noailles–Henri II, July 27th 1554.

28. *Span. Cal.*, XII, pp. 314–20. Figueroa–Charles V, July 26th 1554.

29. The account of Philip's arrival at Southampton, meeting with the Queen, etc., and of their marriage is drawn from:

Span. Cal., XII, pp. 319–22. Figueroa–Charles V, July 26th 1554.
Tyler, Letter relating to Philip's voyage and marriage, July 1554.
John Elder's 'Letter' in Chron. of Queen Jane, App. X, p. 136 et seq. See also:
Martin Hume, 'The visit of Philip II, 1554', English Historical Review, VII, 1892, pp. 253 et seq.

30. Tyler. Letter relating to Philip's voyage and marriage, July 1554.
31. Narr. of the Reformation. Edward Underhill's Narrative, pp. 170–1.
32. ibid.
33. Tyler, loc. cit.
34. ibid. Queen Mary–Charles V, August 15th 1554.
35. ibid. Gomez–Eraso, August 12th 1554.
36. ibid. Letter of a Gentleman . . . to a friend at Salamanca, August 17th 1554.
37. ibid. Gomez–Eraso, July 29th 1554.
38. ibid.
39. ibid. Letter of a Gentleman ut sup.
40. Chron. of Queen Jane, pp. 78–9.
41. Tyler. Ambassador of Savoy–Granvelle, November 24th 1554. Machyn, p. 76.
42. Tytler, II, p. 462. Mason–the Council, December 25th 1554.
43. Tyler. Eraso–Gomez, November 29th 1554.
44. ibid. Letter relating to Philip's voyage, July 1554.
45. Ambass., III, pp. 294–9. Noailles–Henri II, August 1st 1554.
46. Tyler. Renard–Charles V, September 18th 1554.
47. ibid. Letter of a Spanish Gentleman, October 2nd 1554.
48. ibid. Renard–Charles V, September 18th 1554.
49. Chron. of Queen Jane, p. 81.
50. Tyler. Ambassador of Savoy–Granvelle, September 19th 1554.
51. ibid. Letter of a Spanish Gentleman, October 2nd 1554.
52. ibid. Renard–Charles V, July 29th 1554.
53. ibid. Negotiations of Paget, November 14th 1554.
54. ibid. Renard–Charles V, November 23rd 1554.
55. Narr. of the Reformation. Edward Underhill, p. 146.
56. Beccatelli, Life of Cardinal Pole, pp. 26–8.
57. Ven. Cal., VI, i, 614. Pole–Card. Farnese, [September 15th 1556].
58. Beccatelli, loc. cit., pp. 132–3.
59. Ven. Cal., V, 805. Pole–Queen Mary, October 2nd 1553.
60. ibid., 772. Information for Charles V, [? August 20th] 1553.
61. ibid., 836. Pole–Queen Mary, December 1st 1553. Cf. Span. Cal., XI, pp. 419–22. Memoir of Pole–Queen Mary.
62. Span. Cal., XI, p. 312. Renard–Charles V, October 23rd 1553.
63. Ven. Cal., V, 946. Pole–King Philip, September 21st 1554.
64. Tyler. King Philip–Eraso, November [14th–15th] 1554.
65. Tytler, II, pp. 451–7. Mason–the King and Queen, November 9th 1554.
66. Machyn, pp. 75–6. Greyfriars, pp. 52–3.
67. Tyler. Renard–Charles V, November 23rd 1554.
68. Ven. Cal., V, 966. Pole–Julius III, November 30th 1554.
69. Strype, Ecc. Mem., III, i, pp. 323–4.
70. Narr. of the Reformation, Edward Underhill, p. 158.

CHAPTER XVII (pp. 289–306)

1. *Chron. of Queen Jane*, App. x, p. 164. John Elder's 'Letter'.
2. Tyler. Renard–Charles V, November 6th 1554. *Ambass.*, IV, pp. 153–6. Noailles –the Constable, January 20th 1555.
3. Tyler. Renard–Charles V, December 21st 1554.
4. *Ven. Cal.*, VI, i, 67. Michiel–the Doge, April 29th 1555.
5. Stone, p. 346, quoting *Archives des Affaires étrangères. Angleterre*, I, p. 827. Paris.
6. Foxe, VIII, p. 621.
7. Allen, *Political Thought in the Sixteenth Century*.
8. Dixon, IV, p. 368.
9. Strype, *Ecc. Mem.*, III, i, p. 586.
10. Pococke, 'Condition of Morals and Religious Belief in the Reign of Edward VI', *English Historical Review*, VII, 1895, p. 417.
11. Dixon, IV, pp. 206–7. The words in [...] are from a second version.
12. *Narr. of the Reformation*, Underhill, p. 171.
13. Strype, *Ecc. Mem.*, III, ii, pp. 152–5.
14. Foxe, VI, p. 592.
15. Tyler. Embassy–Charles V, August 8th 1554.
16. Foxe, VII, p. 70. Wriothesley, II, pp. 127–8. Machyn, pp. 84–5.
17. Foxe, VII, p. 733.
18. *Ambass.*, IV, pp. 23–8. Noailles–Henri II, November 30th 1554.
19. Maitland, *Essays*, p. 123.
20. ibid., pp. 50 and 47.
21. ibid., pp. 99–105.
22. ibid., pp. 90.
23. Cf. Garrett. *Marian Exiles*. Intro., p. viii.
24. *Papiers d'État*, IV, pp. 402–5. Renard–Charles V, [February 1555].
25. Maitland, *Essays*, p. 79, quoting Strype, *Life of Parker*.
26. *Span. Cal.*, XII, p. 152. Renard–Charles V, March 14th 1554.
27. ibid., p. 200. Same–same, April 3rd 1554.
28. Foxe, VI, p. 704.
29. *Papiers d'État*, IV, pp. 402–5. Renard–Charles V, [February 1555].
30. Foxe, VII, pp. 100 and 104.
31. ibid., p. 86.
32. *Chron. of Queen Jane*, App. x. Elder's 'Letter'.
33. Strype, *Ecc. Mem.*, III, ii, pp. 482–510.
34. Foxe, VII, p. 91.
35. Forneron, *Philippe II*, I, pp. 56–8.
36. *Ven. Cal.*, VI, 1, 132. Michiel–the Doge, June 11th 1555.
37. ibid., VI, 2, 884, p. 1056. Michiel Report, May 13th 1557.
38. *Papiers d'État*, IV, pp. 399–402. Renard–King Philip, [February ? 1555].
39. Cf. Harbison, *Rival Ambassadors*, pp. 224–7, 257–9.
40. *Ven. Cal.*, VI, 2, App., 136. Collier, *An Ecclesiastical History of Great Britain*, 1714, II, p. 371.
41. Foxe, VII, p. 86.
42. B. White, *Mary Tudor*, p. 351, quoting Pole, *Epistolae*, v.
43. *Ven. Cal.*, VI, 2, 884, p. 1056 ut sup.

CHAPTER XVIII (pp. 307–325)

1. *Papiers d'État*, IV, pp. 432–3. Renard–Charles V, [June 27th 1555].
2. Foxe, VII, p. 126.
3. *Ambass.*, IV, pp. 225–7. Noailles–the Constable, March 10th 1555.
4. *Ven. Cal.*, VI, 1, 42. Michiel–the Doge, April 2nd 1555.
5. Tytler, II, p. 469.
6. *Ven. Cal.*, VI, 1, 72. Michiel–the Doge, May 6th 1555.
7. Tytler, II, pp. 469–70. Mason–Petre, May 3rd 1555.
8. *Ven. Cal.*, VI, 1, 89. Michiel–the Doge, May 21st 1555.
9. *Ambass.*, IV, pp. 341–3. Noailles, Avis, May 29th 1555.
10. *Ven. Cal.*, VI, 2, 884, p. 1060. Report of Michiel, May 13th 1557.
11. *For. Cal.*, 383. Hoby–Mason, June 6th 1555. ibid., p. 390. Mason–Petre, June 24th 1555.
12. Foxe, VII, p. 126.
13. Maitland, *Essays*, p. 112.
14. *Papiers d'État*, IV, pp. 432–3 ut sup.
15. ibid.
16. *Ven. Cal.*, VI, 1, 162. Badoer–the Doge, July 21st 1555.
17. Stone, p. 351.
18. *Ven. Cal.*, VI, 1, 200. Michiel–the Doge, August 27th 1555. ibid., 204. Same–same, September 3rd.
19. *Ambass.*, V, pp. 122–8. Noailles, Avis, September 9th 1555.
20. *Ven. Cal.*, VI, 1, 309. Badoer–the Doge, December 5th 1555.
21. ibid., 200 ut sup.
22. ibid., 213. Michiel–the Doge, September 13th.
23. ibid., 232 and 238. Badoer– the Doge, October 2nd and 5th.
24. ibid., 251. Michiel–the Doge, October 21st 1555.
25. *Ambass.*, V. pp. 146–52. Noailles–the Constable, October 6th.
26. *Ven. Cal.*, VI, 1, 288. Badoer–the Doge, November 24th.
27. *Ambass.*, V, pp. 201–4. Noailles–d'Oyssel.
28. *Ven. Cal.*, VI, 1, 245. Badoer–the Doge, October 13th 1555.
29. *Ambass.*, V, pp. 169–73. Noailles, Avis, October 22nd 1555.
30. *Ven. Cal.*, VI, 1, 257. Badoer–the Doge, October 27th 1555.
31. Stone, p. 341, quoting *A Portfolio of a Man of Letters*.
32. *Ven. Cal.*, VI, i, 289. Michiel–the Doge, November 25th 1555.
33. *Ven. Cal.*, VI, 1, 473. Marc Antonio Faitta–friend in Italy, April 4th 1556.
34. Strype, *Ecc. Mem.*, III, ii, 482–510.
35. *S.P. Dom.*, 11, 7, No. 6. Mason–Devonshire.
36. Schenk, *Reginald Pole*, p. 144.
37. Dixon, IV, pp. 521–3.
38. ibid., pp. 534–5.
39. Foxe, VIII, p. 307.
40. *Ven. Cal.*, VI, 1, 460. Badoer–the Doge, April 19th 1556.
41. ibid., 416. Same–same, March 1st 1556.
42. ibid., 256. Pole–Philip, [October 26th] 1555.
43. ibid., 309. Badoer–the Doge, December 5th 1555.
44. ibid., 318. Same–same, December 18th 1555.
45. ibid., 332. Same–same, December 29th 1555.

46. *Ven. Cal.*, VI, I, 353. Same–same, January 16th 1556.
47. Baschet, *Trans.*, 3, 22. Noailles–the Constable, June 30th 1556.
48. *Ambass.*, V, pp. 169–73. Noailles, Avis, October 22nd 1555.

CHAPTER XIX (pp. 326–343)

1. *For. Cal.*, 218. Mason–the Council, June 11th 1554.
2. *Ambass.*, IV, pp. 116–19. Noailles–Henri II, January 10th 1555.
3. *Ven. Cal.*, VI, I, 91. Soranzo–the Doge, May 23rd 1555.
4. *Ambass.*, V, pp. 25–34. Noailles–Henri II, June 10th 1555.
5. *Ven. Cal.*, VI, I, 154. Michiel–the Doge, July 9th 1555.
6. ibid., 258. Same–same, October 27th 1555.
7. Baschet, *Trans.*, 3, 21. Noailles–the Constable, February 17th 1554. Cf. Harbison, *Rival Ambassadors*, pp. 19–25.
8. Tytler, II, p. 289. Wotton–the Queen, February 12th [1554].
9. *Ambass.*, III, pp. 240–5. Noailles–the Constable, May 24th 1554.
10. *For. Cal.*, 240. Cheke–Petre, July 22nd 1554.
11. Hooker, *Life of Carew*, p. 65.
12. *Ven. Cal.*, VI, i, 429 and 434. Michiel–the Doge, March 17th and 24th 1556.
13. *S.P. Dom.*, 11, 8, No. 70. Examination of William Crowe.
14. ibid., No. 38. Confession of J. Daniel.
15. ibid., No. 64. Questions to be put to Dethick.
16. Harbison, *Rival Ambassadors*, pp. 273–4.
17. *S.P. Dom.*, 11, 7, No. 31. Confession of Richard Uvedale. Cf. *Ven. Cal.*, VI, i, 495. Michiel–the Doge, May 26th 1556. Harbison, loc. cit.
18. *Span. Cal.*, XII, p. 213. Renard–Charles V, April 7th 1554. *Ven. Cal.*, VI, i, 466. Michiel–the Doge, April 28th 1556.
19. *S.P. Dom.*, 11, 8, No. 46. Statement by Sir R. Peckham.
20. ibid., 7, No. 47. Confession of Thomas White.
21. *Ambass.*, III, pp. 305–7. Noailles–the Constable, August 18th 1554.
22. *Papiers d'État*, IV, p. 695. Renard–King Philip, September 14th 1556.
23. Baga de Secretis. Pouch XXXIV. Printed in *4th Report of the Deputy Keeper of the Public Records*, App. II, p. 252 et seq.
24. *S.P. Dom.*, 11, 7, No. 48. Deposition of Thomas White.
25. ibid., No. 66. Examination of John Throckmorton.
26. *For. Cal.*, 496. Wotton–the Queen, April 12th 1556.
27. *S.P. Dom.*, II, 7, No. 37. Confession of Sir Thomas White.
28. ibid., 8, Nos. 2 and 3. Examinations of Sir A. Kingston.
29. ibid., 7, No. 42. Confession of William Hinnes.
30. ibid., No. 44. Notes on Hinnes's Confession.
31. ibid., No. 52. Deposition by Bedell.
32. ibid., 8, No. 6. Confession of J. Daniel.
33. ibid., No. 38. Confession of J. Daniel, [? May 24th].
34. *For. Cal.*, 496 ut sup. *4th Report of the Deputy Keeper of the Public Records*, App. II, pp. 252 et seq.
35. *S.P. Dom.*, 11, 7, No. 31. Confession of Richard Uvedale.
36. ibid.
37. ibid., No. 63. Notes from Deposition of Rossey.

38. *S.P. Dom.*, 11, 7, No. 46. Statement of William Hinnes.

39. ibid., 8, No. 53. Confession of Henry Peckham.

40. ibid.

41. ibid., No. 21. Notes of Interview between the Dean of St. Paul's and Throgmorton, April 23rd 1556.

42. ibid., No. 53 ut sup.

43. ibid., No. 38. Confession of J. Daniel.

44. ibid., No. 58. Memoranda by one of the conspirators.

45. *Ven. Cal.*, VI, 1, 477. Michiel–the Doge, May 5th 1556.

46. *S.P. Dom.*, 11, 8, No. 70. Examination of William Crowe.

47. *Ambass.*, V, pp. 352–8. Noailles–Henri II, 7 May 1556. *Ven. Cal.*, VI, i, 467. Soranzo–the Doge, May 1st 1556.

48. *S.P. Dom.*, 11, 8, No. 16. Devonshire–Mason, April 18th 1556.

49. ibid., No. 52. Confession of Henry Peckham.

50. *Ven. Cal.*, VI, 1, 461. Michiel–the Doge, April 21st 1556.

51. *S.P. Dom.*, 11, 8, No. 80. Examination of Battista Castiglione.

52. *Ambass.*, V, pp. 298–300. The Constable–Noailles, February 7th 1556.

53. *Ven. Cal.*, VI, 1, 510 and 514. Michiel–the Doge, June 9th and June 16th 1556.

54. *S.P. Dom.*, 11, 5, No. 9. Basset–Devonshire, May 3rd 1555.

55. Tytler, II, pp. 477–8. Martyn–Devonshire, May 31st 1555.

56. *S.P. Dom.*, 11, 5, No. 42. Devonshire–Abergavenny, June 30th 1555.

57. ibid., No. 45. Same–Thomas Smith, July 1st 1555.

58. ibid., No. 44. Same–the Marchioness of Exeter, July 1st 1555.

59. *Ven. Cal.*, VI, 1, 173 and 187. Badoer–the Doge, August 4th and August 18th 1555.

60. *S.P. Dom.*, 11, 6, Nos. 38 and 42. Basset–Devonshire, October 30th 1555. Devonshire–Basset, November 2nd 1555.

61. ibid., No. 67. Same–Lady Barkley, November 23rd 1555.

62. ibid., 7, No. 59. Examination of Martin Dare.

63. *Papiers d'État*, IV, pp. 580–9. Renard–King Philip, May 31st 1556.

64. *S.P. Dom.*, 11, 9, No. 22. Mason–Devonshire, July 19th 1556.

65. *For. Cal.*, 537. Vannes–Queen Mary, September 8th 1556.

66. *Ven. Cal.*, VI, 2, 729. Motion of the Council of Ten, November 26th 1556.

CHAPTER XX (pp. 344–355)

1. Baschet, *Trans.*, 3, 22. Noailles–Henri II, October 18th 1556.

2. *Ven. Cal.*, VI, 1, 328. Deposition of Marco Pisano, December 24th 1555.

3. Baschet, *Trans.*, 3, 22. Noailles–the Constable, August 30th 1556.

4. *Ambass.*, V, pp. 361–3. Same–same, May 11th 1556.

5. Baschet, *Trans.*, 3, 22. Noailles–Henri II, July 19th 1556. *Ambass.*, V, pp. 369–71.

6. *Ven. Cal.*, VI, 1, 570. Michiel–the Doge, August 4th 1556.

7. *Ambass.*, V, pp. 361–3 ut sup.

8. ibid., pp. 186–91. Noailles–the Constable, October 31st 1555.

9. *For. Cal.*, 333. Mason–Petre, March 3rd 1555.

10. Strype, *Ecc. Mem.*, III, ii, lxxx, p. 534. Pole–Queen Mary.

11. Baschet, *Trans.*, 3, 22. Noailles–Henri II, July 19th. Same–the Constable, October 5th.

12. *For. Cal.*, 297. Gresham–the Council, November 30th 1554.

13. *For. Cal.*, 429. Same - Queen Mary, October 27th 1555.

14. *Ven. Cal.*, VI, 1, 594. Michiel–the Doge, September 2nd 1556.

15. *Acts of the P.C.*, N.S., VI. Many entries in autumn of 1557. Cf. *S.P. Dom.*, 11, 11, Nos. 44, 45, 49, etc.

16. *Ven. Cal.*, VI, 1, 347. Navagero–the Doge, January 11th 1556.

17. ibid., 587. Badoer–the Doge, August 27th 1556.

18. ibid., 415. Navagero–same, February 28th 1556.

19. ibid., 459. Same–same, April 18th 1556.

20. ibid., 425 and 484. Navagero–the Doge, March 14th, and Badoer–the Doge, May 16th 1556.

   Baschet, *Trans.*, 3, 22. Noailles–the Constable, June 30th 1556.

21. *Ven. Cal.*, VI, 2, 808. Soranzo–the Doge, February 1st 1557.

23. *Acts of the P.C.*, N.S., VI, p. 64.

24. *Papiers d'État*, V, p. 62. King Philip–Granvelle, April 2nd 1557.

25. Harbison, *Rival Ambassadors*, pp. 323–5.

26. *Ven. Cal.*, VI, 2, 866. Soranzo–the Doge, April 26th 1557.

27. *Papiers d'État*, V, p. 71. King Philip–Granvelle, May 4th 1557.

28. Strype, *Ecc. Mem.*, III, ii, pp. 31–9.

29. Beccatelli, *Life of Cardinal Pole*, pp. 115–16.

30. *Ven. Cal.*, VI, 2, 928. Navagero–the Doge, June 10th 1557.

31. ibid., 937. Same–same, June 18th 1557.

32. ibid.

33. ibid.

34. ibid.

35. ibid., 991. Navagero–the Doge, August 14th 1557.

36. *For. Cal.*, 587. Wotton 'Advertisement' [before April 14th] 1557.

37. *Ven. Cal.*, VI, 2, 870. Surian–the Doge, April 29th 1557. *For. Cal.*, 593. Wotton–Queen Mary, April 27th 1557.

38. Strype, *Ecc. Mem.*, III, ii, lxxi, p. 515.

39. *Ven. Cal.*, VI, 2, 896, p. 1106. Soranzo–the Doge, May 21st 1557.

40. ibid., 873. Surian–the Doge, May 6th 1557.

41. ibid., 891. Same–same, May 17th 1557.

42. *Archives curieuses . . . de France*, 1ᵉ serie, t. 3, p. 213.

43. *Ven. Cal.*, VI, 2, 883. Soranzo–the Doge, May 11th 1557.

44. ibid., 927. Same–same, June 9th 1557.

CHAPTER XXI (pp. 356–367)

1. Lettenhove, *Relations . . .* , I, p. 86. Bedford–Cecil, September 3rd 1557.

2. For the whole description of the Pale I have relied on C. Dillon's 'Calais and the Pale', *Archaeologia*, 53, ii, 1893, pp. 289–388.

3. *L. and P.*, XV, 316. Commission appointed to inquire into religion in Calais. March 1540. ibid., 473. Henry VIII–the Commissioners, April 8th 1540.

4. *Ven. Cal.*, VI, 1, 127. Badoer–the Doge, June 8th 1555.

5. Muller, *Gardiner and the Tudor Reaction*, Ch. XXXIII, n. 17, quoting Parsons, *Domestical Difficulties*.

6. *For. Cal.*, 496. Wotton–Queen Mary, April 12th 1556.

7. *S.P. Dom.*, 11, 9, No. 26. Further Confession of Killigrew, August 26th 1556.

8. *For. Cal.*, 553. Wotton–Queen Mary, October 29th 1556.

9. ibid., 558. Same–same, November 17th 1556, and p. 560. Wotton–Petre, November 30th 1556.

10. *S.P. Dom.*, 11, 9, No. 51. Select Council–the King, November [22nd] 1556. *Ven. Cal.*, VI, 2, 743. Michiel–the Doge, December 1st 1556.

11. *For. Cal.*, 570. Wotton–Queen Mary, January 21st 1557. *Ven. Cal.*, VI, 2, 752. Michiel–the Doge, December 7th 1556.

12. Hardwicke, *State Papers*, I, p. 103. Council of Calais–Queen Mary, May 23rd 1557.

13. *For. Cal.*, 633. Grey–Queen Mary, June 14th 1557.

14. *Acts of the P.C.*, N.S., VI, pp. 91, 93 and 113–14.

15. ibid., p. 134.

16. ibid., pp. 147–8.

17. *Ven. Cal.*, VI, 3, 1108. Michiel–the Doge, December 15th 1557.

18. *Ambass.*, I, Intro., p. 37.

19. 'Discours de la Prinse de Calais', *Archives curieuses de l'histoire de France*, Ie serie, t. 3, p. 239.

20. *Ven. Cal.*, VI, 3, 1112. Michiel–the Doge, December 19th 1557.

21. ibid., 1116 and 1123. Same–same, December 25th 1557, and January 3rd 1558.

22. *For. Cal.*, 695. Grey–Queen Mary, December 22nd 1557.

23. ibid., 697. Wentworth–Queen Mary, December 26th 1557.

24. Hardwicke, *State Papers*, I, pp. 104–6. *For. Cal.*, p. 698. Grey and Wentworth–Queen Mary, December 27th 1557.

25. For the siege and fall of Calais I have drawn upon the following: Arber, *English Garner*, Ed. Pollard, pp. 312–17. John Highfield's Account, ibid., pp. 290–301. George Ferrer's Account, ibid., pp. 308–11. Wentworth–Queen Mary, January 2nd 1558. *Ven. Cal.*, VI, 3, 1124, 1129, 1130, 1131, 1137, 1142, 1161. Surian and Michiel–the Doge, January 5th to February 6th 1558. *Archives Curieuses . . . de la France*, Ie serie, t. 3, pp. 239–47. 'Discours de la Prinse de Calais.'

26. *For. Cal.*, 706. Wentworth–Queen Mary, January 1st 1558.

27. *Grey, . . . Services . . .* , App. pp. 51–2.

28. For the siege and fall of Guisnes I have used the following: Arber, *English Garner*, pp. 321–30, Thomas Churchyard. Arthur Grey, *Services of Lord Grey of Wilton.* (*v.* also Holinshed). *Ven. Cal.*, VI, 3, 1161. Surian–the Doge, February 6th 1558.

29. *Ven. Cal.*, VI, 3, 1161 ut sup.

30. *Grey, . . . Services . . .* , p. ix.

CHAPTER XXII (pp. 368–383)

1. Arber, *English Garner*, VI, pp. 290–301. George Ferrers, *Loss of Calais.*

2. Lettenhove, *Relations . . .* , I, p. 119. King Philip–the Council. *Ven. Cal.*, VI, 3, 1159 and 1268. Michiel–the Doge, February 4th 1558. Surian–the same, October 16th 1558.

3. ibid., 1161. Michiel–the Doge, February 6th 1558.

4. ibid.

5. ibid.

6. Arber, *English Garner*, VI, pp. 312–17. Highfield.

7. ibid., pp. 308–11. Wentworth–Queen Mary, January 2nd 1558.

8. ibid., Highfield ut sup.

9. Arber, *English Garner*, VI, pp. 321–30. Churchyard.

10. *Ven. Cal.*, VI, 3, 1161 ut sup.

11. *For. Cal.*, 699. Queen Mary–the Deputy of Calais, December 29th 1557.

12. ibid., 701. Same–same, December 31st.

13. *S.P. Dom.*, 11, 12, No. 3. Minute of a letter, January 2nd 1558.

14. ibid., No. 5. Instructions to Valentine Brown, January 6th 1558.

15. Machyn, p. 162.

16. *S.P. Dom.*, 11, 12, No. 6. Queen Mary–the gentlemen in every shire, [? January 7th] 1558.

17. ibid., No. 12. Queen Mary–William Woodhouse, January 9th 1558.

18. *Acts of the P.C.*, N.S., VI, pp. 233–8.

19. Machyn, p. 162.

20. Arber, *English Garner*, VI, pp. 290–301. Ferrers.

21. *S.P. Dom.*, 11, 12, No. 20. Queen Mary–[lieutenants of some Counties], January 13th 1558.

22. ibid., No. 22. Queen Mary–the Duke of Norfolk, etc., January 17th 1558.

23. ibid., No. 30. Cheyne–Queen Mary, January 23rd 1558.

24. ibid., No. 40. Queen Mary–Norfolk and Rich, January 3rd 1558.

25. Lettenhove, *Relations . . .* , I, pp. 108–9. d'Assonleville–King Philip, November 26th 1557.

26. Strype, *Ecc. Mem.*, III, ii, p. 96.

27. *S.P. Dom.*, 11, 13, No. 7. Montague–Queen Mary, May 17th 1558.

28. ibid., 12, No. 67. Instructions. Bedford–Justices of the Peace.

29. Stow, *Annales*, pp. 1071–3.

30. *S.P. Dom.*, 11, 13, No. 62. Jernigan–Queen Mary, August 31st 1558.

31. *Chronicle of Calais*, p. xxx.

32. Foxe, VIII, p. 625.

33. *Ven. Cal.*, VI, 2, 884, p. 1050. Michiel's Report, May 13th 1557.

34. Machyn, pp. 152–3.

35. *Ven. Cal.*, VI, 1, 316 and 327. Michiel–the Doge, December 16th and December 23rd 1555. *Acts of the P.C.*, N.S., V, p. 305.

36. Hakluyt, *Principal Navigations, Voyages and Discoveries . . .* , 1587, p. 282.

37. ibid., p. 283.

38. Stow, *Annales*, pp. 1065–6. *Acts of the P.C.*, N.S., VI, pp. 54–5. Machyn, p. 130.

39. Lettenhove, *Relations . . .* , I, pp. 66–7. de Courteville–Viglius, April 28th 1557.

40. ibid., pp. 161–2. Fresneda–the Queen of England, March 16th 1558.

41. *Span. Cal.*, XI, pp. 361–2. Sebastian Cabot–Charles V, November 15th 1553.

42. *S.P. Dom.*, 11, 11, No. 35. List of ships serving, [? July] 1557.

43. ibid., 9, No. 26. Further Confession of Killigrew, August 26th 1556.

44. Lettenhove, *Relations . . .* , I, pp. 127–30. Feria–King Philip, February 2nd 1558.

45. *Ven. Cal.*, VI, 3, 1142. Surian–the Doge, January 15th 1558.

46. Lettenhove, *Relations . . .* , I, pp. 179–81. Feria–King Philip, May 1st 1558.

47. ibid., pp. 171–2. Same–same, April 7th 1558.

48. *Ven. Cal.*, VI, 1, 504. Soranzo–the Doge, June 1st 1556.

49. ibid., VI, 2, 775. Same–same, December 27th 1556.

50. MS. Cott. Tit. B. 2, f. 109. Queen Mary–King Philip. Printed in Strype, *Ecc. Mem.*, III, ii, p. lvi, p. 418, without interlineations and dated 1556.

51. *Ven. Cal.*, VI, 3, 1274. Surian–the Doge, October 29th 1558.

52. Lettenhove, *Relations* . . . , I, pp. 171–2. Feria–King Philip, April 6th 1558.

53. James Rae, *Deaths of the Kings of England*. London, 1913.

54. *Ven. Cal.*, VI, 3, 1274 ut sup.

55. Lettenhove, *Relations* . . . , I, pp. 272–4. d'Assonleville–King Philip, November 6th 1558. *Ven. Cal.*, VI, 3, 1279. Surian–the Doge, November 12th 1558.

56. Lettenhove, *Relations* . . . , pp. 273 and 277. d'Assonleville–King Philip, November 6th and November 7th 1558.

57. Stone, App., p. 507 et seq. Also in Madden, *P.P. Exs.*, App. IV.

58. ibid.

59. Lettenhove, *Relations* . . . , I, p. 279. Tytler, II, pp. 496–9. Feria–King Philip, November 13th or November 14th 1558.

60. *Jane Dormer*, pp. 69–80.

61. ibid.

Index